EXPLORING THE
BOUNDARY WATERS

EXPLORING THE BOUNDARY WATERS

A Trip Planner and Guide to the BWCAW

Daniel Pauly

University of Minnesota Press
Minneapolis | London

The maps in this book are for information only. Do not use these maps as guides for navigation.

See the book's companion Web site at http://www.BoundaryWatersGuide.com
for route updates and additional useful information.

Published by the University of Minnesota Press
111 Third Avenue South, Suite 290
Minneapolis, MN 55401-2520
http://www.upress.umn.edu

Library of Congress Cataloging-in-Publication Data

Pauly, D. (Daniel)
     Exploring the Boundary Waters : a trip planner and guide to the
BWCAW / Daniel Pauly.
        p.   cm.
     Includes bibliographical references and index.
     ISBN 0-8166-4216-8 (pb : alk. paper)
     1. Canoes and canoeing—Minnesota—Boundary Waters Canoe Area
Wilderness—Guidebooks.   2. Boundary Waters Canoe Area Wilderness
(Minn.)—Guidebooks.   I. Title.
     GV776.M62B685 2005

                                                        2004026466

Printed in the United States of America on acid-free paper

The University of Minnesota is an equal-opportunity educator and employer.

12 11 10 09 08 07   10 9 8 7 6 5 4 3 2

To Laura, Matthew, and Garrett

CONTENTS

- - - - - - - - - - - -

PREFACE

The Boundary Waters Canoe Area Wilderness (BWCAW), along with neighboring Quetico Provincial Park, is renowned as the finest canoeing area in the world. No other place offers such an exceptional combination of expansive and varied wilderness canoe routes, intact natural ecosystems, and fascinating human history.

A journey through the Boundary Waters is a trip across water and time. In one week you might paddle past a beaver lodge built three summers ago, portage through cedar groves that were old long before the American Revolution, run your hand along billion-year-old granite, and awaken to timeless loon calls. In addition, the human history in this wilderness area is remarkable: the portage trails often follow prehistoric paths used by generations of Native Americans, and the surrounding forests once hosted mineral prospectors, big-pine loggers, and remote fishing lodges.

The purpose of this guidebook is to help you explore and discover the Boundary Waters, whether you are planning your first trip or have already visited fifty times. One of the great joys of wilderness travel is the satisfaction of discovery and exploration as wild lands unfold before you. This guide has been written to help you discover the BWCAW for yourself and has been designed with a number of basic principles to help accomplish that goal. First, it gives you an overview of each entry point to the Boundary Waters and important considerations for planning a trip from that entry. Second, it provides detailed discussions of more than one hundred specific routes (including portages you will encounter), plus advantages and disadvantages of changes in the routes. Third, it offers a natural and historic context for your journey, revealing fascinating information about some of the geologic forms and natural sites you will see, and historic human activities that have occurred along the routes. Fourth, and finally, the routes have been laid out to facilitate designing your own journeys, however long, hard, or complex you wish them to be. The thorough index will help you in this regard, as will the many descriptions of alternative routes and optional side trips.

In addition to the detailed content in this book, the companion Web site www .BoundaryWatersGuide.com presents information that can be downloaded as you plan your trip, including gear lists, overview maps, and route updates. These materials will not replace what you find here but instead are a useful accompaniment and aid in making your plans. Links to other helpful sites, including the Boundary Waters Reservation Center and the Superior National Forest, are also provided.

The content of this book has been assembled since my first trip to the Boundary Waters more than twenty years ago but was primarily acquired during a systematic visit and revisit to hundreds of lakes during the past seven years. I have visited every portage and lake described in this guide unless noted otherwise, and many lakes were visited repeatedly. The Boundary Waters is, however, a constantly changing ecosystem, and you should anticipate that natural fluctuations in water levels, vegetation, and visitor usage will modify the characteristics of some of these routes. To maintain your safety and maximize your enjoyment in the BWCAW, keep alert for changes in these routes.

Another objective of this guidebook is to provide users with the tools to visit the Boundary Waters in a low-impact manner, to avoid overused routes, and to come away with greater affection for this unique treasure. When visitors have an increased understanding and appreciation of the wilderness communities through which they travel, they are more likely to give those communities the respect and care that they need.

Finally, I hope your next trip to the Boundary Waters inspires you to get involved in its long-term protection. Visitors often assume that the Boundary Waters has always been a remote haven free of modern intrusions and damage, and that efforts to "protect" it are now complete. Both assumptions are false. The Boundary Waters has experienced human impacts for thousands of years, including extreme changes involving logging, dam building, road construction, and resort development.

In many aspects the Boundary Waters is much more wild today than it was fifty or one hundred years ago, when loggers traversed the portages and dozens of homes and lodges dotted the interior lakes. The work of many dedicated people preserved the large expanses of roadless canoe country—and also resulted in the removal of dozens of resorts and private cabins from the present-day BWCAW, a task that took years to accomplish and required great sacrifice from those who owned and loved those resorts and cabins.

Even with these advances, the Boundary Waters continues to face threats, including damage from reckless campers. Take it upon yourself to leave your campsites pristine, not only free of garbage but also unaltered by careless collection of firewood, improper positioning of tents, or senseless harm to plants and animals. Also take the time to understand current issues affecting the BWCAW, and take a stand to protect it. Invasive species, airborne mercury pollution, and global warming all pose real dangers to the Boundary Waters. Extensive logging occurs right up to the edge of the wilderness, and development of homes and resorts continues on its borders. Certainly other unknown threats will emerge in coming years and will require a new generation of people willing to work to protect it.

ACKNOWLEDGMENTS

I would like to thank the many people who helped make this guide possible. Research for the manuscript required dozens of trips in the BWCAW over a number of years to gather accurate information for describing the many portages, lakes, and streams. I could not have completed this research without the help of friends willing to head out on strenuous expeditions that focused far more on data collection than simply relaxing, fishing, or swimming. My wife, Laura Walvoord, was a wonderful companion on many of those challenging trips. The great assistance of Dan McGarry and Jade Anderson, who each took more than one long journey researching this book, contributed tremendously to this effort. Dave Hartman and John Hartman were also essential, retracing and updating portages after the 1999 blowdown and carefully measuring the length of dozens of portages. Cyndee Krenos transcribed and revised many of my notes and manuscript drafts, offering important edits along the way.

Numerous other people gave critical input on content for this guide. The friendly assistance of Superior National Forest personnel is much appreciated, including help from Barb Soderberg and Jo Barnier on visitor rules and suggestions, Christina Boston for visitor usage data, Walt Oksted for human history data, and Kendall Cikanik for cartographic data. Joseph Geiss, Minnesota Department of Natural Resources regional fisheries supervisor, provided a professional's view of catch-and-release fishing recommendations. Amy Wilkenloh of the Friends of the Boundary Waters Wilderness was a good contact on leave-no-trace camping principles.

Later, as the manuscript was in its final stages, outfitters Steve Piragis of Piragis Northwoods Company and Bill Hansen of Sawbill Canoe Outfitters (among others) reviewed portions of the text and offered excellent suggestions. I am also grateful to the staff at the University of Minnesota Press, especially editor Todd Orjala, who had the patience to stick with this book from conception to completion, even through false starts and substantial revisions.

Finally, I wish to express my deep gratitude to Boyd Larson, Bill Boecker Sr., Gary Corpron, Larry Rich, and Gary Brown. They were leaders of the Boy Scout troop in Chaska, Minnesota, in which I was active as a boy, and they took the time to introduce me and many others to the joys of wilderness camping. Those introductions included my first ventures into the Boundary Waters. Every young person should be so fortunate to have such fine guides and mentors.

THE NATURAL AND
HUMAN HISTORY OF
THE BOUNDARY WATERS

This chapter provides an introduction to the natural and human forces that have shaped the present-day Boundary Waters Canoe Area Wilderness (BWCAW) over a period of three billion years. During this time, mountains rose from an ancient seabed, volcanoes erupted across the region, and sheets of glacial ice scoured the rocky surface. As the glaciers receded, plants and animals rapidly colonized exposed soil and rock.

The natural history section covers the fascinating geologic and glacial history of the Boundary Waters, describes ecosystems that arose 10,000 years ago after the retreat of the last glaciers, briefly introduces some of the plants and animals you may encounter, and gives guidance on sources to learn more about them.

Humans first came to this region after the glaciers receded, probably following caribou and other game into new habitats. The earliest humans had limited impacts on the lake country, but the arrival of the first people of European descent nearly four centuries ago quickly changed the relationship between the environment and humans. By the 1700s humans had become a major force of change in canoe country. The human history discussion provides an introduction to the many people who have called this region home, and describes some of the heroic efforts of people to preserve the Boundary Waters for later generations to appreciate and enjoy.

Natural History

Boundary Waters Geology

The Boundary Waters is perched atop rock that is among the oldest on Earth, including portions estimated to be nearly three billion years old. Exposed bedrock is located throughout the Boundary Waters, making the area a fascinating history exhibit of billions of years of geology. This history includes formation of massive mountains, eruption of lava-spewing volcanoes, and scouring of glacial ice sheets. Each of these geologic transformations has left its mark on the landscape, and an informed eye can decipher these marks while paddling and portaging the wilderness waterways.

Once you have an appreciation for the geology of the Boundary Waters, you will never see a portage the same way. Many of the routes in this guide describe the bedrock you will encounter, and the following section will help you to understand these descriptions. In addition, you can learn more about the geology of the Boundary Waters by reading *Minnesota's Geology* by Richard W. Ojakangas and Charles L. Matsch, which is an excellent guide to the state's geology.

To understand the geology of the Boundary Waters, you should first consider two essential aspects of how all rock was formed and the minerals contained within it. All rock is formed by one of three different processes: cooling of liquid magma to form *igneous rock,* deposition and aggregation of particles or chemicals to form *sedimentary rock,* or pressure cooking of existing rock to form *metamorphic rock.* If you understand these three processes of rock formation, you will have a solid foundation for learning about the geologic history of the Boundary Waters.

The first of these processes, the cooling of molten magma to form *igneous rock,* is a consequence of the immense heat and pressure under the earth's crust. The heat and pressure are so intense that they melt rock deep within the earth to form magma. Rocks of different characteristics are formed depending on where the magma cools and what types of minerals are within the magma. When the magma cools deep under the earth, it usually cools slowly and can form large crystals within its structure. When the magma cools at the earth's surface, such as from volcanoes, it usually cools rapidly and forms small or fine crystals. Thus, by looking at the crystal size of bedrock containing the same minerals you can gain an idea of how quickly the rock cooled and how close to the surface it was when it cooled.

Thousands of igneous rocks have been identified around the world, but for the purposes of this geology introduction you need be concerned with only four types: granite, rhyolite, gabbro, and basalt. These rocks all vary depending on where they were formed and their mineral content, all are found in the Boundary Waters, and all are encountered on routes in this guide.

The first two types of igneous rocks, granite and rhyolite, are "cousins" formed of similar low-density materials. The difference between them is that granite formed deeper inside the earth than rhyolite, which formed near the surface. As expected, slow-cooling granite has relatively large crystals (of quartz), while fast-cooling rhyolite has relatively small crystals.

The second pair of igneous rocks, gabbro and basalt, are also "cousins," this time formed of similar high-density materials. The difference between them is that gabbro formed deep under the earth's surface while basalt formed near the surface. As you might expect, gabbro has large crystals, while basalt has small crystals. Because basalt is very dense, it is no surprise that it forms most of the ocean floor (which is low lying), while relatively light granite forms most of the continents (which are, obviously, higher than the ocean floor).

When molten magma hardens deep underground, it is called an *intrusive* igneous rock. When molten magma reaches the earth's surface, it forms an *extrusive* igneous rock. Thus, granite and gabbro are examples of intrusive igneous rocks, while rhyolite and basalt are examples of extrusive igneous rocks.

Igneous Rock Properties

Rock	Density	Cooling	Crystals
granite	low	slow	large
rhyolite	low	fast	small
gabbro	high	slow	large
basalt	high	fast	small

- -

The second major type of rock is sedimentary rock. Over time, all exposed rock is eventually weathered away. This weathering sometimes forms bits and pieces of particles, such as sand, while at other times weathering forms dissolved salts. When these small particles and salts accumulate and solidify over millions of years, they form sedimentary rock.

Sedimentary rocks frequently form along ocean and lake basins, in riverbeds, and at deltas. Any place where water or wind carries bits and pieces of eroded rock can eventually form sedimentary rocks. Interestingly, the conditions under which sediments were deposited can be learned by examining the rocks. For example, under some circumstances, heavier erosion components will settle out before the light components, thereby creating layered beds. Common sedimentary rocks include sandstone, shale, and limestone.

The third major type of rock to be discussed in this introduction to Boundary Waters geology is metamorphics, which are rocks that had an igneous or sedimentary origin but subsequently were forced underground and heated under intense pressure to form a new type of rock. Examples of metamorphic rocks include slates and greenstones, both of which are found in the Boundary Waters and referred to often in this guide.

Now that you have this quick introduction to rock formation, you can use it to understand Boundary Waters geology. Geologists believe that approximately 2.7 billion years ago, around what is now Ely, crevasses opened in a section of crust far below the surface of an ancient ocean. Molten magma flowed from these crevasses into the salty seawater. The magma rapidly cooled, forming dense, fine-grained basalt having a "pillowed" texture much like a head of cauliflower. Geologists speculate that the basalt cooled at depths of 1,000 meters or more, because it does not contain gas cavities that would have formed if it had emerged in lower-pressure shallow waters. The basalt formed layers as thick as 5,000 meters.

Massive volcanoes erupted, and lava flows piled on top of the pillowed basalt in the ensuing millions of years. These flows were also initially underwater, but over time they gained sufficient height to break the surface of the ancient ocean. Unlike the dense basalt, these flows were rhyolite, the lightweight extrusive cousin of granite.

Some of the rhyolite was formed when magma and hardened rock were expelled from volcanic vents. The expelled material was spread for great distances, and it is possible to identify the approximate center of the ancient volcanic activity by locating the largest expelled boulders, since these would generally not have flown as far as smaller expelled rocks.

During this period of volcanism, and particularly after the volcanic matter extended above the water surface, erosion gradually attacked the exposed rock surfaces. Waters eroded the rhyolite and deposited it in beds at low spots along the ocean floor. As is often the case, these deposits separated into graded beds with large particles on the bottom and small particles on top. Many of these beds were formed in what is now the central and eastern Boundary Waters. The sedimentary beds were subsequently metamorphosed at high temperatures and pressures to form the Knife Lake Group underlying most of the BWCAW lakes between Sea Gull and Snow Bank. The shores of such famous lakes as Kekekabic, Ogishkemuncie, Gabimichigami (north shore), Knife, Moose, and Birch contain extensive exposures of the Knife Lake Group originating in metamorphosed sedimentary rocks.

In subsequent years the older basalt and rhyolite rock underwent a period of intense folding from massive geologic forces. First, enormous bodies of granitic magma penetrated and deformed the older volcanic-sedimentary deposits. Fault lines formed, and earthquakes likely shook this ancient world. Unlike the preexisting deposits, the granitic magma cooled and hardened deep below the surface.

The rise of these granites coincided with sinking of the surrounding basalt, rhyolite, and sedimentary rocks. As they slowly sank into the earth, the rocks came in contact with the new flows of granitic magma. This hot magma metamorphosed the surrounding rocks. The ancient pillowed basalt flows that had formed on the ocean floor transformed into a meta-basalt, much of it greenish in color. Today, this rock is commonly referred to as "greenstone" or "Ely greenstone," and can be found in deposits in the general vicinity of Ely.

All of this folding, faulting, and magma intrusion led to formation of a great mountain range 2.5 billion years ago over what is now northern Minnesota. The newly formed mountains were slowly attacked by the elements, wearing away exposed rock. In addition, some evidence exists that glaciers may have also worn away at the ancient rock surface.

While the mountains were undergoing dramatic erosion, a transforming process was occurring in the oceans of the world that would have tremendous implications for northeastern Minnesota more than two billion years later: formation of huge iron ore deposits. By a process that is apparently not yet completely understood, many sedimentary deposits throughout the world became enriched with an abundance of iron. Today, these deposits account for almost all of the commercial reserves of iron ore on Earth, including those in northern Minnesota.

What could have caused these concentrated deposits of iron in a relatively narrow band of sedimentary rocks? A leading theory is premised on the belief that these iron minerals were deposited at the same time that photosynthesizing plants were first beginning to fill the earth's oceans. These plants—simple algae—consumed carbon dioxide and released oxygen. For the first time ever, large quantities of oxygen would have been present in the atmosphere and oceans. This oxygen would have reacted with dissolved iron that had accumulated in the oceans from hundreds of millions of years of erosion, and iron oxides would have been chemically precipitated in shallow waters as hematite (Fe_2O_3), magnetite (Fe_3O_4), iron carbonate ($FeCO_3$), and iron silicates.

Although the BWCAW is not commonly known for iron ore deposits, the Gunflint Iron Formation was created during this period and runs east-west from Gabimichigami Lake up toward Magnetic Lake, Gunflint Lake, and North Lake. Without this iron formation the Paulson Mine, described later, would probably never have been undertaken, and the Gunflint Trail not completed to its current end. Similarly, the iron mines around Ely would not have existed, and perhaps even Ely would have risen and fallen as a short-lived lumber town rather than the more prosperous and longer-lived mining center that is now a recreational destination.

Geologically speaking, these iron deposits were laid down in a very short period of time—a matter of a few million years. The erosion and sedimentation that preceded the iron formation continued after the iron was deposited. In the Boundary Waters an extensive area of bedrock known as the Rove Slate Formation was deposited at this time along what is today the far eastern BWCAW, including Clearwater, Alder, Pine, Caribou, Little Caribou, West Pike, and East Pike lakes. Originally sand and mud, these deposits eventually hardened into various sedimentary rocks, including slate, shale, argillite, and graywacke.

Approximately 1.1 billion years ago another great period of igneous rock formation occurred in what is today the BWCAW. A series of massive magma intrusions known as the Duluth Complex formed along the southeastern BWCAW. These intrusions formed rock similar to the basalts originally forming the Ely greenstone. However, unlike the quick-cooling basalts that gave rise to the greenstone, the Duluth Complex magma slowly cooled underground into a large-grained gabbro (more properly known as diabase). Huge expanses of the southeastern BWCAW are covered by this gabbro.

In the far northeastern BWCAW, the gabbro intruded into the sedimentary Rove Formation, metamorphosing the sedimentary rocks and at the same time forming sills penetrating between layers of the sedimentary rocks. Over millions of years these layers of intrusive Duluth gabbro and metamorphosed Rove Formation were tilted by shifting of the continental plates into an upright position. When glaciers arrived 10,000 years ago, they made short shrift of the slate, carving it out while only relatively scratching the gabbro.

Glaciation of the Boundary Waters

Although the bedrock of the Boundary Waters was deposited, fractured, and redeposited repeatedly during the past 2.5 billion years, the series of events that most dramatically shaped this area as we know it today started just 2 million years ago when temperatures around the world gradually cooled to start the Great Ice Age, also known as the Pleistocene Epoch.

Ice sheets formed as snows fell during the winter but failed to melt during the cool summers. Over time the accumulation of snow reached epic proportions and formed a massive ice sheet known as the Laurentide. This ice sheet was centered in Hudson Bay and expanded and contracted across central North America over a period of hundreds of thousands of years. Geologists studying the movements of the Laurentide ice sheet have divided its advances into four general periods of glacial expansion followed by warm periods of glacial retreat. These periods of expansion have been classified as the Wisconsin, Illinoisan, Kansan, and Nebraskan glaciations, listed from most recent to oldest.

Glaciers altered the landscape in two general manners: glacial erosion and glacial deposition. The massive weight of glacial ice sheets has a scouring effect on the ground they pass over. Loose rock is pulled from the ground and dragged along with the advancing ice sheets. The carried-along rocks dig into and form scratches and grooves in the bedrock over which they pass. These scratches, termed *striae,* can be spotted along many of the lakes of the BWCAW. Look for sets of parallel lines scratched into the rock face. The scratches typically have varying depths. Another form of glacial erosion is the removal of large rocks from the surrounding bedrock to create blunt-nosed hills known as *whalebacks* that form when a glacier moves across a bedrock irregularity or protrusion. Glacial ice is able to essentially climb up and over the front of the protrusion, but it often freezes to and rips loose the back side of the protrusion, creating an irregular shape.

Glacial deposition is the other major impact of glaciation and may be of either fine-grained powdered bedrock or larger boulders. These deposits may be made far from their origins—even hundreds of miles away. Transported rocks, known as *erratics,* are useful for determining the direction and extent of glacial ice travel. Glacial erratics are carried along until the glacier stops advancing and are left behind when the glacial ice melts. In some cases, the load is deposited as a pile of rocks known as a *moraine.* In the Boundary Waters, you will sometimes notice places in which mounds of boulders have been deposited, forming small moraines.

Take a little time when you see moraines and boulders to observe how well they match surrounding bedrock. You will be surprised how often noticeable differentiation can be found. Pay attention to bedrock changes when you are going from north to south on a route. You will, on occasion, see that some of the bedrock of northern lakes has ended up as moraines and erratics along southern portages and lakes. I have found this to be especially evident near Saganaga Lake. Distinctive pinkish granite with black spots (technically tonalite) originating around Saganaga often shows up along portages miles to the south.

In addition to the massive sheets of glacial ice that formed on the present-day Boundary Waters, enormous Glacial Lake Agassiz also covered much of the western Boundary Waters about 11,000 years ago. Lake Agassiz stretched as far east as present-day Basswood Lake, leaving behind clay deposits along its ancient shoreline, high above the current shores of Basswood. Interestingly, the ancient shores of Lake Agassiz are where some of the oldest artifacts are found in this area.

Emergence of Evolving Ecosystems

With the final retreat of the Rainy-Superior Lobe of the Late Wisconsin glaciation, the Boundary Waters landscape was exposed for the first time in millennia to colonization by plants and animals. According to U.S. Forest Service information, northeastern Minnesota was probably free of glacial ice as early as 13,000 BC, at a time when western Minnesota was still covered by sheets of ice, as was the Lake Superior basin to the east. The initial Boundary Waters environment after the glaciers receded was probably a wet tundralike environment with occasional shrubs, grasses, and sedges similar to those present today around Hudson Bay, Canada. Caribou were probably present in large numbers.

A reasonably detailed picture of the Boundary Waters ecosystem during the millennia since the ice sheets receded can be obtained by looking at lake sediment cores taken in northern Minnesota. Notably, Lake of the Clouds, located in the BWCAW just west of Saganaga, provides an interesting record of the plants that first colonized the postglacial landscape. Over 9,000 years of annual layers of lake sediment have been recovered from the depths of Lake of the Clouds, making it a remarkable historical repository of pollen and charcoal for most of the time since the glaciers receded. The information gathered at Lake of the Clouds and other locations indicates that it is likely that birch and spruce were common here by 8000 BC.

Around 7000 BC the weather started to warm and get somewhat drier in the area encompassed by the present-day Boundary Waters. Tundra plants gradually gave way to white pine and red pine, and large mammals, including moose, became more common.

Temperatures fluctuated over the past few thousand years, contributing to changes in plant communities. At this time forest fires probably became the defining force of nature. The research of the late Miron Heinselman, a Superior National Forest ecologist, shows that fires probably burned frequently throughout the forest. Smaller trees would have been killed by these fires, but the larger red and white pine could survive low-intensity fires and become a source of seeds for another generation of pine.

Today the BWCAW is considered to be part of a "southern boreal forest" between the larger boreal forest to the north and the temperate deciduous forest to the south. You will find plants such as black spruce, balsam fir, aspen, birch, and jack pine that are common to boreal forest, as well as white pine and red pine common (at least before logging) in more temperate forests.

One of the great misunderstandings regarding the BWCAW is that it is a homogeneous northern forest. Today about 20 percent of the Boundary Waters is comprised of lowland, nonlake areas; 60 percent is comprised of upland, nonlake areas; and the rest is comprised of water. Most of the upland areas have shallow glacial till deposits, with less than 40 inches to bedrock.

I strongly recommend that you learn how to identify the most common plants of the Boundary Waters. Once you start to identify them, and especially once you understand a bit about their biology, you will likely be hooked for life on trying to understand the many different plants. I recommend getting *Canoe Country Flora: Plants and Trees of the North Woods and Boundary Waters* by Mark Stensaas. This book is full of fascinating plant facts. The pictures are not very useful for identification, but the other great aspects of this book more than make up for the limited illustrations.

If you are new to the north woods and wondering where to start your education on the plants of canoe country, I recommend that you learn how to identify the coniferous trees that are so common: red pine, white pine, jack pine, balsam fir, tamarack, black and white spruce, and white cedar. In addition, you should learn to identify aspen, birch, and maples. Being able to identify these plants will give you a window into forest distribution and age, and allow you to follow forest succession more intelligently and have a better appreciation for how human activity has influenced plant communities. Once you have covered these basic plants, learn more about the orchids, water lilies, lichens, mosses, ferns, shrubs, and other plants that make the Boundary Waters such a fascinating place to explore.

The Boundary Waters also provides habitat for hundreds of species of animals, ranging from insects and spiders up to the mighty moose. Indeed, at least forty species of mammals, mostly smaller rodents such as shrews, chipmunks, squirrels, voles, and mice, have been identified. Besides the moose, other large mammals include white-tailed deer, beaver, timber wolf, brown bear, otter, and lynx. Eagles, ospreys, gulls, loons, mergansers, vultures, jays, ravens, and dozens of other birds are regular visitors or inhabitants here. The number of different reptile species is relatively small, but snapping and painted turtles are rather common. That they can survive even though ice covers their water homes approximately half the year is amazing. Read *Canoe Country Wildlife: A Field Guide to the North Woods and Boundary Waters* by Mark Stensaas to learn more about these animals and many others native to the Boundary Waters.

Will you see any of these animals on your trip? The short answer is absolutely, because no designated campsite in the Boundary Waters is without a resident raiding chipmunk and at least one supervising squirrel. Gulls always seem to show up when one is cleaning fish, and larger lakes have at least one pair of common loons. If you hope to see other animals, you will need to be alert, perceptive, and quiet. Moose tracks can be spotted on many portages, and they will not be mistaken for anything else. Spotting beaver lodges and dams is also an everyday event in the Boundary Waters. You may also come upon moose feeding in shallows, otters bobbing curiously in the water ahead of your canoe, and beavers rippling along the surface of lakes, ponds, and streams. Deer, too, are frequently seen, perhaps a sign of their relative abundance.

Many of these animals are most active at dawn and dusk. Get into the habit of scanning all the shoreline visible from your camp during these hours. You might be treated to the sight of a moose far off in the distance or perhaps one poking around by your canoes. Similarly, beavers seem to be most active late in the day.

Look for otters throughout the lakes and streams of the BWCAW. Their curious heads have bobbed up at me randomly throughout the wilderness, most commonly while I have been paddling down meandering rivers and streams, or in modest-sized lakes. Here, too, is where beavers are most at home. Some beavers make their homes on larger lakes, but they are most common in more constrained areas of moving water and in smaller ponds.

After moose, timber wolves are perhaps the animals most Boundary Waters visitors would love to see. Unless you are lucky, you might spend years in the Boundary Waters with hardly a glimpse of a wolf. You might find tracks and wolf scat on a portage if you are in a pack's territory, especially in early spring, and many visitors have heard their haunting howls carrying across these northern lakes. Only once have I had the good fortune of viewing wolves in the Boundary Waters, on a winter camping trip when I watched two wolves pursue and bring down a deer on the east side of Three Mile Island in Sea Gull Lake. Amazingly, the wolves finally caught up with and killed their prey just 80 feet from my campsite. My camera had frozen up (it was 34°F below zero), but I was able to capture the end of the hunt on video, incontrovertible proof to counter my doubting friends. I certainly do not expect to see such a sight again.

One of the more interesting biology stories out of the Boundary Waters in recent years has involved the lynx. In the 1990s researchers began hearing reports that lynx had been spotted in the Superior National Forest. By 2000, the reports had become more common, and hair samples collected from the wilderness confirmed that lynx had returned. A couple dozen lynx, or more, probably now inhabit the Superior National Forest. Forest Service scientists have also collected the first scientific evidence of hybridization between bobcats and Canada lynx in the wild. Superior National Forest biologists collected tissue and hair samples from nineteen cats believed to be Canada lynx. Two of the cats had external physical characteristics resembling both species, and DNA tests later showed that three of the cats were hybrids from male bobcats mating with female lynx.

The excellent habitat of the Boundary Waters along with the regional recovery of the bald eagle population make it very possible that you will see one or more of these great birds, especially if you are out for a longer trip. Scan the shoreline for watchful eagles perched in trees. The white heads of mature birds will often stand out, but also look for darker silhouettes of brown-headed immature eagles. The osprey, also known as the "fish eagle," is rather common in the Boundary Waters. Smaller than an eagle, its raccoonlike banded eyes are a giveaway for identification. This is a great bird to pause and observe because you might be lucky enough to see one hover high over a lake, only to plunge talons first underwater to grab a fish. Kingfishers, while comparably tiny, are also frequently seen in the BWCAW.

Loons also prosper in the Boundary Waters, although not nearly as well as they would if they could get a 5 percent royalty payment on every loon doll, T-shirt, postcard, mug, paperweight, napkin holder, and pencil sharpener sold each summer north of Duluth. Loons will occasionally surface very near your canoe, and I have had one swim just under my canoe. If you are motionless, you may be treated to a few minutes of floating together with these great birds, only to have them vanish underwater in a flash with a dip of their head and a roll of their bodies. Loons rarely go ashore (they cannot take off to fly from land) except to tend to their eggs. You should never approach a loon onshore, because it is probably at its nest. These northern birds can be skittish, and you want to make sure you do not cause one to abandon its eggs.

I highly recommend *The Boundary Waters Wilderness Ecosystem* by Miron Heinselman to learn more about BWCAW plants and animals. Written by a great field ecologist and leading researcher on the impacts of wildfires (as well as a leader in efforts to preserve the BWCAW), no other book pulls together the natural history of this area better.

Human History

The first humans probably arrived in the Boundary Waters as the last glaciers retreated, and are known today as the Paleo-Indians. Archaeologists believe the Paleo-Indians were probably nomadic hunters who pursued mammoths, mastodons, and other now extinct large mammals at the edge of the receding glaciers, as well as herds of caribou. Paleo-Indian spear points have been found at various locations in the BWCAW, including at Knife Lake and South Fowl Lake, and their stone quarries have been found at more than one location on Knife Lake. Interestingly, even though most of the lakes we visit today would have already formed when Paleo-Indians lived in the Boundary Waters, the few Paleo-Indian artifacts found in the wilderness were located near hilltops with clear views of surrounding areas for spotting caribou herds. Canoes had not yet been invented, water travel would have been difficult, and fishing techniques still limited. Thus, these earliest inhabitants of the lake country probably did not rely on the lakes for much of their subsistence or for travel. Archaeologists do surmise, however, that hunters would have used water to their advantage as a natural barrier, driving caribou toward water during hunts and to slow them down so they could be overtaken and killed.

Paleo-Indians probably lived in small groups. They hunted with spears thrown using an atlatl, which is a device that effectively lengthens the thrower's arm. The atlatl allowed farther throws and higher velocities for the spear, an important innovation because these hunters had not yet adopted the bow and arrow. Their hunting techniques and the game supply probably did not support large, centralized settlements. Forest Service archaeologists have recovered artifacts dating back as early as the late Paleo-Indian period near the Fall Lake campground and at the junction of the Cross River and Gunflint Lake, as well as at other places in the Boundary Waters. Additional artifacts have been found scattered throughout northeastern Minnesota.

Approximately 8,000 years ago northeastern Minnesota experienced a significant and prolonged warming. This warm period helped initiate the Archaic period, which started around 5000 BC and continued for more than 5,000 years. Archaic people probably lived in larger groups than their Paleo-Indian predecessors and made major advances in tool-forming techniques and materials, including grooved axes, complex spearheads, and even copper points. Many of the copper artifacts, as well as various stone implements, can be traced back to origins in Wisconsin deposits, indicating that at least some regional exchange of goods was occurring. The Archaic people also created fishing-related tools, an indication of significant dependence on aquatic resources that sharply contrasts with the Paleo-Indians terrestrial focus.

Archaeologists theorize that the Archaic people produced dugout canoes from red and white pines, making routine lake travel possible. No such boats have been found in northern Minnesota, but their presence has been inferred by finds of axes and other tools particularly well suited to hollowing out a tree trunk. These dugouts would have required an incredible amount of work to produce, but once completed they would have lasted years. Although not readily movable between most lakes, they would have had been tremendously useful on larger lakes such as Basswood, Knife, and Lac La Croix.

Lake levels were lower in northeastern Minnesota during most of the Archaic period, and therefore many habitation sites were submerged in later years when lakes rose to their current levels. I sometimes wonder, paddling through big lakes such as Basswood, Lac La Croix, and Saganaga, whether I am floating over 5,000-year-old camps of Archaic hunters and also whether the hills above me hold artifacts and memories of even earlier Paleo-Indians.

At the end of the Archaic period, the weather again began to cool and become moister, returning to a wetter climate much like what exists today. Around 500 BC this warming period helped initiate changes in the inhabitants of northeastern Minnesota, beginning a time now known as the Woodland period. Woodland people made a number of important innovations, including creation of functional pottery and the adoption of the bow and arrow. They also began to have an increased reliance on plant foods, including wild rice and berries. Many artifacts from the Woodland period have been found near historic wild rice harvesting areas. Pottery was probably an important innovation that allowed wild rice to be blanched and preserved for extended periods, as well as to be used in cooking and storage.

Wild rice became an important dietary staple for the Woodland people, but the short northern Minnesota growing season probably precluded significant agriculture, just as it does today. The eastern Boundary Waters may have been less heavily populated at this time than the western areas because significantly less rice grows in the deeper, hard-bottomed lakes of the east.

By about AD 1000 Native Americans had developed the first birch-bark canoes. These canoes reflect a remarkable sophistication in material selection, design, and manufacture. Amazingly lightweight, efficient, and durable, the birch-bark canoe remains one of the most impressive nautical innovations of all time. Perfectly matched to its task of transporting goods and people over inland lakes connected by rugged portages, the Native American birch-bark canoe is still echoed in the many lightweight canoes paddled through the BWCAW each year.

The Dakota people, also known as the Sioux, inhabited northeastern Minnesota for unknown generations before AD 1500. However, sometime between 1400 and the early 1600s they were forced out by the Anishinabe arriving from the east. The Anishinabe are sometimes referred to as the Ojibwe or Chippewa. The Anishinabe probably moved seasonally to take advantage of changing food supplies. In the late spring they would gather together to tap maples, birches, and other trees to collect sugar sap. Families maintained permanent summer villages where they raised some food and also fished and gathered berries and other plants. Late in the summer and through the fall the Anishinabe would have harvested wild rice.

In 1854 the Anishinabe signed the Treaty of La Pointe, ceding much of northeastern Minnesota to the U.S. government and opening the area to European settlement. The Grand Portage Band of the Lake Superior Chippewa, the Bois Fort Band of the Lake Superior Chippewa, and the Fond du Lac Band of the Lake Superior Chippewa all participated in this treaty. The Treaty of La Pointe also established the Grand Portage Reservation, located in the extreme northeastern corner of Minnesota, east of the BWCAW.

While traveling through the Boundary Waters, you may have an opportunity to view one of a handful of pictograph sites painted by the Anishinabe or their predecessors the Dakota on exposed rock walls. At least some of the pictographs are probably from historic times, because they appear to reference images relating to voyageurs and Europeans, including guns and voyageur canoes, although other pictographs may predate the arrival of Europeans.

I have always marveled at how long these simple paintings have survived, exposed to temperature fluctuations that can exceed 130°F over a single season, and to hard driven snow and drenching rains. The secret may be the elegant simplicity of their medium: powdered red ochre containing iron ore mixed with fish oils, perhaps from sturgeon. This composition stained the rock, with the iron in the ochre remaining long after the organic oils had degraded. Some of the finest pictographs in the BWCAW are located on Crooked Lake just north of Lower Basswood Falls, and on North Hegman Lake off the Echo Trail. Other pictographs can be seen in various locations within the Boundary Waters. Where appropriate, they are identified in the routes described in this guide.

The Voyageurs

The first Europeans and people of European descent to arrive in significant numbers in northeastern Minnesota came in the 1700s. French fur traders heavily used the Boundary Waters from 1732 to 1756, establishing posts at Moose, Saganaga, and Basswood lakes in the current BWCAW. In 1736 the Frenchman Bourassa built a small fort on Little Vermilion Lake. These traders were interested in animal furs of many types, but beaver pelts were particularly prized.

English fur traders arrived in the Boundary Waters region in the 1760s after northeastern Minnesota was transferred to British hands by the Treaty of Paris, which concluded the French and Indian War between France and Great Britain. By

1768 the Englishman John Askin had built a crude post in the vicinity of present-day Grand Portage, but not until 1779 was the North West Company organized and a depot built at Grand Portage, connected by the 8.5-mile-long Grand Portage trail to the inland post of Fort Charlotte.

The Grand Portage came alive each summer when North West Company crews headed east, hauling bundles of valuable furs from as far away as the Rocky Mountains, and crews headed west with important trade goods destined for smaller, more remote posts. Fort Charlotte was generally a temporary storage location, while the much larger Grand Portage depot had a large enclosed stockade area with nearly twenty buildings and space for many people to establish a temporary camp outside the depot's walls.

"Northmen" from the North West Company and voyageurs from the west would arrive with plentiful furs from the winter harvest season and exchange them with the traders at the depot. The Northmen transported their furs to Fort Charlotte in canoes that were about 25 feet long and had room for a crew of four to six men and almost 4,000 pounds of gear. These canoes could be portaged by two men but were still cumbersome. Fortunately the canoes did not need to be portaged down the Grand Portage itself. Only the furs and trade goods were carried across the trail, the canoes being left at Fort Charlotte. Large Montreal canoes were then used to transport European trade goods from Montreal to Grand Portage in the spring, returning with loads of furs after the rendezvous. The Montreal canoes were about 36 feet long and 6 feet wide, with space for a crew of eight to ten men and up to 8,000 pounds of cargo. These craft were certainly big by canoe standards but still tiny for the cold waters of Lake Superior.

The North West Company was divided into posts based upon location, and each post would take about a week to get their gear down the Grand Portage. On the way out they would leave in waves to avoid overcrowding at western portages and intermixing of goods. This was perhaps the beginning of the quota system for the Boundary Waters! The packs used to carry the furs and trade goods weighed about 90 pounds each. Legends remain of men who are said to have carried three or even four packs up the portage. We cannot be certain of the truth of such stories, but historical records do reveal that the portage had sixteen "poses," or rest stops, where a voyageur would pause with his load and smoke a pipe. The portage usually required a full day to cover.

From 1779 until 1803 the route through the border lakes from Grand Portage to Rainy Lake was one of the most important trade routes in the interior of North America. The first reasonably accurate maps were produced of the Boundary Waters around this time by David Thompson, an employee of the North West Company.

The fur trading business played itself out in these parts rather quickly, both as a result of diminishing animal populations and changing political realities. Notably, the American Revolutionary War brought much of northern Minnesota clearly in control of the U.S. government. British fur traders were not welcome, and by 1804 the North West Company had all but stopped using the Grand Portage, relocating north to Fort William on the Kaministiquia River in Canada to avoid U.S. customs charges. The area known as the Boundary Waters was relatively quiet for much of the next century up until the 1880s and 1890s. In 1858 Minnesota entered the union as the thirty-second state, at which time it gained ownership of the lake beds under all navigable waters.

In the 1970s the Minnesota Historical Society undertook an endeavor known as the Underwater Archaeology Project. Using careful archaeological techniques, crews found and documented fascinating remnants of the hundreds of years of activity along these routes. Much of the research occurred at Fort Charlotte, but a great deal was undertaken at other notable sites, some within the Boundary Waters. The divers discovered little organic matter, and the most substantial finds were early European artifacts from the fur trading era. Today the Grand Portage remains accessible, and an occasional sturdy modern voyageur still carries a canoe over the mud and rock trail. Rarely does anyone attempt to carry two, much less three, of the 90-pound bundles carried by their predecessors, but the memory lives on.

As the age of the voyageur ended, an interesting new chapter in history unfolded as the United States and England tried to map the exact boundary between the United States and Canada. Despite heavy commerce along the present-day border lakes in the 1700s, the exact location of the border had never been agreed on. Disputes concerning the border originated with the treaty that settled the Revolutionary War between the United States and Great Britain (which retained present-day Canada). At that time the heart of North America was still relatively unmapped, and diplomats were at a loss to find a precise geographic feature that could be used to establish the border. The few available maps of that period showed an elongate body of water known as "Long Lake" extending from Lake Superior toward Lake of the Woods. With little else to go on, diplomats chose to set the border as this "Long Lake" and its water communication to Lake of the Woods. The only problem with their choice is that no single identifiable "Long Lake" connects Lake Superior to Lake of the Woods, effectively leaving a great deal of uncertainty as to the proper border.

The United States and Great Britain argued at length over the location of "Long Lake" in the decades that followed the end of the Revolutionary War. The British suggested that it was the St. Louis River in Duluth, while the United States proposed the Kaministiquia waterway near Thunder Bay in present-day Canada. Either choice would have dramatically altered the border location by hundreds of miles. After much debate, the issue was resolved in 1842 when the Webster-Ashburton Treaty established the boundary as the historic route from the Pigeon River through the long chain of lakes that extends through Gunflint Lake and past Saganaga Lake, Knife Lake, Basswood Lake, Crooked Lake, and Lac La Croix on to Rainy Lake.

The Webster-Ashburton Treaty established the rough boundary, but it would take nearly eighty more years to precisely map and mark it. Most of this work took place in the early 1900s by the International Boundary Commission, whose survey crews carefully mapped the connecting waterways. These crews established the boundary as a series of straight lines, which are much easier to survey and calculate than curves.

Also, the border was established so that it generally runs through water and avoids intersecting islands. You can observe these facts by looking at your BWCAW maps, which show jagged straight lines, none of which split any islands.

The boundary was precisely marked by a total of 1,279 short bronze markers positioned along the border, numbered consecutively from west to east. These markers are still in place in their original locations and still get occasional maintenance by International Boundary Commission crews. Even-numbered markers are generally placed in the United States, odd-numbered markers in Canada. Each marker extends 7 inches aboveground and has a buried 10-inch-round shank. Three portages (Swamp/Monument, Height of Land, and Watap) have larger boundary monuments (numbered one to nine from west to east). These boundary markers are either 5-feet-tall bronze obelisks or short, conical bronze posts. When traveling the border lakes, keep your eyes open, and you are all but certain to see these interesting and historic markers. Pull over and view a few close up, and you will see interesting identifying marks and information.

Mining near the Boundary Waters

After the demise of much of the fur-trapping commerce in the late 1700s, the Boundary Waters generated relatively little interest for nearly a century. That changed with the Lake Vermilion gold rush of 1865–66, bringing thousands of miners to northeastern Minnesota. These miners found very little gold to satisfy their ambitions but did uncover the Vermilion Iron Range, one of the greatest iron ore deposits in the world. In the late 1880s and early 1890s iron mines opened at Soudan and Ely. The first iron was shipped out in 1884 on the Duluth and Iron Range Railroad from Tower to Two Harbors.

Most iron mining activities occurred well south of the present-day BWCAW, but iron ore was also discovered along Gunflint Lake as early as 1850 by a geological survey team. In 1886 iron deposits were found to the west of Gunflint Lake by Henry Mayhew, one of the most colorful and historically important figures along the Gunflint Trail. Mayhew was already well known in these parts for constructing a winter road to Rove Lake, where he operated a trading post and trapping business. Mayhew received assistance in creating a mining company from John Paulson and other industrialists, who named the venture the Paulson Mine.

The Gunflint Trail was little more than a rough wagon road that ended twenty miles away near Rove Lake at the time Mayhew discovered iron ore west of Gunflint Lake. Mayhew gradually succeeded in getting the road extended all the way to Gunflint Lake, often using government dollars for a road that had few uses other than his commercial endeavors. The road was extended as far as Paulson Mine in 1893, the same year basic mining activity came on line.

Mayhew also strongly advocated for construction of a rail line into the Paulson Mine site. Canadians were already building the Port Arthur, Duluth, and Western railroad (the PAD&W) toward North Lake, and the Paulson Mine investors convinced the PAD&W officials to extend the rails across the border into the mine site. The Paulson Mine investors did not need to twist too many arms, because the railroad was desperately looking for cargo of any sort, and the iron ore seemed like a solution to their problems.

Most of the PAD&W was built through Canadian forest, with the last few miles skirting the northern shore of North Lake and Gunflint Lake before crossing the international border at the narrows between Gunflint and Magnetic lakes, terminating at the Paulson Mine site five miles away. Plans called for the railroad to eventually head another twenty miles to Fraser Lake. This route was surveyed, although no tracks were ever laid. Indeed, connection all the way to Ely was contemplated but of course never completed.

The PAD&W was built to standards that would have allowed millions of tons of iron ore to be transported along its rails. A thousand-foot trestle bridge even extended along the shore of North Lake, a serious engineering feat at the time. In this regard the railway was much different from subsequent short-lived logging railroads built through the wilderness, some of which were built only for seasonal use.

Concurrent with the dreams of a huge find at the Paulson Mine, a flurry of development occurred all around Gunflint Lake. A number of small villages sprang up along the PAD&W Railroad, including a little village named Leeblain on the north-central Canadian shore of Gunflint Lake. Ambitiously named little Gunflint City arose on the American side in the vicinity of the Paulson Mine and Mine Lake. By 1893 Gunflint City was served by the PAD&W Railroad line extending all the way to Lake Superior (through Canada), by a rough Gunflint Trail to Grand Marais, a U.S. customs post, and (according to local historians) an infamous brothel.

Numerous test pits and two relatively shallow mine shafts were sunk at Paulson Mine, seeking both iron and nickel ore. Enthusiasm ran high, with visions of a mining center growing up in the forest. The mines in Ely were in similarly early stages, and locals easily imagined Gunflint City growing into a large border community. These dreams were dashed by an international economic panic in 1893 that dried up capital and created generally unfavorable economic conditions. Efforts to revive the mine in future years failed when the iron ore never proved sufficient in quantity or quality to commercially mine and transport. Almost as rapidly as the mining and railroad communities had sprung up, they shrank down to ghost towns and were then reclaimed by the forest.

All that remains today of the Paulson Mine are a few partially filled mine shafts just off the Kekekabic Trail, easily reachable from a small parking lot on the south side of the Gunflint Trail. My wife and I hiked through this area on our honeymoon and never found any of the mining equipment that is rumored to exist in these woods. Exploring this area is a sober reminder that even the best-formed, most ambitious, and enthusiastic plans often go awry. I tried not to dwell on that on our honeymoon hike. An alternative hike for honeymooners starts a few miles away on the Gunflint Trail and leads to Magnetic Rock, which provides a more comforting metaphor of timeless, unwavering attraction.

Logging in the Northern Forests

By the end of the nineteenth century, as dreams were fading at the Paulson Mine, another dramatic change had begun in the forests of the border lakes: logging for red pine and white pine. A wave of lumberjacks soon arrived and would have an impact that is still noticeable a century later in the Boundary Waters. Most of the rich pine forests of Michigan and Wisconsin had already been heavily logged, and demand for high-grade lumber brought logging companies and their thousands of employees to northern Minnesota, which still held tens of thousands of acres of fine pine forests.

Most of the logging activity was focused on areas outside of the current Boundary Waters, in part because much of the present-day BWCAW had been burnt by wildfires in the 1800s that destroyed or damaged large expanses of pine forest. However, the loggers did make major inroads into large areas of what is now the central and eastern BWCAW.

One of the first, and largest, logging operations within the current Boundary Waters was focused on the shores of Basswood Lake, which had plentiful lumber that could easily be floated across this huge lake to access points in its southern bays. In 1901 a four-mile logging railroad from Fall Lake into Hoist Bay of Basswood Lake was completed along what is now the Four Mile Portage. Swallow and Hopkins logging company would haul an astounding 350 million board feet of pine over this portage railroad during the next ten years. The railroad was used for another decade by the St. Croix Lumber Company and then stripped of its rails and abandoned. Logging had removed almost all red and white pine from the American shore of Basswood, although the Canadian side was still heavily forested.

Other logging operations were also undertaken within the present-day Boundary Waters, and a handful of small logging railroads were built to haul supplies in and logs out. One of the more interesting railroad systems was built and maintained from 1918 to 1929 by the General Logging Company, a subsidiary of Weyerhaeuser. General Logging Company extended an old Alger-Smith logging railroad throughout much of the Gunflint Trail region. Spurs were built to East Bearskin, Alder, Caribou, and Deer lakes. These tracks ran generally in a line cutting between Hungry Jack and Flour lakes, split into spurs reaching Clearwater Lake, and followed the north shore of Flour Lake to Moon, Deer, and Caribou lakes. The rails apparently never extended much past the western end of Caribou. Of course, they did not need to extend much farther because the frozen surface of Caribou would have provided easy winter access to areas significantly farther to the east.

Hiking along the Deer–Caribou portage and the western Caribou–Clearwater portage, you can observe large numbers of moss-covered stumps along the trail. These stumps are remnants of the great white pines that once reigned over the hills here. The loggers do not appear to have reached much to the east of these trails, because just a mile away on the north shore of Alder Lake are great stands of old white pine. These trees may have been spared for a number of reasons, including the discovery that much of the pine in this portion of the border country suffered from extensive heart rot from fires decades earlier, fires in the Brule lakes area in 1929 that decreased the logging companies' profits, and the Great Depression, which undercut lumber prices and demand, diminishing the attractiveness of the remaining red and white pines of northeastern Minnesota.

Saving the Boundary Waters

As the 1800s came to an end, awareness began to grow that the lake country of northern Minnesota was a special resource worthy of protection for its aesthetic value, as well as for its potential for wilderness recreation. One of the first public officials to speak out in favor of preserving some of the lake country was Minnesota's forestry commissioner Christopher Andrews. Andrews advocated that a half million acres of public land in northeastern Minnesota be withdrawn from public sale. This land contained virgin forest, but much of it had been partially or wholly burned by a series of fires in the late 1800s and thus had little value to loggers seeking large stands of unblemished lumber.

In 1905, septuagenarian Andrews canoed a long stretch of the international boundary from Basswood Lake to Crane Lake, heading through the very same island-studded lakes that had carried voyageurs two centuries earlier and carry modern canoeists today. The many magnificent tree-covered islands of Basswood Lake, Crooked Lake, and Lac La Croix awed Andrews, and upon returning from this journey, he persuaded the General Land Office to withhold another 141,000 acres of land along the Canadian border.

By the end of the decade the natural value of this area was gaining a national audience, and on February 13, 1909, President Theodore Roosevelt formed the million-acre Superior National Forest. A similar reserve was established north of the border as Quetico Provincial Forest and Game Reserve, and the state of Minnesota created the Superior Game Refuge, which covered most of the Superior National Forest, in an effort to save the declining moose and woodland caribou populations.

This national forest designation by Roosevelt formed the nucleus of the future BWCAW but was of only limited protective value because it did not significantly limit uses within the forest, and because it failed to extend all the way to the Canadian border. Also, the important border areas of Basswood Lake, Knife Lake, and Trout Lake were left outside of the new national forest.

A plan for how to use and benefit from the forest had yet to be established ten years after formation of the Superior National Forest. That job would first fall to Arthur H. Carhart, a landscape architect hired by the U.S. Forest Service. Conventional wisdom at the time was that the forest should be opened to the public with a series of major roads, but Carhart proposed a plan that would have relied on water transport along existing waterways. Carhart's proposal also included prohibitions against logging within 400 feet of lakeshores to preserve the aesthetic qualities of the countryside, and a series of lodges and cabins on interior lakes.

Carhart was hired by the Forest Service to help develop the recreational potential of the national forests. His efforts were in some regards a response to the popularity of the newly created National Park Service. Many areas under Forest Service control had been recommended for transfer to the National Park Service, and the Forest Service sought to minimize any losses in land to the Park Service.

Carhart's plan had two significant elements: first, no major additional roads would be constructed into the interior of the wilderness; second, a series of lodges and cabins would be constructed on key canoe routes to provide recreational opportunities for the thousands of visitors who were expected in the coming decades. The Carhart proposal has been praised as a bold step forward in wilderness management but also criticized as a mere aesthetic plan that was more concerned with appearances than ecosystem integrity, solitude, or conservation. It is probably only fair to judge it in the context of its times, in which case it is quite impressive.

The most important aspect of Carhart's proposal was what it excluded: roads. Carhart was in favor of major recreational development, but he opposed the use of roads within the wilderness to accomplish this goal. This anti-road view was in conflict with what was desired by most northern Minnesotans and indeed was in conflict with the desires of the Forest Service, which argued that roads were necessary to manage the forest and properly patrol the wilderness and control forest fires.

Carhart's proposal to use the lakes as an aquatic highway was not just romantic: he advocated a series of tows between the portages to move large numbers of people and supplies through the wilderness. A series of small, wilderness hotels would be established along the border from Lac La Croix to Saganaga Lake. Carhart saw these hotels both as an opportunity to widen the audience of visitors beyond the young and fit to include older individuals, and also as staging points for short trips into the surrounding wilderness by canoe. A series of fourteen chalets would also be constructed along the Kawishiwi and Isabella rivers east of Farm Lake. Carhart's plan was never adopted, although portions of his proposals did coincide with future preservation efforts, including restrictions on logging within 400 feet of lakeshores.

Just a few years after Carhart proposed a substantially roadless interior to the Superior National Forest, the Forest Service adopted essentially the opposite policy and created plans for major roads out of Ely, including one across the heart of the forest to connect with the Gunflint Trail at Sea Gull Lake, and westerly roads toward Echo Lake, Lac La Croix, and Trout Lake. Environmentalists rallied in opposition to the road proposals, leading the first sustained grassroots efforts to protect the border lakes as a wilderness area. After vigorous opposition, the trail program was dramatically scaled back in a compromise plan approved by Secretary of Agriculture W. M. Jardine. The comprise included construction of what is now the Echo Trail, along with expansions of the Fernberg Road to Snowbank Lake and expansion of the Gunflint Trail to Sea Gull Lake. However, the most damaging route, from the Fernberg Road to Sea Gull Lake was dropped. The compromise also abandoned plans for roads into Lac La Croix and Trout Lake.

Had these road proposals gone through in their entirety, the BWCAW as we know it would probably have been impossible to create. The road between Ely and Saganaga would have created a new route to the Canadian border and Lake Superior. Although the road would have started modestly, economic and political forces would have made it all but impossible to close, if for no other reason than a perceived safety need to have two routes in and out of the interior lakes.

In the 1920s and 1930s, just as the road question was being resolved, wealthy lumberman Edward W. Backus introduced a plan to create a series of dams along the border lakes from Rainy Lake to Saganaga. Backus proposed damming as many waterways as possible along the border. He hoped to bring economic prosperity to northern Minnesota and its residents (or at least himself) by increasing hydro-electricity for growing industry, while also helping log the idle trees sitting along the many unproductive lakes and rivers.

The result would have been astounding: Saganaga Lake, at Entry Point 55, would have risen 15 feet. Camp on any island in Saganaga, and imagine the water 15 feet higher. Crooked Lake, covered in Routes 23B and 24C, would have risen in depth by the same amount. Loon Lake in the western BWCAW would have been a full 30 feet deeper, making Route 12B a trip along a lake, not a river. Most astonishingly, Little Vermilion Lake at Entry Point 12 would have risen by 80 feet. The great border waterfalls of the western Boundary Waters, including Basswood Falls, Curtain Falls, Rebecca Falls, and Birch Falls, would have all vanished.

The overall result would have been to create massive reservoirs covering large areas of existing forest, enlarging the lakes and drowning many of the most popular campsites. It would also have merged numerous lakes. For example, Agnes Lake would have become a southern bay of Lac La Croix. The islands of southern Saganaga Lake would have been submerged, creating a large open bay. On Basswood Lake, United States Point would have been cut off from the mainland and would now simply be United States Island.

Landowners throughout northeastern Minnesota hotly contested the Backus plan. At the time Backus made his proposal, the actual border lakes were not a part of the Superior National Forest, and much of the land along the border was owned by the state of Minnesota and county governments, with some owned by private individuals. Backus and his opponents tried to rally supporters near and far, while also taking the struggle to the courts. The project was ultimately defeated with the Shipstead-Newton-Nolan Act of 1930, which prohibited logging within 400 feet of lakeshores, prohibited alteration of natural water levels with dams, and withdrew federal land from subsequent homesteading.

Significant credit for winning this battle goes to Ernest C. Oberholtzer, known by many as "Ober," and called by his Ojibwe friends "Atisokan," or "legend." Born in 1884 in Davenport, Iowa, Oberholtzer was ill most of his childhood, diagnosed with a terminal heart condition, and given just months to live. He persevered through illness and was eventually educated at Harvard. After graduation Oberholtzer ventured into northern Canada on an epic paddling journey that shaped much of his affection for the northern lakes and forests. Ober lived much of his life on Mallard Island in Rainy Lake, from where he fought the Backus plan.

Although the Backus plan was rejected, a number of smaller dams were constructed in the BWCAW prior to the Shipstead-Newton-Nolan Act, mostly during the big-pine logging around 1900 to raise water elevations for moving logs. Most of these dams were small, simple boulder or log dams that have either naturally deteriorated or been removed by the Forest Service at the urging of environmental organizations, including the Friends of the Boundary Waters Wilderness. For example, the two small dams at Little Gabbro Lake no longer maintain the elevations of Gabbro and Bald Eagle lakes.

One exception to the trend to remove dams or allow their natural deterioration has been the Prairie Portage dam connecting Sucker Lake with Basswood. This concrete dam, owned by the U.S. Department of Agriculture, controls the elevation of Moose, Newton, and Sucker lakes. Fall Lake, south of Basswood, is also controlled by a dam, this one outside the wilderness. The only other dam still regulating water levels in the BWCAW is at South Fowl Lake. The dam itself is outside the Boundary Waters on private land, although it raises water levels upstream in a small portion of the BWCAW.

In the 1930s the Forest Service began its first major expansions of the Superior National Forest since its original creation, acquiring cutover timberland and land that went into tax forfeiture during the tough Depression years. Areas along Basswood, Knife, and Trout lakes were all acquired during this time, but resources were insufficient for large-scale acquisition of other private holdings. In 1938 the Forest Service officially designated three sections of the Superior National Forest as Superior Roadless Primitive Areas, including the newly acquired land along the border. These roadless primitive areas correspond closely to the current BWCAW. Logging and motorboats were permitted throughout these roadless areas.

In 1942 the Lac La Croix Research Natural Area was formed, protecting large stands of red and white pine from the Boulder River and Boulder Bay into Lady Boot Bay of Lac La Croix. In 1980 the research natural area was declared a National Natural Landmark. This area, now within the BWCAW, remains important for researching northern forests.

During the early 1940s the nation was preoccupied with World War II, but as the war ended a robust economy demanded increased pulpwood and lumber. Logging had never stopped since the turn of the century. The end of large-scale commercial white and red pine logging had occurred decades earlier, but at the end of the 1940s the Forest Service began a series of timber sales of historic proportions. The most famous of these was the now infamous logging contract known as the Tomahawk Sale to Tomahawk Timber Company in 1945. Nearly 130 square miles of forest and lakes north of Lake Isabella were opened to logging, and a small logging town called Forest Center was established at the end of the road. Over the next two decades dozens of small roads would fan out from Forest Center. See "Entry from Highway 1 and the Tomahawk Road" for a description of this interesting town.

The Rise of Recreational Use

The convergence of rising affluence and improved transportation after World War II brought visitors to northern Minnesota seeking the splendor of a wilderness vacation. Up until World War II the impact of visitors had been somewhat tempered by the continuing difficulty of getting into and out of the border lakes. Ever greater numbers of visitors began to arrive by floatplane, and development of land within the Boundary Waters took on a feverish pitch. Although no roads were being constructed for public use (as opposed to logging roads, which were still being built through officially "roadless" areas), advances in private aviation made the entire Boundary Waters accessible by floatplane. Resorts sprang up all over the interior, even on lakes that had never been considered for possible road access.

Basswood Lake soon became a popular location for resort operations. In 1928 two small resorts had been built on Basswood, but by 1942 that number had grown to fourteen. A number of private homes were also located on the shores and islands of Basswood.

Alarmed by the steady development of interior lakes, the Izaak Walton League and a corps of environmentalists fought to roll back the new fly-in activities. Their efforts bore fruit on two critical fronts: first, Congress passed the Thye-Blatnik Act of 1948, which provided the most money to date for acquiring private holdings that "impair[ed] or threaten[ed] the unique qualities and natural features of the remaining wilderness canoe country." Ultimately nearly four dozen resorts and more than one hundred cabins were acquired using funds allocated by the Thye-Blatnik Act and subsequent appropriations. Second, in 1949, Harry Truman issued a presidential order prohibiting aircraft from flying below 4,000 feet above sea level over the roadless areas of the Superior National Forest.

The combination of the Thye-Blatnik Act and President Truman's airspace reservation was critical to preserving the long-range wilderness qualities of the Boundary Waters. In the near term, Truman's actions dramatically reduced the amount of mechanized intrusions into the wilderness and would make expansion of existing resorts and homes far less attractive. In the long term, the Thye-Blatnik Act allowed the Forest Service to meaningfully reduce the amount of private land within the roadless areas. As long as these landholdings existed within the wilderness there would be a constant pressure for development.

As required by the U.S. Constitution, landowners were provided compensation for all land acquired under the Thye-Blatnik Act. Paradoxically, and arguably unjustly, the government is said to have asserted that Truman's airspace reservation diminished the value of land holdings because the holdings were no longer accessible. Place yourself in the circumstances of these landowners, and it is certainly easy to appreciate why they felt they were getting a raw deal. How, they must have asked, could the government take actions to diminish their property values and then use its condemnation power to acquire this property at lower prices? Whether anyone actually was paid below market prices is not clear.

A number of resorts bitterly fought Truman's airspace reservation, and a few undertook acts of civil disobedience. Two resort owners even built an unauthorized road from the Echo Trail to Crooked Lake on the Canadian border. This primitive road followed partly along an old railroad grade but then extended past the old railroad beds along a trail carved out using heavy equipment. In 1956 a federal court of appeals ruled that these resort owners had no fundamental right to reach their holdings by anything other than traditional methods of boat, canoe, and portage. With this ruling came the bitter end to the fly-in lodge business inside the Superior Roadless Area.

One of the best-known and most appreciated resort owners was the legendary Dorothy Molter of Knife Lake. Dorothy and the Forest Service spent the better part of three decades arguing over if, and when, she would move from her home and small resort on the Isle of Pines. Ultimately they struck a compromise in 1975 that allowed Dorothy to continue the rest of her life on the Isle of Pines for a cash settlement and agreement not to maintain her resort business. Instead, Dorothy supported herself by an enterprise that provided canoeists with homemade root beer. Dorothy did not charge for her root beer, but donations were certainly encouraged! In a typical summer she would use hundreds of pounds of sugar for the famous brew given to a steady stream of visitors.

Dorothy's legend grew over the final two decades of her life, and today her memory is cherished by the thousands of visitors fortunate enough to have sipped a root beer at her isolated outpost. To learn more about Dorothy, stop by her relocated cabins at the Dorothy Molter Museum on the east end of Ely. Also, you will paddle past her legendary Isle of Pines on various routes out of Moose Lake. Her cabins and personal property are long gone, but the memories and a few holdover garden perennials remain. The island took a hit in the 1999 windstorm but remains beautiful.

Other changes were underway at the same time that the Forest Service was initiating land purchases in northeastern Minnesota. In 1958 the Forest Service formally named the roadless areas the Boundary Waters Canoe Area (BWCA), a move that was criticized at the time as merely whitewashing the fact that this was no longer a roadless area, because logging roads were penetrating deep into the wilderness, particularly near Lake Isabella from the Tomahawk Sale.

By this time the Boundary Waters had been subject to decades of hard-fought battles over its future, and a cadre of defenders had risen to protect the wilderness from a world hungry for it. Dams had been stopped, roads resisted, and airplanes banned. But big fights were still to come, particularly over the use of motorized craft, including boats and snowmobiles, within the wilderness.

The 1950s and early 1960s saw an explosion in the number of motorboats and snowmobiles entering the Boundary Waters, in particular smaller boats that could be carried or pulled over portages into large lakes such as Trout and Basswood. Again the battle lines were drawn, this time first culminating in the National Wilderness Act of 1964. The Wilderness Act explicitly included the Boundary Waters and offered it at least nominal protections, but the law was ambiguously crafted and appeared to preserve the right to operate motorboats, a use that was abhorred by those seeking to preserve the canoe country as an oasis of silence and simplicity.

One of the most influential leaders of the effort to preserve the Boundary Waters, and certainly its most loved author, was Sigurd Olson. Born and raised in rural Wisconsin, Olson became a voice for the wilderness in the decades after he moved to Ely as a young man in the 1920s. His writings in the 1950s, 1960s, and 1970s were important well-received efforts to share the essence of this wonderful wilderness. Two of his most famous works are the *Singing Wilderness* and *Listening Point,* both of which captured the magnificent natural rhythms and made them accessible to a public increasingly waking up to the loss of wild places and the hazards of modern, industrialized life. These books should be mandatory reading for anyone making a journey into the wilderness. The canoe country of the Boundary Waters has perhaps never had a stronger voice than that of Olson. He, along with a band of peers, was among its most outspoken advocates.

As for the Boundary Waters, the only thing the Wilderness Act of 1964 settled is that nothing had been settled. The decade after passage of the Wilderness Act was one of pitched battles on many fronts between the numerous parties attached to the Boundary Waters. Finding loopholes in the myriad laws and regulations governing the wilderness proved to be a passion for all sides. For example, resorts often found it beneficial to keep motors and boats on both sides of long portages. After all, no one wants to portage a 100-pound Evinrude outboard motor every time they go fishing on the neighboring lake. The Forest Service responded by banning the caching of boats on federal land. Clever boat owners soon responded by mooring their boats in lakes a few feet off shore, which were under the jurisdiction of the state of Minnesota, or on some of the plentiful state-owned land near many of the portages. Minnesota authorities soon closed this loophole, using their jurisdiction over the lake surfaces and their state land to further prohibit caching of boats. As a side note, today it is still illegal to cache gear in the BWCAW for future trips. There appears to be no such restriction enforced on Superior National Forest lands outside of the BWCAW. This is evident, for example, at the Wood Lake entry point, where a few aluminum canoes and boats are often stashed just outside the BWCAW boundary, ready for that next trip.

After 1964, conservationists wanting absolutely minimal human impact on the wilderness fought businesses interested in opening the Boundary Waters to recreational development and natural resource harvesting, as well as local residents who did not want limits on exploration of their "backyards." Many of these battle lines were perceived as being drawn between local interests seeking development and outside interests seeking conservation. However, this distinction was never completely accurate, because numerous local residents also favored restrictions on development and were active in the efforts to protect the wilderness.

The next major legislation to involve the Boundary Waters came in 1978 with passage of the BWCA Wilderness Act, which eliminated logging and restricted mining within the BWCAW. The act prohibited snowmobiling with the exception of a corridor into Canada from Saganaga, and motorboats were allowed on only one-fourth of the BWCAW water surface area.

One of the most ardent activists supporting the 1978 legislation was Miron "Bud" Heinselman, a longtime Forest Service ecologist. Heinselman was already well known for his thorough research into the fire history of the border lakes region. During his career he constructed detailed maps of the fire history of this area, some of it extending back to 1595. In 1974 he took an early retirement from his job with the Forest Service to work full-time to save the wilderness. Heinselman was instrumental in forming the Friends of the Boundary Waters Wilderness and served as the first chair of the group when it was formed in 1976. Heinselman is regarded by many of his contemporary conservationists as the "linchpin" in the efforts leading to passage of the 1978 act.

Opponents challenged the BWCA Wilderness Act from 1979 to 1989 in federal court, but the Eighth Circuit Court of Appeals ultimately upheld it. In 1986 the Forest Service produced the "Superior National Forest Land and Resource Management Plan," which led to further litigation culminating in a settlement that produced the "1993 BWCAW Management Plan and Implementation Schedule." The 1993 plan is a crystallization of key legislation and earlier agreements. The plan was written in standard regulatory prose and is no threat to Sigurd Olson's *Singing Wilderness*, although copies are free. Nevertheless, there is plenty of interest in this document.

You cannot miss the big issues addressed by the 1993 plan. The BWCAW is managed as four distinct areas depending on primitiveness, ranging from pristine areas free of portages and developed campsites (the "primitive management areas" described later in this guide) to semiprimitive motorized areas along the BWCAW's edge. The plan also covers fire management, acceptable transportation systems, visitor quotas, and regulation of outfitters and guides.

The plan includes numerous management details, many of which are rather obvious. For example, you will not be allowed to build cabins and/or dig mines on your next visit. Do not even ask about building dams—the Forest Service is quite content with the two the government owns on Basswood Lake and Fall Lake.

Other details are less obvious. Portage paths between motorized lakes shall have a 3-foot-wide path, while portage paths between nonmotorized lakes shall be kept to just 18 inches. Only native fish can be stocked in BWCAW waters. However, non-native fish can be restocked if they were previously stocked before 1964. I call this the "smallmouth bass" provision. Smallmouths are non-native species introduced by Sigurd Olson and others in the 1930s, although the provision also applies to brook trout populations in some lakes. Finally, you are not allowed to bring food and beverage cans into the BWCAW *unless* you are traveling through Saganaga Lake on your way to a residence in Canada. Even then, common sense warrants that you keep those beer bottles out of sight to prevent thirsty fishermen from boarding your craft.

One persistent issue was whether motorboats could be pulled by trucks and trailers along a number of "truck portages." Controversy continued through the 1990s, with disputes over the motorized truck portages warming from simmer to boil, and culminating in a rider to a federal transportation bill that kept the truck portages in operation on Trout Lake and at the Prairie Portage (leading to Basswood Lake). That same year the first user fees were collected, with revenue going to maintenance and management of the BWCAW.

A Changing Forest

As you paddle the waters of the Boundary Waters, it is worth pondering what we will find here in ten years, fifty years, and one hundred years. The struggles of all those who fought for this wilderness, from Andrews to Oberholtzer to Olson, have allowed a wonderful legacy to be passed on for today's visitors.

The blowdown of July 4, 1999, came just as a century of human intrusions and preservationist efforts was closing, and led to another round of discussions about the best response by federal and local authorities. Opinions ranged from letting nature run its course by doing nothing to logging within the wilderness to remove the downed trees. Ultimately the decision was made to make extensive prescribed burns in large portions of the Superior National Forest, including thousands of acres within the BWCAW.

Change has long been the norm in the Boundary Waters. In the past one hundred years the Boundary Waters has gone from a remote northern forest to the most popular wilderness area in the United States. Legendary struggles over logging, road building, and motorized boats have been fought, and fought again. If history tells us anything, it is that the Boundary Waters is a sacred retreat for thousands upon thousands of people, but those people do not agree on how this area should be enjoyed and protected.

The BWCAW is now involved in a number of pressing new issues. Mercury contamination is a real and significant problem for most of the BWCAW lakes. Most of this mercury is from airborne sources, so any solution must go far beyond the border. Lead contamination from fishing gear is probably a smaller threat, but one that each of us can address each time we enter by bringing lead-free tackle. Invasive species (besides humans) are now of great concern. These include armored crawfish, invasive water plants, and topsoil-destroying earthworms. The Forest Service is even struggling with the fact that some of the boardwalks and small bridges in the BWCAW were constructed with preserved lumber that may be a new, albeit modest, environmental concern. Acid rain, also generated outside of the BWCAW, is another issue for these hard-bottomed lakes, which cannot effectively buffer the incoming acids.

Perhaps most importantly, global warming may do more to alter the forests and lakes than anything in the past one hundred years. Will lake trout populations fall as water temperatures rise? Will the lynx that have recently returned soon be forced north again, this time by a loss of cold-weather habitat? Will invasive insects take advantage of longer growing seasons to disrupt the natural equilibrium in the forests, as they are believed to have done in Alaska? Will precipitation changes bring long droughts and lower water levels?

The next chapters in the human history of the BWCAW are now being written by each of us who visits this wilderness and cares about it, both by what we do to protect and care for it as well as by what we fail to do. Hopefully that history will be one for which future visitors are thankful.

PLANNING YOUR TRIP

T he Boundary Waters Canoe Area Wilderness (BWCAW) is a nearly 1.3-million-acre portion of the Superior National Forest managed by the U.S. Forest Service as a wilderness area. It includes more than 1,000 lakes and steams, more than 1,500 miles of canoe routes, and almost 2,200 designated canoe campsites.

The BWCAW offers unmatched opportunities to escape hectic modern life and paddle the silent waters of an incomparable wilderness canoe area. You can journey deep into secluded lakes over ancient portage trails that see more moose traffic than human. Alternatively, you can have a simple trip to the edge of the Boundary Waters, foregoing portaging while you enjoy a few luxuries, such as camp chairs or a cooler. This guidebook is appropriate for visitors planning trips at both ends of this spectrum, as well as for the many people planning trips somewhere in between.

You will have much to do when planning your trip, especially if you are making your first visit to the Boundary Waters. Essential tasks include selecting an entry point, learning about the rules and regulations, choosing a time to visit, outfitting yourself with gear, and planning your route.

Entry Points, Permits, and Quotas

The first thing to know about visiting the Boundary Waters is that *you must always have a permit to enter,* even if just for an afternoon of paddling. If you enter from May 1 through September 30 for an overnight trip, you are required to have a Forest Service–issued permit, typically one reserved months in advance. The availability of these overnight permits is limited by a quota system controlling exactly where and when you may enter the Boundary Waters. The quota system was implemented in an effort to preserve the wilderness qualities of the Boundary Waters and has undergone various changes over the years.

If you are entering before May 1 or after September 30, you do not need an advance permit issued by the Forest Service but instead can issue your own permit at each entry to the wilderness. Similarly, from May 1 to September 30, if you are on a day trip that does not involve overnight camping or a motor, you can issue your own permit when you enter the wilderness. If you will have a motor from May 1 to September 30, you must have a Forest Service–issued permit, even for day trips.

The Forest Service has established fifty-six water access entry points for canoeists and has set a precise quota for the number of groups that may use each entry point per day. The primary factor determining the quota of available permits is the ability of lakes near an entry point to accommodate travelers. Numerous permits are available for big lakes with many campsites, such as Trout Lake or Saganaga Lake. Fewer permits are available for small lakes or streams with only a couple of campsites nearby, such as Larch Creek.

Map 1 shows all of the canoeing entry points to the BWCAW and the number of permits available per day. The entry points appear to have been numbered in random order, but using this map you can get a general idea of entry locations. Entry points that are designed for hikers are not shown on this map.

Most entry points and permits allow free travel anywhere within the Boundary Waters, but six entries have special permits that limit where you are allowed to camp. These six entry points (Little Vermilion Lake, Entry Point 12; Mudro Lake, Entry

- -

BWCAW Permit Requirements

Type of Trip	Entering May 1 to September 30	Entering October 1 to April 30
Overnight paddle	Quota permit, picked up at Forest Service ranger station or permit issuing station, typically reserved in advance	Self-issuing permit obtained by visitor at entry point kiosk
Overnight motor	Quota permit, picked up at Forest Service ranger station or permit issuing station, typically reserved in advance	Self-issuing permit obtained by visitor at entry point kiosk
Day-use paddle	Self-issuing permit obtained by visitor at entry point kiosk	Self-issuing permit obtained by visitor at entry point kiosk
Day-use motor	Quota permit, picked up at Forest Service ranger station or permit issuing station, typically reserved in advance	Self-issuing permit obtained by visitor at entry point kiosk

Point 22/23; Snowbank Lake, Entry Point 27; Brule Lake, Entry Point 41; Sea Gull Lake, Entry Point 54; and Saganaga Lake, Entry Point 55) have two types of permits with different travel rules controlling the geographic areas that may be visited. The specific restrictions for each of these entries are described later in this guide under the introduction to each entry. In general you should get an unrestricted permit for these lakes, if available.

Forest Service regulations allow a maximum of nine people and four watercraft per permit. At no time may a group in the Boundary Waters ever exceed nine people. Thus, it is illegal to get two permits so that eighteen people can camp together, or even ten people. In past years large groups have pooled together under a number of permits and camped near each other on the same lake. For example, six people might camp on one site, six people on another, and then they would meet up during the day to travel and cook. This is now illegal. To avoid excess resource degradation, you must observe the nine-person limit at all times in the wilderness, not just upon entering. Similarly, everyone entering the wilderness on the same permit must camp at the same site.

If your group approaches a portage landing and observes another group on it, you must wait until the other group departs if your combined group would have more than nine people. Although that sounds overly strict, the rule exists because large groups make big impacts: eighteen people crowding a landing are likely to spread their gear and canoes into the surrounding woods as they unload, thus damaging the forest in those areas. In contrast, two sequential groups of nine people can occupy half as much area and make less of an impact. Take a look around portages on busy routes, and you will notice how years of use by large groups have expanded the impact zones. Attention to this rule will allow regeneration of vegetation in these disturbed areas, as well as at overused campsites.

Your permit may be picked up 24 hours prior to the day you will be starting your trip and must be picked up in person. You will pick it up either at the nearest Forest Service district ranger station or at a private cooperator authorized by the Forest Service to issue permits. Dozens of outfitters and lodges offer this service. At the time you reserve your permit, you will select where you wish to pick it up. If you plan to use an outfitter or guide, you will probably want to pick up the permit at their location and may even ask them to reserve your permit. If you will be traveling without help from an outfitter, or don't know which outfitter you will be using, then you are probably best served by requesting to pick up the permit at the nearest ranger station.

At the time of reserving your permit you will have to identify your group leader as well as one or more alternate leaders if appropriate. Personal identification of the group leader or an alternate is required to pick up your permit, a rule implemented to prevent people from reserving blocks of permits and then giving (or selling) them to others. To avoid problems, list a couple of alternate leaders so that you don't lose your reservation if the primary leader has to cancel.

A copy of the permit or other form of identification will be issued for each watercraft in the party, and this allows members of a party to enter at different times on

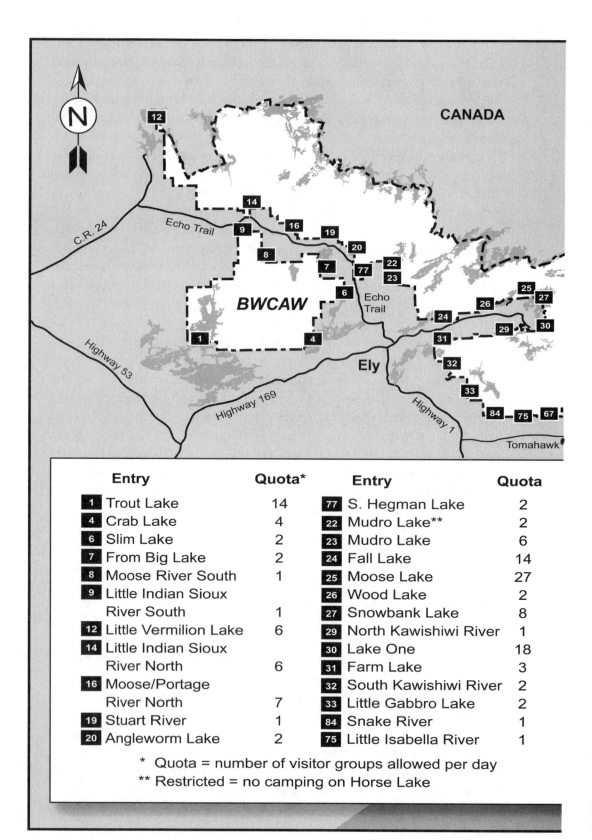

Entry	Quota*	Entry	Quota
1 Trout Lake	14	77 S. Hegman Lake	2
4 Crab Lake	4	22 Mudro Lake**	2
6 Slim Lake	2	23 Mudro Lake	6
7 From Big Lake	2	24 Fall Lake	14
8 Moose River South	1	25 Moose Lake	27
9 Little Indian Sioux River South	1	26 Wood Lake	2
12 Little Vermilion Lake	6	27 Snowbank Lake	8
14 Little Indian Sioux River North	6	29 North Kawishiwi River	1
16 Moose/Portage River North	7	30 Lake One	18
19 Stuart River	1	31 Farm Lake	3
20 Angleworm Lake	2	32 South Kawishiwi River	2
		33 Little Gabbro Lake	2
		84 Snake River	1
		75 Little Isabella River	1

* Quota = number of visitor groups allowed per day
** Restricted = no camping on Horse Lake

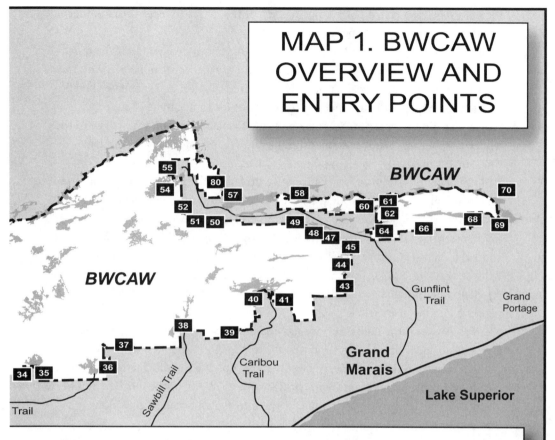

MAP 1. BWCAW OVERVIEW AND ENTRY POINTS

Entry		Quota	Entry		Quota
67	Bog Lake	2	50	Cross Bay Lake	3
34	Island River	3	51	Missing Link Lake	5
35	Isabella Lake	3	52	Brant Lake	4
36	Hog Creek	5	54	Sea Gull Lake	11
37	Kawishiwi Lake	9	55	Saganaga Lake	17
38	Sawbill Lake	14	80	Larch Creek	1
39	Baker Lake	3	57	Magnetic Lake	3
40	Homer Lake	2	58	South Lake	3
41	Brule Lake	7	60	Duncan Lake	4
43	Bower Trout Lake	1	61	Daniels Lake	1
44	Ram Lake	1	62	Clearwater Lake	4
45	Morgan Lake	1	64	East Bearskin Lake	5
47	Lizz and Swamp Lakes	4	66	Crocodile Lake	1
48	Meeds Lake	3	68	Pine Lake	1
49	Skipper and Portage Lakes	2	69	John Lake	1
			70	North Fowl Lake	2

the *same* day. However, a party entering on a different day to meet with another party must have a separate permit.

Reserve your permit well in advance of your visit to give yourself the most choices for the entry point and date you desire. Reservations can be made on the Internet, by phone, or by mail. You will be required to select an exact date and entry location for your permit, and neither the date nor location can be changed without reserving a different permit. You may be asked to state how long you will be in the wilderness, but this number is not binding, and you can stay longer than whatever time you estimate.

Internet and telephone reservations are preferred because they give you real-time confirmation of availability. Internet reservations are made at the Web site www.BWCAW.org, and telephone reservations are made by calling toll-free 877-550-6777. International reservations can be made by calling 518-885-9964. The mailing address for a reservation application is BWCAW Reservation Center, P.O. Box 462, Ballston Spa, NY 12020. This mailing address reflects the current reservation service provider and may change in coming years, which is one more reason to reserve your permit by phone or Internet.

In recent years the Forest Service has conducted a lottery each January to allow everyone an equal chance to get entry points that are in the greatest demand. Lottery rules change from time to time, so be sure to get up-to-date information from the BWCAW Permit Reservation Center at www.BWCAW.org or the toll-free number given above. Currently, applications for the lottery can be submitted as early as November.

Reservations for available entries and dates can be made after the lottery drawing, normally in the second half of January. All permits after the lottery are reserved on a first-come basis. Most entry points will still have good availability throughout the winter, but favorites such as Moose Lake and Lake One can fill up early, as can popular weekend dates around the fishing opener in May and during peak travel in July and August.

The cost for reserving a permit was $12 at the time this book was published. The Forest Service also charges a user fee to generate revenue to help preserve the Boundary Waters and provide visitor services, such as portage maintenance. This fee is $10 per adult per trip. Youth under the age of eighteen and Golden Passport and Golden Access cardholders are charged $5 per trip. You can buy a single-person season pass for one person for $40 that allows an unlimited number of visits during the year ($20 per season for youth and Golden Passport/Access cardholders). Season pass owners must still obtain a permit for each visit, and the permit reservation charge still applies.

What should you do if you have waited too long to get a permit for any entry points on the day you intend to visit? You can change your date of arrival, hoping to have more luck with availability. Generally Monday through Thursdays have the most availability. Also, you can consider a canoe trip outside of the Boundary Waters but still within the Superior National Forest. Go to the Superior National Forest

Web site at www.superiornationalforest.org for more information on these non-BWCAW trips.

This book is focused on visitors who will be exploring the BWCAW, which is a unit within the Superior National Forest. However, you may also wish to plan a trip into Quetico Provincial Park in Canada, north of the BWCAW. You must get a separate permit for entering the Quetico, available up to five months before your departure date. In addition, you will generally need a Remote Area Border Crossing (RABC) authorization, which is essentially a way to clear customs by mail before you enter the wilderness. You should apply for your RABC at least six weeks before your expected departure date. More information on the Quetico can be obtained from the Ontario government at www.Ontarioparks.com. Without an RABC authorization you are not allowed to camp on any Canadian territory on a Boundary Waters trip. Thus, even on border lakes you may not sleep on the Canadian side and may not fish on the Canadian side without an appropriate Ontario fishing license.

Accommodations before Entering the Boundary Waters

As stated above, your permit to enter the Boundary Waters identifies a single day on which you may enter the wilderness. You can pick up your permit the day before you will be entering the Boundary Waters, in which case you will need accommodations for a night. You are *not* allowed to camp at parking lots near entries. Numerous outfitters, lodges, and hotels on the edge of the wilderness cater to visitors entering the Boundary Waters. Ely and Grand Marais both have good hotels, and many outfitters and lodges have comfortable, inexpensive accommodations, often allowing your party to share a large "bunkhouse" room with multiple beds for a reasonable rate. See the list of outfitters and lodges later in this guide for local tourism organizations that provide directories of accommodations, or go to www.BoundaryWatersGuide .com for additional information. In addition, the Forest Service operates numerous campgrounds throughout Superior National Forest. A complete list of campgrounds is provided later in this guide.

Selecting Maps and Navigating through the Boundary Waters

With thousands of lakes, ponds, marshes, islands, bays, and points, the Boundary Waters is a complicated place to navigate a canoe. Early voyageurs chopped off the lower branches of prominent trees, creating "lob trees" that guided their trips. You won't make a lot of friends if you create your own set of lob trees, so be prepared with a good set of maps. *The maps shown throughout this book are not sufficient to navigate in the Boundary Waters and are provided only for trip planning. It is essential that you purchase a set of high-resolution maps for the areas you plan to visit.*

W. A. Fisher Company, McKenzie Maps, and Voyageur Maps are three companies that produce Boundary Waters maps showing locations of campsites and portages in addition to all navigable lakes and streams and surrounding topography. Bring at least two copies of each map for the route you will be covering; that way you will still be able to navigate if you lose one set of maps. Better yet, bring one complete set of maps for each canoe, which maximizes safety if your canoes are separated from one another and also increases the pleasure of traveling through the wilderness.

The choice between Fisher, McKenzie, and Voyageur maps is often an issue of personal preference. All three sets of maps are printed on waterproof paper, an essential improvement over traditional paper maps printed by the U.S. Geological Survey, which are not recommended for canoe travel. Maps from all three companies contain similar topographic information. In addition, all three companies have worked with the Forest Service to confirm the accuracy of their maps, although each set of maps has its own unique errors.

You will find that the portage distances are not the same on all portages on all of these maps, because each company independently measured the portages, and also because portage distances sometimes change over time as trails are moved or water levels shift. Voyageur maps were produced concurrently with the production of this guide, and therefore all portage distances in this book are the same as will be found on Voyageur maps. If you are using maps other than Voyageur maps, you will notice differences in portage distances from those described in this guide. In most cases the distance measurements are similar enough that that you will be able to correctly identify routes.

If you plan on fishing, you may prefer either the McKenzie or Voyageur maps, which show lake depths on significantly more lakes than the Fisher maps. Voyageur maps also show the results of fish surveys from the Minnesota Department of Natural Resources (DNR) and indicate which fish inhabit each lake—useful data if you intend to fish on your trip. McKenzie maps are laid out at 2 inches per mile, while Fisher and Voyageur maps are laid out at 1.5 inches per mile. Although the scale is different, topographic resolution is identical.

Voyageur maps also indicate the locations of various "historic" portages that are no longer maintained, the location of additional historic points of interest, including old railroads and logging camps, and the boundaries of Primitive Management Areas. Naturalists will enjoy all three sets of maps, although Voyageur maps also give basic information about geology, forest fire history, and prescribed burn locations from the 1999 windstorm (useful for gauging forest regeneration).

As is always the case, these maps are occasionally revised and reissued, and it may serve you well to visit the company Web sites to determine which maps best suit your interests and trips you will be taking: www.FisherMapsMN.com; www.McKenzieMaps.com; and www.VoyageurMaps.com.

In addition to good maps, you should always bring along a compass, which can be helpful for navigation through islands and on days when the sun is not shining. You may be tempted to bring along a GPS unit, and new models with built-in maps are useful. However, even if you have a GPS unit, you must bring along maps. GPS units can get lost, break, or run out of batteries. Also, existing GPS units fail to show the level of detail on quality paper maps and also do not show the specific information about campsites and portages on traditional maps.

Leave No Trace

In recent years the Superior National Forest has been a strong advocate of the "leave-no-trace" wilderness ethic. The leave-no-trace ethic involves seven criteria designed to minimize impacts on the wilderness and other visitors. These criteria, as applied to the BWCAW, include adequate planning of your trip, camping at designated campsites, proper disposal of all waste, minimizing campfire impacts, respecting wildlife, being considerate to other visitors, and leaving what you find. You will find these principles advocated in the various recommendations provided in this guide, and in Forest Service rules and recommendations. For more information on leave-no-trace camping, visit www.LNT.org.

Making Camp

Canoeists may camp only at designated sites identified by a cast-iron fire grate and a pit latrine unless expressly authorized on their permit by the Forest Service to camp elsewhere. The Boundary Waters is a wilderness area with minimal human-made structures, so campsites do not have any other *improvements,* such as bear-proof boxes, wells, picnic tables, and so on. From time to time the Forest Service closes campsites if they show signs of excessive damage or if visitor encounter levels exceed established standards. Make sure you have current maps reflecting any changes in campsites.

You can stay as long as you would like in the BWCAW unless you are damaging resources or breaking any rules and regulations, but may not stay more than fourteen days at any one campsite. Storage of boats or equipment is not allowed, except for those items used in conjunction with a current visit. I have encountered Forest Service personnel searching for renegade gear on a number of occasions at the end of long portages, where regular visitors sometimes stash old canoes to avoid portaging them into the wilderness on each trip. Such gear is seized by law enforcement agencies, the owners are fined if they can be tracked down, and the gear is often eventually sold at auction.

As mentioned above, every designated campsite has a latrine. Old-timers will remember when most of these latrines were wooden boxes that made perfect microhabitats for wasps. The wood made good nest-building material, while other insects that were attracted to the habitat made good prey for the wasps. Fortunately, these old latrines have been replaced by better designed, more durable plastic units that do not have the same problems.

What should you do if you are out on a portage or away from camp and need to use a bathroom? The Forest Service recommends that you dig a small hole 6 to

8 inches deep at least 150 feet back from the water's edge. When finished, fill the hole and cover with needles and leaves. You can bring along a cheap, lightweight plastic trowel for these emergencies.

Campfires

Unless fire restrictions are in place, campfires are allowed within the Boundary Waters at cast-iron fire grates at designated campsites or as specifically approved by your permit. The Forest Service recommends that you bring a small camp stove because they are quicker, cleaner, and lower impact than cooking over a fire. Also, stoves come in handy during rainy weather and may be essential if fire restrictions are in effect.

In recent years fire restrictions have often been in place for all or part of the BWCAW, especially the eastern half of the Boundary Waters that was most heavily hit by a major windstorm in 1999. These restrictions are for your safety and to reduce the threat of large, dangerous wildfires. You should check on fire restrictions before entering the wilderness. Your permit issuer should tell you of any restrictions, but ask if you are not told. Also, you can contact any Superior National Forest district office, forest headquarters at 218-626-4300, or the Superior National Forest Web site at www.fs.fed.us/r9/superior.

If you build a fire, you may only burn dead wood found lying on the ground. Do not burn trash, and collect all firewood away from campsites. It is recommended that you paddle down the shore and walk into the woods, where you will find wood more abundant. Never collect wood from beaver dams or beaver lodges, and do not peel bark off birch trees for fire starters because you will kill the tree. You may not cut live vegetation for any reason.

When you are done with your fire, drown it with water until all embers, rocks, and sticks are wet. Stir the remains, then add more water until the fire is extinguished and cool to the touch. Do not bury coals, as they can smolder for days and then break into flames long after you have left. Be sure your campfire is completely extinguished before you leave your site, even for a short time!

Law enforcement agencies are very serious about enforcing fire regulations, especially after the 1999 windstorm created so much fuel. In 2002 an individual was sentenced to serve four months in the custody of the Federal Bureau of Prisons for his role in the 41-acre Katherine Lake fire (outside the BWCAW), caused when he left a fire without completely extinguishing it. Fireworks of all kinds are strictly prohibited, even if they are a kind legal in the rest of Minnesota.

Drinking Water

The Boundary Waters contains thousands of crystal clear lakes, but do not assume water from these lakes is safe to drink without either bringing it to a boil or properly filtering it to remove giardia. Some research indicates that giardia may be killed at temperatures below boiling, and that the cysts settle out in deep water. However, the greatest assurance of safety is obtained by momentarily reaching boiling or by filtering. Many travelers disregard warnings without ill effect for years, but to do so is to play a dangerous game of roulette. Anyone who has suffered from giardia's painful cramps and intestinal distress can attest to the wisdom of treating your water supply.

Cooking, Cleaning, and Garbage

Everything that you carry into the BWCAW must be carried out unless it is consumed during your stay. No one wants to come across a campsite with cigarette butts or aluminum foil in the fire pit. It is BWCAW custom to haul out any garbage you find in the wilderness. In this way the few slackers who fail to do their part do not cause a lingering eyesore. In addition, you should keep your campsite clean to avoid bear problems. Nothing will bring the bears in better than a buffet of food scraps. Place your food out of reach between meals, and clean everything carefully when you are done eating.

Cans and bottles are not allowed in the BWCAW, except containers of fuel, insect repellent, medicines, and personal toilet articles. Other items that are not foods or beverages are allowed in cans and bottles. Disposable plastic containers are permitted but must be packed out. Garbage should never be thrown in latrines. Extra food should always be packed out, as should cigarettes, cotton swabs, and plastic feminine products.

One of the greatest hazards to the clean, low-nutrient waters of the Boundary Waters is pollution from dish soap and shampoo. These lakes cannot absorb the fertilizing properties of soaps (including biodegradable soaps) without degrading water clarity. Therefore, do all of your cleaning as far from shore as possible. I prefer to wash my dishes at camp in a pan, keeping all of the soap contained, which can then be spread back in the woods far from shore.

Similarly, you should never use soap and water to clean yourself in a Boundary Waters lake. I use a bucket of water (sometimes warmed on my stove) to lather up and rinse away from the shore. Alternatively, some Boundary Waters guides recommend going for a swim and then lathering up on shore and forming a bucket brigade with your fellow travelers to get rinsed off away from the water's edge.

Safety, Cell Phones, and Communications

You should enter the Boundary Waters Canoe Area Wilderness prepared for all reasonable contingencies. In much of the Boundary Waters it is possible to go days without seeing another party, so be prepared to take care of yourself if problems arise. Bring along quality gear and have it packed properly, take along enough food for your trip plus a couple days of emergency rations, and always travel with a good first aid kit. If you are not certain about your equipment or skills, select a conservative route or work with an outfitter to make sure you are ready for a trip.

One question you may have is whether your cell phone will work in the Boundary Waters. The short answer is maybe. Cell phones work in parts of the Boundary Waters, but coverage is spotty and unpredictable. As of 2004, the best reception is on lakes nearest Ely. The Gunflint Trail lakes generally do not have cell phone reception, although that may change in coming years. Phones are most likely to work when the sun is down or setting, especially from open areas along shore or on rocky hills. Your battery will probably drain much more quickly in the wilderness than in developed areas because signals are weaker, so you probably do not want to leave your phone in standby mode for extended periods of time.

Even the thought of bringing a cell phone into the Boundary Waters raises impassioned objections from many diehard visitors, who view them as improper concessions to modern life. Why get away from it all if you are calling home each night? I think there is some truth to this view, but I also believe communication equipment can be critical if a life-and-death circumstance arises, such as a lightning strike or heart attack, or if someone in your party has an unpredictable medical condition.

In recent years a number of outfitters have begun offering rental of satellite phones on daily and weekly plans, and these phones are probably the best option for anyone desiring a reliable way to reach the outside world. The basic rates are pretty reasonable if you intend to keep the phone as an emergency tool, although even a short call will be pricey.

Primitive Management Areas

The BWCAW contains a dozen remote interior areas that are defined under the BWCAW Management Plan as Primitive Management Areas, or PMAs, and that are maintained in a "pristine environment" free from any maintained human structures. These areas are wild, rugged, and remote. For the most part they are locations with small, shallow lakes that are long distances apart, generally with nothing more than a moose path connecting them, if that. I have heard some people refer to visits to PMAs as "backpacking with a canoe," although even that description is generous because the portages are often so rough as to hardly even exist. Bushwhacking with a canoe is more accurate in most cases.

No campsites are maintained within the PMAs, and there are no latrines or fire grates. Overnight access into PMAs is regulated by the Superior National Forest, and you must have authorization from the local ranger station to stay within a PMA overnight. You are allowed much greater flexibility on where you can camp, as long as you use minimum-impact practices. As alluded to above, the portage trails are not maintained and can become very overgrown in just one season.

A journey into a PMA should only be attempted by diehard visitors who are looking for an extreme challenge. Expect a tough trip with very difficult travel in most PMAs. Also, due to the blowdown of 1999, some of the PMAs have become especially difficult and potentially hazardous, most notably eastern PMAs, such as the Hairy Lake PMA, Mugwump PMA, Pitfall PMA, and Spider Lake PMA.

You will find references to some of the PMAs at various points in this guide, especially at a couple points where the described routes cross next to PMAs or, rarely, through them. If a PMA has any reasonable routes into and out of it, this guide seeks to at least call that to your attention. Some PMAs and parts of PMAs are so remote and rugged that they get few, if any, visitors each year. Such PMAs are generally not described in this guide. If you plan on entering a PMA, consider using Voyageur maps, which show the boundaries of each PMA. The locations of the dozen PMAs are not shown on current Fisher and McKenzie maps.

In conclusion, PMAs are exceedingly rugged and remote areas. Most visitors will have little interest in the leg-scratching, eye-poking, mosquito-biting, log-climbing challenges. However, if you are so inclined and have strong wilderness skills, give PMAs a thought.

Your Canoe: Regulations and Advice

Most visitors to the BWCAW travel by canoe, or in the case of motorized lakes, in small boats with outboard motors. Sailboats, sailboards, and other watercraft designed for propulsion by wind are not allowed. Watercraft with rowing devices that were in regular use in the BWCAW prior to 1979 are permitted, and kayaks are allowed.

You will find all types of canoes in the Boundary Waters, from fine handcrafted wood and canvas models to the newest ultralights, such as those made with high-performance synthetic fibers. Picking a good canoe is both an art and a science. You will want to keep such things in mind as stability, paddling efficiency, capacity, and weight. If you don't own a canoe, dozens of outfitters on the edge of the BWCAW can rent one to you for a reasonable rate and will even haul it right to your entry point if necessary. I recommend renting a model before you purchase to find out whether it will meet your needs.

Most outfitters carry two lines of canoes: low-cost, durable models made of aluminum or synthetic materials and weighing about 75 pounds or more, and ultralight canoes weighing about 40 pounds or less. I prefer ultralight canoes for journeys that will involve long portages, but the heavier canoes are usually more durable. If you do not intend to portage your canoe, such as on a trip through Saganaga or Brule lakes, weight is not much of a factor. However, I think most visitors will appreciate the relative ease with which ultralight canoes can be portaged. Even 20 pounds of weight can make a big difference on a portage, especially during the sometimes awkward process of lifting a canoe onto your shoulders and setting it back down.

You will need to carry your canoe over most portages in the Boundary Waters. Make absolutely certain your canoe has a good yoke in the middle to comfortably hold the canoe on your shoulders when portaging. All canoes from outfitters will come with a yoke, but the model that comes out of your neighbor's garage might not be equipped with one. Don't find out on the first portage that your canoe doesn't have a yoke. Portaging a canoe without a yoke will make even a modest portage seem like torture. One alternative I have seen people try is to portage with two people, having one person take each end of the canoe. This is OK on short portages, but the awkward weight of a canoe makes it difficult to carry in this manner for very far.

If you are concerned about the ability of your group to portage canoes, make your first trip one that has few portages and also consider renting an ultralight canoe. Once you are better able to gauge your strength and stamina, you can design your next trip to be more challenging. Also don't forget to ask your outfitter for a five-minute lesson on how to pick up and set down a canoe without injury to back or bow.

Carts, wagons, and wheels, sometimes called portage wheels, can be used to transport your canoe only on the international boundary and along a few lakes where motors are allowed. For the most part, portage wheels are useless in the Boundary Waters because the rough portage trails are impassible by wheeled vehicles.

Don't forget that your canoe must display a valid watercraft license, one issued by Minnesota or another state. Check to make sure that your neighbor's canoe that you are borrowing, the one without a yoke, at least has a current license. If you are coming to Minnesota from a state that does not require watercraft licenses on canoes, either register your canoe at home as a motorized craft or license the canoe in Minnesota. You can reach the Minnesota Department of Natural Resources License Center at 1-800-285-2000.

Under Minnesota law you must also carry a lantern or flashlight in your canoe from sunset to sunrise. If you are in a motorized craft, it must comply with the more stringent requirements of red and green bow lights and a white stern light.

On a further watercraft note, Forest Service rules prohibit use of pontoons in the BWCAW, and you cannot bring watercraft designed for habitation, such as houseboats. This rule seems obvious to anyone who has taken even a single portage in the BWCAW but is directed to people who might want to take such boats into large, road-accessible lakes such as Moose, Brule, Sea Gull, or Saganaga. Even without this rule, I think you would stand a much better chance of seeing three wolves playing tiddledywinks with a moose than seeing a houseboat on an interior BWCAW lake.

Bears

Nothing concerns some Boundary Waters visitors more than the thought of having a black bear visit their campsite looking for a quick meal. Fortunately, any bear that comes to a BWCAW camp is almost certainly interested in your food supply rather than you as a food supply. Nevertheless, a bear that associates humans with food is a dangerous bear, and you must make every reasonable effort to keep bears from getting food at your campsite.

Bears have an exceptional sense of smell. It is all but futile to try to keep them at bay by simply putting food in a cooler at camp. Even an old bear with a bad cold will quickly smell past such primitive defenses. The traditional way to stop bears from getting your food is to keep it out of their reach by hanging it at least 10 feet off the ground and 5 feet from the nearest branch. I recommend bringing a 50-foot-long,

⅜-inch-diameter polypropylene rope to use as a "bear rope." These strong ropes are readily tossed over high branches.

Everyone in and around the BWCAW seems to have advice on how to hang your food pack. The task is easy in campsites that have a big, old white pine with a high isolated branch. Those sites are in the minority, and I have often found myself trying to hang my pack at dusk in a campsite of smallish spruce trees with itty-bitty branches that broke off every time I tried to haul up my pack. A number of commercial pulley systems have been designed to hoist gear up between two trees, and the garbage bags you can get from the Forest Service show an idealized way to string up your gear in such situations. The Forest Service drawings make it all look so easy, but of course the federal government also says it should take about 75 minutes to do your taxes. I am not convinced any system works flawlessly, but with a little patience and creativity most stands of trees will provide an opportunity to hang your pack.

Consider packing your food into a bear-proof container made for backpacking if you are traveling in an area with heavy tree damage from the 1999 windstorm. Some outfitters are also now selling and renting large bear-resistant packs. I highly recommend them. These bear-proof containers are a good alternative to trying to hang your pack up in a tree, even assuming such trees are readily available.

If a bear does enter your camp seeking food, the general recommendation is to deter your unwelcome visitor by banging pots and pans and tossing stones or branches at it from a good distance. Don't do anything to corner a bear, and don't be overly aggressive. A good bluff will normally keep all but the most persistent bears away. Today's campers generally keep a good, clean camp, and bears are finding less of interest in most campsites. Still, a bad berry year can bring out hungry bruins seeking a free meal. You should relocate camp and inform Forest Service officials of the situation as soon as possible if a bear ignores your efforts to dissuade it.

Fishing in the Boundary Waters

You will need a Minnesota fishing license anywhere you fish in the BWCAW, and all seasons, limits, and regulations are established by the Minnesota Department of Natural Resources (DNR). Your license must be in your possession when fishing and cannot be left in your vehicle or back at camp. Be sure to get a copy of the Minnesota Fishing Regulations booklet at your license issuer, or download one from www.dnr.state.mn.us.

The Minnesota DNR now has an electronic license system that allows you to get your license over the Internet or by phone, and then have it mailed to you. The main DNR Internet site, identified above, can direct you to this program. Also, you will need a trout stamp when fishing any trout lake or stream. A number of such lakes are identified in this guide, so go prepared.

McKenzie and Voyageur maps are probably best suited for Boundary Waters fishing because both sets of maps contain depth contours for most lakes. Current Fisher maps show contours on significantly fewer lakes. In addition Voyageur maps show fish species present in each lake, as well as some basic data on lake structure and stocking history.

Minnesota has increasingly implemented special regulations directed to individual fish species and lakes. For example, in recent years limits on the size of northern pike have been implemented in Basswood and Saganaga lakes. Be certain to check up-to-date regulations before entering the wilderness. Your Minnesota Fishing Regulations book that comes with your license explains what special regulations are in place.

In recent years the Minnesota DNR has started encouraging the use of nontoxic alternatives to lead sinkers and jigs. Such tackle is often made of steel, tin, bismuth, or plastic. In the BWCAW it is especially appropriate to use these alternatives because it limits lead poisoning of eagles, osprey, loons, and other wildlife.

Eating part of your catch is always a treat, but keep in mind that many of these cold, nutrient-poor lakes have slow fish-growth rates and are unable to sustain extensive harvests. According to local DNR and Forest Service officials contacted during research for this guide, many of the lakes within the BWCAW actually receive relatively heavy fishing pressure relative to their low nutrient levels, and would benefit from limited fish harvests. Fortunately, catch-and-release fishing has increasingly taken hold in northern Minnesota, with many visitors consuming just one or two meals on a week-long trip. My crude fishing skills have generally prevented me from eating more meals than this, but even good fishermen and fisherwomen should show restraint in their harvest. If this attitude continues to take hold, we can all expect bigger fish and more of them in the Boundary Waters in years to come.

You are allowed to transport a limited amount of fish home with you, but this is impractical for most visitors—you will likely end up with spoiled meat and wasted fish. If you intend to transport any fish home, refer to Minnesota fishing regulations for possession limits (usually one daily limit) and how your fish must be cleaned to permit identification of the fish species by law enforcement officers.

Finally, the disposal of fish remains is a challenge that has no obvious solution. I have heard the supervisor of the Superior National Forest speak on this issue, and he agrees there is no simple answer. Current recommendations by the Forest Service are that fish remains be disposed of by burying them at least 150 feet from the lakeshore or by cutting them into small pieces and placing them on a rock away from camp for wildlife consumption, typically by a hoard of hungry gulls. Leaving the fish remains for wildlife changes animal behavior and is arguably not consistent with leave-no-trace principles. If the remains are not consumed by wildlife at the time camp is broken, they must be buried well back from camp and shore. It is illegal to dispose of remains within lakes.

Invasive Species

Introduction of non-native species is an important issue for the Forest Service nationally, including in the Superior National Forest. Many non-native plants and animals have already been introduced to the Superior National Forest by humans, intentionally or not. For example, smallmouth bass had their range dramatically extended by stocking programs. In addition, logging introduced non-native plants to parts of the wilderness, often by seeds brought in with hay for feeding horses. Early resorts and inhabitants also planted various ornamental plants that still grow in a few remote sites. Such limited incursions are of less concern than major infestations of more troublesome species.

One damaging species is the common earthworm, or night crawler, used for fishing bait. Earthworms consume so much biological material on the forest floor that they can do significant damage to native flora and fauna. You should never release extra earthworms on the shore. Non-native minnows also are a problem and must never be released. Designated trout lakes prohibit the use and possession of any live minnows whatsoever. The rusty crawfish is a non-native invader now present in many lakes and outcompetes native crawfish without providing as favorable forage for fish. Never transport crawfish between lakes. Milfoil has not yet been reported in the BWCAW. Be sure your canoe or boat is clean and free of plant matter before you enter and leave the Boundary Waters. Remove all weeds stuck to your watercraft, don't bring in straw for bedding (such as in the winter, for dogs), and don't release excess minnows and worms back into the ecosystem.

The 1999 Blowdown: Changes and Challenges

On July 4, 1999, a windstorm of historic proportions tore through the Superior National Forest, especially the north-central and northeastern Boundary Waters. Winds of more than 90 miles an hour blew down millions of trees over a 350,000-acre area. Hundreds of campsites and portages were hit hard, and a heroic effort by hundreds of rescue personnel, Forest Service staff, and volunteers evacuated everyone from affected areas and cleared trails and campsites. Miraculously, no one was killed by the storm, a fact that is hard to believe when you view the scale and extent of the damage.

This incredible storm changed the wilderness for years to come. It has created the opportunity for new experiences but raises new risks for BWCAW visitors. One of the most significant risks posed by the blowdown is that fuel loads in the forest have dramatically increased. A Forest Service team examining the storm area found that fuel loads on the forest floor increased from 5 to 20 tons per acre to 50 to 100 tons per acre over many thousands of acres.

The Forest Service also concluded that lightning strikes will be more successful at igniting wildfires in the blowdown, and that fires are more likely to exhibit extreme behavior. Because of the expected fire intensities and flame lengths in the dense fuels, fires will be much more difficult to control during a wider range of weather conditions. Fires will be larger and will spread more quickly under more moderate weather conditions because of the high fuel density, the potential for plume-dominated fire, and the difficulty in controlling wildfires in the blowdown.

According to Forest Service analyses, the elevated risk of extreme fires and of a wildfire exiting the BWCAW will remain for a number of years. Under natural decay processes, dead and down woody fuel currently on the forest floor will not return to pre-blowdown conditions for fifteen years or more in hardwood stands, and thirty years or more in conifer stands. The Forest Service Fuels Risk Assessment states that it is highly likely that wildfires will occur in many of these areas before the downed materials have completely decayed.

Wildfires that occur within the blowdown will have the potential to become plume-dominated fires that are driven by extreme fire behavior, creating more challenges for firefighters and extreme hazards for anyone in the vicinity of such fires. According to the Forest Service fire experts, plume-dominated fires create their own weather, potentially producing smoke columns reaching 30,000 to 50,000 feet high, strong in-drafts on the fire perimeter that can quickly change to downdrafts of as much as 40 miles per hour, fire whirls along the fire perimeter, high rates of fire spread, and development of spot fires up to 3 or more miles away from the main fire.

If you are traveling in areas that were heavily affected by the 1999 blowdown, which is primarily the central and eastern portions of the BWCAW, you need to be extra vigilant about preventing fires and prepared to respond if a fire does occur near you. If you see or smell smoke, don't panic. The Forest Service recommends that you follow these steps:

- *Watch the weather.* Most fires travel east and north. Make sure you have a safe route to follow in case the wind direction changes. Embers can blow more than a mile, possibly starting new fires. As humidity increases in the early morning and late evening, fire activity may decrease. Travel may be safer at these times. Also, tall smoke plumes indicate a very hot fire. If you see a tall smoke plume upwind of you, seek a point of refuge, such as a lake.
- *Make a new plan.* Look at maps, alternative routes, and your proximity to a large body of water. Stay close to water. If there is a safe way around the fire, with broad expanses of water, consider traveling from the area. If you must travel through burned areas, watch for burning stump holes and hot embers. Burned trees can easily fall.
- *Seek safety.* If you feel threatened, get on a large lake. Stay upwind, but be aware that large fires can burn unpredictably in any direction. If a fire is upon you, take your canoe into the water. Put on your life jacket, paddle to the middle of the lake, tip over your canoe, and go under it. You can breathe the cool, trapped air under the canoe until the fire passes.

The Forest Service has approved prescribed burns to reduce fuel loads to prevent an extreme wildfire from engulfing large areas inside or outside the BWCAW. The prescribed burns should be completed by the end of 2007. The total area burned within the BWCAW will be about 75,000 acres (almost 120 square miles). The most significant burns within the Boundary Waters will be near the end of the Gunflint Trail, mostly south and west of Sea Gull Lake and extending toward Tuscarora Lake. In addition, various pockets of smaller fires will be scattered through the most heavily affected areas of blowdown between Ely and the end of the Gunflint Trail. Most of these fires will be large broadcast burns, typically initiated with burning material ejected from helicopters.

The 1999 windstorm had a great impact on the area south of Sea Gull Lake to Tuscarora Lake, and much of this area was the target of the prescribed burns by the Forest Service in 2002 and 2003. The forest on the west side of Magnetic Lake was burned by a prescribed fire in September 2002. The forest in the general vicinity of Jap Lake east of Sea Gull was burned in the Honker Lake prescribed burn of 2003, extending from Jap Lake to around Glassy and Elusion lakes, to Glee Lake, and toward Bingshick and Honker lakes.

In the far eastern BWCAW a series of much smaller burns is being conducted, mostly "fuel patch burns" to remove understory material without destroying the canopy-forming trees. Areas in which you may see the remains of such fires are along the southwestern end of Pine Lake and around Duncan, Douglas, and Rose lakes.

Some prescribed burns will also occur in the western BWCAW. The area around Crab Lake was generally only modestly affected by the 1999 windstorm. There are sufficient downed trees, however, that the Forest Service has planned a series of small-scale prescribed burns on the southwestern side of Crab, extending toward Clark, Saca, and Battle lakes. The area around the Little Indian Sioux River south of the Echo Trail is also scheduled for limited prescribed burns.

The extensive blowdown and any subsequent fires will provide visitors with a special opportunity to view the forest changing and regenerating. The storm has made the forest an even more dynamic place where visitors can watch plants and animals adapt to the changes. I can recall one of my first trips into the Boundary Waters after the 1999 blowdown, a late-summer trip to Brule Lake. The storm had leveled the thick forest around the portage to Juno Lake. I came across hundreds of bunchberry plants along the portage trail, and they were in full bloom as if they were experiencing spring all over again. I surmise that the removal of the tree canopy mimicked spring before the trees had leafed out, and the bunchberries were prompted to bloom for a second time that summer.

You also will have an opportunity to view changes in the forest, whether it be fireweed growing up after a prescribed burn, perhaps a burgeoning moose population, or an explosion of woodpeckers arriving to feed on insects colonizing millions of dead trees. According to the Forest Service, initial forest regeneration will likely include aspen stands sprouting from surviving roots, and jack pine and black spruce seedlings, both of which have seeds that are released and activated by the heat of fire.

For the first three or four decades after a fire, the new trees will grow into prime habitat for a wide range of native species, including timber wolves, lynx, moose, deer, and snowshoe hares. As the forest matures, we can expect fir seedlings to begin to prosper, and white cedar and birch will probably become more prominent, depending on seed sources.

If you find a favorite lake and expect to return repeatedly in future years, take a few pictures of the same location on each trip, which will give you a photographic history of regeneration. You should also become familiar with some of the primary colonizers of regenerating land, including fireweed and jack pine.

Miscellaneous Rules

You can have dogs in the BWCAW, but they must be under voice or leash control at all times. Give careful thought to how well your dog will travel in the Boundary Waters before bringing it along. One particular hazard of big dogs in small canoes is that if they get nervous, they can quickly tip you over by shifting from side to side.

You may be surprised to learn that hunting is also allowed in the BWCAW, and grouse hunters go there each fall. Moose and other game are also hunted in the wilderness but under strict controls. Most hunting occurs after the main paddling season is over, but don't be surprised to encounter a hunter on an autumn trip.

Choosing a Time to Visit

The most popular time to travel in the Boundary Waters is during the open-water seasons from early May until late October. In a typical year the ice breaks up on large lakes in early May, and by late October it has already returned to the smaller lakes. In theory the canoeing season extends from ice-out to ice-in. In reality most canoeists limit their travel to the middle of May until the end of September. October can also be an interesting time to enjoy the north woods, but the weather is less predictable, it can be quite cold, and snow is possible.

There is no "best" time to canoe the Boundary Waters. If you go in early May, you may be the first human visitor many lakes and portages have seen in at least six months. Portages tend to get plenty of winter use by deer, wolf, and moose, and you are likely to see signs of their activities—everything from abundant wolf droppings to perhaps the sparse remains of a deer or moose killed by wolves. You will also encounter more than your share of downed trees along portages that obstruct your trail until you can find a way around, under, or over. If spring comes late, you might experience iced-over lakes even in the middle of May, and measurable snow is possible all month.

The second half of May is also relatively quiet but attracts people fishing for lake trout, northern pike, and walleye. Some of the best fishing in the Boundary Waters is from the mid-May fishing opener through June. This is a particularly good time to seek lake trout, and waters with established "laker" populations are popular soon after the opener, even lakes deep in the interior of the BWCAW. You are also likely to be treated to the distant drumming sound of ruffed grouse seeking mates.

Although use of motorboats is limited in the Boundary Waters, the majority of all motor permits are issued in May and June, no doubt a correlation with fishing activities. In most years motorboat use in August is a third of what it is in May. Many visitors to the Boundary Waters want to avoid lakes where motorized boats are allowed. Fortunately, even motorized lakes are far quieter than most Minnesota lakes because no jet skis and ski boats rule these wilderness waters. If you are one of the many visitors to the BWCAW who want to completely avoid motorboats, then you should restrict your travels to those lakes that do not allow motors. Whether a lake allows motorboats is information included throughout this guide.

Memorial Day weekend marks the start of the busiest paddling season in the Boundary Waters, and the activity continues through Labor Day weekend at the beginning of September. These three months account for over 75 percent of the travelers that enter the Boundary Waters each year. June provides the best chance to see young loons, moose calves, and deer fawns. It is also a time during which many wildflowers are in bloom, including wild iris and the pink lady slipper orchid. If you intend to go swimming, the lake water is still quite cold, and you will have to be hardy to brave the depths. Air temperatures rise throughout the month, with average lows in the 40s, and highs in the 60s.

In early to mid-June blackflies come out in droves, typically for a two-week period that can be a bit earlier or later depending on whether spring came early or late. These small flies swarm around your head, biting exposed skin and causing an extreme nuisance when they are at their worst. Bringing a bug net to cover your head is definitely recommended during blackfly season. Most outfitters sell them.

While on the topic of insects, I suggest you bring along plenty of insect repellent, and dress properly to ensure the best protection. I always bring a repellent with low levels of DEET in it, which is a very effective ingredient for keeping mosquitoes at bay. Most efficacy tests I have seen show that you do not need pure DEET, which should be used somewhat sparingly due to health concerns about overexposure. Bring a long-sleeve shirt and long pants to wear when the bugs are biting, especially at dawn and dusk. Light-colored clothing is also recommended.

You should also be aware of Lyme disease, which is caused by the corkscrew-shaped bacterium *Borrelia burgdorferi*. The bacteria are transmitted through the bite of deer ticks, which are tiny ticks just a couple millimeters wide, making them much smaller than the common wood tick, which is closer to the size of a flat match head. Lyme disease can cause serious problems involving the heart, joints, eyes, and nervous system. According to the Center for Disease Control, common symptoms of Lyme disease are a "bull's-eye" rash with a dark red center and lighter exterior, accompanied by nonspecific symptoms such as fever, malaise, fatigue, headache, muscle aches, and joint aches. You should consult a healthcare professional if these symptoms develop, although to date the incidence of Lyme disease appears to have been relatively low in the BWCAW.

By July the lakes have usually warmed, and the fishing cooled. Summer is in full swing, and you might see loons and mergansers fishing with their newly expanded families. Don't be surprised to find thick swarms of mosquitoes ready for your arrival. The days are long, and temperatures typically range from the 50s to the 80s. In both June and July temperatures can drop to the 40s and 50s, as well as hit the 90s, so be prepared for temperature swings.

By August the days have shortened significantly but are still plenty long, and the lakes reach their warmest temperatures of the year. The first two weeks of August are historically the most heavily traveled in the Boundary Waters. Air temperatures are just a tad cooler than July, still in the range of the 50s to the 80s. If you are lucky, you will happen upon a blueberry patch (and won't have to share it with a bear). The mosquito population drops throughout August and is usually manageable without repellent by Labor Day (but bring some to be safe). August and September are prime months for amateur mycologists seeking edible mushrooms, as long as there has been adequate rainfall (but don't eat anything you are not absolutely certain is safe).

In September the number of human visitors drops, and many of the animals that head south for the winter start their journeys. Loons flock together to fly to their winter homes on the Gulf Coast. Moose begin a loud and active dating game, and you might hear their bellowing from up to a mile away. The forests begin a subtle, yet magnificent color change: aspen and tamarack turn golden yellow, while the occasional maple lights up the shoreline in brilliant red. The time for maximum foliage color can vary across the Boundary Waters from west to east, but generally the peak color is observed around the last ten days of September through the first week of October.

From October until November's arrival of complete ice-in, deciduous trees lose their leaves, abandoning the pines, spruce, and firs to reign over the woods. During this time the greatest solitude is found by canoeists, as well as the shortest days and coldest winds. This is absolutely not a time for the unprepared or inexperienced to venture into canoe country but is a wonderful change of pace for the experienced Boundary Waters traveler who can handle potentially winterlike conditions.

In recent years, a small but increasing number of hardy campers have ventured into the Boundary Waters year-round. These travelers head into the winter wilderness on snowshoes or cross-country skis, or by dogsled. Winter can be a magnificent time to enjoy the Boundary Waters and is one of my favorite times to visit. Discussion of winter camping is outside the scope of this canoeing book, but descriptions of the lakes and portages are still useful to the winter traveler, as are the natural history and human history sections.

If you desire more detailed information about winter camping, read *Winter Camping* by Stephen Gorman, which describes in detail how to camp with modern gear in winter conditions. I also highly recommend reading *The Snow Walkers Companion* by Garrett and Alexandra Conover. The Conovers practice traditional winter camping with canvas tents and compact wood-burning stoves. Their book is the definitive source on traditional winter travel gear, shelter, transportation, and food. The tents used by the Conovers, such as the well-made Snow Trekkers produced

Five Statements You Are Likely to Regret
When Planning a Boundary Waters Trip

1. "I don't need a long-sleeve shirt—it's July." Even at the height of the summer, the low temperatures in the Boundary Waters are frequently below 50°F. There is no time of year when you won't want a long-sleeve shirt, at least as a backup.

2. "Skip the sunscreen. I never burn." In late June the Boundary Waters gets eighteen hours of sunlight a day. Compound this with reflection off the water surface, and you are likely to get a tremendous dose of sun that necessitates strong sunscreen and UV-blocking sunglasses.

3. "Who needs a filter? This water is crystal clear." The Boundary Waters, for all its pristine beauty, is not without waterborne parasites, the worst of which include giardia. Bring a suitable filter and use it.

4. "Don't pack the noodles. I'll fish for dinner." Boundary Waters fish can be as fickle as the weather, and I have been on many trips where nary a bite was felt. In addition, the low-nutrient lakes of the Boundary Waters cannot support heavy extractive fishing, so you should instead plan on practicing catch and release most of the time. One or two meals per trip are reasonable. A meal of fish is a luxury, not a way to put food on the table.

5. "Of course I'm bringing a cooler. What's an extra 20 pounds?" Remember, every pound has to be carried over rocky, muddy, hilly portages.

- -

in Wisconsin by Empire Canvas Works, can keep you surprisingly warm even when temperatures drop to 30°F below zero or colder.

Equipment for a Canoe Trip into the Boundary Waters

A trip to the Boundary Waters requires that you have proper equipment to explore the wilderness safely and enjoyably. Inexperienced campers tend to bring far too much gear, then realize the gear they do have is not well suited to the elements. In the Boundary Waters your packing challenges are increased by the variability of the weather and the need to portage everything you bring. Even in the middle of summer temperatures can range from hot to quite cool. The following basic gear list has been developed over the years and has served me well under a wide range of conditions experienced in the canoe country during paddling season. A copy of this gear list can be downloaded in Adobe Acrobat format (PDF) from www.BoundaryWaters Guide.com and can be sent by e-mail to each of the people on your trip.

Canoeing Gear and Transportation
entry permit

canoe

waterproof maps (at least one per canoe for your whole route)

life jackets (one per person)

paddles (plus one extra)

portage packs (see below)

Clothing
long pants

shorts

T-shirts

long-sleeve shirt

socks

underwear

hat with visor

gloves or mittens

sweater or fleece pullover

rain gear

footwear (two pair with good traction)

Shelter and Sleeping Gear
sleeping bag

sleeping pad

tent

ground cloth

rain fly (optional)

Cooking and Food Preparation
food pack, optionally bear-proof

cooking kit containing at least

> two large saucepans
>
> frying pan
>
> cups
>
> plates
>
> bowls
>
> silverware

water filter

backpacking stove

stove fuel

waterproof matches and spares

biodegradable dish soap

"bear rope" (50 feet of ⅜-inch-diameter braided nylon)

Personal Hygiene and Safety

toilet paper

toothbrush and toothpaste

first aid kit

biodegradable soap and shampoo

sunscreen (SPF 15 or higher)

lip balm

Insect Protection

mosquito repellent

bug net (optional)

Miscellaneous

pocketknife

flashlight and spare batteries

fishing gear:

> Minnesota fishing license
>
> poles and reels
>
> lures
>
> leeches or minnows
>
> fillet knife (optional)
>
> stringer (optional)

nature guides

compass

camera

How much will all this fancy gear cost? If you buy all of it at once and choose quality equipment, you will easily spend a couple thousand dollars on a canoe, tent, rain gear, lightweight stove, water filter, sleeping bags, and a top-quality, but remarkably reasonably priced, guidebook. But don't let cost keep you out of the Boundary Waters! You can rent some or all of your gear from one of many excellent outfitters for reasonable prices. Outfitters stock quality equipment that has been field tested, is rugged, and is generally well maintained. A quality canoe is essential, and if you don't own one, outfitters have many options from which to choose. I am partial to ultralight canoes, but many good, old aluminum and fiberglass models remain popular and are certainly durable. Also consider going with a friend who has extra gear and can show you the ropes.

If you are going to splurge on anything for your trip, I would make it quality rain gear. Nobody wants to be the person wearing a garbage bag on the portages after his or her four-dollar plastic poncho tore into shreds. Not just dignity is at stake: when you are wet, you are usually cold, so good rain gear is also an insurance policy for staying warm. You should also be certain to buy or rent a life jacket that you will be comfortable wearing. I believe it is important to always wear your life jacket when paddling over these cold lakes, even if you can swim. Other high-priority items, in my opinion, are a good fleece top, a warm sleeping bag, and a comfortable sleeping pad.

Working with an Outfitter

You may want to work with an outfitter when planning a trip into the Boundary Waters. Dozens of high-quality outfitters are located along the edges of the Boundary Waters, with the biggest concentrations near Ely and along the Gunflint Trail. Most outfitters offer a wide range of services, including everything from complete guided trips to selling maps and basic fishing tackle. I have found outfitters to be well informed and friendly. Most will gladly give you a tip or two, even if you are not using their services. However, I feel it is appropriate to patronize their businesses if you are seeking their advice.

Most outfitters will also help reserve your permit for the Boundary Waters and can give you guidance on selecting an entry point. Outfitters can arrange at the time of reserving your permit to have it picked up at their location. You can also arrange pickup at an outfitter when you reserve your permit yourself.

Many, but not all, outfitters offer complete guided trips. These trips are generally led by an experienced Boundary Waters guide and include all the gear and food you will need for your trip. Guided trips are great if you have limited camping and canoeing experience, or if you want the benefit of traveling with someone who knows the route well, can share fishing "hot spots," and can suggest the best areas to view wildlife or explore interesting natural areas.

In addition to guided trips, most outfitters offer both complete and partial equipment outfitting packages. In complete packages you are generally provided a canoe, tent, sleeping bag, cooking gear, food, maps, and virtually everything other than clothes. You can also choose partial outfitting to rent a canoe, tent, sleeping bag, cooking gear, or just about any other type of camping equipment. Most rentals are by the day, with discounts given for full week.

In addition to renting gear, outfitters can shuttle you and your vehicles between entry points so that your vehicles are waiting for you when you exit the wilderness. If you are using a complete outfitting package, this service is often provided in your costs. You will want to reserve your shuttle in advance with your outfitter because their schedules can get quite hectic.

On a number of large lakes outfitters offer tow services either to the edge of the Boundary Waters or across motorized portions of the BWCAW. Some of the more popular tow options are available on the Moose Lake chain (Entry Point 25) toward Prairie Portage and Birch Lake, along Little Vermilion Lake and Lac La Croix (Entry Point 12, and across Saganaga Lake as far as American Point (Entry Point 55). Additional tow services operate on Sea Gull Lake down the east side of Three Mile Island (Entry Point 54), across Burntside Lake to the Crab Lake portage (Entry Point 4), and across Snowbank Lake (Entry Point 27).

Finally, if you are flying to northern Minnesota for a canoe trip, you can make arrangements to have an outfitter pick you up at a regional airport. Air travel options change from year to year, but Ely generally has summer air service from at least one regional carrier, and Hibbing (about 70 miles south of Ely) has year-round scheduled service. You will need to fly through the Minneapolis–St. Paul airport for scheduled service to either Ely or Hibbing. Grand Marais, Tofte, and other towns along the north shore of Lake Superior have not had scheduled air service in recent years. In addition, good air service is offered to Duluth, which is just over 100 miles from both Ely and Grand Marais. The costs of having an outfitter pick you up in Hibbing or Duluth can be considerable because you are paying for a driver, vehicle, and fuel. An alternative in either of these locations is to rent a car.

A good place to get a list of outfitters is at the Superior National Forest Web page, www.SuperiorNationalForest.org. Their list of Boundary Waters permit issuing stations shows all outfitters that are authorized to issue BWCAW permits. For additional links, you can visit the companion site to this guide (www. BoundaryWaters Guide.com), or see the Web sites for the Ely Chamber of Commerce (www.ely.org), Gunflint Trail Association (www.gunflint-trail.com), Crane Lake Visitor and Tourism Bureau (www.visitcranelake.com), and Lutsen-Tofte Tourism Association (www.61north.com).

Planning Your Route

The following section provides information to consider in planning a route in the Boundary Waters. It is followed by a comprehensive description of more than a hundred recommended routes. These recommended routes include nearly every navigable lake in the BWCAW. Use these descriptions to select one of the recommended routes, or use the lake and portage descriptions in conjunction with the index to design your own route.

The BWCAW provides the finest wilderness canoeing opportunities in the United States, if not the world. The Boundary Waters are wonderful in any dose, but with an area of nearly 1.3 million acres and 1,500 miles of canoe routes, even the most ambitious canoeist can find a lifetime of beauty, relaxation, and challenges. Whether you are merely paddling in for a day from one of the Forest Service group campgrounds or planning a three-week trip along the border and down the Grand Portage, you are in for a wonderful adventure.

Every group traveling to the Boundary Waters has different skills and objectives. Some people like to cover as many miles as possible, while others would just as soon stop at the first campsite they find and set up camp for five days. The objective of this guide is to facilitate and enrich the travels of all types of visitors. All routes are described with regard to total miles and total length of portages. I conservatively estimate that a group of canoeists in the Boundary Waters will be able to comfortably travel between 6 and 9 miles during a typical day. Having said that, the number of miles any individual group can travel is widely variable. Fit groups who want to cover a lot of miles can sometimes cover 20 miles in a good day, while other groups might struggle to do 5. In an effort to assist you in planning your visits, the following five factors are identified as the biggest modifiers of trip difficulty, travel times, and travel distances: portages, gear, weather, ability, and attitude. Keep these considerations in mind as you review routes or design your own.

Portages

The biggest variable in the distance visitors can cover in one day is the number and length of portages. For the unacquainted, a portage is the traditional voyageur term for an overland trail connecting two bodies of water. Portages are still measured in terms of "rods," 1 rod corresponding to 16.5 feet, or 5 meters. There are 320 rods per mile. To convert portages into miles, multiply the number of rods by .0031. To convert portages to kilometers, multiply the number of rods by .005.

A typical canoe party will travel about 2 miles an hour on smooth water with no headwind. Once you factor in the unloading, carrying, and reloading of gear, that same party is likely to travel just a half mile an hour on portages (taking a half hour to cover a 160-rod portage).

The most important thing to realize about portages is that they are not created equal. Length, trail conditions, changes in elevation, and landing characteristics all make a big difference in portage difficulty. Some long portages are easy, some short portages are nearly impassable. To assist trip planners, this guide ranks most portages on a scale of 1 to 10. The most difficult, long portages are given a high difficulty rating number (L10), while the easiest, shortest portages are given a low difficulty rating number (L1). Some portages do not have rankings, typically because they are of average difficulty for their length.

In addition to length and difficulty of a portage, the number of portages is a major factor in route difficulty. Three short portages are typically far more work and will take much more time than one long portage of the same total length. The increased difficulty arises because of the energy and time required to land, unload, and reload your canoe. For this reason, this guide has been prepared assuming that a group can comfortably cover from four to seven average 50-rod portages in a day, and that all but the easiest portages require a minimum of 15 minutes to cross completely.

Amount of Gear

The amount of gear you bring with you is the second critical factor determining how much distance you can cover on a Boundary Waters trip. The biggest way to increase the miles you can explore is to travel light enough to do all of your portages in a single trip. If the people in each canoe in your party can carry all their gear and their canoe across a portage in one trip, you will cut your portage distances by two-thirds because you only have to cover each portage once from start to finish, rather than three times (start to finish, back to the start, and then to the finish again).

The key to traveling light is traveling smart. If you want to be mobile, bring only what you need to be safe and reasonably comfortable: a good lightweight tent, compact sleeping bags, mostly dry foods, a small stove, and so on. A complete list of recommended gear is provided in this guide and downloadable at www.Bound aryWatersGuide.com. Pack like you are going backpacking rather than car camping. If you are bringing a stove, which you should, make it a backpacking model, not the two-burner suitcase style. If you want a chair, sit on a log or bring a lightweight collapsible chair that utilizes your sleeping pad. If you travel in this manner, the portages will be much, much easier. There is nothing wrong with bringing along a larger stove, chair, roll-up table, and so on. But just remember that every ounce of gear in your canoe has to go across every portage. That 15-pound cot can quickly transform from your pride and joy to the bane of your existence.

Plan your gear in accordance with your trip objectives, and you will be a happy camper. I remember a trip a few years ago on the Isabella River. A father and his son decided to head north for a weekend of canoeing. They brought along far more gear than they needed, and after about two portages, they realized that the trip wasn't as much fun as they had planned. Seeking to save some trouble and avoid portaging the extra gear, they started shooting rapids to save time and effort.

My traveling companion and I met them as we were putting our canoe in at a portage landing. We saw the son floating in the river yelling for help, and he said that his dad was upstream with their capsized canoe. We quickly fished the boy out of the river and headed by shore to the overturned canoe, which was being righted by the father and pushed downstream. Everyone was safe and uninjured, but much of their gear was lost, what remained was soaked, and their maps were history. We gave them a spare map and made sure they had all the gear they needed to be safe. They learned their lesson the hard way—but you don't have to. Bring only what you need to be safe and are willing to carry, and then don't take unnecessary risks in the wilderness.

Weather

Another important factor in determining travel is the weather, in particular strong headwinds and rain. The larger lakes in the Boundary Waters are mostly west-east oriented, which makes them perfectly situated to develop large rolling waves on days when the wind is howling out of the west. Such popular large lakes as Brule, Gunflint, Pine, and Saganaga can become all but impassable to canoe traffic in the afternoon (or any other windy period). You should keep this in mind and allow adequate time to travel large lakes. On most days the wind does not really pick up until after noon. Cool morning hours before the sun has significantly heated the atmosphere are prime travel times on the big lakes of the Boundary Waters.

The other weather condition that can wreak havoc on trip planning is rain. Naturally it can rain any time on a trip to the Boundary Waters. If you are prepared, it really shouldn't have any impact on your travels. If you are not prepared, you are likely to lose an entire day of travel as you sort through wet pancake boxes and try to dry out your clothes, or puzzle over how synthetic sleeping bags can mildew. You have a lot of control over how you handle rain in the Boundary Waters. Come prepared and rain can be another way of experiencing the rich and varied beauty of the north woods.

Many experienced campers make the best of rain and use it as their time to travel. Canoeing to your next destination during rain maximizes the chance you will be able to enjoy drier weather in camp when it returns. If you are well prepared, rain won't slow you down and traveling is a lot better than cowering under a tarp at camp. Of course, never travel during thunderstorms or when thunderstorms even threaten. Any time you can hear thunder or see lightning you must immediately leave the lake, even if it appears to be miles away or is confined to the upper atmosphere. Lightning strikes have killed BWCAW visitors in the past, so use utmost caution.

Ability and Attitude

The final travel factors that I have seen significantly affect canoeists are their ability and attitude. The Boundary Waters continues to draw young and old of every experience level and physical condition. With good communication, planning, and teamwork, anyone can enjoy a canoe trip in the Boundary Waters. However, the type of trip you take and the distance you cover is still closely related to your experience level, strength, and stamina. If your group includes inexperienced campers, consider making modest travel plans, such as spending five or six days to cover a route normally estimated to take three or four days. Also, look for routes that are easily modified to make them longer or shorter depending on how your trip is going. The labyrinth of lakes and portages that makes up the Boundary Waters allows you to plan a couple of possible routes that start and end at the same location.

Over the years I have talked to numerous people whose first trip in the BWCAW was with seasoned travelers who planned an aggressive route, not taking into account how much of a mental and physical challenge it would be for the first-time visitors. The first-timers are often not prepared for the hard struggle, and I think much less likely to attempt wilderness travel again. Introduce people to the BWCAW with a moderate trip so they come back hungry to return.

Perhaps even more important than ability is attitude. The Boundary Waters is rough, wild country. You are not staying at the Holiday Inn: the mosquitoes can be overwhelming, the wind biting cold, and the ground rock hard. Come ready for a challenge, and you will leave satisfied.

Recommended Routes

Most of the remainder of this guide is dedicated to thorough discussions of each entry point to the BWCAW and recommended routes from each entry. The entry points are grouped by location rather than by entry number:

- entries south of the Echo Trail
- entries north of the Echo Trail, starting in the west
- entries along the Fernberg Road east of Ely
- entries along the southern portion of the central BWCAW area reachable by Forest Service roads off Highway 1
- entries reachable from the Sawbill Trail and State Highway 61
- routes along the Gunflint Trail starting south or west of the trail
- routes along the Gunflint Trail starting north and east of the trail
- the far eastern BWCAW accessed from the end of the Arrowhead Trail

Each portage and every lake described on the following routes was visited during research for this guide, and you should find the descriptions to be accurate and informative. However, visitors should appreciate that the BWCAW is a wilderness area subject to natural changes and fluctuations that will alter routes and travel times. Do not be surprised if some of these routes require changes due to downed trees, beaver activity, forest growth, high or low water, and so on. Plus, from time to time the Forest Service makes changes in campsite and portage locations. You can visit www.BoundaryWatersGuide.com, the companion Web site to this guide, to learn about changes in these routes or to report changes.

You will find that this guide includes more routes for entry points with a high permit quota than for infrequently traveled entries with low quotas. For example, the Forest Service can issue as many as twenty-seven permits per day to enter at Moose Lake, but issues only one permit every other day to paddle down the Little Indian Sioux River South. Therefore, this guide provides more routes for Moose Lake than the Little Indian Sioux River South.

Many of the most popular and practical routes through the Boundary Waters are included in this guide, such as border routes and well-traveled loops. A fair number of truly challenging routes are also included that will appeal to only the most diehard visitors, such as the long, remote portages north of Cummings Lake. Those portages are not for everyone, but I am sure they will appeal to a few crazy canoeists.

To keep this guide from becoming enormous, an emphasis has been placed on making sure as many lakes and portages are described as possible, allowing visitors to easily plan their own routes. Therefore, this guide seeks to be well suited for visitors who want to design their own trip. Use the suggestions provided for each entry point and the planning maps and index to design your own route.

If you are designing your own route consider the following suggestions:

- Lakes near the edge of the BWCAW are usually the busiest. To seek out greater isolation, head deeper into the wilderness from the entries.
- Long portages, typically those greater than 100 rods, and certainly those greater than 200 rods, keep all but the most adventurous away. If you want isolation, head to a lake that can be reached by only one or more long portages. On this note, look for easy "back roads" into lakes. A lake

that is accessible over a long portage from one route (such as Vista, from Morgan Lake) might be easily reached from a different entry point (such as Vista, from Lizz Lake).

• Most people prefer loop routes for the sake of variety. Also consider loops within loops that allow you to shorten your planned journey, if necessary, due to weather or slow travel.

• Some areas are best suited for one-way trips (such as the entries along the Isabella River). These trips are easiest with two vehicles, so that one can be left at the finish point. If you are a small group bringing just one vehicle, you can work with an outfitter to leave your car at your finish location. I once had an outfitter drive my car 50 miles down the Gunflint Trail so that I could paddle all the way from Sea Gull Lake to Lake Superior. Alternatively, arrange to have an outfitter pick you up at the end of your trip. I prefer to leave my vehicle at the finish rather than get picked up because it gives more flexibility in timing my exit. Your cell phone will not work in much of the Boundary Waters, so don't plan on calling your outfitter to change your pickup date or location.

• Underestimate how far you can travel in a day. Although 15 miles might look easy on the maps, it can take a lot longer than expected. Most visitors are probably happy traveling 10 or fewer miles per day.

• Don't be afraid to seek advice from outfitters. They know the BWCAW as well as anyone, and most have an area in which they are experts. If you are going to use their free advice, be certain to reward them with your business, whether renting canoes or at least buying maps.

• It is all but impossible to bushwhack significant distances through the dense forests of the Boundary Waters, particularly with a canoe and gear. Even a distance of a quarter mile through the thick brush and trees can take hours when you are hauling gear. Commercial maps of the BWCAW all show numerous lakes with no apparent portage connection, as well as streams that appear completely unexplored but enticing. In general you will find it very hard going to reach these remote lakes and to navigate these streams. Many of the streams of main travel routes are too shallow and narrow to navigate and are usually completely obstructed by fallen trees.

A number of conventions are used to explain various aspects of each route described in this guide.

First, all routes are described in terms of difficulty, from easy to intermediate to challenging. An *easy* route covers well-traveled lakes near the edge of the Boundary Waters. Easy routes are suitable for less experienced canoeists who have a good understanding of safety, navigation, and leave-no-trace camping principles. An *intermediate* route is about average for wilderness travel and can be covered by most experienced canoeists who are physically fit. Intermediate routes may involve challenging navigation and crossing into infrequently traveled lakes. Portages can be difficult, but are less numerous or less difficult than challenging routes. A *challenging* route is very difficult and should be taken by experienced crews of fit individuals. It may go into exceedingly remote areas that receive few visitors, and cross seldom-maintained portages.

Second, the total miles for each leg of each journey are described, including a combination of the portage distance (if taking the portage once) and the paddling distance. In general these distances are measured taking natural, reasonable routes along the lakes and rivers of the Boundary Waters but are not necessarily the shortest distance. When a leg stops at a large lake, unless otherwise noted the distance is measured into center or interior bays of the lake, which approximates the distance an average traveler might paddle to reach a campsite on that lake.

The length of portages is provided in the conventional unit of a rod, which corresponds to 16.5 feet. The difficulty level of each of the portages is also given on a scale of L1 to L10, with an L1 being extremely easy, and an L10 being oppressively hard. Many visitors will want to avoid an L9 or L10 portage, and an L7 or an L8 will still be a good, sweat-breaking haul. This subjective scale is provided based on the author's examination of each portage and is given because portage length does not always correspond well to difficulty. Some long portages are relatively easy despite their length. Other portages are terribly hard even though much shorter. The difficulty levels are designed to factor in criteria such as elevation changes, condition of the trail with regard to mud, rock, and roots, and challenges in landing and launching your canoe. Although these difficulty numbers are neither perfect nor entirely objective, they will provide you a basic difficulty parameter besides distance that is based on one person's comparison of hundreds of portages.

Finally, you will find that the portage distances in this guide often differ from those you will see on McKenzie and Fisher maps. The reason for these differences is that most of the portages in this guide were remeasured to correct errors that have been propagated from generation to generation of maps. Portage distance measurement is not a precise art, and reasonable methods can differ by 10 or 15 percent on some portages. In most cases, however, I believe these distances are more accurate than earlier reported measurements.

ENTRY SOUTH OF THE ECHO TRAIL

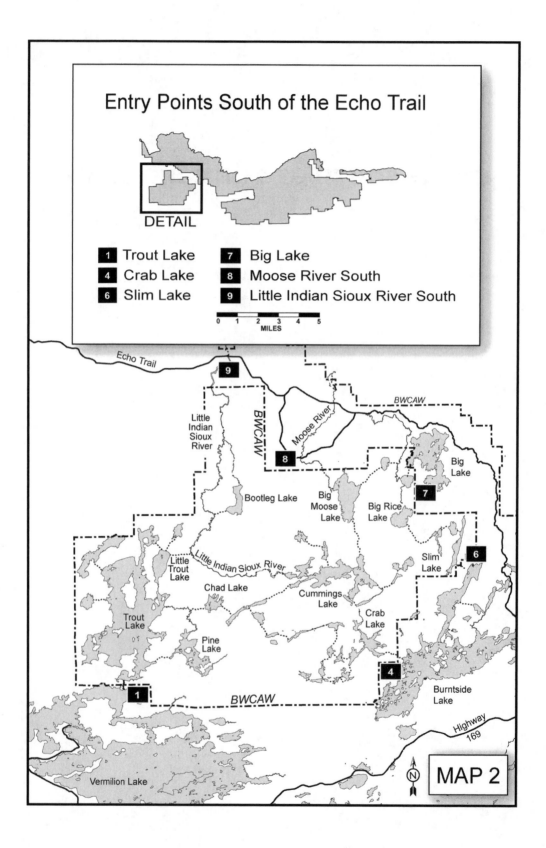

Entry Points South of the Echo Trail

DETAIL

1 Trout Lake
4 Crab Lake
6 Slim Lake

7 Big Lake
8 Moose River South
9 Little Indian Sioux River South

0 1 2 3 4 5
MILES

Echo Trail

9

BWCAW

Little
Indian
Sioux
River

BWCAW

Moose River

8

Big
Lake

Bootleg Lake

Big
Moose
Lake

Big Rice
Lake

7

Little Indian Sioux River

Little
Trout
Lake

Slim
Lake

6

Chad Lake

Cummings
Lake

Trout
Lake

Crab
Lake

Pine
Lake

4

Burntside
Lake

BWCAW

Highway
169

Vermilion Lake

N

MAP 2

ENTRY SOUTH OF THE ECHO TRAIL

As shown on Map 1 earlier in this guide, the BWCAW is divided into three discontinuous areas separated by the Echo Trail in the west and the Gunflint Trail in the east. One of these areas is the portion of the BWCAW south of the Echo Trail and north of Highway 169. This area is shown in greater detail on Map 2, which contains an overview of all of the BWCAW between these two roads.

Six entry points are located in the portion of the BWCAW south of the Echo Trail, but most visitors start at either Trout Lake or Crab Lake. These two entries account for the overwhelming majority of all available and issued permits. Trout Lake (Entry Point 1) is a fine entry in many regards but is not advised for novice canoeists, because it is an enormous lake that can be difficult to traverse in high winds and because it is reached only by crossing the big waters of Lake Vermilion. Motorized watercraft are allowed on Trout Lake, which is also a reason some canoeists find it less attractive. Crab Lake (Entry Point 4) is generally more attractive to canoeists and leads to excellent interior lakes. You will need to portage a mile to get to Crab Lake along a new portage trail that was first established in 2003 (but is *much* harder than the old one). Slim Lake (Entry Point 6) is another entry south of the Echo Trail. Slim is well suited for easy short trips, but only a handful of lakes are easily accessible beyond it. Big Lake and the Moose River South (Entry Points 7 and 8) are also OK entries but offer limited trip options because you must cross almost impassable portages if you want to visit more than one or two lakes. The final entry is Little Indian Sioux River South (Entry Point 9), which is a rugged gateway for hard-core adventurers.

A number of considerations should come into play when planning a trip south of the Echo Trail, particularly if you are deviating from one of the routes described below. First, if you seek isolation, consider routes out of the northern entries (6, 7, 8, or 9), which have far fewer visitors than the southern entries (1 and 4). Second, one-way trips from one entry to another will often be challenging because of the difficult interior portages. In particular, travel from the main northern entries (6, 7, and 8) to the southern entries (1 and 4) is not advised for most groups, because of the long, hard central portages that are involved. Third, trips across the south are feasible, such as from Trout to Cummings or Crab, and good loops can be made between these large lakes. These routes will be challenging journeys through central areas that do not get many visitors, although much less challenging than long trips from north to south.

Entry Point 1, Trout Lake (Map 3)

Daily permit quota: 14
Permit availability: easy

Trout Lake is one of the most famous entry points to the BWCAW and is the most heavily used entry point south of the Echo Trail. In fact, this entry has more permits available and has more permits issued than the other five local entry points combined. The Trout Lake entry is reached by water from Lake Vermilion. In recent years the entry has been the subject of intense controversy over whether a "truck portage" should be allowed to haul boats to Trout from Vermilion. This issue was settled, at least for now, in 1997 by legislation that kept this portage and the Prairie Portage between Moose Lake and Basswood Lake open to trucks hauling boats, partially in exchange for removing motors from Alder and Canoe lakes in the eastern BWCAW.

You will need to paddle across at least part of Lake Vermilion to reach Trout Lake, or you can contract with an outfitter to tow you and your gear to the portage landing on the north side of Vermilion. You can start on Vermilion from numerous locations, but it is best to depart from one of the northern landings that do not require crossing Big Bay, on the lake's south side. I prefer the Moccasin Point landing, reached by taking Highway 169 southwest out of Ely for 22 miles before turning north (right) onto County Road 77 for 10 miles, then heading to the left at County Road 929 for the last 1.5 miles. Moccasin Point Resort has a pay parking lot next to the landing and provides a good spot to keep your vehicle.

From the Lake Vermilion landing on Moccasin Point, paddle north about 1.5 miles before curving east to paddle 2 more miles to the Trout Lake portage. You will be crossing big open water on your way to the portage, so it is a good idea to start early in the morning before the winds pick up, and of course wear your life jacket.

Consider staying at Bear Head Lake State Park, off Highway 169 between Lake Vermilion and Ely, if you need a place to spend the night before entering the wilderness.

Route 1A: Exploration of Trout Lake and Its Neighbors (Map 3)

Difficulty: intermediate due to big, open-water crossing
Number of days: 2 or more

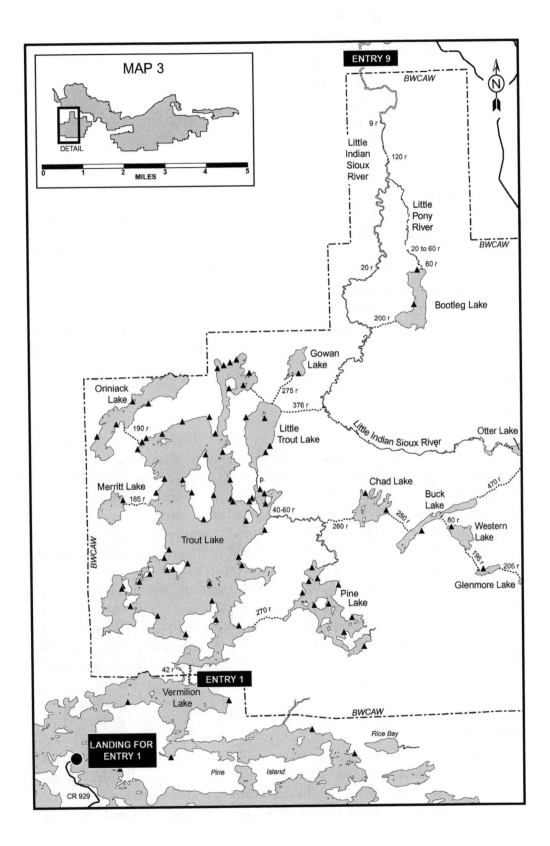

MAP 3

0 1 2 3 4 5
MILES

DETAIL

ENTRY 9

BWCAW

N

Little
Indian
Sioux
River

9 r

120 r

Little
Pony
River

20 to 60 r

20 r

60 r

200 r

Bootleg Lake

BWCAW

Gowan
Lake

275 r

Oriniack
Lake

376 r

190 r

Little
Trout Lake

Little Indian Sioux River

Otter Lake

470 r

Merritt Lake

185 r

p.

Chad Lake

Buck
Lake

250 r

80 r

Western
Lake

195 r

205 r

40-60 r

260 r

Trout Lake

Glenmore Lake

Pine
Lake

270 r

42 r

ENTRY 1

Vermilion
Lake

BWCAW

Rice Bay

LANDING FOR
ENTRY 1

Pine   Island

CR 929

Total miles (approx.): 10 or more
Number of portages: 2
Total portage rods: 84
Greatest portage difficulty: 42 rods (L4)
Navigation maps: Voyageur 3
                  Fisher F1, F8
                  McKenzie 15

This little route is a great introduction to the BWCAW for capable canoeists. It takes you to giant Trout Lake, where you will have an opportunity to explore over 10 square miles of lake surface and to stay at one of thirty-five designated campsites. In addition, you are able to easily get off the beaten track by heading to one of five neighboring lakes that are just one or two portages away. Trout Lake is one of the few lakes remaining in the Boundary Waters to permit motors, and you should expect to see motorized fishing boats on any trip to Trout. This route, like the others to Trout Lake, is less desirable for novice canoeists due to the big waves you may encounter on the wide stretches of open water, making for dangerous conditions for inexperienced paddlers.

Detailed Route

Paddle across Lake Vermilion for 4 miles, portage 42 rods (L4) to Trout Lake. Paddle from the Lake Vermilion landing to Trout Lake and head across the easy 42-rod portage at the end of the narrow bay north of Pine Island. If you want more exercise, take the 160-rod (L6) portage a quarter mile to the east, but expect to share it with motorboats being hauled to Trout Lake. This second portage is the "truck portage" that has been challenged in court over the years. It remains open and is used by a private business to move boats by truck and trailer between Vermilion and Trout lakes.

Once on Trout Lake you have arrived at a big and feisty Boundary Waters jewel. Huge stretches of water are punctuated by a couple of large islands and numerous small ones. Trout offers many opportunities to explore interesting bays, peninsulas, and islands. You can also wet a line for walleye or northern pike and, of course, lake trout. The latter is stocked by the Minnesota DNR in Trout Lake but curiously does not show up in recent fish surveys.

Optional Extensions

In addition, you may consider one of the following short excursions out of Trout Lake.

Little Trout Lake and Gowan Lake: A journey northeast to Little Trout Lake and optionally on to Gowan Lake can be an excellent day trip or an easy extension of a stay on Trout Lake. Little Trout is accessible from Trout Lake by a small creek that requires a short pull-over in dry conditions. Four campsites are located on Little Trout, but you may face competition for them during busy visitor periods. If you head on to Gowan, you will have to take a seldom-used 275-rod portage. Gowan has a maximum depth of 13 feet but does contain walleye and northern pike. A single campsite is located on the south shore.

185-rod (L6) portage to Merritt Lake: If you find Trout Lake to be too busy for your liking, a journey to Merritt Lake might be a good remedy. Merritt is a uniformly shallow lake, with its greatest depth being just 8 feet. Historically this lake was known to hold northern pike, but no surveys have been done in twenty-five years. The lone campsite is found on the east shore just north of the portage from Trout. The portage is not heavily used, so it is prone to being a bit overgrown, with portions of the trail near the Trout side having been heavily hit by the 1999 windstorm.

190-rod (L5) portage to Oriniack Lake: An excellent excursion out of Trout Lake takes you over a 190-rod portage to Oriniack Lake, which has four campsites along its shore. The surrounding forest sustained a bit of damage in the 1999 windstorm but much less than the damage to nearby Merritt Lake. This area is not heavily traveled and provides nice solitude. Although Oriniack is fairly large, nearly 800 acres, it is shallow, with a maximum depth of 17 feet in the northeast corner. Northern pike and walleye are both present.

Route 1B: Short Loop through Pine Lake (Map 3)

> Difficulty: intermediate
> Number of days: 3 or more
> Total miles (approx.): 24
> Number of portages: 4
> Total portage rods: 394
> Greatest portage difficulty: 270 (L7)
> Navigation maps: Voyageur 3
> > Fisher F1, F8
> > McKenzie 15

On this route you will skirt the eastern shore of Trout Lake and then travel a winding creek to Pine Lake. The only disadvantage with Pine is that it is the most popular escape out of Trout for canoeists. If you want to avoid motorboats and want even more isolation, look at Route 1C.

Detailed Route

Paddle and portage 7.5 miles across Lake Vermilion to the interior of Trout Lake, including a portage of 42 rods (L4). You will take the same route to Trout Lake as described in Route 1A. Spend a night at one of the many campsites on Trout Lake, or continue immediately up the eastern shore of Trout until you reach the mouth of Pine Creek.

Paddle and portage 7.5 miles from Trout Lake to Pine Lake, including a portage of 40 to 60 rods (L5) to Pine Creek. A relatively easy portage leads up the shore of Pine Creek from Trout Lake but can have a muddy landing on the east end. This portage changes in difficulty and distance depending on water levels. When water is high, you will probably be able to paddle farther up Pine Creek from Trout Lake, shortening a 60-rod portage to 40 rods. This portage is not shown on recent McKenzie maps but is located just east of Cramer Island, where Pine Creek meets Trout Lake. McKenzie maps show buildings at this location, but they have been gone for decades. This is believed to be the location where Leslie Beatty built a logging camp around 1895 to log red and white pine. Historians recognize the camp as one of the earliest sites of logging activity in what is now the BWCAW.

Paddle upstream on Pine Creek toward Pine Lake. The creek winds back and forth along a shallow channel that can be a good place to spot moose and waterfowl. The creek contains no major rapids, but shallows halfway to Pine Lake may require that you pull your canoe through a rocky stretch. Once on Pine Lake you can camp at one of ten campsites. Although Pine is not a huge lake, it provides good privacy among its many bays and islands, even during peak summer travel.

Paddle and portage 8.75 miles to your starting point on Moccasin Point of Lake Vermilion, including portages of 270 rods (L7) from Pine Lake to Trout Lake, and 42 rods (L4) to Lake Vermilion. The portage from Pine Lake to Trout Lake is long but otherwise not particularly difficult. If you would rather not take such a long portage, you can paddle back down Pine Creek and retrace your steps on the shorter portage to Trout Lake, which will add about 3 miles to your total paddling distance.

Route 1C: Loop East through Cummings Lake (Map 3)

> Difficulty: challenging
> Number of days: 5 or more
> Total miles (approx.): 36
> Number of portages: 16
> Total portage rods: 1,780 rods
> Greatest portage difficulty: 470 (L10)
> Navigation maps: Voyageur 3
> Fisher F1, F8, F9
> McKenzie 15, 16

This challenging route takes you into some of the most remote and least traveled areas of the southwest BWCAW. You will start your travels on Lake Vermilion and head to Trout Lake before moving deep into the interior lakes east of Trout. Your eventual destination is fantastic Cummings Lake, where you can relax, fish, and explore. A number of great side trips can be made out of Cummings. The recommended return route is a northern course through the Little Indian Sioux River, but an equally nice return can be made along a southern path through Lunetta, Schlamn, and Glenmore lakes. You will want to have at least four days to cover this journey, and five or more are recommended to enjoy and explore the many great lakes along the way.

This route is geared to the seasoned traveler who is fit and travels light. It requires that you cross long stretches of open water on Lake Vermilion and Trout Lake, and then adds in a number of difficult portages. Your hard work will be rewarded with unmatched variety: huge lakes but also a winding river; a portage wide enough for cars but also overgrown, muddy, long ones; and the bustle of motorboats on Vermilion but also tremendous isolation when you venture into the remote interior.

Map 3 shows the first half of this route, and Map 4 shows the second half. In addition, the entire route can be seen in overview on Map 2.

Detailed Route

Paddle and portage 7.5 miles across Lake Vermilion to the interior of Trout Lake, including a portage of 42 rods (L4). Take the same route to Trout Lake as described in Route 1A, and either spend a night on one of the many campsites on Trout or continue immediately up the eastern shore until you reach the mouth of Pine Creek.

Portage 40 to 60 rods (L5) to Pine Creek, paddle 1 mile on Pine Creek, portage 260 rods (L8) to Chad Lake. Head across the portage from Trout Lake to Pine Creek, and then paddle up meandering Pine Creek to the long portage to Chad Lake, which will be on your left. The Chad Lake portage marks something of a frontier. Only diehard campers cross this long portage into the BWCAW interior, so prepare for a challenging wilderness experience. As you continue to head east on this route, you may notice that the portages get a bit tougher and seem more rugged. That is because fewer visitors enter this area each year, but also because you are entering a Forest Service management area that is intentionally kept more primitive than the area around Trout Lake. You may want to camp on Chad Lake, especially if the day is getting late; otherwise, press on toward Buck Lake.

Paddle and portage 6 miles from Chad Lake to the interior of Cummings Lake, including portages of 250 rods (L8) from Chad Lake to Buck Lake, and 470 rods (L10) from Buck to Cummings Lake. The portage to Buck Lake is tough, climbing steadily before finally dropping steeply to the shores of the lake. The difficulty in reaching Buck makes for a fine, remote lake that gets even less use than Chad Lake. Buck has one campsite.

The portage from Buck to Cummings is a long, tough trail that is prone to being muddy in patches and gets relatively few travelers, even though it leads to popular Cummings Lake. When you reach Cummings, you will be treated to a fine lake with over a dozen campsites and plentiful game fish. Cummings is probably the most popular interior destination (excluding Trout and Crab, which are on the edge of the BWCAW) of all the lakes south of the Echo Trail but is still not heavily visited. It is certainly the type of lake where you can base camp for a few days of fishing

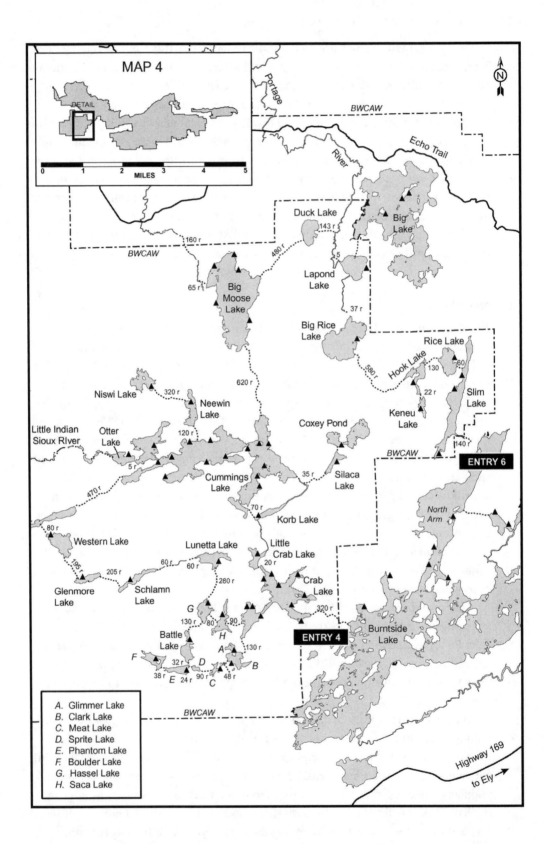

MAP 4

0 1 2 3 4 5
MILES

BWCAW

Echo Trail

Portage

River

Duck Lake
143 r

Big Lake

Lapond Lake

BWCAW

160 r

480 r

65 r

Big Moose Lake

5

37 r

Big Rice Lake

Rice Lake

580 r

Hook Lake

130

60

Niswi Lake

320 r

Neewin Lake

22 r

Slim Lake

Keneu Lake

620 r

Little Indian Sioux River

Otter Lake

120 r

Coxey Pond

BWCAW

5 r

470 r

Cummings Lake

35 r

Silaca Lake

140 r

ENTRY 6

70 r

Korb Lake

North Arm

80 r

Western Lake

Lunetta Lake

Little Crab Lake

195 r

60 r

60 r

20 r

205 r

Glenmore Lake

Schlamn Lake

280 r

Crab Lake

320 r

Burntside Lake

G

130 r

80

90

ENTRY 4

H

Battle Lake

A

F

32 r

D

130 r

B

38 r

E

24 r

90 r

C

48 r

BWCAW

Highway 169

to Ely

A. Glimmer Lake
B. Clark Lake
C. Meat Lake
D. Sprite Lake
E. Phantom Lake
F. Boulder Lake
G. Hassel Lake
H. Saca Lake

and exploration of its 1,100 acres. Cummings has a reputation as a good small-mouth bass lake and decent northern pike lake, but has very few walleye according to DNR fish surveys and personal accounts. Numerous spur and loop routes lead out of Cummings, and they are described next in this guide along with the Crab Lake entry, which is Entry Point 4. I recommend that you spend at least a day on Cummings before regaining the energy to return to Trout Lake.

Paddle 2 miles across Cummings Lake (longer if you camped on the east end of Cummings), portage 5 rods (L3) to Otter Lake, paddle and portage 6 miles down the Little Indian Sioux River, including eight portages totaling 300 rods. Head out through the west end of Cummings Lake by crossing the easy 5-rod portage to Otter Lake (which also has a campsite), and begin down the Little Indian Sioux River. You will be covering only about 6 miles before reaching the long portage to Little Trout Lake, but allow at least 6 hours to complete the journey. (Note: An alternative way back to Trout is via a southern route through Little Crab Lake and Lunetta Lake on to Schlamn Lake and Buck Lake. See Route 4D for details on these lakes and portages if you want to modify this route.)

Be prepared for shallow stretches as you travel down this narrow section of the Little Indian Sioux River. You will start with five portages separated by short segments of river. The longest of these portages is 120 rods, but the rest are all fewer than 50 rods. You will then reach a 2.5-mile stretch without portages, followed by three more portages of 40 or fewer rods. These three portages lead through an area that was heavily hit by the windstorm of 1999. This entire stretch of river experiences variation in water levels with the seasons and is likely to have beaver dams built along stretches. You will be traveling through the narrow headwaters of the Little Indian Sioux River, so I recommend checking with an outfitter or the Forest Service to confirm that water levels are adequate to make the river passable. Most of the portages are reasonably level but somewhat difficult due to a relative lack of use, and are occasionally challenging to find. These factors combine to make it essential that you allow plenty of time to travel this segment.

Portage 376 rods (L9) to Little Trout Lake. After the final portage on the Little Indian Sioux River, keep your eyes open for the long 376-rod portage to Little Trout Lake. You should have no problem spotting the landing on the west side of the river. The first half of this long portage covers low-lying ground, in particular the first 15 rods, which can be quite muddy. After 150 rods the portage climbs for another 70 rods before leveling and dropping to Little Trout Lake. Except for the first portion, this is a quite nice trail.

Paddle and portage 12 miles from Little Trout Lake to your start on Lake Vermilion, including a portage of 42 rods (L4) from Trout Lake to Lake Vermilion. Head south out of Little Trout Lake through the creek leading to Trout Lake, and then paddle down Trout to the same portage to Lake Vermilion that you took earlier in the trip. Finally, paddle west to Moccasin Point and your waiting vehicle. This last segment is best taken early in the morning, when the chances of strong winds and high waves are the lowest.

Entry Point 4, Crab Lake (Map 4)

> Daily permit quota: 4
> Permit availability: moderate

The Crab Lake entry point is a favorite of many Boundary Waters paddlers. You must take a long portage to get to Crab Lake, but the trail should be in good shape. Once on Crab you can either head through the northwest corner to Little Crab Lake and routes beyond, or you can head south toward Clark Lake. Most groups either stay put right on Crab or head toward Little Crab. The journey to Clark Lake is also quite interesting and much less busy. Historically the long portage to Crab Lake has made permits readily available for this entry, with the exception of the first couple of weeks in August. As always, however, you should get your permit reserved as early as possible and as soon as you select your date and destination.

An important change at Crab Lake occurred in 2003, when a dispute between the Forest Service and a local landowner resulted in relocation of the portage from Burntside to Crab. The portage is now located about a half mile south of its former location. If your maps were printed before 2003, ask your permit issuer to mark them with the correct portage location.

Five routes from Crab Lake are described in this guide, including a basic trip to explore Crab Lake (Route 4A), a nice journey to Cummings Lake by way of Little Crab Lake (Route 4B), and a loop to Clark Lake (Route 4C). The first two routes are well suited for BWCAW novices, while the trip to Clark is only moderately difficult. More experienced paddlers may be attracted to the final two routes: one to Trout Lake (Route 4D), and the other to Big Moose Lake (Route 4E). These last two routes can be rewarding journeys but are very demanding due to the condition and length of the portages encountered along the way.

Crab Lake is located west of Ely across Burntside Lake, which lies at the southern edge of the Boundary Waters. The easiest access to Crab is from Highway 169, about 4 miles south of Ely. Turn north off Highway 169 onto County Road 88, and drive 2.4 miles until you reach County Road 404 (Van Vac Road). An excellent DNR landing is located about a mile down on the right (north) side of the Van Vac Road.

Overnight lodging is available at numerous hotels in Virginia and Ely and at a good public campground at Bear Head Lake State Park, which is located 8 miles south of Highway 169 east of Burntside Lake. This state park is a popular destination in the summer, so make sure you reserve a site in advance.

Route 4A: Exploration of Crab Lake (Map 4)

> Difficulty: easy to moderate
> Number of days: 2 or more
> Total miles (approx.): 8

Number of portages: 2
Total portage rods: 640
Greatest portage difficulty: 320 (L9)
Navigation maps: Voyageur 3
                        Fisher F9
                        McKenzie 16

This pleasant route takes you across legendary Burntside Lake and over a long portage to Crab Lake. The portage will be a tough challenge for anyone with excessive or poorly packed gear, but otherwise this is a great route and a nice introduction to the BWCAW.

This route can easily be covered in just two days: one to get to Crab Lake, and one to return to Burntside. It is certainly more enjoyable, however, if you allow yourself an extra day or more to enjoy Crab Lake, possibly going on day trips to interesting lakes to the north and south.

Detailed Route

Paddle 4 miles across island-studded Burntside Lake, portage 320 rods (L9) to the interior of Crab Lake. The portage to Crab Lake was created in 2003 to replace an established portage that ran over private land. The old portage is to the north and is the only one marked on older Fisher and McKenzie maps. A sign at the old portage informs you it is closed, and you should paddle south to the landing for the new portage.

Crab Lake contains nine designated campsites, which get heavy use during the busiest months of the summer. I recommend reaching Crab early in the day so that you have time to head to Cummings Lake if the Crab Lake sites are full. Crab is known for its smallmouth bass population but also contains northern pike and some rock bass. Walleye are present only in very small numbers, if at all.

An interesting aspect of the forest around Crab Lake, in particular the area to the north and sections on the east side of Little Crab Lake, is that it was logged in the 1920s to remove most large red and white pine. But unlike the usual practice at areas logged at that time, the "slash," consisting of branches and tips of the trees, was burned in small fires as the loggers advanced. The result was that this area was spared the huge, hot fires so common in cutover lands of northern Minnesota, and a healthy population of young red and white pine survived logging without being incinerated. These pine are now growing along much of the northern shore of Crab.

If you reach Crab Lake and are still hungry for adventure, consider connecting to either Route 4B (to Cummings Lake) or Route 4C (to Clark Lake and Phantom Lake). Route 4B will take you to a beautiful, large BWCAW lake, while Route 4C sends you to an infrequently traveled loop of remote, small lakes.

Paddle and portage 4 miles and 320 rods back to Burntside Lake. Your return trip is simply the reverse of your route to Crab Lake. Be cautious on Burntside Lake if the winds are blowing—the lake can be quite rough. If you find yourself wind bound, consider camping at the Forest Service campsite located just north of the portage landing on Burntside.

Route 4B: Cummings Lake Excursion (Map 4)

Difficulty: intermediate
Number of days: 3 or more
Total miles (approx.): 14
Number of portages: 6
Total portage rods: 750
Greatest portage difficulty: 320 (L7)
Navigation maps: Voyageur 3
                  Fisher F9
                  McKenzie 16

A journey to Cummings Lake can be an unforgettable wilderness adventure. The route sends you across Burntside Lake and over the mile-long portage to Crab Lake. You then navigate a number of smaller bodies of water and easy portages to Cummings, which is known as a fine bass-fishing lake. Although some walleye are present, they are not very common. Most paddlers can reach Cummings in one day, but an overnight on Crab is a nice start. Also consider staying on Crab the night before leaving the wilderness so that you can get an early morning start on Burntside before the winds pick up.

Consider taking at least three days for this trip: one to get to Cummings, one or more to explore or fish on Cummings and its neighboring lakes, and one to return to your vehicle on Burntside. However, this trip is easily extended to a week-long journey in which you spend an extra day or two on Crab Lake, and a day or two exploring lakes around Crab and Cummings.

Detailed Route

Paddle 4 miles across island-studded Burntside Lake, portage 320 rods (L9) to the interior of Crab Lake. Your journey starts with the same lakes as in Route 4A, crossing Burntside Lake and then hauling your gear over the long portage to Crab Lake. If it is late in the day, you may want to spend the night at one of the sites on Crab; otherwise continue over the easy portage to Little Crab Lake.

Paddle and portage 5 miles from Crab Lake to Cummings Lake, including portages of 20 rods (L2) to Little Crab Lake, and 70 rods (L5) or 35 rods (L4) to Cummings Lake. The short portage from Crab Lake to Little Crab is a nice trail and should be in good shape during all seasons. Little Crab has a single campsite in a good south-facing location, but it is often occupied. Head to the east and into the Korb River, and then to Korb Lake. A reasonably good 70-rod (L5) portage drops to Cummings Lake, or you can travel up to the northeast corner of Korb Lake and rejoin the Korb River. After one-half mile on the Korb River, take a short, 35-rod portage to Cummings.

On Cummings Lake you have a number of options for side trips and exploration. A trip from the west end to Otter Lake is easy and involves just a 5-rod portage. You can also take a 120-rod portage north to Neewin Lake, which is within the Canthook Primitive Management Area (PMA). To camp on Neewin, you need special written authorization from the Forest Service, available from the LaCroix Ranger Station in Cook (218-666-0020). Just one group can stay in the PMA per night. The trail from Cummings to Neewin is not particularly well used, is not maintained by the Forest Service, and is likely to be overgrown. Old maps show a designated campsite on Neewin Lake, but the fire grate and latrine have been removed consistent with the pristine nature of PMAs, which do not have any maintained campsites or portages. In theory, a 320-rod portage leads from Neewin to Niswi Lake; however, this long, dead-end portage appears to be entirely unused and would require extensive bushwhacking through a mile of downed trees. I don't recommend attempting this long portage, which appears essentially impassable, but if you must, then at least bring your survival pack and make sure someone knows where you are going. You can also take long, tough portages to Buck Lake or Big Moose Lake. These are described in Routes 1C and 4E, respectively. Cummings Lake, Crab Lake, and Korb Lake all have healthy populations of smallmouth bass and decent populations of northern pike.

A spur out of Korb Lake to Silica Lake and Coxey Pond is another side trip worthy of consideration. Well off the beaten path, this diversion gets relatively few visitors, but the condition of the portage trails indicates at least occasional use. This area is of some historic significance. A small logging camp and sawmill were constructed on the north end of Silica near the portage to Coxey Pond in the early 1940s. The short-lived logging operation probably focused on red pine for use as timbers in the Ely iron mines during World War II.

Paddle across Cummings Lake, paddle and portage 9.5 miles on Korb Lake, Little Crab Lake, Crab Lake and Burntside Lake, including portages of 70 rods (L5) or 35 rods (L4), 20 rods (L2), and 320 rods (L7) to Burntside Lake. Your return trip is simply the reverse of your route to Cummings Lake.

Route 4C: Loop through Crab, Clark, and Boulder Lakes (Map 4)

> Difficulty: challenging
> Number of days: 3 or more
> Total miles (approx.): 17
> Number of portages: 10
> Total portage rods: 1,394
> Greatest portage difficulty: 280 (L9)

Navigation maps: Voyageur 3
                   Fisher F9
                   McKenzie 16

This route takes you to a wonderful corner of the Boundary Waters that is well worth exploring but rarely visited. The journey circles a small loop of lakes that lie south of the main travel routes from Crab Lake to Cummings Lake and Trout Lake. You will pass through or past eleven small lakes, each with only one campsite (on Sprite Lake, none). There is no better chance to "own" a Boundary Waters lake for a weekend than on this trip to small, remote lakes.

The string of small lakes you will encounter on this journey makes it well suited to setting your own camping objectives for each night. Most of this journey is through infrequently traveled lakes, so you shouldn't have much problem finding open camp-sites after you pass through Crab Lake.

Detailed Route

Paddle 4 miles across island-studded Burntside Lake, portage 320 rods (L9) to the interior of Crab Lake. This first stretch to Crab Lake is exactly the same as Route 4A. The route then breaks off the common northerly travel path through Crab and turns south to much less frequented lakes.

Paddle 1.3 miles across Crab Lake, paddle and portage 3 miles to Boulder Lake, including portages of 130 rods (L5) from Crab to Clark Lake, 48 rods (L5) from Clark to Meat Lake, 90 rods (L6) from Meat to Sprite Lake, 24 rods (L4) from Sprite to Phantom Lake, and 38 rods (L4) from Phantom to Boulder Lake. The portage from the south arm of Crab Lake to Clark Lake is a neat trail with a wonderful stand of medium-aged red and white pine trees. Enjoy the reasonably good path, which climbs steeply from Crab before moving through the pine grove and dropping to Clark.

Camp on Clark if you are so inclined. You may also want to give a thought to camping on Glimmer Lake, which is reached by a steep climb from the north shore of Clark along a 15-rod (L5) portage. It is possible to hike to the campsite on Glimmer from the portage without putting in on Glimmer because a trail extends along the ridge between Glimmer and Clark. The Glimmer campsite is in a nice stand of red pine.

The forest south and west of Crab Lake is only lightly managed by the Forest Service. Expect portage trails to be narrower, overgrown, and perhaps have a few downed trees, compared to earlier portages on this route. In accordance with the BWCA Wilderness Management Plan, Forest Service maintenance crews come this way less than once a year to remove downed trees and obstacles.

From Clark you have a 48-rod portage to Meat Lake. Meat has become a smaller, leaner lake in recent years, losing about 3 feet in depth. This shrunken lake now requires a pull-over portage between a small eastern bay and the main body of the lake, where you will find a compact campsite that looks like it gets little use. The next portage is to Sprite Lake. Some older maps misidentify the start of the portage—it is in the first small bay north of the southernmost bay, not in the larger southernmost bay. An incorrect trail heads out of the southernmost bay but quickly leads off into oblivion.

Sprite is a small lake with no campsites, so head over the easy 24-rod portage to Phantom Lake, where you have an option to camp or push onward to the interesting island campsite on Boulder Lake after taking a 38-rod portage (which sustained a bit more wind damage than other lakes in this area).

In the 1950s a small logging camp, known as the Palmquist Camp, was constructed along the portage between Phantom Lake and Battle Lake. A number of spur roads were built in this area, heading east toward Sprite Lake but also much farther north and west of Battle Lake into a stretch of land owned by the State of Minnesota. Indeed, a small sawmill was in operation for a few years along the road west of Battle Lake. Today, forest growth has obscured most of the roads in this area, although it is still possible to identify a spur trail near the Phantom–Battle portage, which appears to be along the route of one of the old roads. Similarly, a very overgrown trail skirts the shore between Sprite and Glimmer Lakes. If you decide to do any trail exploration in this area, you must be extra careful to keep yourself well oriented. It is easy to get turned around in the thick forest, and the trails in this area are not maintained.

Paddle and portage 6 miles to Crab Lake, including portages of 32 rods (L4) from Phantom to Battle Lake, 130 rods (L7) from Battle to Hassel Lake, 280 rods (L9) from Hassel to Lunetta Lake, and 20 rods (L2) from Little Crab to Crab Lake. After Phantom Lake this route heads north, first over a 32-rod portage to Battle Lake. Battle has a campsite, and the waters contain pike, walleye, bass, and reportedly even bluegill. Continue out of Battle and head to Hassel Lake by a 130-rod portage. This route then takes you over the 280-rod portage to Lunetta Lake, but an alternative is a pair of 80- and 95-rod portages back to Crab Lake by way of Saca Lake. The Lunetta portage is the hardest you will have on this entire route. Once on Lunetta Lake, you can paddle down narrow Lunetta Creek to Little Crab Lake. Lunetta Creek is usually deep enough to paddle through, although it may require a couple of pull-overs. From Little Crab head south to the easy portage to Crab Lake.

Paddle 2.7 miles across Crab Lake, portage 320 rods (L7) to Burntside Lake, paddle 2 miles to your landing. Head back the way you arrived.

Route 4D: Trout Lake Loop (Map 4)

      Difficulty: very difficult

      Number of days: 5 or more

      Total miles (approx.): 37

      Number of portages: 23

      Total portage rods: 2,581 (approx. 8 miles)

Greatest portage difficulty: 376 rods (L9)
Navigation maps: Voyageur 3
Fisher F1, F8, F9
McKenzie 15, 16

This is the longest, most challenging route south of the Echo Trail described in this guide. You will start by traveling though popular Crab Lake, head to big Cummings Lake, and then travel the seldom-visited Little Indian Sioux River before heading to Trout Lake. Your return is through a series of small southern lakes. If you are fit and traveling light, this is a premier Boundary Waters route that can produce a lifetime of memories.

Map 4 shows the first half of this route, and Map 3 shows the second half. In addition, the entire route can be seen in overview on Map 2.

Detailed Route

Paddle and portage 8 miles from Burntside Lake to Cummings Lake, including portages of 320 rods (L9) to Crab Lake, 20 rods (L2) to Little Crab Lake, and 70 rods (L5) or 35 rods (L4) to Cummings Lake. Your journey starts with the same lakes as in Routes 4A and 4B, paddling across Burntside Lake, and then hauling your gear over a long portage to Crab Lake. If it is late in the day, you may want to spend the night at one of the sites on Crab; otherwise continue to the easy 20-rod portage to Little Crab Lake. I recommend that you spend at least a day on Cummings Lake before heading to Trout Lake.

Paddle and portage 10 miles from Cummings Lake to Little Trout Lake, including a portage of 5 rods (L3) to Otter Lake, followed by eight portages totaling 300 rods down the Little Indian Sioux River, and concluding with a 376-rod (L9) portage to Little Trout Lake. Head out of Cummings Lake by crossing the easy 5-rod portage to little Otter Lake, and begin down the Little Indian Sioux River. If you are taking the river during a dry summer, call the LaCroix Ranger Station in Cook (218-666-0020) to confirm that the river is passable. You will be traveling along the small river's headwaters, so be prepared for shallow stretches and allow yourself plenty of travel time.

Some of the best wild rice stands in the BWCAW grow along the Little Indian Sioux River. This is a neat place to look for some of the animals and plants that thrive near wild rice. Certainly keep your eyes open for waterfowl, but smaller inhabitants are also of interest. A tiny spider called the long-jawed orb weaver inhabits rice stands and has a body that looks almost identical to a grain of rice. Look closely at a few rice stems, and you might see these intriguing creatures. When you are paddling through rice stands, the tiny spiders often fall into your canoe and appear like little walking rice grains.

You will need to take at least eight portages on the Little Indian Sioux River and must navigate through a couple more rocky rapids. You start with five portages separated by short stretches of river. The longest of these portages is 120 rods, but the rest are all fewer than 50 rods. You will then reach a 2.5-mile stretch without portages, followed by three more portages of 40 or fewer rods. These final three portages lead through an area that was heavily hit by the windstorm of 1999. Many of the portages are somewhat difficult due to relative lack of use and are challenging to find, conditions that make it essential that you allow plenty of time for the route.

Once you have paddled the Little Indian Sioux River, you will take the long portage to Little Trout Lake. The first half of this 1-mile-plus portage is low lying, especially the first 15 rods, which can be somewhat muddy. After about 150 rods, the trail climbs up for 70 rods, levels, and then drops to Little Trout Lake. Except for the first portion this is a quite nice trail. You may want to camp on Little Trout Lake, which has four campsites, but they get a fair amount of use from people paddling out of Trout Lake.

Paddle and portage 5.5 miles across Little Trout Lake to Chad Lake, including portages of 40 to 60 rods (L5) to Pine Creek, and 260 rods (L8) to Chad Lake. Paddle south through Trout Lake to the portage from Trout Lake to Pine Creek, which is likely to be from 40 to 60 rods in length depending on water levels, and then paddle down meandering Pine Creek to the 260-rod portage to Chad Lake, which will be on your left. The Chad Lake portage marks something of a frontier—only diehard campers cross this long portage into the interior BWCAW. You may have seen other campers on Trout Lake, but you will now be heading into remote interior lakes with far fewer visitors. If the day is wearing on, you may want to camp on Chad Lake; otherwise press on toward Buck Lake.

Paddle and portage 1.5 miles across Chad Lake to Buck Lake, including a portage of 250 rods (L8). The portage to Buck Lake is tough, climbing steadily before finally dropping steeply at its end. The difficulty in reaching Buck makes it a fine, remote lake that gets even less use than Chad Lake. The single campsite on Buck can be a nice, isolated place for a night or two of relaxation.

Paddle and portage 6 miles from Buck Lake to Lunetta Lake, including portages of 80 rods (L6) from Buck to Western Lake, 195 rods (L8) from Western to Glenmore Lake, 205 rods (L9) from Glenmore to Schlamn Lake, and two portages of 60 rods to Lunetta Lake. The next leg of this route heads down the portage from Buck Lake to Western Lake, which is surrounded by a "sunken forest" of dead spruce trees. Most people will choose to paddle past the campsite on Western and head right down the 195-rod portage to Glenmore Lake. From Glenmore, a 205-rod portage leads to Schlamn Lake. Both Glenmore and Schlamn have single campsites. You must then paddle and portage to Lunetta Lake. Old maps show a 100-rod portage between these lakes, but you should be able to avoid the first 40 rods and then paddle along the creek connecting the two lakes. Next, paddle about one-third of a mile to an overgrown landing that will lead to the second 60-rod portage, this one ending on Lunetta.

Paddle 1.8 miles across Lunetta Lake, Lunetta Creek, and Little Crab Lake; portage

20 rods (L2) to Crab Lake. Cross Lunetta Lake and paddle down Lunetta Creek to Little Crab Lake. Lunetta Creek is narrow but usually deep enough to paddle through, although it may require a couple of pull-overs. From Little Crab, head to the south exit to Crab Lake.

Paddle and portage 4 miles from Crab Lake to your starting location on Burntside Lake, including a portage of 320 rods (L9) to Burntside Lake. Head back the way you arrived.

Route 4E: Big Moose Lake Loop (Map 4)

> Difficulty: challenging
> Number of days: 3 or more
> Total miles (approx.): 32
> Number of portages: 12
> Total portage rods: 2,605 (more than 8 miles)
> Greatest portage difficulty: 620 rods (L10)
> Navigation maps: Voyageur 3
> Fisher F1, F8, F9
> McKenzie 12, 16

This route leads from Crab Lake through Cummings Lake to Big Moose Lake by way of long portages, and then to the north side of Burntside Lake. The three longest portages total 1,680 rods (5.25 miles) along challenging trails that are likely to have numerous downed trees and be overgrown with vegetation. These low-priority portages get little maintenance by the Forest Service. Bring lots of insect repellent, pack good maps and a compass, and prepare yourself for a real battle. This is one of the hardest routes in this book. Reasonable pacing for this route is to spend the first night on Crab Lake or Cummings Lake, the second night on Big Moose Lake, and the third night on Big Rice Lake or Hook Lake.

Detailed Route

Paddle 2 miles across Burntside Lake, portage 320 rods (L9) to Crab Lake, paddle 5 miles from Crab Lake to Cummings Lake, including portages of 20 rods (L2) to Little Crab Lake, and 70 rods (L5) or 35 rods (L4) to Cummings Lake. Your journey starts with the same initial lakes of Route 4B, requiring crossing of Burntside Lake and then hauling your gear over the long portage to Crab Lake. If it is late in the day, you may want to spend the night at one of the sites on Crab; otherwise continue over the easy 20-rod portage to Little Crab Lake and then on to Cummings. The long portage to Crab Lake will be a mere warm-up for what comes after Cummings. If this portage whets your appetite for bigger challenges, then continue on the next leg to Big Moose Lake. If you find yourself crying or cursing on this first portage, don't even consider the far more difficult portion of this route to Big Moose, and perhaps revise your plans to take Route 4B or 4C.

Paddle and portage 4 miles from Cummings Lake to central Big Moose Lake, including a monster portage of 620 rods (L10). The portage from Cummings Lake to Big Moose is probably the hardest one on this route and absolutely one of the toughest in the BWCAW. This portage is never easy but will be especially tough in the spring before other campers or the Forest Service has removed downed trees. This portage is not a high priority for Forest Service maintenance crews, so assume it will be in tough shape. If you are double portaging, this portage will take most of a day. The biggest challenge of this trail is that it will probably be relatively overgrown. In addition, a couple of low spots can make for muddy going.

Once you reach Big Moose you will have the thrill of knowing you conquered a monster portage that appears to be traveled just a few times a year. Your emotions may flag as soon as you notice other campers on Big Moose Lake. You will wonder how they could have gotten there without leaving tracks on the huge portage you just took! The answer is that these resourceful souls probably took the easy route from the Moose River South entry (see Entry Point 8 and Map 6). If you are the jealous type who also likes shortcuts, skip the backbreaking portage and reserve your permit for Entry Point 8. Big Moose can be a nice place to spend an evening, particularly because you have more than 500 rods of portaging before you get to the next campsite on Lapond Lake. Get a good night's rest. The next day is just as tough.

Paddle and portage 7 miles from Big Moose Lake to Big Rice Lake, including portages of 480 rods (L10) to Duck Lake, and 143 rods (L8) to the Portage River; paddle to Lapond Lake (with a seasonal 5-rod portage along the way), and paddle to Big Rice Lake, crossing a 37-rod (L3) portage just before you enter Big Rice Lake. The way out of Big Moose Lake is not any easier than the way in: you have a very tough portage to Duck Lake along another rarely used trail. Trail conditions indicate that this portage gets a bit more use than the one connecting Big Moose to Cummings but is still infrequently used. It will likely have quite a few downed trees along the trail in the spring, with fewer later in the year as the trail is cleared.

Once on Duck Lake the route eases and takes a long portage and a short seasonal portage to Lapond Lake. Lapond has a campsite, but it is an attractive destination for visitors coming from Big Lake to the north. You should assume that it will be occupied when pacing yourself through these lakes, and allow yourself time to get to Big Rice Lake. Whether or not you camp on Lapond, the route next follows the Portage River to Big Rice Lake, which also has one campsite. The campsites on Lapond and Big Rice are the only sites readily accessible from the Big Lake entry, so they may be occupied by groups entering from Big Rice Lake. If they are occupied, head down the grueling 580-rod portage to Hook Lake.

Paddle and portage 13 miles from Big Rice Lake to your origin on the southeast side of Burntside Lake, including portages of 580 rods (L10) to Hook Lake, 130 rods (L7) to Rice Lake, 60 rods (L5) to Slim Lake, and 140 rods (L5) to Burntside Lake. The portage from Big Rice Lake to Hook Lake is another whopper, much of which is poorly marked, and some of which is quite wet. This is the final tough portage of this route. Continue over two more portages to Rice Lake and Slim Lake, both of which will be a breeze after the long portage to Hook. Your trip concludes with a portage to North Arm Road (County Road 644) on the shore of Burntside Lake, where you can paddle back to your starting point on Burntside, or go to your car if you left it at the Slim Lake parking lot. Pat yourself on the back upon finishing this route; you've traveled one of the most demanding trips in the BWCAW!

Entry Point 6, Slim Lake (Map 5)

> Daily permit quota: 2
> Permit availability: moderate

The BWCAW contains two lakes named Slim: one to the west of Burntside, and one near Lac La Croix. This entry is for the lake near Burntside, which is a narrow stretch of water 3 miles long and covering nearly 300 acres. Most visitors to Slim Lake appear to go no farther than Slim itself, but relatively easy passage can also be made to Rice Lake and Hook Lake. Beyond these lakes you will need to take a tremendously difficult portage to Big Rice Lake, which is a lake of only moderate interest for most visitors and is much easier to reach from Entry Point 7. Unless you want to take the tough portage to Big Rice (plus two other long portages), Slim offers no opportunities for large loop trips.

To get to the Slim Lake entry, go east from Ely for 1.5 miles, then turn north (left) onto County Road 88. Continue down County Road 88 about 2.3 miles to the Echo Trail, which is County Road 116. Turn right onto the Echo Trail, and travel approximately 9 miles to North Arm Road (County Road 644), which is located about 1.5 miles past the Fenske Lake campground. Turn left on North Arm Road, and drive 4.3 miles to the parking lot for Slim Lake. The parking lot is about one-half mile past a YMCA camp. The Fenske Lake campground is a great place to spend the night, but get a reservation during busy summer months because it is one of the few (and the most popular) public campgrounds on the Echo Trail.

Route 6: Exploration of Slim Lake with Side Trip to Hook Lake (Map 5)

> Difficulty: easy to intermediate
> Number of days: 2 or more
> Total miles (approx.): 3 to 6, depending on options
> Number of portages: 2 to 6
> Total portage rods: 280 to 660
> Greatest portage difficulty: 140 rods (L5) or 130 rods (L7)

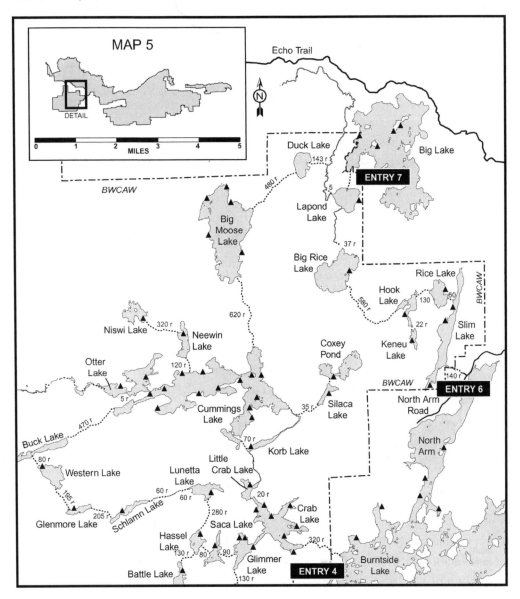

Navigation maps: Voyageur 3
Fisher F9
McKenzie 16

This nice little route takes you to long, narrow Slim Lake, where you may choose to relax and base camp. You also have the option to head to Rice Lake, Hook Lake, and even Keneu Lake. These additional lakes are relatively easy to get to and take you progressively farther from civilization.

Detailed Route

> *Portage and paddle 1.5 miles, including portaging 140 rods (L5) to central Slim Lake.*
> The 140-rod portage to Slim Lake starts from the parking lot and travels west through a deep valley. It is not heavily traveled, but the location at an entry point makes for a reasonable trail. Three designated campsites are provided on Slim, and they make nice places to spend a weekend, where you can also troll the depths for walleye, which have been repeatedly stocked in recent years. Northern pike are also present in average numbers, according to Minnesota DNR fish surveys.

> *Optionally paddle and portage 2 miles to Hook Lake, including portages of 60 rods (L5) to Rice Lake and 130 rods (L7) to Hook.* If you decide to press on past Slim Lake, take the 60-rod portage to Rice Lake from the northwest shore of Slim. This portage gets considerably less use than the earlier portage to Slim but is still along a decent trail. Camp at the designated site on the eastern shore of Rice, or perhaps take the more challenging 130-rod portage to Hook Lake. This 130-rod portage appears to be used rarely, so you should be prepared for it to be overgrown with occasional downed trees, especially in the spring. You are not likely to see another soul on Hook, but in the unlikely event that the lone designated campsite is taken, consider heading down the 22-rod portage to Keneu Lake, which gets even fewer visitors but is hidden at the south end of Hook. A ski trail appears to lead out of the south end of Keneu to Slim, but it was not explored during research for this guide.

> If you really want to test your endurance, take the grueling 580-rod (L10) portage from Hook Lake to Big Rice Lake. This is among the hardest portages in all of the BWCAW and is particularly difficult if a Forest Service crew has not cleaned it out recently, which is probable. Big Rice is very large but less than 5 feet deep, with only one designated campsite. Also, although you need to take a massive portage from the south to get to Big Rice, a much easier route from the north is possible by way of Big Lake (Entry Point 7), so do not assume Big Rice will be free of other visitors.

> *Paddle and portage approximately 3 miles to Burntside, including portages of 130 rods to Rice Lake, 50 rods to Slim Lake, and 140 rods to the parking lot.* Your return to Slim Lake is simply the opposite route from the way you arrived.

Entry Point 7, From Big Lake (Map 5)

> Daily permit quota: 2
> Permit availability: easy

Big Lake is one of the least popular entry points to the BWCAW, probably because only two shallow lakes are accessible without taking long, overgrown portages. In addition, the challenging portages lead you to lakes that are much easier to reach from other directions. Thus, all of your hard work on these tough portages won't get you any more seclusion than if you had taken an easier route from the south. Typically, fewer than a hundred groups enter here per year.

This guide includes one easy route to Big Rice Lake, which is a good retreat where you will see few other visitors. If you would like the challenge of the longer portages, review Route 4E and Route 6, which describe other portages and destinations in the vicinity of Big Lake. Be forewarned, if you head west, that the two long portages in and out of Big Moose Lake are among the nastiest in all of the BWCAW: long and infrequently used. Expect to encounter downed trees and mud on both portages, especially the Big Moose to Cummings portage.

To reach Big Lake, head east from Ely for 1.5 miles, then turn left onto County Road 88. Continue down County Road 88 for about 2.3 miles to the Echo Trail, which is County Road 116. Take the Echo Trail for 17.4 miles, then turn south (left) onto Forest Service Road 1027. About 0.2 mile down Forest Service Road 1027 you will come to the public access and parking lot for Big Lake.

The Fenske Lake campground on the Echo Trail (on your way from Ely) is a fine place to camp the night before entering the Boundary Waters, or you can stay at one of the four Forest Service campsites on Big Lake. The four campsites on Big Lake do not require a permit and are often occupied by people who are not entering the Boundary Waters. If you need to rent gear, the Big Lake Wilderness Lodge and Lodge of Whispering Pines are both located on Big Lake and can be a convenient source for equipment and advice.

Route 7: Exploration of Big Rice Lake (Map 5)

Difficulty: moderate
Number of days: 2 or more
Total miles (approx.): 12
Number of portages: 4
Total portage rods: 84
Greatest portage difficulty: 37 rods (L3)
Navigation maps: Voyageur 3
       Fisher F9
       McKenzie 16

This route sends you south across Big Lake to Lapond Lake, and then on to Big Rice Lake. Both lakes are very shallow and can be heavily covered in weeds much of the year. However, the relative lack of visitors makes for a pleasant getaway and change of pace.

Detailed Route

Paddle and portage 6 miles from Big Lake to Big Rice Lake, including paddling across Big Lake to the narrow creek feeding into the Portage River, paddling upstream through the creek and river, crossing a seasonal 5-rod (L2) portage to Lapond Lake, and portaging 37 rods (L3) to Big Rice Lake. Head across Big Lake and paddle into the Portage River, and then on to Lapond Lake. The short portage to Lapond varies in length depending on water levels but should be relatively easy. If you want to avoid paddling the Portage River, you can take a 160-rod portage from Big Lake directly to Lapond. Most people appear to use the river route, and it is certainly far easier to avoid this long, rarely used portage. Once on Lapond Lake, you can either camp at the single site on the east shore or continue farther upstream on the Portage River to the easy 37-rod portage to Big Rice Lake, where there is also a campsite. Big Rice contains a population of northern pike, but it is not clear whether shallow Lapond also contains game fish.

Paddle and portage 6 miles from Big Rice Lake to your starting point on Big Lake, including portages of 37 rods (L3) and seasonally 5 rods (L2). Your return trip doubles back across your incoming route.

Entry Point 8, Moose River South (Map 6)

> Daily permit quota: 1
> Permit availability: moderate

Moose River South (Entry Point 8) leads south from the Echo Trail to Big Moose Lake, and is one of the best entry points for solitude near the edge of the BWCAW. Moose River South has just one permit available each day, and these permits often go unused. When reserving your permit, don't mistakenly make your reservation for Moose River North (Entry Point 16), which takes you north of the Echo Trail.

Typically just three or four groups enter the Big Moose Lake by way of Moose River South each week. In addition, the only other routes in and out of Big Moose Lake travel a pair of the longest, most difficult portages in the entire Boundary Waters. Few people head to Big Moose along these portages, so you probably won't have visitors from the south or east. Therefore, if you want relative peace and quiet but don't want to cover a lot of miles, this is a wonderful entry.

To get to the Moose River, head east from Ely for 1.5 miles, then turn north (left) onto County Road 88. Continue down County Road 88 for about 2.3 miles to the Echo Trail, which is County Road 116. Turn right onto the Echo Trail and travel 22.2 miles to Forest Service Road 464, where you will turn south (left) and travel 3.6 miles on a narrow road past a small landing pad labeled "Heliport 4," for emergency helicopters, to a little parking lot and landing on the Moose River.

You can camp the night before at the Fenske Lake campground (with fourteen campsites), which is on the Echo Trail on the way from Ely (17 miles from the Moose River), or head to the west another 12 miles to the Lake Jeanette campground (with twelve campsites).

Route 8: Exploration of Big Moose Lake (Map 6)

> Difficulty: easy to intermediate
> Number of days: 2 or more

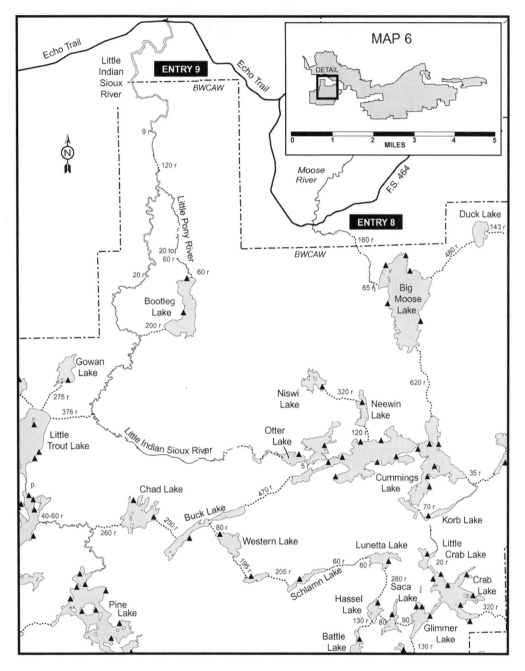

Total miles (approx.): 8

Number of portages: 4

Total portage rods: 450

Greatest portage difficulty: 160 rods (L8)

Navigation maps: Voyageur 3

Fisher F9

McKenzie 12, 16

Everything about this route feels remote: the rustic access road, the small landing, and the winding river to Big Moose Lake. This is a great journey for anyone looking for relative isolation on a trip that can be done over a weekend. Although quite short, this trip has one relatively long portage, making its overall difficulty somewhere between easy and intermediate.

Detailed Route

Paddle and portage 4 miles down the Moose River to the interior of Big Moose Lake, including portages of 160 rods (L8) and 65 rods (L6). After you push off from the landing on the Moose River, paddle for 2 miles up the winding Moose River, which gradually narrows, before coming to a 160-rod portage around a long series of rapids. The portage has two hills but is not too challenging considering how relatively little use it gets. Continue up river another mile, where a final 65-rod portage diverts around additional rapids before dropping to Big Moose Lake. Enjoy your stay on Big Moose Lake, and consider wetting a line for walleye, which DNR sampling indicates to be relatively abundant.

Paddle and portage 4 miles back to your starting point, including portages of 65 rods (L6) and 160 rods (L8). Your return trip is simply the reverse of how you arrived.

Entry Point 9, Little Indian Sioux River South (Map 6)

Daily permit quota: 1 every 2 days
Permit availability: difficult

Little Indian Sioux River South has the most restricted entry point quota in the entire BWCAW. Just one permit is issued every two days. The primary reason for this relative exclusivity is that designated campsites are rare in the vicinity of the entry. Just two campsites are located within 10 paddling miles of the start, both on Bootleg Lake, so this area can't handle many groups. The lack of other visitors and the wonderful terrain make this a great entry if you love paddling narrow little streams and hope for a moose sighting. Be certain to reserve your permit as early as possible.

Trips up the Little Indian Sioux River are best started early in the morning to give yourself plenty of time to travel the river to a good designated campsite. The river can become low during dry periods, so I recommend that you make a call to the LaCroix Ranger Station (218-666-0020) to confirm that water levels are adequate for the trip, and give yourself plenty of travel time. Even in high water, travel will be slow.

To reach the entry, head east from Ely for 1.5 miles, then turn north (left) onto County Road 88. Take County Road 88 about 2.3 miles to the Echo Trail, which is County Road 116. Turn right onto the Echo Trail and travel approximately 29 miles until you cross over the Little Indian Sioux River, which is marked by a small sign. Just after the bridge is a small parking lot on the north side of the road. Carry your gear across the Echo Trail, and you will find a sloped rock landing at the river edge where you can launch your canoe.

The closest public camping for the night is located 4.5 miles farther west on the Echo Trail at Lake Jeanette campground, which is a decent place to spend a night before entering the wilderness. The Echo Lake campground is also nearby, 10 miles farther past Lake Jeanette campground.

Route 9A: Exploration of Bootleg Lake (Map 6)

Difficulty: intermediate
Number of days: 2 or more
Total miles (approx.): 24
Number of portages: 8
Total portage rods: 598
Greatest portage difficulty: 200 rods (L7)
Navigation maps: Voyageur 3
Fisher F8, F16
McKenzie 12, 15

This route heads south along the slowly meandering Little Indian Sioux River to the Little Pony River and then to Bootleg Lake. Your return route is either the reverse of your route to Bootleg or a loop that heads over a 200-rod portage to reconnect to the Little Indian Sioux River before heading north. This route doesn't look much longer than 15 miles on most maps, but you will find that the numerous bends and curves make it approximately 24 miles long.

Detailed Route

Paddle and portage 10 miles up the Little Indian Sioux River and Little Pony River to Bootleg Lake, including portages of 9 rods (L3) around Sioux Falls and 120 rods (L7) along the Little Indian Sioux River, and 20 to 60 rods (L4 to L6) and 60 rods (L6) along the Little Pony River. The first 5 miles of this route wind upstream along a relatively wide stretch of the meandering Little Indian Sioux River to Sioux Falls, a 10-foot tumbling cascade. A simple 9-rod portage leads up and around the falls. Continue less than a mile to the longest portage of the day: a 120-rod trail past impassable rapids and shallows. Soon after this portage you should look for the small spur into the Little Pony River, which will be on your left (east). The Little Pony River becomes quite rocky the farther south you travel, and you should not be surprised if you need to walk your canoe through stretches. You will come to two more portages before reaching Bootleg Lake. The first of these can be as short as 20 rods during high-water levels, or as long as 60 rods during low-water periods. The second portage is 60 rods and drops you right to Bootleg Lake.

The Forest Service has established two designated campsites on Bootleg Lake. Only one group is permitted to enter at Little Indian Sioux River South every two days, but there can be some competition for these campsites on Bootleg because paddlers occasionally come to Bootleg from neighboring entry points, in particular from Trout Lake. You may find yourself in the awkward position of asking to share a campsite if both locations are occupied. If you find the campsites on Bootleg are occupied and want to press on farther, I recommend heading to Cummings Lake along Route 9B, but this is a long, hard journey that is difficult to cover in one day. An alternative is to head over the 376-rod portage to Little Trout Lake and Trout Lake. Sites on Little Trout are in high demand because they are the most accessible, nonmotorized campsites in the Trout Lake region, but sites on Trout Lake should always be available.

Returning to your start: Paddle and portage 14 miles from Bootleg Lake back to your starting point, including portages of 200 rods (L7), 20 rods (L3), 120 rods (L7), and 9 rods (L3). The long portage to the Little Indian Sioux River from Bootleg Lake is not as bad as one would expect considering its remote location. It has a generally good, dry trail with considerable exposed bedrock. However, be prepared for a fairly steep climb, particularly on the Bootleg Lake side. Once on the Little Indian Sioux River, head north toward your starting location. A 20-rod portage leads you around a stretch of rapids, after which you paddle downstream to your starting location by way of two more portages that you have already taken.

Route 9B: Cummings and Big Moose Loop (Map 6)

> Difficulty: challenging
> Number of days: 3 or more
> Total miles (approx.): 31.5
> Number of portages: 17
> Total portage rods: 1,303
> Greatest portage difficulty: 620 rods (L10)
> Navigation maps: Voyageur 3
>   Fisher F8, F16
>   McKenzie 12, 15, 16

This remote route follows the Little Indian Sioux River south to Cummings Lake and then heads north to Big Moose Lake before exiting the BWCAW on the Moose River. This great adventure through remote wilderness will satisfy visitors looking for a real challenge. Most of the trip is along the rugged Little Indian Sioux River, but you will also press over a grueling portage to Big Moose Lake. This is one of the toughest portages in the entire BWCAW, so be prepared for hard work. You will need two vehicles for this route, or else you will need to have an outfitter drop you off at the start.

Important Warning: You should not start this trip unless you are confident that you can finish it without having to turn back. If you have just one vehicle, and it is left at the end of this route, you will have a long hike to get to it if you don't complete the whole route.

Detailed Route

Paddle and portage 10 miles up the Little Indian Sioux River and Little Pony River to Bootleg Lake, including portages of 9 rods (L3) around Sioux Falls and 120 rods (L7) along the Little Indian Sioux River, plus 20 to 60 rods (L4 to L6) and 60 rods (L6) along the Little Pony River. This journey starts along the same course as Route 9A, paddling and portaging to Bootleg Lake for a first night of rest and perhaps a bit of fishing.

Paddle and portage 13.5 miles to Cummings Lake, including portaging 200 rods (L7) to the Little Indian Sioux River, and taking nine portages along the river and Otter Lake to Cummings Lake. The second day of travel starts with a long portage to the Little Indian Sioux River along a decent trail. The next few miles of river are among the least traveled in all of the BWCAW. Keep your eyes open for moose and the plentiful beaver that thrive in this area. After about 3 miles, you paddle past the portage to Little Trout Lake. Continue the last 6 miles up the river to Otter Lake. Your paddling activities will be interrupted at least eight times for short portages and perhaps a few more times for beaver dams. Once you reach Cummings Lake, you are at one of the finest interior lakes in the BWCAW, but you will probably see at least a few other campers who have arrived from Crab Lake to the southeast. Campsites are plentiful, but keep to the western bays if you want maximum privacy.

Paddle and portage 4 miles from Cummings to Big Moose Lake, including a portage of 620 rods (L10). I recommend staying on Cummings Lake for at least one evening. The stay on Cummings is worthwhile for the remote beauty and the quiet relaxation it offers, but is equally valuable to gain your strength for the 2-mile portage to Big Moose Lake. As discussed earlier, in the description of Route 4E, this is a long, remote portage. Expect it to be overgrown and absolutely grueling, particularly during peak mosquito season. If you pack poorly and will make multiple trips, or the trail has not been recently maintained, this portage will take most of a day. Plan your trip so that you can spend a night on Big Moose Lake. This large lake gets relatively few visitors, and it is worth wetting a line there for walleye and the occasional northern pike. Big Moose can also have fantastic sunrises and sunsets across its big main bay.

Paddle and portage 4 miles to your takeout point, including portages of 65 rods (L6) and 160 rods (L8). Wind up your trip by paddling and portaging north to the landing on Forest Service Road 464, where you should have a vehicle waiting (and keys for it). Otherwise, you have an 8-mile-long walk back to your starting point.

ENTRY NORTH OF THE ECHO TRAIL

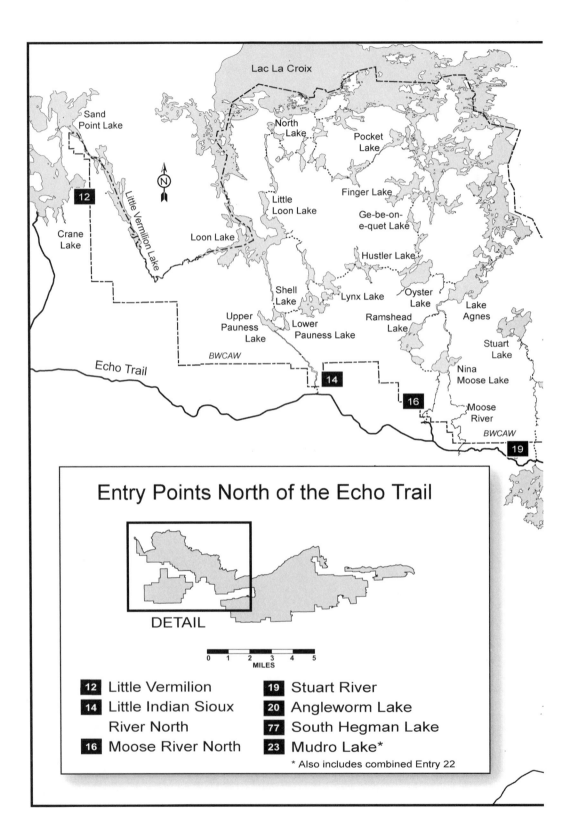

Lac La Croix

Sand
Point Lake

North
Lake

Pocket
Lake

Finger Lake

Little
Loon Lake

Ge-be-on-
e-quet Lake

Crane
Lake

Loon Lake

Hustler Lake

Shell
Lake

Lynx Lake

Oyster
Lake

Lake
Agnes

Upper
Pauness
Lake

Lower
Pauness Lake

Ramshead
Lake

Stuart
Lake

Echo Trail

BWCAW

Nina
Moose Lake

Moose
River

BWCAW

Entry Points North of the Echo Trail

DETAIL

0 1 2 3 4 5
MILES

12 Little Vermilion

14 Little Indian Sioux
River North

16 Moose River North

19 Stuart River

20 Angleworm Lake

77 South Hegman Lake

23 Mudro Lake*

* Also includes combined Entry 22

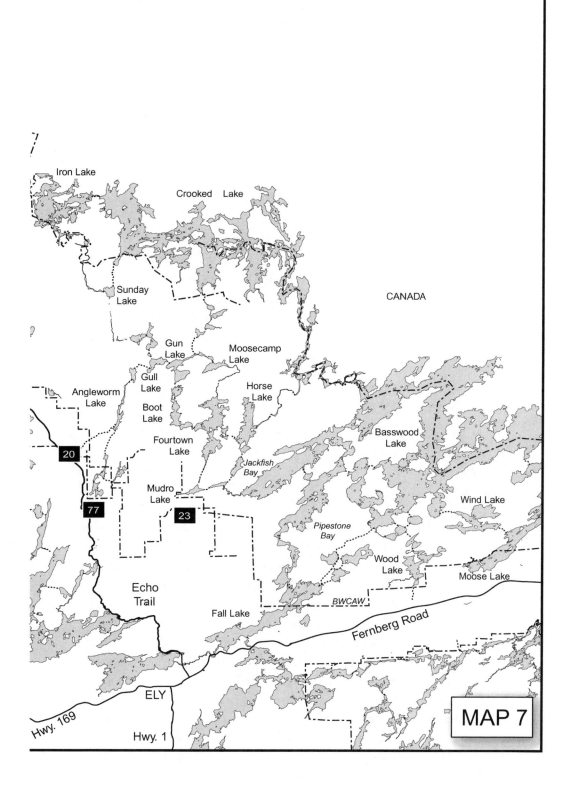

Iron Lake

Crooked   Lake

CANADA

Sunday
Lake

Gun
Lake

Moosecamp
Lake

Gull
Lake

Angleworm
Lake

Horse
Lake

Boot
Lake

Basswood
Lake

Fourtown
Lake

20

Jackfish
Bay

Mudro
Lake

Wind Lake

77

23

Pipestone
Bay

Wood
Lake

Moose Lake

Echo
Trail

BWCAW

Fernberg Road

Fall Lake

ELY

Hwy. 169

Hwy. 1

MAP 7

ENTRY NORTH OF THE ECHO TRAIL

- -

Seven overnight paddling entry points, shown on Map 7, are located north of the Echo Trail, stretching from the west at Little Vermilion Lake (Entry Point 12) to the east at Mudro Lake (Entry Points 22 and 23). This area encompasses legendary Lac La Croix and Crooked Lake on the Canadian border and numerous smaller lakes and rivers. Lakes closest to the Echo Trail are generally quite small, but all the entry points provide access to deep into the wilderness and to larger border lakes.

The most popular entries north of the Echo Trail are Little Indian Sioux River North (Entry Point 14), Moose River North (Entry Point 16), and Mudro Lake (Entry Points 22 and 23). These entry points offer ready access to nice lakes and also have options for big trips and long loops. You will probably see a fair number of other visitors at the lakes closest to these entry points, but a day's worth of travel from any of them can place you into seldom-traveled territory that will satisfy even the most reclusive visitors.

South Hegman Lake (Entry Point 77), another popular entry, is an easy portage from excellent Native American pictographs. These pictographs attract large numbers of visitors on short day trips, so this entry is less than ideal if you wish to see few other people. Little Vermilion Lake (Entry Point 12) gives you easy access to Lac La Croix without too much portaging. Finally, Stuart River (Entry Point 19) and Angleworm Lake (Entry Point 20) are also excellent entries, but only if you are an experienced visitor and willing to start with very long portages. Stuart River, in particular, offers opportunities to get off the "beaten track" into great remote lakes.

All seven of these entries allow wonderful wilderness trips. General considerations useful in planning a journey north of the Echo Trail include the following points. First, expect to find the greatest isolation in the "middle-ground" lakes between the Canadian border and the Echo Trail. These lakes are more difficult to reach than those adjacent to the Echo Trail, which keeps visitor numbers down, and they are not big, long lakes like Lac La Croix and Crooked Lake, which attract people interested in long border travels. Second, with the exception of Little Vermilion

Lake, all of these entries are reasonably well suited for one-way trips starting and ending at different entries. If you have two vehicles, you can easily drop one at your takeout location. Numerous area outfitters also provide services to drop you at one entry and your car at another. Third, the eastern entries, especially Mudro Lake, are well suited to loops to lakes farther east toward Basswood, Fall, and even Moose lakes.

Entry Point 12, Little Vermilion Lake (Map 8)

> Daily quota: 14
> Permit availability: easy

Little Vermilion Lake is the most westerly of all BWCAW entry points and is located on a finger of protected land and water extending from the main body of the BWCAW. All Boundary Waters routes from Little Vermilion head to the east, starting along a common course through Crane Lake and Little Vermilion Lake toward the Loon River and Loon Lake. Once on Loon Lake you have nice exploration options, including going to Lac La Croix or toward the Little Indian Sioux River, both of which are described below.

Entry Point 12 has a total quota of fourteen permits per day, but the quota is divided into two groups: Entry Point 12, which has six permits per day and allows you to camp anywhere in the BWCAW reachable from Little Vermilion Lake; and Entry Point 12A, which has eight permits per day but restricts camping to Lac La Croix. However, this distinction is usually of no importance because on most days not even the six permits for Entry Point 12 are depleted. In 2003 only *one* permit was issued for Entry Point 12A during the *entire* summer because enough permits were available for Entry Point 12.

Entry Point 12 is not a first choice for many canoeing visitors to the BWCAW, because it offers relatively few route options, area lakes are traveled by motorboats, and these lakes do not necessarily provide the same remote wilderness atmosphere of most of the BWCAW. Indeed, two popular portages have short, primitive railroads for carrying boats or canoes! If you are seeking silent isolation, this is not your best entry. However, if you are more flexible, this can be a really excellent entry and is a good choice if you are too late to get a permit for more rustic starting points.

To reach Little Vermilion Lake, you must enter by water from Crane Lake. Crane Lake is located off County Road 24 on the very western end of the BWCAW. From Ely take the Echo Trail 47 miles to its end at County Road 24. Turn right (north) and drive 6 miles on County Road 24 until you reach County Road 425. Turn right onto 425 and drive about 1.5 miles to a public boat launch on Crane Lake. Paddle through Crane Lake and King Williams Narrows to get to Little Vermilion Lake, as described below in Route 12A. A good place to spend a night before heading into the wilderness is at the Echo Lake campground near the west end of the Echo Trail. In addition, a number of resorts on Crane Lake and in the vicinity offer bunkhouse facilities.

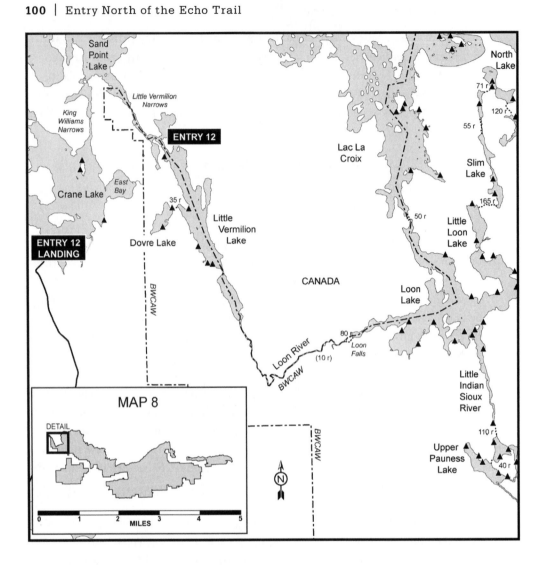

Route 12A: Exploration of Little Vermilion Lake (Map 8)

        Difficulty: easy
        Number of days: 2 or more
        Total miles (approx.): 18
        Number of portages: 0
        Total portage rods: 0
        Greatest portage difficulty: N/A
        Navigation maps: Voyageur 1
                            Fisher F15, F22
                            McKenzie 14

This route is a perfect match for anyone looking for an easy trip with a minimum of portaging who doesn't mind occasional motorboats. It takes you to Little Vermilion Lake, where the fishing can be quite good, without so much as a single portage.

Detailed Route

Paddle 9 miles through Crane Lake, King Williams Narrows, Sand Point Lake, and Little Vermilion Narrows to Little Vermilion Lake. Your journey starts outside of the Boundary Waters on Crane Lake, which is a gateway to both Voyageurs National Park and the western BWCAW. Boating traffic converges in King Williams Narrows but drops off considerably once you head east toward Little Vermilion Narrows. You enter the BWCAW while passing through Little Vermilion Narrows, after which you cross into Little Vermilion Lake.

Once on Little Vermilion you can camp on one of five designated campsites on the U.S. side and can also climb a 35-rod portage to Dovre Lake, which has two additional campsites. Without a Remote Area Border Crossing permit you are not allowed to camp on the Canadian side. Although Little Vermilion is in a protected wilderness area, it may feel less remote than most locations in the BWCAW because motorboats are allowed. Also, this long, narrow lake serves as a channel for traffic into and out of Lac La Croix, giving you less solitude. You won't have much trouble making it to Little Vermilion in just a few hours, so if you want a greater challenge, consider continuing down the Loon River to Loon Lake, described in Route 12B.

A dam-building plan from the early 1900s would have raised the level of Little Vermilion Lake by 80 feet to generate hydropower for papermaking and to facilitate logging. Fortunately, this plan was never implemented, although it would have eliminated the portage to Dovre!

Paddle 9 miles through Little Vermilion Lake, Little Vermilion Narrows, Sand Point Lake, King Williams Narrows, and Crane Lake. Return to Crane Lake by the same route you took to Little Vermilion Lake.

Route 12B: One-Way to Little Indian Sioux River (Map 8)

Difficulty: easy/intermediate
Number of days: 3 or more
Total miles (approx.): 29.5
Number of portages: 6
Total portage rods: 255
Greatest portage difficulty: 110 rods (L8)
Navigation maps: Voyageur 1
   Fisher F15, F16, F22
   McKenzie 12, 14

This route is a continuation of Route 12A and goes all the way to the Little Indian Sioux River on the Echo Trail. It expands on Route 12A by allowing you to cover new territory without backtracking through Little Vermilion Lake. This route will hold more appeal to most BWCAW visitors than Route 12A because it pushes deeper into the wilderness and eventually escapes the motorboat traffic along the border. This is an ideal journey for avid paddlers because it has little portaging yet miles of high-quality paddling.

Your trip starts by paddling across Crane Lake, through Little Vermilion Lake, and then on to the Loon River and Loon Lake. Be alert on the Loon River because it is traveled by high-speed boats shuttling fishermen and lodge visitors to Loon Lake and beyond to the Canadian side of Lac La Croix. At Loon Lake you continue south to the Pauness lakes and on to the Little Indian Sioux River to your takeout point on the Echo Trail. Comfortable pacing is to spend the first night on Little Vermilion Lake, the second night on Loon Lake, and the third night on Upper Pauness Lake or Lower Pauness Lake.

This journey generally requires two vehicles because your starting point is a 20-mile drive from your finish. Some outfitters and resorts on Crane Lake offer drop-off services to drive your vehicle to your takeout point if you will be traveling with one vehicle.

Map 8 shows most of this route, and Map 9 shows the remainder. In addition, the entire route can be seen in overview on Map 7.

Detailed Route

Paddle 20 miles through Crane Lake, King Williams Narrows, Sand Point Lake, Little Vermilion Narrows, Little Vermilion Lake, and the Loon River to Loon Lake, including portages of 10 rods (L2) and 80 rods (L4). Your journey starts outside of the Boundary Waters on Crane Lake, along the same course as Route 12A. Boating traffic from Voyageurs National Park and the Boundary Waters converges in King Williams Narrows, which can be busy with boats.

Once on Little Vermilion Lake you have an opportunity to camp on one of five campsites on the U.S. side of Little Vermilion and can also climb a 35-rod portage to Dovre Lake, which has two additional campsites, described in Route 12A. You may want to camp on Little Vermilion; otherwise continue straight to the Loon River if it is not too late in the day.

The Loon River is one of the most attractive stretches of any Boundary Waters river and has a rich forest pressed against the shoreline. Contrast this area with the dramatically different (boggy) shoreline you will paddle through later in this trip on the Little Indian Sioux River, where the forest is far back from the water's edge.

After about 3 miles on the Loon River, you will come to a seasonal 10-rod portage around a set of rapids. Just after the 10-rod portage is the 80-rod Loon Lake portage around Loon Falls. A manually operated small-gauge marine railroad is used to pull motorboats (and occasionally canoes) around the falls for a fee. This railroad is one of only two such railroad systems I know of that still join BWCAW lakes, the other one being located at the Beatty Portage on the north end of Loon Lake. Remnants of similar systems can be found at other points along the international border, such as between Gunflint and North lakes on the Gunflint Trail, and a similar system is used outside of the BWCAW at Triangle Lake near the North Kawishiwi River. The Loon

Lake "railroad" apparently continues in use because the Ontario side of the border is not protected wilderness.

Paddle 4.5 miles across Loon Lake and up the Little Indian Sioux River, portage 110 rods (L8) to Lower Pauness Lake, portage 40 rods (L5) to Upper Pauness Lake. A 110-rod portage leads from the Little Indian Sioux River into Lower Pauness Lake, following a trail that has a steep climb over much of its length. This portage is quite difficult for its length, warranting a high difficulty rating of L8. Along the portage is the raging Devil's Cascade, which is well worth a second look. A trail leads down near the cascades from the main portage in a partial clearing. A nice, but popular, campsite is located just off the portage trail. Upper and Lower Pauness lakes have a total of eight campsites. The easiest way between the two lakes is over an excellent 40-rod (L5) portage in the middle of the lakes, but a 15-rod (L5) portage in the south can also be taken. However, this 15-rod portage is up and over a steep, rocky hill, and the 40-rod portage is likely to be easier for most visitors.

Paddle and portage 4 miles along the Little Indian Sioux River, including portages of 65 rods (L5) and 40 rods (L5). Continue down the Little Indian Sioux River. A good 65-rod portage diverts you around a set of impassable rapids. The trail is quite nice, with a first quarter that is rocky but otherwise in great shape. Paddle the last 1.5 miles to the final portage, which has a rocky landing and leads over exposed bedrock that is slippery when wet. You should have a vehicle at this parking lot or have arranged for a pickup here by an outfitter.

Route 12C: Lac La Croix Adventure (Map 8)

> Difficulty: challenging
> Number of days: 7 or more
> Total miles (approx.): 82
> Number of portages: 17
> Total portage rods: 1,080
> Greatest portage difficulty: 200 rods (L8)
> Navigation maps: Voyageur 1, 2
> Fisher F15, F16, F22, F23
> McKenzie 13, 14, 32

The first half of the trip is quite easy, heading along the historic voyageurs' highway to Lac La Croix, where you will travel for miles with minimal portages. The second half of the trip is much more arduous, taking you away from the busy border into small, remote interior lakes.

You can easily shorten or lengthen this route. The easiest way to shorten your trip is to visit just western Lac La Croix, turning into the southern corner of Snow Bay on Lac La Croix and paddling through North Lake and to Slim Lake before returning to Loon Lake. Alternatively, continue farther on Lac La Croix past Forty One Island to the portage to Takucmich Lake and then on to Loon Lake. To lengthen the trip, paddle the entire length of Lac La Croix and drop south to Lake Agnes before returning through Oyster and Hustler lakes.

Map 8 shows most of this route, and Map 9 shows the remainder. In addition, the entire route can be seen in overview on Map 7.

Detailed Route

Paddle and portage 20 miles from Crane Lake to Loon Lake, traveling through King Williams Narrows, Sand Point Lake, Little Vermilion Narrows, Little Vermilion Lake, and the Loon River, taking a seasonal 10-rod (L2) portage if necessary, and portaging 80 rods (L4) around Loon Falls to Loon Lake (see Map 8). The first two days of this trip are the same as Route 12B. Your journey starts outside of the Boundary Waters on Crane Lake, which is a gateway to both Voyageurs National Park and the western Boundary Waters, and gets a good volume of motorboat use. Little Vermilion is a nice place to spend your first night. Camp at one of the five campsites on the U.S. side of Little Vermilion, or climb the 35-rod portage to Dovre Lake, which has two additional campsites and no motorboats.

From Little Vermilion Lake paddle down the Loon River about 3 miles until you come to a 10-rod portage around a set of rapids. During high water these rapids can be paddled through without too much trouble. Just after the 10-rod portage is an 80-rod portage around Loon Falls. A manually operated small-gauge railroad is used to pull motorboats (and occasional canoes) around the falls for a fee. This railroad is one of only two active marine railroad systems that join BWCAW lakes, the other one being located at the Beatty Portage on the north end of Loon Lake.

Paddle 5.5 miles across Loon Lake, portage 50 rods (L4) to lower Lac La Croix (see Map 8). The easy 50-rod portage over the Beatty Portage, which is also served by a primitive railroad, should be no problem. This portage is believed to be named after James Beatty, an early logger in this area who had a well-known logging camp on Trout Lake in the late 1800s.

Paddle and explore for 17 miles to the eastern side of Lac La Croix. Once on Lac La Croix you are in one of the most famous Boundary Waters border lakes, forming a jagged arc along some 40 miles of the border. Lac La Croix's 34,000 acres hold healthy populations of most north-country fish, including walleye, pike, and lake trout. According to Minnesota DNR fish surveys, the west side of the lake contains generally larger fish than the east side, but the east-side fish are more common.

It is probably impossible to visit Lac La Croix without being awed by its magical bays and islands. You will not be the first to be impressed by the magnificence of these waters. General Christopher C. Andrews was the first Minnesota forestry commissioner, serving from 1902 to 1908. Andrews visited Lac La Croix during those years while he was in his late seventies, and he is said to have been tremendously inspired by the unrivaled beauty of Lac La Croix. After his visit Andrews continued efforts to preserve the wilderness and sought to stop the sale of millions of acres of public land. The efforts by Andrews were an early, important part of preserving the

Boundary Waters by seeking to keep large expanses of the land in public ownership. It would have been much more difficult to form the present-day BWCAW if more of the land had been privately owned.

Motorboats are not allowed on the U.S. side of Lac La Croix past Snow Bay, but most of the Canadian side is open to them. Indeed, there are a number of resorts on the Canadian side, including famous Zup's Resort (on an island just a couple miles north of the Beatty Portage), a seaplane base, and the Neguaguon Lake Indian Reservation. Zup's Resort was built on Lac La Croix after being forced to relocate from Crooked Lake in the 1950s.

Campsites abound on Lac La Croix, but remember you are allowed to camp only on the U.S. side unless you have a Remote Area Border Crossing permit to go into Canada. Similarly, you need an Ontario fishing license to fish Canadian waters. A good place to spend a first night can be on one of the ten campsites scattered around the peninsula projecting into Snow Bay. Some of these sites are very nice, but you will be certain to hear and see motorboat traffic.

Significant forest fires burned through areas south of Lac La Croix in 1863 and 1864. This area also saw large fires in 1894. Although many big red and white pines survived the fires, their reduced numbers and burn scars made them less attractive to loggers in the late 1800s and early 1900s. In contrast, areas to the east around Basswood Lake had not been recently burned. As a consequence, extensive pine logging took place in large stretches of the BWCAW around Basswood Lake, but the area around Lac La Croix saw significantly less logging activity.

On this route you paddle east into the large central body of Lac La Croix and south toward Lady Boot Bay. The area south of Coleman Island is probably the most appealing portion of Lac La Croix for paddlers because it is free of motorized watercraft (see Maps 9 and 10). This might be your most satisfying choice if you plan to base camp on Lac La Croix for a few days of fishing. I also recommend paddling to the east side of Lac La Croix for a view of pictographs and Warrior Hill, marked on BWCAW maps. According to legend, young Ojibwe braves raced to the top of Warrior Hill to demonstrate their strength and speed.

Another fine place for exploration is the forest between Boulder Bay and Lady Boot Bay, which contains great stands of red and white pine. These trees were protected from logging in 1942 when the U.S. Forest Service created the Lac La Croix Research Natural Area, later designated by the National Park Service in 1980 as a National Natural Landmark. This important designation as a research area prevented logging similar to that which occurred up to the 1960s on other Forest Service lands in the "roadless" areas.

Paddle and portage 19 miles from eastern Lac La Croix to Loon Lake, canoeing through a dozen small lakes connected by twelve portages with a total of 845 rods and a maximum length of 200 rods (L8) (see Maps 9 and 8). Your journey will now send you west through the most isolated stretch of wilderness in the far western BWCAW. You will travel south of the traffic on Lac La Croix but north of the main routes near the Little Indian Sioux River and Moose River entry points. This entire stretch is too arduous for most paddlers to cover in one day, so I recommend breaking the trip into at least two days of travel. Nearly thirty campsites are scattered along this portion of the route, and you will typically have no problem finding a nice place to stay. In particular, Beartrack, Little Beartrack, and Eugene lakes are all nice mid-trip lakes with campsites and come as a welcome reward after the 200-rod portage to Beartrack.

This segment starts with two short portages of 20 rods (L3) and 18 rods (L3) along Pocket Creek. Like many river and creek portages in the BWCAW, these two tend to change in length depending on water levels, which are greatly affected by rainfall and beaver activity. The second portage can sometimes be skipped altogether. Pocket Lake is an attractive little lake with four designated campsites. Do not be surprised if these sites are occupied, because Pocket Lake is accessible from the west, south, and east. You may want to paddle past Pocket Lake along Finger Creek, particularly if you intend to get all the way to Loon Lake the following day. About a mile down Finger Creek the shore closes in and leads to a 90-rod (L7) portage to Finger Lake. Finger Lake can also be a nice place to spend a night, and its deep, clear waters contain some elusive northern pike.

Press on from Finger over a 1-rod (L1) portage to Thumb Lake, camping there if you are so inclined, and then head to the 200-rod (L8) portage to Beartrack Lake. This long portage is the hardest on the route, primarily due to its length and almost constant climb during the first 100 rods. All things considered, this portage is not too bad if you can make it across in one trip. Once on Beartrack Lake, you are in the heart of a wonderful stretch of deep, clear lakes bordered by steep hills and cliffs. The hills appear particularly impressive looming over beautiful wild lakes and certainly kindle appreciation for the many people who have worked so hard to keep them wild and protected.

Paddle across Beartrack Lake, and take the 30-rod (L4) portage to Little Beartrack, and the 30-rod (L4) portage to Eugene Lake. Six campsites are available on these lakes, and one on Fat Lake can be reached by taking a 60-rod (L7) portage from Eugene Lake. This portage to Fat Lake sees little use or maintenance and is quite overgrown. Search carefully for it if this off-the-beaten-path destination appeals to you.

Next, you climb up a 45-rod (L4) portage to Steep Lake but then have a generally downhill 120-rod (L6) portage to South Lake. Some McKenzie maps erroneously mark the distance from Steep Lake to South Lake as 20 rods. The correct distance is 120 rods!

A 71-rod (L6) portage leads you next to Section 3 Pond, apparently named by one of the less creative explorers of this region. Section 3 Pond connects to Slim Lake by way of a narrow creek, where you will need to take a 55-rod portage. The south end of Slim Lake has the last portage of any great difficulty. This 165-rod (L7.5) portage to Little Loon Lake requires a modest climb before a long downhill. This portage is likely to be a bit muddy in stretches but otherwise is not too bad.

Paddle and portage 20 miles from Loon Lake to Crane Lake, covering portages of 80 rods (L4) and 10 rods (L2) along the Loon River (see Map 8). This leg returns you from Loon Lake to your starting point on Crane Lake along a segment you covered on the first day of this route.

Entry Point 14, Little Indian Sioux River North (Map 9)

>Daily permit quota: 6
>Permit availability: difficult

Little Indian Sioux River North is one of the main gateways to the far western BWCAW and allows relatively easy access to Lac La Croix and the Canadian border. Little Indian Sioux River North and Moose River North (Entry Point 16) account for most of the paddle visitors to the far northwest BWCAW. Get your permit early for this entry; the full quota is used most days during the summer, and during peak August travel every permit is likely to be used.

Possible routes from Entry Point 14 vary considerably, but a few considerations should come into play when you are planning to enter from Little Indian Sioux River North. First, according to the BWCA Wilderness Management Plan, the corridor from the Moose River north through Nina Moose Lake and Lake Agnes is managed as semiprimitive wilderness, while areas to the west and east are managed as primitive wilderness. The result is that portages are more developed and maintained, as well as more heavily used, in the semiprimitive wilderness area than in the primitive wilderness area. Second, if you want a classic BWCAW experience devoid of motorboats but don't crave absolute isolation, then consider taking route 14A or 14B. Both offer great experiences but follow popular routes near the edge of the wilderness. Third, if you are taking a longer trip and want complete isolation, head to the interior area north of Upper Pauness and Lower Pauness lakes but not so far north as to reach more popular Lac La Croix. Route 14C is ideal for such a trip.

To get to Entry Point 14, take the Echo Trail 31 miles out of Ely, where you will find a well-marked turnoff to the north (right), which quickly leads to a parking lot and portage to the river. Consider staying at the Echo Lake campground the night before entering the wilderness, which has twenty-four campsites and also accepts reservations.

Route 14A: Exploring the Pauness Lakes (Map 9)

>Difficulty: easy
>Number of days: 2 or more
>Total miles (approx.): 8
>Number of portages: 6
>Total portage rods: 290
>Greatest portage difficulty: 65 rods (L5)
>Navigation maps: Voyageur 1
>   Fisher F16
>   McKenzie 14

This easy route paddles down the Little Indian Sioux River for about 3.5 miles to the shores of Upper Pauness Lake, which has an easy connection to Lower Pauness Lake,

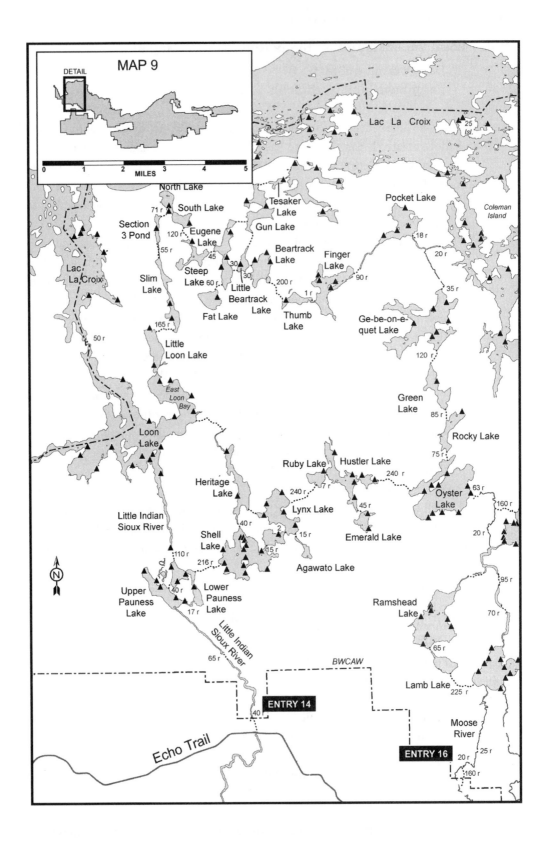

MAP 9

DETAIL

0 1 2 3 4 5
MILES

Lac La Croix

25 Isl

Coleman Island

North Lake

South Lake

71 r

Section 3 Pond

120 r

Eugene Lake

55 r

45

Tesaker Lake

Gun Lake

Beartrack Lake

Finger Lake

Pocket Lake

18 r

20 r

Slim Lake

Steep Lake 60 r

30

30

Little Beartrack Lake

200 r

90 r

35 r

Lac La Croix

Fat Lake

1 r

Thumb Lake

Ge-be-on-e-quet Lake

165 r

50 r

Little Loon Lake

120 r

East Loon Bay

Green Lake

85 r

Rocky Lake

Loon Lake

75 r

Ruby Lake

Hustler Lake

240 r

Oyster Lake

63 r

160 r

Heritage Lake

Little Indian Sioux River

240 r

7 r

Lynx Lake

45 r

Emerald Lake

20 r

40 r

2

15 r

Shell Lake

15 r

Agawato Lake

95 r

110 r

216 r

Upper Pauness Lake

40 r

Lower Pauness Lake

17 r

Ramshead Lake

70 r

65 r

Little Indian Sioux River

65 r

BWCAW

Lamb Lake

225 r

ENTRY 14

40

Moose River

Echo Trail

ENTRY 16

20 r

25 r

160 r

N

and then paddles back up the Little Indian Sioux River at the end of your trip. This easy route is suitable for visitors of all skill levels.

Detailed Route

Paddle and portage 4 miles to Lower Pauness Lake, including portages of 40 rods (L5) and 65 rods (L5) along the Little Indian Sioux River, and 40 rods (L5) to Lower Pauness Lake. The first portage from the parking lot scurries over a section of inclined bedrock. This rocky face can be slippery, especially on the start of your trip before your nimble "portage" legs have fully formed.

Paddle north along the nice, wide Little Indian Sioux River. This section of river has a good channel lined by marsh plants. After 1.5 miles you will reach a 65-rod portage along a generally good trail, the last quarter of which is over a rock base. Continue along the Little Indian Sioux River to Upper Pauness Lake. This lazy stretch can be good country for spotting moose, and you may also come across beavers, otters, and ducks. Two alternative portages connect Upper and Lower Pauness lakes. You can take either portage, although the level 40-rod trail on the north is probably preferable to the rough, hilly 17-rod trail to the south.

Both Upper Pauness and Lower Pauness are nice lakes but weedier than most in the BWCAW. Most of Upper Pauness is downright swampy. However, some nice pike reside in those weedy shallows. The deep north bay of Lower Pauness provides the most weed-free areas.

As is often the case with lakes near popular entries, the campsites on the Pauness lakes tend to be under more visitor pressure than interior sites. If all nine campsites are taken, head to either Loon Lake or Shell Lake, which are more likely to have empty sites.

The north bay of Lower Pauness leads to a portage around the Devil's Cascade, a granite gorge through which the Little Indian Sioux River tumbles. When water levels are high, the cascades are spectacular, but even during drier seasons it is worth a trip to hike the portage.

Paddle and portage 4 miles back up the Little Indian Sioux River, including portages of 40 rods (L5), 65 rods (L5), and 40 rods (L5) to the parking lot. Your return trip is simply a reversal of your way to the Pauness lakes down the Little Indian Sioux River.

Route 14B: One-Way to Nina Moose Lake (Map 9)

> Difficulty: moderate
> Number of days: 3 or more
> Total miles (approx.): 22
> Number of portages: 19
> Total portage rods: 1,318
> Greatest portage difficulty: 240 rods (L9)
> Navigation maps: Voyageur 1

Fisher F16

McKenzie 12, 13, 14

This excellent route travels from Entry Point 14 to the Moose River (Entry Point 16) by way of great wilderness lakes. Although some of the portages are long, even first-time visitors can enjoy this route if they pack light, and even the toughest portages are along generally good trails. Many of the lakes on this route are relatively popular and offer limited isolation. However, a few suggestions are provided on how to turn off the main route and seek greater solitude.

Map 9 shows most of this route, and Map 10 shows the remainder. In addition, the entire route can be seen in overview on Map 7.

Detailed Route

Paddle and portage 4 miles to Lower Pauness Lake, including portages of 40 rods (L5) and 65 rods (L5) along the Little Indian Sioux River, and 40 rods (L5) to Lower Pauness Lake. You should have no problem reaching the Pauness lakes in two or three hours, following the same course as Route 14A. The first portage from the parking lot to the river is well traveled, and the next portage is an easy 65 rods along a generally good trail, the last quarter of which is over a rock base.

Continue along the Little Indian Sioux River to Upper Pauness Lake. With luck you will spot a moose feeding along the river, or perhaps a beaver or family of otters. Both Upper Pauness and Lower Pauness are nice lakes but weedier than most BWCAW lakes. You can take either one of two portages between the Pauness lakes, although I prefer the level 40-rod trail on the north to the rough, hilly 17-rod trail to the south.

Portage 216 rods (L7) to Shell Lake. The 216-rod portage to Shell Lake follows an excellent trail but is likely to be a bit muddy on either end. A short boardwalk across the middle helps pass a muddy low spot. The portage also crosses over the Sioux Hustler Hiking Trail. Shell Lake makes an excellent location for a first night in the BWCAW. Ten designated campsites are located on Shell, including four on islands. Shell Lake is much shallower than subsequent lakes along this route and holds a nice population of walleye and northern pike. You can expect this lake to warm up faster in the spring than other area lakes, and can plan accordingly if you will be fishing. When the bite is off on Shell, it well might be on at either Little Shell or Lynx Lake, which are much deeper and thus likely to warm later in the spring and cool later in the fall. Once on Shell you have the option of heading to Heritage Lake by way of a 40-rod portage along a rocky trail that is not well traveled. The two Heritage Lake sites are nice destinations if you want more isolation than you are getting so far along this route. Heritage seems to get relatively few visitors because of the longer portages you must take to exit through its north end.

Paddle 4 miles from Shell Lake to Hustler Lake, including portages of 15 rods (L3) to Little Shell Lake, a seasonal 2 rods (L2) to Lynx Lake, 240 (L8.5) rods to Ruby Lake, and 7 rods (L1.5) to Hustler Lake. Head out through the eastern end of Shell Lake over an easy 15-rod portage to Little Shell Lake. Next, a simple beaver dam pull-over is all you are likely to encounter between Little Shell and Lynx lakes, although some older maps show a 4-rod portage. Consider staying on Lynx Lake for a night; the deep waters hold a good population of pike and walleye.

You can make an interesting side trip from Lynx Lake to Agawato Lake by way of a 15-rod (L4) portage on the south end of Lynx. The portage is not well used and leads to a forest partially submerged by beaver activity along the northern bay of Agawato. One seldom-used campsite is on the eastern shore. Agawato is a good option if you want greater isolation than is otherwise possible on this route.

When leaving Lynx, portage your gear over the 240-rod trail to Ruby Lake. This is a long portage that passes through a stand of old-growth white and red pine. Finally, an easy 7-rod portage leads to Hustler Lake, which is also a nice place to spend an evening. Another escape off the main route can be found by going south from Hustler Lake to Emerald Lake, which has two campsites. The 45-rod (L5) portage is well hidden and starts a bit north of the end of the southern bay of Hustler.

Paddle 1.5 miles across Hustler Lake, portage 240 rods (L9) to Oyster Lake. A good, well-drained 240-rod trail leads to Oyster Lake and is easy but long. Oyster Lake is a Boundary Waters jewel and well worth a night's stay. The most popular campsites are on the long peninsula, but the east shore is also quite nice and has some fine, sandy beaches!

Paddle and portage to Lake Agnes, including portaging 63 rods (L4) to the Oyster River, paddling 2 miles with a 20-rod portage down the Oyster River, or paddling 1 mile with a 160-rod portage to Lake Agnes. This route takes you out of Oyster Lake by way of a relatively easy 63-rod portage that is modestly hilly but also has a number of really nice red and white pines. The portage ends at the Oyster River, which connects with the Nina Moose River south of Lake Agnes.

The Oyster River is marginal for canoeing during dry years, particularly in the southern sections, where the channel is narrow, shallow, and easily lost. During these dry periods you may have to take the 160-rod portage to Agnes. This 160-rod portage is a bit boggy on the Oyster River side and makes a steep climb out of the river valley. However, the trail soon flattens and then drops to a nice sandy beach on Agnes. Consider taking the Oyster River all the way to the Nina Moose River if water levels permit. If you take the full Oyster River, you will have one more portage (in addition to occasional beaver dams) of 20 rods. Once you reach the Nina Moose River, turn north to paddle a short distance into Lake Agnes, which is an excellent place to spend the night.

Lake Agnes is one of the most attractive lakes in this portion of the BWCAW, but it is also a popular destination for travelers entering on the Moose River. Do not expect to be the only campers on Agnes, even during early spring and late fall. This route does not require that you pass through the northern reaches of Agnes, but I highly recommend at least a detour to the short portage leading to Boulder Bay. The forest in this vicinity was burned in the recent past, leaving a stand of old red and white pines mostly unharmed. Birch and aspen have taken off in the cleared under-story below the old pines. These old pines are now a source of seedlings that will grow up under the aspen-birch forest and perhaps someday replace that forest.

Lake Agnes probably looks today much like it has for at least five thousand years, but in the early 1900s lumber baron Edward E. Backus hoped to change this area forever. Backus dreamed of building a series of dams along the border to generate hydropower and facilitate logging. This plan would have dramatically altered this area, including raising the water levels on Lac La Croix 16 feet, sufficient to merge it with its smaller neighbor Lake Agnes. Backus's plan was fought tooth and nail by early environmentalists, most notably Ernest C. Oberholtzer, a fearless ally of wilderness for much of his life, and arguably the grandfather of the effort to preserve the Boundary Waters. Eventually the Backus plan was rejected. It is due to the efforts of Oberholtzer (and many others) that you are visiting Lake Agnes, and not Agnes Bay or the Agnes Bay Resort and Dam!

Paddle 4.5 miles south along the Nina Moose River with portages of 95 rods (L5) and 70 rods (L5) to Nina Moose Lake. Continue south from Lake Agnes to Nina Moose, which is a nice but well-traveled lake. You should not assume that there will be available campsites on Nina Moose unless you get a very early start in the morning or are visiting during early spring or late fall.

The west shore of Nina Moose Lake burned in May 1971 in the Little Sioux fire, which consumed over 14,000 acres of forest straddling the Echo Trail. The portage to Lamb Lake from Nina Moose is within the fire perimeter and is a worthwhile hike to see the regenerating forest. The Little Sioux fire was the largest fire within the BWCAW in the last half of the twentieth century. Nothing else of similar size occurred in the Boundary Waters after 1910, when major fire suppression activity started in the Superior National Forest. The work of Miron Heinselman, a pioneer in forestry and fire history, showed that the dearth of fires in the twentieth century reflects a major change from the prior three hundred years, and has significantly changed forest succession. See Heinselman's book *The Boundary Waters Wilderness Ecosystem* for more information on this topic.

Paddle 3.25 miles along the Moose River with portages of 25 rods (L2), 20 rods (L1), and 160 rods (L5). The final southern stretch of the Moose River is easy traveling. The first, 25-rod portage is a good trail but a bit rocky; the second, 20-rod portage is exceedingly easy and passes over only one small low spot, where a boardwalk has been constructed. Between these two portages is a small stretch of rocky shallows with an optional 2-rod portage, but most people succeed in paddling or pulling their canoe through these shallows without taking the portage.

Route 14C: Interior Loop South of Lac La Croix (Map 9)

        Difficulty: challenging

        Number of days: 7

        Total miles (approx.): 44

> Number of portages: 28
> Total portage rods: 1,970 (approx. 6 miles)
> Greatest portage difficulty: 290 rods (L9)
> Navigation maps: Voyageur 1, 2
> Fisher F16
> McKenzie 12, 13, 14

This route takes you to a wonderful set of small lakes south of Lac La Croix and offers you some of the greatest isolation to be found in the western BWCAW. You will travel far enough into the wilderness to avoid most visitors, who stay close to the entries, but will not go so far as to hit Lac La Croix and the more numerous visitors that are sometimes found there.

Map 9 shows the start of this route, and Map 10 shows the remainder. In addition, the entire route can be seen in overview on Map 7.

Detailed Route

Paddle and portage 4 miles down the Little Indian Sioux River to Lower Pauness Lake, including portages of 40 rods (L5) and 65 rods (L5) to Upper Pauness Lake, and 40 rods (L5) to Lower Pauness Lake. You should have no problem reaching the Pauness lakes in two or three hours, following the same course as Route 14A. The first portage from the parking lot to the river is well traveled, and the next portage is an easy 65-rod trail along a generally good path, the last quarter of which is over a rock base.

Continue along the Little Indian Sioux River to Upper Pauness Lake and Lower Pauness Lake. This lazy stretch of river can be good country for spotting moose, and you may come across beavers, otters, and ducks. Both Upper Pauness and Lower Pauness are nice lakes but weedier than most in the BWCAW. You can take either of two portages between the lakes, although I prefer the level 40-rod trail on the north to the rough, hilly 17-rod trail to the south.

Portage 216 rods (L7) to Shell Lake. The 216-rod portage to Shell Lake follows an excellent trail but is likely to be a bit muddy on either end. A short boardwalk across the middle helps pass a muddy low spot. The portage also crosses over the Sioux Hustler Hiking Trail. Shell Lake makes an excellent location for a first night in the BWCAW. Ten designated campsites are located on Shell, including four on islands.

Shell Lake is much shallower than subsequent lakes along this route and holds a nice population of walleye and northern pike. You can expect this lake to warm up in spring faster than other area lakes, and can plan accordingly if you will be fishing. When the bite is off on Shell, it well might be on at either Little Shell or Lynx Lake, which are much deeper and thus likely to warm later in spring and cool later in fall. Once on Shell you have the option of heading to Heritage Lake by way of a 40-rod portage along a rocky trail that is not well traveled. Heritage gets fewer travelers than Shell and is an option for a bit more solitude than you will find on the main route.

Paddle and portage 4 miles from Shell Lake to Hustler Lake, including portages of 15 rods (L3) to Little Shell Lake, a seasonal 2-rod (L2) portage to Lynx Lake, 240 (L8.5) rods to Ruby Lake, and 7 rods (L1.5) to Hustler Lake. Head out through the eastern end of Shell Lake over an easy 15-rod portage to Little Shell Lake. A simple beaver dam pull-over is all you will likely need between Little Shell and Lynx lakes, although older maps show a 4-rod portage. Consider staying on Lynx Lake for a night; the deep waters hold a good population of pike and walleye.

An interesting side trip from Lynx Lake can be made by taking a 15-rod (L4) portage on the south end of Lynx into Agawato Lake. The portage is not well used and leads to a forest partially submerged by beaver activity along the northern bay of Agawato. One seldom-used campsite is on the eastern shore of Agawato. This diversion is a good option if you want to seek out greater isolation than is otherwise possible on this route. When leaving Lynx, portage your gear over the 240-rod portage to Ruby Lake. This is a long portage that passes through a nice stand of old-growth white and red pines. Finally, an easy 7-rod portage leads to Hustler Lake, which is also a nice place to spend an evening. Another nice escape off the main route can be found by going south from Hustler Lake to Emerald Lake, which has two campsites. The 45-rod (L5) portage is well hidden and starts a bit north of the end of the southern bay of Hustler. Emerald clearly gets fewer visitors than Hustler.

Paddle and portage 2.5 miles across Hustler Lake and on to Oyster Lake, including a 240-rod (L9) portage. A good, well-drained 240-rod trail leads to Oyster Lake and is easy but long. Oyster Lake is a Boundary Waters treasure and well worth a night's stay. The most popular campsites are on the long peninsula, but the east shore is also nice and has some small sand beaches.

Paddle and portage 5 miles through Oyster Lake to Ge-be-on-e-quet Lake, including portages of 75 rods (L5) to Rocky Lake, 85 rods (L6) to Green Lake, and 120 rods (L8) to Ge-be-on-e-quet Lake. Head north from Oyster Lake and on to Ge-be-on-e-quet Lake by way of Rocky and Green lakes, which are beautiful small lakes with steep shorelines. You should find this area feels even more remote and peaceful than the southern lakes you passed through earlier in this route. Rocky is a pretty lake with one marginal campsite and is much shallower than Green Lake, which also has one campsite. Rocky Lake has pictographs located along the west-central shore, about 6 feet above the water surface along a cliff, showing distinct vertical marks plus a cross that may be a simple human figure. Finally, the 120-rod portage from Green Lake to Ge-be-on-e-quet climbs gradually for about 90 rods before dropping steeply to Ge-be-on-e-quet. Ge-be-on-e-quet is an excellent destination lake and is said to be fine bass water in its many little bays.

Paddle and portage 2.5 miles from Ge-be-on-e-quet Lake to Pocket Lake, including portages of 35 rods (L9) to Ge-be-on-e-quet Creek and 18 rods (L3) along Pocket Creek to Pocket Lake. The 35-rod portage from Ge-be-on-e-quet Lake to Ge-be-on-e-quet Creek is a rough, steep, rocky trail that drops considerably along its relatively short length. This is one of the toughest short portages in the BWCAW when coming from the north; fortunately you have a downhill route from the south. The 18-rod portage is much easier.

This route keeps you south and west of Lac La Croix, which is just a short portage and paddle to the east. If you want to make a diversion to Lac La Croix, you will find plenty of interest on its massive, island-studded surface. See Route 12C for more information on Lac La Croix, including such interesting sites as Warrior Hill and the red and white pines designated by the National Park Service as a National Natural Landmark.

Paddle and portage 16 miles from Pocket Lake to Loon Lake, canoeing through a dozen small lakes connected by ten portages with a total of 757 rods and a maximum length of 200 rods (L8). Your journey will now send you through some of the most isolated wilderness in the far western BWCAW. You are south of the traffic on Lac La Croix but generally north of the main routes near the Little Indian Sioux River and Moose River entry points. Once you head beyond Pocket Lake, you are venturing into some of the most remote lakes of this north-woods wilderness. This entire stretch is too arduous for most paddlers to cover in one day, so consider breaking the trip into at least two days of travel. Nearly thirty campsites are scattered along this portion of the route, so you should have no problem finding a nice place to stay. Beartrack Lake, Little Beartrack Lake, and Eugene Lake are all nice mid-trip lakes with campsites and will come as a welcome reward after the long portage to Beartrack.

Paddle out the southwest end of Pocket Lake, and about a mile down Finger Creek the shore closes in and leads to a 90-rod (L7) portage to Finger Lake. Finger Lake can be a nice place to spend a night, and its deep, clear waters contain some elusive pike. Press on from Finger over the 1-rod (L1) portage to Thumb Lake.

The 200-rod portage (L8) to Beartrack Lake is the hardest on this route, primarily due to its length and a tough climb for the first 100 rods. Once on Beartrack Lake, you are in the heart of a wonderful stretch of deep, clear lakes bordered by relatively steep hills and cliffs. The hills appear particularly impressive looming over these smaller lakes. Along peaceful stretches of remote lakes such as these it is easy to feel appreciation for the many people who have worked so hard to keep them wild and protected. Paddle through Beartrack Lake, and take the 30-rod (L4) portage to Little Beartrack, and the 30-rod (L4) portage to Eugene Lake. Six designated campsites are located on these lakes, and one on Fat Lake can be reached by taking a 60-rod (L7) portage from Eugene Lake.

Pressing onward from Eugene, you must climb up a 45-rod (L4) portage to Steep Lake, but you will then have a generally downhill 120-rod portage to South Lake. Some McKenzie maps erroneously mark the distance from Steep Lake to South Lake as just 20 rods rather than the proper 120 rods. From South Lake a 71-rod (L6) portage leads to Section 3 Pond. Section 3 Pond connects to Slim Lake by way of a narrow creek, where you take a 55-rod portage. The south end of Slim Lake has one of the last portages of any great difficulty on this route. This 165-rod (L7.5) portage requires a modest climb before a long downhill to Little Loon Lake and is likely to be a bit muddy in stretches but otherwise not too bad.

Paddle 5.5 miles across Loon Lake and up the Little Indian Sioux River, portage 110 rods (L8) to Lower Pauness Lake, portage 40 rods (L5) to Upper Pauness Lake. A 110-rod portage leads from the Little Indian Sioux River into Lower Pauness Lake, following a trail that has steep climbs throughout much of its length. Along the west shore is the raging Devil's Cascade, which is well worth a second look. A trail from the main portage leads to near the cascades. Upper and Lower Pauness lakes have a total of eight campsites. The easiest connection between the two lakes is over a 40-rod (L5) portage in the middle of the lakes, but a 17-rod (L5) portage in the south can also be taken. However, this 17-rod portage is up and over a rocky hill, and I consider the longer 40-rod portage to be easier.

Paddle 4.5 miles along the Little Indian Sioux River from Upper Pauness Lake to your starting location, including portages of 65 rods (L5) and 40 rods (L5) to the landing and parking lot. Continue on the Little Indian Sioux River. A nice 65-rod portage diverts you around a set of impassable rapids. The trail is generally quite easy, with a first quarter that is quite rocky but otherwise in great shape. Paddle the last 1.5 miles to the final portage, which has a rocky landing and leads over exposed bedrock, which can be slippery when wet.

Entry Point 16, Moose/Portage River North (Map 10)

Daily permit quota: 7
Permit availability: difficult

The Moose River and the neighboring Portage River are a combined entry that is among the most popular in the BWCAW. Nina Moose Lake and Lake Agnes are close to the entry and appeal to many people. Just beyond these well-known lakes are magnificent Lac La Croix and the Canadian border. Four different routes are proposed below: a short trip to Nina Moose Lake, a trip through Agnes into Lac La Croix, and loops to the west and to the east. Some of these routes are reasonably well traveled and will not give you the same level of isolation you will find in other areas in this guide. Fortunately, a few recommended spurs to isolated lakes allow you to find very secluded areas.

You can start Entry 16 at either the Moose River or the neighboring Portage River, but most people enter by the Moose River, which is accessible by a 160-rod portage. The Moose River is reached by following the Echo Trail just over 23 miles from Ely to Forest Service Road 206, which is well marked with a sign to the Moose River entry. Take Forest Service Road 206 for a mile to a large parking lot (with overflow capacity). The parking lot has a good area to unload your gear, and outhouses, but you will have to move your car to the long-term parking area before departing.

If you would rather enter at the Portage River, you can do so by starting about 2 miles closer to Ely, where the Echo Trail crosses the river. A small turnout is on the

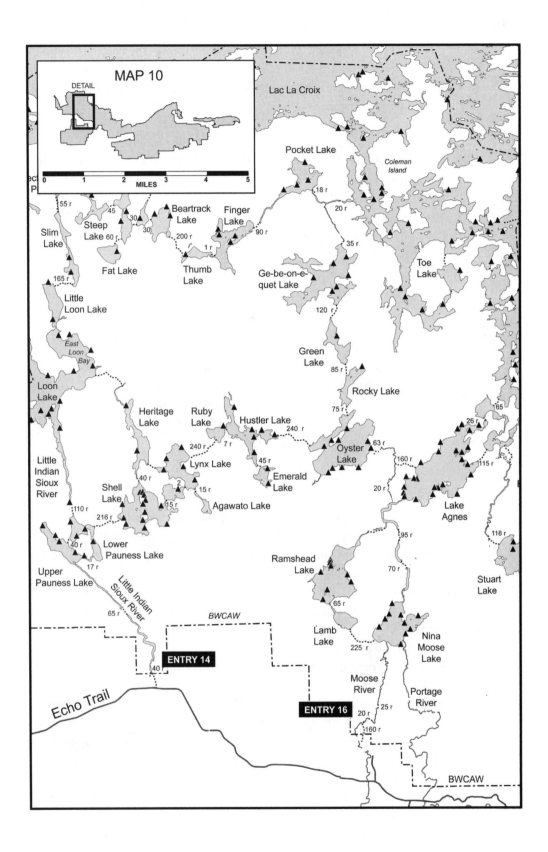

south side of the road, although it is not suitable for parking. The Portage River is a permissible entry, but the stretch to Nina Moose Lake is not regularly maintained for canoeing. Travel along the Portage River is likely to be a serious challenge with downed trees obstructing parts of it.

Route 16A: Exploration of Nina Moose with Optional Extensions (Map 10)

Difficulty: easy
Number of days: 2 or more
Total miles (approx.): 7
Number of portages: 8
Total portage rods: 414
Greatest portage difficulty: 160 rods (L5)
Navigation maps: Voyageur 1
                  Fisher F16
                  McKenzie 12

This easy route takes you to Nina Moose Lake, which is a famous Boundary Waters gem with eight designated campsites. You will certainly see other campers on Nina Moose and crews paddling through on their way to or from more remote lakes. If you seek more solitude, greater isolation is easy to find by crossing a demanding portage to Lamb Lake and on to Ramshead Lake.

Detailed Route

Paddle and portage 3.5 miles to Nina Moose Lake, including portages of 160 rods (L5), 20 rods (L1), optional 2 rods (L1), and 25 rods (L2.5). The greatest challenge to this route is the initial 160-rod portage that travels down a good trail to the edge of the Moose River. This portage is long but easily managed on its excellent trail. Once you put in on the Moose River, you will soon have a very easy 20-rod portage along another good trail. A low-lying muddy section on this portage has been bridged by a short boardwalk.

After the 20-rod portage, you will paddle through a small, rocky channel where an optional 2-rod portage can be taken but can generally be avoided with nice canoe work through some rocky shallows. A final, 25-rod portage lies ahead, again follow-ing a good trail, but one that is more rocky than others along this route. After this final portage, you will paddle up the Moose River to where it drops into Nina Moose Lake. This easy stretch of river may have a couple beaver dams but soon widens into a broad bed of wild rice opening into Nina Moose Lake. I have seen otters through here on more than one trip.

Nina Moose has a number of very nice campsites. Unless you are visiting in January, expect at least some of them to be occupied by other visitors, and some could be occupied in January as well! Your proximity to the entry point makes it possible that you will have difficulty getting a site in the peak of the summer paddling season. Based on Forest Service data and my own experience, campsite availability on this lake can sometimes be a problem.

Nina Moose is also of interest to people curious about forest regeneration. The west shore of Nina Moose burned in the Little Sioux fire in May 1971, which scorched over 14,000 acres of forest straddling the Echo Trail east of the Little Indian Sioux River. Much of the forest between Nina Moose Lake and Ramshead Lake also burned in this fire, including the forest surrounding Lamb Lake. A hike along the portage from Nina Moose to Lamb Lake takes you through a maturing forest of aspen and birch, with an undergrowth of conifers, which should plunge through the aspen and birch as they die off in coming decades. This regenerating forest may be a good indication of how areas burned after the 1999 windstorm will look three decades after the storm. Take a hike to Lamb Lake on the 225-rod portage to see this regeneration up close.

Paddle and portage 3.5 miles back to the entry, including portages of 25 rods (L2.5), optional 2 rods (L1), 20 rods (L1), and 160 rods (L5) along the Moose River. Your return from Nina Moose is simply the reverse of your paddle up the Moose River. Be alert when leaving Nina Moose Lake so that you head south down the Moose River rather than the Portage River, which is found a half mile to the east. The mouths of both rivers are in the same broad wild rice beds on the south side of Nina Moose and can be confused if you don't carefully watch your position.

Optional Extensions

As already mentioned, if you want more isolation on this route, head out over the 225-rod (L9.5) portage to Lamb Lake and then on to Ramshead Lake by way of a 65-rod (L7) portage. The first portage to Lamb Lake is difficult to find but starts at a concealed landing just to the north of a large light-colored boulder on the west shore of Nina Moose. The trail is rocky in stretches and not well traveled—watch your step on this long haul. Paddle through Lamb Lake and then hike over the 65-rod portage (not 150, as shown on older maps) to Ramshead Lake. Ramshead has numerous campsites to choose from, none of which get much use. You may want to stalk the waters for northern pike, which are said to be plentiful.

Route 16B: Lac La Croix Express (Map 10)

> Difficulty: easy
> Number of days: 4 or more
> Total miles (approx.): 28
> Number of portages: 12
> Total portage rods: 792 rods
> Greatest portage difficulty: 160 rods (L5)

Navigation maps: Voyageur 1, 2
Fisher 16
McKenzie 12, 13

If your main objective is to get to Lac La Croix, then this is one of your best choices and is certainly the easiest way into eastern Lac La Croix. You will follow a popular route though Nina Moose Lake and then on to Lake Agnes, both of which are fine destinations in their own right, before finally reaching Boulder Bay of Lac La Croix.

Detailed Route

Paddle and portage 3.5 miles to Nina Moose Lake, including portages of 160 rods (L5), 20 rods (L1), optional 2 rods (L1), and 25 rods (L2.5). This journey follows the same first leg to Nina Moose Lake as Route 16A. The greatest challenge is the initial 160-rod portage to the edge of the Moose River. Once you put in on the Moose River, you will quickly reach a very easy 20-rod portage along another good trail. A short boardwalk has bridged the only significant muddy section. After the 20-rod portage, you will paddle through a small, rocky channel where an optional 2-rod portage can be taken but is usually avoidable by paddling through the shallows. A final, 25-rod portage lies ahead, again following a good trail. After the 25-rod portage, you will paddle up the Moose River to where it drops into Nina Moose Lake. This easy stretch of river may have a couple beaver dams but soon widens into an expanse of wild rice opening into Nina Moose Lake. Nina Moose is a very popular lake, so get there early if you want to spend the night.

Paddle 4.5 miles along the Nina Moose River to Lake Agnes, including portages of 70 rods (L5) and 95 rods (L5). You will take two portages to get to Lake Agnes from Nina Moose, both of which are about average in difficulty. Perhaps the most remarkable sight on either trail is a monster white pine on the east side of the first portage. Once on Lake Agnes you are at one of the main paddling intersections in the western BWCAW, with options to explore in every direction. Agnes is also a wonderful destination or stopover in its own right and has a number of fine red and white pine stands. I highly recommend spending a day or two on Agnes at one of the seventeen designated campsites located along its shores before pressing on to Lac La Croix. Lake Agnes holds healthy populations of pike and walleye.

Paddle and portage 6 miles to Lac La Croix, including portages of 26 rods (L5) to the Boulder River and a short 2-rod (L1) portage around rapids. You have a couple of good options for getting to Boulder Bay of Lac La Croix from Lake Agnes. As shown on Map 10, you can take a 26-rod portage to the Boulder River and then either portage 65 rods to Boulder Bay or paddle a circuitous route along the Boulder River. Alternatively, take a 115-rod portage from the east side of Agnes and paddle the lower stretches of the Boulder River north to Boulder Bay. The 115-rod option starts at a sandy beach on Agnes and follows a flat, well-drained trail to Boulder Bay. This long portage can be a bit mucky on the Boulder Bay side.

The 26-rod portage is a rocky climb up around a set of rapids but not too difficult. One advantage of this option is that you see an interesting area of burned forest east of the portage. You will notice that many large red and white pines survived the fire, with an understory of birch and aspen now growing in beneath and between the pines. After the 26-rod portage, you can take a 65-rod (L7.5) portage right to Boulder Bay, but this is a hard trail that has a tough uphill followed immediately by a steep downhill along a fairly rocky path. If you want an easier, longer route, take the Boulder River in a loop to the south and around to Boulder Bay. You will need to pass around one set of rapids that requires an easy lift-over.

Once on Boulder Bay you can paddle northwest into the island-studded expanse of Lac La Croix. Your options are plentiful on Lac La Croix for campsites and fishing. In addition, you should paddle up the Canadian side of Irving Island to take a glimpse at Warrior Hill, and paddle to pictographs, marked on BWCAW maps, about 4 miles north of Boulder Bay. See Route 12C for more information about this remarkable lake.

Paddle 14 miles back to your start, including portages of 26 rods (L5) to Lake Agnes, 95 rods (L5) and 70 rods (L5) along the Nina Moose River, and portages of 25 rods (L2.5), 20 rods (L1), and 160 rods (L5) along the Moose River. Return to your starting point by the same route you arrived, or for a change, loop back to Lake Agnes by one of the other alternative portages described above.

Route 16C: Oyster, Ge-be-on-e-quet, Lac La Croix Loop (Map 10)

>   Difficulty: challenging
>   Number of days: 6
>   Total miles (approx.): 38.5
>   Number of portages: 19
>   Total portage rods: 1,415
>   Greatest portage difficulty: 160 rods (L8.5)
>   Navigation maps: Voyageur 1, 2
>   Fisher F16, F23
>   McKenzie 12, 13

This is the first of two challenging loops recommended out of Nina Moose, and takes you up to Lake Agnes before turning west to hit Oyster Lake and Ge-be-on-e-quet Lake on your way to Lac La Croix. This trip is remarkable for its beauty, which is enhanced by the numerous groves of red and white pine that you will paddle past or portage through. Indeed, this route takes you through some of the best virgin forest in the BWCAW, much of it dating back to the early 1800s. Route 16D is similar in difficulty but heads east from Agnes.

Map 10 shows most of this route, and Map 9 shows the portion of the route that extends farther west. In addition, the entire route can be seen in overview on Map 7.

Detailed Route

Paddle and portage 3.5 miles to Nina Moose Lake, including portages of 160 rods (L5), 20 rods (L1), optional 2 rods (L1), and 25 rods (L2.5). This journey follows the same start to Nina Moose Lake and Lake Agnes as Route 16B. The 160-rod portage travels down a high-quality trail to the edge of the Moose River. Once you put in on the Moose River, you will soon have a very easy 20-rod portage along another good trail. A short boardwalk has bridged the only significant muddy section. After the 20-rod portage, you will paddle through a small, rocky channel where an optional 2-rod portage can be taken but is usually avoidable. A final, 25-rod portage lies ahead, again following a good trail, but one that is more rocky than others along this route. After this final portage, you will paddle up the Moose River to where it drops into Nina Moose Lake. This easy stretch of river may have a couple beaver dams but soon widens into Nina Moose Lake, which will make a fine place to spend a first evening.

Paddle 4.5 miles along the Nina Moose River to Lake Agnes, including portages of 70 rods (L5) and 95 rods (L5). You will take two portages to get to Lake Agnes, both of which are about average in difficulty. Lake Agnes is one of the main paddling intersections in the western BWCAW, with options to explore in every direction. Agnes is also a wonderful destination or stopover in its own right. Seventeen campsites are positioned along its shores, and the waters hold healthy populations of pike and walleye. Consider spending a day or two on Agnes before pressing on to Oyster Lake.

Paddle and portage 2.5 miles from Lake Agnes to Oyster Lake, including portages of 160 rods (L8.5) and 63 rods (L4). Take the 160-rod portage from Lake Agnes to the Oyster River. Alternatively, you can paddle up the length of the Oyster River, taking a 20-rod portage along the way. The 160-rod portage is probably a superior route because it is along a nice trail. In contrast, the southern mile of the Oyster River can be difficult to navigate in all but very high water levels. Indeed, it can even be hard to find where the Oyster River splits with the Nina Moose River. Fortunately, the northern half of the Oyster River (reached from the 160-rod portage) is much easier to navigate than the southern half and leads to the final, 63-rod portage to Oyster Lake.

You may want to spend a day or two on Oyster Lake, and I recommend checking out any of the three peninsula campsites, of which the middle one is highly regarded for its fine perch looking east over the main bay of Oyster. This area has some of the oldest red and white pines in the BWCAW. You won't find solid stands of such trees, but you will find numerous groves of mixed-age trees, some more than two hundred years old. The southern and eastern campsites on Oyster are also nice, a few having decent sandy shorelines for swimming.

Paddle and portage 5 miles from Oyster Lake to Ge-be-on-e-quet Lake, including portages of 75 rods (L5) to Rocky Lake, 85 rods (L6) to Green Lake, and 120 rods (L8) to Ge-be-on-e-quet Lake. Head north from Oyster Lake and on to Ge-be-on-e-quet Lake by way of Rocky and Green lakes. This is a beautiful stretch of small lakes with steep shorelines and is more peaceful than the southern lakes you passed through earlier in this route. Rocky is a pretty lake with a marginal campsite and a small display of pictographs on the western shore. Shallow Green Lake also has one campsite. The 120-rod portage from Green Lake to Ge-be-on-e-quet climbs gradually for about 90 rods before dropping steeply down to Ge-be-on-e-quet Lake, which is an excellent destination lake. It can be a fine bass water in its many little bays.

Paddle and portage 2.5 miles from Ge-be-on-e-quet Lake to Lac La Croix, including portages of 35 rods (L7) to Ge-be-on-e-quet Creek and 20 rods to Lac La Croix. The 35-rod portage from Ge-be-on-e-quet Lake to Ge-be-on-e-quet Creek is a rough, steep, rocky trail that drops considerably along its relatively short length—certainly a portage you will be happy to take from the south.

Once on Lac La Croix, you can explore what seems like an ocean of islands and bays. Motorboats are permitted on all of the Canadian side of Lac La Croix, and a few tow services travel all the way across Lac La Croix to Bottle portage on the far eastern edge of the lake. The area south of Coleman Island is about 2 miles into the U.S. side of the lake, so it is relatively peaceful, as is all of Lady Boot Bay and the area around Boulder Bay. The area between Lady Boot Bay and Boulder Bay was designated the Lac La Croix Research Natural Area in 1942, which prevented logging of its extensive stands of red and white pine. This protection was significant because at the time federal law allowed extensive logging within the current BWCAW except within 400 feet of recreational waters. The Ontario walleye fishing opener is usually a week later than the Minnesota opener (the third Saturday rather than the second Saturday of May), which can be used to your benefit to avoid motorized traffic. You will see significantly fewer boats on the Canadian side of Lac La Croix before the walleye season opens.

Paddle 12.5 miles across Lac La Croix, and portage 115 rods (L7) to Lake Agnes. Once you are in Boulder Bay, you can paddle southeast to Lake Agnes, a journey of about a dozen miles. The 115-rod portage to Lake Agnes is along a fine trail; otherwise take the much shorter 26-rod portage, described in Route 16B.

Paddle 8 miles from Lake Agnes to your starting point, including portages of 95 rods (L5.5) and 70 rods (L5.5) to Nina Moose Lake, and 25 rods (L2.5), 20 rods (L1), and 160 rods (L5) along the Moose River.

Route 16D: Agnes, Iron, Stuart Loop (Map 10)

Difficulty: challenging
Number of days: 5 or more
Total miles (approx.): 34.5
Number of portages: 22
Total portage rods: 1,822
Greatest portage difficulty: 288 rods (L8)

Navigation maps: Voyageur 1, 2
Fisher F16
McKenzie 12, 13

This route is the second of the two challenging loops out of Nina Moose. It takes you out the east side of Lake Agnes and on to Lac La Croix, Iron Lake, and Stuart Lake. Route 16C is similar but heads out the west side of Agnes.

Map 10 shows the first legs of travel on this route, and Map 11 shows the eastern areas. In addition, the entire route can be seen in overview on Map 7.

Detailed Route

Paddle and portage 6.5 miles to Nina Moose Lake, including portages of 160 rods (L5), 20 rods (L1), an optional 2 rods (L1), and 25 rods (L2.5); then paddle 3 miles along the Nina Moose River to Lake Agnes, including portages of 70 rods (L5.5) and 95 rods (L5.5). This journey follows the same start to Nina Moose Lake and Lake Agnes as Route 16B. Nina Moose Lake makes a fine place to spend a first evening, assuming its high-demand sites are available.

Paddle and portage 9.5 miles from Lake Agnes to Iron Lake, including portages of 115 rods and 2 rods to Boulder Bay, and the 80-rod (L9) Bottle portage to Iron Lake. When leaving Agnes on your way to Boulder Bay, you have a number of portage options, all of which are described in Route 16B. This route includes the flat 115-rod portage from Agnes, but you can easily take the 26-rod portage described in Route 16B. Paddle through Boulder Bay and east toward Bottle Lake and the Bottle portage. The Bottle portage crosses through Canada to avoid raging rapids on the Bottle River. This portage is not long but tends to be very muddy and is relatively rocky. During wet years you can step in mud pits up to your knees along stretches, and even in dry years the portage is a challenge.

Although the Bottle portage is in Canada, you are entitled to use it under the Webster-Ashburton Treaty of 1842, which established the boundary between the two countries. The treaty explicitly allowed all portages along the border from Lake Superior to Lake of the Woods to be freely used by U.S. and Canadian citizens. However, don't forget, you still cannot camp in Canada without advance authorization, involving a Remote Area Border Crossing permit, and a Quetico permit if you will be entering Quetico Provincial Park. The alternative to the Bottle portage is a long 321-rod portage on the U.S. side, which generally has a better trail but also has a couple of muddy marshy sections. Most people appear to take the shorter Bottle portage.

Paddle and portage 4.5 miles from Iron Lake to Stuart Lake, including portages of 75 rods (L6) to Dark Lake, 67 rods (L6) to Rush Lake, 64 rods (L6) to Fox Lake, and 288 rods (L8) to Stuart Lake. Once you leave Iron Lake, you will be paddling through the Stuart Lake area, which is much less visited than the country through which you have already traveled. You will paddle and portage by way of three small lakes: Dark, Rush, and Fox. Each of these three lakes is relatively shallow and has one campsite. The most desirable of these three lakes for camping is certainly Rush Lake, which has a decent island campsite. Rush is also the only one of these three lakes with a good game-fish population, which includes walleye and northern pike. The portage to Stuart Lake is long but reasonably flat and should be pretty free of mud except after heavy rains. Its remote location and length make it more likely to have some downed trees along its length.

Paddle and portage 6 miles from Stuart Lake to Lake Agnes, including portages of 118 rods (L6) to the Dahlgren River, 153 rods (L6) to the Boulder River (L7), and 115 rods (L6) to Lake Agnes. Three portages greater than 100 rods now lead you to Lake Agnes, none of which is particularly difficult considering their length. The first, 118-rod portage follows through a nice old stand of pine, while the longer, 153-rod portage heads along a trail that is also quite good. When viewing a detailed topographic map of this area, you might think that you can paddle around the 153-rod portage, but there is no navigable channel through the lower stretches of the Dahlgren River. The final, 115-rod portage to Agnes is relatively flat and along a good trail.

Paddle 8 miles from Lake Agnes back to your starting point, including portages of 95 rods (L5.5) and 70 rods (L5.5) to Nina Moose Lake, and 25 rods (L2.5), 20 rods (L1), and 160 rods (L5) along the Moose River. Return to your starting point by retracing your route through Lake Agnes, or alternatively loop back into Agnes by one of the other alternative portages.

Entry Point 19, Stuart River (Map 11)

> Daily permit quota: 1
> Permit availability: difficult

The Stuart River entry starts with a stunning 480-rod portage, one of the longest in the entire BWCAW. This entry is not for anyone who refuses to leave his or her Coleman cooler behind. The long portage and visitor quota keep visitors to a minimum, and long portages to Stuart Lake from other directions make this a great entry to an isolated part of the BWCAW. The trail on the long portage to Stuart is relatively good, and its difficulty is mostly an issue of total portage length.

One route is described in this guide for the Stuart River entry, and it takes you along a nice loop to Iron Lake and then around through Boulder Bay of Lac La Croix and back to Stuart. Other routes are possible that hit neighboring areas of the BWCAW, all of which are described elsewhere in this guide and indexed at the end. The easiest extensions out of Stuart Lake head to the west toward Lake Agnes and Lac La Croix and offer many great opportunities to add to your trip. You can also head east toward Nibin, Bibon, and Sterling lakes toward Sunday Lake. However, be advised that this eastern route is very challenging and can be all but impassable, especially when water levels are low. None of the portages between Stuart and Sunday lakes are maintained, and they lie in the Sundial Lake Primitive Management Area. Go this way if you are interested in tough bushwhacking, although I strongly discourage first-time visitors from attempting such a route. If you intend to spend the night on any one of these lakes, you will need written authorization from the Superior National Forest, available from the Kawishiwi Ranger Station (218-365-7600) on a limited basis.

To reach the Stuart River entry, take the Echo Trail 17.5 miles from Ely to the relatively spacious parking lot on the right side of the road (just after the Big Lake turnoff on the left). A good place to camp the night before you enter the BWCAW is at the small Fenske Lake campground, which has sixteen campsites and takes advance reservations.

Route 19: Stuart River, Iron Lake Loop (Map 11)

      Difficulty: challenging
      Number of days: 4 or more
      Total miles (approx.): 37
      Number of portages: 19
      Total portage rods: 2,407
      Greatest portage difficulty: 480 rods (L10)
      Navigation maps: Voyageur 2, 3
                        Fisher F9, F16
                        McKenzie 12, 13

This route takes you along an interesting little loop. Much of the travel is challenging, with many portages, some of which are very long. The greatest challenges are along a set of isolated lakes and rivers, but you will also hit popular Iron Lake and even famous Lac La Croix.

Detailed Route

Paddle and portage 10 miles to Stuart Lake, including portages of 480 rods (L10) to the Stuart River, and 85 rods, 55 rods, 68 rods, 19 rods, and 74 rods along the Stuart River. This first day of traveling is challenging. The initial portage is very long but follows a relatively good path, especially for the first half. The second half can be a bit wet because it is low lying and gets less maintenance.

After the long initial portage, you will paddle down the winding Stuart River to Stuart Lake and will have another five portages along the way. If you are using McKenzie maps, note that one of the longer portages is misidentified as being 14 rods, but it should be 68 rods long. The marshy lowlands through which you are traveling have plentiful beavers, which may add a few dams to the river. You will paddle along a magnificent sedge meadow on this fine stretch. The relatively light visitor

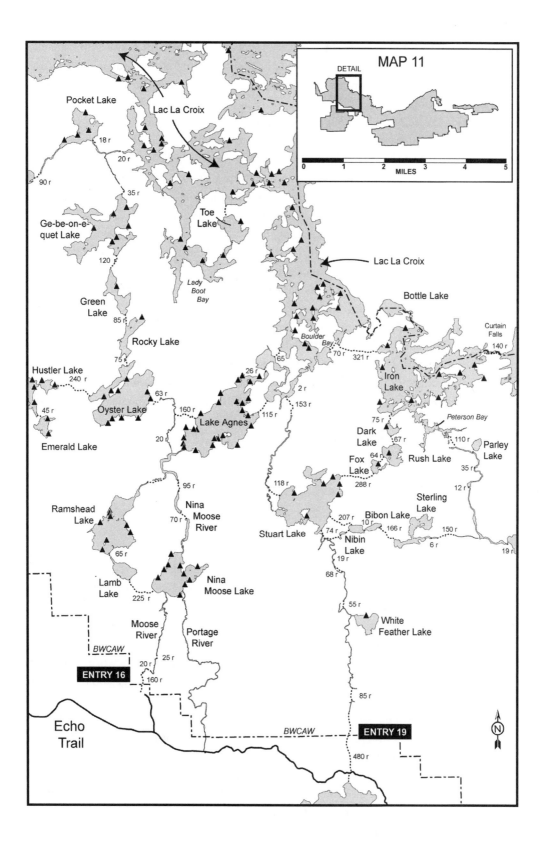

MAP 11

DETAIL

0 1 2 3 4 5
MILES

Pocket Lake

Lac La Croix

18 r

20 r

90 r

35 r

Ge-be-on-e-quet Lake

Toe Lake

Lac La Croix

Bottle Lake

Curtain Falls

120

Lady Boot Bay

140 r

Green Lake

85 r

Boulder Bay

70 r

321 r

Rocky Lake

75 r

65

Iron Lake

Peterson Bay

Hustler Lake

240 r

26 r

2 r

75 r

110 r

Parley Lake

45 r

63 r

160 r

153 r

Dark Lake

67 r

Rush Lake

35 r

Oyster Lake

115 r

Lake Agnes

Fox Lake

64 r

12 r

Emerald Lake

20

Sterling Lake

Ramshead Lake

95 r

Nina Moose River

118 r

207 r

Bibon Lake

10 r

166 r

150 r

70 r

Stuart Lake

74 r

Nibin Lake

6 r

19 r

65 r

19 r

Lamb Lake

Nina Moose Lake

225 r

68 r

55 r

Moose River

Portage River

White Feather Lake

BWCAW

ENTRY 16

20 r

25 r

160 r

85 r

Echo Trail

BWCAW

ENTRY 19

480 r

N

use will give you a better chance of seeing beavers or perhaps moose. Almost 5,000 acres of forest east of the Stuart River and west of Sunday Lake burned in a forest fire in 1996 and now provide an interesting natural history laboratory for examining regenerating forest.

Paddle and portage 4.5 miles from Stuart Lake to Iron Lake, including portages of 288 rods (L8), 64 rods (L6), 67 rods (L6), and 75 rods (L6). Continue on from Stuart Lake to Iron Lake. You may want to stop and spend a night on Rush Lake, which is the nicest of the three small lakes on this stretch. Fox also has a designated campsite but is quite shallow and less attractive than Rush.

Paddle and portage 6.5 miles from Iron Lake to Boulder Bay in Lac La Croix, including a portage of 80 rods (L9) along the Bottle portage. If you are lucky, the Bottle portage will be relatively dry and easily passable. It is far more likely that this short, but tough, portage will be a mucky slog warranting its L9 difficulty rating.

Paddle and portage 6 miles to Stuart Lake, including portages of 153 rods (L6) from Boulder Bay to the Dahlgren River, and 118 rods (L6) to Stuart Lake. Take the 153-rod portage from Boulder Bay to the Dahlgren River. Maps appear to show a stream channel that avoids this portage, but it is not navigable. On the 118-rod portage you will cover a nice trail. Be sure to stick your head out from under your canoe to take a look at some of the old red pine stands you will pass along the way.

Paddle and portage 10 miles from Stuart Lake to your starting point, including portages of 74 rods, 19 rods, 68 rods, 55 rods, 85 rods, and 480 rods. Reverse your first day's travel to return to your starting point.

Entry Point 20, Angleworm Lake (Map 12)

> Daily permit quota: 2
> Permit availability: moderate

Angleworm is a beautiful little lake that offers a great chance to get off the beaten track—specifically, about 640 rods off the beaten track! That is the length of the first portage from the parking lot to the shores of Angleworm, making it one of the longest portages in the entire BWCAW. This trail is typically in quite nice shape, but its length will dissuade most visitors. I know of one local outfitter who will equip you for any trip into the western BWCAW except one starting at Angleworm Lake. It has been their experience that you will be overwhelmed by the portage and blame them for the bad trip. Consider yourself fully informed.

In truth, Angleworm is a great entry for the right people: those who have visited the BWCAW before, pack light, and want a challenge. This is also a good place to visit if you want to combine your paddling with hiking, because the Angleworm Trail around Angleworm Lake is beautiful, easily hiked in half a day, and accessible from some of the canoeing campsites. Ironically, in spite of the long portage, Angleworm Lake is not necessarily a great place for complete isolation, because of the relative popularity of the hiking trail, which brings in visitors for day hikes and overnight trips. The hiking trail overlaps the long portage, so you may see one or more groups of hikers as you are walking to or from Angleworm Lake with your canoe and gear.

To get to the Angleworm Lake entry, head east from Ely for 1.5 miles, then turn north (left) onto County Road 88. Take County Road 88 for about 2.3 miles to the Echo Trail, which is County Road 116. Turn right onto the Echo Trail, and travel 13.1 miles, where you will come to a small turnout labeled "Angleworm Hiking." This is also the starting point for the portage, although it is long enough to warrant the title "hike."

Route 20: Exploration of Angleworm (Map 12)

  Difficulty: challenging
  Number of days: 2 or more
  Total miles (approx.): at least 6
  Number of portages: 2
  Total portage rods: 1,280
  Greatest portage difficulty: 640 (L10)
  Navigation maps: Voyageur 4
         Fisher F9
         McKenzie 11

This route may have almost as much portaging as paddling, so travel light. You will be rewarded for your work with a stay on a wonderful little lake. If you are interested in extending your trip beyond Angleworm, you can easily take the 40-rod portage to Home Lake, and from there go to Gull Lake by way of a 277-rod portage. Less arduous routes to Gull are also possible from other entry points, so the result might not be worth the effort.

Detailed Route

Portage 2 miles, 640 rods (L10), to the shore of Angleworm Lake. From the parking lot, head east down the portage trail to Angleworm. The first portion of this portage is outside of the BWCAW and has a higher level of maintenance than the portion within the BWCAW. After about 200 rods, you will pass a sign telling you that you are now in the designated wilderness area. Continue along the trail until you reach Angleworm Lake. Near the end of the portage is an area that might be a bit wet, depending on beaver activity.

You have four designated paddling campsites to choose from on Angleworm. In addition, there are a number of campsites designated for people hiking the Angleworm Trail encircling Angleworm Lake. Consider hiking the 11-mile loop around Angleworm, which is one of the finest hikes in the BWCAW and easily done in less than a day. On the west side is a rocky hill that once held the Angleworm lookout

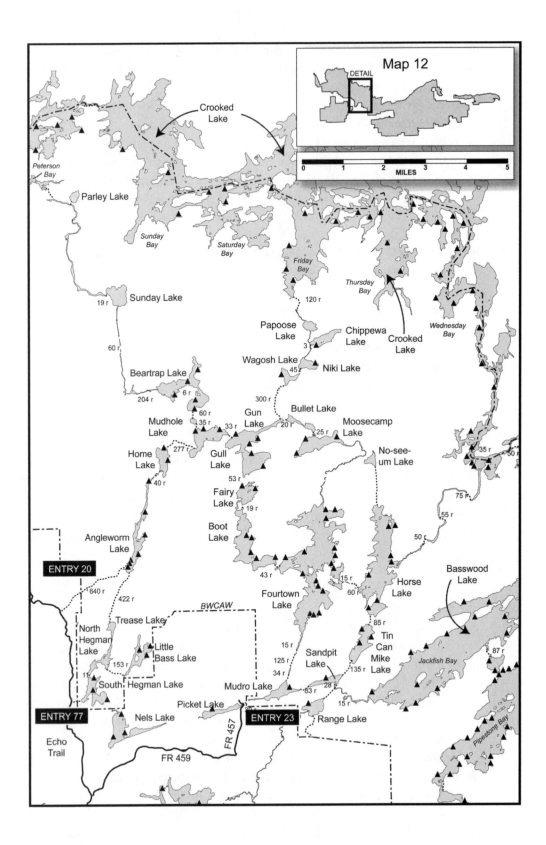

Map 12

DETAIL

0 1 2 MILES 3 4 5

Crooked Lake

Peterson Bay

Parley Lake

Sunday Bay

Saturday Bay

Friday Bay

Thursday Bay

Crooked Lake

Wednesday Bay

Sunday Lake

19 r

60 r

Papoose Lake

Chippewa Lake

120 r

3

Wagosh Lake

45

Niki Lake

Beartrap Lake

204 r

6 r

300 r

Bullet Lake

Moosecamp Lake

60 r

Gun Lake

Mudhole Lake

35 r

33 r

20 r

25 r

No-see-um Lake

277 r

Home Lake

Gull Lake

35 r

40 r

53 r

Fairy Lake

19 r

75 r

55 r

Boot Lake

Angleworm Lake

Basswood Lake

50 r

43 r

15 r

Horse Lake

60

Fourtown Lake

ENTRY 20

640 r

422 r

BWCAW

85 r

Tin Can Mike Lake

Trease Lake

North Hegman Lake

Little Bass Lake

15 r

Sandpit Lake

Jackfish Bay

87 r

153 r

125 r

135 r

11

34 r

28

South Hegman Lake

Mudro Lake

83 r

ENTRY 77

Picket Lake

15 r

Nels Lake

ENTRY 23

Range Lake

Pipestong Bay

Echo Trail

FR 457

FR 459

tower, used by the Forest Service to spot forest fires. The tower was one of just four within the current boundaries of the BWCAW, the others being located north of the Devil's Cascade on the Little Indian Sioux River, on the south side of Kekekabic Lake, and by Brule Lake. The Angleworm tower has been gone for years, but remnants of the trail to the peak remain.

The east side of Angleworm was once reached by a simple logging railroad built in the early 1900s. The railroad extended from Jackfish Bay of Basswood Lake to Fourtown and Horse lakes, and then all the way to the west shore of Gun Lake. A spur led to the east side of Angleworm and was reportedly used for years by the Forest Service to reach Angleworm by way of a small gasoline-powered "pusher" railcar.

Portage 2 miles, 640 rods (L10), to your start. When your time comes to leave Angleworm, simply portage back to your starting location.

Entry Point 77, South Hegman Lake (Map 12)

Daily permit quota: 2
Permit availability: difficult

South Hegman Lake, Entry Point 77, is famous for providing easy access to some of the finest pictographs in the entire Boundary Waters and Quetico region. Although the visitor quota is just two overnight permits per day, many people visit South Hegman Lake on self-issuing day permits that do not need a reservation. Thus, South Hegman gets relatively heavy use considering its limited size, and will likely feel less remote than most other BWCAW lakes. However, it is an excellent entry point for first-time visitors.

Three designated campsites are located on South Hegman, and another three can be reached by covering a pair of portages to Little Bass Lake, which will take you off of the main traffic routes. South Hegman offers very limited options for longer trips unless you want to make at least two long portages: one of 422 rods to Angleworm Lake, and another of 277 rods to Gull Lake.

To reach South Hegman Lake, take the turnoff to the right (east) from the Echo Trail 10.9 miles out of Ely (about 2 miles after the road surface turns to gravel). An 80-rod (L5) portage leads downhill on an occasionally rocky trail to a staircase and a small rock landing on South Hegman. This portage is interesting because the surrounding forest was subject to a prescribed burn in the 1990s. The regenerating forest is a fine example of how fire affects forest diversity.

Route 77: Exploration of South Hegman Lake and Pictographs (Map 12)

Difficulty: moderate
Number of days: 2 or more
Total miles (approx.): 6

Number of portages: 6
Total portage rods: 488 rods
Greatest portage difficulty: 153 rods (L7)
Navigation maps: Voyageur 4
Fisher F9
McKenzie 11

South Hegman is a fantastic entry point, and a lot of people know it. Visitors in a steady flow enter South Hegman during all seasons to see the pictographs at the junction of North Hegman and Trease lakes, so do not expect isolation along this route like that you will find in most of the BWCAW.

Detailed Route

Portage 80 rods (L5) to South Hegman Lake. The portage to South Hegman is well traveled and likely to be in good shape, with a steep final drop down a long wooden staircase to the lakeshore. The surrounding forest is regenerating from a modest controlled burn in the late 1990s. Once on South Hegman you can stay at one of three campsites along its shores. Alternatively, continue to Little Bass Lake by way of North Hegman Lake, where three designated campsites have been established.

Paddle 1 mile across South Hegman Lake, portage 11 rods (L2) to North Hegman Lake. The portage to North Hegman is simple and fairly flat. This trip is not complete without a journey to the pictographs in the channel between North Hegman Lake and Trease Lake. The pictographs are positioned on the west shore and easily spotted.

Paddle and portage 2 miles from North Hegman Lake to Little Bass Lake, including a portage of 153 rods (L7). If you are continuing on to Little Bass Lake, you will need to head over a 153-rod portage, which will certainly be your hardest portage of the trip because it is twice as long as the initial carry and gets much less use. Little Bass is a good escape from the busier corridor along South Hegman and North Hegman.

Paddle and portage 3 miles back to your start, including portages of 153 rods (L7), 11 rods (L2), and 80 rods (L5). Return to your start by retracing your travels.

Optional Extension

If you are eager for a real challenge, take the 422-rod (L9) portage to Angleworm Lake. This trail is not heavily used but is in decent shape. The trail starts on the north end of Trease Lake and then climbs during the first third before dropping gradually to the shore of Angleworm Lake. Keep in mind that you will still need to get out of the wilderness, and your only options will be the 640-rod portage to the Angleworm parking lot, back across the 422-rod portage, or out to the northeast through Home Lake and a 277-rod portage to the interior of the Boundary Waters.

Don't take this route with a first-time visitor to the BWCAW, unless you hope that they never visit again.

Entry Points 22 and 23, Mudro Lake (Map 13)

> Daily permit quota: 8
> Permit availability: very difficult; early reservations essential

Mudro Lake is a popular entry, perhaps because it provides relatively easy access to remote lakes west of Basswood Lake. Your landing on Mudro is only a half day's travel from Jackfish Bay on Basswood Lake, Fourtown Lake, or Horse Lake. From these lakes numerous good routes funnel you right to the Canadian border, including upper and lower Basswood Falls. Thus, you have plenty of good travel options from Mudro.

When planning a trip out of Mudro, factor in that journeys to the east and northeast (toward Basswood Lake and Horse Lake) will likely encounter more people than trips west and north (toward Boot Lake and beyond). Also, in accordance with the BWCA Wilderness Management Plan, portages generally east of Mudro get significantly more maintenance than those to the northwest. Many of the portages north of Boot Lake receive scheduled maintenance less than once a year, while those to the east are maintained more than once per year. If you want the most rugged experience possible, head west from Mudro; if you prefer a less challenging experience, head east.

Mudro Lake is served by two official entries: Entry Point 22, which does not allow camping on Horse Lake, and Entry Point 23, which is unrestricted as to where you can camp. Six permits are available per day for Entry Point 23, and two per day for Entry Point 22. Reserve a permit for Entry Point 23 if one is available in order to keep your travel options open. Entry Point 22 is also a fine entry, and the prohibition from camping on Horse Lake will not be much of a problem for most visitors. Both of these permits are in very high demand, and you will definitely want to get your reservation well before May to ensure a permit is available.

To reach Mudro Lake, head east out of Ely for 1.5 miles, then turn north (left) onto County Road 88. Take County Road 88 for about 2.3 miles to the Echo Trail, which is County Road 116. Turn right onto the Echo Trail, and travel 7 miles until you reach Forest Service Road 459, and turn right (northeast). Drive another 5 miles to Mudro. The way is well marked, with your only turn at the top of a T intersection where you take the well-traveled road (FR 457) to the left rather than the infrequently traveled road to your right. You will drive past the landing to Picket Lake, and catch a glimpse of the pilings of a logging bridge from an old rail line through this area—the same one that used to extend all the way to Angleworm Lake.

Soon after the Picket Lake landing is the landing to Mudro Lake. You must take a short portage to the creek leading to Mudro. Most people park at the Chainsaw

Sisters Saloon, which is on a small parcel of private land adjacent to the entry point and charges a modest fee for parking. You don't have a lot of parking alternatives because there is no official Forest Service parking lot, and you are not allowed to park on the road within a mile of the landing. I recommend taking advantage of the Chainsaw Sisters' hospitality and parking in their lot for the required fee.

Route 23A: Loop through Fourtown and Horse Lakes (Map 13)

Difficulty: easy
Number of days: 2 or more
Total miles (approx.): 11
Number of portages: 12
Total portage rods: 625
Greatest portage difficulty: 125 (L8)
Navigation maps: Voyageur 4
                     Fisher F9, F10
                     McKenzie 11

This route is an excellent trip for first-time visitors to the Boundary Waters. It takes you through classic canoe country while avoiding the largest lakes and hardest portages. Your route will circle through Horse Lake and then to Fourtown Lake before returning to your start at Mudro. This can be a very leisurely trip if done in two or three days, but it even makes a fine weekend getaway.

I recommend that you take this circular route in a counterclockwise manner because it first takes you through lakes with a limited number of campsites (Horse) and then to lakes (Fourtown) with a much greater number of campsites. In this way you can choose to camp at one of the more isolated spots on Tin Can Mike or Horse Lake (if you enter at Entry Point 23), but if these are occupied, you can move on to Fourtown or to Gun Lake if necessary. If you go the opposite direction, you risk passing open sites on Fourtown only to find that Horse Lake and Tin Can Mike are occupied, leaving you no choice but to backtrack to Fourtown or even head out to Mudro.

Detailed Route

Paddle and portage 2.5 miles from Mudro Lake to Tin Can Mike Lake, including portages of 30 rods (L3) to Mudro, 83 rods (L7 to L9) to Sandpit Lake, and 135 rods (L4) to Tin Can Mike Lake. Your trip starts with an easy, short portage to the narrows on the west side of Mudro Lake. Warm up and stretch as you glide across Mudro. You will want to be limber for the climb up and descent down to Sandpit Lake by way of an 83-rod portage. You will be going in the primarily downhill direction, but this is still a quite challenging portage. Once on Sandpit paddle straight across to the landing in the northeast corner for the 135-rod portage to Tin Can Mike Lake. A fine trail will

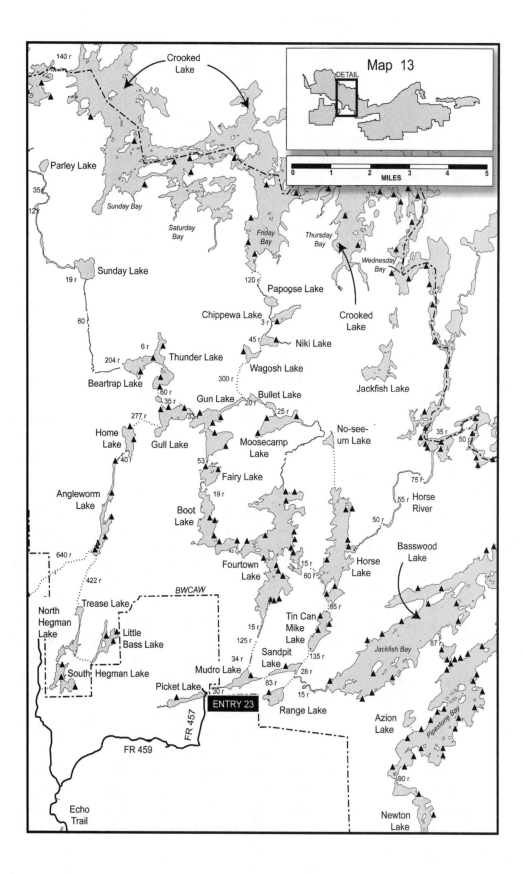

Map 13

DETAIL

0 1 2 3 4 5
MILES

140 r

Crooked Lake

Parley Lake

35 r

12 r

Sunday Bay

Saturday Bay

Friday Bay

Thursday Bay

Wednesday Bay

Crooked Lake

Sunday Lake

19 r

60

Papogse Lake

120 r

Chippewa Lake

3 r

45 r

Niki Lake

Jackfish Lake

204 r

6 r

Thunder Lake

Wagosh Lake

300 r

Beartrap Lake

60 r

35 r

Gun Lake

Bullet Lake

20 r

25 r

277 r

33

No-see-um Lake

Home Lake

Gull Lake

Moosecamp Lake

40 r

53

35 r

50

Angleworm Lake

Fairy Lake

19 r

75 f

Horse River

55 r

Boot Lake

50 r

Basswood Lake

640 r

43

Fourtown Lake

15 r

60 f

Horse Lake

422 r

BWCAW

Treake Lake

North Hegman Lake

Little Bass Lake

85 r

Tin Can Mike Lake

Jackfish Bay

87 r

South Hegman Lake

15 r

125 r

Sandpit Lake

135 r

34 r

28 r

Mudro Lake

83 r

15 r

Picket Lake

30 r

ENTRY 23

Range Lake

Azion Lake

Pipestone Bay

FR 457

FR 459

90 r

Echo Trail

Newton Lake

take you to Tin Can Mike with minimal trouble. One of the best boardwalks in all of the Boundary Waters is at the north end of this portage. Not only is it sturdy and wide, but it even includes a passing lane after about 70 rods!

Paddle and portage 2.5 miles from Tin Can Mike Lake to central Horse Lake, portaging 85 rods (L5). Head north on Tin Can Mike Lake. Consider camping at one of the three designated campsites along the way if they are open. From Tin Can Mike take the 85-rod portage to Horse Lake. This is an easy trail with good landings. Modest hills rise up on each end of the portage, but the central portions are quite level. You may want to camp at one of the seven campsites on Horse Lake, but these tend to fill up quickly. Remember, if you are entering with a permit for Entry Point 22, you cannot camp on Horse Lake. Keep your eyes on the west shore as you are paddling through the narrows connecting the southern bay on Horse Lake to the main body of the lake. In the narrows you will see an old iron ring embedded in the bedrock. This ring appears to have been used to fasten ropes pulling rafts of logs south across Horse Lake. A campsite was located here long before creation of the Boundary Waters (and is shown on old maps of the area), and the site remains in use today as a designated Forest Service campsite.

If you are carrying older maps, you may see a portage from the north end of Horse Lake into No-see-um Lake, but that portage receives no maintenance because it is within the Tick Lake Primitive Management Area (PMA). In 2002 the portage location could not even be located despite careful searching. It is possible that the portage still exists in some form, but it is clearly exceedingly rugged. If you wish to attempt to explore the area to No-see-um, as challenging as that might be, consult with the Kawishiwi Ranger Station for a Tick Lake PMA permit.

Paddle and portage 2 miles from Horse Lake to the interior of Fourtown Lake, including short portages of 60 rods (L5) and 15 rods (L4), and optionally 10 rods (L2) and 3 rods (L1). Heading to Fourtown Lake is not hard but can be time consuming because you take at least two portages, and perhaps four, depending on water levels and your paddling skills. The first portage is the longest: a 60-rod carry over an improved trail. You will put in on a very small pond and then need to paddle through a tiny channel to a modestly larger pond, from where you will take a 15-rod portage that is also along a decent trail but requires a pretty good climb and descent to what I call the "Bay of Six-Foot Stumps." Hundreds of old stumps are a visible remnant of the old logging days, most likely in the years during and after World War II, when significant logging occurred in this area. You may have yet another easy 10-rod portage (L2) around a small stretch of rapids when water levels are low, but under most conditions these easy rapids are passable without taking the little used portage. Finally, shoot to the northwest, and you have only one last portage, a simple 3-rod (L1) carry that can also often be avoided. Fourtown Lake is a fine place to spend an evening.

Paddle and portage 4 miles from Fourtown Lake to Mudro Lake, including portages of 15 rods (L4), 125 rods (L8), and 34 rods (L5). This journey next follows a deep gorge on the south end of Fourtown Lake that has a distinctly mountainous feel to it. The first, 15-rod portage (L4) is short but reasonably hard considering its length. It involves a lot of hill climbing for a 15-rod portage and doesn't afford a good landing on the Fourtown side. Continue past this portage, and take the 125-rod (L8) trail on the west side of the valley, which is a tough route but has recently been upgraded by the Forest Service to improve the walking surface. It had perilous sections in years past that skirt some high drop-offs. The final portage is only 34 rods but is difficult because it tends to be rocky and muddy.

Paddle across Mudro Lake, portage 30 rods (L3) to your exit. Continue back through Mudro to the landing at the Chainsaw Sisters.

Route 23B: Iron Lake Loop (Map 13)

Difficulty: challenging
Number of days: 6 or more
Total miles (approx.): 48
Number of portages: 27
Total portage rods: 1,720
Greatest portage difficulty: 300 rods (L8)
Navigation maps: Voyageur 2, 4
Fisher F9, F10, F16, F17
McKenzie 11, 12, 13, 29

This route sends you through Fourtown Lake and on to Iron Lake along the Canadian border, and then southeast through Crooked Lake and back through Fourtown Lake by way of the great Moosecamp River. The route permits easy changes along the way because it can be shortened with an early detour to Moosecamp Lake or lengthened with extensions through the Horse River or even Basswood Lake.

Map 13 shows most of this route, and Map 11 shows the western portions. In addition, the entire route can be seen in overview on Map 7.

Detailed Route

Paddle and portage 4 miles from Mudro to Fourtown Lake, including portages of 30 rods (L3), 34 rods (L5), 125 rods (L8), and 15 rods (L4). Start with the easy portage to the west end of Mudro Lake. Paddle across Mudro, and begin the journey to Fourtown Lake. This stretch is a challenge, with three portages separated by quite short paddles. The route follows a deep gorge that has a distinctly mountainous feel to it, among the most impressive terrain any BWCAW portages pass through. These three portages follow north through an ancient fault or crack in the bedrock. This crack formed sometime after the bedrock was created more than a billion years ago. Not until glaciers swept through just 10,000 years ago did it get carved into the present gorge.

The first portage from Mudro is only 34 rods long but is difficult for its length because it is rocky and tends to be muddy. Continue past this portage, and take the 125-rod trail on the west side of the valley. This tough haul road was recently upgraded by the Forest Service to improve the walking surface. The trail was quite perilous in years past as it skirts some high drop-offs. Continue on to a final, 15-rod portage that involves a lot of hill climbing for a short portage and doesn't afford a good landing on the Fourtown side.

Paddle and portage 6 miles from Fourtown Lake to Gull Lake, including portages of 43 rods (L4) to Boot Lake, 19 rods (L2) from Boot to Fairy Lake, 53 rods (L4) from Fairy to Gun Lake, and 33 rods (L5) from Gun to Gull Lake. Fourtown Lake is usually a fine place to spend a night, and typically a fair number of the fifteen campsites are open. The only drawback is the fact that the campsites are clustered together in little groups. Fortunately even most of the close sites are not visible from one another. When it comes time to leave, take a level, easy 43-rod portage to Boot Lake. You may also want to camp at one of five designated campsites on Boot.

When your time comes to leave Boot Lake, go across the easy 19-rod portage to Fairy Lake. This is a relatively flat portage even though you gain about 10 feet in elevation along the trail. Fairy Lake also has two designated campsites, and they appear to get much less use than those on Fourtown or even Boot.

Camp on one of Fairy Lake's two campsites, or continue moving on to Gun Lake. The 53-rod portage to Gun is not exactly exciting—just a basic flat portage that collects a bit of water in the spring. This route takes you directly over the "handle" of Gun Lake to Gull Lake. The 33-rod portage from Gun gradually climbs to Gull Lake. It was significantly eroded in 2002 but is easily passable.

Paddle and portage 2 miles from Gun Lake to Beartrap Lake, including portages of 35 rods (L3) to Mudhole Lake, 60 rods (L6) from Mudhole to Thunder Lake, and 6 rods (L1.5) from Thunder to Beartrap Lake. Continue on up through Gull, Mudhole, and Thunder lakes. The 35-rod portage to Mudhole is quite flat, while the 60-rod trail from Mudhole to Thunder has moderate hills on either end (but a good path). The 6-rod portage to Thunder Lake diverts around rapids that drop about 4 feet in elevation (and do not have any navigable channel). You may want to camp on one of these lakes, which have thirteen designated campsites. These sites see much fewer visitors than the lakes closer to Mudro. Once you leave Thunder Lake, you have only one campsite before Iron Lake, which is 10 miles away, so plan accordingly.

Paddle and portage 3.5 miles from Beartrap Lake to Sunday Lake, including portages of 204 rods (L8) and 60 rods (L6). Portage out the west end of Beartrap Lake along the 204-rod trail. This is not a heavily traveled portage and gets limited scheduled maintenance under the BWCA Wilderness Management Plan, so expect this portage to be somewhat overgrown. It is also a bit hilly (particularly when coming from the river) and tends to be wet in parts near the Beartrap River.

Continue down the Beartrap River. You will come across a massive beaver dam just before you turn north into the main channel (assuming the hard-working beavers have maintained it since this guide was written). After about a mile you will come to a 60-rod portage on the west shore around a set of rapids. This trail is reasonably level and would warrant a difficulty of L4 if it were not seldom used and overgrown. You may be tempted to divide this portage up into two 20-rod carries with a small pond in between. You will likely gain only frustration by doing so because you will have to load and unload your canoe an extra time just to save 20 rods.

A bit farther up ahead (about a half mile) is a small rapids that is likely to be canoeable to most canoeists (but scout it first). The forest in this area burned in the 1990s and is now starting to show good regrowth of young pine, particularly opportunistic jack pine. You will soon be dropped into Sunday Lake, which does not have any designated campsites.

Paddle and portage 6 miles from Sunday Lake down the Beartrap River to Iron Lake, including portages of 19 rods (L2), 12 rods (L1), 35 rods (L3), and 110 rods (L7). Continue out the west end of Sunday Lake, and take the easy 19-rod portage on the north shore of the Beartrap River. Paddle farther down the Beartrap River. If you are designing your own route, you can branch off to Sterling Creek after about 0.8 mile, and then head in toward Sterling Lake, which is in the midst of the Sundial Lake Primitive Management Area (PMA). Portages and campsites are not maintained within the PMA. Old maps show portages connecting to Sterling, Nibin, and Bibon lakes, but they are all very challenging considering their length. Also, you will need special authorization in advance from the Forest Service to camp within the PMA.

Your next portage, assuming you do not detour into Sterling Lake, is a good 12-rod trail along the Beartrap River around impassable rapids, soon followed by a little used 35-rod portage around the west side of mild rapids. Your map may also show a portage to Parley Lake, but I searched unsuccessfully for it in 2002. If this portage ever did exist, it is now so infrequently used that it is all but impossible to find. The final, 110-rod portage has a challenging trail to Peterson Bay of Iron Lake. The hardest part of this portage is the difficult rock-face landing dropping to Peterson Bay. You will need to be a bit acrobatic placing and loading your canoe. This is not a portage you want to take in the fading light of dusk!

Paddle 3 miles across Iron Lake, and portage 140 rods (L7) around Curtain Falls to Crooked Lake. Iron Lake provides camping opportunities at ten designated campsites on the U.S. side of the lake, and good fishing. The 140-rod portage to Crooked Lake is an ancient route that is still much used today. You will have a healthy initial climb out of Iron Lake, but then the excellent trail flattens out and ends just after passing Curtain Falls. These are some of the most beautiful falls in the border country. They lack huge free falls (like Johnson Falls in the far eastern BWCAW) but have a surging power all their own. Nearly a hundred years ago a hydroelectric dam was proposed for this very site. It would have dammed Curtain Falls to fulfill the dreams of lumberman Edward E. Backus, who dreamed of harnessing the border lakes for his own hydropowered papermaking empire. Crooked Lake would have risen some 15 feet in depth, a significant amount in such flat terrain, drowning countless historic sites and flooding thousands of acres of forest.

Paddle and portage 8 miles across Crooked Lake to Friday Bay. Continue down

Crooked Lake for a great stretch of portage-free paddling. This historic trail takes you past the famous pictographs on Crooked Lake, which you will find marked on your maps south of Curtain Falls. Continue east across Crooked and turn south at Friday Bay to head through Chippewa Lake back to Gun Lake.

Today, a journey from Gun Lake to Friday Bay of Crooked Lake is a peaceful, quiet paddle and portage journey. In 1954 this route was the front line of the battle for the future of the BWCAW. Two resorts were located on Crooked Lake at that time. One, run by the Zupancich family, was east of Curtain Falls, and the other, run by the Perkos, was at Friday Bay. For a short time these resorts hauled supplies to Crooked Lake from Gun Lake using an old amphibious vehicle known as a "weasel." In late 1954 the resort owners even used a bulldozer to carve out a rough road. The resort owners were responding to a court order forbidding them from flying guests and supplies into their resorts by floatplane. The federal district court quickly banned the use of this road, and it was soon abandoned. The exact route for this short-lived road is obscured by history and trees but appears to have covered some of the same portages now in use between Friday Bay and Gun Lake. Both resorts were eventually bought by the U.S. government, and the Zupancich family built a well-known resort farther west, on the Canadian side of Lac La Croix.

Paddle and portage 3 miles from Friday Bay of Crooked Lake to Wagosh Lake, including portaging 120 rods (L5) to Papoose Lake, paddling to Chippewa Lake, optionally portaging 3 rods (L2) from Chippewa to Niki Lake, and portaging 45 rods (L8) from Niki to Wagosh Lake. A 120-rod portage curves up from Friday Bay to Papoose Creek with only a gradual uphill. Head down Papoose Creek to Papoose Lake and then on to Chippewa Lake, which is connected by a small stream to Niki Lake. You will likely have to take a 3-rod portage to lift over a beaver dam along the stream. Finally, take the tough 45-rod portage to Wagosh Lake. Although this is not a long portage, it is quite strenuous because the first 35 rods are mostly uphill, much of which is steep. Paddle across Wagosh, camping in the one designated site, if you choose and it is open.

Paddle and portage 8 miles from Wagosh Lake to Fourtown Lake by way of the Moosecamp River, including portages of 300 rods (L8) to Gun Lake, 20 rods (L3) to Bullet Lake, 25 rods (L4) to Moosecamp Lake, and paddling down the Moosecamp River to Fourtown Lake. The portage from Wagosh to Gun Lake is one of the finest long portages in the Boundary Waters and in some ways is easier than the preceding, far shorter portage to Wagosh Lake. You will travel over modest hills on either end, but the trail is generally smooth, flat, and relatively dry. A 20-rod portage (not 10 rods, as shown on some maps) will then take you to Bullet Lake. The rocky little portage travels around impassable shallows of rocks and downed trees. You are now certainly off the well-traveled routes, and your next 25-rod portage to Moosecamp Lake is likely to be a bit overgrown compared to portages you have been on so far. You have three campsites to choose from on Moosecamp, or you can head immediately out the east end along the Moosecamp River, which is about 3 miles long. This is a shallow, mostly soft-bottomed stream that is normally passable to canoe travel.

You will have a few lift-overs, most notably around a log obstruction after three-quarters of a mile and again a mile later at a massive beaver dam. Excellent cliffs loom up from the east at a couple of points on the lower half of the river.

Paddle and portage 4 miles back to Mudro Lake, including portages of 15 rods (L4,) 125 rods (L8), and 34 rods (L5). Your trip now concludes with the journey south across Fourtown Lake and then back across the three valley portages to Mudro.

ENTRY FROM THE FERNBERG ROAD

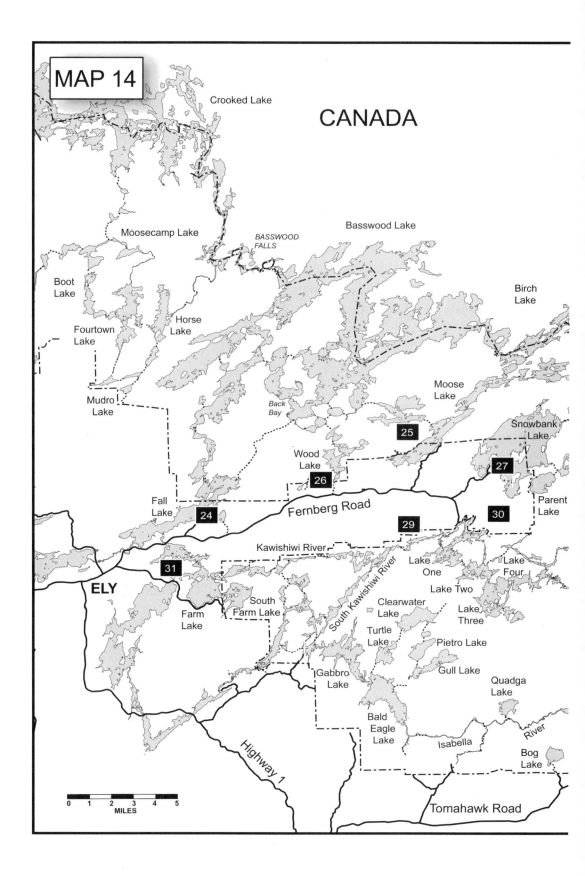

MAP 14

Crooked Lake

CANADA

Moosecamp Lake

BASSWOOD
FALLS

Basswood Lake

Boot
Lake

Birch
Lake

Horse
Lake

Fourtown
Lake

Moose
Lake

Mudro
Lake

Back
Bay

Snowbank
Lake

Wood
Lake

25

27

26

Fall
Lake

24

Fernberg Road

Parent
Lake

29

30

Kawishiwi River

Lake
One

Lake
Four

31

Lake Two

ELY

South
Farm Lake

Clearwater
Lake

Lake
Three

Farm
Lake

Turtle
Lake

Pietro Lake

Gull Lake

Quadga
Lake

Gabbro
Lake

Bald
Eagle
Lake

Isabella

River

Bog
Lake

Highway 1

Tomahawk Road

0   1   2   3   4   5
MILES

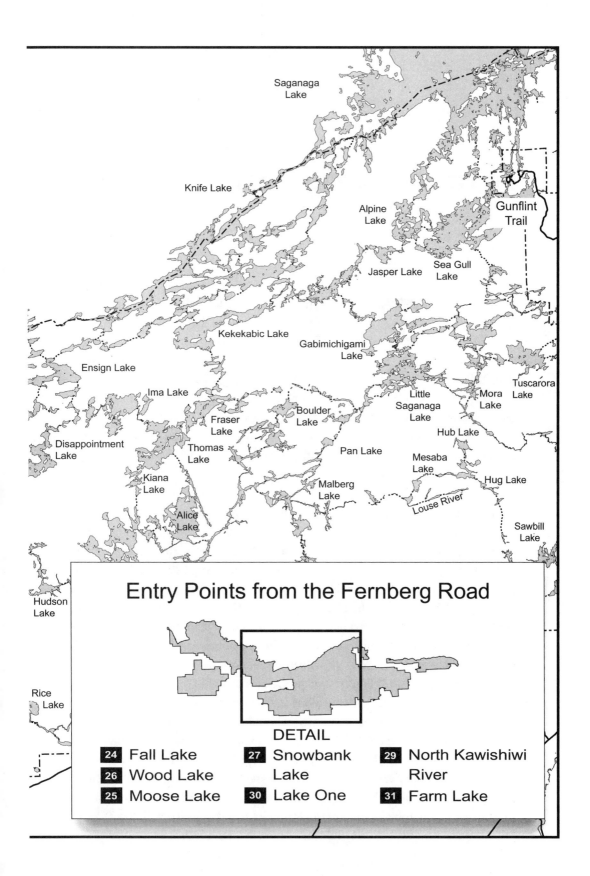

Saganaga
Lake

Knife Lake

Alpine
Lake

Gunflint
Trail

Jasper Lake

Sea Gull
Lake

Kekekabic Lake

Gabimichigami
Lake

Ensign Lake

Ima Lake

Boulder
Lake

Little
Saganaga
Lake

Mora
Lake

Tuscarora
Lake

Fraser
Lake

Hub Lake

Disappointment
Lake

Thomas
Lake

Pan Lake

Mesaba
Lake

Hug Lake

Kiana
Lake

Malberg
Lake

Louse River

Alice
Lake

Sawbill
Lake

Hudson
Lake

Rice
Lake

Entry Points from the Fernberg Road

DETAIL

24	Fall Lake	**27**	Snowbank Lake	**29**	North Kawishiwi River
26	Wood Lake	**30**	Lake One	**31**	Farm Lake
25	Moose Lake				

ENTRY FROM THE FERNBERG ROAD

The Fernberg Road extends for 18 miles from the outskirts of Ely east to Lake One. Lakes accessible from the Fernberg Road have long been regarded as some of the finest canoe waters in the world. Indeed, lakes in this area figured prominently in one of the earliest plans for preserving and protecting a wilderness area. From 1919 to 1922, Arthur H. Carhart prepared a plan for recreational development of the Superior National Forest. Carhart was a landscape architect employed by the U.S. Forest Service, and he recommended that the Superior National Forest be largely preserved as a canoeing wilderness with restrictions on road building and lakeshore development.

Carhart's focus on preservation and water travel was a significant departure from contemporary management of national forests, although his plan allowed significantly more development than currently exists in the BWCAW. The preliminary plan called for a canoeing loop to be established along the Kawishiwi and Isabella rivers, reachable from entry points off the Fernberg Road. Carhart's plan also identified Alice and Insula lakes for their beauty, both of which are accessible from the Fernberg Road. When traveling through these lakes, it is easy to imagine you are paddling with Carhart and exploring the potential of this area as a wilderness preserve. Unlike Carhart, you reap the benefit of more than eight decades of hard-fought battles to preserve this wilderness and can see it in a condition that is arguably even more wild than enjoyed by Carhart himself.

Seven entry points are scattered along the length of the Fernberg Road and the spur roads off of it, including the two most popular entries in the BWCAW: Moose Lake (Entry Point 25) and Lake One (Entry Point 30). These two entries have a combined permit quota of a whopping forty-five groups per day, which is remarkable considering many other BWCAW entries allow just one or two groups per day. On your first day of travel from either entry you will inevitably see other groups of visitors. Fortunately, many routes can be crafted from each of these entries, and with proper planning excellent trips are possible for visitors of all interests.

Two additional popular entries from the Fernberg Road are Snowbank Lake (Entry Point 27) and Fall Lake (Entry Point 24). Snowbank Lake is a big, deep Boundary Waters legend offering numerous good tripping options, while similarly large Fall Lake is often used by people looking to reach Basswood Lake and beyond. The final entries from the Fernberg Road are Wood Lake (Entry Point 26), North Kawishiwi River (Entry Point 29), and Farm Lake (Entry Point 31), all of which take you to smaller lakes and less busy areas than other Fernberg Road entries.

Entry Point 24, Fall Lake (Map 15)

> Daily permit quota: 14
> Permit availability: moderate

The Fall Lake entry is one of the most convenient gateways to fantastic Basswood Lake and also the entry point closest to Ely. Fall Lake is over 200 acres in size and lies mostly outside of the Boundary Waters. Motors are allowed on the entire lake, with an outboard maximum size restriction of 25 horsepower on the northern quarter of the lake within the BWCAW. The ease of entry to Basswood and the right to use motors (with the proper permit) makes it one of the higher-demand Boundary Waters entries, especially for the month after the fishing opener in the middle of May and again in early August.

A few points should be considered when contemplating a trip from Fall Lake. First, because most of the lake surface area accessible from Fall Lake allows motorboats, this entry may not be right for visitors strongly opposed to sharing a lake with motorboats. Second, Fall Lake leads to large lakes with big stretches of open water that can be hazardous in high winds, so be prepared for rough water. Third, the Fall Lake landing is a long hike (about 6 miles) from the nearest other BWCAW entry point, so it works best to have two cars or to be dropped off by an outfitter if you are doing a one-way trip.

To get to Fall Lake, take the paved Fernberg Road east for 5 miles from Ely, and turn left onto County Road 182. The Fall Lake campground is 1.5 miles down CR 182 and includes a sizable parking lot and a canoe landing. If you are arriving late, consider reserving one of the sites at the campground to spend the night before entering the wilderness.

Route 24A: Exploration of Basswood Lake (Map 15)

> Difficulty: easy
> Number of days: 2 or more
> Total miles (approx.): 14 or more
> Number of portages: 4
> Total portage rods: 380 rods
> Greatest portage difficulty: 90 rods (L5)

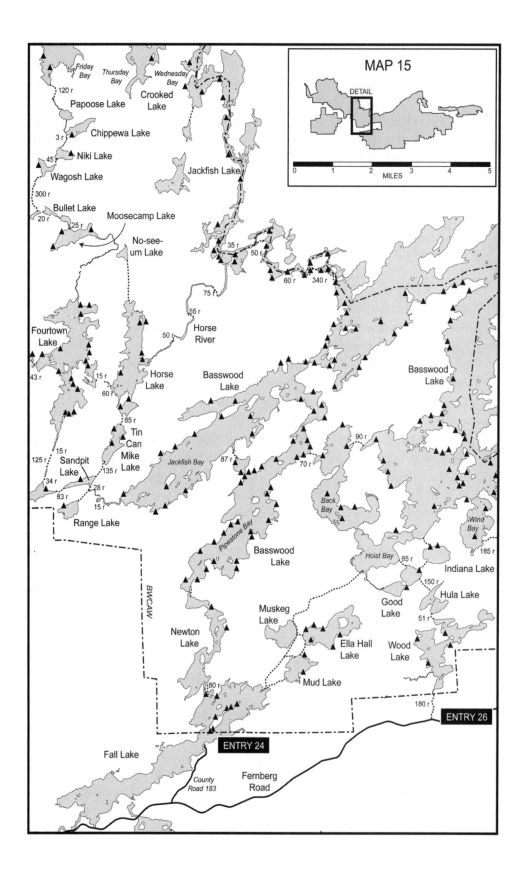

MAP 15

DETAIL

0 1 2 3 4 5
MILES

Friday Bay
Thursday Bay
Wednesday Bay
Crooked Lake
120 r
Papoose Lake
Chippewa Lake
3 r
Niki Lake
45 r
Wagosh Lake
Jackfish Lake
300 r
Bullet Lake
Moosecamp Lake
20 r
25 r
No-see-um Lake
35 r
50 r
60 r
340 r
75
55 r
50
Horse River
Fourtown Lake
Basswood Lake
Basswood Lake
43 r
15 r
Horse Lake
60 r
85 r
90 r
Tin Can Mike Lake
Jackfish Bay
87 r
70 r
15 r
125 r
Sandpit Lake
135 r
34 r
28 r
83 r
15 r
Back Bay
Wind Bay
Range Lake
185 r
Pipestone Bay
Basswood Lake
Hoist Bay
85 r
Indiana Lake
150 r
Hula Lake
Muskeg Lake
Good Lake
51 r
Newton Lake
Ella Hall Lake
Wood Lake
BWCAW
80 r
Mud Lake
180 r
ENTRY 26
ENTRY 24
Fall Lake
County Road 183
Fernberg Road

Navigation maps: Voyageur 4
                  Fisher F10
                  McKenzie 9, 10, 17

This is a great route for canoeists who want to visit big, beautiful lakes with a minimum of portaging, and who don't mind sharing a lake with motorboats. You have just two portages to get to Pipestone Bay on Basswood Lake, from where you can try your hand fishing waters that produced the state record northern pike, do a day trip to Basswood Falls, or seek out motor-free waters on the northern side of Basswood (although you will need a remote border crossing permit if you are going into the Canadian side). Basswood can quickly cast a spell on you, drawing you back year after year. Don't make this your first journey, lest you find paddling nirvana and have no further need for this guide!

Detailed Route

Paddle and portage 7 miles from Fall Lake to Pipestone Bay of Basswood Lake, including portages of 80 rods (L4) to Newton Lake and 90 rods (L5) to Pipestone Bay. Start from the Fall Lake landing at the Forest Service campground. Eight designated campsites are located on the northern quarter of Fall Lake, and these sites are great for a first or last night in the wilderness. They are often occupied during busy times in the summer, so plan to arrive early if you want to stay at one. You leave Fall Lake by heading north to the portage a mile from the Fall Lake campground. This 80-rod portage is one of the smoothest in the BWCAW, and you may see small fishing boats being pulled across on portage wheels placed beneath their hulls. Few canoeists use portage wheels, although they are legal on this portage.

Pay attention to the changing bedrock geology exposed intermittently along the shores and at the portages along this route. On Fall Lake you are well within the boundaries of the ancient Knife Lake Group of slates and similar metamorphic rocks formed by heating of existing bedrock millions of years ago. Moving north over Newton Lake, you are in a transition zone of pyroclastic rocks that started as fluidized flows up rock fragments. Once you reach Pipestone and Jackfish bays, the rock changes to being predominantly granites, which are among the most recent rock formations on this route and were created deep underground by cooling magma. Even an inexperienced observer will be able to find interesting differences among the exposed bedrock.

Wind your way through the islands and curves of Newton Lake, and camp at one of the two designated campsites, or head on to the 90-rod portage that drops to Pipestone Bay of Basswood Lake. This is another excellent portage over a smooth trail. Once on Basswood you have almost unlimited places to explore and camp and can certainly spend many days on this huge lake.

One of your immediate options is to travel west to famous Jackfish Bay. No portage is usually necessary for paddlers because they can wind through the little swamp connecting the middles of the two bays (you can also take an 87-rod (L5) portage). This route is favored by paddlers but typically impassable to motorboats. Alternatively, paddle north to the end of Pipestone Bay and then circle back to the southwest to get to Jackfish. At the north end of Pipestone and Jackfish bays you can also keep going toward Basswood Falls. You will escape motorized traffic once you pass through the convergence of Jackfish Bay and Pipestone Bay because motorboats are not allowed past the narrows.

Alternatively, you can head east over a fine 70-rod portage (L3) to Back Bay. From Back Bay the eastern side of Basswood Lake is accessible by heading south to Hoist Bay or over an infrequently traveled 90-rod (L6) portage on the northeast side of Back Bay. Unless you are in a hurry, this 90-rod portage is not necessary, but it does avoid the paddle to Hoist Bay. The portage is modestly rocky and will probably have only minimal mud—really not too bad considering its relative lack of use. Hoist Bay is named after a logging hoist constructed there by the Swallow and Hopkins Logging Company in the early 1900s. A century ago this bay was bustling with activity as lumberjacks rafted logs across Basswood to the logging hoist, which loaded them onto railroad cars to be hauled by a wood-burning locomotive to Fall Lake.

Paddle and portage at least 7 miles from Basswood Lake to Fall Lake, including portages of 90 rods (L5) to Newton Lake and 80 rods (L4) to Fall Lake. To return to the start, backtrack down the portages through Newton Lake to Fall Lake. Alternatively, consider Routes 24B or 24C for great extensions out of Basswood Lake.

Route 24B: Horse Lake Loop (Map 15)

Difficulty: intermediate
Number of days: 5 or more
Total miles (approx.): 39.5 or more
Number of portages: 14
Total portage rods: 1,233
Greatest portage difficulty: 340 rods (L9)
Navigation maps: Voyageur 4
Fisher F9, F10
McKenzie 10, 17

This route takes you into the heart of canoe country through some of the most storied areas in the Boundary Waters, including the popular fishing grounds of Jackfish Bay of Basswood Lake, through Horse Lake, and along the Horse River. You will then curve around to beautiful Basswood Falls and back to Fall Lake. This journey passes through areas long inhabited by Native Americans, ventured through by voyageurs, logged by lumberjacks, and coveted for the dam-building dreams of an early industrialist. This wonderful route has relatively few portages, but one long portage must be taken around Basswood Falls. Also, be prepared for the potential challenges of crossing the wide-open expanses of Jackfish Bay and Pipestone Bay on Basswood Lake.

Detailed Route

Paddle and portage 7 miles from Fall Lake to central Pipestone Bay of Basswood Lake, including portages of 80 rods (L4) to Newton Lake, and 90 rods (L5) to Pipestone Bay. The first few miles of this trip are identical to Route 24A and involve traveling the popular route from Fall Lake to Pipestone Bay of Basswood. You may want to spend an evening on Pipestone Bay or head across to Jackfish Bay. A portage connects these two bays, but you should be able to paddle through a channel in the shallow marsh connecting the two. Timing on this stretch of the trip is not entirely under your control because a brisk southwest or northeast wind can bring up rollers that all but shut down Basswood canoe travel, so allow yourself leeway in your schedule in the event you get wind bound for a day.

Paddle and portage 9.5 miles from Pipestone Bay of Basswood Lake to Horse Lake, including portages of 15 rods (L3) and 28 rods (L3) to Sandpit Lake, 135 rods (L4) to Tin Can Mike Lake, and 85 rods (L5) to Horse Lake. Continue to the southwest corner of Jackfish Bay and head into the channel just to the southwest of the campsite located there. The channel narrows until you must take an easy 15-rod portage, after which you continue through another narrows until you reach the 28-rod portage to Sandpit Lake. This portage is quite easy, although it is low lying and sometimes muddy. The portage branches at the top of a T that connects to the left (south) to Range Lake, and to the right (north) to Sandpit. For this route make sure you turn right and head north to Sandpit Lake, which is very close. Portage left all the way to Range Lake if you want to get off the beaten track. If you are taking this alternative route, stay at the single campsite on the southwest shore of Range. You may want to hike the trail first without your gear to see if anyone is occupying the Range Lake site, rather than risk having to haul your gear there and back.

Paddle along the eastern shore of Sandpit Lake to the portage landing in the northeast corner. Some Fisher maps erroneously show a portage continuing along this shoreline. In fact, the trail ends abruptly after about 20 rods when you come to a cliff, so don't waste your time trying to portage around Sandpit Lake unless you've brought your climbing gear. After paddling across Sandpit, you will find a fine trail that will take you right to the shore of Tin Can Mike Lake with minimal trouble. One of the finest boardwalks in all of the Boundary Waters is at the north end of this portage. Head north on Tin Can Mike Lake, where you might want to camp at one of the three designated campsites. From Tin Can Mike you take the 85-rod portage to Horse Lake. This is an easy trail with good landings. Modest hills are located on either end of the portage, but the central portions are quite level.

You may want to camp at one of the seven designated campsites on Horse Lake, or alternatively head to neighboring Fourtown Lake (see route 24C). Horse Lake is very popular, so you should arrive early in the day if you hope to find an open campsite. In August, which is typically peak travel time in the BWCAW, the sites on Horse are rarely open.

The bedrock under both Fourtown and Horse is primarily pinkish granite that weathers to a much lighter gray. If you find recently cracked boulders or rocks, you will see that the interior is typically somewhat pink. This granite, particularly that on the west side of Fourtown Lake, is sometimes referred to as Lac La Croix granite. The bedrock under both of these lakes is crossed by ancient north-south faults, and these areas of weak rock were carved into lake beds by the last glaciers 10,000 years ago. Interestingly, narrow Tin Can Mike Lake to the south of Horse Lake lies along a fault line in the granite bedrock, a fact easily appreciated when looking at a map. Yet another fault line runs northeast from Sandpoint to Mudro to Picket to Nels Lake, also apparent from an overview map showing these lined-up lakes.

Paddle and portage 5 miles from Horse Lake down the Horse River, with portages of 50 rods (L4), 55 rods (L4), and 75 rods (L6), and three other shallow rapids potentially requiring you to walk your canoe through the shallows. Keep your eyes on the west shore as you are paddling through the narrows connecting the southern bay on Horse Lake to the main body of the lake. In the narrows you will see a decades-old iron ring believed to have been used to string ropes hauling rafts of logs down Horse Lake. A campsite was located here long before creation of the Boundary Waters (and is shown on old maps of the area). The site remains in use today as a Forest Service designated campsite.

If you are not staying on Horse Lake, paddle into the main body of Horse and then down the Horse River. Give yourself plenty of time on the Horse River. Depending on your abilities and the river's water levels, you will take at least three portages and are likely to come across three additional shallow areas that you will either have to portage around or pole through. The first of these portages comes just a quarter mile into the Horse River at a rapids and beaver dam. An easy 15-rod portage (L3) is available on the west shore. Soon thereafter another 16-rod (L3) portage threads down the east shore around shallow rapids. The next set of rapids is about a half mile farther and cannot be navigated in a canoe, so take the easy 50-rod portage (L4), which has a boardwalk through a marshy central area. An optional portage is found a third of a mile later. Take the short portage on the east side of the river if you are uncomfortable paddling this shallow stretch. Two final portages remain. The first one is 55 rods (L4) along a decent trail with some rocks. The second portage is 75 rods (L6) along a fine trail but with a fair amount of hill climbing and descent.

Visit Lower Basswood Falls, paddle and portage 4.5 miles to Basswood Lake, including portages of 50 rods (L5), 60 rods (L6), and 340 rods (L9). The Horse River will drop you in a wide bay of the Basswood River. This is one of the most scenic and popular parts of the Boundary Waters, so don't assume that you will get one of the campsites in this stretch. Also, remember you cannot camp on the Canadian side without a permit from Canadian authorities. I recommend heading across this bay to view and photograph Lower Basswood Falls, which can be done from the 35-rod

(L3) portage on the north side of the river. These are formidable, perilous falls, so show caution when landing your canoe (there are plenty of safe landing spots back from the falls).

After stopping at Lower Basswood Falls, continue upstream (east) along the Basswood River to Basswood Lake. Every portage remaining before Basswood Lake is along the border, and these portages or ones close to them have been used for at least hundreds of years. Existing maps can be somewhat inexact on the placement of portages, but the following description should work well. Your first portage is a 50-rod carry around Wheelbarrow Falls at an island. The main falls are on the west channel of the island, and this portage along the south channel follows a relatively straight chute of smaller rapids. The portage is well traveled but somewhat rocky. You can also portage up the Canadian side, but it seems to be a much less frequently traveled trail.

Turn south after the Wheelbarrow portage, and canoe about a mile until you get to a 60-rod portage (L6) on the Canadian side. This portage is initially a relatively steep climb, then levels out and can be a bit muddy before dropping steeply again to the Basswood River.

Continue a quarter mile up the river, and you will find a landing for the final portage on the south shore. This final portage is about 340 rods long and certainly one of the easiest long portages you will ever experience. The trail is mostly level and in nice shape. The trail includes a number of spurs to the left that lead to camp-sites or put-ins on the river. I saw a canoe wrapped around a rock in a pile of logs the last time I was through this area. You don't want to add your canoe or yourself to the debris collection. Besides, you are not likely to save much time by breaking this portage into smaller chunks because you will spend so much time getting in and out of your canoe.

Important warning: Don't try to take a shortcut along these spurs. This stretch of the Basswood River can be hazardous and sadly seems to claim the life of a visitor every few years. This stretch of river and falls has probably taken more lives than any other in the BWCAW. Keep yourself and your party alive for future trips, and take the full 340-rod portage! Also, never swim in this section of the Basswood River. The unpredictable currents are deadly. Even if you are wearing a life jacket, you can be caught in the churning waters and drown.

Portage and paddle 13.5 miles across Basswood Lake though Pipestone Bay and Newton Lake to Fall Lake, including portages of 90 rods (L5) and 80 rods (L4). From Basswood Lake continue south toward Pipestone Bay, and return to Fall Lake, re-tracing the early portions of this route. On your way south you may paddle past a tiny little building on an island about 3 miles south of Basswood Falls and won-der what this tiny cabin or huge outhouse is doing in such a remote location. This building is identified as a "gauging station" on most maps and is used to measure the water levels at Basswood Lake. The information is gathered for the International Joint Commission, which has regulatory control over the Prairie Portage dam on the east end of Basswood. This structure is just one of a handful of buildings still maintained in the Boundary Waters. Consider breaking this segment into at least two pieces, allowing yourself time to enjoy more of Basswood Lake.

Route 24C: Loop though Iron Lake (Map 15)

> Difficulty: challenging
> Number of days: 10
> Total miles (approx.): 75
> Number of portages: 27
> Total portage rods: 1,753
> Greatest portage difficulty: 340 rods (L9)
> Navigation maps: Voyageur 2, 4
>   Fisher F9, F10, F16, F17
>   McKenzie 10, 11, 17

This challenging route out of Fall Lake rewards a traveler with some of the finest of the Boundary Waters: lakes of all shapes and sizes, routes off the beaten path, and long stretches of portage-free paddling. You will be covering a long distance, some of it in very remote areas with rarely maintained portages and challenging navigation, so this route is best suited to seasoned visitors.

Map 15 shows most of this route, and Map 12 shows the western portions.

Detailed Route

Paddle and portage 7 miles from Fall Lake to Basswood Lake, including portages of 80 rods (L4) to Newton Lake, and 90 rods (L5) to Pipestone Bay of Basswood Lake; then paddle and portage 7 miles from Pipestone Bay to Sandpit Lake, including portages of 15 rods (L3) and 28 rods (L3). The first part of this route is identical to Route 24B all the way to Sandpit Lake. Remember to be cautious about winds and waves on Basswood. See Routes 24A and 24B for more information about this stretch.

Paddle and portage 1 mile to Mudro Lake, including a portage of 83 rods (L9). On Sandpit Lake your path will diverge from that of Route 24B by heading west toward Mudro Lake rather than north to Tin Can Mike Lake. The 83-rod portage to Mudro is one of the toughest medium-length portages in the Boundary Waters. You have a steep, tough climb along a rock trail from Sandpit Lake for about 60 rods before leveling briefly and then dropping steeply for another 30 rods. Even die-hard voyageurs may want to make two trips on this one!

Paddle and portage 4 miles from Mudro Lake to Fourtown Lake, including portages of 34 rods (L5), 125 rods (L8), and 15 rods (L4). The journey to Fourtown Lake is a challenge, with three portages separated by quite short paddles, but this is beautiful country and enjoyable even on a tough portage. The first carry is only 34 rods but is reasonably difficult. Continue past this portage and take the 125-rod trail on the west side of the valley, which is a tough route but has been upgraded by the Forest

Service to improve the walking surface. The final, 15-rod portage is short but reasonably hard considering its length. It involves a lot of hill climbing for a short portage and doesn't afford a good landing on the Fourtown side.

Paddle and portage 5 miles from Fourtown Lake to Gun Lake, including portages of 43 rods (L4) to Boot Lake, 19 rods (L2) to Fairy Lake, and 53 rods (L4) to Gun Lake. Fourtown Lake is usually a fine place to spend a night, and typically a fair number of the fifteen designated campsites are open. The only drawback is the fact that the campsites are clustered together in little groups. Fortunately, most of the sites are not visible from one another.

A reasonably level and easy 43-rod (L4) portage leads from Fourtown to Boot Lake, followed by an easy 19-rod portage from Boot to Fairy Lake. This is a relatively flat portage even though you gain about 10 feet in elevation along the trail. Camp on one of Fairy Lake's two campsites, or continue moving on to Gun Lake. The 53-rod portage from Fairy to Gun is just a basic flat portage that collects a bit of water in the spring.

Gun Lake has five designated campsites. This peaceful little lake was the center of a significant battle over the use and protection of the Boundary Waters in the 1950s, when two resort owners sought to build a road from Gun Lake to their resorts on Crooked Lake. Their efforts were an extreme, but perhaps understandable, response to a federal court ruling that they could no longer fly guests by floatplane to their Crooked Lake resorts. Using amphibious vehicles, and reportedly even a small bulldozer, the resort owners carved out a trail from Gun Lake to Friday Bay. Even in the 1950s, when other parts of the current BWCAW were being heavily logged, the unauthorized use of bulldozers on federal lands was frowned upon. The federal district court quickly imposed another injunction. The resort owners both put up a formidable fight to preserve the viability of their resorts but were eventually bought out by the federal government. One of the resorts was relocated to Canada and is today Zup's resort on the western side of Lac La Croix. When enjoying the quiet beauty of this area, it is worth reflecting on the fact that this solitude came at a personal price to folks who lost a way of life. Changing rules and regulations forced them from their resorts and businesses, and it should come as no surprise that they fought these changes aggressively.

Paddle and portage 3 miles from Gun Lake to Beartrap Lake, including portages of 33 rods (L5) to Gull Lake, 35 rods (L3) to Mudhole Lake, 60 rods (L6) to Thunder Lake, and 6 rods (L1) to Beartrap Lake. This route now takes you directly over the "handle" of Gun Lake to Gull Lake, but you can also head into the "barrel" to Bullet Lake (see Route 23B). The 33-rod portage to Gull gradually climbs a trail that showed significant erosion in 2002 but is easily passable.

Continue through Gull, Mudhole, and Thunder lakes. The 35-rod portage to Mudhole is quite flat, while the 60-rod trail from Mudhole to Thunder has moderate hills on either end (but a good path). The 6-rod portage to Thunder Lake diverts around a wooded rapids that drops about 4 feet in elevation (and does not have a navigable channel). You may want to camp on one of these lakes. Once you leave

Thunder Lake you have only one campsite before Iron Lake, which is 10 miles away, so plan accordingly. If it is late in the day and you are looking for a campsite, hope that the Beartrap Lake site is open, because a 200-rod portage and miles of paddling lie between you and the next campsite.

Paddle and portage 3.5 miles from Beartrap Lake to Sunday Lake, including portages of 204 rods (L8) and 60 rods (L6). Portage from the west end of Beartrap Lake to the Beartrap River. This is not a heavily traveled area, so expect this 204-rod portage to be somewhat overgrown. It is also a bit hilly and tends to accumulate water on the trail near the Beartrap River. After the portage, continue down the Beartrap River. You are likely to come across a massive beaver dam just before you turn north into the main channel.

After about a mile you will come to a 60-rod portage on the west shore of the Beartrap River, leading around a set of rapids. This trail is reasonably level and would warrant a difficulty of L4 but for the fact it is rarely used or maintained, making it somewhat overgrown. You may be tempted to divide this portage up into two 20-rod carries with a small pond in between, but you will gain only frustration by doing so. A bit farther ahead (about a half mile) is a small rapids likely to be shootable or walkable to most canoeists (but scout them first). This entire area was burned by a wildfire in the 1990s but is now starting to show good regrowth of young pine, particularly jack pine.

Paddle and portage 6 miles down the Beartrap River from Sunday Lake to Iron Lake, including portages of 19 rods (L2), 12 rods (L1), 35 rods (L3), and 110 rods (L7) on the Beartrap River. Continue out the west end of Sunday Lake, and take the easy 19-rod portage on the north shore of the Beartrap River where it leaves Sunday Lake. Your next portage is a good 12-rod trail around impassable rapids, which is soon followed by a little-used 35-rod portage around the west side of quite easy rapids. The final, 110-rod portage has a challenging trail to Peterson Bay of Iron Lake, with the hardest part being the difficult rock-face landing dropping to Peterson Bay. You need to slide your canoe down a long, steep rock face and then carefully load and enter it, a challenging little series of ballet moves. I am sure many visitors have taken an unexpected swim at this location. Iron Lake provides camping opportunities at ten designated campsites on the U.S. side of the lake, and good fishing. Remember, you can't camp on the Canadian side without approval from Canadian authorities.

Paddle and portage 3 miles from Iron Lake to western Crooked Lake, including portages of 140 rods (L7) around Curtain Falls to Crooked Lake. The portage to Crooked Lake is an ancient route that is still much used today. You will have a healthy initial climb, but then the excellent trail flattens out and ends just after passing Curtain Falls. These are some of the most beautiful falls in the border country. Early in the twentieth century industrialist Edward Backus hoped to dam Curtain Falls to provide power and water transportation. His plans would have raised water levels here by 15 feet and inundated at least hundreds of acres of forest, but were vigorously fought by Ernest Oberholtzer and other conservation pioneers. In the middle of the twentieth century a resort was operated on the east end of the falls (see Route 23B for information about this resort).

Paddle 18 miles along Crooked Lake to Lower Basswood Falls. Ah, the easy life without portages! You will likely want to camp at least one night on Crooked Lake and should consider more. Numerous campsites are scattered across the islands and peninsulas, but make sure you have a good map and compass along. This is easy country to find yourself turned around. You will have the option of heading south at Friday Bay to paddle through Chippewa Lake back to Gun Lake (a course described in Route 23B), but this route takes you past Friday Bay, Thursday Bay, and Wednesday Bay to the Basswood River.

Very adventurous visitors may seek to break from this route and head south toward Jackfish Lake, which is enticingly remote. Jackfish Lake and its surroundings are part of the Tick Lake Primitive Management Area (PMA) administered by the Kawishiwi Ranger District (reachable at 218-365-7600). As discussed at the start of this guide, PMAs have no maintained portages or campsites and require written authorization from the local ranger district to camp within them. Thus, the portages south from Wednesday Bay and Thursday Bay toward Jackfish Lake are both very overgrown, although the portage through Wabosons Lake was somewhat open in 2002. It is probable that these portages will become increasingly difficult in future years until they return to a native state of deadfalls, brush, and mud. Old maps show other portages fanning out from Jackfish Lake to Sauna Lake and Maingan Lake, but investigation in 2002 found no evidence of these portages. On a related note, you can also attempt to enter the Tick Lake PMA from the south via Horse Lake, but the portage from Horse to Tick appears to have returned entirely to nature and is not passable without a herculean effort.

As you pass through Wednesday Bay and turn south, you will come across Table Rock, which was a major stopping point for voyageurs. Continuing south, you will come across a set of fine pictographs along the west shore of the lake. These pictographs are marked on most BWCAW maps.

Paddle and portage 4.5 miles to Basswood Lake, including portages of 35 rods (L3), 50 rods (L5), 60 rods (L6), and 340 rods (L9). Take the well-traveled 35-rod portage trail around Lower Basswood Falls. These falls are not huge yet remain absolutely magnificent. Perhaps the relative silence of paddling a canoe makes ears more sensitive to roaring water. Or perhaps the visual simplicity of unbroken forest and flat water is such a contrast to raging falls. Whatever the reason, paddling and portaging to wilderness waterfalls cleanses the sensory pallet, allowing you to really enjoy them in a way that non-wilderness falls will never match.

Now your journey will rejoin route 24B around the upper reaches of the Basswood River and onward to Basswood Lake. You should continue upstream (east) along the Basswood River. Existing maps are somewhat inexact on the placement of portages in this area, but the following description is based on my travels. Your first portage is a 50-rod carry up around Wheelbarrow Falls. The main falls are on the west channel of an island near these falls, and this portage along the south channel is along a relatively straight chute of rapids. The portage is well traveled but somewhat rocky. Alternatively, take the portage up the west side of the rapids on the Canadian side and then paddle around the island. Turn south after the Wheelbarrow portage, and travel about a mile until you get to a 60-rod portage on the Canadian side. This portage is initially a relatively steep climb, then levels out and can be a bit muddy before dropping steeply again to the Basswood River.

Continue a quarter mile up the river, and you will find a landing for the final portage on the south shore of the river. This final portage is about 340 rods long and one of the easiest portages of this length in the wilderness. The trail is mostly level and in nice shape. A number of spurs in the road to the left lead to campsites or put-ins on the river.

Important warning: Don't try to take a shortcut along these spurs. This stretch of the Basswood River can be hazardous and sadly seems to claim the life of a visitor every few years. It has probably taken more lives than any other in the BWCAW and is never safe for swimming or canoeing. Keep yourself and your party alive for future trips, and take the full 340-rod portage.

Paddle and portage 13.5 miles from Basswood Falls back to your start on Fall Lake, including portages of 90 rods (L5) and 80 rods (L4). From Basswood Lake continue south toward Pipestone Bay, and return to Fall Lake, retracing the early portions of this route.

Entry Point 26, Wood Lake (Map 16)

> Daily permit quota: 2
> Permit availability: difficult

Wood Lake is a fine entry point for a quick trip into the Boundary Waters, or for anyone interested in seeking the peace and quiet of nonmotorized lakes in an area surrounded by the motorized waters of Basswood, Fall, and Moose lakes. You can stick to the handful of neighboring lakes that do not allow motors, hook up to the west with any of the routes out of Fall Lake (Entry Point 24), or travel east along any of the routes out of Moose Lake (Entry Point 25). To keep this guide light enough to take into the wilderness, only the route to Basswood Lake is described below.

To get to Wood Lake, take the Fernberg Road east from Ely for 12.6 miles. An excellent parking lot with space for more than twenty vehicles is located on the north side of road. The Fall Lake campground, north of the Fernberg Road on County Road 182, 5 miles from Ely, is a good place to spend an evening before entering the wilderness.

Route 26: Wood Lake to Basswood Lake (Map 16)

> Difficulty: intermediate
> Number of days: 2 or more
> Total miles (approx.): 11 or more
> Number of portages: 8

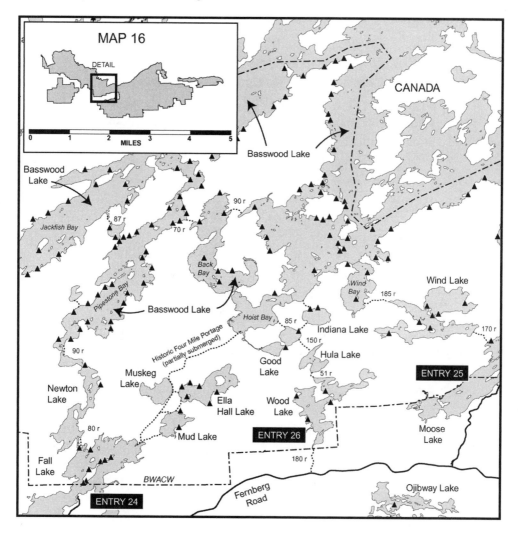

Total portage rods: 932
Greatest portage difficulty: 150 rods (L8)
Navigation maps: Voyageur 6
Fisher F10
McKenzie 9, 17

This trip heads from Wood Lake through small neighboring lakes to Hoist Bay on Basswood Lake. Wood Lake and its nearest neighbors (Hula and Good lakes) received extensive damage during the 1999 blowdown yet are still very nice destinations. Once on Basswood you have many opportunities to explore its thousands of acres, possibly seeking out fishing opportunities or simply exploring its many bays and islands.

Detailed Route

Paddle and portage 5.5 miles from Wood Lake to Hoist Bay on Basswood Lake, including portages of 180 rods (L5) to Wood Lake, 51 rods (L4) to Hula Lake, 150 rods (L8) to Good Lake, and 85 rods (L7) to Hoist Bay. From the Wood Lake parking lot take the gently rolling trail to Wood Lake. This entire portage is outside of the Boundary Waters and well maintained. A fine bridge extends over the one extensive low area, and a second, smaller bridge crosses a small intermittent stream.

On Wood Lake you can either stay at one of the five campsites or head farther to Hula Lake. If you choose to move past Wood Lake, you have only two more campsites to choose from before reaching Basswood. The portage to Hula is generally in good shape. The 150-rod portage to Good Lake is mainly a soft-bottomed trail that is prone to becoming muddy in the spring and during wet periods, warranting the difficulty level of L8, which is high for a portage of 150 rods. Finally, the portage to Hoist Bay is also soft bottomed and tends to be relatively muddy except during extended dry periods. A shorter portage leads out of the west side of Good Bay but is sometimes impassable due to low water levels.

Once on Basswood you will want to head for a campsite and can paddle either west to Back Bay or east toward Lincoln Island. The majority of Basswood's campsites are located to the east, although this huge lake has good campsites scattered in every direction. Basswood Lake looms large in the history of the Boundary Waters; see Route 25C to learn more about this great lake and its interesting history.

Paddle and portage 5.5 miles, plus your distance on Basswood, back to the Wood Lake parking lot, including portages of 87 rods, 150 rods, 51 rods, and 180 rods.

Entry Point 25, Moose Lake (Map 17)

Daily permit quota: 27
Permit availability: moderate to difficult

More permits are issued for travel though the Moose Lake entry than any other entry to the Boundary Waters. Easy access to Basswood Lake and to Quetico Provincial Park in Ontario gets much of the credit for the popularity of Moose Lake. In addition, Moose and Basswood both allow motorboats, which attract some visitors but repel others.

Moose Lake and its immediate neighbors, Newfound Lake and Sucker Lake, can be reached without portages and provide access to almost forty campsites. In addition, taking the easy 20-rod Prairie Portage to Basswood Lake gives you access to dozens of other campsites. All of the routes from Entry Point 24, Fall Lake, are easily reachable from Moose Lake by way of Basswood Lake. In addition, many of the routes from Entry Point 27, Snowbank Lake, are easy extensions from Moose Lake. You will also find that visitors use Moose Lake to gain access to Quetico Provincial

Park in Canada, for which a special permit is needed, as described in "Planning Your Trip," earlier in this guide.

Dozens of different trips can be designed out of Moose Lake. To keep the size of this guide manageable, only relatively short routes from Moose Lake to the nearest lakes are described. Route 25A describes options for exploring Moose Lake, Newfound Lake, and Sucker Lake. Route 25B describes options for heading to Wind Lake. Route 25C takes you on a short loop to Basswood Lake and then back through Wind to Moose. Finally, Route 25D takes you east to Ensign Lake and a number of other interesting lakes. These routes describe just about every portage and lake reachable by canoe in the immediate Moose Lake vicinity, so if you can't find the perfect route below, mix and match them to create a trip that best fits your interests and objectives.

If you would like to press farther afield, use overview Map 14 in addition to more detailed Map 17 and the index to this guide to craft your own route. Based on personal experience as well as Forest Service surveys and the BWCA Wilderness Management Plan, I recommend that you keep the following considerations in mind when selecting a route from Moose Lake. First, expect relatively numerous visitors on Moose, Newfound, and Sucker lakes. These visitors will be canoeists and many overnight motorboats and day-use motorboats. Second, the easiest way to break away from the other paddlers heading up Moose is to go west to Wind Lake and toward Hula, Good, and Wood lakes. Third, if you head east from Moose, the best isolation is found south of the border lakes, as far into the interior as possible. Lakes such as Vera, Missionary, and Skoota (all south of Knife Lake) are beautiful, remote gems.

Moose Lake is served by numerous good outfitters, located on the shores of Moose Lake or in the vicinity, and almost every outfitter in Ely will take you to Moose Lake and pick you up at the end of your trip. If you are driving to the lake yourself, take the Fernberg Road (County Road 18) east from Ely for 15.5 miles, and then take a left onto Moose Road (County Road 183) for 2.5 miles. A parking lot with space for dozens of vehicles will be on your left. Consider camping at the Fall Lake campground before entering the wilderness, or stay at one of the hotels or motels in Ely.

Route 25A: Exploration of Moose Lake (Map 17)

> Difficulty: easy
> Number of days: 2 or more
> Total miles (approx.): 3 or more
> Number of portages: 0
> Total portage rods: N/A
> Greatest portage difficulty: N/A
> Navigation maps: Voyageur 6
>   Fisher F10
>   McKenzie 17

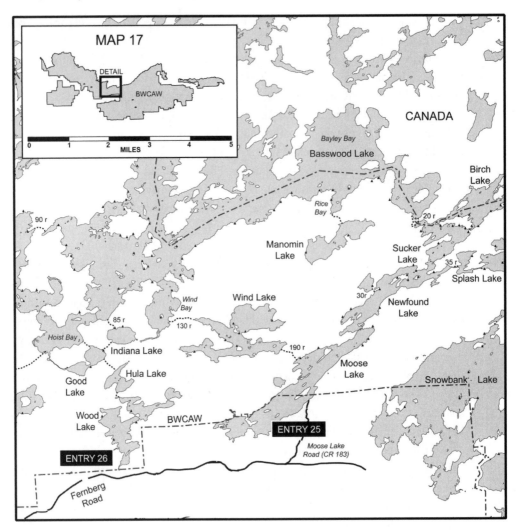

A few days on Moose Lake, with optional side trips to neighboring lakes, make a great introduction to the BWCAW for new campers and also a perfect getaway for the seasoned veteran. Even in the dead of winter these lakes get occasional visitors, so expect to see other people on your trip.

Detailed Route

Put in on Moose Lake and paddle north. Moose Lake is very popular, so you will not be alone on this journey. If this is your first trip into remote wilderness, having a few other folks around can provide a certain sense of comfort. For this reason, plus the lack of portages, this is a fine introduction to the BWCAW. As you paddle from the landing or when relaxing at camp, pause to ponder the fascinating history of this lake. Moose Lake lies just south of the main voyageurs' highway, but at least as early as the mid-1700s French fur traders had established a post along its shore. In 1763 northeastern Minnesota came under British control pursuant to the Treaty of Paris ending the French and Indian War. Within years the British-organized North West Company built their great depot at Grand Portage, and a way station or wintering post at Moose Lake. Countless canoes full of furs and voyageurs traveled through Moose Lake, heading to the good west-east route from Rainy Lake to Lake Superior.

Nearly a hundred years after the fur trade faded, loggers arrived at Moose Lake, as well as neighboring lakes such as Basswood and Knife, seeking wealth in the rich stands of red and white pine. To help facilitate logging operations, various small dams were built to control water levels, as well as the much larger Prairie Portage dam between Sucker Lake and Basswood Lake, originally constructed in 1902. The Prairie Portage dam raised the water levels in Sucker and Newton lakes, connecting them to larger Moose Lake.

In the 1920s and 1930s this area came into its own as a fishing destination. The biggest recorded northern pike ever caught in Minnesota (49 pounds, 12 ounces) was taken next door on Basswood Lake in 1929. The fisherman who caught that monster may have traveled up Moose Lake to get to Basswood, hoping to catch "the big one." Best of luck if you hope to travel up Moose Lake seeking "the even bigger one."

Few people have traveled up and down the length of Moose Lake more times than the late Dorothy Molter, aka "The Root Beer Lady," whose cabin was located at the Isle of Pines on nearby Knife Lake. Dorothy was the last person to make her permanent residence in the Boundary Waters. In that regard, she was the last person to head home by paddling north on Moose Lake. Of course, in other regards, today we are all going home when we travel north on Moose!

You can seek out one of the five campsites on Moose Lake or travel 2.5 miles to the narrows leading to Newfound and Sucker lakes, all without ever taking a portage. On Newfound and Sucker you have numerous designated campsites from which to select. On all three lakes you have the opportunity to seek out walleye and northern pike, as well as smallmouth bass.

At camp, or when trolling along shore, pause to take a look at any exposed bedrock you come across. According to the Minnesota Geological Survey, most of the ancient stone under Moose, Newfound, and Sucker lakes started as layered sand and mud that eroded from ancient volcanoes. These deposits were later pressed and heated three billion years ago to form the exposed rock visible today.

If you want some solitude, an easy 30-rod portage from Newfound Lake heads over a short rise to Found Lake. The trail is not heavily traveled but is short and easy. One campsite exists on Found Lake, but walk the portage first to see if it is open before hauling all your gear across. Alternatively, you can take a 35-rod portage from the far eastern bay of Newfound Lake to little Splash Lake, where you will also find one campsite. This campsite is on the opposite shore from the portage landing but is visible across the lake.

Return to the landing the same way you came. If you want to head in farther, check out routes 25B to 25D with great excursions to the west, north, and east!

Route 25B: Exploration of Wind Lake (Map 17)

> Difficulty: easy
> Number of days: 2 or more
> Total miles (approx.): 8
> Number of portages: 2
> Total portage rods: 380
> Greatest portage difficulty: 190 rods (L5)
> Navigation maps: Voyageur 6
>   Fisher F10
>   McKenzie 17

This route provides another short trip from Moose Lake and quickly takes you off the motorboat route with a portage to Wind Lake. It is a fine extension of Route 25A that will appeal to visitors of all experience levels, yet provides an opportunity to see an interesting lake that most Moose Lake visitors paddle right past.

Detailed Route

Paddle and portage 4 miles from Moose Lake to Wind Lake, portaging 190 rods (L5). From the landing on Moose Lake, head north around a cluster of islands to a shallow bay on the northwest side of the lake. You will find an excellent trail that doglegs to Wind Lake. The path is well maintained and likely to be in good shape, with the only challenge coming in the first 50 rods as you climb up the moderate hill from Moose. This portage was heavily hit by the 1999 windstorm. Many trees are down along this and subsequent portages to Basswood Lake, but the portages were all completely reopened. Also, pay attention to the geology. You will notice on the shores of Moose Lake that the exposed bedrock is a tilted slate, while up on the ridges it is a much harder igneous rock.

On Wind Lake you can choose from seven designated campsites to spend the night. If these sites are taken, head over the 130-rod portage to Wind Bay of Basswood Lake, which will give you access to numerous additional campsites. You will encounter motorized boats on Basswood, but this huge lake still offers great opportunities to explore, fish, and relax.

Paddle and portage 4 miles back to Moose Lake, including a portage of 190 rods (L5). Return to your starting point the same way you arrived.

Route 25C: Basswood–Wind Lake Loop (Map 17)

> Difficulty: intermediate
> Number of days: 3 or more
> Total miles (approx.): 23.5
> Number of portages: 3

Total portage rods: 360
Greatest portage difficulty: 190 rods (L5)
Navigation maps: Voyageur 6
　　　　　　　　　Fisher F10
　　　　　　　　　McKenzie 17

If you are looking for a bigger challenge than routes 25A and 25B and are interested in exploring a legendary Boundary Waters lake, this route may be for you. It covers the same initial path of route 25B to Wind Lake but then continues on to Basswood Lake, where you can explore and camp among dozens of bays, islands, and campsites. The route subsequently follows along the U.S.-Canadian border east over the Prairie Portage to Sucker Lake, where you will return back to your start through Newfound and Moose lakes. But for the potentially rough waters of Basswood Lake, this fine route would be classified as easy in difficulty.

Detailed Route

Paddle across Moose Lake; travel 6.5 miles, including a portage of 190 rods (L5) to Wind Lake and 130 rods (L5) to Basswood Lake. From the landing on Moose Lake, paddle to a shallow bay on the northwest side of Moose. You will find an excellent trail that gently winds up to Wind Lake. The trail is well traveled and likely to be in good shape, with the only challenge coming in the first 50 rods as you climb up from Moose. Camp on one of Wind Lake's seven campsites, or immediately head over the portage to Wind Bay of Basswood Lake. This portage to Wind Bay is mostly downhill and is also quite well traveled, although not as well traveled as the route from Moose to Wind. Seek out a campsite on Basswood, where you are likely to have numerous options. Travel west to Hoist Bay and Back Bay if your schedule permits, or turn northeast and head along the border, where you will also find good campsites, but remember that you can't camp on the Canadian side without a Quetico permit and RABC authorization.

Basswood Lake arguably looms larger in the long history of the Boundary Waters than any other lake. This lake is at the center of the BWCAW, leaving you free to head out and explore great areas to the west and east, and to the north if you have a Quetico permit. Like its smaller neighbor Moose Lake, Basswood has long attracted humans. It has probably been at least periodically inhabited for thousands of years. Its fine fishing would have helped sustain Native American populations, and at least as early as the 1800s United States Point was periodically burned by the Ojibwe to promote blueberry growth.

Extensive logging operations took place a century ago along the shores of Basswood Lake, where loggers harvested thousands of red and white pines. Loggers undertook elaborate efforts to move the logs across Basswood to southern sawmills. In fact, a simple logging railroad line was constructed from Hoist Bay to Fall Lake along what is now the Four Mile Portage. Millions of board feet of lumber were driven into Hoist Bay and then transported by railcar south to Fall Lake. At the end of the logging years, Hoist Bay is said to have had so much pine bark on its bottom that wild rice did not grow for decades.

Eventually the rails were pulled up from the Four Mile Portage, and for decades the grade was used as a truck portage to haul boats to and from Basswood. Endless legal wrangling persisted over this portage, with environmentalists trying to remove the trucks. Not until the 1990s was the controversy resolved by an act of Congress prohibiting motorized vehicles from using the portage. That same act preserved the truck portage at Prairie Portage on the northeast side of Basswood and a truck portage between Vermilion Lake and Trout Lake.

Many visitors to the wilderness don't know that Basswood Lake was also home to the Quetico-Superior Wilderness Research Center north of Hoist Bay, founded by conservationist Frank Hubachek, who was one of the major activists striving to preserve the Boundary Waters.

By the 1950s numerous resorts had also sprung up along the shores of Basswood. Heated battles ensued for decades over land ownership, access, and resource use. Eventually all of the resorts were purchased or closed, with existing residents given life estates that allowed them to stay on their land until they passed away. At the start of the twenty-first century, one private inholding still existed, a pair of cabins owned by the descendants of Henry Chosa, to be used until his current descendants pass away. Once these descendants have died, the cabins will be removed, and the sites rehabilitated to their natural state.

Enjoy your time on Basswood, which was home to the largest northern pike ever captured in Minnesota (49 pounds, 12 ounces). Be observant of geology on Basswood, and you will notice subtle changes in exposed bedrock between your start on Moose Lake and the main bays of eastern Basswood Lake. The rock changes from layered, folded gray deposits on Moose, including some flaking slates, to more uniform granite on Basswood. The explanation for these differences is that ancient sand and mudflows around Moose Lake hardened under heat and pressure when flows of molten rock pressed against them nearly three billion years ago. The mudflows became the rock beneath Moose Lake. The molten rock became granite under Basswood.

If you are looking for a diversion, you can head over a 120-rod portage to Manomin Lake, located a couple miles west of Prairie Portage. Two Forest Service campsites are located on Manomin. This portage gets few visitors, following a mostly grassy trail to its terminus on Manomin.

Paddle and portage 17 miles across Burntside Lake and over the 20-rod Prairie Portage, and back to your start on Moose Lake. When your time comes to leave Basswood, head out its eastern end to Sucker Lake. You will need to go over the 20-rod Prairie Portage, located on the north (Canadian) side of the Prairie Portage dam.

A much longer portage to the south (American) side is used to pull motorboats between Sucker and Basswood lakes.

Route 25D: Eastern Loop through Ensign Lake and Beyond (Map 17)

> Difficulty: challenging
> Number of days: 6
> Total miles (approx.): 44.5
> Number of portages: 13
> Total portage rods: 758
> Greatest portage difficulty: 200 rods
> Navigation maps: Voyageur 5, 6, 7
> Fisher F10, F11
> McKenzie 8, 9

This route takes you east from Moose Lake to Ensign Lake and then on to a set of interior lakes that generally get relatively few visitors. This route intentionally avoids some of the most popular areas east of Moose Lake to give you interesting alternatives that are relatively infrequently traveled.

Map 17 shows the first portion of this route, and Map 18 shows the remainder. The entire route is shown in overview on Map 14.

Detailed Route

Paddle and portage 9 miles from Moose Lake to Ensign Lake, including paddling north from Moose Lake to Newfound Lake, and portages of 35 rods from Newfound to Splash Lake, and 10 rods from Splash to Ensign Lake. The first leg of this journey takes you to Ensign Lake, which is a large lake that has three dozen designated campsites along its spruce- and aspen-covered shores. Ensign is a relatively popular destination out of Moose Lake, and you will certainly see other visitors on it. Not until the next leg will you get into more remote areas.

Paddle and portage 6.5 miles from Ensign Lake to Missionary Lake, including portages of 168 rods from Ensign to Vera Lake, 82 rods from Vera to Trader Lake, and 33 rods from Trader to Missionary Lake. You will now press east to Missionary Lake. Travel is just south of the border in areas that appear to get significantly fewer visitors, based on portage conditions, than the border lakes just to the north. You will first take a 168-rod portage from Ensign to Vera that is uphill and long and has very significant damage from the 1999 windstorm. Fortunately the trail has been completely reopened, and the blowdown will not affect your travels. Next, an 82-rod portage leads along a moderate uphill path from Vera to Trader. You will need to press on from Trader since it does not have any designated campsites.

Take the 33-rod portage from Trader to Missionary, which also has significant blowdown. You will be happy that you weren't portaging along this trail during the monster storm of 1999 that took down these trees. If you want to try a side trip, you can head up a 64-rod trail to Neglige Lake, along a *very* tough trail that is all but impassable due to blowdown. Alternatively, go 30 rods to Explorer Lake along a significantly better, though still not easy, trail. Missionary Lake has just one designated campsite, so allow yourself time to press on in the event it is occupied. All of Missionary Lake was hit hard by the 1999 windstorm.

Paddle and portage 4 miles from Missionary Lake to Spoon Lake, including portages of 200 rods from Missionary to Skoota Lake, 29 rods from Skoota to Dix Lake, and 21 rods from Dix to Spoon Lake. The 200-rod portage from Missionary Lake to Skoota Lake is a long, difficult portage. Although it gets some trail maintenance, it will likely be much more overgrown than any other portage encountered so far on this journey. Your reward will be reaching even more remote lakes than the wild waters you have already passed through. After that 200-rod portage, subsequent portages to Dix and Spoon will be quite easy.

Paddle and portage 2 miles from Spoon Lake to Sema Lake, including a portage of 19 rods from Spoon to an unnamed pond, and portages of 15 rods and 28 rods to Sema Lake. The second portage is on the north side of a stream along a rarely traveled trail, and drops you into a marsh area. The 28-rod portage to Sema Lake is also rarely traveled. The lone campsite on the northeast shore can make a wonderful place to spend a day or two.

Paddle and portage 6.5 miles from Sema Lake to the South Arm of Knife Lake and then west through most of Knife Lake, including a portage of 131 rods from Sema to the South Arm of Knife Lake. The 131-rod portage from Sema Lake starts out great from a sand and gravel beach but then becomes a quite challenging twisted-root, rock-strewn test of ankle strength before dropping you to another nice gravelly beach. Paddle west from the South Arm of Knife Lake.

Paddle and portage 7.5 miles from western Knife Lake to Birch Lake, including portages of 73 rods and 11 to 33 rods to Seed Lake, 21 rods from Seed to Melon Lake, 24 rods from Melon to Carp Lake, and 44 rods from Carp to Birch Lake. The portages from Knife to Birch are all well traveled and should be in good condition.

Paddle and portage 9 miles from Birch Lake to your starting point on Moose Lake. Head back to your starting point by paddling west through Birch Lake, perhaps camping on the American side along the way, and then south to Sucker, Newfound, and Moose lakes.

You can also, should you choose, head to Frog and Trident lakes from Birch Lake. This detour is longer and more difficult but interests people who want to explore areas that most people simply paddle past! The 87-rod portage from Birch Lake to Frog Lake is mostly uphill, yet toward the middle there is an area that accumulates water. During research for this guide I found that the central section had shin-deep muddy areas without ready alternatives around the mud. Pressing on along this extension, the 72-rod portage from Frog to Trident is uphill, ending at a marsh on the Trident end. You will probably need to walk your canoe at least partway through this marsh before launching. Indeed, when coming from Trident to Frog, this portage might be hard to find. The 117-rod portage from Trident to Ensign Lake is also uphill and tends to be a bit more overgrown than other portages in this area. Head out through Ensign Lake to Splash Lake to return to your starting point.

Entry Point 27, Snowbank Lake (Map 18)

> Daily permit quota: 9
> Permit availability: moderate to difficult

Snowbank Lake is a popular starting point for canoeists heading to the remote interior of the Boundary Waters and provides flexibility in trip planning because so many routes can be formed out of Snowbank. Motors up to 25 horsepower are allowed on all of Snowbank, and motors of all sizes are allowed outside the BWCAW on the southwest half of Snowbank, although none of the neighboring lakes allows motors. These deep, cold waters are well known for lake trout, so you might want to take a shot at catching them, particularly in early spring when they aggressively feed in the shallows.

One of the more interesting natural history aspects of Snowbank Lake is that its deep waters are rumored to contain elusive "silver pike." These legendary northwoods Nessies are said to be a northern pike color variant that is almost metallic in appearance, lacking most of the green coloration and spots of normal northern pike. Parent and Disappointment lakes are also said to contain silver pike. Adding credibility to these sightings is a report that Minnesota DNR fisheries personnel captured one in 1997 while surveying Parent Lake's fish population.

When planning a trip from Snowbank, you can take portages southeast to Disappointment and Parent lakes, or head northeast through Boot Lake and on to either Ensign or Ima lakes, giving you access to the Canadian border or the east-central Boundary Waters. Based on Forest Service information and my own experience, the larger lakes closest to Snowbank are all frequently visited. Not only do visitors travel from Snowbank to these lakes, but some visitors from Moose Lake head toward Snowbank. Fortunately, the maze of lakes east of Snowbank allows many great routes.

When reserving your permit, make sure you get one for Entry Point 27, which is a standard permit allowing you to travel beyond Snowbank Lake, rather than a permit for Entry Point 28, which allows camping only on Snowbank. Eight permits are allowed per day for Entry Point 27, with just one set aside for Entry Point 28. In the event you cannot get a permit for Entry Point 27, then Entry Point 28 may be a decent backup. Either spend all your time on Snowbank, or do day trips to neighboring lakes.

To reach Snowbank Lake, take the Fernberg Road 18.5 miles out of Ely, and turn north onto the Snowbank Lake Road for another 3.25 miles to the public access. If you need a place to sleep the night before, you can stay at the Fall Lake campground 5 miles east of Ely or at one of the numerous motels and hotels in Ely.

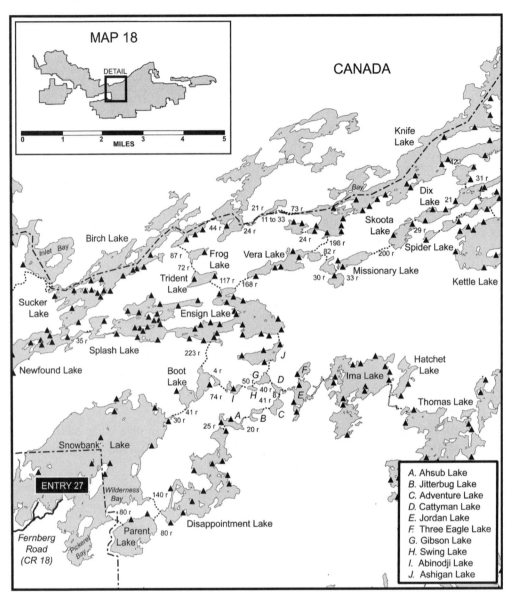

Route 27A: Loop through Parent and Disappointment Lakes (Map 18)

> Difficulty: easy
>
> Number of days: 2 or more
>
> Total miles (approx.): 17
>
> Number of portages: 13
>
> Total portage rods: 519
>
> Greatest portage difficulty: 74 rods (L7)
>
> Navigation maps: Voyageur 7
>
> Fisher F31
>
> McKenzie 9

This is a great loop that takes you from Snowbank Lake to Boot Lake and on through a series of small lakes before passing through Parent Lake and returning to your starting point on Snowbank. This route starts with a long crossing of big open water, which typically is best made in the early morning before winds pick up. If you arrive at Snowbank and find the weather uncooperative, consider reversing the route and head along the protected southern shore to Parent Lake. If you are an inexperienced paddler, you should consider hiring an outfitter to tow you and your gear by motorboat to the Boot Lake portage.

Good pacing for this trip is to spend a first night on Snowbank, Boot, or Abinodji lakes; paddle to Disappointment Lake for a second night, and then head back to Snowbank for a third night or to leave the wilderness. All of these lakes are also well suited for a longer stay, and great extensions to eastern lakes are possible.

Detailed Route

Paddle and portage 4 miles from Snowbank to Boot Lake, including portages of 30 rods (L5) and 41 rods (L5). Your journey starts on Snowbank Lake, which makes a fine place to spend a first night, particularly if you are arriving late in the day. Snowbank is huge, so be prepared for potentially large waves. On a lake of this size it always makes sense to start early in the day, when the winds and waves are usually smallest. Don't forget to *wear* your life jacket. The shore will never seem farther away than when you capsize on this huge, cold lake!

Portage to Boot Lake by way of two modest portages divided by a small pond. Older maps show this route having a longer portage that can avoid the pond, but the longer portage was obscured by downed trees during the 1999 windstorm and does not appear to have been cleared afterward. The first portage is near a log landing that once served the heavy motorboat traffic in this area. This trail is well traveled and in reasonably good repair, dropping you to a little pond. Paddle across the small, shallow pond to the second portage, which is 41 rods long. Boot Lake makes a fine place to spend the night if one of its two campsites is available. Boot's proximity to Snowbank makes these campsites popular, so give yourself time to press on if necessary.

Paddle and portage 1.5 miles from Boot Lake to Abinodji Lake, including portages of 4 rods (L1) to Haven Lake and 74 rods (L7) to Abinodji. From Boot Lake, take the easy 4-rod pull-over to Haven Lake, continuing on to Abinodji by way of a difficult 74-rod portage. This second portage climbs uphill for most of the distance from Haven, partially over exposed rock, before dropping to Abinodji over the final 20 rods. Many canoeists coming through Boot Lake head to Ensign Lake, so by heading east to Abinodji you are venturing into a less frequented area.

Look for exposed beds of metamorphic rock, particularly on the Abinodji landing, which are evidence of the extreme temperatures and pressures applied to the sediments deposited in an ancient ocean some three billion years ago. Paddle through Abinodji, and you can spend the night on the single designated campsite if it is available. If the campsite on Abinodji is taken, you will need to head farther down this route and consider portaging to Ashigan Lake or Jordan Lake, both of which are more likely to have open campsites.

Paddle and portage 1.5 miles from Abinodji to Cattyman Lake, including portages of 50 rods (L4) from Abinodji to Swing Lake, 40 rods (L3) from Swing to Gibson Lake, and 26 rods (L4) from Gibson to Cattyman Lake. When leaving Abinodji, take the 50-rod portage to Swing Lake, which is quite flat and has few obstacles. The only difficult portion is the landing on the Swing Lake side, which is likely to be slightly muddy. Continue across Swing Lake until you reach the 40-rod portage leading to Gibson Lake. This portage is fairly level and has two good landings.

Paddle across Gibson to its southeast corner, where you take an interesting 26-rod portage on the north side of a creek and waterfall to Cattyman Lake. The portage is nearly entirely uphill with extensive exposed rock formations of metamorphic Knife Lake deposits. The landing on the Cattyman side makes an excellent place for a snack or lunch if no other visitors are in the area, with an extensive rock shelf to sit on and time for a stroll to the little waterfall beside the portage. You will also note the extensive old windblown trees caught above the falls. Many are cut off in clean, horizontal lines at their base and are perhaps lost logs of a long-ago lumberjack who was unable to drive them down the falls.

Paddle and portage 3.25 miles from Cattyman to Disappointment Lake, including portages of 8 rods (L2) to Adventure Lake, 41 rods (L3) to Jitterbug Lake, 20 rods (L3) to Ahsub Lake, and 25 rods (L4) to Disappointment Lake. Continue to the southern tip of Cattyman. An 8-rod portage leads past a shallow stretch of water that is often little more than a pull-over to Adventure. The portage trail is relatively flat and easy. Paddle across Adventure to the landing for the portage to Jitterbug. This is also an easy portage, with the exception of a somewhat muddy landing on the Jitterbug side. You will have to navigate through a small labyrinth waterway before entering the main body of Jitterbug.

Jitterbug is an interesting lake, with extensive stands of spruce and tamarack on its low-lying shores. On the western shore you will find a 20-rod portage to Ahsub Lake. The landing on the Jitterbug side is likely to be quite soft, but you can pass through by scampering along the logs tossed on one side of the landing to provide somewhat solid footing.

You may want to consider camping on Ahsub Lake, which is a designated trout fishing lake and contains two campsites. It is illegal to fish outside of trout season or without a trout stamp, even if you are fishing for other species. Live minnows are also unlawful to possess or use on Ahsub. Paddle across Ahsub, and perhaps stay on one of the two designated canoe campsites. The 25-rod portage to Disappointment Lake is up and over a small hill, and you will cross the Old Pines Hiking Trail along the way.

Paddle and portage 6.5 miles from Disappointment Lake to Snowbank Lake, including portages of 80 rods (L6) to Parent Lake and 80 rods (L6) to Snowbank. A relatively easy 80-rod portage connects to Parent Lake along a flat trail that crosses over a small stream. This trail is not too heavily traveled. Follow the 80-rod portage from Parent to Snowbank. This trail is mostly downhill and somewhat rocky. If you would rather skip Parent Lake, you can head directly from Disappointment to Snowbank along a 140-rod (L7) portage that is more heavily traveled than either 80-rod portage.

Route 27B: Northern Loop from Snowbank (Map 18)

Difficulty: challenging
Number of days: 6 or more
Total miles (approx.): 52
Number of portages: 29
Total portage rods: 1,402
Greatest portage difficulty: 223 rods (L8)
Navigation maps: Voyageur 5, 6, 7, 8
Fisher F4, F10, F11
McKenzie 8, 9, 26

This high-quality route takes you out of Snowbank Lake to the Canadian border and legendary Knife Lake. From Knife you will circle around to Kekekabic Lake and to Fraser, Thomas, and Ima lakes before returning to your starting point on Snowbank.

Map 18 shows most of this route, and Map 43 shows the lakes on the far eastern end. In addition, the entire route can be seen in overview on Map 14.

This route minimizes portages and maximizes long stretches of paddling, and you will have many opportunities to explore remote side lakes that are seldom visited. Parts of this route will take you through areas that were heavily damaged by the 1999 windstorm, but don't let this dissuade you from visiting (unless there is severe fire danger). The forest is regenerating and offers a unique opportunity to see up close the results of the storm and the subsequent regrowth. Consider bringing a bear-proof container for your food pack in the event a suitable tree cannot be found to hang your pack.

Detailed Route

Paddle and portage 4 miles from Snowbank Lake to Boot Lake, including portages of 30 rods (L5) and 41 rods (L5). Your journey starts on Snowbank Lake, which is a fine place to spend a first night, particularly if you are arriving late in the day. Follow the same two initial portages as Route 27A. The first portage is near a log landing built years ago, before construction of such "improvements" was discontinued by the Forest Service. Over time the Forest Service has gradually reduced the human imprint on the wilderness, removing almost all signs and even taking down "portage rests," log resting spots along long portages for holding your canoe, which were still in use as recently as the 1980s. These two portages are well traveled and in reasonably good repair. Boot Lake makes a fine place to spend the night if one of the two campsites is available; otherwise head on to Abinodji, which also has a campsite.

Paddle and portage 2 miles from Boot Lake to central Ensign Lake, including a portage of 223 rods (L8). Paddle across Boot Lake to the 223-rod portage leading to Ensign Lake. This popular portage to Ensign follows an average trail that parallels a beaver pond and dam. The last time I traveled this way the dam was in great shape, and I even spotted an otter feeding on a fish it had caught. It is a rewarding sight to actually watch a river otter feed! After halfway the trail leaves the pond and heads sharply north to Ensign. While the path is easy to follow, a couple of low, wet spots are likely in spring or during a wet summer.

Ensign is a beautiful lake surrounded by nearly forty designated campsites. Don't expect isolation on Ensign, since it can be reached with relative ease by the hordes heading north out of Moose Lake (with only two short portages). It makes a great destination and excellent location for the first night of your journey.

Paddle and portage 8 miles from Ensign Lake to west-central Knife Lake, including portages of 168 rods (L7) from Ensign to Vera Lake and 198 rods (L8) from Vera to Knife Lake. This route now takes you in a broad loop to the Canadian border and back through Kekekabic Lake to Snowbank. Head over the 168-rod portage to Vera Lake, and then over the 198-rod portage to Knife Lake. Both of these portages are relatively well traveled but require a bit of climbing. The 168-rod portage to Vera was particularly heavily hit by the July 4, 1999, windstorm, but the trail has been well cleared. The portage from Vera to Knife is steep at both ends and relatively flat along a middle section of exposed bedrock.

Once on Knife Lake you have dozens of campsites to explore at the crossroads of the western and eastern BWCAW. To reach a less frequented campsite, make a detour over the 24-rod portage from Knife Lake to Portage Lake. The flat trail is on the north side of a marsh, not the south side as indicated on some maps of this area. Two designated campsites are located on Portage Lake.

Huge Knife Lake has a special place in the hearts of many visitors, not just because of its prominent position on the voyageurs' highway or its fine fishing, but as home for fifty-six years to Dorothy Molter, the last year-round resident in the BWCAW. Dorothy lived on the Isle of Pines on the west end of Knife Lake from 1930 to 1986, where she ran a small fishing lodge for many years before closing under government pressure. She lived out her years on Knife Lake, serving root beer to thousands of annual visitors, earning her the nickname "the Root Beer Lady." She remains an inspiration to thousands, many of whom visit her reconstructed cabin in Ely. See "The Natural and Human History of the Boundary Waters" earlier in this guide for further discussion about Dorothy.

Much of Knife Lake, especially the South Arm, was among the areas heaviest hit by the July 4, 1999, windstorm. Maps of the damage from that storm are imprecise and make many generalizations of severity. However, there is no need to be imprecise about what happened to much of this area: it got walloped, and large stretches seem to have lost nearly every tree. Take an opportunity to explore as much of this damage as you can from the convenience of your canoe. You will likely never again have a chance to view such widespread impact from a windstorm. Consider photographing a few scenes to document the stage of forest rejuvenation, and then returning in later years to rephotograph and observe the same area.

Knife Lake provides some of the longest stretches of portage-free paddling in the BWCAW, and you can easily design your own route through Knife. All of Knife Lake is relatively popular with visitors, who can arrive from Moose, Snowbank, and Saganaga with relatively little trouble. Fortunately, this long, strung-out lake provides room for everyone. If you want to get off the beaten path, navigate to the small lakes south of Knife Lake or to a cluster of little lakes at the east end before Saganaga. Keep north of Ensign, Kekekabic, and Ogishkemuncie if you want the most isolation.

Paddle and portage 11 miles from Knife Lake to Kekekabic Lake, including portages of 30 rods (L6) to Eddy Lake, and portages through the Kekekabic ponds of 18 rods, 10 rods, 20 rods, 15 rods, and 10 rods to Kekekabic Lake. Head into the South Arm of Knife Lake and then to Eddy Lake. The portage from Knife is uphill to Eddy around a set of raging rapids and is primarily difficult because of the fairly steep and constant climb. Paddle through Eddy Lake, and then take a series of portages through the Kekekabic ponds to Kekekabic Lake. The first portage from Eddy to the Kekekabic ponds had a major blowdown of cedar trees into the creek adjacent to the portage, but the trail is clear. The second portage can sometimes be skipped, depending on water levels. The 15-rod portage is probably the most difficult due to another fairly constant climb. Still, these portages are short and not very challenging.

Kekekabic is a fine, deep remote lake known for its lake trout. Although it is far into the interior of the BWCAW, it still gets frequent visitors because it is such a great destination. If you are entering at a busy time and desire more isolation, take the 78-rod portage to Pickle Lake, where you will find considerably more isolation on Pickle and the other small lakes between Kekekabic and Knife lakes. Maps show a portage from Pickle Lake to Kettle Lake, where a campsite is believed to be located, and a portage to Spider Lake from Kettle, where another campsite is located. However, the blowdown was so severe on the south end of Pickle that the portage could not be located during research for this guide. Forest Service maps of the blowdown area show that these two campsites were searched after the storm, but they are not identified as being inhabitable. Thus, even if your maps show a portage to Kettle and then on to Spider, you are likely to have trouble reaching either lake.

The Kekekabic Trail runs across the wilderness south of Kekekabic Lake, having originally been built for fire control. A lookout tower was built on the prominent hill south of the east bay of the lake, and a Forest Service cabin was built on the south shore of Kekekabic for crews staffing the tower. The tower was removed decades ago.

If you have time to explore Kekekabic, be sure to circle the two largest islands on the western bay, and then paddle to the southern shore of the lake. You will notice a significant difference in geology on this paddle. The islands are made of granite (formed by slowly cooling molten magma) that is rare in this part of the BWCAW, while most of the rest of Kekekabic is mud and sand deposits that were formed into rock by heat and pressure. Differences in rock shape, color, and texture are readily observable.

Paddle across Kekekabic, and head to Fraser Lake, paddling and portaging 6.5 miles, including portages of 85 rods (L8) to Strup Lake, 10 rods (L2) to Wisini Lake, 90 rods (L7) to Ahmakose Lake, 30 rods (L6.5) to Gerund Lake, and 15 rods (L2) to Fraser Lake. The 85-rod trail to Strup climbs immediately uphill for about 50 rods before gently flattening out. This trail is good but challenging for its length. The 10-rod portage from Strup to Wisini is rather easy. The shores of Wisini, like those of many lakes around here, were very heavily hit by the July 4, 1999, windstorm. This would be a great lake to pause for photos of the changed lakeshore. Try to take a picture from a set location so that you can come back in the future and take an identical picture of the regenerating forest. You have another nice trail on the 90-rod portage between Wisini and Ahmakose. This trail also has a substantial hill climb for the first half. The trail from Ahmakose to Gerund drops down a steep path that tends to become a raging stream after heavy rains, while the final, 15-rod portage to Fraser is short, flat, and easy.

Paddle 4.3 miles across Fraser Lake, and paddle 2.5 miles across Thomas Lake. Fraser Lake connects without a portage to Thomas Lake by a narrow cliff-lined channel. You won't be disappointed camping along either of these lakes. The next stage of this trip takes you through great lakes you will love visiting, plus they are not quite as busy as Knife and Ensign lakes.

Paddle and portage 3 miles from Thomas Lake to Ima Lake, including portages of 7 rods from Thomas to a small pond, 30 rods, 20 rods, and 15 rods to Hatchet Lake, and 28 rods from Hatchet to Ima Lake. The first portage from Thomas Lake is just 7 rods over a very easy portage to a small pond on the west side of Thomas. You will then take a 30-rod portage and 20-rod portage, both of which are easier than average for their length. Fisher maps incorrectly show a single 60-rod portage, but I believe you will have to take this as two portages. You will soon take a 15-rod portage around a set of rapids at the southeast elbow of Hatchet Creek. After this portage go toward Hatchet Lake. Some maps show a 15-rod portage just before the entrance to Hatchet, but you should be able to avoid this portage except when water levels are very low. Finally, take a 28-rod portage to Ima Lake, which ends with a difficult 10-rod descent down a rough trail to a narrow, rocky landing on Ima.

Paddle and portage 2.5 miles from Ima Lake to Cattyman Lake, including portages of 5 rods (L1) from Ima to Jordan Lake and 50 rods (L3) from Jordan to Cattyman Lake. The portage from Ima to Jordan is very easy, followed by a paddle along some interesting overhanging cliffs on the shore of Jordan. The portage from Jordan to Cattyman is fairly easy. A pond is located in the middle, and you can paddle along it to cut down on your actual portage distance. However, the time saved is likely to be minimal, and you double your effort at loading and unloading your canoe. Considering how easy the trail is, skip the pond and portage straight to Cattyman Lake.

Paddle and portage 3.25 miles from Cattyman Lake to Disappointment Lake, including portages of 8 rods (L2) to Adventure Lake, 41 rods (L3) to Jitterbug Lake,

20 rods (L3) to Ahsub Lake, and 25 rods (L4) to Disappointment Lake. Continue to the southern tip of Cattyman. When you leave Cattyman at its south end, you will come to an 8-rod portage that leads past a shallow stretch of water that is often little more than a pull-over to Adventure. The portage trail is relatively flat and easy. Paddle across Adventure to the landing for the portage to Jitterbug. This is also an easy portage, with the exception of a somewhat muddy landing on the Jitterbug side. You will have to navigate through a small labyrinth waterway before entering the main body of Jitterbug. This is an interesting lake, with extensive stands of spruce and tamarack on its low-lying shores. On the western shore you will find a 20-rod portage to Ahsub Lake. The landing on the Jitterbug side is likely to be quite soft, but you can pass through by scampering along the logs tossed on one side of the landing to provide somewhat solid footing.

You may want to consider camping on Ahsub Lake, which is a designated trout fishing lake and contains two campsites. It is illegal to fish outside of trout season or without a trout stamp on Ahsub, even if you are fishing for other species. Live minnows are also unlawful to possess or use on Ahsub. Paddle across Ahsub, and perhaps stay on one of the two designated canoe campsites. The 25-rod portage to Disappointment Lake is up and over a small hill, and you will cross the Old Pines Hiking Trail along the way.

Paddle and portage 6.5 miles from Disappointment Lake to your starting point on Snowbank, including portages of 80 rods (L6.5) to Parent Lake and 80 rods (L6.5) to Snowbank Lake. A relatively easy 80-rod portage connects to Parent Lake along a flat trail that crosses over a small stream. This trail is not too heavily traveled. Then take the 80-rod portage from Parent to Snowbank. This trail is mostly downhill and somewhat rocky. If you would rather skip Parent Lake, you can head directly from Disappointment to Snowbank along a 140-rod (L7) portage that is more heavily traveled than either 80-rod portage.

Route 27C: Southern Loop from Snowbank (Map 19)

> Difficulty: challenging
> Number of days: 5 or more
> Total miles (approx.): 38
> Number of portages: 19
> Total portage rods: 836
> Greatest portage difficulty: 140 rods (L7)
> Navigation maps: Voyageur 5, 7, 8
>   Fisher F4, F5, F10, F11
>   McKenzie 8, 9, 18, 19

This is the second long route out of Snowbank Lake in this guide, and it takes you through a rich assortment of lakes to the south of Snowbank. No other route in this guide will probably challenge your navigation skills more than the twists and turns

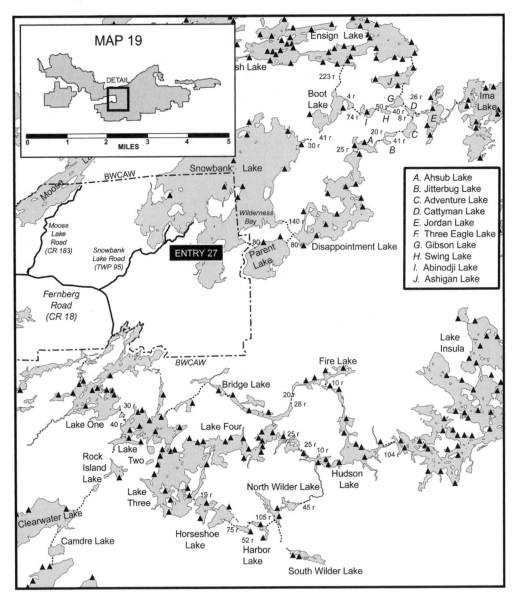

you will find on the lakes along this journey. This classic BWCAW trip will produce memories for a lifetime.

Map 19 shows the first portion of this route, and Map 20 shows the eastern segments. In addition, the entire route is shown in overview on Map 14.

Detailed Route

Paddle and portage 6 miles from Snowbank Lake to Disappointment Lake, including a portage of 140 rods (L7). A good portage trail leads from Snowbank to Disappointment Lake. Even if you are not a geology buff, read the geology section earlier in this guide, and track the geologic clues you encounter on this route. The bedrock you climb over is fascinating because it moves from the ancient Knife Lake Group to the Duluth Complex. Snowbank Lake lies along an ancient geologic boundary. Underlying Snowbank Lake is a mixture of relatively old rock from the Knife Lake Group, mostly layered slates and similar bedrock. This bedrock is estimated to be nearly three billion years old. However, just south of Snowbank Lake lies the Duluth Complex, a massive area of molten rock that forced up against the Knife Lake Group about a billion years ago. Ima, Insula, and Alice lakes are all formed on top of the Duluth Complex, while Snowbank and Disappointment are carved out of the Knife Lake Group.

Paddle and portage 6 miles from Disappointment Lake to Ima Lake, including portages of 25 rods (L4) from Disappointment to Ahsub Lake, 20 rods (L3) from Ahsub to Jitterbug Lake, 41 rods (L3) from Jitterbug to Adventure Lake, 8 rods (L2) from Adventure to Cattyman Lake, 50 rods (L3) from Cattyman to Jordan Lake, and 5 rods (L3) from Jordan to Ima Lake. The first section of this route is the opposite of the final segments of Route 25B.

Paddle and portage 3.25 miles from Ima Lake to Thomas Lake, including portages of 28 rods from Ima Lake to Hatchet Lake; 15 rods, 20 rods, and 30 rods from Hatchet Lake through Hatchet Creek; and then 7 rods to Thomas Lake. See Route 25B for details about these portages.

Paddle and portage 6.5 miles from Thomas Lake to central Lake Insula, including portages of 35 rods to Kiana Lake and 185 rods from Kiana to Lake Insula. From the southwest corner of Thomas, head over a 35-rod portage (not 25, as indicated on Fisher maps) along a trail that is mostly uphill yet not too taxing. Good landings are found on both ends. Wind your way through the labyrinth of peninsulas that make up Kiana Lake, and then head over the 185-rod portage to Lake Insula.

Lake Insula is a wonderful destination, rivaling any other lake in the BWCAW for beauty. It has over three dozen campsites, some of which have relatively rare sand beaches. Today's visitors to Lake Insula will agree that it is a marvelous canoeing masterpiece. Insula appears to have made the same impression nearly a century ago on Arthur Carhart, who prepared a recreation plan for the Superior National Forest in 1922. Carhart's plan called for preserving much of the forest as a canoeing wilderness free of automobile roads (albeit with significantly more development than we would find acceptable today). Carhart pictured a camp on Insula as the cover to his preliminary report, no doubt aware of what an inspiring lake it is.

Visitors to the BWCAW usually think of it as a huge federally owned land of trees and water. In fact, much of the land is owned by the State of Minnesota and local counties. The state and counties have relatively little control over the use of the lands, because of federal laws that preempt nonwilderness uses. However, a few little vestiges of state control remain, including in the southeast corner of Insula, where you will find the Insula Lake State Forest. The trees are not any different here, although Minnesota does have a well-concealed little DNR administrative cabin on the shores of Insula.

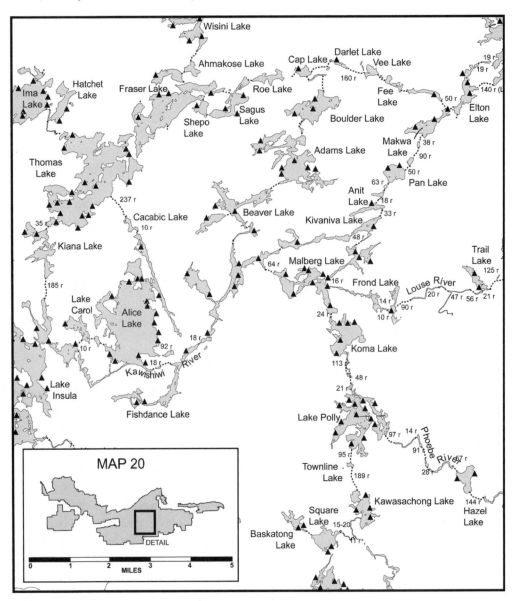

Most traffic through Insula follows along the southern and eastern shores. If you want maximum privacy, head to islands on the west side of the lake. Consider exploring the depths for walleye and northern pike, both of which are present in good numbers. If you are out exploring, you might also want to check out Williamson Island on the north bay. Carved into an exposed rock face is the name "Williamson," with no other identification of who Williamson was or when the name was carved. The island's name shows up at least as early as the 1950s on maps of the area.

Paddle and portage 8 miles from Lake Insula to Lake Four, including portages of 104 rods from Insula to Hudson Lake, and portages of 10 rods, 25 rods, and 25 rods through ponds and creeks to Lake Four. The 105-rod portage between Insula and

Hudson Lake is well traveled and relatively mild for a portage of this length. It begins from a small inlet on Insula, takes a fairly sharp incline, flattens out, and then continues with another fairly steep decline into a small inlet of Hudson. The first portage after Hudson Lake toward Lake Four is 10 rods long and follows a flat, well-traveled trail on the east side of rapids. Just downstream is a 25-rod portage that descends along the east side of severe rapids that are not navigable by canoe. The portage is also well traveled and follows in part along a large exposed rock face. The trail ends at a scenic small lake, which you will paddle across to the northwest corner and make another nice 25-rod portage to Lake Four. This portage is located on the northeast side (right) of the rapids.

Once you are on Lake Four you have arrived at the "number chain" comprising Lakes One, Two, Three, and Four. Of these lakes, Two, Three and Four really amount to separate bays of one big lake rather than four distinct lakes. It took a bit of creativity by any early lake-naming explorer to see this area as being four separate lakes, although that creativity did not extend to the picking of the numerical names. Fortunately, these four lakes are spectacular no matter what they're called. They are a great destination with dozens of campsites, healthy fish populations, islands scattered about from north to south, and connections to interesting neighboring lakes. The biggest drawback to these lakes is the many visitors, up to eighteen groups per day from the Lake One entry alone, as well as visitors heading in from neighboring locations. Campsites are sometimes hard to find during peak summer travel months, so be certain to look early for a site. See Entry Point 30 for more information on extensions from Lakes One to Four.

Paddle and portage 7.5 miles from Lake Four to Lake One and your exit, including portages of 40 rods (L2) and 30 rods (L2) from Lake Two to Lake One. Paddle west through Lake Four to Lake Three and Lake Two, and then portage to Lake One. The two portages from Lake Two to Lake One are heavily traveled. During the peak canoeing season they amount more to freeways than portages. Both are relatively flat, although numerous rocks project into the trail. Neither portage should pose much difficulty, and both have extensive landings, although they are fairly rocky. On Lake One you should exit the wilderness by paddling to the northeast around a large peninsula, avoiding a pair of portages farther west. Your exit on Lake One is about 3.5 miles from your start on Snowbank. Drive or walk back to your start.

Entry Point 30, Lake One (Map 21)

> Daily permit quota: 18
> Permit availability: difficult

Lake One provides easy access to some of the most beautiful areas of the BWCAW, so it should come as no surprise that this entry is among the most popular, typically ranking second to Moose Lake in total permits issued per year. With minimal portaging you can paddle through beautiful lakes full of pine-covered islands and quiet bays. The many peninsulas, islands, and bays will confuse even the most experienced traveler, making navigation the hardest part of a journey through Lake One. The beauty of Lake One and its neighbors, along with their easy access, makes this entry perfect for inexperienced visitors who want a quality introduction to the BWCAW.

Lake One and its neighbors figured prominently in one of the earliest plans for preserving and protecting what is today the BWCAW. Arthur H. Carhart drafted the plan for recreational development of the Superior National Forest in 1922. Carhart was a landscape architect employed by the Forest Service, and he recommended that much of the Superior National Forest be preserved as a canoeing wilderness with restrictions on road building and lakeshore development. His plan was a radical departure from contemporary plans for national forest areas, although it had significantly more development than currently exists in the BWCAW.

The three routes starting at Lake One described below emphasize lakes that will give you a bit of isolation. Route 30A is a basic, but popular, route to the number chain, traveling from Lake One to Lake Four. Route 30B is significantly more difficult, taking you into the most rugged areas immediately accessible from Lake One, including a journey south to Clear Lake. Route 30C sends you farther east to North Wilder Lake for a wonderful detour off the main travel routes. The combination of these three routes covers the majority of all lakes and portages readily accessible from Lake One in a day or two of travel. In addition, many crews will want to explore even farther afield. Reverse Route 27C for a good trip to Lake Insula, where you can head even farther into the wilderness. You can also use the index to find descriptions of most other lakes and portages east of Lake One, and design your own long adventure.

To get to Lake One, take the Fernberg Road for 19 miles to its termination at Lake One. A good place to spend the night before entering the BWCAW is at the public campground on Fall Lake or at a hotel in Ely.

Route 30A: Exploring the Number Chain (Map 21)

      Difficulty: easy
      Number of days: 2 or more
      Total miles (approx.): 15
      Number of portages: 4
      Total portage rods: 140
      Greatest portage difficulty: 40 rods (L2)
      Navigation maps: Voyageur 7
                      Fisher F4, F10
                      McKenzie 18, 19

Does the idea of fishing, swimming, and relaxing appeal to you more than paddling and portaging? Will you have a good time even if you see a dozen canoes paddle past your campsite? Do you pack too much gear and hate to portage? Then take this route

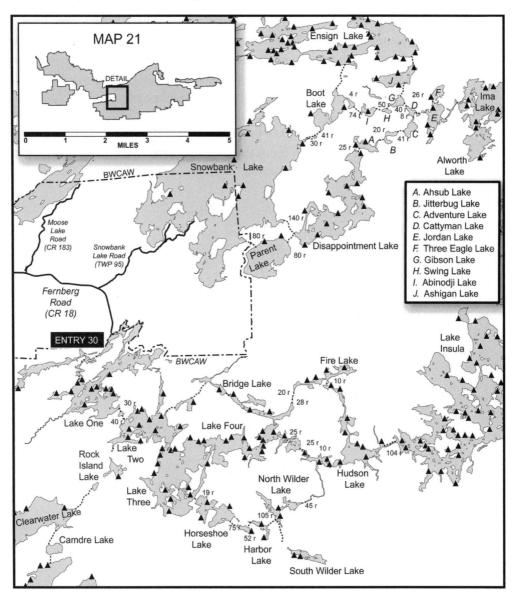

and go no farther than Lake One to Lake Four, which gives you access to over four dozen designated campsites and thousands of acres of lake surface with just two easy portages.

Detailed Route

Enter Lake One, paddle 7.5 miles, and take portages of 30 rods (L2) and 40 rods (L2) to Lake Two, Lake Three, and Lake Four. Head northeast from the landing on Lake One, and paddle through a narrow channel before turning south through another narrow channel into the main body of Lake One. If you are continuing on to Lake

Two, you will have two portages, both of which are among the most commonly traveled portages in the BWCAW. Perhaps only the Prairie Portage to Basswood Lake sees more visitors each year. If you don't see anyone else near these portages, you are probably either lost or visiting in January.

You can paddle from Lake Two to Lake Three and then Lake Four without taking another portage. You have dozens of designated campsites along the way, including many that are on islands and tucked into remote bays. The fishing can be excellent in these lakes, particularly for walleye. Catch-and-release fishing is particularly important on these busy waters, and consider limiting your consumption to one or two meals of fish per trip.

Paddle and portage 7.5 miles back to your starting location on Lake One, including portages of 40 rods (L2) and 30 rods (L2). Your return trip is back along the same route that you took on your way into the wilderness. If you would like more adventure, continue along one of the following routes.

Route 30B: Clear Lake Loop (Map 21)

> Difficulty: intermediate
> Number of days: 2 or more
> Total miles (approx.): 25
> Number of portages: 14
> Total portage rods: 643
> Greatest portage difficulty: 210 rods (L10)
> Navigation maps: Voyageur 7
>   Fisher F3, F4, F11
>   McKenzie 18, 19

Most paddlers going far beyond Lake One will head east toward Lake Insula and Alice Lake. This "contrarian" route heads west, avoiding more popular areas and taking you along some interesting narrow waterways with relatively easy portages.

Map 21 shows the start of this route, and Map 22 shows the western portion. In addition, the entire route is shown in overview on Map 14.

Detailed Route

Paddle and portage 5 miles from Lake One through Confusion Lake to the intersection of the Kawishiwi River and South Kawishiwi River, including portages of 16 rods, 30 rods, and 5 rods. Head west from the Lake One landing, and continue to where the Kawishiwi River and South Kawishiwi intersect. The first portage along this route is 16 rods, followed by a 30-rod trail and a 5-rod trail. All three portages are well used and maintained.

An interesting side trip can be made to Conchu Lake by way of an easy 18-rod portage. Conchu is regularly stocked with brook trout and is a designated trout lake requiring that your fishing license have a trout stamp. This little lake is 67 feet deep, which explains why it can support a trout population. One small campsite is on the south shore of Conchu, and another one is just over the portage on the Kawishiwi River side.

Paddle and portage 6 miles west along the Kawishiwi River to Clear Lake, including portages along the Kawishiwi River of 210 rods (L9), 16 rods (L3), and 10 rods (L1), and a portage of 175 rods (L7) from the Kawishiwi River to Clear Lake. Head west along the Kawishiwi River to the 210-rod portage just after Conchu Lake. This first portage, the most difficult on this route, can be challenging because it tends to be a bit muddy and rocky. Fortunately it is mostly downhill in this direction.

You will probably need to continue to Clear Lake or on to the South Kawishiwi River to find a campsite. Along the way there are two short portages of 16 rods and 10 rods and a final, 175-rod portage to Clear Lake. For the first portage you will have a short climb on the north shore that leads up and over a hill, followed by another short portage on the west shore of the Kawishiwi around a patch of rapids before paddling to the landing for the long Clear Lake portage. The 175-rod portage to Clear Lake is relatively flat with nothing more than a slight incline toward the center. The trail is heavily traveled and relatively free of obstruction, with the one exception of a low-lying spot toward the center of the trail that may be muddy during parts of the year. You are likely to find a few logs placed in the mud to provide a firmer footing. Clear Lake, with five designated campsites, is a nice place to spend an evening. Portage and campsite conditions indicate that it sees fewer visitors than the main travel corridors along the Kawishiwi River and South Kawishiwi River. The moderately long portages to and from Clear Lake probably keep most people away. Clear Lake has average populations of walleye and northern pike and has been regularly stocked with walleye fry in past years.

Paddle and portage 6.5 miles from Clear Lake through the South Kawishiwi River, including portages of 70 rods to the South Kawishiwi, and portages along the South Kawishiwi of 30 rods, 15 rods, and 15 rods to the intersection of the Kawishiwi River and South Kawishiwi River. Your next segment paddles past numerous designated campsites scattered along the South Kawishiwi, which are nice places to spend a night or two. This leg starts with a 70-rod portage from Clear Lake to the Kawishiwi River. The portage is likely to be in good shape with minimal elevation change. Parts of the trail are covered by broken rock, but this should be only a minor obstacle. Next, the 1-rod portage shown on many maps along the Kawishiwi is not a portage at all and can be canoed over with no difficulty most of the year.

Pressing on, take a 30-rod portage on the South Kawishiwi that bypasses a stretch of extensive rapids. The portage climbs steeply up one side and then down another. Fortunately, the trail is in good shape and not too long. A rock landing has been constructed on the downstream side. This portion of the South Kawishiwi is the Boundary Waters at its finest. The shoreline includes substantial bedrock outcroppings, and the forest is a mixture of both conifers and deciduous trees. You will see plenty of birch and more red and white pines than in many other areas of the

Boundary Waters. You will have two more easy 15-rod portages before arriving at the north end of the South Kawishiwi where it meets with the Kawishiwi River south of Triangle Lake.

Paddle and portage 5 miles along the Kawishiwi River to Lake One, including portages of 5 rods, 30 rods, and 16 rods. Return the way you arrived.

Route 30C: North Wilder/Fire Lake Trip from Lake One (Map 21)

Difficulty: easy to intermediate
Number of days: 3 or more
Total miles (approx.): 22
Number of portages: 12
Total portage rods: 496
Greatest portage difficulty: 105 rods (L6)
Navigation maps: Voyageur 7
Fisher F4, F10
McKenzie 18, 19

If you seek out back roads instead of the interstate highway, then this may be the best route for you out of Lake One. Many visitors to Lake One and its neighbors like to take the well-worn route from Lake One all the way through Lake Four and on to Hudson Lake and Lake Insula. They do this for good reason: the portages are easy and the scenery unbeatable. Just off this busy route, however, is a great detour loop to Horseshoe Lake, North Wilder Lake, and Fire and Bridge lakes that is just as beautiful but relatively rarely traveled.

Detailed Route

Enter Lake One, and paddle and portage 6.5 miles, including portages of 30 rods (L2) and 40 rods (L2) to Lake Two and Lake Three. Head northeast from the landing on Lake One, and paddle through a narrow channel before turning south through another narrow channel into the main body of Lake One. See Route 30A for details on this first stretch.

Paddle and portage 1.5 miles from Lake Three to Horseshoe Lake, including a 19-rod portage. The portage from Lake Three to Horseshoe Lake is flat and well traveled with few obstructions other than small protruding rocks. Look around on this portage, and you will notice you are walking through a substantial grove of old-growth white cedars. The shoreline of Horseshoe is covered primarily by cedars and spruce with occasional white pines and red pines. Rocky outcroppings are remarkably fewer than what you found on Lake Three.

The bedrock around these lakes is generally part of the Duluth Complex of coarse-grained gabbro that formed some 1.1 billion years ago as a great rift opened in the middle of North America, allowing magma to erupt at the surface as volcanoes, forming much of the modern Minnesota shore of Lake Superior. Deep beneath these volcanoes, slowly cooling magma was able to form the gabbro exposed here.

Paddle and portage 2 miles from Horseshoe Lake to North Wilder Lake, including portages of 75 rods (L5) from Horseshoe to Brewis Lake, 52 rods (L4) from Brewis to Harbor Lake, and 105 rods (L6) from Harbor to North Wilder Lake. Continue on to the 75-rod portage from Horseshoe to Brewis Lake. The trail is not frequently maintained and therefore is likely to be somewhat overgrown. Of interest at the halfway point is a massive, ancient white pine that has fallen over the trail. From the pieces that are scattered in the woods, it is clear that this big tree came down in a bang. Brewis Lake is low lying with few rocky outcroppings. It has one campsite and spruce-lined shores. On the east side of Brewis is a 52-rod portage to Harbor Lake, and this portage is also slightly overgrown. The trail begins with a gradual uphill for most of the distance and then descends to Harbor Lake. Finally, the 105-rod portage from Harbor Lake to North Wilder Lake is reasonably flat with only a gradual uphill and a gradual downhill from one end to the other.

North Wilder Lake is low lying and surrounded by an almost exclusively spruce forest. Parts of the lake are so low lying that they are characterized by the stunted, pencil-like spruce common north of the BWCAW. A significant amount of blow-down occurred in this area, especially on the portage from Harbor to North Wilder. Historically North Wilder contained both walleye and northern pike, although no DNR survey has been conducted in recent years.

Paddle and portage 4 miles from North Wilder Lake to Lake Four, including portages of 45 rods from North Wilder to the south arm of Hudson Lake, and portages of 10 rods, 25 rods, and 25 rods from Hudson Lake to Lake Four. The 45-rod portage leaving North Wilder Lake is fairly flat and relatively wide-open. Paddle north to Hudson Lake and then continue back toward Lake Four. The first portage from Hudson Lake toward Lake Four is 10 rods long and follows a flat, well-traveled path on the east side of the rapids. Just downstream is a 25-rod portage. This portage travels along the side of severe rapids that are not navigable by canoe. The trail ends at a scenic small lake, which you will paddle across to the northwest corner and make another 25-rod portage.

Paddle and portage 8 miles from Lake Four to Lake One, including portages of 40 rods and 30 rods. You can now paddle west back into the main body of Lake Four and then on to Lake Three, Lake Two, and your starting location on Lake One. You will have a 40-rod portage and a 30-rod portage along the way, both of which are wide-open and easy.

Optional Extensions

Are you looking for another extension off the beaten path? Loop north from Lake Four to Fire Lake and then west and south through Hudson Lake. First you will take a 28-rod portage along the right-hand side of a small creek running through a shady little valley. The landing on the far side is in a scenic, narrow waterway bordered by two large bedrock faces on either side, both of which are partially covered by caribou moss and other lichens. Iris bloom in this little backwater, and an old, possibly abandoned beaver lodge is located here. Next, a 20-rod portage continues at a second narrows along this same creek. This trail appears to get frequent use and is fairly open but will have a much wilder feel compared to what you are used to on the number lakes. Although the trail climbs a slight incline, it is primarily flat and should pose no difficulty. Finally, take a 10-rod portage found on the south side of a small bay bordered on the west side by a tamarack swamp and on the east side by a large, exposed bedrock face.

Entry Point 29, North Kawishiwi River (Map 22)

Daily permit quota: 1
Permit availability: difficult

Entry Point 29, North Kawishiwi River, gives access to some of the most beautiful areas of the BWCAW, including stretches of the Kawishiwi River and nice lakes and rivers east of the entry. Just one permit is issued per day through this entry, and it is in high demand. The North Kawishiwi River entry is just a short paddle from the second busiest entry to the BWCAW (Lake One), so expect to see other visitors on the lakes and rivers accessible from this entry.

Numerous options exist for travel out of Entry Point 29, and an excellent loop known as the Kawishiwi Triangle is described below as Route 29. In addition, all of the routes starting at Entry Point 30 are possible by paddling east to Lake One. Routes out of Entry Points 31, 32, and 33 are also well suited to anyone starting at the North Kawishiwi, which is perhaps one of the reasons this entry is in such high demand.

To reach the North Kawishiwi River, you will need to paddle through Ojibway Lake and Triangle Lake, both of which are outside of the BWCAW. The parking lot and landing on Ojibway are reached by taking the Fernberg Road (County Road 18) east from Ely for 15 miles and turning right onto a small spur road. Continue just over a half mile south to the public landing on Ojibway Lake, taking the western (right) fork of the one T intersection along the way. Consider camping at the Fall Lake campground before entering the wilderness, or stay at one of the hotels or motels in Ely. Also, one campsite is located on Ojibway Lake, and one is located on Triangle Lake. These sites are identical to standard Boundary Waters campsites, with fire grates and latrines, but do not require an advance reservation because they are not within the BWCAW. As always, you are not allowed to camp at the entry parking lot.

Route 29: Kawishiwi Triangle Loop (Map 22)

Difficulty: intermediate
Number of days: 2 or more

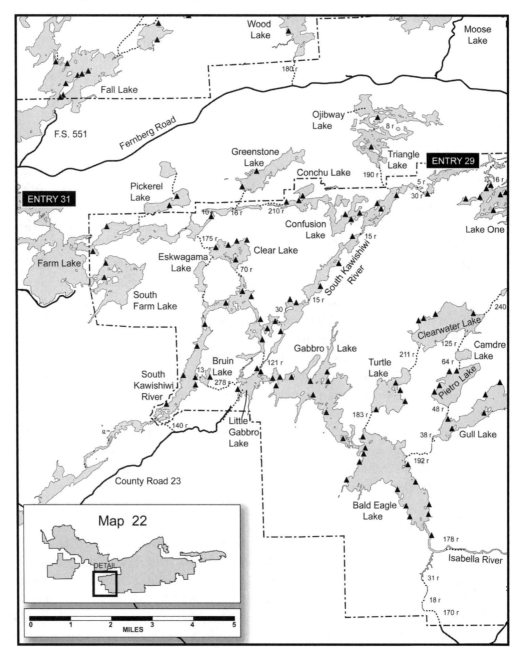

Total miles (approx.): 18.5

Number of portages: 13

Total portage rods: 952

Greatest portage difficulty: 210 rods (L9)

Navigation maps: Voyageur 7

Fisher F3, F4, F10

McKenzie 18

This short route takes you south from your start on Ojibway Lake into the Boundary Waters at the North Kawishiwi River, then loops counterclockwise through Clear Lake and the South Kawishiwi River. This easy route is suitable for visitors of all experience levels, but a couple of long portages make it essential that you travel light to maximize enjoyment of this journey.

Detailed Route

Paddle 1 mile across Ojibway Lake, take an optional 8-rod (L2) portage to Triangle Lake, paddle 1 mile across Triangle Lake, and portage 190 rods (L9) to the North Kawishiwi River. The short portage from Ojibway Lake to Triangle Lake can often be avoided simply by carefully navigating your canoe through the channel between the two lakes. A 190-rod portage connects Triangle Lake with the North Kawishiwi River and is relatively flat and tends to be muddy. The combination of length and mud can make this portage a bit difficult.

Once on the North Kawishiwi River you should have a number of campsites from which to choose. This is one of the most beautiful portions of the BWCAW, with its narrow, twisting path providing constantly varying scenery. An interesting side trip can be made to Conchu Lake by way of an easy 18-rod portage. Conchu is regularly stocked with brook trout and is a designated trout lake, requiring that your fishing license have a trout stamp. Conchu has one small campsite on its south shore.

Paddle 3.5 miles west along the North Kawishiwi River, portage 210 rods (L9), and paddle and portage 3 miles, including portages of 16 rods (L3), 10 rods (L1), and 175 (L7) rods to Clear Lake. Head west toward the 210-rod portage just after Conchu Lake. This long portage can be challenging because it tends to be a bit muddy. Fortunately the trail is mostly downhill in this direction. Continue to Clear Lake, and along the way take two short portages and a final, 175-rod portage. First you will have a short 16-rod climb on the north shore that ascends over a hill, followed by a short 10-rod portage on the west shore around a patch of rapids. Finally, paddle to the landing for the 175-rod trail to Clear Lake. This portage is relatively flat with nothing more than a slight incline toward the center. The trail is well traveled and relatively free of obstructions, with the one exception of a low-lying spot toward the center of the trail that might be muddy. You are likely to find a few pine logs placed in the mud to provide a firmer footing.

Paddle 1 mile across Clear Lake, portage 70 rods to the South Kawishiwi River, continue paddling and portaging 3.5 miles along the Kawishiwi River, including portages of 30 rods, 15 rods, and 15 rods. The 70-rod portage from Clear Lake to the Kawishiwi River is likely to be in generally good shape. Many maps next show a 1-rod portage a mile south where the Kawishiwi narrows. Most of the year this is not a portage at all and can be canoed over with no difficulty.

Continue along the Kawishiwi to a 30-rod portage that bypasses a short stretch of extensive rapids that are not navigable by canoe. The portage climbs steeply up one side and then down the other. Fortunately the trail is in good shape and not too long. A decent rock landing has been constructed on the downstream side. The portion of the South Kawishiwi you travel next is some of the Boundary Waters at its finest. The shoreline includes substantial bedrock outcroppings, and the forest is a mixture of both conifers and deciduous trees. You will see plenty of birch trees and more red and white pines than in many other areas of the Boundary Waters.

Paddle and portage 5.5 miles back to your start on Ojibway Lake, including portages of 190 rods (L9) and 8 rods (L2). Finish this route by heading through the South Kawishiwi to Triangle Lake and Ojibway, which is the same leg that started the trip.

Entry Point 31, Farm Lake (Map 23)

> Daily permit quota: 3
> Permit availability: difficult

The Farm Lake entry gives you access to the Kawishiwi River and beyond, and to South Farm Lake, from which there are no farther extensions. Most people take the North Kawishiwi River from Farm Lake, which gives numerous options for routes.

As is often the case, you will find the greatest isolation by heading into lakes that are deep in the Boundary Waters interior or that require long portages. In the vicinity of Farm Lake your first option for relative isolation is to head to Clear Lake and Eskwagama Lake, which are south of the main travel route along the North Kawishiwi River. If you desire greater isolation, then work your way farther east toward Turtle Lake, Clearwater Lake, Pietro Lake, and Gull Lake. These four lakes require long portages from all directions and therefore are significantly more secluded than other local lakes. You can also head south toward Gabbro and Bald Eagle lakes. You can even take the Isabella River 30 miles to the Hog Creek entry. In such circumstances you will need two vehicles, because no lakes connect to the north along the Isabella, or to arrange to have an outfitter drop you off or pick you up.

To reach Farm Lake, take the Fernberg Road 1.6 miles east from Ely, then turn southeast (right) onto the Section Thirty Road (County Road 16). Drive 4.2 miles down the Section Thirty Road until you come to a spur on your left with signs to the public landing on Farm Lake.

The most convenient place to camp the night before entering the Boundary Waters is at the Fall Lake campground, located a few miles back down the Fernberg Road. You can also spend a night at one of the hotels or motels in Ely.

Route 31: Kawishiwi River Triangle (Map 23)

> Difficulty: easy to intermediate
> Number of days: 3 or more

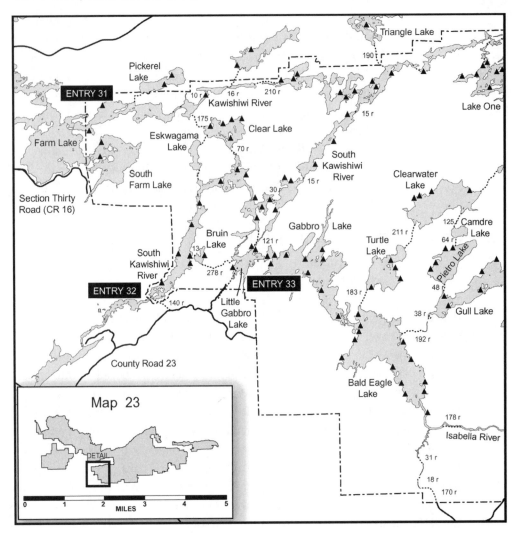

Total miles (approx.): 21
Number of portages: 8
Total portage rods: 541
Greatest portage difficulty: 210 (L9)
Navigation maps: Voyageur 7
                  Fisher F3, F4, F10
                  McKenzie 18

This easy route covers the most natural journey out of Farm Lake and is very well
suited to first-time visitors. You will take minimal portages as you travel along an
area of exceptional beauty. You will almost certainly see other campers each day of
this trip, but the natural beauty of both branches of the Kawishiwi River will provide
memories of a lifetime.

Detailed Route

Enter at Farm Lake, and paddle and portage 9 miles along the Kawishiwi River to the junction with the South Kawishiwi River, including portages of 10 rods (L2), 16 rods (L3), and 210 rods (L9). Your first day's journey takes you from the landing on Farm Lake to the Kawishiwi River. Motorboats are allowed on Farm Lake, which is outside of the BWCAW and has no restrictions on motor size. Paddle east across Farm and head out the northeast corner to the entrance to the Kawishiwi River, which feels more like a wide lake than a river. Only in the narrows are you likely to detect much of a current.

This portion of your journey passes along a wonderful stretch of forest, and your paddling will be interrupted only three times by portages, although one of these portages is long and difficult. The first two portages are relatively easy, getting a fair amount of use. The final, 210-rod portage is very challenging because it follows a trail that tends to be somewhat muddy and is also fairly rocky. Only a handful of campsites are scattered along the first 8 miles of travel, so it may be difficult to shorten this day's travel if campsites are taken along the way. If you are visiting during June or July, start early in the day to avoid trouble finding a nice campsite.

Paddle and portage 7 miles along the South Kawishiwi River to Clear Lake, including portages of 15 rods, 15 rods, 30 rods, and 70 rods. The second day of travel on this trip takes you along the South Kawishiwi River to Clear Lake. All the portages along this section should be in reasonably nice shape. The longest, a 70-rod haul to Clear Lake, is along a good trail with only moderate elevation changes. Unlike the first day of travel, you will pass by many campsites along the South Kawishiwi, and you may want to make camp at one of them. This beautiful stretch of river attracts paddlers from the many entry points around it, so don't be surprised to see other visitors. If you are having trouble locating a campsite, your luck is likely to improve on Clear Lake, which appears to get fewer visitors than either the Kawishiwi or the South Kawishiwi rivers.

Paddle and portage 6 miles from Clear Lake to Farm Lake, including a portage of 175 rods (L7). A long portage leads you from Clear Lake to the North Kawishiwi, after which you will travel back along the way you arrived. This portage is somewhat challenging due to its length, but the steepest hill is on the North Kawishiwi side, and you will be heading downhill over it.

Optional Extensions

If you would like to modify this route, a simple addition is to continue to Eskwagama Lake on your second day rather than going straight to Clear Lake. The amount of wear on the portage to Eskwagama indicates that this route is less popular than the shortcut to Clear Lake. Alternatively, you can shoot down a spur route to Gabbro and Bald Eagle lakes if you would like to spend time on larger border lakes. This involves nothing more than taking a simple, well-traveled 121-rod portage out of the south end of the South Kawishiwi River. See Entry Point 33 for information on adjacent lakes and portages.

ENTRY FROM HIGHWAY 1
AND THE TOMAHAWK ROAD

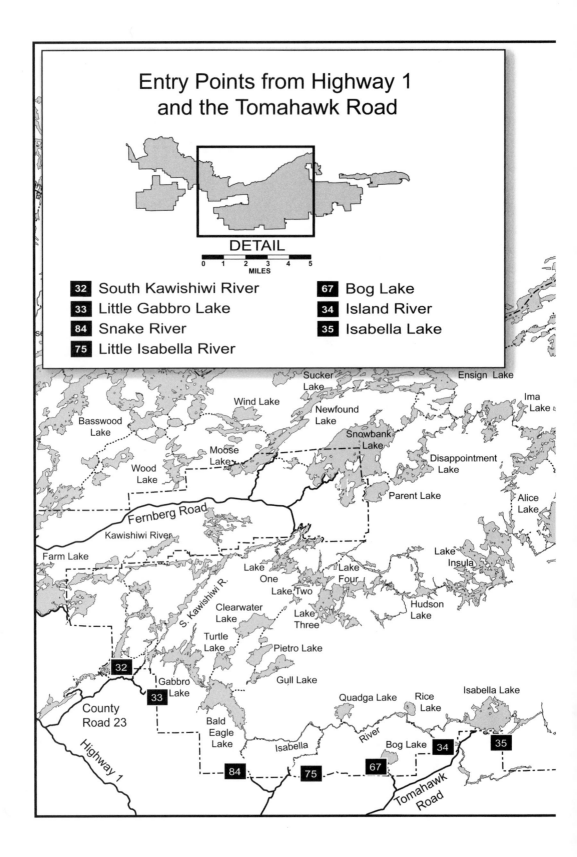

Entry Points from Highway 1 and the Tomahawk Road

DETAIL

0 1 2 3 4 5
MILES

32 South Kawishiwi River

33 Little Gabbro Lake

84 Snake River

75 Little Isabella River

67 Bog Lake

34 Island River

35 Isabella Lake

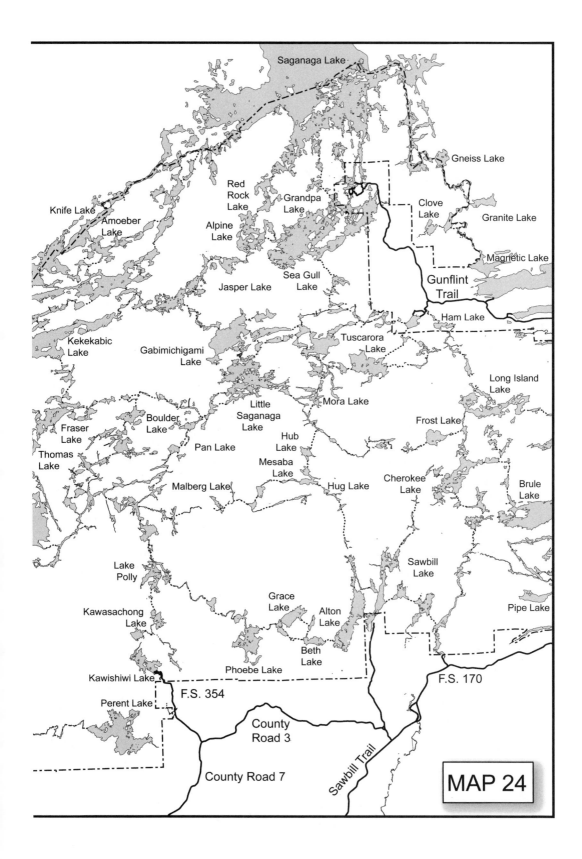

MAP 24

ENTRY FROM HIGHWAY 1
AND THE TOMAHAWK ROAD

Highway 1 runs from Ely southeast to Lake Superior. This all-season paved road provides immediate access to two nice entry points: South Kawishiwi River (Entry Point 32) and Little Gabbro Lake (Entry Point 33). These two entries combine for a quota of just seven permits per day.

In addition, the Tomahawk Road (Forest Service Road 377) extends from Highway 1 along the southern border of the Boundary Waters and has five entry points along its length: Snake River (Entry Point 84), Little Isabella River (Entry Point 75), Bog Lake (Entry Point 67), Island River (Entry Point 34), and Isabella Lake (Entry Point 35). With the exception of Bog Lake, the entries from the Tomahawk Road give access to the Isabella River and lakes on either end of the Isabella River and along its length. The Isabella River starts in the east at Isabella Lake and then heads west to Bald Eagle and Gabbro lakes. Few loop trips are possible along the Isabella River, but excellent out-and-back routes can easily be designed, as well as nice one-way trips that can be taken if you have two vehicles or hire an outfitter to drop you off or pick you up. Bog Lake is a limited entry that gives access only to Bog Lake.

The best source for official information about entries from Highway 1 and the Tomahawk Road is the Tofte Ranger Station (218-663-7280) along Lake Superior in the town of Tofte. The nearest location for picking up visitor permits is the Forest Service work station in the tiny town of Isabella, located along Highway 1 almost halfway between Lake Superior and Ely. The work station (218-323-7722) makes Isabella a convenient starting point for trips to the south-central Boundary Waters.

The Tomahawk Road and the logging operations it led to were a battleground in the 1950s and 1960s over the future of the Superior Roadless Area, as the present-day BWCAW was then known. At that time a branch of the Duluth, Mesabi, and Iron Range Railroad ran from Isabella to a terminus at the logging town of Forest Center, just south of Isabella Lake.

Forest Center was constructed as a logging town for the Tomahawk Timber

Company from Wisconsin, which purchased timber rights to tens of thousands of acres of federal land within the present-day Boundary Waters. The Tomahawk Sale, as this purchase was known, included logging operations fanning out from Forest Center as far as the south side of Lake Insula, almost to Alice Lake, and over to Malberg and Mesaba lakes. Interesting accounts of life at Forest Center are included in the book *By Water and Rail: A History of Lake County, Minnesota* by Hugh Bishop. In addition, Miron Heinselman's *The Boundary Waters Wilderness Ecosystem* includes an extended discussion of how these logging operations affected forest composition and regeneration.

Almost nothing remains of the town of Forest Center today except for a few clearings where homes and town buildings once stood. You will still see Forest Center marked on some maps, including canoeing maps made by Fisher and McKenzie that have not been recently updated. If you are using these old maps, don't arrive expecting to see a town, village, or even a house. The railway tracks have long been pulled up, and you might not even know such a town existed if you had not been told. Indeed, the areas reached by the Tomahawk Road are some of the most remote in the entire BWCAW, isolated by miles of lakes and forests from the paved roads of Ely and the Gunflint Trail. The road is mostly free of lodges and developments along its length, with little private property along it.

If you are arriving late at night or want a place to camp before heading into the Boundary Waters, you will find a number of options at Forest Service campgrounds off Highway 1. The Little Isabella campground has eleven sites, the McDougal Lake campground has twenty-one sites, the South Kawishiwi campground has thirty-two sites, and the Birch Lake campground and Divide Lake campground provide additional sites (although they are a bit farther from Isabella). All of these campgrounds charge a modest fee. Only the South Kawishiwi River and Birch Lake campgrounds take advance reservations.

Entry Point 32, South Kawishiwi River (Map 25)

> Permit quota: 2
> Permit availability: difficult

The South Kawishiwi River (Entry Point 32) is an excellent gateway to the central Boundary Waters. Although the South Kawishiwi is nominally a river, the current is almost undetectable along most stretches, becoming apparent only where the river narrows. It is well suited to trips of all experience levels, but this area is somewhat less remote than other areas of the wilderness farther east along the Tomahawk Road.

Most visitors entering the BWCAW at the South Kawishiwi River travel northeast along the main channel of the Kawishiwi, but less frequented spurs can be taken east to Bruin, Eskwagama, and Clear lakes. An easy diversion to Gabbro Lake is also possible by way of a 121-rod portage. Alternatively, you can continue up the South Kawishiwi toward Lake One. Only one route is described below, but this area is ideally suited for designing your own course using the maps and index.

You have two options for entering the Kawishiwi River. The most popular is by way of a 140-rod portage off County Road 23 just after it crosses Filson Creek. Your other option is to put in farther west along the Kawishiwi at a landing that does not require a long initial portage but does have a series of shorter portages. I recommend taking the 140-rod portage.

To reach the parking lot for Entry Point 32, take County Road 23 east from Minnesota Highway 1. If you are coming from the south on Highway 1, travel 45 miles up the highway from Illgen City (on Lake Superior) to the exit for County Road 23, which will be on your right. The turnoff is just a half mile before the bridge over the South Kawishiwi River, so you have gone too far on Highway 1 if you cross the South Kawishiwi bridge. If you are coming from the west on Highway 1 from Ely, travel about 11.5 miles along Highway 1 until just after it crosses the South Kawishiwi, and then turn left. Either way, travel 4 miles on County Road 23 until you reach a small parking area for the portage down to the river.

Ely's many hotels are a perfect place to spend the night before you enter the wilderness, as is the South Kawishiwi River campground, which you will drive past on County Road 23 on your way to the entry. The campground has thirty-two campsites, charges a fee, and accepts reservations.

Route 32: Loop through Clearwater Lake and Lake One (Map 25)

Difficulty: intermediate
Number of days: 5 or more
Total miles (approx.): 37
Number of portages: 22
Total portage rods: 1,510
Greatest portage difficulty: 240 rods (L10)
Navigation maps: Voyageur 7
Fisher F3, F4, F11
McKenzie 18, 19

This fine loop takes you from the scenic South Kawishiwi River to relatively remote Pietro and Clearwater lakes, before heading to ever popular Lake Two and Lake One. This is an excellent route for anyone seeking relative solitude in the busy Kawishiwi Triangle area and not afraid of hitting a few long portages. This route is easily modified and shortened, so you should have no problem altering your travel plans if you so desire.

Map 25 shows most of this route, and Map 19 shows the northeastern section. The entire route is shown in overview on Map 24.

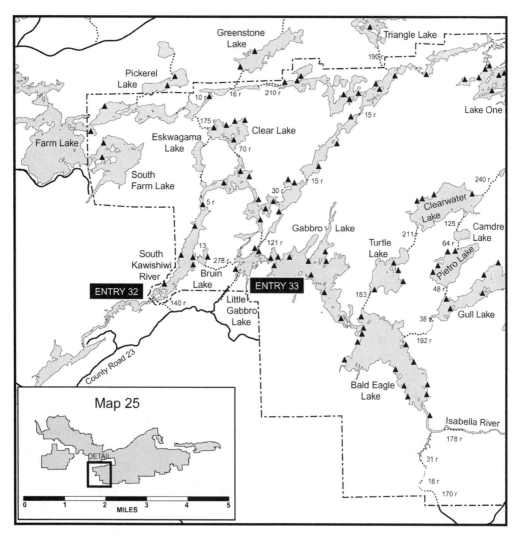

Detailed Route

> *Paddle and portage 7 miles along the South Kawishiwi to Little Gabbro Lake, includ-*
> *ing portages of 140 rods (L6) from the parking lot to the South Kawishiwi, an optional*
> *5 rods (L1) along the South Kawishiwi, and 121 rods (L4) to Little Gabbro Lake. The*
> first, 140-rod portage is along a moderate trail starting at the parking lot off County
> Road 23. You may be able to forego the 5-rod portage if water levels permit. Paddle
> along the South Kawishiwi, winding through a stretch of magnificent river bends,
> islands, and peninsulas. Finally, a 121-rod portage climbs along a nice trail and
> places you on Little Gabbro Lake, which has three campsites and easy access to
> more campsites to the east on Gabbro and Bald Eagle lakes.
>
> > *Paddle and portage 9.5 miles from Little Gabbro Lake to Clearwater Lake. You*
> > *will first paddle to Gabbro Lake and then take a short portage to Bald Eagle Lake,*

followed by two portages of 192 rods (L8) and 38 rods (L3) from Bald Eagle to Gull Lake, 48 rods (L4) to Pietro Lake, 64 rods (L4) to Camdre Lake, and 125 rods (L5) to Clearwater Lake. From Little Gabbro you will paddle to Gabbro Lake and Bald Eagle Lake and then head toward Clearwater Lake by way of Gull Lake and Pietro Lake, both of which are also nice destinations in their own right. This area was partially burned in the early 1990s and offers an interesting natural history laboratory for observing the regenerating forest.

The portage from Bald Eagle Lake to Gull Lake starts at the northern side of a small, low-lying island. Take a minute to survey the island, and you will notice it is covered by a mixed forest dominated by white cedar. However, large numbers of stumps are scattered across the island, remaining evidence of the logging activity on this edge of the wilderness nearly a century ago. Another remnant of that logging is the remains of an old rock dam on the northeast bay of Little Gabbro leading to the South Kawishiwi River. This dam kept water levels elevated to permit log transport on the lake surface. In particular, this dam kept water high enough to float logs between Gabbro and Bald Eagle lakes.

The portage from Bald Eagle to Gull begins with a long moderate uphill. A number of rocks and roots and the occasional downed tree obstruct portions of the trail, which then winds through the forest with modest hills before emptying into a small stream connecting to Gull Lake. The first couple of rods of the stream are strewn with dark, slightly submerged boulders lurking for your canoe. Keep alert. The stream soon straightens out and goes through an interesting first section in which small tamarack trees, mostly no more than 8 to 10 feet tall, sprout from the aquatic vegetation. Take this stream about a quarter mile before you head down a moderate 38-rod portage that will deposit you on Gull Lake. You may want to spend an evening at one of the five campsites located on Gull Lake; otherwise continue immediately on toward Pietro Lake.

The 48-rod portage from Gull Lake to Pietro Lake is almost perfectly level. During the rainy season the trail is prone to becoming fairly muddy. Fortunately the portage is not too long. Pietro Lake is in the middle of an area of interesting geologic formations from the Duluth Complex. Most of the rock is igneous gabbro that rapidly cooled during formation, and you will notice intrusions where molten rock penetrated into distinctly different "country" rock. Stay alert and you will find many such exposures.

Next, take the 64-rod portage to Camdre Lake. The portage very gradually climbs 50 feet along a relatively easy trail. This portage is not heavily traveled, so it may be overgrown compared to portages earlier on this journey. Paddle across little Camdre Lake and perhaps pause to observe the fascinating bog life, including pitcher plants common along parts of the shore. A final, 125-rod portage to Clearwater Lake gently rolls along a reasonably good trail.

Clearwater Lake is fittingly named, with waters that seem clearer than most in the BWCAW. You have four campsite options on Clearwater, all of which provide opportunities to fish for northern pike and lake trout (the latter is present but not identified in recent DNR field surveys). Some storm damage occurred on the south shore of Clearwater in 1999, but this area is already showing significant evidence of regrowth.

Portage and paddle 4 miles from Clearwater Lake to Lake Two, including portages of 240 rods (L10) and 62 rods (L5) to Rock Island Lake, and 95 rods (L6) to Lake Two. The 240-rod portage from the north end of Clearwater Lake is the toughest along this route, being the most rugged and unused. You may have to jostle around downed trees and thick brush. This is definitely not a portage to take if you hate a bit of bushwhacking or have a ton of gear. While there are no long uphills and only a few low muddy areas, the trail rises and falls throughout, and in numerous places the path narrows. Eventually you will reach a nameless, shallow little pond. It is possible that this little pond might dry up during a very dry year, effectively lengthening the 240-rod portage. Most years you will be able to paddle across this pond.

After the pond, continue down a tough 62-rod portage to Rock Island Lake. At Rock Island Lake you will enter a flat, marshy area with an opening of water in the center. Before reaching the open water, you will have to navigate about 5 rods through a flat, floating bog with precarious footing. Watch your step because the muck is very deep. Pause a moment to take a look at the trees around you. The nearest trees are predominantly tamarack and can be identified by their lighter color and clustered needles. Behind them is a predominantly black spruce forest of thin pencil-like trees. The tamarack and spruce are classic boreal lakeshore inhabitants. Many maps show a campsite on Rock Island Lake, but the latrine and fire grate appear to have been removed, and the site closed by the Forest Service because this area is within the Weasel Lake Primitive Management Area (PMA). You will need special authorization, in writing, from the Forest Service to stay on Rock Island Lake, and only one group is permitted to enter the PMA per day for an overnight stay. Contact the Kawishiwi Ranger District (218-365-7600) to obtain a permit for staying on Rock Island Lake within the PMA.

The 95-rod portage leading to Lake Two from Rock Island begins with a steep 2-rod climb, then meanders along a seldom-used portage trail that is somewhat overgrown. You might have to twist around a couple of trees and large logs that obstruct portions of the trail. Partway through you will descend to a boulder field with a couple of nice mud pits and then cross a flat section for the last few rods before Lake Two. Lake Two makes a fine place to spend an evening or two, and you can paddle west to Lake Three and Lake Four without portaging. Look at routes from Entry Point 30 (Lake One) for more ideas on exploring this scenic chain of lakes, especially Routes 30A and 30B.

Paddle and portage 2 miles from Lake Two to Lake One, including portages of 40 rods (L2) and 30 rods (L2). This route next takes you west toward Lake One. The two portages from Lake Two to Lake One are heavily traveled. During the peak canoeing season they amount more to freeways than portages. Both are relatively flat, although numerous rocks project into the trail. Neither portage should pose much difficulty, and both have extensive landings, although they are fairly rocky.

Paddle and portage 7 miles along the South Kawishiwi River, including portages of 45 rods and 25 rods to the Kawishiwi River, followed by portages west along the Kawishiwi of 30 rods, 5 rods, 15 rods, and 15 rods. From Lake One you will take two easy portages to the Kawishiwi River, then head straight west along the river before coming to an easy 30-rod portage and a 5-rod portage. Continue southwest to the South Kawishiwi River, where you will have two additional short portages, each just 15 rods long. A number of excellent campsites are scattered along the Kawishiwi and South Kawishiwi, but they are quite popular much of the year, so allow yourself plenty of time to find a site if you are traveling during peak visitor usage periods, such as late July and early August.

Paddle and portage 7 miles along the Kawishiwi River back to your starting location, including portages of 30 rods and 5 rods (L1) along the South Kawishiwi River and 140 rods (L6) to your starting point. The final stretch of your journey travels back up the South Kawishiwi to your starting point. The 30-rod portage bypasses a short stretch of extensive rapids that are too difficult to shoot in a canoe. The portage goes steeply up one side and then down another. Fortunately the trail is in good shape and not too long. A rock landing has been constructed on the downstream side. After this portage, head back along the same stretch of river you took on the first day of travel.

Entry Point 33, Little Gabbro Lake (Map 25)

> Permit quota: 2
> Permit availability: difficult

Little Gabbro Lake is a very attractive entry. It requires a long initial portage but then gives you access to Gabbro and Bald Eagle lakes, which have plentiful campsites. You can also easily explore off the main travel corridors toward Clearwater Lake, or head east along the Isabella River as far as Perent Lake. The large, accessible lakes reached from Little Gabbro are entirely motor-free and less traveled than areas to the north on Lake One and its neighbors.

Two routes are described below: Route 33A is a nice trip to Gabbro and Bald Eagle lakes and can be a short a weekend getaway or a much longer stay to explore the many bays, reefs, and backwaters, seeking walleye and northern pike. Route 33B takes you on a longer trip up the South Kawishiwi River and through the Kawishiwi Triangle to Clear Lake before returning to Little Gabbro by way of Bruin Lake.

Take County Road 23 east from Minnesota Highway 1 to reach the parking lot for Entry Point 33. If you are coming from the south on Highway 1, travel about 45 miles up the highway from Illgen City (on Lake Superior) before reaching the exit for County Road 23. If you are coming from the west on Highway 1 from Ely, travel about 11.5 miles along Highway 1 until just after it crosses the South Kawishiwi River. Take County Road 23 just over 5 miles until you get to Forest Service Road 1474, which you will take north (left) for 0.6 mile to a parking lot for Little Gabbro Lake.

Ely's many hotels are a perfect place to spend the night before you enter the wilderness, as is the South Kawishiwi River campground, which you will drive past on County Road 23 on your way to the entry. The campground has thirty-two campsites, charges a fee, and accepts reservations.

Route 33A: Exploration of Gabbro and Bald Eagle Lakes (Map 25)

Difficulty: easy to intermediate
Number of days: 2 or more
Total miles (approx.): 10 or more
Number of portages: 2
Total portage rods: 480
Greatest portage difficulty: 240 rods (L7)
Navigation maps: Voyageur 7
                   Fisher F3, F4
                   McKenzie 18

This short route takes one long portage to reach Little Gabbro Lake, from where you will be able to explore hundreds of acres of Gabbro and Bald Eagle lakes. Although it starts with a long portage, the trail is decent and the destination well worth the carry. After this initial portage, you will head east to Gabbro Lake and Bald Eagle Lake, where you will find numerous designated campsites.

Detailed Route

Portage 240 rods (L7) to Little Gabbro Lake, and then paddle about 5 miles to the interior of Gabbro Lake and Bald Eagle Lake. The first half of the 240-rod portage follows an old logging road and is likely to be in good condition. The second half is a bit rocky and hilly but still not too bad. A few short sections of the route can be a bit muddy, but in general the trail has excellent drainage.

Once on Little Gabbro you can paddle to the main body of Gabbro Lake without portaging. Fourteen campsites are located on these two lakes, and another twelve are on Bald Eagle Lake, which is accessible by a short pull-over portage. This chain of pretty lakes holds good populations of walleye and northern pike. An interesting excursion can also be made to the north end of Little Gabbro Lake, where the remains of two old logging dams are visible. The first dam is in the large island-studded bay on the northwest corner of Little Gabbro and includes a row of logs that were placed across the channel and are still visible when water levels are low. The remains of the second dam are on the northeast end of Little Gabbro in the channel to the north of the landing of the 121-rod portage to the Kawishiwi River. This rock dam has been opened to allow lake levels to drop about a meter to their natural levels.

Paddle 5 miles from Gabbro and Bald Eagle lakes to Little Gabbro Lake, and portage 240 rods (L7) to your starting point. Your trip back to the starting point is simply the reverse of your route to Gabbro and Bald Eagle.

Route 33B: Loop through the Kawishiwi River Triangle (Map 25)

> Difficulty: intermediate
> Number of days: 3 or more
> Total miles (approx.): 19
> Number of portages: 12
> Total portage rods: 1,023
> Greatest portage difficulty: 210 rods (L9)
> Navigation maps: Voyageur 7
> Fisher F3, F4
> McKenzie 18

This route takes you up the beautiful South Kawishiwi River and through the Kawishiwi Triangle to Clear Lake before returning to Little Gabbro. The first part of this journey is along a popular route, where you will probably encounter other visitors, but the middle of this journey to Gull, Pietro, and Clearwater lakes is quite isolated and gets far fewer visitors. The last third of the journey takes you through Lake Two, Lake One, and the Kawishiwi River, all of which are also quite popular.

Detailed Route

Paddle and portage 2 miles to the South Kawishiwi River, including portages of 240 rods (L7) to Little Gabbro Lake and 121 rods (L4) to the South Kawishiwi River. The first portage, to Little Gabbro Lake, starts from the parking lot with about 120 rods of trail down an old logging road and is in good condition. The second half is a bit rocky and hilly but still not too bad. A few short sections of the route can be a bit muddy, but in general the path is well drained.

Once on Little Gabbro, spend the night or immediately head out through the northeast end along the 121-rod portage to the South Kawishiwi River. Old maps show alternative 8-rod and 10-rod portages along a stream out the northwest bay of Little Gabbro, but I don't recommend taking this "shortcut." The portages are rarely used, and the fast-moving stream can be hazardous during high water. It is definitely no quicker to take this northwest route. In contrast, the 121-rod portage from Little Gabbro to the South Kawishiwi River is well maintained. There's a bit of up and down, but the trail is in good shape and should not be too challenging. You may want to stop about 150 yards after the beginning of the portage and look down on the Kawishiwi River, where you will see the remains of an old stone dam. The middle has been knocked out to permit the water level on Gabbro Lake to return to its natural elevation.

Upon entering the South Kawishiwi River, you may notice that the bedrock along the river is substantially different from the bedrock on Gabbro Lake. The pinker-colored stone, exposed in many spots, is granitic in nature and reflects the fact that you are now leaving the Duluth Complex of gabbro rock and entering a more ancient area known as the Giants Range Batholith, a huge area of granite. A particularly nice granite outcropping is located on the left-hand side of the South Kawishiwi as you approach the end of the 121-rod portage.

Paddle and portage 5 miles to the North Kawishiwi River, including portages of 30 rods, 15 rods, and 15 rods. Head northeast along the South Kawishiwi River, where you will take three portages. The 30-rod portage bypasses a short stretch of extensive rapids that are too difficult to shoot in a canoe. The portage trail rises steeply up one side and then down another. Fortunately the trail is in good shape and not too long. A rock landing has been constructed on the downstream side. Move along over two more portages of 15 rods.

Paddle and portage 6.5 miles along the Kawishiwi River to Clear Lake, including portages of 210 rods (L9), 16 rods (L3), 10 rods (L1), and 175 (L7) rods. Head west toward the 210-rod portage on the Kawishiwi River. This long portage can be challenging because it tends to be a bit muddy and rocky and is certainly long. This is the most difficult portage on this route, but fortunately it is mostly downhill in this direction.

You may need to continue to Clear Lake to find a campsite. Along the way you will cover two short portages and a final, 175-rod portage to Clear Lake. For the first short portage you will have an easy climb on the north shore that tracks up and over a hill. The second short portage is on the west shore of the river around a patch of rapids. Next, paddle down to the landing for the long Clear Lake portage. This 175-rod portage is generally flat with nothing more than a slight incline toward the center. The trail is relatively free of obstruction, with the one exception of a low-lying spot toward the center of the portage that tends to be muddy during parts of the year.

Paddle and portage 5.5 miles from Clear Lake to your start on Little Gabbro Lake, including portages of 70 rods to the South Kawishiwi River, 121 rods from the South Kawishiwi to Little Gabbro, and 240 rods (L7) to the parking lot. The 70-rod portage from Clear Lake to the South Kawishiwi River is a good trail with minimal elevation change. Parts of the trail are covered by broken rock, but this should only be a minor obstacle. A 1-rod portage is shown on many maps along a narrows as you are heading south. Most of the year this is not a portage and can be canoed over with no difficulty. Finally, head back over the 121-rod portage to Little Gabbro Lake and the long 240-rod portage to the parking lot.

Entry Point 84, Snake River (Map 26)

> Daily permit quota: 1
> Permit availability: difficult

The Snake River, Entry Point 84, provides easy access to Bald Eagle and Gabbro lakes and good opportunities to reach more remote lakes such as Clearwater and Pietro.

The Snake River is also a fine start for a trip on the Isabella River, providing opportunities to search for some of the moose that call this area home.

Two routes originating at the Snake River are described below. The first is a pleasant trip down the Snake River to Bald Eagle Lake. This easy journey will pose few problems for most visitors. The second route is a loop into the less traveled area north of Bald Eagle Lake, including Pietro and Clearwater lakes, which gives more solitude but requires much longer portages.

To reach the parking lot for Entry Point 84, take Forest Service Road 377 (the Tomahawk Road) east from Minnesota Highway 1. If you are coming from the south on Highway 1, travel 36 miles up Highway 1 from Illgen City (on Lake Superior) to the exit for the Tomahawk Road. Take Forest Service Road 377 just over 6 miles until you get to Forest Service Road 381, which you will take north (left) for 1.8 miles until you reach a Y. Take the left fork (known as Forest Service Road 381E) for 1.3 more miles until you reach the end of the road, where parking is available. The final portions of this drive down 381 and 381E are narrow and lightly maintained, so drive carefully.

Consider camping at the South Kawishiwi River campground if you need a place to spend the night before entering the wilderness, located just off of Highway 1, 8 miles north of Forest Service Road 377. As always, no camping is allowed at the entry point parking lot.

Route 84A: Exploration of Bald Eagle Lake (Map 26)

> Difficulty: easy to moderate
> Number of days: 2 or more
> Total miles (approx.): 5 or more
> Number of portages: 6
> Total portage rods: 438
> Greatest portage difficulty: 170 (L6)
> Navigation maps: Voyageur 7
>   Fisher F3, F4
>   McKenzie 18

This easy route is perfect for a short journey into the Boundary Waters. You reach Bald Eagle and Gabbro lakes quickly, and both are top-quality wilderness destinations with significantly fewer people than you will encounter on many other close-in lakes, such as Lake One and Snowbank. However, this route starts with a half-mile portage, making it a bit challenging for some first-time visitors. Check out Entry Point 33 (Little Gabbro Lake) if you want an alternative option for reaching Gabbro and Bald Eagle lakes.

Detailed Route

Paddle and portage 5 miles down the Snake River to Bald Eagle Lake, including portages of 170 rods (L6), 18 rods (L2), and 31 rods (L2). To get to Bald Eagle

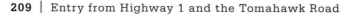

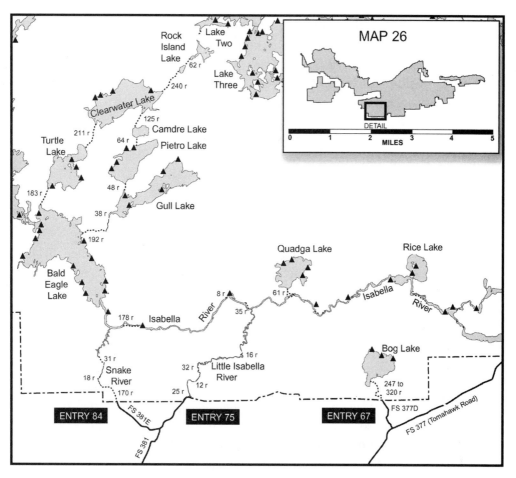

you will start by taking a 170-rod portage down an abandoned logging road. This road was developed in the 1960s as part of the Tomahawk timber sale. After about 140 rods, you will double back along a bridge and end up in a clearing where a small logging camp was once located. A simple landing gives access to the Snake River, which you will take for another mile, punctuated by two simple, short portages before Bald Eagle Lake. The total distance covered will be a bit more or less than 5 miles depending on where you stop on Bald Eagle Lake.

Bald Eagle is a large lake with more than 1,200 acres and a maximum depth of 36 feet. You can choose from thirteen designated campsites on Bald Eagle and an additional thirteen designated campsites to the west on easily accessible Gabbro Lake. Healthy populations of northern pike and walleye are present, and crappies and perch also inhabit this lake. See Route 84B for ideas on routes heading north to Clearwater Lake for a good extension of this route.

Paddle and portage 5 miles to your start, including portages of 31 rods (L2), 18 rods (L2), and 170 rods portage (L6). Your return trip is the reverse of the way you came.

Route 84B: Clearwater Lake Loop (Map 26)

> Difficulty: intermediate to challenging
> Number of days: 3 or more
> Total miles (approx.): 20.5
> Number of portages: 13
> Total portage rods: 1,300
> Greatest portage difficulty: 211 rods (L8)
> Navigation maps: Voyageur 7
>   Fisher F3, F4
>   McKenzie 18

This route starts with the same lakes as Route 84A, and then follows north from Bald Eagle Lake to Gull Lake and on to Clearwater Lake before looping back to Bald Eagle and the Snake River. This journey builds on Route 84A by giving you more challenges and the opportunity to see interesting, less traveled areas.

Detailed Route

Paddle and portage 5 miles to Bald Eagle Lake, including portages of 170 rods (L6) to the Snake River, and portages of 18 rods (L2) and 31 rods (L2) along the Snake River before arriving at Bald Eagle Lake. To get to Bald Eagle you will start by taking the 170-rod portage down an abandoned logging road developed in the 1960s as part of the Tomahawk timber sale, and two simple, short portages along the Snake River. Consider spending a night or two on Bald Eagle Lake and perhaps also exploring west to Gabbro Lake. Both of these huge lakes are known for good walleye fishing.

Paddle and portage 2.5 miles from Bald Eagle Lake to Gull Lake, including portages of 192 rods (L8) and 38 rods (L3). The portage from Bald Eagle Lake starts just north of a small, low-lying island. You may want to take a minute to survey the island and note that it is presently covered by a mixed forest dominated by white cedar. Large numbers of stumps are scattered across the island, evidence of the logging activity at this edge of the wilderness. These stumps probably date from early logging activity in this area in the early 1900s. Subsequent logging operations from the Tomahawk Sale after World War II also occurred in this area, but loggers were prohibited from cutting trees within 400 feet of navigable waters, making it probable that these stumps predate the Tomahawk logging.

Pressing on, the 192-rod portage from Bald Eagle to Gull begins with a long, moderate uphill with a number of rocks and roots and the occasional downed tree obstructing portions of the trail, winding through the forest with modest hills before emptying into a small stream connecting to Gull Lake. The first couple rods of the stream are strewn with dark, slightly submerged boulders lurking for your canoe, so paddle with care. The stream straightens out and goes through a first section in which small tamaracks, mostly no more than 8 to 10 feet tall, sprout from the shore.

Take this stream about a quarter mile before you head down a moderate 38-rod portage that drops to Gull Lake, which has five designated campsites and is another excellent place to spend an evening, especially after the long portage you have taken from Bald Eagle.

Paddle and portage 3 miles from Gull Lake to Clearwater Lake, including portages of 48 rods (L4) to Pietro Lake, 64 rods (L4) to Camdre Lake, and 125 rods (L5) to Clearwater Lake. The portage from Gull Lake to Pietro Lake is almost perfectly level. During the rainy season this flatness becomes a liability because the trail is relatively low lying and prone to becoming fairly muddy. Nevertheless, it is not too long and should always be traversable.

Next, the 64-rod portage to Camdre Lake gradually climbs 50 feet along a relatively easy trail. This route is not heavily traveled, so the trail may be overgrown compared to portages on busier routes. Paddle across little Camdre Lake and perhaps pause to observe the fascinating bog life, including pitcher plants common along parts of the shore. The final, 125-rod portage to Clearwater Lake gently rolls along a reasonably good trail.

Clearwater Lake is fittingly named, with waters that seem clearer than most in the BWCAW. You have four designated campsite options, all of which provide opportunities to fish for northern pike and lake trout (the latter is present but not identified in the most recent DNR field survey from the 1970s). Some storm damage occurred on the south shores of the lake in 1999, but this area is already showing significant evidence of regrowth.

Paddle and portage 5 miles from Clearwater Lake to Bald Eagle Lake, including portages of 211 rods (L8) from Clearwater to Turtle Lake, and 183 rods (L8) from Turtle to Bald Eagle. The portage from Clearwater Lake to Turtle Lake follows a fairly rocky trail, with the southern half likely to be muddy if it has recently rained. The landing on the Turtle Lake side is generally quite mucky, as is Turtle Lake itself. You have the option of camping on four designated sites on Turtle Lake. These campsites are likely to be available even if Clearwater is full because Turtle Lake attracts fewer campers. From Turtle Lake continue south over the 183-rod portage to Bald Eagle Lake.

Paddle and portage 5 miles from Bald Eagle Lake to the Snake River, including portages of 31 rods (L2), 18 rods (L2), and 170 rods (L6). Your return trip is simply a paddle and portage back the way you came.

Entry Point 75, Little Isabella River (Map 27)

Daily permit quota: 1
Permit availability: difficult

Entry Point 75, Little Isabella River, provides easy access to the meandering rivers and streams of the south-central Boundary Waters. This area gets few visitors and provides a wonderful, relaxed introduction to the wilderness. From Entry Point

75 you will paddle north along the Little Isabella River until it flows into the larger Isabella River. You can choose to head east along the Isabella River toward Quadga Lake, which provides a nice weekend destination and the potential to hike a part of the Pow Wow Trail. This journey is described in Route 75A. Alternatively, go west along the Isabella River to Gabbro Lake in a great one-way trip to the South Kawishiwi River, described in Route 75B.

The Little Isabella River does not allow any moderate-sized complete loops, although you can cut short the western journey and head up the Snake River to Entry Point 84, in which case you will have just a 2-mile walk back to your car. If you would like a longer journey, you can also paddle all the way east to Perent Lake and the Hog Creek entry point, but you will need two vehicles or a drop-off from an outfitter.

To reach the parking lot for Entry Point 84, take Forest Service Road 377 (the Tomahawk Road) east from Minnesota Highway 1. If you are coming from the south on Highway 1, travel 36 miles up the highway from Illgen City (on Lake Superior) before reaching the exit for 377. Take 377 just over 6 miles until you get to Forest Service Road 381, which you will take north (left) for 1.8 miles until you reach a Y. Take the right fork for 1.1 more miles until you reach the trailhead parking lot at the end of the road. The final portion of this drive on 381 is narrow and poorly maintained, so drive carefully.

If you need a place to spend the night before entering the wilderness, consider camping at the South Kawishiwi River campground, located just off of Highway 1, 8 miles north of Forest Service Road 377.

Route 75A: Quadga Weekend (Map 27)

    Difficulty: easy
    Number of days: 2 or more
    Total miles (approx.): 10
    Number of portages: 10
    Total portage rods: 292
    Greatest portage difficulty: 61 rods (L5)
    Navigation maps: Voyageur 7
                     Fisher F4
                     McKenzie 18

This pleasant route travels down the Little Isabella River to its junction with the Isabella River and then heads east for a short distance to the portage to Quadga Lake. The portages along this route are all relatively short and easy, and the winding rivers provide an enchanting paddling highway. This journey is well suited for beginners and experienced campers alike.

Detailed Route

Paddle and portage 5 miles down the Little Isabella River to Quadga Lake, including portages along the Little Isabella of 25 rods (L3), 12 rods (L3), 32 rods (L4), and

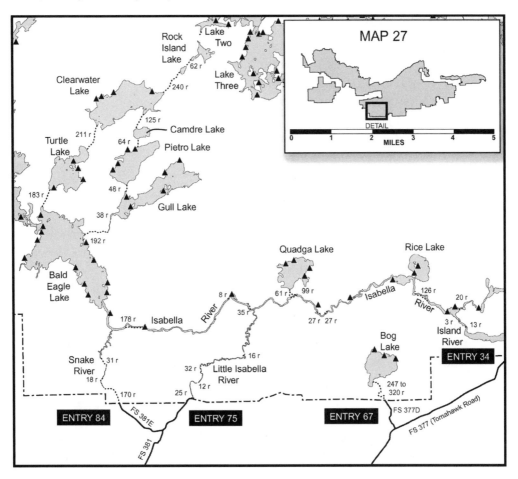

16 rods (L3) to the Isabella River, and finally 61 rods (L5) from the Isabella River to Quadga Lake. Start at the landing, put in, and head down the Little Isabella River. Your canoe steering skills will be tested on the meandering river, and you should also expect a beaver dam or two across the route. Keep alert: you may startle a moose along these two rivers, as well as ducks, beavers, otters, and various shorebirds. Although the portages on the Little Isabella River are not heavily used, they do get regular visitors.

Quadga Lake has four campsites. The neighboring Isabella River has relatively few campsites, so Quadga Lake is an attractive destination for a number of neighboring entry points. An early arrival on Quadga is well advised if you are traveling in June or July. If all the sites are occupied, you will still have plenty of time to head east toward Rice Lake or west toward Bald Eagle Lake. Quadga is relatively shallow (maximum depth of 36 feet) and has populations of both walleye and northern pike.

Paddle and portage 5 miles from Quadga Lake back to your starting point on the Little Isabella, including portages of 61 rods (L5), 16 rods (L3), 32 rods (L4), 12 rods (L3), and 25 rods (L3). Your return trip is simply the reverse of the route you took to Quadga.

Route 75B: One-Way to the South Kawishiwi River (Map 27)

Difficulty: moderate

Number of days: 3 or more

Total miles (approx.): 17

Number of portages: 10

Total portage rods: 737

Greatest portage difficulty: 278 rods (L8)

Navigation maps: Voyageur 7

Fisher F3, F4

McKenzie 18

This fantastic trip offers a wonderful progression from the tiny Little Isabella River to the larger Isabella River and on to large Bald Eagle and Gabbro lakes before heading out the South Kawishiwi River. The first half of this journey should offer excellent solitude on the river stretches, while the second half is along scenic lakes known for good fishing. You will need two vehicles for this journey, or should have an outfitter drop you off or pick you up if you are using just one vehicle.

Map 27 shows the first half of this route, and Map 25 shows the western half. In addition, Map 24 shows an overview of the entire route.

Detailed Route

Paddle and portage 4 miles down the Little Isabella River to the Isabella River, including portages of 25 rods (L3), 12 rods (L3), 32 rods (L4), and 16 rods (L3). Begin your trip heading down the Little Isabella along the same stretch covered in Route 75A. All of these portages along the Little Isabella River are relatively easy and should not pose problems other than occasional standing water and perhaps a bit of overgrown forest along the paths.

Paddle and portage 4.5 miles to Bald Eagle Lake, including portages of 35 rods (L3 to L4), an optional 8 rods (L2), and 178 rods (L7); then paddle 5.5 miles to Little Gabbro Lake. The first portage west of the junction of the Little Isabella and Isabella Rivers is located at a bend just after their confluence. This portage is likely to be in fairly good shape, although portions of it can be muddy after a rain. The downstream side is sandy and includes a nice clearing that makes a good spot for a short break if it fits into your schedule and the mosquitoes cooperate. After this 35-rod portage, the Isabella River begins to widen and deepen, and the current becomes less apparent. You will next paddle to a small rapids, which most visitors paddle through (or you can take a short 8-rod portage). This portion of the river is quite scenic.

The forest closes in a little tighter, and the water deepens and darkens after these two portages. You will notice that the spruce forest begins to diversify with occasional balsam fir and jack pine. Even the black spruce that are present appear much more robust than those found on the earlier backwaters.

The final, 178-rod portage leading from the Isabella River to Bald Eagle Lake is likely to be in decent shape and follows the south side of the Isabella River. This portage avoids a long stretch of substantial rapids. Entry to the portage is just before the rapids on the south side. Be careful not to land at the campsite just before the portage. You should paddle downstream 50 yards past the campsite to find the real entry to the portage on your left. This is a fairly long portage and the longest one on the Isabella River. The trail includes a number of ups and downs, although none of them is extreme.

Bald Eagle Lake makes an excellent place to spend the night and may have the first open campsites you come to if the two designated sites along the Isabella River are occupied. Otherwise, continue across Bald Eagle to Gabbro Lake, which is connected by a small portage that can often be avoided by paddling through a shallow narrows. If you want a longer diversion, head to Turtle Lake or Gull Lake to make a loop through Clearwater Lake. This extension takes you to areas that get significantly fewer visitors than Bald Eagle and Gabbro (see Route 84B).

Gabbro is a beautiful Boundary Waters gem carved directly out of the underlying diabase (gabbro) bedrock. You will see the exposed rock along most of the shoreline. This bedrock is of igneous (molten magma) origin and formed over a billion years ago as part of the Duluth Complex. Notice that the rock is deposited in large, massive folds.

On the southwest shore of Gabbro about a mile or mile and a half past the entry from Bald Eagle Lake is a fine swimming beach with a relatively large sandy shore. While this isn't Waikiki Beach, it is pretty good compared to the typical boulder-strewn Boundary Waters shore. Portions of the northwest shore of Gabbro display evidence of a forest fire that raged through here in the early 1990s. The shoreline of Gabbro Lake also shows evidence of the shifts in water level over the years, in particular the 3-foot drop in depth when the rock dam to the Kawishiwi River was opened.

Paddle and portage 3 miles from Little Gabbro Lake to your exit at the South Kawishiwi River, including portages of 278 rods (L8) from Little Gabbro to Bruin Lake, 13 rods portage (L2) from Bruin to the South Kawishiwi River, and 140 rods (L6) to the parking lot. Head to the far western end of Gabbro Lake to Little Gabbro Lake (reached without a portage), and take the 278-rod portage to Bruin Lake. This long portage begins at a little bay to the northwest of the campsite on Little Gabbro. It does not start at the location shown on many Fisher maps, but is rather a well-traveled landing to the northwest, so don't be confused. Next, an easy 13-rod portage drops you to the South Kawishiwi River from Bruin. Paddle south along the river, and head up the 140-rod portage to the parking lot for the South Kawishiwi River entry (Entry Point 32), where you should have left a second vehicle or arranged to be picked up by an outfitter.

Entry Point 67, Bog Lake (Map 27)

Daily permit quota: 2
Permit availability: easy

Entry Point 67, Bog Lake, is the only entry in the BWCAW that connects to just one lake. Tucked along the edge of the Boundary Waters, Bog Lake is relatively small and shallow. You will need to take a long portage of at least 247 rods to reach the lake. This portage is often longer in the spring when rising water levels sometimes close the last quarter mile of road.

Bog Lake's dead-end nature is an issue only if you want to cover multiple lakes. Numerous BWCAW visitors never paddle beyond their entry lake, so the inability to go beyond Bog is not necessarily a problem. Only about fifty groups enter Bog Lake during an entire year, so you might not see a single other party, making this a potentially excellent option if you seek maximum solitude.

To reach Bog Lake from Highway 1, take the Tomahawk Trail (Forest Service Road 377) east from its junction with Highway 1 for just over 13 miles until you come to a spur (Forest Service Road 377D) to your left and a sign for Bog Lake. Take this spur for about .75 mile until you reach the parking lot and trailhead. You may need to park farther back on this spur road if water levels are high. (You can also reach Bog Lake from the south along Trappers Lake Road and Northwest Road, but this route is much more confusing and probably no quicker.)

Overnight options near Bog Lake are very limited, but you can camp at McDougal Lake campground off Highway 1, about 11 miles west of Isabella, or continue all the way to Ely. If you are arriving from the north shore of Lake Superior, you may want to spend the night at one of the Minnesota state parks along Highway 61.

Route 67: Bog Lake Weekend (Map 27)

> Difficulty: intermediate
> Number of days: 2 or more
> Total miles (approx.): 3
> Number of portages: 1
> Total portage rods: 494 to 640 rods (longer if wet)
> Greatest portage difficulty: 247 to 320 rods (L8)
> Navigation maps: Voyageur 7
> Fisher F4
> McKenzie 19

Portage to remote and isolated Bog Lake. This route is most pleasant late in the canoeing season, such as in August and September when mosquito populations are on the decline and the road to the portage is not partially submerged. A spring trip has the potential to be quite uncomfortable, particularly if you need to extend the portage a quarter mile and hike over a submerged or soggy roadbed. Also, the plentiful swampy areas around Bog Lake can produce mammoth mosquito hatches. Neither mud nor insects should be much problem by early August.

Detailed Route

Portage 247 rods (L7) or 320 rods (L9) to Bog Lake, and paddle 1 mile to a campsite. If you are arriving during the second half of the summer, which is usually quite dry, the 247-rod portage should be firm and relatively easy. However, if you are visiting in the spring, be prepared for the last quarter mile of road to the trailhead to be submerged, in which case you may need to extend the portage by approximately 80 rods to get to the "official" start. If the trailhead is submerged, you will need to walk through ankle- to knee-deep water, which is likely to be quite cold. Bringing waterproof boots is a good idea during such conditions. The entire portage, whether the official 247 rods or the seasonal 320 rods, is along a nice trail.

Once on Bog Lake you will be treated to a true wilderness experience, one where you will see only one or two other parties and perhaps none. Some old maps show four campsites on Bog Lake, but the Forest Service confirms that only three sites are available for use, with the campsite on the southwest shore now closed. The shallow waters of Bog Lake reach a maximum of just 16 feet, but they contain a decent population of walleye and perch.

Paddle 1 mile, and portage 247 rods (L7) or 320 rods (L9) to your start. Your return trip is simply the reverse of your way to Bog Lake.

Entry Point 34, Island River (Map 27)

> Daily permit quota: 3
> Permit availability: moderate to difficult

The Island River, Entry Point 34, is a "sister" entry to neighboring Entry Point 35 at Isabella Lake, which is just a short paddle away. The same routes can easily be taken from both entry points, and many of the same trip options available for other routes off the Tomahawk Road are also available. The two routes described below are a one-way trip west to Quadga Lake (Route 34A) and a one-way trip east to Perent Lake (Route 34B). The Island River does not provide for any long loops, but numerous Ely outfitters will be happy to park your car at one of the many destinations along the Isabella River if you want a nice, long one-way route.

To reach the Island River, take Forest Service Road 377 (the Tomahawk Road) east from Minnesota Highway 1. If you are coming from the south on Highway 1, travel 36 miles up the highway from Illgen City (on Lake Superior) to the exit for 377. Take 377 about 17 miles until you reach a bridge over the Island River, where you will find a small parking lot and landing.

If you need a place to spend the night before entering the wilderness, consider camping at the South Kawishiwi River campground, located just off Highway 1, 8 miles north of Forest Service Road 377.

Route 34A: One-Way to Quadga Lake (Map 27)

> Difficulty: moderate to easy
> Number of days: 2 or more
> Total miles (approx.): 15
> Number of portages: 12
> Total portage rods: 590
> Greatest portage difficulty: 126 rods
> Navigation maps: Voyageur 7
> Fisher F4
> McKenzie 18, 19

This easy route paddles down the Island River to the Isabella River, continuing west to Quadga Lake, and offers a decent chance to spot a moose along the way. This is an easy journey for paddlers of all ability levels as long as they have packed well. Otherwise the relatively numerous short portages will be quite challenging.

Detailed Route

Paddle and portage 7.5 miles to Quadga Lake, including portages of 13 rods, 3 rods, 126 rods, 27 rods, 27 rods, and 99 rods. Your travels will start with easy 13- and 3-rod portages down the Island River before you reach the larger Isabella River. Next, the 126-rod portage on the Isabella River just before Rice Lake is relatively flat except for a gradual uphill and downhill on the second half. The trail is clear of obstructions, and in one location a small wooden footbridge crosses a streambed. In a couple of other locations boardwalks are in place to traverse muddy spots. The portage bypasses a series of rapids that seem relatively minor from the topside, but halfway through the portage you begin to hear raging water from the rapids on your right. The length of the rapids and the relatively large amount of water flowing through them make it very hazardous to canoe these rapids. You are absolutely advised to take the easy portage. The portage terminates on the downstream side of the rapids and is notable for a small but excellent growth of cedars.

Consider camping on Rice Lake if you are not in a hurry to get to Quadga. You should also give thought to camping at one of the other designated campsites along the Isabella River before you reach Quadga Lake. Relatively few campsites in the BWCAW are along narrow little rivers like the Isabella, and these sites offer a nice contrast to typical lakeshore camping. This early portion of the Isabella River meanders through narrow flats in which the far shores are covered by a low-lying forest predominated by spruce with an occasional birch.

A campsite is located on the right (north) side of the Isabella River approximately a mile and a half past Rice Lake. Just after this campsite is a short rocky stretch that can typically be paddled through by most experienced canoeists. If you are uncomfortable canoeing these rapids, take the short portage on the right-hand side.

The next two portages are both 27 rods long, the first of which is relatively flat with only a few large boulders obstructing portions of the middle of the trail. Both the put-in and take-out positions are small, sandy beaches. The second 27-rod portage, just around a bend from the first, bypasses a short area of fast water. The portage is on the north side of the river along a relatively steep and rocky trail. After this second portage, the river remains approximately 3 rods wide, but the spruce forest presses in more closely along the shores.

The Isabella River continues to another series of major, hazardous rapids south of Quadga Lake. Portage on the north side of the rapids, and fork to the right and take the 99-rod trail to Quadga Lake. Quadga has four designated campsites and offers a nice base to test the depths for walleye and northern pike.

Paddle and portage 7.5 miles back to the Island River, including portages of 99 rods, 27 rods, 27 rods, 126 rods, 3 rods, and 13 rods. Retrace your route back to the Island River, stopping to camp a night or two at one of the campsites along the way, if time permits.

Route 34B: One-Way to Perent Lake (Map 27)

Difficulty: moderate (many short portages)
Number of days: 2
Total miles (approx.): 20.5
Number of portages: 17
Total portage rods: 414
Greatest portage difficulty: 57 rods (L4)
Navigation maps: Voyageur 7, 8
                      Fisher F4, F5
                      McKenzie 19, 20

This route is the "mirror image" of Route 34A, taking you east instead of west from the Island River. Ideal pacing for this route might be to spend a first night on one of the many designated campsites on Isabella Lake, and then cover the many little portages on the Perent River to Perent Lake to spend another night (or more) before exiting via Hog Creek. You will need two vehicles or a lift from an outfitter for this route. This trip is best suited for returning visitors because the numerous little portages could be a harsh introduction for less experienced campers.

Map 27 shows the first portion of this route, and Map 28 shows the remainder. The entire route is shown in overview on Map 24.

Detailed Route

Paddle and portage 5.5 miles to Isabella Lake, including portages of 13 rods, 3 rods, 20 rods, and 28 rods. From the landing on the Island River, take two short, easy portages to the Isabella River, and then head east toward Isabella Lake. Once on the Isabella

River, a 20-rod portage takes you into a stretch of river bordered predominantly by a spruce forest with the classic boreal characteristics of thin, almost dead-looking, pencil-like spruce with an occasional white cedar scattered along the shore. Next, a 28-rod portage on the west end of Isabella Lake passes around a series of rapids that are not navigable by canoe. The Forest Service has constructed a footbridge where the Pow Wow Trail crosses the Isabella River and heads to the interior of the Boundary Waters. This bridge is in the same location as was a bridge used by the Tomahawk Timber Company to gain access to log stands in the Superior Roadless Area in the 1950s and 1960s.

Once on Isabella Lake you can camp at one of the thirteen designated campsites. Isabella Lake is also reachable directly by way of Entry Point 35, so don't expect the luxury of complete solitude. A half century ago this lake would have been visited by residents of the short-lived logging village of Forest Center on its southwest shores, described in greater detail earlier in this section.

Paddle and portage 10.5 miles from Isabella Lake to Perent Lake, including portages of 16 rods, 19 rods, 36 rods, 24 rods, 22 rods, 21 rods, 29 rods, 18 rods, 47 rods, 29 rods, 29 rods, and 57 rods. Now the fun starts! You will have a long day ahead of you on the Perent River. This is a good day to pack your gear into as few bundles as possible, making it easy to load and unload your canoe quickly. Fasten that water bottle to your backpack, keep the sunscreen accessible but secure, lash fishing poles together, and so on. As always, wear your life jacket.

Most of the portages on this stretch of river bypass deceptively hazardous rapids. You will be heading upstream, so it is unlikely you will be tempted (or able) to paddle through many of them. The last time I passed this way I came to the end of one of these portages to find a man bobbing in the water beside his empty canoe, asking for help, and wondering if we happened to have any spare maps. Fortunately for him, we were carrying a spare map of the Superior National Forest that had enough detail to get him to Isabella Lake and his way out.

Once you reach Perent Lake you will have the satisfaction of knowing you have just one short portage remaining on the route. Hopefully your schedule allows you to spend a night or two at one of the twenty designated campsites on this fine lake, which is known for having a good walleye population.

Paddle and portage 4.5 miles to the Hog Creek parking lot, including a portage of 3 rods and probably a number of beaver dam pull-overs. The final leg of this journey takes you to your exit by way of Hog Creek on the east end of Perent Lake. This winding stretch of creek is far more twisty than anything you will have seen on the Isabella River or Perent River, but it has only one short portage. You should expect, however, to come across at least a couple beaver dams along the way necessitating pull-overs. Have a vehicle waiting for you at the Hog Creek parking lot, or arrange to be picked up there by an outfitter.

Entry Point 35, Isabella Lake (Map 28)

Daily permit quota: 3
Permit availability: difficult

The area around Isabella Lake is one of the most peaceful in the Boundary Waters, feeling much more remote than most entries along the Gunflint Trail, Echo Trail, and Fernberg Road. However, a half century ago this area was home to an epic battle against widespread logging within the boundaries of the present-day wilderness. At issue was the sale of logging rights for over 100 square miles of forest extending west, north, and east from Isabella Lake. This logging concession, known as the Tomahawk Sale, resulted in the clear-cutting of acre after acre of virgin forest. In an age before environmental impact statements and mandatory government disclosure, the full extent of this logging was kept somewhat secret by the Forest Service.

According to the Forest Service, from 1949 until 1964 the village of Forest Center was located on the shores of Isabella and had as many as 250 residents and fifty-three homes. The village also had a small school, a recreation hall with a restaurant, a lumber mill, and a small store. Loggers worked the area with as many as 112 horses, cutting 100,000 to 150,000 cords of wood per year. Upon the conclusion of logging in the 1960s, the village buildings were moved or dismantled, and many residents relocated in Isabella and other area communities. Today little evidence of the village site remains.

To reach Isabella Lake, take Forest Service Road 377 (the Tomahawk Road) east from Minnesota Highway 1. If you are coming from the south on Highway 1, travel 36 miles up the highway from Illgen City (on Lake Superior) to the exit for 377. Take 377 just over 18 miles until its termination at a parking lot in the former location of Forest Center.

If you need a place to spend the night before entering the wilderness, consider camping at the South Kawishiwi River campground, located just off of Highway 1, approximately 8 miles north of Forest Service Road 377.

Route 35A: Exploration of Isabella Lake (Map 28)

       Difficulty: easy
       Number of days: 2 or more
       Total miles (approx.): 2 or more
       Number of portages: 2
       Total portage rods: 70
       Greatest portage difficulty: 35 (L2)
       Navigation maps: Voyageur 7
                          Fisher F4
                          McKenzie 19

This simple excursion to Isabella Lake is a fine introduction to the wilderness, offering opportunities to fish, explore, and reflect on the fascinating history of this lake.

Detailed Route

Portage 35 rods (L2) to Isabella Lake. This route, confined to a single lake, is certainly one of the easiest in the BWCAW. Take the easy 35-rod portage to the shores of

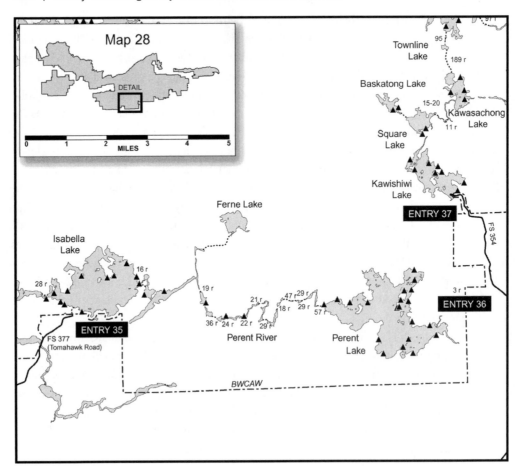

Isabella Lake, and then stay at one of the eleven campsites scattered along the shore and islands. Without taking any significant portages, you can extend this route to the west by looping over to the Island River, taking four portages along the way, and then walking back to your vehicle (see Route 34B).

One of the wonders of this route is imagining all the activity on this lake decades ago when the small town of Forest Center still existed at what is now the parking lot. Imagine the men and equipment heading north along a gravel road to the west end of Isabella, crossing over the narrow Isabella River, and then traveling north to the cuttings of the Tomahawk Lumber Company. The occasional rumble of locomotives would also have been heard, as trains pulled into Forest Center with supplies and departed with loads of logs for southern mills. No doubt Isabella Lake would have been a draw to the people of Forest Center, for skating in winter and fishing in all seasons. The lumberjacks and their families are long gone from this lake, and it is getting harder and harder to see where the old roads and train tracks ran. This area is certainly far more wild than it was two or three generations ago and becomes more wild every year.

Portage 35 rods (L2) back to the parking lot. When your journey is over, simply paddle back to the portage leading to the parking lot.

Route 35B: One-Way to the South Kawishiwi River (Map 28)

Difficulty: intermediate
Number of days: 4 or more
Total miles (approx.): 28.5
Number of portages: 14
Total portage rods: 1,057
Greatest portage difficulty: 278 rods (L9)
Navigation maps: Voyageur 7
                  Fisher F3, F4
                  McKenzie 18, 19

This route takes you west to the South Kawishiwi River (exiting at Entry Point 32) along some of the best river paddling in the Boundary Waters. This journey can be easily shortened by stopping at one of six other entries along the way to the South Kawishiwi. This moderate route is well suited to competent canoe campers looking for an alternative to the primarily lake travel in most of the BWCAW.

This route starts on Map 28 and continues westward onto Map 27 and then onto Map 25. The entire route is shown in overview on Map 24.

Detailed Route

Paddle and portage 1.5 miles from the parking lot to central Isabella Lake, including a portage of 35 rods (L2). Start this route by heading to Isabella Lake, where you might want to spend an evening. As described earlier for Route 35A, one of the pleasures of staying on Isabella Lake is imagining all the activity on this lake decades ago, when the small town of Forest Center still existed at what is now the parking lot at the start of the 35-rod portage.

Paddle and portage 5 miles from Isabella Lake to Rice Lake, including portages of 28 rods, 20 rods, and 126 rods along the Isabella River. When you are ready to leave Isabella Lake, take the 28-rod portage on the west end, which passes around a series of rapids. The Forest Service has constructed a footbridge over the Isabella River where the Pow Wow Trail crosses the river and heads to the interior of the Boundary Waters. This bridge is in the same location as was a bridge used by the Tomahawk Timber Company to gain access to log stands in the Superior Roadless Area in the 1950s and 1960s. Next, the 20-rod portage is likely to be in relatively good condition. You will then take a 126-rod portage on the Isabella River just before Rice Lake that is relatively flat except for a gradual uphill and downhill on the second half. The trail is clear of obstructions, and in one location a small wooden footbridge crosses a streambed. In a couple of other locations boardwalks are in place to traverse muddy spots.

The 126-rod portage bypasses a series of rapids that seem relatively minor from the topside, but halfway through the portage you begin to hear raging water from the rapids. The length of the rapids and the relatively large amount of water flowing through them would make it hazardous to canoe these rapids under all but the best conditions. You are absolutely advised to take the easy portage. The portage terminates on the downstream side of the rapids and is notable for a small but excellent growth of cedars.

Consider camping on Rice Lake if you are not in a hurry to get to Quadga. You should also give thought to camping at one of the other designated campsites along the Isabella River before you reach Quadga Lake. Relatively few campsites in the BWCAW are along little rivers like the Isabella, and these sites offer a nice contrast to typical lakeshore camping. This early portion of the Isabella River meanders through a narrow plain in which the far shores are covered by a low-lying forest predominated by spruce with an occasional birch.

Paddle and portage 5 miles from Rice Lake to Quadga Lake, including portages of 27 rods, 27 rods, and 91 rods. A campsite is located on the right (north) side of the Isabella River approximately a mile and a half past Rice Lake. Just after this campsite is a short rapids that can typically be paddled through by most experienced canoeists. If you are uncomfortable canoeing these rapids, take the short portage on the right-hand side.

The next two portages are both 27 rods long, the first of which is relatively flat with only a few large boulders obstructing portions of the middle of the trail. Both the put-in and take-out positions are small, sandy beaches. The second 27-rod portage, just around a bend from the first, bypasses a short area of fast water. The portage is on the north side of the river along a relatively steep and rocky trail. After this second portage, the river remains approximately 3 rods wide, but the spruce forest presses in more closely along the shores.

The Isabella River continues to another series of major, hazardous rapids south of Quadga Lake. Portage on the north side of the rapids, fork to the right, and take the 99-rod trail to Quadga Lake. Quadga has four designated campsites and offers a nice base to test the depths for walleye and northern pike.

Paddle and portage 8 miles from Quadga Lake to central Bald Eagle Lake, including portages of 61 rods, 35 rods (L3 to L4), an optional 8 rods, and 178 rods (L7). The first portage after Quadga takes you down a nice 61-rod trail to the Isabella River. Continue west past the junction of the Little Isabella and Isabella rivers, where you will find a 35-rod portage located at a bend just after their confluence. This portage is likely to be in fairly good shape, although portions of it can be muddy after a rain. The downstream side is sandy and includes a clearing that makes a good spot for a short break if it fits into your schedule and the mosquitoes cooperate. After this 35-rod portage the Isabella River begins to widen and deepen, and the current becomes less apparent. You will next paddle to a small rocky section of the river, which most visitors paddle through (or you can take a short 8-rod portage).

The forest closes in a little tighter, and the water deepens and darkens after these two portages. You will notice that the spruce forest begins to diversify with occasional balsam fir and jack pine. Even the black spruce that are present appear much more robust than those found on the earlier backwaters.

The final, 178-rod portage leading from the Isabella River to Bald Eagle Lake is likely to be in decent shape and follows the south side of the Isabella River. This portage avoids a long stretch of substantial rapids. Entry to the portage is just before the rapids on the south side of the river. Be careful not to land at the campsite just before the portage. You should paddle downstream 50 yards past the campsite to find the real entry to the portage on your left. This is a fairly long portage, and the longest one on the Isabella River. The trail includes a number of ups and downs, although none of them is extreme.

Paddle and portage 9 miles from Bald Eagle Lake to your exit at the South Kawishiwi River, including portages of 278 rods (L9) from Little Gabbro to Bruin Lake, 13 rods portage (L2) from Bruin to the South Kawishiwi River, and 140 rods to the parking lot. Move on to Gabbro Lake when you are done exploring Bald Eagle. Gabbro is a beautiful Boundary Waters gem carved directly out of the underlying diabase (gabbro) bedrock. You will see exposed rock along most of the shoreline. This bedrock is of igneous (molten magma) origin and formed over a billion years ago as part of the Duluth Complex. Notice that the rock is formed in large, massive folds. On the southwest shore of Gabbro about a mile or mile and a half past the entry from Bald Eagle Lake is a fine swimming beach with a relatively large sandy shore. While this isn't Waikiki Beach, it is pretty good compared to the typical boulder-strewn Boundary Waters shore. Portions of the northwest shore of Gabbro display evidence of a forest fire that raged through here in the early 1990s. The shoreline of Gabbro Lake also shows evidence of the shifts in water level over the years, in particular the 3-foot drop in depth when the simple stone logging dam over to the Kawishiwi River was opened.

Head to the far western end of Gabbro Lake to Little Gabbro Lake (reached without a portage), and take the 278-rod portage to Bruin Lake. This long portage begins at a little bay to the northwest of the campsite on Little Gabbro. It does not start at the location shown on many Fisher maps, but is rather a well-traveled landing to the northwest, so don't be confused. Next, an easy 13-rod portage drops you to the South Kawishiwi River from Bruin. Paddle south along the river, and head up the 140-rod portage to the parking lot for the South Kawishiwi River entry (Entry Point 32), where you should have left a second vehicle or arranged to be picked up by an outfitter.

ENTRY NORTH OF HIGHWAY 61

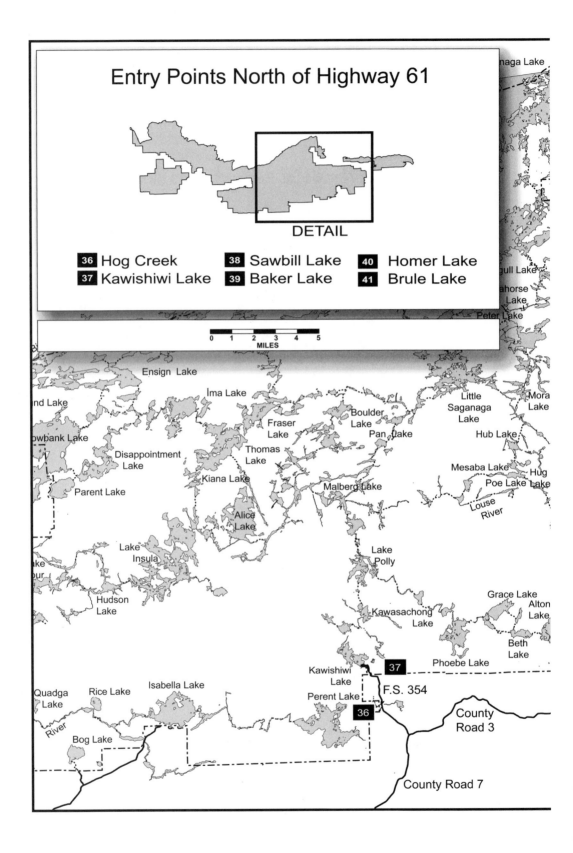

Entry Points North of Highway 61

DETAIL

36 Hog Creek   38 Sawbill Lake   40 Homer Lake

37 Kawishiwi Lake   39 Baker Lake   41 Brule Lake

0 1 2 3 4 5
MILES

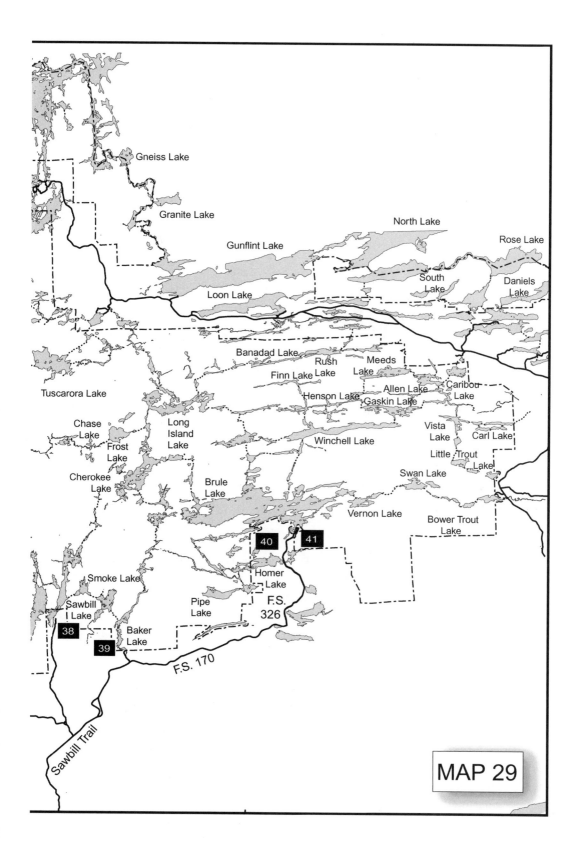

Gneiss Lake

Granite Lake

Gunflint Lake

North Lake

Rose Lake

South Lake

Daniels Lake

Loon Lake

Tuscarora Lake

Banadad Lake

Rush Lake

Finn Lake

Meeds Lake

Allen Lake

Caribou Lake

Henson Lake

Gaskin Lake

Chase Lake

Long Island Lake

Frost Lake

Winchell Lake

Vista Lake

Carl Lake

Little Trout Lake

Cherokee Lake

Brule Lake

Swan Lake

Vernon Lake

Bower Trout Lake

40

41

Smoke Lake

Homer Lake

Sawbill Lake

Pipe Lake

F.S. 326

38

39

Baker Lake

F.S. 170

Sawbill Trail

MAP 29

ENTRY NORTH OF HIGHWAY 61

Minnesota Highway 61 runs along the north shore of Lake Superior from Duluth to the Canadian border, passing through Two Harbors, Tofte, Grand Marais, and other small towns. Six entries to the BWCAW are best reached by taking spur roads off of Highway 61. The most popular of these entries is Sawbill Lake (Entry Point 38), located at the end of the Sawbill Trail. In addition, Baker Lake (Entry Point 39), Brule Lake (Entry Point 41), and Kawishiwi Lake (Entry Point 37) are all great starting points and offer excellent loop routes as well as fine one-way trips. Hog Creek (Entry Point 36) is also a good entry, giving relatively easy access to large Perent Lake but no moderate-length loop trips. Homer Lake (Entry Point 40), the final entry point off of Highway 61, is a great location for a weekend trip into the wilderness or a longer journey to Brule Lake.

When planning a trip out of these entry points, keep in mind that the big waters of Brule can be quite rough and are best left to your second or third trip into the BWCAW unless you are a very proficient canoeist. In addition, you will find that many of the lakes in this part of the BWCAW are joined by multiple portages, offering you the opportunity to tailor a route to fit your own preferences. If designing your own route, keep in mind that many visitors avoid the longest portages. Take these tough portages, and give yourself a chance to explore the remote interior of the BWCAW in nearly complete solitude.

Entry Point 36, Hog Creek (Map 28)

> Daily permit quota: 5
> Permit availability: easy to moderate

Hog Creek (Entry Point 36) provides a unique opportunity to combine travel down a narrow, twisty stream with a beautiful, large destination lake of islands and peaceful bays. Good canoe-steering skills will be helpful on Hog Creek, but otherwise this entry is suitable for first-time visitors. Hog Creek gives you easy access west to

Perent Lake, and then you can follow a series of small rivers to Isabella Lake, Rice Lake, Quadga Lake, and eventually Bald Eagle and Gabbro lakes. This entire area is beautiful, and travel along these narrow streams and rivers is much different from the lake-to-lake travel in most of the BWCAW.

Two routes are described below. The first, Route 36A, takes you on a short journey to explore Perent Lake a few miles west of the Hog Creek entry. The second, Route 36B, is a longer journey over the Perent River to Isabella Lake. You will need two cars for this journey or will have to arrange with an outfitter for your pick-up or drop-off. Many local outfitters offer this service. If you want to press on farther past Isabella Lake, look at route 35B, which goes from Isabella Lake all the way to the South Kawishiwi River.

To reach Hog Creek, take Forest Service Road 172 for 12 miles from the tiny village of Isabella on Highway 1 until you come to the intersection of County Road 7. Turn left (north) onto County Road 7, and drive about 11.5 miles until you reach the intersection of Forest Service Road 354, where you will turn left (north) and go another 2 miles until you reach a turnout on the west side of the road for the parking lot for Hog Creek.

A small campground is located at Kawishiwi Lake, just 2.5 miles farther north on Forest Road 354. No fees are charged to stay at the campground, and all five sites are available only on a first-come basis. A much larger campground at Sawbill Lake to the east has fifty campsites. It also does not accept advanced reservations, but sites are generally available all summer long.

Route 36A: Exploration of Perent Lake (Map 28)

      Difficulty: easy
      Number of days: 2 or more
      Total miles (approx.): 9
      Number of portages: 2
      Total portage rods: 6
      Greatest portage difficulty: 3 rods (L1)
      Navigation maps: Voyageur 8
                      Fisher F5
                      McKenzie 19, 20

This easy route takes you down Hog Creek to Perent Lake. Although you will cover just one official portage, be prepared for further pull-overs at beaver dams along the way. This route is suitable for first-time visitors to the BWCAW, assuming they do not mind getting a bit wet hauling their canoe over beaver dams.

Detailed Route

Paddle and portage 4.5 miles to central Perent Lake, including a portage of 3 rods (L1). Hog Creek is approximately two canoe lengths in width at the entry point landing.

After about a quarter mile you will come to a short 3-rod portage that is not shown on many maps. Alternatively, in high water you can navigate through two short, relatively mild rapid runs. Hog Creek winds back and forth along a narrow channel that is often just a few feet wide. The remainder of Hog Creek can typically be covered without portaging and requires only an occasional pull-over at intermittent beaver dams. During high water, you will be able to float over many of these dams without a problem.

The last half mile of Hog Creek widens out before it enters a small bay on Perent Lake. Perent Lake lies in a relatively shallow depression, and the shoreline has a few rock outcroppings. Perent Lake has twenty designated campsites, of which six are located on islands. Perent is a fine destination in its own right, and the depths are regarded as fine walleye waters. Your options for tripping beyond Perent Lake are limited to paddling west out the Perent River toward Isabella Lake, described in route 36B.

Route 36B: One-Way to Isabella Lake (Map 28)

> Difficulty: intermediate
> Number of days: 2 or more
> Total miles (approx.): 16.5
> Number of portages: 13
> Total portage rods: 350
> Greatest portage difficulty: 57 rods
> Navigation maps: Voyageur 7, 8
>   Fisher F4, F5
>   McKenzie 19, 20

This route is a natural extension to Route 36A, heading out the west end of Perent Lake and traveling on to Isabella Lake. It is a great route along the meandering Perent River, which requires that you take a dozen portages along the way. So you should not only pack light but pack well so that your gear is easily portable in as few bundles as possible. This route can easily be extended at Isabella Lake (Entry Point 35) by taking Route 35B another 28 miles west to the Kawishiwi River.

Detailed Route

Paddle and portage 4.5 miles to Perent Lake, including an easy portage of 3 rods (L1). Hog Creek is approximately two canoe lengths in width at the entry point landing. After less than a quarter mile you will come to a short 3-rod portage not shown on most maps. Alternatively, in high water you can navigate through two short, relatively mild rapid runs. The remainder of Hog Creek winds back and forth along a narrow channel to Perent Lake. Much of the year the rest of Hog Creek can be covered without portaging and requires only an occasional pull-over at intermittent beaver dams. During high water, you will be able to float over many of these dams without a problem. The last half mile of Hog Creek widens out before it enters a small bay on Perent Lake.

Perent Lake lies in a relatively shallow depression. This fine lake has twenty designated campsites, of which six are located on islands, and it makes an excellent place to spend one or more nights before forging on toward Isabella Lake. Perent is known as a decent walleye fishing lake and appears to attract significant numbers of fishermen. The condition of the portages to and from Perent Lake indicates that most visitors entering from Hog Creek go no farther than Perent Lake.

Paddle and portage 12 miles from Perent Lake to Isabella Lake, including portages of 57 rods, 29 rods, 29 rods, 47 rods, 18 rods, 29 rods, 21 rods, 22 rods, 24 rods, 36 rods, 19 rods, and 16 rods. Press on from Perent Lake along the Perent River to Isabella Lake. You will travel past five designated campsites along the way, so you can break this leg into two segments if necessary. However, you should start your travels early in the morning in the event that all of these sites are occupied, in which case you will need to press on all the way to Isabella Lake.

Your route out of Perent Lake starts with a 57-rod portage along a flat trail that receives sufficient use that it is not excessively overgrown. You canoe approximately a half mile down the Perent River around an oxbow to reach the next portage, which is about 29 rods long and also relatively flat and well maintained. Paddle on and canoe a quarter mile, and you cover another easy 29-rod portage. The next portage is 47 rods long and, like most of the portages on this route, circumvents a series of misleadingly hazardous rapids. The last time I passed this way I came to the end of this portage to find a man bobbing in the water beside his empty canoe, asking for help, and wondering if we happened to have any spare maps. Fortunately for him, we were carrying a spare overview map of the Superior National Forest that had enough detail to get him to Isabella Lake and his way out. This portage is a little bit more uphill and rocky than the others covered so far on this route, although it too poses little challenge. This portage passes between two magnificent old white pines toward the end of the portage just before reentering the Perent River. They are a good place to pause for a rest after putting your canoe in, to ponder their age and size.

You will then come to a short 18-rod portage and move on to a 29-rod carry. This final portage also bypasses a series of rapids. It begins with a very gradual uphill followed by a long, sloping downhill, neither of which is particularly difficult to travel. Paddle on to a 21-rod portage that empties into a broad area of the river covered by wild rice.

The remainder of the Perent River before Boga Lake alternates between large ponds filled with wild rice and short portages. The 24-rod portage shown on most maps is traversable much of the year without portaging. A couple of designated campsites are located along this section, and they are fairly good sites considering the low-lying land provides few options.

After about 12 miles of travel from Perent Lake you will arrive on the shores of Isabella Lake, which is the largest lake between Perent and Bald Eagle lakes. Isabella is now a peaceful and remote wilderness retreat, but in the decades immediately after World War II the surrounding area was bustling with logging activities from the Tomahawk timber sale, which resulted in creation of the short-lived village of Forest Center on the southwest end of Isabella Lake. Refer to "The Natural and Human History of the Boundary Waters" in this guide, and the discussion in the section for Entry Point 35, for more information on Forest Center and the contentious logging activities.

Optional Extensions

If you want to extend this trip from Isabella Lake, take Route 35B from Isabella all the way to the South Kawishiwi River. You will need two vehicles to complete this journey, leaving one at your start and one at the finish. If you want a more modest extension, continue along Route 35B but stop at the Island River, Little Isabella River, or Snake River, all located along the way to the South Kawishiwi. If you have an old Fisher or McKenzie map, you may see a mile-long portage to Ferne Lake, northeast of Isabella Lake. Indeed, some old maps show campsites on Ferne Lake. However, the portage to Ferne is no longer maintained and appears to be all but impassable. The start of the portage could not even be located during research for this guide.

Entry Point 37, Kawishiwi Lake (Map 30)

> Daily permit quota: 9
> Permit availability: moderate

Kawishiwi Lake (Entry Point 37) provides direct access to the heart of the east-central BWCAW and is well suited for first-time visitors to the Boundary Waters because it allows a nice short trip as far north as Kawasachong Lake with minimal portaging and no large open bodies of water to cross. Great trips can also be made to more remote interior lakes.

Three trips are described below. First is an up-and-back trip to explore Lake Polly (Route 37A), second is a loop to the west to Alice Lake (Route 37B), and third is a long journey to Little Saganaga Lake (Route 37C). The first route is well suited to first-time visitors, while the second loop is significantly more difficult. The final route is a great challenge for adventurous visitors.

To reach Kawishiwi Lake, take Forest Service Road 172 for 12 miles from Isabella on Highway 1 until you come to the intersection of County Road 7. Turn left (north) onto County Road 7, and drive about 11.5 miles until you reach the intersection of Forest Road 354, where you turn left (north) and go another 4.5 miles until you reach the Kawishiwi Lake campground and boat access.

A small campground is located at the Kawishiwi Lake landing, with five camp-sites. No fees are charged to stay at the campground, and all sites are available only on a first-come basis. A much larger campground at Sawbill Lake to the east has fifty

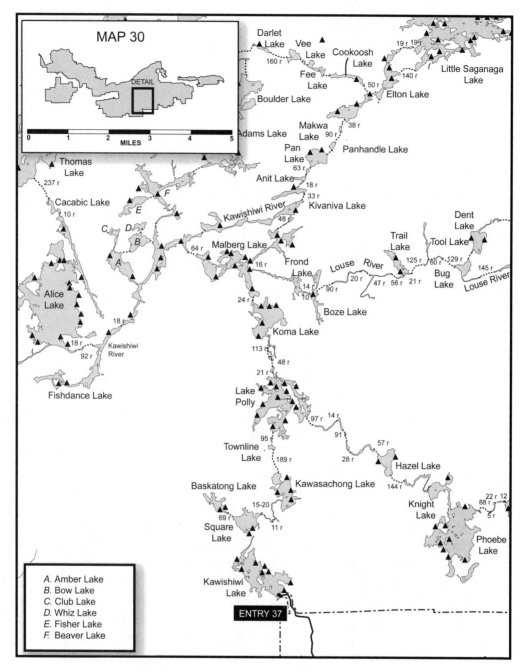

MAP 30

DETAIL

0 1 2 3 4 5
MILES

A. Amber Lake
B. Bow Lake
C. Club Lake
D. Whiz Lake
E. Fisher Lake
F. Beaver Lake

Darlet Lake
Vee Lake
Cookoosh Lake
160 r
Fee Lake
Boulder Lake
50 r
Elton Lake
19 r 19 r
140 r
Little Saganaga Lake
Makwa Lake
38 r
90 r
Adams Lake
Pan Lake
63 r
Panhandle Lake
Anit Lake
18 r
33 r
Kivaniva Lake
Kawishiwi River
48 r
Dent Lake
Trail Lake
Tool Lake
Thomas Lake
237 r
Cacabic Lake
10 r
F
E
C D
B
A
64 r
Malberg Lake
16 r
Frond Lake
Louse River
125 r
60 r
129 r
14 r
20 r
90 r
47 r 56 r 21 r
Bug Lake
145 r
Louse River
Alice Lake
18
18 r
92 r
Kawishiwi River
24 r
10
Boze Lake
Koma Lake
113 r
48 r
Fishdance Lake
21 r
Lake Polly
97 r 14 r
91
57 r
Hazel Lake
Townline Lake
95
189 r
28 r
144 r
Baskatong Lake
Kawasachong Lake
Knight Lake
22 r 12
88 r
5 r
69 r
15-20
Square Lake
11 r
Phoebe Lake
Kawishiwi Lake

ENTRY 37

campsites. It also does not accept advance reservations, but sites are generally available all summer long.

Route 37A: Exploration of Lake Polly (Map 30)

Difficulty: average

Number of days: 2 or more

> Total miles (approx.): 13
> Number of portages: 8
> Total portage rods: 630
> Greatest portage difficulty: 189 rods (L7)
> Navigation maps: Voyageur 8
>   Fisher F5
>   McKenzie 20

This easy route is an excellent introduction to the BWCAW. It travels through gener-ally moderate-sized lakes, and the portages encountered are all well maintained and likely to be in good shape. The biggest disadvantage to this route is that some of the lakes are quite popular, including Polly, so you should expect to see other paddlers on the entire route. Most people can easily reach Lake Polly in half a day of traveling, but get an early start to allow adequate time to find a campsite during busy times of the paddling season.

Detailed Route

Paddle and portage 6.5 miles from Kawishiwi Lake to Lake Polly, including paddling from Kawishiwi Lake to Square Lake, and portages of 15 to 20 rods (L2) and 11 rods (L2) from Square to Kawasachong Lake, 189 rods (L5) from Kawasachong to Townline Lake, and 95 rods (L5) from Townline to Lake Polly. Your journey starts at the land-ing on Kawishiwi Lake, which has eight designated campsites and makes a fine place to spend a first night or two before heading north to Lake Polly. Paddle across Kawishiwi on your way up to Square Lake. Although no maintained portages are located between Kawishiwi and Square lakes, don't be surprised to find one or more beaver dams. As always, try not to damage any beaver dams you encounter. They are an important part of the natural system. In prior years some visitors have tried to cut channels through wilderness beaver dams, but such activities are absolutely illegal and completely at odds with leave-no-trace camping.

Square Lake is quite shallow but has two designated campsites if you choose to spend a night along its shores. You can make an excellent detour by taking a moder-ate 69-rod (L4) portage to Baskatong Lake from Square Lake. Baskatong has two campsites and is said to have a healthy population of small northern pike, yet is not as popular as other lakes on this route. However, it still gets regular use due to its proximity to the Kawishiwi Lake entry point.

Continue on to Kawasachong Lake along the narrow Kawishiwi River, taking two portages along the way. The first portage will vary from about 15 to 20 rods in length depending on water levels (it is 5 rods shorter during high water). The landing is a bit rocky on the Square Lake side, but otherwise this portage is pretty easy. Farther down the river is an 11-rod portage that circumvents a shallow stretch of water. The trail follows the eastern shore along a rocky path. Kawasachong Lake has four designated campsites, which also make a nice place to spend the night. According to the Minnesota Historical Society, *kawasachong* means "mist" or "foam" lake.

You will next head from Kawasachong to Townline Lake, named for its position straddling two townships when this land was surveyed and plotted in the late 1800s. The 189-rod portage is likely to be in good shape in most places. The trail is almost entirely downhill, and the final 80 rods are particularly easy (this portage is a long, tough haul in the opposite direction). Townline Lake is a little pond with spindly black spruce along the shore. Paddle across this tiny lake, and take the 95-rod portage to Lake Polly. The trail is relatively flat with an occasional up and down. The landing on the Townline side is likely to be a bit muddy, while the landing on the Polly side is strewn with large rocks.

This route terminates on Lake Polly, which is a fine walleye lake. Koma and Malberg to the north are also good fishing lakes and are both reachable on day trips. Polly has long had a reputation as home to pack-snatching rogue bears. It is hard to say with certainty that Polly has consistently worse bear problems, but you will want to be extra careful to properly stow your food pack on Polly and adjacent lakes.

Paddle and portage 6.5 miles back to your starting point on Kawishiwi Lake, including portages of 95 rods (L5), 189 rods (L7), 11 rods (L2), and 15 to 20 rods (L2). Your return journey requires simply backtracking the way you traveled to Polly. Your return will be a bit more difficult than your arrival because you will have a noticeable climb up the 189-rod portage from Townline Lake to Kawasachong Lake.

Route 37B: Alice Lake Loop (Map 30)

> Difficulty: challenging
> Number of days: 7
> Total miles (approx.): 49
> Number of portages: 36
> Total portage rods: 1,921
> Greatest portage difficulty: 237 rods (L10)
> Navigation maps: Voyageur 7, 8
>   Fisher F5, F11, F12
>   McKenzie 8, 19, 20

This challenging route takes you in a long loop north and west of Kawishiwi Lake, including a side trip to faint, but remarkable, Native American pictographs. You will then travel to Alice Lake, on to mighty Thomas and Fraser lakes, and then over smaller lakes through Malberg Lake on your way to your starting point. This route is best suited for experienced wilderness paddlers who are physically fit and travel light.

Map 30 shows most of this route, and Map 25 shows the remainder. The entire route is shown in overview on Map 29.

Detailed Route

Portage and paddle 6.5 miles from Kawishiwi Lake to Lake Polly, including paddling to Square Lake, and portages of 15 to 20 rods (L2) and 11 rods (L2) from Square to Kawasachong Lake, 189 rods (L5) from Kawasachong to Townline Lake, and 95 rods (L5) from Townline to Lake Polly. The first leg of this trip follows the same path as Route 37A. Your journey starts at the landing on Kawishiwi Lake. If you are getting a late start, you might want to camp right on Kawishiwi. Next, paddle up to Square Lake. Although no portages are located between Kawishiwi and Square lakes, don't be surprised to find one or more beaver dams requiring a pull-over. Square Lake is quite shallow but has two designated campsites if you choose to spend a night there. A moderate 69-rod portage leads from Square Lake to Baskatong. Baskatong has two campsites and is said to have a healthy population of small northern pike.

Continue along a short stretch of the narrow Kawishiwi River to Kawasachong Lake, taking two portages along the way. The first portage will vary from about 15 to 20 rods depending on the water level (it is 5 rods shorter during high water). The landing is a bit rocky on the Square Lake side but otherwise pretty easy. Farther down the river is an 11-rod portage that avoids a shallow stretch of water leading to Kawasachong.

The 189-rod portage from Kawasachong Lake to Townline Lake is in reasonably good shape in most places. The trail is almost entirely downhill, and the final 80 rods are particularly easy. Townline is little more than a pond lined by spindly spruce. Paddle across, and take the 95-rod portage to Lake Polly. The trail is relatively flat with an occasional up and down. The landing on the Townline side is likely to be a bit muddy, while the landing on the Polly side is strewn with large rocks.

Paddle and portage 3.75 miles from Lake Polly to Malberg Lake, including portages of 21 rods (L1), 48 rods (L3), and 113 rods (L5) to Koma Lake, and 24 rods to Malberg. The trip to Malberg is along an excellent stretch of good portages. The first, 21-rod portage is flat and wide, bypassing rapids leading to a small pool. Head across the small pool to the 48-rod portage, which is also fairly flat and wide-open, having just a few obstructions and two good landings. Point your canoe north, and continue across another pool in the Kawishiwi to a 113-rod portage to Koma Lake. This portage is very easy considering its length, with a path that climbs over a very slight hill and then descends along the side of the river before gradually climbing another hill and making the final descent to Koma.

Finally, a 24-rod portage leads from Koma to Malberg Lake. Malberg is known as a good walleye lake, as are the dark waters of Polly and Koma. A quick look at a map of this area shows that Malberg is in a commanding crossroads location in the south-central BWCAW. Travel from Malberg can take you in four different directions. The heaviest used route to and from Malberg is certainly the portage between Koma and Malberg, probably because it is closest to an entry point. In addition, the popular loop from Sawbill Lake through Beth, Grace, and Phoebe lakes travels this way. The western exit from Malberg over the 64-rod portage (described below) is also commonly traveled. Although it is likely to be muddy, this gateway to Alice, Insula, and Thomas is worth the trouble. The two least traveled exits from Malberg are north to the Kawishiwi River and east to Frond Lake. They take you to rugged areas of challenging portages, and so get fewer visitors than the western and southern portages. If you want to design your own route to these areas, see Routes 50C and 38C, respectively.

Paddle and portage 7 miles from Malberg Lake to Alice Lake, including portages of 64 rods (L7) to the Kawishiwi River, and 18 rods, 92 rods (L6), and 18 rods (L4) along the Kawishiwi River. When your time comes to leave Malberg Lake, take the 64-rod portage to the Kawishiwi River. The portage is short but can be exceedingly muddy, sometimes even well underwater. Be prepared for considerable standing water on this portage and then be pleasantly surprised if the trail is dry.

Once on the Kawishiwi River you will paddle west before wrapping south and taking an 18-rod portage that gives you access to Fishdance Lake. Well-faded pictographs are located up on a cliff running along the western shore of Fishdance. Although they are faint, you should be able to make out a number of interesting figures, including what appears to be a moose. Two designated campsites are located on the south end of Fishdance, and they appear to get significantly less use than many other campsites in this area, making them a nice place to seek isolation.

When you leave Fishdance Lake, paddle north and take the 92-rod and 18-rod portages to the south end of Alice Lake. The 92-rod portage trail diverts along a stretch of impassable rapids, climbing out of the Kawishiwi River, leveling for most of its length, and then dropping steeply again to the river. The 18-rod portage is also relatively hilly, diverting around two cataracts in the Kawishiwi.

Once on Alice Lake you are in the heart of a group of large, interior lakes. Alice has over a dozen designated campsites scattered along its shore, and a healthy population of walleye inhabits the depths. Paddlers from the busy Lake One and Snowbank Lake entries can reach Alice Lake without too much trouble, so expect to see other visitors.

Alice Lake is a modestly historic destination in that the earliest wilderness recreation plan for the Superior National Forest, written from 1919 to 1922 by landscape architect Arthur Carhart, displays a picture of the Kawishiwi River near Alice Lake and also shows a photograph of a portage east of Alice. Carhart's plan proclaimed the Superior National Forest one of the few great canoe countries of the world, a conclusion that would be greeted with unanimous approval by anyone who has visited in the eight decades since his proposal. The interim years have seen many threats to this great wilderness, and all modern visitors should be grateful that Carhart and countless others worked hard to preserve this area as a wonderful wilderness canoe country.

Paddle and portage 7.5 miles from Alice Lake to Fraser Lake, including portages of 10 rods (L2) to Cacabic Lake, and 237 rods (L10) from Cacabic to Thomas Lake, concluding by paddling through a narrow channel from Thomas to Fraser Lake. You will now move on from Alice Lake toward Fraser Lake. First, take a 10-rod portage out of the narrow north arm of Alice Lake. The portage is quite easy, giving you no foreshadowing of the challenge that awaits you on the 237-rod portage to Thomas Lake. This long portage would be tough enough due to its length but is made even tougher by the fact that you cross very muddy low spots along the trail. Tie your shoes on tight—you don't want to lose one if you should slip into hip-deep mud. The best thing about this portage is probably the sandy beach on the Thomas side, where you will be able to rinse off any extra mud you have acquired along the trail. If you have an aversion to mud, consider taking a longer route to Thomas Lake by way of Alice to Insula to Kiana, described in Route 27C.

Once on Thomas you may be lured into spending a few nights among its many islands and bays. When it comes time to move on, paddle through a wonderful narrow rock-walled channel joining up with Fraser Lake. This glacial-scoured channel, funneling traffic through such major lakes, has probably seen visitors for thousands of years. Perhaps the people who painted the cliffs at Fishdance Lake, viewed earlier in this journey, traveled this way.

On Fraser Lake you will be deep in the wilderness, days of travel from most entry points, yet with easy access to seemingly countless lakes of every size and shape. You will come across some of the first significant stands of windblown trees from the 1999 storm. You are at the southern edge of the most severe storm damage, so the impact was spottier here than on lakes just to the north. Five designated campsites are scattered along Fraser's shores, along with even more remote campsites accessible on Gerund Lake and Shepo Lake by way of short portages. See Route 27B for descriptions of portages to Gerund and other lakes northwest of Fraser.

Paddle and portage 8.5 miles from Fraser Lake to Makwa Lake, including portages of 68 rods (L4) from Fraser to Sagus Lake, 32 (L4) rods from Sagus to Roe Lake, 61 rods (L4) from Roe to Cap Lake, 186 rods (L8) from Cap to Ledge Lake, 160 rods (L9) from Ledge to Vee Lake, 80 rods (L6) from Vee to Fee Lake, 47 rods (L5) from Fee to Hoe Lake, and finally 86 rods (L5) from Hoe to Makwa Lake. You will now press on from Fraser Lake into some of the most remote wilderness in the BWCAW. You will first portage to Sagus Lake along a 68-rod trail that overlooks great moose habitat. This longer trail is superior to the alternative route of going from Fraser to Shepo by way of a 10-rod portage and then from Shepo to Sagus by way of a 20-rod portage. The 10-rod portage isn't bad, but the 20-rod trail is along a low-lying cedar swamp that is quite rooty and likely to be very wet much of the year. Sagus has three campsites, none of which appears to get much use.

Next, portage from Sagus to Roe Lake along an easy 32-rod trail. North of Roe Lake is seldom-visited Raven Lake, which is in the Mugwump Primitive Management Area (PMA). PMAs, described in "Planning Your Trip" in this guide, do not include any maintained portages or campsites, making them much more difficult to travel through and camp within. In addition, if you want to stay in a PMA, you must get written authorization from the local district office of the Superior National Forest in addition to your regular permit. The Mugwump PMA is administered by the Tofte Ranger District (218-663-8060). Raven Lake is said to contain lake trout, a claim supported by a DNR survey from the 1970s and the lake's maximum depth of 56 feet. You will need to take two nonmaintained portages to Raven Lake: one of 48 rods and one of 16 rods, both of which are very overgrown. These portages were challenging before the blowdown, when they were investigated for this guide, and are likely to be even more difficult in coming years because they get no maintenance from the Forest Service, and this area was heavily hit by the 1999 windstorm. The north side of Raven previously held a designated campsite, but the fire grate and latrine have been removed consistent with the pristine management principles of the PMA in which it is located.

Continue on from Roe Lake to Cap Lake over a 61-rod portage. Many maps of this area overestimate the length of this portage, but unless water levels are very low, it should be just 61 rods because you can paddle along a swampy channel for much of the distance between Roe and Cap. Cap Lake has one designated campsite, which appears to be a little-used outpost for the infrequent visitors to this area. When leaving Cap Lake, you may be confused by the numerous trails in and out of its south and east shores. This confusion is aggravated by the misleading representations made on some maps, which show a long, narrow lake just south of Cap Lake. This "lake" is actually a very shallow marsh that appears to have dried up years ago with the failure of an old beaver dam. Don't be misled into thinking this detour provides a good shortcut. You should take the 186-rod (L8) portage directly to Ledge Lake, which follows a gentle trail having few obstructions although an occasional wet spot. This portage has significant blowdown along much of its length. Ledge Lake also has a campsite on it, another potential place to spend an evening.

From Ledge Lake take the 160-rod portage to Vee Lake. This portage can also be quite mucky. A few footbridges have been built along the trail, but they are quite deteriorated. Look for young white pine in this area, reproducing since the last fire here, a great sight to see in the BWCAW. Paddle across Vee Lake to Fee Lake, which is reached over a flat 80-rod trail, which also can be muddy. Fee Lake has a boggy shore surrounded by a ghostly forest of black spruce.

Continue on from Fee Lake to Hoe Lake, taking another flat trail, which will be easy unless there has been significant rainfall. Hoe Lake has a number of attractive moss-covered cliffs. Your last portage of this leg is a good downhill trail to Makwa Lake. Makwa is not a heavily visited lake, but due to its location as a junction allowing connections in three directions, it probably gets more visitors than any other lake on this route since Fraser. Pay attention to the exposed bedrock on Makwa, especially an interesting large cliff with layers of intruded gabbro.

Paddle and portage 5.5 miles from Makwa Lake to Malberg Lake, including portages of 38 rods and 90 rods to Panhandle Lake, 50 rods to Pan Lake, 63 rods to Anit Lake, 18 rods to Kivaniva Lake, 33 rods to the Kawishiwi River, and 48 rods to Malberg Lake. The stretch from Makwa to Malberg Lake is a great journey through remote little lakes. You will not see many people on any of these lakes. The first leg, from Makwa to Panhandle Lake, involves a 38-rod portage (mislabeled as 60 rods on some maps) and a 90-rod portage. Neither is well traveled but should be in OK shape. Next paddle 50 rods to Pan Lake, which has two campsites. From Pan Lake you will travel by way of a single, 63-rod portage to Anit Lake. Some older maps show two portages split by a pond, but this pond appears to have permanently dried up and is unlikely to be navigable during any time of the year. A short 18-rod portage carries you from Anit Lake to Kivaniva, and a final, 33-rod portage takes you to the Kawishiwi River, where you will navigate into a small bay with a 48-rod portage back to Malberg Lake.

Paddle and portage 10.25 miles from Malberg Lake to Kawishiwi Lake, including portages of 24 rods from Malberg to Koma Lake, 113 (L5), 48 (L3), and 21 (L1) rods from Koma to Lake Polly, 95 rods (L5) and 189 rods (L5) from Polly to Kawasachong Lake, 11 rods (L2) and 15 to 20 rods (L2) to Square Lake, and a paddle to Kawishiwi Lake. The last leg of this journey takes you south to your starting point on Kawishiwi Lake. As described earlier in this route, there are numerous good places to spend the night between Malberg and Kawishiwi lakes, but arrive early if you want a campsite on Lake Polly.

Route 37C: Little Saganaga Loop (Map 30)

Difficulty: challenging
Number of days: 8
Total miles (approx.): 57
Number of portages: 44
Total portage rods: 3,424
Greatest portage difficulty: 460 rods (L9)
Navigation maps: Voyageur 6, 8
Fisher F5, F11, F12
McKenzie 7, 8, 20

This long, tough journey takes you all the way to Little Saganaga Lake and then heads south to Mesaba Lake before taking you down the remote Louse River to Malberg Lake on your way back to Kawishiwi Lake. This route differs from Route 37B in that it travels to the northeast of Kawishiwi Lake, while Route 37B travels to the northwest of Kawishiwi Lake. This route is best suited to experienced visitors.

Map 30 shows the majority of this route, and Map 31 shows the remainder. An overview of the entire route is shown on Map 29.

Detailed Route

Portage and paddle 6.5 miles to Lake Polly, including paddling to Square Lake, portages of 15 to 20 rods (L2) and 11 rods (L2) to Kawasachong Lake, 189 rods (L5) from Kawasachong to Townline Lake, and 95 rods (L5) from Townline to Lake Polly. Your journey starts at the landing on Kawishiwi Lake and follows the same course to Lake Polly as taken by Route 37A. You will paddle across Kawishiwi Lake on your way toward Square Lake. If you are getting a late start, you might want to camp right on Kawishiwi Lake and consider the detour to Baskatong Lake described in Route 37A. Continue on to Kawasachong Lake along the narrow Kawishiwi River, taking two portages along the way. The first portage will vary from about 15 to 20 rods depending on the water level (it is 5 rods shorter during high water). The landing is a bit rocky on the Square Lake side but otherwise pretty easy. Farther down the river is an 11-rod portage that circumvents a shallow stretch of water that you may be able to pull through during high water. The 189-rod portage leading from Kawasachong Lake to Townline Lake is in good shape in most places and fairly well traveled. The 95-rod portage to Lake Polly is relatively flat with an occasional up and down. The landing on the Townline side is likely to be a bit muddy, while the landing on the Polly side is strewn with large rocks.

Paddle and portage 3.75 miles to Malberg Lake, including portages of 21 rods (L1), 48 rods (L3), and 113 rods (L5) to Koma Lake, and 24 rods to Malberg. The trip to Malberg is also along a well-maintained route. The first, 21-rod portage is flat and wide, bypassing rapids. Head across the small pool on the Kawishiwi River to the 48-rod portage. Point your canoe north and continue across another pool in the Kawishiwi. This 113-rod portage to Koma Lake is easy considering its length. The path climbs over a slight hill when leaving Polly and then descends along the side of the river before gradually climbing another hill and making the final descent to Koma.

Paddle and portage 5.5 miles from Malberg Lake to Makwa Lake, including portages of 48 rods from Malberg to the Kawishiwi River, 33 rods from the Kawishiwi River to Kivaniva Lake, 18 rods from Kivaniva to Anit Lake, 63 rods from Anit to Pan Lake, and 50 rods, 90 rods, and 38 rods from Pan to Makwa Lake. This stretch of paddling is the most remote segment of the BWCAW you will cover on this journey, and it is well off the busiest segment you will have just passed through to Malberg Lake. In addition, the smaller lakes from Malberg to Makwa have ten campsites scattered between them, allowing ample opportunities for a secluded place to spend one or more days with greater isolation than you will get along the rest of this route. If you are traveling early in spring or after Labor Day, you have a good chance of having complete solitude on these lakes.

Start by taking the 48-rod portage from Malberg to the Kawishiwi River, and then take the 33-rod portage to Kivaniva. This portage is not heavily traveled but gets enough use from day-trippers out of Malberg and occasional through-trippers that it should be in decent shape. One designated campsite is located on Kivaniva, and it can be a good base from which to fish this pretty little lake. Follow up with the short portage to Anit Lake, and a 63-rod portage from Anit to Pan. If you are using older maps, you will notice that the Anit to Pan segment appears to be two portages separated by a small pond. However, this pond is now essentially overgrown with vegetation and doesn't look to be navigable at any time of year, making this a single portage. Finally, portage and paddle from Pan Lake to Makwa along two relatively infrequently used portages.

Paddle and portage 4 miles from Makwa Lake to Little Saganaga, including portages of 50 rods (L4) from Makwa to Elton Lake, and 19 rods (L4) and 19 rods (L2) from Elton to Little Saganaga Lake. The trail from Makwa to Elton follows along a streambed with a nice path. As you travel from Elton Lake to Little Saganaga you have two options: either a 140-rod (L7) single portage or two shorter portages of 19 rods each. The long portage from Elton to Little Saganaga follows a reasonably smooth trail, but has a long climb and similarly long descent that are steep and slippery in parts. The two shorter portages appear to be the more popular route. The first 19-rod (L4) portage climbs above a stream before dropping to a bog. Wind through this bog to the second 19-rod (L2) portage down an easy trail.

Little Saganaga is an island-studded masterpiece. Few lakes in the BWCAW can compare with a misty morning on Lil' Sag, the islands floating before your campsite like a drifting pine flotilla. Twenty-four designated sites are available for camping, but even these can fill with the numerous canoeists coming in from the entry points at Missing Link, Brandt, and Cross Bay lakes. The spectacular scenery along with the nice side trips attract campers during the busy summer months. The northwest shore of Little Saganaga was hit by the 1999 windstorm, but most of the lake was relatively undamaged.

Little Saganaga's beauty would be sufficient to make it a popular destination, but this crossroads lake is also popular because it allows paddlers so many options to explore neighboring territory. Many visitors come to Little Saganaga by way of Gabimichigami and Agamok to the west, often starting at Sea Gull Lake. Entry from Mora Lake to the southeast is also popular, especially when starting at one of the three entries originating near Round Lake (Entries 50, 51, and 52). Less popular is the portage to Virgin Lake, but this is a good route to hit Fern, Peter, and French lakes. Finally, the least popular portage out of Little Sag is probably to Elton Lake. This is not a bad portage but appears to get few visitors.

Paddle and portage 8 miles from Little Saganaga east to Mesaba Lake, including portages of 40 rods (L4) from Little Saganaga to Mora Lake, 96 rods (L5) from Mora to Whipped Lake, 16 rods (L2) from Whipped to Fente Lake, 300 rods (L7) from Fente to Hub Lake, and 105 rods (L5) from Hub to Mesaba Lake. The first portage of this segment, from Little Saganaga to Mora Lake, diverts around an impassable rapids. These rapids are extremely perilous and cannot be shot safely in a canoe. The trail skirts to the north side of the rapids. Although the portage has portions of relatively steep incline, it is easily traveled with few obstructions and provides a number of good views of the raging rapids.

Next, the portage from Mora Lake to Whipped Lake is well maintained. Only an occasional deadfall is likely to obstruct you and your load. The portage from Whipped Lake to Fente is flat and relatively clear of obstacles. The 300-rod portage between Fente and Hub is likely to be a pleasant surprise. Although long and starting with a tough initial hill, this is one of the best trails you will find on a portage. Nothing will make this easy if you are overloaded, but a well-packed and fit crew should have no problem. The final portage to Mesaba from Hub Lake is straight and smooth although likely to be a bit overgrown. Mesaba Lake is a wonderful remote wilderness lake. It is just a few portages from busy Sawbill Lake, but one of these portages is over a mile long, which keeps all but the most determined visitors away.

Paddle and portage 2.25 miles from Mesaba Lake to Zenith Lake, including portages of 74 rods from Mesaba to Hug Lake, 10 rods from Hug to Duck Lake, and 64 rods from Duck to Zenith Lake. Head out the east end of Mesaba Lake, and paddle and portage along three moderate portages to Zenith Lake. None of these portages is heavily maintained, so expect them to be somewhat overgrown. No designated campsites are located on either Hug or Duck lakes, so you will need to press on to Zenith for the night, which has one campsite, or continue down the long portage to Alton.

Paddle and portage 5.75 miles from Zenith Lake to central Alton Lake, including a portage of 460 rods (L9) from Zenith to Lujenida Lake; paddle to Kelso Lake, and portage 10 rods (L1) from Kelso to Alton Lake. This journey will next send you across a long portage to Lujenida Lake. The 460-rod portage between Zenith and Lujenida begins with a long gradual uphill, after which the trail becomes rolling up and down. A fair number of canoeists take this route out of Sawbill Lake, so the trail is likely to be in decent shape. The early portion of the trail is fairly free of obstructions, and there should be few rocks causing you much trouble. After about 150 rods the trail will fork to the left and the right. The fork to the left leads to a swamp that will allow you to break the portage into smaller segments if water levels are high.

From Lujenida Lake, head south to the Kelso River, which is low lying and meanders through a sphagnum bog. Look for fascinating bog plants such as pitcher plants. Continuing on to Kelso Lake, head to the right (west) at the fork on the southern end of the lake, and you paddle past a campsite to a 10-rod portage to Alton Lake. The 10-rod portage is flat, following a well-traveled trail, and should be no problem to traverse. The landing on Lujenida is a bit rocky.

Alton is a big, relatively low-lying lake and provides you with a choice of sixteen designated campsites. Trout, northern pike, walleye, and bass are all located beneath its 1,000-plus acres. While sixteen campsites are plenty for most areas, the busy Sawbill Lake entry point is just an easy portage away, and it attracts large numbers of canoeists. You should get an early start to Alton if traveling in July or August.

Paddle and portage 6.5 miles from Alton Lake to Phoebe Lake, including portages of 147 rods (L4) from Alton to Beth Lake, 280 rods (L8) from Beth to Grace Lake, and four portages of 12 (L1), 22 (L3), 5 (L2), and 88 rods (L5) from Grace to Phoebe Lake. The easy 147-rod portage from Alton to Beth Lake receives frequent use, and the majority of the trail is level. It has a couple of plank footbridges over low areas and climbs a short, steep hill before leveling off again before the Beth Lake landing. When you go over the top of the hill, you are crossing the Laurentian Divide. Water falling on the south side of the divide eventually flows to the Atlantic Ocean by way of the Lake Superior drainage and St. Lawrence River. Water falling on the north side eventually drains into the Arctic Ocean by way of Hudson Bay.

Next, a 280-rod portage to Grace Lake rises and falls along the south shore of a marshy area. Don't be misled by your map; this portage is high and dry. If you are observant, you will notice that the exposed rock on this portage is much different from the rock surrounding Sawbill and Alton lakes. On Grace the rock is primarily a distinctly reddish granite, much different from the weathered gray gabbro you find in most of the southeastern Boundary Waters. According to the Minnesota Geological Survey, the gray rock underlying Sawbill and Alton was formed deep underground some 1.3 billion years ago by slowly cooling magma. Later, new flows of magma penetrated this gray rock, cooled, and formed the pink granite beneath Beth Lake and Grace Lake.

Take the 280-rod portage directly to Grace Lake rather than the 93-rod and 151-rod portages by way of Ella Lake. The longer portage appears to be more popular than the two shorter portages based on the condition of the trails. You don't save much distance by splitting the connection into two portages, you must deal with an extra load and unload of your canoe, and you have to canoe an extra mile and a half on Grace Lake to Phoebe. If you take the Ella Lake route, you will find the 93-rod portage is lower lying and less traveled than the 280-rod portage to the south. Expect significant amounts of mud along the trail. Ella Lake is peaceful, with a nice mixed forest and a fair number of young white pines surrounding the lake, particularly near the Grace Lake portage. The final, 147-rod portage to Grace from Ella Lake is fairly rocky, and portions of it are muddy. In addition, the landing on the Grace Lake side is rocky, all of which is why this route gets significantly less traffic than the single-portage southern route. Grace is a great place to camp for a night, a weekend, or a week. You have seven campsites to choose from and can jig for walleye or cast for northern pike.

When you leave Grace Lake, head down the Phoebe River to Phoebe Lake, taking four short portages along the way. The first portage starts on the western corner of Grace and is a flat, well-traveled path. The Phoebe River is very rocky, shallow, and slow moving most of the year. You will need to cautiously pick your path through this rocky obstacle course to the 22-rod portage, which is flat and dry most of the year. Continue along through a tamarack swamp past various bog plants to the 5-rod portage bypassing a 2-foot waterfall. On the upstream side you will notice an excellent exposure of dark gray gabbro that has been intruded by a subsequent lighter gray granitic rock. The intruding granite is readily apparent as inch-wide bands.

Next, an 88-rod portage to Phoebe has a few ups and downs but is generally not too strenuous. The most difficult portion is a short stretch where you must scurry down a rock face for a few feet. Exposures of intruded gabbro are also evident at numerous places. As you reach the Phoebe landing, a small waterfall cascades through the woods on your left. A trail leads to the falls, a great place to refresh yourself and soothe any mosquito bites you may have picked up along the way. Well-loved Phoebe Lake has eight campsites scattered across the west shore and on three islands. The depths of Phoebe are home to walleye and northern pike, and the shore is surrounded by an early growth forest of birch and aspen.

Paddle and portage 8.5 miles from Phoebe Lake to central Lake Polly, including portages of 144 rods (L6), 57 rods (L4), 28 rods (L2), 91 rods (L6), 14 rods (L1), and 97 rods (L4). To leave Phoebe, paddle through the channel on the north side of Phoebe and enter Knight Lake. The eastern shores of Knight are low lying and covered by a mixture of birch and spruce. Knight has a secluded little campsite on its small northern bay, where it might be worth spending a night if you are so inclined. From Knight, paddle up the peaceful Phoebe River until you see a portage on your left side. Stretches of the river are quite shallow, so keep alert for rocks. You will be passing through fine beaver country and should keep your eyes peeled for their signs. You will have no problem spotting beaver lodges along the way but should also look for less obvious marks such as skinned branches and matted-down grassy spots on the edge of the river where beavers have recently fed.

A 144-rod trail leads to Hazel Lake from Knight Lake and is fairly level and free of most obstacles as it passes through an aging aspen forest. Stretches of thick underbrush may make this portage feel somewhat overgrown and rugged if it has not been cleared recently. Head across Hazel Lake, or spend an evening at one of the three designated campsites.

You next travel by way of the Phoebe River to Lake Polly. Five portages must be crossed along the way. The 57-rod portage starts at a clear rock landing just to the right of the spot where the Phoebe River starts its journey from Hazel Lake. The portage covers a smooth flat trail and soon winds down to the right and drops abruptly to a gravel landing. The Phoebe River then broadens out through a tamarack swamp. Interesting glacial erratics deposited in the last ice age stick up from the riverbed at various points.

Continue through shallow pools to the 28-rod portage, which is also flat and well traveled. The 91-rod portage climbs a very gradual hill before once again dropping down to the river. The 14-rod portage bypasses a short series of non-navigable rapids. Expect a simple portage with only a few exposed roots and rocks. The upstream landing is a bit challenging because you will be scampering up an inclined rock face. The final portage is a straight 97-rod path through a spruce forest before a descent to a rocky landing on Lake Polly.

Paddle and portage 6.5 miles back to your starting point on Kawishiwi Lake, including portages of 95 rods (L5), 189 rods (L7), 11 rods (L2), and 15 to 20 rods (L2). Your return journey requires simply backtracking the way you traveled to Polly. Your return will be a bit more difficult than your arrival because you will have a noticeable climb up the 189-rod portage from Townline Lake to Kawasachong Lake.

Entry Point 38, Sawbill Lake (Map 31)

> Daily permit quota: 14
> Permit availability: Difficult

Sawbill Lake is a bustling center of canoeing activity every summer and certainly the most active entry point in the southeastern Boundary Waters. Not only is Sawbill a popular BWCAW entry, but it has a large public campground and the well-established

Sawbill Canoe Outfitters, both of which draw campers who also use neighboring entry points.

Sawbill Lake is an excellent destination in its own right and gives ready access to Alton Lake, a large lake just west of Sawbill. From these two lakes it is possible to plan numerous excellent routes, including one-way trips west to Kawishiwi Lake or east to Baker and Brule lakes. Good loops can also be crafted to include Lake Polly, Malberg, Little Saganaga, and Cherokee lakes, as well as longer loops to other interior lakes.

Three routes are described below. First is an easy trip to Alton Lake, suitable for all skill levels and great for a weekend or a week (Route 38A). Second is a popular loop directly north to wonderful Cherokee Lake and then on to the Temperance lakes and south to Kelly Lake, before heading west over Flame and Smoke lakes back to Sawbill (Route 38B). Third is a challenging loop west toward Lake Polly and then north to remote interior lakes before descending south through Lujenida, Kelso, and Alton (Route 38C). This third route partially travels through a chain of lakes that sees relatively few visitors but also has some quite tough portages, making it best suited for experienced campers. Also, do not hesitate to design your own route if the ones described don't suit your fancy. The three routes described cover all of the major route segments out of Sawbill, and descriptions of more distant lakes and portages can be found by consulting the index.

If you design your own route out of Sawbill, keep the long portage from Lujenida to Zenith Lake in mind (northwest of Sawbill). This portage is one of the longest in the Boundary Waters, but it has a reasonably good trail and can sometimes be broken into a couple smaller segments. This length appears to dissuade most visitors, who prefer the easier travel west of Beth Lake or toward Cherokee Lake. If you include this long portage in your route, you will be sure to leave most other visitors behind as you head to lakes such as Mug, Dent, and Wine. The other three exits from Alton and Sawbill are west to Beth Lake, north to Ada Lake on the way to Cherokee Lake, and east to Smoke Lake. All three of these exits are quite popular and have good, well-maintained portages.

To get to Sawbill Lake, take the Sawbill Trail (County Road 2) from its start on Highway 61 at the town of Tofte about 23 miles to its end at Sawbill Lake. A good place to pick up your permit is at the ranger station in Tofte, or you can also get it from Sawbill Canoe Outfitters. A fine place to spend a night is at the campground on the south end of Sawbill Lake. It has fifty campsites, does not accept reservations, and charges a fee. The campsite rarely is full, and extra room can be made along the edges to stay.

Route 38A: Exploration of Alton Lake (Map 31)

> Difficulty: easy
> Number of days: 2 or more
> Total miles (approx.): 3 or more
> Number of portages: 2

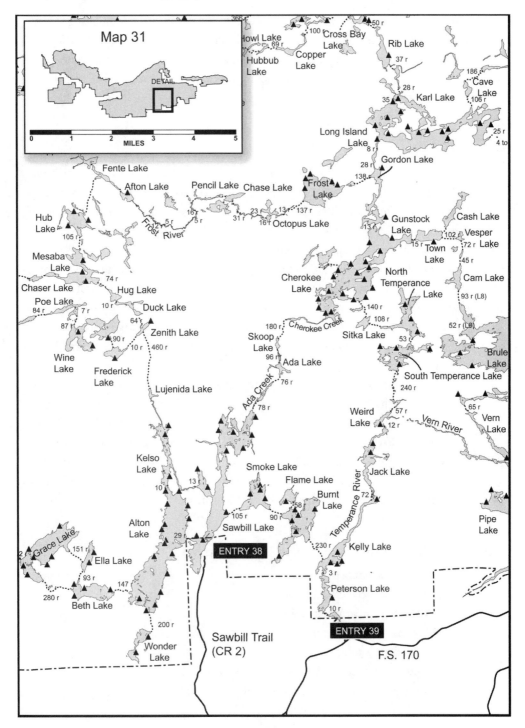

Total portage rods: 58
Greatest portage difficulty: 29 rods (L2)
Navigation maps: Voyageur 8
                  Fisher F5
                  McKenzie 20, 21

This route will appeal to anyone interested in a less physically demanding journey than most trips described in this guide. It is about as easy as BWCAW trips get, having just one short portage, which you will take twice. The ease of this route makes it ideal for someone traveling with limited physical ability or small children, or anyone simply seeking a route with minimal difficulty.

Detailed Route

Paddle and portage about 1.5 miles from the Sawbill boat access to central Alton Lake, including a portage of 29 rods (L2). This short trip is confined to travel through Sawbill and Alton lakes. You won't be disappointed spending a few days exploring these two lakes. The portage to Alton is very well maintained and easy to find. It should be in decent shape year-round.

Alton Lake is big and relatively low lying, and provides you with a choice of sixteen designated campsites. Northern pike, walleye, and bass are all located beneath its 1,000-plus acres. While sixteen campsites are plenty for most areas, the busy Sawbill entry point is just a portage away, and Alton attracts large numbers of canoeists. You would be well advised to get an early start to Alton if traveling in July or August.

You can make a nice day trip by paddling a loop north to Kelso Lake and then around through Sawbill back to Alton again. Also, the portage from Lujenida to Zenith Lake, being well over a mile in length, can make for a pleasant hike to stretch your legs, spot wildflowers, or perhaps cross paths with a grouse or two. Look at Route 38C to learn more about the many fine lakes to the west and north of Alton.

Paddle and portage 1.5 miles back to Sawbill, taking the 29-rod portage from Alton to Sawbill. Simply return to Sawbill Lake the same way you came.

Route 38B: Loop through Cherokee Lake (Map 31)

        Difficulty: intermediate
        Number of days: 3 or more
        Total miles (approx.): 23
        Number of portages: 14
        Total portage rods: 1,156
        Greatest portage difficulty: 230 rods (L10)
        Navigation maps: Voyageur 8
                        Fisher F5, F6, F12
                        McKenzie 7, 20, 21

This loop circles northeast from Sawbill to Cherokee Lake and then down along the Temperance River to Kelly Lake and back to Sawbill. This 23-mile journey is a great trip that will produce memories for a lifetime. It is probably a bit aggressive for people without wilderness canoeing experience, but well-outfitted visitors with a trip or two under their belts will enjoy this little expedition.

Detailed Route

Paddle and portage 9 miles from Sawbill Lake to Cherokee Lake, including portages of 78 rods (L4) from Sawbill to Ada Creek, 76 rods (L4) from Ada Creek to Ada Lake, 96 rods (L5) from Ada Lake to Skoop Lake, and 180 rods (L7) from Skoop to Cherokee Creek. The first leg of this journey is along a popular route to Cherokee Lake. The first portage, 78 rods from Sawbill Lake to Ada Creek, is relatively flat, free of obstructions, and well traveled because it is a main gateway out of the busy Sawbill entry point. The 76-rod portage from Ada Creek to Ada Lake is also not too difficult.

Next you will cover a 96-rod portage between Ada Lake and Skoop Lake. This portage was historically a long, muddy, nasty trail, but in recent years it was modified by the Forest Service to be longer but much less muddy. If you have an old map, it might show two separate portages connected by a small marsh. In recent years this marsh became impassable after loss of a beaver dam, and the two shorter portages were joined to become the current 96-rod portage. It might be possible during high water to take this long portage as two shorter carries. Finally, a 180-rod portage leads from Skoop Lake to Cherokee Creek. You will find few Boundary Waters portages as clear as this path. Small footbridges have been constructed across the few low areas along the trail, making this a great all-weather crossing even though it has frequent short hills along the way. Paddle down Cherokee Creek until you arrive at the heart of Cherokee Lake.

Cherokee Lake holds a special place in the hearts of many visitors to the BWCAW. Its large, island-studded surface includes nineteen designated campsites, and easy extended route connections can be made to four neighboring lakes. Cherokee hosts an average northern pike population and some lake trout, although walleye are absent according to Minnesota DNR lake surveys. Cherokee is a popular destination for visitors from Sawbill Lake and Brule Lake, so don't expect complete solitude along its shores. Fortunately, the many bays and islands give a great feeling of isolation.

Paddle and portage 3.5 miles from Cherokee Lake to South Temperance Lake, including portages of 140 rods (L8) from Cherokee to Sitka Lake, 108 rods (L5) from Sitka to North Temperance Lake, and 53 rods (L3) from North Temperance to South Temperance Lake. The 140-rod portage from Cherokee to Sitka will get your heart pumping with hill climbs and a bit of fancy footwork on a quite rocky path. Still, this long carry is just a bit harder than average for a portage of this length.

Next, the portage to North Temperance Lake will come as a pleasant surprise after you have carried to Sitka from Cherokee. Not only is it almost a third shorter, but the trail is relatively flat, free of rocks, and is likely to be dry most of the year. Finally, the portage from North Temperance to South Temperance is a relatively easy 53-rod trail that poses few obstacles other than the fact that you are likely to have little solitude much of the year—this is a busy trail on a busy route. Either of the two Temperance lakes makes a nice place to spend an evening or two.

Paddle and portage 6 miles from South Temperance Lake to Kelly Lake, including portages of 240 rods (L8) from South Temperance to a pool in the Temperance River, 57 rods (L5) from the pool to Weird Lake, 12 rods (L2) from Weird to Jack Lake, and 72 rods (L3 to L5) from Jack to Kelly Lake. The 240-rod portage from South Temperance Lake is the longest on this route and follows one of the flattest and smoothest paths. The east side of the trail still bears evidence of a forest fire from 1996 and provides a great chance to view the natural regeneration and growth of the forest.

The final three portages are all relatively short. The 57-rod portage is easy and along a nice trail, but it has a few low spots that are likely to be muddy in spring. The 12-rod portage from Weird Lake to Jack Lake is not difficult and provides plenty of opportunities to relax along the shore of the stream between them. The 72-rod portage from Jack Lake to Kelly Lake is flat and well traveled. However, expect a bit of mud during the spring and after heavy rains, significantly increasing the portage's difficulty during such times.

Paddle and portage 4.5 miles from Kelly Lake to Sawbill Lake, including portages of 230 rods (L10) from Kelly to Burnt Lake, 90 rods (L6) from Burnt to Smoke Lake, and 105 rods (L6) from Smoke to Sawbill Lake. All portages are not created equal, and the 230-rod portage from Kelly to Burnt was created tough. The trail rises over 100 feet above Kelly Lake along a series of ups and downs. Although well-maintained, it is a challenging carry. Once you are on Burnt you should be able to stop and spend the night at one of the six designated campsites. An average difficulty trail leads from Burnt Lake to Smoke Lake, although it is a bit low lying. The portage from Smoke to Sawbill is relatively easy, although the Smoke Lake landing is also low lying.

Route 38C: Loop through Phoebe Lake, Malberg Lake,
and Louse Creek (Map 31)

> Difficulty: challenging
> Number of days: 5 or more
> Total miles (approx.): 40
> Number of portages: 38
> Total portage rods: 2,764
> Greatest portage difficulty: 460 (L9)
> Navigation maps: Voyageur 7, 8
> > Fisher F5, F11, F12
> > McKenzie 7, 8, 20, 21

This interesting, high-quality route will appeal to people who like to see as many lakes as possible. A significant part of this journey is through remote interior lakes that get very few visitors, so expect some of the finest solitude available near Sawbill

Lake. This route is best covered by fit, experienced canoeists because it involves a number of very challenging portages.

Map 31 shows most of this route, and Map 30 shows western portions. In addition, an overview of the entire route is shown on Map 29.

Detailed Route

Paddle and portage 1.5 miles from the Sawbill landing to central Alton Lake, including a portage of 29 rods (L2). The portage to Alton is well used and easy to find. It should be in decent shape year-round. Alton makes a fine place to spend an evening or two.

Paddle and portage 6.5 miles from Alton Lake to Phoebe Lake, including portages of 147 rods (L4) from Alton to Beth Lake, 280 rods (L8) from Beth to Grace Lake, and four portages of 12 (L1), 22 (L3), 5 (L2), and 88 rods (L5) to Phoebe Lake. Alton Lake is big and relatively low lying, and provides you with a choice of sixteen designated campsites. Northern pike, walleye, and bass are all located beneath its 1,000-plus acres. The easy portage from Alton to Beth Lake receives frequent use. The trail is mostly level, with a couple of plank footbridges over low areas, and climbs a short, steep hill before leveling off again near the Beth Lake landing. When you go over the top of the hill, you are crossing the Laurentian Divide. Rain falling on the south side of the divide eventually flows into the Atlantic Ocean by way of the Lake Superior drainage and St. Lawrence River. Water falling on the north side eventually drains into the Arctic Ocean by way of Hudson Bay.

Beth is a clear-water lake of approximately 180 acres, with a maximum depth of 20 feet. Big hills rise up on the south shore and are much taller than most hills that you will come across in this portion of the BWCAW. A 280-rod portage from Beth to Grace Lake rises and falls along the south shore of a marshy area. Don't be misled by topographic lines on your map—this portage is high and dry. If you are observant, you will notice that the exposed rock on this portage is much different from the rock surrounding Sawbill and Alton lakes. The rock is distinctly reddish granite, much different from the gray gabbro you find in most of the southeastern Boundary Waters. According to the Minnesota Geological Survey, the gray rock underlying Sawbill and Alton was formed deep underground some 1.3 billion years ago by slowly cooling magma. Later, new flows of magma penetrated this gray rock, cooled, and formed the pink granite beneath Beth Lake and Grace Lake.

I recommend that you take the 280-rod portage directly to Grace Lake rather than the 93-rod and 151-rod portages by way of Ella Lake. You don't save much distance by splitting the connection into two portages, you must deal with an extra load and unload of your canoe, and you have to canoe an extra mile and a half on Grace Lake to Phoebe. If you take the Ella Lake route, you will find the 93-rod portage is much lower lying and less traveled than the 280-rod portage. Expect significant amounts of mud along the trail. Ella Lake is peaceful with a nice mixed forest and a fair number of young white pines surrounding the lake, particularly near the Grace

Lake portage. The final, 147-rod portage to Grace from Ella Lake is fairly rocky, and portions of it are muddy. In addition, the landing on the Grace Lake side is rocky, all of which is why this segment appears to get significantly less traffic than the single-portage southern route.

Grace Lake is a great place to camp for a night, a weekend, or longer. You have seven campsites to choose from and can fish for walleye or northern pike. When you leave Grace Lake, you will head down the Phoebe River to Phoebe Lake, taking four short portages along the way. The first portage, 12 rods long, starts on the western corner of Grace and follows a flat, well-traveled path. The Phoebe River is very rocky, shallow, and slow moving most of the year. You will need to cautiously pick your path through this obstacle course to the second portage, which is a flat, typically dry 22-rod carry. Continue through a tamarack swamp past various bog plants to a 5-rod portage bypassing a 2-foot waterfall. On the upstream side you will notice an excellent exposure of dark gray gabbro that has been intruded by a subsequent lighter gray granitic rock. The intruding granite is readily apparent as inch-wide bands.

Finally, an 88-rod portage to Phoebe has a few ups and downs but is generally not too strenuous. The most difficult portion is a short stretch where you must scurry down a rock face for a few feet. Exposures of intruded gabbro bedrock are evident at numerous places. As you reach the Phoebe landing, a small waterfall cascades through the woods on your left. A trail leads back to the falls and is a great place to refresh yourself and soothe any mosquito bites you may have picked up along the way. Phoebe Lake has eight designated campsites scattered across the west shore and on three islands. The depths of Phoebe are home to walleye and northern pike, and the shore is surrounded by an early growth forest of birch and aspen.

Paddle and portage 8 miles from Phoebe Lake to Lake Polly, including portages of 144 rods (L6), 57 rods (L4), 28 rods (L2), 91 rods (L6), 14 rods (L1), and 97 rods (L4). To leave Phoebe, paddle through the channel on the north shore and enter Knight Lake. The eastern shores of Knight are low lying and covered by a mixture of birch and spruce. Paddle up the peaceful Phoebe River until you see a portage on your left side. Stretches of the river are quite shallow, so keep alert for rocks. You will be passing through fine beaver country and should keep your eyes peeled for their signs. You will have no problem spotting beaver lodges along the way, but you should also look for less obvious marks such as skinned branches and matted-down grassy spots on the edge of the river.

The 144-rod trail to Hazel Lake is fairly level and free of most obstacles. Stretches of fairly thick underbrush may make it feel somewhat overgrown and rugged if it has not been cleared recently. Head across Hazel Lake, or spend an evening at one of the three designated campsites available for your use.

You next travel by way of the Phoebe River to Lake Polly. Five portages must be crossed along the way. The 57-rod portage starts at a clear rock landing just to the right of the spot where the Phoebe River starts its journey from Hazel Lake. The portage covers a smooth, flat trail and soon winds down to the right and drops abruptly to a gravel landing. The Phoebe River then broadens out through a tamarack swamp.

Interesting glacial erratics deposited in the last ice age stick up from the riverbed at various points.

Continue through shallow pools to the 28-rod portage, which is also flat and well traveled. Next, a 91-rod portage climbs a gradual hill before once again dropping down to the river. The 14-rod portage bypasses a short series of non-navigable rapids. Expect a simple portage with only a few exposed roots and rocks. The upstream landing is a bit challenging because you will be scampering up an inclined rock face. The final portage is a straight 97-rod path through a spruce forest before a descent to a rocky landing on Lake Polly.

Beautiful Lake Polly is another wonderful lake on this great route. Dozens of islands dot its surface, and it has fifteen designated campsites. Arrive early because many visitors entering from Kawishiwi Lake make Polly their destination after their first day of paddling. Walleye and northern pike inhabit these depths, and even sunfish can be caught, according to Minnesota DNR lake surveys.

Paddle and portage 3.75 miles from Lake Polly to Malberg Lake, including portages of 21 rods (L1) and 48 rods (L3), and then 113 rods (L5) to Koma Lake, and 24 rods from Koma to Malberg Lake. The trip to Malberg is along an excellent stretch of good portages. The first, 21-rod portage is flat and wide, bypassing rapids. Head across the small pool to the 48-rod portage, which is also fairly flat and wide open, having just a few obstructions and two good landings. Point your canoe north, and continue across another pool in the Kawishiwi to a 113-rod portage to Koma Lake. This portage is easy considering its length, with a path that climbs over a slight hill and then descends along the side of the river before gradually climbing another hill and making the final descent to Koma. Finally, a 24-rod portage leads from Koma to Malberg Lake. Malberg is known as a good walleye lake, as are the dark waters of Polly and Koma leading to Malberg. A quick look at a map of this area shows that Malberg is in a commanding crossroads location in the south-central BWCAW.

Paddle and portage 5 miles from Malberg Lake to Trail Lake, including portages of 16 rods, 10 rods, 14 rods, 50 rods, 90 rods, 20 rods, 47 rods, 56 rods, and 21 rods. You will now venture into the fantastic interior of the Boundary Waters. If you have packed light and well, you will find this stretch interesting and enjoy the rhythm of alternating short stretches of paddling and portaging. If you have packed too much gear and packed it poorly, then this stretch will be interesting but for different reasons. The Louse River gets relatively few visitors and has prime habitat for moose and many other north-woods animals.

You will start this leg with the 16-rod portage to Frond Creek, which is mismarked on some commercial maps of the area. The correct location for the start of the portage is in a little bay just south of a campsite. An apparent landing on the south side of the bay is the beginning of an old portage route and has now grown over. Instead, canoe a few rods into the bay and find the landing on your right. During periods of sufficient water you will be able to paddle upstream for the few rods of shallow water.

Frond Creek travels through a number of beautiful small pools and narrow channels. Portions of the creek are fairly shallow, and you may need to push your canoe through a number of stretches. Frond Lake is a small but scenic and secluded expanse of water. Next you will come to 10-rod and 14-rod portages. The 10-rod portage is on the north bank of the creek, while the 14-rod portage is on the south bank. Both portages climb up steep inclines and then drop down steep declines. Soon thereafter you will come to a 50-rod portage that follows a trail relatively free of obstructions, but don't be surprised if it is slightly overgrown because this stretch receives relatively little traffic. The 90-rod portage puts in upstream from the rapids, which you have just bypassed. In front of you will be a classic tamarack-spruce swamp. Notice along the grassy shores an abundance of tamarack trees and, farther in, the spindly spruce. If you haven't yet had a chance to spot a carnivorous pitcher plant, this is a perfect opportunity.

Pressing on, a 20-rod portage goes up the right side of the creek where it becomes too narrow to paddle. The portage receives infrequent use relative to other portages in this vicinity. The next portage is 47 rods up a gradual incline. The real challenge on this portage, however, is the fact that it is infrequently used and therefore likely to be both somewhat overgrown and occasionally blocked by downed trees. You will follow up with a 56-rod portage passing to the north of another low spot in the stream, and a 21-rod portage dropping to Trail Lake, which has two designated campsites.

Paddle and portage 6 miles from Trail Lake to Wine Lake, including portages of 125 rods (L7), 60 rods (L5), 129 rods (L7), 145 rods (L9), 84 rods (L8), 7 rods (L3), and 87 rods (L7). The first portage you will take is 125 rods, crossing a generally flat trail with a few rocky spots along the way. Halfway through you will have to scamper down an inclined rock face into a little gully and then back up the other side. This rock is likely to be slippery when wet. Paddle ahead and you will come to a 60-rod portage. Be careful not to miss it: turn to the right (east) where the river forks both left and right. If you paddle too far, you will head to Tool Lake and need to backtrack to the portage. This portage begins with a steep uphill for the first 15 rods and then flattens out before beginning a more gradual climb to a large flat rock landing at the head of a series of rapids.

Continue on and take the 129-rod portage to Bug Lake. This portage also begins with a steep uphill that tapers off but continues at a substantially uphill pace for much of the way. The low water and rapids that you are avoiding will be to your left. The rapids drop a substantial distance over the length of this portage, and you may wish to backtrack after dropping off your gear to give them a second look.

Next, a 145-rod portage leads to Louse Lake. This portage is no yellow brick road. At least two-thirds of the trail is through a field of boulders ranging from toaster size to washing-machine size. These boulders are piled on top of one another to create the trail along the left bank of the river. Grasses have grown up between many of the boulders, so it is not always possible to tell exactly where to find firm footing. This portage will give you a vivid feeling of what it must be like for an ant to scurry along a gravel pile—especially an ant carrying a crumb half its weight over its head, if you are carrying a canoe. Much of the trail that is not covered by boulders is covered by mud. Good luck.

After hiking the boulder-strewn portage to Louse Lake, you will take an 84-rod portage from Louse to Poe Lake. This portage is similar but shorter than the portage from Bug Lake to Louse Lake. Most of the trail follows the north side of the creek running between the two lakes. You will find the going rocky, although not much of it should be muddy. A short stretch in the middle has a small intermittent stream entering from the north that may create a mud pool at that location. This is not a route on which you will want to make repeat portages. Poe Lake, like most lakes on this route, has substantial numbers of birch and jack pine along its shore. No designated campsites are located on Poe, so push on in the direction of Wine Lake.

From Poe Lake you take a short portage south toward Mug Lake. This portage is mismarked on some old maps. To find the proper location just paddle along the south shore of Poe until you hear the water percolating through from Mug Lake. You have to scamper up the rocks and put in at a beaver dam, which has an elevation approximately 10 feet higher than Poe Lake. Mug Lake is a jewel in the rough. The shore on most sides is covered by exposed rock sloping up approximately 20 feet. In the southwest corner, a small waterfall cascades 20 feet down an exposed rock face into a little pool.

The last leg of this trip is an 87-rod portage from Mug Lake to Wine Lake. The trail begins with a very steep climb of which the first 2 rods are a scramble over a broken rock face. The trail continues upward for another 15 rods, flattens out, and follows the side of a small swamp before descending to Wine Lake. Wine is very pretty and has noticeably more old pines and spruce than the other lakes leading to it. Three designated campsites can be found on the lake. Wine Lake and its neighbors are probably among the least visited lakes in the eastern BWCAW, making for some of the most remote country in an already remote wilderness.

Paddle and portage 9 miles from Wine Lake to Sawbill Lake, including portages of 90 rods from Wine to Frederick Lake, 10 rods from Frederick to Zenith Lake, and 460 rods (L9) from Zenith to Lujenida Lake; paddle to Kelso, and portage 10 rods from Kelso to Alton Lake, and 13 rods from Alton to Sawbill Lake. You will now head south to reconnect to Sawbill Lake. The 90-rod portage leading to Frederick Lake begins with a sharp uphill and then flattens out. The portage is not heavily traveled and is otherwise unremarkable. From the eastern shore of Frederick, a 10-rod portage leads to a channel connecting to Zenith. This portage is mismarked on many older maps. It follows along the right side of the channel and bypasses two beaver dams and a stretch of low water.

The 460-rod portage between Zenith Lake and Lujenida Lake begins with a gradual uphill, after which the trail becomes rolling up and down for a long stretch. The early portion of the trail is generally free of obstructions, and there should be few rocks causing you trouble. After another 30 rods the trail forks to the left and the right. The fork to the left leads to a swamp and is a shortcut that can cut a bit off the portage distance, although you will still have to portage again later.

From Lujenida Lake head south to the Kelso River. The Kelso River is low lying and meanders through a bog. Look along the shore for interesting bog plants such as pitcher plants and sundews. Continuing on to Kelso Lake, head to the right (west) at the fork on the southern end of the lake. You will paddle past a campsite to a 10-rod portage to Alton Lake. Finally, take an easy 3-rod portage to Sawbill Lake, and paddle back to your starting location.

Entry Point 39, Baker Lake (Map 32)

Daily permit quota: 3
Permit availability: moderate

Baker Lake is another fine entry to the south-central Boundary Waters and is well suited for a first trip into the Boundary Waters because it allows exploration and camping with a few easy portages. If you want to make a long journey out of Baker Lake, you will need to take at least one lengthy, challenging portage.

Two routes are described below starting at Baker Lake. The first is a simple and easy trip (Route 39A) north to explore Kelly and Baker lakes. The second route is a longer loop to Cherokee Lake (Route 39B). This route is similar to Route 38B, but it circles the loop in the opposite direction. In addition, Baker is a half-day's travel from Sawbill Lake to the west (Entry Point 38) and about a day's travel from Brule Lake to the east (Entry Point 41), making many routes from these two entries natural extensions out of Baker. Indeed, you can easily extend Route 39A into a much longer journey by adding western loops (Route 38A), northern loops (Route 38C), and eastern loops (Route 41B).

To reach Baker Lake, take the Sawbill Trail for about 17 miles from Tofte on Lake Superior until you come to the junction of Forest Service Road 170, which you take northeast for another 4.75 miles until you see a turnoff on the left for Baker Lake, which is just down a short spur road that will drop you at a small parking lot.

A good place to spend a night before entering the wilderness is at the small Baker Lake campground at the entry point, although its five campsites cannot be reserved in advance and may not be available on busy summer weekends. Otherwise, head over to Sawbill Lake campground on Sawbill Lake, about 11 miles by road to the west. Sawbill Canoe Outfitters are located adjacent to the campground and are a good place to rent anything from tents to canoes. They also provide a shuttle service to and from Baker Lake and other area entry points.

Route 39A: Exploration of Burnt Lake (Map 32)

Difficulty: easy to moderate
Number of days: 2 or more
Total miles (approx.): 7

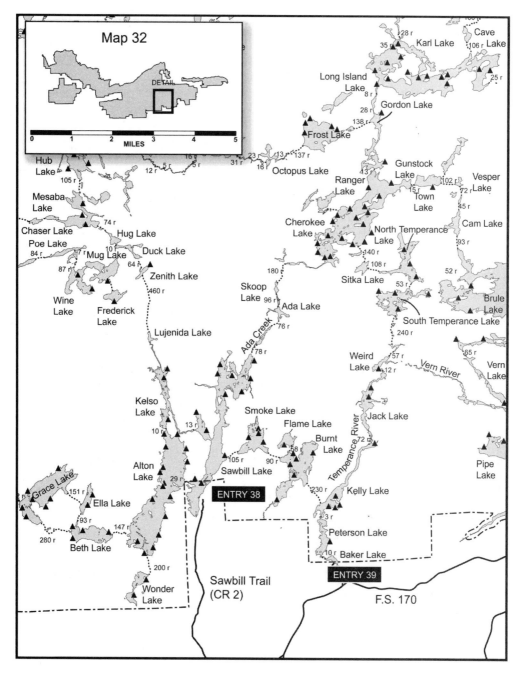

Number of portages: 6
Total portage rods: 486
Greatest portage difficulty: 230 rods (L10)
Navigation maps: Voyageur 8
                   Fisher F6
                   McKenzie 21

This route travels from Baker Lake to Peterson Lake and then to Burnt Lake. This trip into the southern Boundary Waters provides a nice weekend retreat. Depending on where you decide to stop, you will travel across a long, strenuous portage, although this can be avoided by slightly shortening the trip.

Detailed Route

Put in at Baker Lake, and paddle and portage 2 miles to Peterson and Kelly lakes, including portages of 10 rods (L1) and 3 rods (L1). You should have no problem portaging over either of the two portages to Kelly Lake. Peterson Lake has one designated campsite, and Kelly has four. Any of these five sites make a nice place to spend one or more nights. This route next heads to Burnt Lake, but you might consider staying on Kelly Lake if you are happy with your campsite and want to avoid the 230-rod portage to Burnt.

Paddle and portage 1.5 miles from Kelly Lake to Burnt Lake, including a 230-rod portage (L10). All portages are not created equal, and this one was created tough. The trail rises over 100 feet above Kelly Lake along a series of ups and downs. Although well-traveled, it is a challenging carry. Fortunately, once you are on Burnt you should be able to stop and spend the night at one of the six designated campsites.

Paddle and portage 3.5 miles back to Baker Lake, including portages of 230 rods (L10), 3 rods (L1), and 10 rods (L1). Your return trip out of Burnt Lake is simply the reverse of your journey in from Baker Lake.

Route 39B: Cherokee Lake Loop (Map 32)

Difficulty: easy to intermediate
Number of days: 4
Total miles (approx.): 26
Number of portages: 18
Total portage rods: 1,563
Greatest portage difficulty: 230 rods (L10)
Navigation maps: Voyageur 8, 9
                        Fisher F5, F12
                        McKenzie 4, 7, 21

This route is a natural loop out of the Baker Lake entry, heading north to Cherokee Lake, then southwest to Sawbill before returning east to the start on Baker. You will not find better scenery anywhere in the BWCAW. The areas you will visit are accessible from a number of different entry points, so this route is well traveled during the peak of summer visitors. Nevertheless, this is a very high-quality loop and a good introductory trip in the BWCAW for experienced campers.

Detailed Route

> *Put in at Baker Lake, and paddle and portage 1.5 miles to Peterson and Kelly lakes, including portages of 10 rods (L1) and 3 rods (L1).* You should have no problem portaging over either of the two portages to Kelly Lake. If you do, then immediately turn around and head back to your car, because this trip will get much tougher.

Once on Kelly Lake you can stay at one of its four designated campsites, all clustered along the south shore. Otherwise, head north toward Jack Lake, paddling through a long, lazy stretch of beautiful water. The northern half of Kelly Lake is rich in wild rice beds. Although shallow, the narrow central channel should normally provide plenty of space and depth for canoe travel except during the driest of years. Paddling through this watery meadow is a wonderful contrast to the rocky shores and islands you will see later on this trip as you reach the Temperance lakes and Cherokee, and one of the reasons this route is such a good introduction to the border country.

> *Paddle and portage 6 miles from Kelly Lake to South Temperance Lake, including portages of 72 rods (L3-5) from Kelly Lake to Jack Lake, 12 rods (L2) from Jack to Weird Lake, 57 rods (L5) from Weird to a small pond, and 240 rods (L8) from the pond to South Temperance Lake.* After paddling to the north end of Kelly Lake, you will cross four portages to reach South Temperance Lake. The first three portages are all relatively short: the portage from Kelly Lake to Jack Lake is flat and well traveled. However, expect a bit of mud during spring and after heavy rains, which significantly increases the portage's difficulty.

The 12-rod portage from Jack Lake to Weird Lake is not difficult and provides plenty of opportunities to relax along the shores of the stream between them. The 57-rod portage you will take from Weird Lake is relatively easy and along a nice trail, but it has a few low spots that are likely to be muddy in spring. Finally, you will take the 240-rod portage to South Temperance Lake. This portage is the longest on this route and fortunately one of the flattest and smoothest paths. The east side of the trail still bears evidence of the fire of summer 1996 and provides a great chance to view the natural regeneration and growth of the forest.

As you plan your trip, you might be tempted to map out a bushwhacking excursion from Weird Lake to Vern Lake. Looking at most maps, this doesn't seem like a bad idea, because a small stream seems to connect the two lakes. In reality this area is all but impassable. With enough time (probably most of a day) it is perhaps possible to portage to Vern, but not without serious struggle, scratched arms, and possibly injury.

> *Paddle and portage 4 miles from South Temperance Lake to Cherokee Lake, including portages of 53 rods (L4) from South Temperance Lake to North Temperance Lake, and 108 rods (L6) and 140 rods (L7) to Cherokee Lake.* The 53-rod portage between the two Temperance lakes is another relatively easy trail that poses few obstacles other than the fact that you are likely to have little solitude much of the year—this

is a busy trail on a busy route because these lakes are reachable from three directions. The 108-rod carry from North Temperance to Sitka Lake is relatively flat, free of rocks, and also likely to be mud-free most of the year. In contrast, the 140-rod portage from Sitka to Cherokee will get the heart pumping with hill climbs and a bit of fancy footwork on the frequently rocky path.

Cherokee Lake holds a special place in the hearts of many visitors to the BWCAW. Its large, island-studded surface includes nineteen designated campsites, and easy extended route connections can be made to four neighboring lakes. Cherokee hosts an average northern pike population and some lake trout, although walleye are absent according to Minnesota DNR lake surveys. This route will take you out the southwest end of Cherokee Lake on to Cherokee Creek. If you want an additional diversion, a loop can be made to Brule Lake by way of Cam and Vesper lakes, but this excursion is very difficult due to the infrequent use of these portages and their extremely rocky conditions. Most portages from Town Lake through Vesper and Cam to Brule are quite rugged and exceedingly rocky. You can also head out the north through Gordon Lake to Long Island, as described in Route 41B.

Paddle and portage 8 miles from Cherokee Lake through Cherokee Creek and on to Sawbill Lake, including portages of 180 rods (L7), 96 rods, 76 rods, and 78 rods. A 180-rod (L7) portage leads from Cherokee Creek to Skoop Lake. You will find few Boundary Waters portages as clear as the path south from Cherokee Creek to Skoop. Small footbridges have been constructed across the few low areas along the trail, making this a great all-weather crossing even though it has frequent short hills along the way.

The 96-rod portage between Ada and Skoop was historically a long, muddy, nasty trail, but in recent years it was modified by the Forest Service to become longer but much less muddy. A 76-rod portage next heads to Ada Creek, followed by a 78-rod portage to Sawbill Lake. This portage from Ada Creek to Sawbill Lake is relatively flat, free of obstructions, and well traveled.

Sawbill Lake lies on the southern edge of the BWCAW and gets relatively heavy visitor use because it serves as a major gateway to the wilderness. You will certainly run across other visitors on Sawbill because as many as thirteen permits per day are issued to enter there, and many of these permits are used by visitors interested in exploring the numerous interesting lakes readily accessible from Sawbill.

Paddle and portage 4.5 miles from Sawbill Lake to Kelly Lake, including portages of 105 rods (L6) from Sawbill to Smoke Lake, 90 rods (L6) from Smoke to Burnt Lake, and 230 rods (L10) from Burnt to Kelly Lake. The portage from Sawbill to Smoke is relatively easy, although the Smoke Lake landing is a bit low lying. An average difficulty trail leads from Smoke Lake to Burnt Lake, although it is also a bit low lying. The real challenge in this segment is from Burnt Lake to Kelly Lake along probably the hardest portage of this route. The trail rises and falls along a series of ups and downs. Although well-traveled, it is a challenging carry. Of course, by this stage in the journey you will have worked out the bugs in your portage skills, so it will not be as taxing as it would have been at the start of the trip.

Paddle and portage 2 miles from Kelly Lake to Baker Lake, including portages of 3 rods (L1) and 10 rods (L1). Your return trip out of Burnt Lake is simply the reverse of your journey in from Baker Lake.

Entry Point 40, Homer Lake (Map 33)

Daily permit quota: 2
Permit availability: moderate

Entry Point 40, Homer Lake, is a gateway to a fascinating area of narrow lakes and lush wildlife. Homer provides a wonderful introduction to the Boundary Waters and allows you to take a minimum number of portages to very interesting, beautiful areas. Depending on your desires, you can seek out peaceful Pipe Lake or journey through the narrows of Vern and Juno lakes to the big water of Brule Lake. Homer is only partially within the Boundary Waters, and the large eastern side is open to motorboats without limits on entry numbers or motor size.

To get to Homer, take County Road 4 (the Caribou Highway) for 19 miles from its start on Highway 61 along Lake Superior until you reach a T at Forest Service Road 170. Turn left onto 170, and take it 3 miles until you reach Forest Service Road 326, and turn right. Continue down 326 for 4 miles until you see a sign directing you to the Homer Lake boat access and parking lot on your left.

A number of campgrounds are located in the general vicinity of Homer Lake for spending a night before entering the BWCAW, although none of them is really close. Two good options are to stay at the Sawbill Lake campground to the west, or at the Two Island Lake campground to the east. Both campgrounds have over three dozen spaces, both charge a nominal camping fee, and neither takes advance reservations.

Route 40A: Exploration of Pipe Lake (Map 33)

Difficulty: easy
Number of days: 2 or more
Total miles (approx.): 9
Number of portages: 8
Total portage rods: 68
Greatest portage difficulty: 20 (L2)
Navigation maps: Voyageur 9
Fisher F6
McKenzie 21

If you are looking for peace and quiet on your next trip, this easy journey to Pipe Lake may be the right choice. This "dead-end" lake is only accessible from the Homer Lake entry point, and thus competition for camping sites is limited by the fact that only two permits are issued per day through Homer. Most visitors to Homer

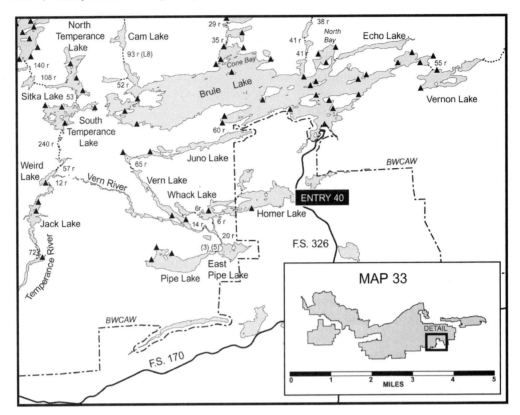

head to Vern Lake or Juno Lake on their way to Brule Lake. Thus, Pipe Lake sees relatively little traffic.

The one negative aspect of this trip is that only three camping sites are available for you on Pipe Lake. You might want to get an early start to provide enough time to backtrack to Vern and Juno in case the sites on Pipe are full. However, this is unlikely except during the heaviest travel periods.

Detailed Route

Paddle and portage 4 miles from Homer Lake to Pipe Lake, including portages of 6 rods (L2), 20 rods (L2), 5 rods (L2), and 3 rods (L2). Head west on Homer Lake, and navigate around the southern islands before heading south into the channel leading to Vern Lake. Homer has three campsites where you can spend the first night. As you head south from Homer, you venture into an interesting low-lying area. A 6-rod portage hugs the western shore and then drops to a small pond. During most of the year you should be able to avoid this portage by pulling over a series of small beaver dams. Continue across the pond and into its southeast corner, where an easy 20-rod portage drops you to East Pipe Lake. Head south and around the small peninsula to the landing for the portages leading to Pipe Lake.

Next a 5-rod portage (L2) leads to a small pond, followed by a 3-rod (L2) portage to Pipe Lake. These portages are flat and easy. Once on Pipe Lake you will find three campsites on the northwestern shore. Both Pipe and East Pipe are shallow lakes, with a maximum depth in Pipe Lake of 33 feet along the southeastern shore. According to Minnesota DNR lake surveys, the only significant population of game fish present is northern pike.

Paddle and portage 4 miles back to your starting point, including portages of 3 rods (L2), 5 rods (L2), 20 rods (L2), and 6 rods (L2). To return to your starting point, just backtrack the way you came.

Route 40B: One-Way to Brule Lake (Map 33)

> Difficulty: easy
> Number of days: 2 or more
> Total miles (approx.): 10.5
> Number of portages: 4
> Total portage rods: 145
> Greatest portage difficulty: 65 rods (L5)
> Navigation maps: Voyageur 9
> Fisher F6
> McKenzie 21

I am a big fan of long narrow lakes—they are wonderful to explore by canoe, allowing you to glide close to shore looking at everything from exposed bedrock formations to beautiful, old twisted cedars. This route is especially attractive in this regard. You will spend almost the entire trip canoeing through long narrow stretches with only a minimum of portaging. This is preferably a one-way trip, so if you have two vehicles make sure to leave one at the landing on Brule Lake. Otherwise, your starting point is just 2 miles from your take-out point, so a short walk is all that is necessary to get back to your vehicle.

This route will be of particular interest to amateur naturalists because it travels through two areas that have recently undergone major environmental changes: first, an area hit by forest fire in the mid-1990s; and second, an area heavily hit by the 1999 windstorm. The result is that much of this trip passes through interesting areas where you can examine the forest regeneration that is underway.

Detailed Route

Paddle and portage 6 miles from Homer Lake to Juno Lake, including portages of 6 rods (L2), 14 rods (L2), and 65 rods (L5). Head west across Homer Lake, choosing from one of the designated campsites if you intend to spend the night. Otherwise, continue to the far western corner of the lake, where you will seek out a short 6-rod portage on a tiny bay just north of a small island. Take the easy 6-rod portage from Homer to Whack Lake, and then immediately continue over the 14-rod portage to Vern Lake.

Vern Lake extends in a narrow northwest line for 3 miles and has two designated campsites available if you would like to spend the night. Northern pike inhabit Vern, which has a maximum depth of 42 feet. A fire swept through this area in the late 1990s, and you can see the forest undergoing a period of rich regeneration. Continue along Vern Lake to the 65-rod portage leading to Juno Lake. This portage is the hardest one of the trip and climbs steeply before dropping along a rocky path to a small bay. The landing on the Juno Lake side can be a bit challenging due to a slippery rock face, but overall this portage is not too bad.

Head to Juno Lake, and camp at one of the three designated campsites along the north shore. The forest fire that burned through this area left little wood untouched, and thus these sites are best suited to cooking on a stove. Juno is host to a nice walleye population, and northern pike are also present in small numbers.

Paddle and portage 4.5 miles from Juno Lake to Brule Lake and your exit, including a portage of 60 rods (L3). This is an easy day of paddling with just one portage on the east end of Juno Lake. This portage is relatively flat and normally in good shape. Although most of the southern Boundary Waters was not heavily affected by the July 4, 1999, windstorm, nearly every tree on this portage was blown down.

The portage from Juno drops you to Brule Lake, which is one of the largest and most famous lakes in the Boundary Waters. The big, unencumbered expanse of western Brule makes for massive waves when the wind is blowing, particularly when it is coming out of the west. Fortunately, on this route you will head east in relatively protected waters. Follow the south shore until you wind around into a bay, where you will find the landing and parking lot for Entry Point 41. Alternatively, you can camp on one of the many Brule campsites, or seek a route to one of the neighboring lakes, such as those recommended in routes 41B, 41C, and 41D.

If you haven't parked a car on Brule, then walk 2 miles down Forest Service Road 326 to the Homer Lake parking lot.

Entry Point 41, Brule Lake (Map 34)

Daily permit quota: 10

Permit availability: difficult to intermediate

Brule Lake is the largest lake in the southeastern BWCAW. It is also the largest entry point lake in the Boundary Waters that does not allow motors on any part of its water surface or lakes connected to it. Thus, this is a huge, motor-free lake. Even a moderate westerly wind on Brule will whip up big waves that can leave even the most experienced canoeist wind bound. In such conditions it can be very difficult to paddle back to the entry point on Brule, making this lake potentially hazardous to inexperienced paddlers. Such folks are probably off better starting at one of the other entries in this area and saving Brule for a later trip.

When reserving a permit, you can request a permit either for Entry Point 41, which has a daily quota of seven permits, or for Entry Point 41A, which has a daily quota of three permits. Both start at Brule Lake, but 41A does not allow you to camp on any lake other than Brule, while 41 has no restrictions on where you can camp. Most visitors prefer a permit for Entry Point 41 rather than 41A since it gives greater flexibility.

Three routes are described below starting at Brule Lake. The first is a portage-free exploration of Brule (Route 41A), the second is a loop north and west of Brule to Long Island Lake (Route 41B), and the third is a loop north and east of Brule through Winchell Lake (Route 41C). In addition, you can reverse Route 40B and go south one-way from Brule to the Homer Lake entry.

A quick review of a map of Brule Lake reveals the existence of seven portages in and out of Brule. Using these portages, you can design numerous interesting trips starting at Brule. The most well-traveled portages are probably the western exit to South Temperance Lake and the two northern exits through South Cone Lake and Lily Lake. Portages also head to the east by way of Vernon Lake and the south by Juno Lake, although these exits do not allow any loop trips and thus seem to get fewer visitors. A portage on the northwest end of Brule heads to Cam Lake. The Cam Lake portage and subsequent portages toward Cherokee Lake are not well traveled because the trails are very rugged and rocky. The alternative route through South Temperance Lake gets you to the same destination with much less trouble, and thus it is much more popular. Consider heading the Cam Lake way if you want to maximize the feeling of isolation and adventure, although camping options are limited to just one site before you get to Cherokee Lake. Finally, a 32-rod portage heads to Echo Lake from Brule's northeast end. Overnight camping is not allowed on Echo Lake, but the easy portage is used by day-trippers from Brule heading to Echo in search of walleye, which are historically relatively common in its shallow waters.

If you are using this guide to design your own route, keep in mind the difficulty of the portages from Cam Lake to Town Lake. Also, all of the routes directly into and out of Davis Lake (north of Brule) are quite strenuous and along rough trails. The two long portages out of Davis are challenging, and the set of four portages from Davis Lake to Winchell Lake get little use. Expect these portages to be somewhat overgrown, in particular the long portage between Pup Lake and Winchell. This portage is so infrequently used that some maps do not even show a portage between Pup and Winchell.

Most lakes in this corner of the BWCAW were not heavily affected by the July 4, 1999, windstorm, although parts of Brule were hit surprisingly hard. In particular, some of the western islands had numerous trees taken down, and on the portage south to Juno Lake almost all trees taller than 8 feet were leveled. If you head to Winchell Lake, you will notice that many trees were also brought down along the

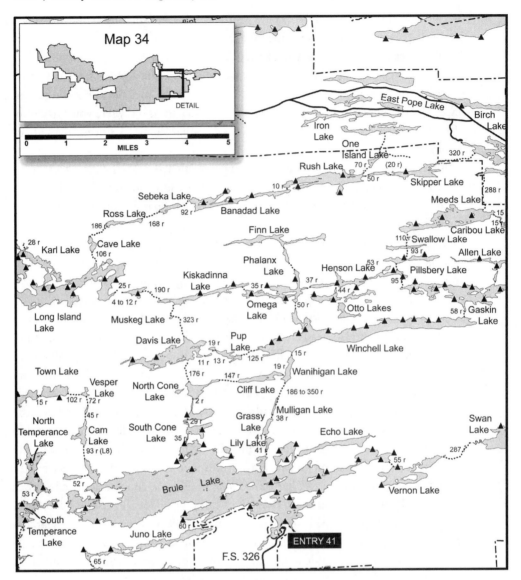

shores of Grassy Lake. However, this damage has not changed any of your route options, and most campsites were not significantly affected. Beyond these areas you will find little storm damage around Brule unless you head east toward Vernon Lake, where you will encounter some additional damage.

To get to Brule Lake, take the Caribou Trail (County Road 4) from its start on Lake Superior just past Lutsen. After 17 miles on the Caribou Trail you will come to a T intersection at Forest Service Road 170. Turn left (west), and go about 1.6 miles and turn right (north) onto Forest Service Road 326. Continue for just over 6 miles down 326 to its end at the large Brule Lake parking lot. No camping is allowed at the Brule Lake landing, but you can spend a night farther west at the small Baker Lake campground or larger Sawbill Lake campground.

Route 41A: Exploration of Brule Lake (Map 34)

> Difficulty: intermediate
> Number of days: 2 or more
> Total miles (approx.): 2 or more
> Number of portages: 0
> Total portage rods: NA
> Greatest portage difficulty: NA
> Navigation maps: Voyageur 9
>   Fisher F6
>   McKenzie 3, 21

This short getaway is great for experienced canoeists wanting to explore magnificent Brule Lake, perhaps to test its depths for its healthy walleye population, small northern pike, and occasional smallmouth bass. You can also explore neighboring lakes on short day trips. Although this trip has no taxing portages, this route is best for visitors who have paddled the BWCAW before or are skilled canoeists, because large rolling waves often develop on Brule.

Detailed Route

Launch your canoe from the excellent public landing on the south end of Brule, and spend a few days exploring this wilderness gem. Brule Lake offers plentiful opportunities to explore many islands and bays and has a nice population of walleye. This trip to Brule is the only short journey in this guide that is not recommended for first-time visitors unless they are seasoned wilderness canoeists. The biggest problem for novice canoeists is the possibility of capsizing in the rough water dished up by Brule on a regular basis.

Brule's great size and beauty have long drawn visitors. The name *Brule* is believed to have originated with Etienne Brule, a Frenchman who explored northern Minnesota in 1624 and 1625, although he is not known to have visited this lake named in his honor. Almost three hundred years later, C. A. A. Nelson is said to have built a wagon trail from Lutsen Resort on Lake Superior along the Poplar River and eventually to Brule Lake. Nelson had a moose hunting camp on Brule, which operated for a couple decades starting in the early 1890s.

Consider making an interesting side trip over the 60-rod portage to Juno Lake on the southwest side of Brule. This portage was all but leveled by the July 4, 1999, windstorm and is now a natural laboratory of forest regeneration. I traveled this route in late summer 1999 after the storm and was amazed to see bunchberries in bloom at a time when they would normally have lots of little fruit. It seems that removal of the tree cover may have replicated the sunny days of spring and tricked the bunchberries into blooming for a second time that summer. In subsequent years I have noticed trees and other vegetation gradually returning. Hike the portage if you have time, and see how much has grown back since 1999.

The geology of Brule may also catch your attention. For example, if you travel the entire lake, you will see a great difference in the exposed rock on the west end compared to the exposed rock on the east end. The west is predominantly basaltic lava flows, part of the same lava flows that formed most of the shore of Lake Superior, and much different from most BWCAW bedrock that hardened deep underground. The east is primarily rhyolite that forced its way into cracks in the basaltic lava flows and hardened. This rhyolite is similar to granite in composition but hardened more quickly and is therefore not nearly as grainy as granite. According to the Minnesota Geological Survey, this rhyolite contains tiny magnetic particles that have reverse polarity, meaning they were formed at a time when the earth's magnetic poles were opposite of their current positions.

A further interesting geologic note about Brule Lake is that all three northern exits lie along ancient fault lines within the underlying bedrock. These three faults run north out of Brule through Cam Lake, the Cone lakes, and Lily Lake. The weak faults appear to have been exploited by glacial ice during the last ice age, which gouged out the bedrock along these fault lines to create depressions for the lakes along them.

Route 41B: Brule to Long Island Loop (Map 34)

> Difficulty: challenging
> Number of days: 4
> Total miles (approx.): 29
> Number of portages: 17
> Total portage rods: 1,427
> Greatest portage difficulty: 323 rods (L10)
> Navigation maps: Voyageur 9
> Fisher F6, F12, F13
> McKenzie 4, 7, 21

This fine trip takes you from Brule Lake all the way to Davis Lake and on to Long Island Lake, then south through Cherokee Lake and back to Brule. It crosses some of the most remote interior portions of the BWCAW. Due to its length and a number of challenging portages, this route is best for experienced wilderness paddlers and returning visitors.

Map 34 shows most of this route, and Map 32 shows the remainder. The entire route is shown in overview on Map 29.

Detailed Route

Paddle and portage 6 miles to Davis Lake, including portages of 35 rods (L2) to South Cone Lake, 29 rods (L1) to Middle Cone Lake, 2 rods (L1) to North Cone Lake, and 176 rods (L8) from North Cone to Davis Lake. This first stretch of paddling will send you north across popular Brule Lake, through the Cone lakes, and up to infrequently visited Davis Lake. The two biggest challenges of this leg are the possibility of significant waves on Brule Lake and the certainty that the 176-rod portage to Davis Lake will be a long, tough haul. Try to make your crossing of Brule early in the morning, when winds are typically low. A wind out of the west will build huge rollers that make north-south traffic impossible to open-topped canoes. To be safe, your schedule should allow for a day of being wind bound on Brule.

After you cross Brule, you will travel through the three Cone lakes to Davis Lake. You reach South Cone from Cone Bay of Brule Lake and can usually paddle or pole up the shallow channel between the lakes. If conditions require that you take the portage, you will find that it is short and flat, following along the western shore. Head through South Cone and on to Middle Cone, taking an easy portage on the east side of the stream connecting these two small lakes. Next, a very easy portage leads to North Cone Lake, although this portage is also one that can normally be paddled or poled through.

From North Cone you will take a tough portage to Davis Lake. This 176-rod trail is infrequently traveled and maintained, resulting in a path that is a bit overgrown. Its difficulty, however, largely stems from the long, steep uphill for the first 50 rods, in which you will climb nearly 100 feet in elevation. Davis Lake has two designated campsites and contains both northern pike and lake trout.

Paddle and portage 1.5 miles from Davis Lake to western Kiskadinna Lake, including a portage of 323 rods (L10). You will soon forget how difficult the portage was to Davis because the mile-long portage out of Davis is much harder and twice as long. This is not a well-traveled portage, but it does get occasional maintenance. The last time I crossed it an exhausted crew of young volunteers was working to clear the trail of obstructions that had accumulated over a long winter.

Paddle and portage 4 miles from Kiskadinna Lake to central Long Island Lake, including portages of 190 rods (L8) from Kiskadinna to Muskeg Lake, 4 to 12 rods (L2) from Muskeg to a small stream, and 25 rods (L4) from this stream to Long Island Lake. The 190-rod portage to Muskeg Lake from Kiskadinna begins with a short uphill that flattens out to a more gradual uphill for the first half of the portage and then drops to Muskeg Lake during the last half of the portage. The Kiskadinna landing is fairly rocky. Overall, this portage receives moderate maintenance, so expect the trail to be fairly wide-open.

Muskeg Lake is surrounded by a rich spruce forest. The one designated campsite on Muskeg is nice because it overlooks a small private bay. Despite the lake's name, its shores are fairly rocky, and this is not a particularly boglike lake. The 4- to 12-rod portage from Muskeg Lake toward Long Island Lake changes dramatically in difficulty depending on water levels. The portage follows a couple of different trails, depending on where you start, but is generally passable. Expect significant roots to hinder your passage, at least along parts of the trail.

You will then paddle down a narrow channel winding through a scenic swamp of tamarack and spruce before you come to a 25-rod portage. This portage leads to

Long Island Lake and has significant rock obstacles on both ends, particularly on the Muskeg Lake side, and slippery rocks along the way. On Long Island, you will put in at a scenic narrow backwater, which you will follow into the main body of the lake.

Long Island Lake is an excellent BWCAW destination for almost every purpose. Caution should be taken on Long Island because it can develop substantial chop and rolling waves during windy days when the wind is coming from the west. Good camping spots are usually available among the fifteen designed sites, and the lake has fine fishing for lake trout and northern pike. Archaeological evidence strongly suggests that Native Americans inhabited or at least had seasonal camps on Long Island Lake for many centuries. This evidence includes an island site on which prehistoric artifacts have been located.

Paddle and portage 3.5 miles from Long Island Lake to Frost Lake, including portages of 8 rods (L2), 28 rods (L3), and 138 rods (L7). When the time comes to move on from Long Island, you will cross the western bay of Long Island and enter the Long Island River. While traveling along the river, you will navigate two portages: a first of 8 rods and a second of 28 rods. The first portage bypasses a series of small rapids and a partially washed-out beaver dam. During high-water periods you should be able to paddle your way through. The 28-rod portage is a bit more difficult to bypass, and you will be wise to take the flat shoreline trail. Don't be surprised to see alder and hazel bushes growing out over the path of this infrequently traveled and maintained portage.

As you head south, the Long Island River widens out and forms a broader body of water known as Gordon Lake. Turn to the west, and take the 138-rod portage to Unload Lake if you would like to spend a night on Frost Lake. The portage from Gordon Lake to Unload Lake is merely 138 rods on the map but will no doubt feel substantially longer. The trail begins with a long, sloping uphill followed by a relatively level path through thick brush that ultimately concludes at the landing to Unload Lake. Just before reaching Unload Lake, on your left side is a small growth of exceptional white cedars—one of which is nearly 2 feet in diameter at chest height. This tree is certainly hundreds of years old and has been spared by the intermittent forest fires by its low-lying, moist environment. These trees are worth the 50-foot hike back from the landing if you happen to reach the end of the portage without noticing these old souls. Head across tiny Unload Lake, and pull your canoe over a beaver dam to Frost Lake.

Frost Lake makes a nice place to spend an evening and has one of the rare sandy beaches in the Boundary Waters on its western shore. This route will now backtrack to Gordon Lake and then down to Cherokee. However, if you want to head farther west along the Frost River, see the description in Route 51B.

Paddle and portage 4 miles from Frost Lake to central Cherokee Lake, including portages of 138 rods (L7) back to Gordon Lake and 13 rods from Gordon Lake to Cherokee. After retracing your path over the 138-rod portage from Frost Lake to Gordon Lake, take the 13-rod portage to Cherokee. Cherokee Lake holds a special place in the hearts of many visitors to the BWCAW. Cherokee hosts an average northern pike population and some lake trout, although walleye are absent according to Minnesota DNR lake surveys. Its large, island-studded surface includes nineteen designated campsites, and easy extended route connections can be made to four neighboring lakes.

Paddle and portage 10.25 miles from Cherokee Lake to your Brule Lake starting point, including portages of 140 rods (L8) from Cherokee to Sitka Lake, 108 rods (L5) from Sitka to North Temperance Lake, 53 rods (L3) from North Temperance to South Temperance Lake, and 9 rods (L1) from South Temperance to Brule Lake. The 140-rod portage to Sitka from Cherokee will get the heart pumping with hill climbs and a bit of fancy footwork on the frequently rocky path. Still, this is just a bit harder than average for a portage of this length. The carry to North Temperance will come as a pleasant surprise after you have carried into Sitka from Cherokee. Not only is it almost a third shorter, but the trail is relatively flat and free of rocks and is likely to be mud-free most of the year. The trail from North Temperance to South Temperance is another relatively easy trail that poses few obstacles. The final short carry to Brule is an easy portage that shouldn't pose any significant problems.

Route 41C: Winchell Lake and the Northeast (Map 35)

> Difficulty: challenging
> Number of days: 4
> Total miles (approx.): 25
> Number of portages: 14
> Total portage rods: 1,275
> Greatest portage difficulty: 323 rods (L10)
> Navigation maps: Voyageur 9
>   Fisher F6, F13
>   McKenzie 3, 4, 21

This route takes you to Winchell Lake from Brule and then onward in a circle northeast of Brule before heading back to your starting point. This route complements route 41B but heads northeast instead of northwest. Many of the lakes on this route are relatively popular, but with good planning and a few suggestions you will find remote lakes. This route is best suited to experienced wilderness paddlers because of the difficulty of a couple of portages and the open-water challenges sometimes posed by Brule Lake.

Map 35 shows the start of this route, and Map 34 shows the rest. The entire route is shown in overview on Map 29.

Detailed Route

Paddle and portage 6 miles from Brule to central Winchell Lake, including portages of 41 rods from Brule to Lily Lake (L3), 41 rods from Lilly to Mulligan Lake (L3),

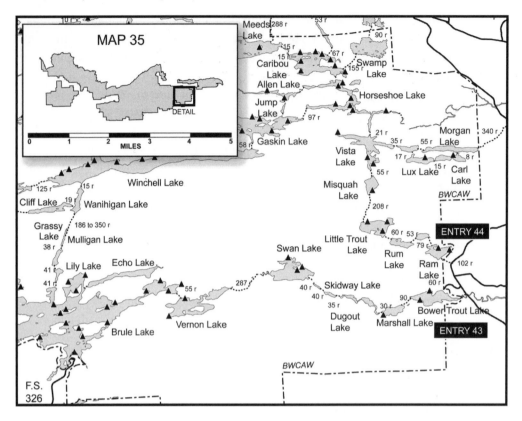

38 rods (L3) from Mulligan to Grassy Lake, 186 to 350 rods (L7 to L9) from Grassy to Wanihigan Lake, and 15 rods (L5) from Wanihigan to Winchell Lake. This route takes you directly north from Brule to Winchell Lake. If possible, try to plan most of your travel on Brule for the morning. Brule often becomes impassable in the afternoon or any time when the wind is howling out of the west. Fortunately, this route does not require that you cross much exposed open water.

The portages through Mulligan and Grassy lakes should be no problem if water levels are high, although the Grassy Lake landing on the 186-rod portage can be a bit muddy. Grassy Lake can become quite shallow and difficult to paddle through if you are visiting late in the summer or when water levels are low. According to a local outfitter, Grassy is now almost never canoeable, so plan on taking a 350-rod portage. In such situations you are better off paddling through the three Cones lakes, 2 miles to the west, and then crossing from North Cone Lake and Cliff Lake to Wanihigan Lake. This easy alternative is described in Route 41B. Ask your permit provider for reports about water levels if you are not sure whether Grassy is open. The final portage from Wanihigan to Winchell is along a rough, rocky trail, but it gets good use and is very short.

Winchell is an exceptionally beautiful lake that you will not soon forget. This long, slender lake is named after N. H. Winchell, who was the Minnesota state geologist in the late 1800s. All of Winchell Lake's campsites stretch along its low-lying north shore. Steep cliffs and palisades rise up along much of the south shore. The deep waters hold a healthy population of lake trout as well as lunker northern pike. Walleye are not believed to be present in any significant numbers. Because of its beauty and location, Winchell is perhaps the most popular destination from Brule, resulting in significant competition for campsites on Winchell during busy weekends. Arrive early in the day to assure yourself of a nice campsite or time to paddle farther if necessary.

Paddle and portage 7 miles from Winchell Lake to Henson Lake, including portages of 58 rods (L4) from Winchell to Gaskin Lake, and 95 rods from Gaskin to Henson Lake. This stretch of paddling along Winchell and Gaskin is wonderful. Excellent campsites are found throughout, and fishing is good in all of these lakes. This area sees frequent visitors from all directions and is a popular destination, so don't expect great isolation until you move past Omega Lake on the next segment. The portages on this stretch are generally in good shape.

Paddle and portage 5.75 miles from Henson Lake to Davis Lake, including portages of 37 rods (L3) from Henson to Omega Lake, 35 rods (L5) from Omega to Kiskadinna Lake, and 323 rods (L10) from Kiskadinna to Davis Lake. The 37-rod portage to Omega Lake is well traveled and maintained, but expect an occasional muddy spot during wet times of the year. Omega Lake is an interesting and scenic border country lake. Numerous bays extend outward from the central axis, providing pleasant vistas for paddlers moving through and greater solitude for those who stay for the night. The shoreline is very rocky, with nice exposed bedrock. Don't expect to find a place on Omega for the night during busy times of the year unless you get there early.

The portage to Kiskadinna Lake from Omega is quite difficult for its length. Although it is fairly short, it climbs steeply uphill and then drops very steeply downhill, with extensive rocks along the way. A portage of this length is rarely more difficult than this one. Kiskadinna is long and narrow with a rocky south shore and a moderately flat north shore, making it feel something like a miniature Winchell. The first campsite has a nice view over the lake from a large rock face sloping into the lake. Unfortunately, there is room for only one tent to be set up comfortably. You can squeeze two more tents into the tight little site, but expect to sleep on a substantial incline.

The final, 323-rod portage of this leg of the journey from Kiskadinna to Davis is very difficult. Few visitors travel over this long portage. It gets some maintenance, but you will still likely encounter a somewhat overgrown trail.

Paddle and portage 6.25 miles from Davis Lake to Brule Lake, including portages of 176 rods (L8) from Davis to North Cone Lake, 2 rods (L1) from North Cone to Middle Cone Lake, 29 rods (L2) from Middle Cone to South Cone Lake, and 35 rods (L2) from South Cone to Brule Lake. Take the 176-rod portage to North Cone Lake, and then head through the three Cone lakes to Brule. As described in Route 41B, some of these three easy portages can be avoided when water levels are high.

ENTRY SOUTHWEST
OF THE GUNFLINT TRAIL

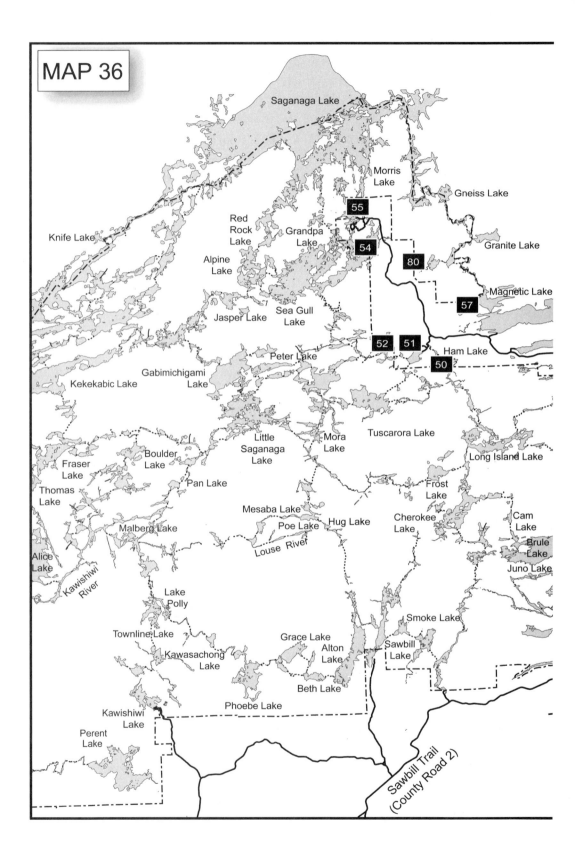

MAP 36

Saganaga Lake

Morris Lake

Gneiss Lake

55

Granite Lake

54

80

Magnetic Lake

57

Knife Lake

Red Rock Lake

Grandpa Lake

Alpine Lake

Jasper Lake

Sea Gull Lake

Peter Lake

52 51

Ham Lake

50

Gabimichigami Lake

Kekekabic Lake

Tuscarora Lake

Long Island Lake

Little Saganaga Lake

Mora Lake

Boulder Lake

Fraser Lake

Pan Lake

Frost Lake

Thomas Lake

Mesaba Lake

Poe Lake

Hug Lake

Cherokee Lake

Cam Lake

Malberg Lake

Louse River

Brule Lake

Alice Lake

Juno Lake

Kawishiwi River

Lake Polly

Smoke Lake

Townline Lake

Grace Lake

Sawbill Lake

Kawasachong Lake

Alton Lake

Beth Lake

Phoebe Lake

Kawishiwi Lake

Perent Lake

Sawbill Trail (County Road 2)

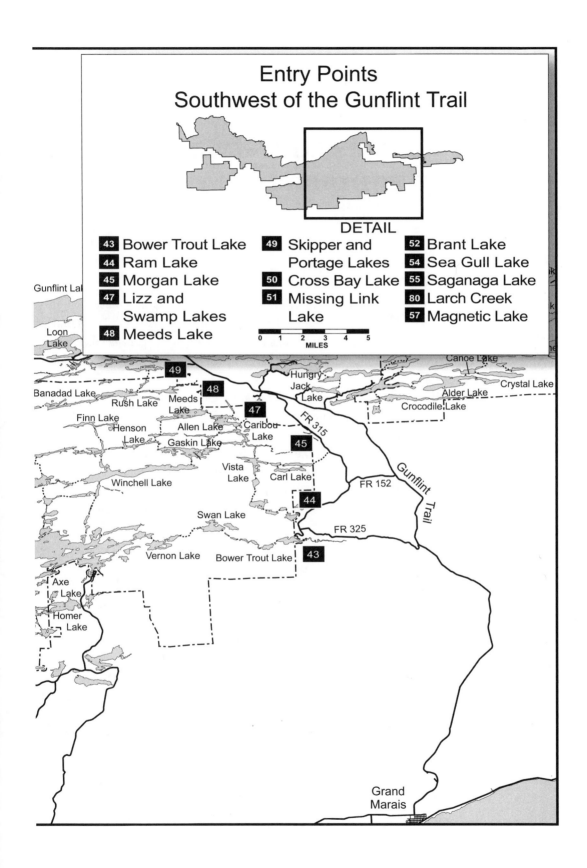

Entry Points
Southwest of the Gunflint Trail

DETAIL

43 Bower Trout Lake
44 Ram Lake
45 Morgan Lake
47 Lizz and Swamp Lakes
48 Meeds Lake

49 Skipper and Portage Lakes
50 Cross Bay Lake
51 Missing Link Lake

52 Brant Lake
54 Sea Gull Lake
55 Saganaga Lake
80 Larch Creek
57 Magnetic Lake

0 1 2 3 4 5
MILES

Gunflint Lal

Loon Lake

Banadad Lake

Rush Lake

Finn Lake

Henson Lake

Winchell Lake

Meeds Lake

Allen Lake

Gaskin Lake

Vista Lake

Swan Lake

Vernon Lake

Caribou Lake

Carl Lake

Bower Trout Lake

Axe Lake

Homer Lake

49

48

47

45

44

43

Hungry Jack Lake

FR 315

FR 152

FR 325

Gunflint Trail

Canoe Lake

Crystal Lake

Alder Lake

Crocodile Lake

Grand Marais

ENTRY SOUTHWEST
OF THE GUNFLINT TRAIL

The Gunflint Trail runs 50 miles from Grand Marais on the shore of Lake Superior to its termination at Trails End campground adjacent to Sea Gull and Saganaga lakes. The entire length of the Gunflint Trail is an all-season paved road, with large expanses of the BWCAW on either side.

The Gunflint Trail has become a popular destination for visitors to northern Minnesota, including many who never enter the BWCAW. You will find far more lodges and resorts along the Gunflint Trail than you will on the Echo Trail, Fernberg Road, or Sawbill Trail. Indeed, only the immediate Ely vicinity competes with the Gunflint in popularity. Numerous outfitters are located along the Gunflint, many of them on lakes leading directly into the Boundary Waters. You certainly won't lack for options to rent gear or find a bunkhouse for the night before you enter the wilderness.

Nineteen paddling entry points are accessible from the Gunflint Trail in two separate segments of the Boundary Waters, allowing travel generally southwest or northeast of the Gunflint. The entries described below are the thirteen that provide access primarily southwest of the Gunflint Trail. The six entries that give access to the northeast are described in the next section.

The most popular entry points south or west of the Gunflint Trail are Saganaga Lake (Entry Point 55) and Sea Gull Lake (Entry Point 54). Saganaga and Sea Gull are big lakes that make fine destinations in their own right. Many people visit these lakes without ever moving beyond them. Almost all of Saganaga is open to motorboats, as is the eastern edge of Sea Gull Lake. Three additional interesting entries originate south of the Gunflint Trail near Round Lake: Cross Bay Lake (Entry Point 50), Missing Link Lake (Entry Point 51), and Brant Lake (Entry Point 52). These three entries offer excellent travel options and have far fewer visitors than Saganaga and Sea Gull. Magnetic Lake (Entry Point 57) is near the end of the Gunflint Trail and is popular with visitors who want a nice one-way trip to Saganaga along the Granite River. Nearby Larch Creek (Entry Point 80) allows travel down a tiny creek to hook up with the Granite River.

Six other entry points southwest of the Gunflint Trail are described in this guide. The first three of these are a cluster of entry points originating in Poplar Lake, including Lizz and Swamp Lakes (Entry Point 47), Meeds Lake (Entry Point 48), and Portage and Skipper Lakes (Entry Point 49). These three entries offer interesting travel options because they allow visitors to start from one entry and exit from another to create a loop that both originates and ends on Poplar Lake. The other three entry points south of the Gunflint are among the most isolated in all of the BWCA: Bower Trout Lake (Entry 43), Ram Lake (Entry 44), and Morgan Lake (Entry 45). Each of these three entrances allows just one group of visitors per day, yet each year many of these permits do not get used. Seek any of these three entries for maximum solitude.

The forest around the Gunflint Trail, in particular much of the wilderness to the south and west, was among the hardest hit by the windstorm of July 4, 1999. Damage from the storm may affect your trip in a number of ways. First, you will have a special opportunity to see an evolving and regenerating wilderness. Parts of this area have been or will be subject to prescribed burns managed by the Forest Service, and natural fires are also likely. The blowdown and burned areas offer a great opportunity to view a regenerating forest. Second, this area will be subject to frequent campfire bans until most of the remaining downed trees burn in small fires or rot away, which could take a generation. Third, some of your camping practices may change as a result of the storm damage, including the manner in which you secure your food pack from bears and the caution you take to keep yourself safe.

Aerial photos taken immediately after the windstorm show enormous swaths of trees that look as if they were cut down by Paul Bunyan and the world's largest scythe. The damage looks unbelievable from above but sometimes appears much less extreme from the vantage point of a canoe. Although from a distance the visual impact of the windstorm is often less than expected, close-up the damage is astounding. You will see broken-off tree trunks, splintered stumps, and a landscape littered with logs. Within three years of the storm the understory trees had already begun to conceal many of the downed trees. Within the first decade a forest of birch and aspen will probably conceal most of the storm damage.

The impact on portages and campsites is also often unbelievable. Some portages were slightly damaged, losing a few trees, while other nearby portages were completely leveled, leaving nothing taller than a few feet. In general the portage trails did not change in terms of difficulty as a result of the storm. However, you will find a fair number of campsites that lost a significant number of trees, often their largest ones, making it difficult to find a tree from which to hang your food pack.

I camped on Sea Gull Lake six weeks before the storm at a magnificent island site full of giant old red pines, only to return after the storm to find every big pine had been leveled. This campsite is one of the few in the wilderness that did not reopen after the storm. In most areas, even the most heavily damaged, you will find a wide variation in the storm's impact, so a campsite that lost most of its trees might be just a quarter mile from a campsite that went unscathed. In addition, lakeshore trees often withstood the forces better than trees in the middle of the forest, perhaps because shoreline trees were already hardened by years of strong winds.

Some of the areas described below will be subject to prescribed burns conducted by the Forest Service during the first decade of the twenty-first century, especially in the area south of the trail from Sea Gull Lake to Tuscarora Lake. The Forest Service is conducting these prescribed burns to avoid a massive fire at the edge of the BWCAW that could spread to the inhabited areas along the Gunflint Trail, and to allow an escape route from western lakes in the event of significant fires.

Make sure you are fully aware of any fire bans that are in place. Your permit issuer should inform you of these restrictions, but ask if you are not told. The tremendous fuel loads are an additional hazard if a fire breaks out. Have a good understanding of lake and portage locations to plan a rapid exit if necessary. Finally, consider renting or buying a bear-proof container to store your food in the event that a good tree is not available for hanging a pack. Numerous outfitters now carry them.

Entry Point 43, Bower Trout Lake (Map 37)

Daily permit quota: 1
Permit availability: difficult to moderate

Bower Trout Lake is tucked into the remote southeast corner of the BWCAW, providing tremendous isolation. Trip options out of Bower Trout Lake are limited because a single chain of lakes leads for about 8 miles to Brule Lake. Once on Brule (Entry Point 41, described earlier) your options multiply, and you have ready access to numerous lakes to the north, west, and even the south.

The most natural loop out of Bower Trout heads west to Brule and then circles north through Winchell Lake, finally returning east to Ram Lake, which is another entry point, just a short walk from your start on Bower Trout Lake. You can also take a one-way trip to Brule Lake, but the layout of area roads makes it difficult to travel by car between the two entry points. If you want an alternative one-way trip, you will do better to head north to Morgan Lake (Entry Point 45), which is just a short drive from the Bower Trout entry.

To reach Bower Trout Lake, follow the Gunflint Trail for 17 miles from Grand Marais, and turn left onto poorly marked Forest Road 325. Take this road for another 6 miles until you reach a Y intersection at Forest Road 152. Turn left onto Forest Road 152, and after about .3 mile take a right onto Forest Road 152H. This final road will lead to the entry point after about a half mile. A 60-rod trail leads from the small parking lot to the shore of Bower Trout Lake.

A good place to spend the night before entering the wilderness is at East Bearskin Lake campground, located north of the Gunflint Trail a few miles past the turnoff for Forest Service Road 325. It has thirty-three campsites, and fees are charged. You will also pass the Kimbell Lake campground on your way up the Gunflint Trail, and it has ten pay campsites. Neither East Bearskin nor Kimbell Lake campgrounds takes

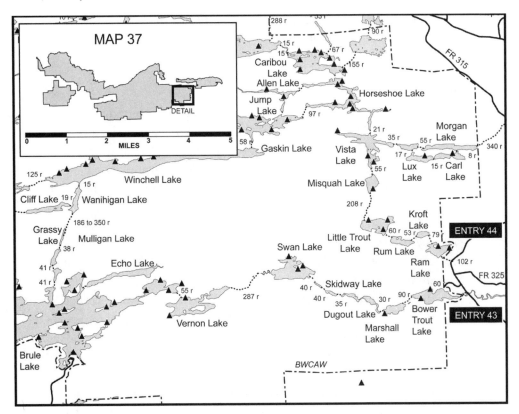

advance reservations. Alternatively, consider staying in Grand Marais, which has a pleasant municipal campground and a number of hotels.

Route 43: Loop to Ram Lake via Brule and Winchell (Map 37)

        Difficulty: challenging
        Number of days: 3 or more
        Total miles (approx.): 29
        Number of portages: 22
        Total portage rods: 1,679
        Greatest portage difficulty: 196 rods (L10)
        Navigation maps: Voyageur 9
                          Fisher F6, F13
                          McKenzie 3, 4, 21

This high-quality route takes you from remote Bower Trout Lake to giant Brule Lake and a popular chain of lakes north of Brule. You then head into a stretch of wild lakes that takes you to your destination at Ram Lake. You will encounter a couple of tough portages on this route, two of which are very long, making this route best

suited for experienced wilderness canoeists or people seeking a challenging introduction to the Boundary Waters.

Detailed Route

This route has plenty of tough portages, so make sure whoever provisions your group
doesn't overdo it. I once took this loop with a good friend whose father was an army
general. The general's son took to heart the old adage that an army marches on its
stomach: we had enough food and drink to last our tiny army a month, even though
we were only taking a three-day trip. The portages certainly become a lot more
memorable when you are carrying an extra 100 pounds of gear.

*Paddle and portage 4.5 miles from Bower Trout to Swan Lake, including portages
of 60 rods (L4) to the shore of Bower Trout, and 90 rods (L7) from Bower Trout to
Marshall Lake, 30 rods (L3) from Marshall to Dugout Lake, 35 rods (L3) from Dugout
to Skidway Lake, 40 rods (L4) to a small pond, and 40 rods (L4) from the pond to
Swan Lake.* The first segment of this trip heads west from Bower Trout to Swan
Lake by way of a series of small lakes and short portages. The parking area at Bower
Trout has evolved over time to include a small lot about 60 rods from the shore of
Bower Trout. The portage trail to Bower Trout tends to get quite wet but is slated for
improvement.

Bower Trout provides a fine place to spend your first evening if you are arriving
late in the afternoon, and you can also camp at Marshall Lake, one portage away.
You should generally find one of these sites available because just one group is allowed to enter per day. Next, the 90-rod portage from Bower to Marshall starts in a
mucky landing but then gets much easier as the portage progresses. Continuing on
you will pass through Dugout and Skidway lakes, both of which had their shorelines
partially burnt by a forest fire in 1995 and are showing good signs of regeneration.
Inspect the revitalized forest carefully, and compare it to blowdown areas you will
see later in this trip on Brule Lake from the 1999 windstorm.

Swan Lake is a good place to spend the first evening, particularly if you are not
yet up for the 287-rod portage to Vernon Lake. The north side of Swan once held
a small logging camp, and a logging railroad ran along the north shore of Swan
Lake and other lakes east to Bower Trout. The area has mostly returned to nature,
with barely a clearing now recognizable where the logging camp was located. The
Minnesota DNR has occasionally stocked Swan Lake with lake trout. These efforts
do not appear to have been a great success, despite the lake's maximum depth of
more than 120 feet, and limited numbers of larger predators.

*Paddle and portage 7 miles from Swan Lake to central Brule Lake, including portages
of 287 rods (L8) from Swan to Vernon Lake, and 55 rods (L8) from Vernon to Brule
Lake.* Pressing on, you will take the long portage to Vernon Lake, covering a nice
trail with gentle elevation changes. It is certainly one of the easiest long portages in
the Boundary Waters. The next portage, to Brule, is only 55 rods long and has nice
landings and a good path, but this portage requires a very steep climb up from the

shore of Vernon, making it seem almost as hard as the 287-rod portage on the opposite side of Vernon.

Once on Brule Lake you are at a legendary destination that attracts returning visitors year after year. Brule is unique in the BWCAW because it is a huge lake reachable by car (Entry Point 41) yet is entirely nonmotorized. Most other similarly large lakes on the edge of the BWCAW (Trout, Saganaga, Sea Gull, Moose, Basswood, Lac La Croix) allow motorized watercraft. A number of private residences were once located on Brule, as was a resort, but they have all been gone for decades. Most were removed in the 1950s and 1960s when the Forest Service purchased numerous private landholdings in what was then the Superior Roadless Area and was later known as the Boundary Waters Canoe Area. Many of these purchases were made against the wishes of the landowners. If you want to carve out a longer route heading south to Homer Lake, west to the Temperance River, or north to such lakes as Long Island, review the information about Brule Lake provided earlier in this guide for Routes 41A and 41B.

Paddle and portage 6 miles from Brule Lake to central Winchell Lake, including portages of 41 rods (L3) from Brule to Lily Lake, 41 rods (L3) from Lily to Mulligan Lake, 38 rods (L3) from Mulligan to Grassy Lake, 186 to 350 rods (L7 to L9) from Grassy to Wanihigan Lake, and 15 rods (L5) from Wanihigan to Winchell Lake. This segment takes you directly north from Brule to Winchell Lake. If possible, travel on Brule in the morning because this big lake often becomes impassable in the afternoon or any time when the wind is howling out of the west. Fortunately, this route does not require that you cover much exposed open water.

The portages through Mulligan and Grassy lakes should be no problem if water levels are high, although the Grassy Lake landing on the 186-rod portage can be a bit muddy. If it is late in the summer or water levels are low, Grassy Lake can become shallow and difficult to paddle across, in which case the portage essentially doubles in length. In such situations you are better off paddling through the three Cone lakes, 2 miles to the west, and then crossing from North Cone Lake and Cliff Lake to Wanihigan Lake. This easy extension is described in Route 41B. Grassy has been perpetually low in recent years, so expect to take the longer portage. Ask your permit issuer about water levels if you are not sure about paddling across Grassy. The final portage from Wanihigan to Winchell is along a rough, rocky trail, but it gets good use and is very short.

Winchell is an exceptionally beautiful lake. All of its campsites stretch along a low-lying north shore, with steep palisades rising along much of the south shore. The deep waters hold a healthy population of lake trout, as well as northern pike. Because of its beauty and location, Winchell is probably the most popular destination from Brule, resulting in significant competition for campsites on Winchell during busy weekends. Arrive early in the day to assure yourself a nice campsite or time to paddle farther on to other lakes if necessary.

Paddle and portage 6.75 miles from Winchell Lake to Vista Lake, including portages of 58 rods (L4) from Winchell to Gaskin Lake, 97 rods (L5) from Gaskin to Horseshoe

Lake, and 21 rods (L3) from Horseshoe to Vista Lake. The stretch of paddling across Winchell, Gaskin, and Horseshoe is among the most beautiful in the Boundary Waters. Excellent campsites are found along this segment, and fishing is good in all of these lakes. This area sees frequent visitors from all directions, so do not expect maximum isolation until you move past Vista on the next segment. The portages on this stretch are generally in good shape and are well traveled.

Paddle and portage 5 miles from Vista Lake to Ram Lake, including portages of 55 rods from Vista to Misquah Lake, 208 rods (L10) from Misquah to Little Trout Lake, 60 rods (L8) from Little Trout to Rum Lake, 53 rods (L5) from Rum to Kroft Lake, 79 rods (L7) from Kroft to Ram Lake, and 102 rods (L5) from Ram to the Ram Lake parking lot. The first portage, from Vista to Misquah, is a bit rocky but will warm you up for the second portage. According to the Minnesota Historical Society, Misquah Lake gets it name from the Ojibwe word for *red,* a reference to the red granite bedrock underlying much of this area. This hard granite forms the Misquah Hills, an area south of Winchell Lake, and Eagle Mountain by Brule Lake, which is the highest point above sea level in Minnesota.

The portage from Misquah to Little Trout Lake is among the toughest in the entire BWCAW and absolutely the hardest portage of this length in the wilderness. Some portages are twice as long and extract their toll slowly. This half-mile portage uses quicker blows to break you down, making you travel an exceedingly rocky trail over two tough hills. Next, the 60-rod haul from Little Trout to Rum is also quite tough, with a big hill in the middle. The final three portages, including the portage back to the Ram Lake entry, will be easy by comparison. Once you reach your exit on Ram Lake, hike the portage to the parking lot and then walk south on Forest Service Road 325 to where you left your vehicle at the Bower Trout parking lot.

Entry Point 44, Ram Lake (Map 37)

> Daily permit quota: 1
> Permit availability: moderate to difficult

Ram Lake is tucked into a corner of the BWCAW that gets relatively few visitors. This sleepy backwater offers great isolation along a chain of small, beautiful lakes. No short loops out of Ram Lake are possible, but excellent out-and-back trips can be made. Two very nice one-way trips are also possible: a short jaunt north to Morgan Lake (Route 44A), and a much longer haul south to Bower Trout Lake (Route 44B). You will want two vehicles for the one-way trip to Morgan Lake (Route 44A), but you can easily walk back to your starting point from Bower Trout if you try Route 44B.

Two portages will play an important role in planning any route out of Ram Lake: the 60-rod portage from Rum Lake to Little Trout Lake, and the 208-rod portage from Little Trout to Misquah Lake. Both of these portages are difficult, the 208-rod portage being among the toughest in the BWCAW. It has numerous exposed rocks, hills, and a generally tough trail. Most journeys out of Ram Lake require you to take at least the first of these portages, making Ram Lake less desirable for first-time visitors, those who bring excessive gear, or people unable to take physically demanding portages.

To reach the Ram Lake entry, follow the Gunflint Trail for 17 miles from Grand Marais, and turn left onto Forest Road 325. Take this road for another 6 miles until you reach a Y intersection, where you will turn right (north) onto Forest Service Road 152. Continue down 152 for about a third of a mile, where you will see a turnout on the left for Ram Lake. Parking is less than ideal here, but you should be able to find adequate space in the rugged parking area and short access road. A 102-rod portage leads to the shore of Ram Lake.

A good place to spend the night before entering the Boundary Waters is at the large East Bearskin Lake campground, located farther up the Gunflint Trail. You will also pass the smaller Kimbell Lake campground on your way up the Gunflint Trail. If you want one last night of civilization, consider staying in Grand Marais at the pleasant municipal campground or one of the various hotels and motels.

Route 44A: One-Way to Morgan Lake (Map 37)

> Difficulty: intermediate/challenging
> Number of days: 2
> Total miles (approx.): 9
> Number of portages: 8
> Total portage rods: 932
> Greatest portage difficulty: 208 rods (L10)
> Navigation maps: Voyageur 9
> Fisher F13
> McKenzie 3

This short route is one of the easiest journeys possible out of Ram Lake yet still includes three difficult portages, one of which is among the hardest in the BWCAW. You will have excellent solitude on this journey, probably seeing few people except when you cross through popular Vista Lake. This is a great trip for light packers who want isolation and are not afraid of challenging portages.

Detailed Route

Paddle and portage 5 miles from Ram Lake to Vista Lake, including portages of 102 rods to Ram Lake, 79 rods (L7) from Ram to Kroft Lake, 53 rods (L5) from Kroft to Rum Lake, 60 rods (L8) from Rum to Little Trout Lake, 208 rods (L10) from Little Trout to Misquah Lake, and 55 rods from Misquah to Vista Lake. Most of these portages are easy, but the 60-rod carry from Rum to Little Trout is relatively difficult due to a steep hill. The following portage, from Little Trout to Misquah, is among the toughest in the BWCAW. This half-mile portage will test you along a rocky trail over two tough hills. A moderate amount of blowdown occurred along the shores of these first lakes in the 1999 windstorm, and the Forest Service has scheduled an understory/patch burn of blowdown from Ram Lake to Little Trout. These fires should be completed by the end of 2005.

Three nice designated campsites are located along the shores of Little Trout Lake, as well as one on Misquah, and three on Vista. You will likely have little trouble getting one of the sites on Little Trout or Misquah, but the Vista Lake sites often attract people coming from the north, south, east, and west. Plan accordingly, and head to Vista only if it is not too late in the day or if you are traveling early in the season (May) or late (September).

Paddle and portage 4 miles from Vista Lake to the Morgan Lake entry, including portages of 35 rods (L3) from Vista to Jake Lake, 55 rods (L4) from Jake to Morgan Lake, and 340 rods (L8) from Morgan to the parking lot (a 5-mile drive or walk from your start on Ram Lake). Your exit from Vista Lake to Morgan Lake is a straightforward trip to the east that culminates in a long portage from Morgan Lake to the parking lot at the Morgan Lake entry. Relatively few visitors enter or leave the BWCAW through Morgan Lake, so you will likely find your exit to be peaceful. The final, 340-rod portage is long but not too difficult. The end of this portage was once one of the muddiest in the wilderness, but a boardwalk was installed in recent years, covering a long, low, wet spot. You might consider staying on either Lux Lake or Carl Lake for an extra night, both of which historically have had good populations of small and medium northern pike. See Route 45A to learn more about these two lakes and the Morgan Lake portage.

Route 44B: One-Way to Bower Trout Lake (Map 37)

Difficulty: challenging
Number of days: 3 or more
Total miles (approx.): 29
Number of portages: 22
Total portage rods: 1,679
Greatest portage difficulty: 196 rods (L10)
Navigation maps: Voyageur 9
 Fisher F6, F13
 McKenzie 3, 4, 21

This long loop extends from Ram Lake to Horseshoe and Gaskin lakes before turning south toward Winchell and Brule lakes. It eventually heads through a remote region to the east of Brule culminating at Bower Trout Lake, just a mile from your starting point. This route is average in difficulty for a journey of this length, but a couple of very tough portages early in the route will test your mettle, making it best suited to experienced campers.

Detailed Route

This route is the opposite of Route 43, so see that route earlier in this guide for detailed information and the possibility of making diversions from the proposed lakes and portages.

Paddle and portage 5 miles from Ram Lake to Vista Lake, including portages of 102 rods (L5) from the parking lot to Ram Lake, 79 rods (L7) from Ram to Kroft Lake, 53 rods (L5) from Kroft to Rum Lake, 60 rods (L8) from Rum to Little Trout Lake, 208 rods (L10) from Little Trout to Misquah Lake, and 55 rods from Misquah to Vista Lake. This first leg starts along an infrequently traveled section of remote lakes and includes a grueling 208-rod portage between Little Trout and Misquah lakes that is among the hardest portages of any length in the BWCAW. When you reach Vista Lake, you will be at a popular crossroads lake and may begin to encounter other visitors.

Paddle and portage 6.75 miles from Vista Lake to Winchell Lake, including portages of 21 rods (L3) from Vista to Horseshoe Lake, 97 rods (L5) from Horseshoe to Gaskin Lake, and 58 rods (L4) from Gaskin to Winchell Lake. Continue through Vista, Horseshoe, and Gaskin lakes along well-maintained trails. Arrive early on Winchell if you are visiting in July or August. This popular lake attracts visitors from every direction.

Paddle and portage 6 miles from Winchell Lake to Brule Lake, including portages of 15 rods (L5) from Winchell to Wanihigan Lake, 186 to 350 rods (L7 to L9) from Wanihigan to Grassy Lake, 38 rods (L3) from Grassy to Mulligan Lake, 41 rods (L3) from Mulligan to Lily Lake, and 41 rods (L3) from Lily to Brule Lake. You have two main options for heading to Brule from Winchell. If water levels are high, the easiest route is through Wanihigan and then straight south by way of Grassy, Mulligan, and Lily lakes. This stretch is described in Route 43. Otherwise, if water levels are low, then the Wanihigan to Grassy portage can stretch to more than a mile in length. Under such conditions, consider heading through the three Cone lakes, described in Route 41B. Either option will take you to Brule Lake, a popular destination in its own right and a great jumping-off point to numerous other lakes.

Paddle and portage 7 miles from Brule Lake to Swan Lake, including portages of 55 rods (L8) from Brule Lake to Vernon Lake, and 287 rods (L8) from Vernon to Swan Lake. When your time comes to leave Brule Lake, head east toward Swan Lake, which was once home to a small logging camp on its north shore. A simple logging railroad ran from Swan east to a major north–south rail line along what is now Forest Service Road 152. The first portage from Brule to Vernon is not long but is surprisingly tough.

Paddle and portage 4.5 miles from Swan Lake to Bower Trout Lake, including portages of 40 rods (L4) from Swan Lake to a small pond, and 40 rods (L4) from the small pond to Skidway Lake, 35 rods (L3) from Skidway to Dugout Lake, 30 rods (L3) from Dugout to Marshall Lake, 90 rods (L7) from Marshall Lake to Bower Trout Lake, and 60 rods (L4) from Bower Trout to the parking lot. Continue along the final stretch of this journey to Bower Trout Lake. Most of the portages are relatively easy and described in greater detail in Route 43.

Entry Point 45, Morgan Lake (Map 38)

Daily permit quota: 1

Permit availability: difficult to moderate

Give the Morgan Lake entry serious consideration if you are not afraid of long portages. You must carry your gear more than a mile on the initial portage to reach Morgan Lake, but the trail is sound, and immediately accessible lakes are lightly visited. A simple loop can circle you through four adjacent lakes that get relatively few visitors, or you can head to Vista Lake to explore the many routes to the north and south.

The Morgan Lake portage used to be among the least welcoming in the BWCAW. It started with a 100-foot-long mud hole that had to be waded through, followed by a 330-rod hike in muddy boots. After the Forest Service started collecting users' fees, one of the first expenditures of funds was for installation of a boardwalk over the low-lying muddy area. Today the start of the portage is quite pleasant, and the remainder of the trail after the boardwalk is a nice walk in the woods. Two routes are described below. First is a simple loop to Morgan Lake's neighbors (Route 45A); second is a longer loop west through Omega and Winchell lakes (Route 45B).

To get to Morgan Lake, take the Gunflint Trail for 21 miles from Grand Marais, then turn west (left) onto Forest Service Road 152 (the Lima Mountain Road), and drive for 2 miles until you reach the intersection of Forest Service Road 315 (at a Y, keep to the right), which you take to the north (right) for another 1.9 miles until you reach the small parking lot and entrance kiosk positioned on the left side of the road.

A good place to spend the night before entering the Boundary Waters is at one of the thirty-three campsites at East Bearskin Lake campground, which is located north of the Gunflint Trail a few miles past the turnoff for Forest Service Road 152. You will also pass the Kimbell Lake campground on your way up the Gunflint Trail, which has ten campsites. You can also stay in Grand Marais, which has a pleasant municipal campground and a number of hotels.

Important warning: Some commercial maps, including those made by Fisher, show three portages north of Morgan Lake along the Brule River draining from Horseshoe Lake. You may be tempted to make a loop through this stretch of the Brule River. I paddled the river during research for this guide and found no sign of these portages, and was forced to bushwhack around difficult rapids. Other rapids appeared without warning, and many trees had fallen across parts of the river. I do not believe this river can be safely navigated and advise against taking it. Unlike Fisher maps, McKenzie and Voyageur maps do not show these phantom portages.

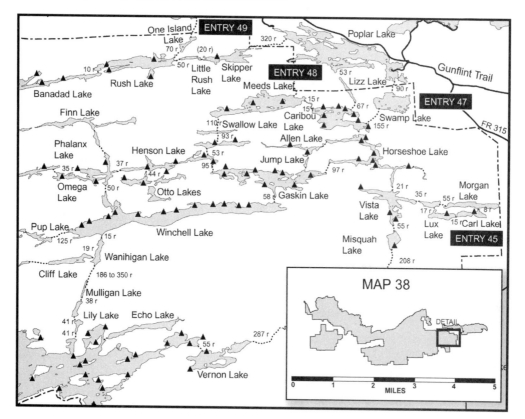

Route 45A: Jake and Lux Lakes Loop (Map 38)

>   Difficulty: moderate
>   Number of days: 2 or more
>   Total miles (approx.): 5.75
>   Number of portages: 6
>   Total portage rods: 775
>   Greatest portage difficulty: 340 rods (L8)
>   Navigation maps: Voyageur 9
>   Fisher F13
>   McKenzie 3

This interesting route is short but pleasant and is a fine weekend escape. You must take a long initial portage, but the trail is likely to be in very good shape and will be manageable for most crews. Once over this portage you are in a peaceful corner of the BWCAW that gets relatively few visitors. Despite its long initial portage, this route is suitable for first-time visitors who do not bring unnecessary gear and are physically fit.

Detailed Route

Portage and paddle 2.5 miles to Carl and Lux lakes, including portages of 340 rods (L8) to Morgan Lake, 8 rods (L3) from Morgan to Carl Lake, and 15 rods (L3) from Carl to Lux Lake. Take the long portage to Morgan Lake and then one or both of the easy portages to Carl and Lux lakes. Your biggest challenge of the day is certainly the initial portage, but it is one of the easiest long portages in the BWCAW. Pack light, and consider renting an ultralight canoe if you don't own one. Neither Carl nor Lux lakes gets many visitors, so with luck you will have your pick between campsites on the two lakes. Both short portages are a bit harder than normal for their length because the first portage can be muddy and the second climbs a short hill.

Portage and paddle 3.25 miles to the Morgan Lake entry, including portages of 17 rods (L2) from Lux Lake to Jake Lake, 55 rods (L4) from Jake to Morgan Lake, and 340 rods (L8) from Morgan to your starting point. Paddle and portage back to your starting point. For variety I recommend circling through Jake Lake, although this requires that you take a longer 55-rod portage. This portage follows a relatively level trail, and the only challenge is likely to be a bit of mud on the Morgan Lake side.

Route 45B: Meeds, Omega, and Winchell Loop (Map 38)

Difficulty: intermediate
Number of days: 4
Total miles (approx.): 28
Number of portages: 17
Total portage rods: 1,430
Greatest portage difficulty: 340 rods (L8)
Navigation maps: Voyageur 9
                  Fisher F13
                  McKenzie 3, 4

This long loop circles through a set of beautiful lakes west of Morgan. Your journey first heads west to Vista Lake and then continues northwest to Horseshoe, Caribou, and Meeds before dropping to Henson, Omega, and finally famous Winchell Lake. You will finish going through Gaskin Lake and then back to Horseshoe and your starting point on Morgan. This route is suitable for relatively inexperienced crews if they are fit, don't overpack, and like a good challenge.

Detailed Route

Paddle and portage 7 miles from the Morgan Lake entry to Caribou Lake, including portages of 340 rods (L8) to Morgan Lake, 55 rods (L4) to Jake Lake, 35 rods (L3) to Vista Lake, 21 rods (L3) to Horseshoe Lake, and 21 rods (L2) to Caribou Lake. This first day of travel is quite easy after the initial portage, and even the first portage is one of the best long trails in the BWCAW. Horseshoe Lake is one of the most popular lakes in this portion of the Boundary Waters, so travelers in the busy months of July and August should arrive early if they hope to spend a night at one of its seven designated campsites.

Paddle and portage 2 miles from Caribou Lake to Meeds Lake, including portages of 15 rods (L4) and 15 rods (L5). You will take two relatively tough little portages to Meeds Lake. The first portage is only 15 rods long but is much harder than most short portages because it essentially follows a riverbed with large rocks and boulders forming most of the trail. During high water expect at least part of the trail to have water running down through these rocks. After this first portage, you paddle through an interesting little marsh with a very narrow channel for canoe traffic, followed by the second short portage. This portage is also rocky but much less so than the first.

Meeds Lake is a fine destination and has three designated campsites along its shores. According to the Minnesota Historical Society, Meeds Lake is named in honor of Alonzo D. Meeds, who was an assistant to N. H. Winchell in the Minnesota Geological Survey at the end of the nineteenth century, for whom Winchell Lake was named.

Paddle and portage 5 miles from Meeds Lake to Omega Lake, including portages of 110 rods (L7) from Meeds to Swallow Lake, 93 rods (L7) from Swallow to Pillsbery Lake, 53 rods (L5) from Pillsbery to Henson Lake, and 37 rods (L3) from Henson to Omega Lake. The 110-rod portage from Meeds to Swallow Lake follows a trail with a couple of muddy sections that have wobbly log bridges over the worst spots, although these bridges are slated for upgrading in the near future. The 93-rod portage from Swallow to Pillsbery is very flat but also very low lying. If it has been a dry summer, you are likely to have few problems with mud, but if it has been a wet summer, expect a fair amount of the trail to be muddy.

Pillsbery Lake is long, narrow, and low-lying. The shoreline is dominated by spruce and a dense population of cedars. A few old white pines puncture this cedar and spruce forest at intervals along the shoreline. Two designated campsites are located on the north shore of Pillsbery, and these are the first campsites since Meeds. You may want to spend an evening on Pillsbery. Also, if you want to do some more exploring, consider taking the 95-rod (L7 to L8) portage east toward Allen Lake, which is a reasonably flat carry following on the north shore of a shallow, intermittent creek bed. Most of the trail is well drained, although its proximity to the creek makes this portage more muddy than average during the rainy season. Allen also has two designated campsites, which get relatively few visitors.

When it comes time to leave Pillsbery, take the 53-rod portage to Henson Lake. The first 20 rods are up a moderately steep and curving trail. The path then levels out and winds through nice terrain before dropping steeply for the last 5 rods to Henson Lake. Camp at one of Henson's five sites if you are so inclined, otherwise take the 37-rod portage to Omega Lake. This portage trail seems to be reasonably well traveled and well maintained. Expect an occasional muddy spot during wet times of the year.

Omega Lake is relatively small but still has four campsites along its shore. Omega's location just a portage from popular Winchell Lake makes this a common destination, more so than many of the other lakes you have already covered. Arrive early in the day to assure yourself a campsite or time to move on to another lake in the event the sites are full.

If you are planning extensions from this route, your other options out of Henson Lake are a 44-rod (L8) portage to the Otto lakes south of Henson, and a 95-rod portage (L7) to Gaskin Lake southeast of Henson. The 44-rod portage to the Otto lakes from Henson Lake is very difficult for its length due to the fact that it climbs steeply uphill and then descends steeply. You will scamper up slippery rock faces and over some sizable boulders. The Otto lakes are interesting and have two designated campsites, neither of which appears to be frequently visited. In contrast, the 95-rod portage to Gaskin Lake is either flat or downhill most of the way before dropping a final steep portion to a clearing and landing on the shores of Gaskin. This portage to Gaskin is the most heavily traveled out of Henson because it connects to a popular lake. The trail itself should be fairly dry in most places, although expect some rocks and occasional rough going.

Paddle and portage 3 miles from Omega to central Winchell Lake, including a 50-rod (L5) portage. The portage to Winchell from Omega is almost completely flat and should be mostly dry except during the wettest parts of the year, but is somewhat rocky. It is also well traveled because Winchell is a popular lake. The second half of the portage climbs over and through a somewhat challenging rock field. These rocks can pose a hazard when wet because they will be slippery, so be thoughtful in your foot placement.

Paddle and portage 6.75 miles from Winchell Lake to Vista Lake, including portages of 58 rods (L4) from Winchell to Gaskin Lake, 97 rods (L5) from Gaskin to Horseshoe Lake, and 21 rods (L3) from Horseshoe to Vista Lake. The next stretch of paddling on this route takes you across Winchell, Gaskin, and Horseshoe lakes. Tall cliffs rise up from the south shore of Winchell, excellent campsites are found throughout the segment, and fishing is good in all of these lakes. The north-central and south-central shores of Winchell Lake were burned in a forest fire in the late 1990s, and this is a good place to watch the regenerating forest. Winchell, Gaskin, and Horseshoe are all popular destinations, so do not expect great isolation until you move past Vista. Also, allow yourself plenty of time to find a campsite on any of these three lakes.

Paddle and portage 4 miles from Vista Lake to your starting point at the Morgan Lake entry, including portages of 35 rods (L3), 55 rods (L4), and 340 rods (L8). Your exit from Vista Lake to Morgan Lake is a straightforward trip to the east that culminates in a long portage from Morgan Lake to the parking lot at the Morgan Lake entry. You might consider staying on either Lux Lake or Carl Lake for an extra night, both of which historically have had good populations of small and medium northern pike.

Entry Point 47, Lizz and Swamp Lakes (Map 38)

Daily permit quota: 4
Permit availability: difficult

Entry Point 47 (Lizz and Swamp lakes), along with Entry Point 48 (Meeds Lake) and Entry Point 49 (Portage and Skipper lakes), is one of three entries starting from Poplar Lake on the edge of the BWCAW south of the Gunflint Trail. All three entries share a common parking lot on the western shore of Poplar, so it is easy to configure a loop that starts at one of these entries and exits at another.

When planning a trip from Entry Point 47, you will enter the BWCAW at either Lizz Lake or Swamp Lake and then progress to Caribou Lake. Most visitors start at Lizz Lake, probably because it involves less portaging and is closest to the landing on Poplar Lake. However, both of these entry lakes are nice options and described below. Once on Caribou Lake you can make loops of various sizes to the west and east. A good moderate loop is to head south toward Gaskin Lake and then work back north through Meeds Lake before returning directly to Poplar Lake from Meeds or back via Caribou Lake (Route 47A). You can also easily extend this route by paddling farther west from Gaskin to Long Island Lake, and then returning to your start by way of Banadad Lake (Route 47B). Similarly, you can use the index to craft loops farther south, as well as southeast toward Morgan or Ram lakes.

To reach Lizz and Swamp lakes, take the Gunflint Trail for 32 miles to a left turn at County Road 92. Drive just over a half mile down CR 92 until you come to the intersection with Forest Road 561, which you take for three-quarters of a mile to the Poplar Lake public access. Adequate parking is available for dozens of cars. The Iron Lake campground, with seven camping spots, is just another 3 miles down CR 92 and is a good spot to spend the night before entering the Boundary Waters. You can make reservations for these sites, which is a good idea to assure yourself a site.

Route 47A: Caribou, Gaskin, Meeds Loop (Map 38)

Difficulty: intermediate
Number of days: 2
Total miles (approx.): 11.5
Number of portages: 5
Total portage rods: 563
Greatest portage difficulty: 288 rods (L9)
Navigation maps: Voyageur 9
Fisher F13
McKenzie 3

This easy route takes you into the Boundary Waters at Swamp Lake and then circles around through Horseshoe Lake, Gaskin Lake, and Meeds Lake before returning to

Poplar Lake. This route is suitable for first-time visitors if they are willing to accept a few challenging portages.

Detailed Route

Paddle and portage 5.5 miles from the Poplar Lake landing to Caribou Lake, including portages of 90 rods (L6) from Poplar Lake to Swamp Lake, and 155 rods (L7) from Swamp to Caribou Lake. As noted above, Entry Point 47 is somewhat unique because you can start from either Lizz or Swamp Lake, although the most common entry is from Poplar to Lizz Lake and then on to Caribou Lake. However, this route makes a nice alternative for people who want to try a more rough and tumble approach by paddling to the eastern side of Poplar Lake and through Swamp Lake and then to Caribou Lake. The Poplar to Swamp portage is mismarked on some Fisher maps as being in the far eastern bay of Poplar (the triangle-shaped bay that looks like its own separate lake). The portage is really located in the middle of the bay one to the west of this "separate" lake. Once you have found the portage, this is a relatively easy trail, mostly dry and free of obstructions, without too much hill climbing. The correction in the location changes the length to about 90 rods, not 100 shown on some maps.

Despite its name, Swamp Lake is quite nice and not very swampy. This is a classic Boundary Waters lake lined by fir, balsam, aspen, and cedar but with very few marshy areas. It is shallow (about 10 feet deep maximum) and does not have any designated camping spots. According to Minnesota DNR fisheries surveys, Swamp Lake has a good population of walleyes, potentially making it an attractive fishing lake to pass through on your way to Caribou. The portage to Caribou Lake is not heavily traveled. Still, it is not a bad portage, with only a little mud on the Swamp Lake side.

Caribou is a pretty lake with eight designated campsites. Campers seem to converge on Caribou in the summer like ants on a picnic, so do not expect solitude on this woodland gem. Visitors used to seeing moose and deer in the Boundary Waters often do not know that woodland caribou occupied these forests until at least the late 1800s, and that they were quite common. Perhaps the explorer who named Caribou Lake came upon a small herd along these shores. Reintroduction of woodland caribou has been discussed from time to time since the 1970s, and the area to the west around Little Saganaga Lake has been considered some of the best habitat for such reintroduction efforts. Some naturalists believe the blowdown of 1999 has diminished this habitat for caribou reintroduction. In addition, the recovery of the wolf population complicates the prospects for caribou reintroduction.

Paddle and portage 2 miles from Caribou Lake to Meeds Lake, including portages of 15 rods (L4) and 15 rods (L3). You will next take two tough little portages to Meeds Lake. The first portage is much harder than most short portages because it essentially follows a riverbed with large rocks and boulders forming most of the trail. During high water expect at least part of the trail to have some running water around these rocks. After this first portage, you paddle through an interesting little marsh with a very narrow channel for canoe traffic, followed by the second 15-rod portage. This portage is also quite rocky but less so than the first portage.

Paddle and portage 4 miles from Meeds Lake to your starting point on Poplar Lake, including a portage of 288 rods (L9). The portage from Meeds to Poplar Lake is not heavily used, probably because other shorter routes to Poplar are possible. A number of slight uphills are found along the way, and you should expect a trail that is somewhat rocky. At least three spots on the second half of this portage are low lying. An old log walkway was constructed through this stretch many years ago, although many of these logs appear fairly well rotted.

Route 47B: Gaskin, Winchell, Long Island, Banadad Loop (Map 38)

Difficulty: challenging
Number of days: 5
Total miles (approx.): 31
Number of portages: 20
Total portage rods: 1,657
Greatest portage difficulty: 320 rods
Navigation maps: Voyageur 9
                  Fisher F13
                  McKenzie 3, 4

This route starts on Poplar Lake and then heads through Lizz Lake in a long loop west through Omega and Kiskadinna lakes on the way to Long Island Lake, before returning east by way of Banadad and Skipper lakes. Most of the lakes on this route are long and very narrow, making them a pleasure to paddle through with the shore close on both sides of your canoe. This route explores sparsely traveled territory, although you are likely to encounter other groups halfway through your journey, on Long Island Lake. This demanding trip is best suited to experienced wilderness canoeists or returning Boundary Waters visitors.

Map 38 shows the eastern portion of this route, and Map 34 shows the western portion. An overview of the entire route is shown on Map 36.

Detailed Route

Paddle and portage 3.5 miles from Poplar Lake to Caribou Lake, including portages of 53 rods (L4) from Poplar to Lizz Lake, and 67 rods (L4) from Lizz to Caribou Lake. Poplar to Lizz is an easy portage. The low-lying Lizz Lake side of the portage has been built up to keep the trail dry during wet years. Lizz has no designated campsites, and halfway down the lake you will officially enter the BWCAW. Lizz Lake has been stocked repeatedly for brook trout, but the trout population has not really prospered. Interestingly, a significant population of pumpkinseed sunfish lives in Lizz Lake, which is unusual for the Boundary Waters. The portage from Lizz to Caribou is quite flat and easy to travel, with a low-lying area on the Lizz Lake side built up with a corduroy log trail and a small log landing (another rarity in the BWCAW). Caribou is a nice place to spend a first evening, but many of the sites will probably be occupied if you are visiting in July or August.

Paddle and portage 2 miles from Caribou Lake to Meeds Lake, including portages of 15 rods (L4) and 15 rods (L3). You will take two tough little portages from Caribou Lake to Meeds Lake. The first portage is only 15 rods long but much harder than most short portages. It essentially follows a riverbed with large rocks and boulders forming most of the trail. During high water expect at least part of the trail to have some water running down through the rocks. After this first portage you paddle through an interesting little marsh with a very narrow channel for canoe traffic, followed by the second portage. This portage is also quite rocky but much less so than the first portage. Meeds Lake is named in honor of Alonzo D. Meeds, who was an assistant to N. H. Winchell in the Minnesota Geological Survey, for whom the larger Winchell Lake was named.

Paddle and portage 5 miles from Meeds Lake to Omega Lake, including portages of 110 rods (L7) from Meeds to Swallow Lake, 93 rods (L7) from Swallow to Pillsbery Lake, 53 rods (L5) from Pillsbery to Henson Lake, and 37 rods (L3) from Henson to Omega Lake. After you depart Meeds Lake, you will venture to a chain of small, west–east oriented lakes that are perfect for exploring by canoe. First, take a 110-rod portage between Meeds Lake and Swallow Lake. Along the portage, approximately 30 rods in from Meeds Lake, is a spectacular old white cedar. The trunk is at least 30 inches in diameter at chest height, making it a very old tree. Seeing a cedar of this size is surprising at an upland site because most cedars of this size are found in wet, low-lying areas spared by the numerous fires that have burned across the border country over the centuries. The portage to Swallow Lake terminates at an opening among a cluster of middle-aged white pines. You can look straight across and see the landing for the portage to Pillsbery Lake. No campsites are located on the long and narrow spruce-lined shores of Swallow Lake.

The 93-rod portage from Swallow Lake to Pillsbery is very flat, although also very low lying. If it has been a dry summer, you are likely to have few problems with mud, but if it has been a wet summer, expect a fair amount of the trail to be muddy. This is an infrequently traveled portage, so the trail tends to be a bit brushy and is somewhat rocky.

Pillsbery Lake is long, narrow, and low lying. The shoreline is dominated by spruce and a dense population of cedar. A few old white pines puncture this cedar and spruce forest at intervals along the shoreline. Pillsbery Lake has two designated campsites on the north shore, and they appear to get relatively little use. The western site is a bit lower lying than the eastern one, but both are reasonably nice. This long, skinny lake can make a fine overnight camping location and is certainly a good destination for visitors wishing to stay away from the more popular north–south routes through Horseshoe Lake.

Next, take the 53-rod portage from Pillsbery to Henson Lake, which begins about 100 yards west of a large rock face on the southern shore of Pillsbery. The first 20 rods are up a moderately steep curving trail. The trail levels out and winds through nice terrain before dropping sharply for the last 5 rods to Henson Lake. Henson is another long, narrow lake, with four designated campsites along its shores. On Henson Lake, opposite the portage to Otto, is a nice stand of white pines. Also, the western side of Henson has a number of well-exposed rock faces on its north shore. This portion of the northwestern shore is notable for a large population of older white pines. One final note on Henson is that some BWCAW maps show a campsite on the north-pointing bay by Creeper Lake. This is an error, and the campsite is actually in the main body of Henson on the north shore about 20 rods west of the north-pointing bay.

Henson is a crossroads lake that allows travel in all directions, including easy access west to Omega Lake or east to Gaskin, and an interesting option south to the Otto lakes. The 44-rod (L8) portage to the Otto lakes from Henson Lake is very difficult for its length due to the fact that it climbs steeply uphill and then descends steeply. You will scamper up slippery rock faces and over sizable boulders. Still, the Otto lakes are quite interesting and have two designated campsites, neither of which appears to be frequently visited. Consider the Otto lakes for a peaceful detour where you will see few other visitors, if any.

Next, the 37-rod portage from Henson to Omega Lake is reasonably well traveled and well maintained. Expect occasional muddy spots during wet times of the year, but these shouldn't be too bad. Consider spending a night on one of four designated campsites on Omega; otherwise press farther west.

Paddle and portage 6 miles from Omega Lake to Long Island Lake, including portages of 35 rods (L6) from Omega to Kiskadinna Lake, 190 rods (L8) from Kiskadinna to Muskeg Lake, and 4 to 12 rods (L2) and 25 rods (L4) from Muskeg to Long Island Lake. This journey now heads west to wonderful Long Island Lake. First, portage from Omega Lake to Kiskadinna along a trail that is fairly short but climbs steeply uphill and then descends very steeply with extensive rocks along the way. A portage of this length is rarely going to be more difficult than this one. Not surprisingly, *kiskadinna* is the Ojibwe word for "steep" or "steep place."

Continue on and take the 190-rod portage from Kiskadinna to Muskeg. This portage appears to get a surprisingly significant amount of use. Most of the trail is not exceptional, but halfway through you will encounter a 20-rod drop that descends 100 feet in elevation. Be cautious along this challenging downhill. The landing on the Kiskadinna side is fairly rocky, while the Muskeg landing is somewhat more open. Muskeg Lake is surrounded by a rich spruce forest. Its one campsite overlooks a small private bay. Despite the name Muskeg, the lake's shores are fairly rocky, and it is not a particularly boggy lake. A 4- to 12-rod portage exiting Muskeg Lake toward Long Island Lake varies in length depending on water levels. As you approach the portage, paddle past the first clear landing to a better spot farther down on the north (right) side. This portage follows a couple of different trails, depending on where you start, but is generally passable. Expect significant roots to hinder your passage along parts of the trail.

Finally, the 25-rod portage to Long Island Lake has significant rock obstacles on both ends, particularly on the Muskeg Lake side, and slippery rocks along the way. On Long Island, you will put in at a scenic narrow backwater, which you will follow to the main body of the lake. Long Island is an excellent BWCAW destination for almost every purpose. Good campsites are usually available among the fifteen designated sites, and it has fishing for lake trout and northern pike. Caution should be taken on Long Island Lake because it can develop substantial chop and rolling waves during windy days. Most of the forested shoreline was not heavily damaged by the windstorm of 1999, although the Forest Service will be conducting prescribed burns on the north shore of Long Island all the way to Sea Gull Lake. Long Island represents the southern border of a large area of lakes to be burned stretching south from Sea Gull to the north shores of Gabimichigami, Tuscarora, and Long Island lakes.

Paddle and portage 8 miles from Long Island Lake to Banadad Lake, including portages of 106 rods from Long Island to Cave Lake, 186 rods from Cave to Ross Lake, 168 rods from Ross to Sebeka Lake, and 92 rods (L8) from Sebeka to Banadad Lake. When it comes time to move on from Long Island Lake, you will head east back toward Poplar Lake. Make sure you don't start this leg late in an afternoon because your next available campsite won't be until you travel across four lakes to Banadad.

Your first task will be the 106-rod portage to Cave Lake along a trail that is largely flat and free of obstructions. Few rocks protrude into the path, and roots are rare. Cave Lake feels completely different from Long Island Lake that you have just left. Unlike the mixed forest and rocky outcroppings of Long Island, Cave is surrounded almost entirely by spruce.

Heading out the north end of Cave, a 186-rod portage to Ross Lake follows along a winding, seldom-traveled trail. The terrain alternates between flat sections and gently rolling hills. Ross Lake is small and narrow but very picturesque. The south side has a number of steeply inclined rock faces dropping off toward the water. In particular, on the far eastern side to the south of the portage is a large palisade rising 70 feet above the forest.

When you leave Ross Lake, you will carry your gear over a 168-rod portage to Sebeka Lake along a trail that is generally free of mud and rocky obstructions. The path winds through a stand of old birch and aspen intermingled with conifers. This infrequently covered portage is likely to feel more remote and overgrown than just about every portage on the first half of this route. It would be quite easy if not for the substantial uphill portion when nearing Sebeka Lake. Sebeka Lake is small and peaceful with numerous birch and aspen back from the shore and spruce lining much of the immediate shoreline, but camping is not allowed anywhere on Sebeka.

After passing through Sebeka, take the 92-rod portage to Banadad Lake. The portage is difficult as well as long. Expect an infrequently maintained trail with some mud and boulder obstructions, as well as a steep climb. At a few points along the way you will make hairpin turns among fairly thick trees while clambering over rough boulders. In addition, you will skirt along the south side of a rock slope, making it necessary to walk along an inclined rock face where footing is difficult when wet. Along the trail you will encounter intermittent spots where crevasses in the rock extend down either right along the trail or just off of it. Watch your footing because these are prime spots to twist a knee or injure an ankle. The relatively low use of this trail heightens the potential that some of these little crevasses will be concealed by brush and warrant additional caution.

Banadad is another long, narrow, and rather infrequently traveled border country lake. Four designated campsites are located on the north side of Banadad, including one on a small island. According to old DNR fish surveys, Banadad contains a limited population of northern pike but no other game fish.

Paddle and portage 6.5 miles from Banadad Lake back to your starting point on Poplar Lake, including portages of 10 rods from Banadad to Rush Lake, 50 rods from Rush to Little Rush Lake, an optional 20 rods from Little Rush to Skipper Lake, and 320 rods from Skipper to Poplar Lake. The 10-rod portage out the east end of Banadad is rather difficult for its length because the last portion is very rocky and difficult to manage with a canoe, and the initial portion is likely to be slightly wet. Next, the 50-rod portage to Little Rush Lake follows through a cedar swamp and is very flat. The down side to this flatness is the extensive roots protruding from the cedars and the likelihood that you will encounter a significant amount of mud along the route. Little Rush Lake is fairly shallow, particularly on the western side.

The portage to Skipper Lake, listed as 20 rods on Fisher maps, is really a pull-over through a shallow, bouldery creek connecting the two lakes. A well-worn portage between the two lakes does not exist, so instead you must carefully pick your way through the rocks or, alternatively, try to beach on the south side and portage 10 or 20 rods along the grassy shoreline. Skipper Lake is low lying and was heavily hit by the 1999 windstorm, yet the convoluted eastern shoreline makes for a pretty border country lake. The Forest Service will be conducting a prescribed patch burn through this area, hoping to reduce the loading of needles and small-diameter woody fuels to about 10 tons per acre (from current levels of up to 50 tons per acre). This patch burn will be on a much smaller scale and less expansive than the major burns farther west along the Gunflint Trail and should be completed by about 2007.

The long portage between Skipper Lake and Poplar Lake is smooth and free of major obstructions. The first half of the trail travels along a needle-covered path that is really easy going. The last half of the trail may be slightly more difficult, particularly the final portion extending to Poplar Lake. This portion is most difficult when coming from the Poplar side since you have to climb slightly in elevation. Even with this in mind, 320-rod portages are rarely this easy. Once on Poplar, paddle back to your starting point on the far western end.

Entry Point 48, Meeds Lake (Map 39)

Daily permit quota: 3
Permit availability: easy

Meeds Lake is one of three entries connecting Poplar Lake with the BWCAW. After a long initial portage you will be in the midst of classic Boundary Waters country of moderate-sized lakes with magnificent forests, interesting bays and islands, and good fishing. This entry is far less popular than neighboring Lizz Lake (Entry Point 47) because it has a much longer first portage.

One route is described in detail below: a loop through Meeds, Horseshoe, and Gaskin (Route 48). However, Meeds Lake is just two short portages from Caribou Lake, which is the first lake reached from Lizz Lake. Therefore all of the routes out of Lizz Lake (Entry Point 47) can be taken on a trip originating out of Meeds with minimal changes in the routes.

To reach Meeds Lake, take the Gunflint Trail for 32 miles to a left at County Road 92. Drive just over a half mile down CR 92 until you come to the intersection with Forest Road 561, which you take for three-quarters of a mile to the Poplar Lake public access. Adequate parking is available for dozens of cars. The Iron Lake campground, with seven camping spots, is just another 3 miles down CR 92 and is a good spot to spend the night before entering the Boundary Waters. You can make reservations for these sites, which is a good idea to assure yourself a spot. As is true at all entry points that do not have campgrounds, no overnight camping is allowed at the Poplar Lake landing.

Route 48: Meeds, Horseshoe, Gaskin Loop (Map 39)

Difficulty: easy/intermediate
Number of days: 3
Total miles (approx.): 18.5
Number of portages: 11
Total portage rods: 820
Greatest portage difficulty: 288 (L9)
Navigation maps: Voyageur 9
                             Fisher F13
                             McKenzie 2, 4

This is the easiest loop possible out of Meeds Lake. It makes a great weekend trip yet can be extended for much longer journeys. The first third of the loop gets the fewest visitors and will provide the best opportunities for isolation. As your trip progresses around to Gaskin and Horseshoe lakes, you are likely to encounter significantly more people but be rewarded with magnificent lakes to travel through and camp along.

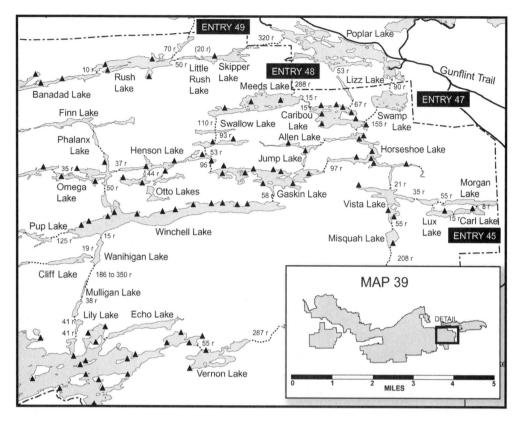

Detailed Route

Paddle and portage 4 miles from Poplar Lake to central Meeds Lake, including a portage of 288 rods (L9). The portage from Poplar Lake to Meeds starts at a little-used rocky landing on the southwest shore of Poplar and then heads up a moderate hill before leveling off on its way to Meeds Lake. At least three spots on the first half of this portage are low lying, and you can expect to encounter some mud during wet times of the year. However, the real challenge comes toward the end of the portage as you cover the last 100 rods. The trail flattens out and descends into a muddy stretch for approximately 20 rods. An old, log walkway was constructed through this stretch many years ago, but many of these logs seem to be fairly well rotted. This portage is probably a prime candidate for an upgrade in coming years.

Meeds is a sizable lake of over 300 acres and contains three designated campsites, including two on islands and one on a far western bay. All three campsites make a nice place to spend a day or two. Although close to Poplar Lake, Meeds appears to get significantly fewer visitors than most lakes to the south and east of Poplar, such as Caribou, Gaskin, and Winchell. The most popular time to visit Meeds seems to be from late May until early July, when the walleye population is a draw to visitors from neighboring Caribou Lake, so visit outside of these months if seeking maximum isolation.

Paddle and portage 3.5 miles from Meeds Lake to Henson Lake, including portages of 110 rods (L7) from Meeds to Swallow Lake, 93 rods (L7) from Swallow to Pillsbery Lake, and 53 rods (L5) from Pillsbery to Henson Lake. After you depart Meeds Lake, you will venture to a chain of small, west–east oriented lakes that are perfect for exploring by canoe. First take a 110-rod portage between Meeds Lake and Swallow Lake. Here, just like on the Poplar to Meeds portage, is a wooden walkway constructed of pine and spruce logs. This one happens to be a little more elevated off the forest floor than the one on the Meeds to Poplar portage. It also has seen better days and warrants great caution lest you injure yourself. Along the portage, approximately 30 rods from Meeds Lake, is a spectacular old cedar. The trunk is at least 30 inches in diameter at chest height, making it a very old tree. It is of some interest that a cedar was able to attain such an old age on this upland site. Most cedars of this size are found in wet, low-lying areas where they have been spared by the numerous fires that have burned across the border country over the centuries.

You cannot camp on Swallow Lake, so press on over the 93-rod portage from Swallow Lake to Pillsbery. The trail is flat although also low lying. If it has been a dry summer, you are likely to have few problems with mud, but if it has been a wet summer, expect a fair amount of the trail to be soggy. The trail tends to be a bit brushy and also has quite a few protruding rocks.

Pillsbery Lake is long, narrow, and low-lying. The shoreline is dominated by spruce and a dense population of cedars. A few old white pines puncture this cedar and spruce forest at intervals along the shoreline. Pillsbery Lake has two designated campsites on the north shore, and they appear to get relatively little use. The western site is a bit more low lying than the eastern one, but both are reasonably nice. This long, skinny lake makes a fine overnight location.

Next, take the 58-rod portage from Pillsbery to Henson Lake, beginning with a small rocky landing on the west end of Pillsbery, about 100 yards west of a large rock face on the southern shore of Pillsbery. The first 20 rods of this portage are up a moderately steep curving trail. The trail levels out and winds through nice terrain before dropping steeply for the last 5 rods to Henson Lake. Alternatively, if you are looking to modify this route, you can take a 95-rod (L7 to L8) portage on the east end of Pillsbery Lake to Allen Lake. This, too, is a reasonably flat path following the north shore of a shallow, intermittent creek bed. Most of the trail is well drained, although its proximity to the creek makes this portage more muddy than average during rainy months.

Henson Lake is another long, narrow lake, with four designated campsites. On Henson, opposite the portage to Otto, is a nice stand of white pines, many of which are fairly mature. The western side of Henson has interesting exposed rock faces on its north shore. This portion of the northwestern shore is also notable for a relatively large population of older white pines. One further note on Henson is that some BWCAW maps show a campsite on Henson in the north-pointed bay by Creeper Lake. This is an error; the campsite is actually in the main body of Henson on the north shore about 20 rods west of the north-pointed bay.

Henson is a crossroads lake that allows travel in all directions, including easy access west toward Omega Lake or east to Gaskin, and an interesting option south to the Otto lakes. The 44-rod (L8) portage to the Otto lakes from Henson Lake is very difficult for its length due to the fact that it climbs steeply uphill and then descends steeply. In between you will scamper up slippery rock faces and over some sizable boulders. Still, the Otto lakes are quite interesting and have two designated campsites, neither of which appears to be frequently visited.

Paddle and portage 3 miles from central Henson Lake to central Gaskin Lake, including a portage of 95 rods (L7). The 95-rod portage to Gaskin Lake is flat or downhill most of the way before dropping a final steep portion to a clearing and landing on the shores of Gaskin. This portage is more heavily traveled than the other ones covered to this point in the trip and is clear evidence of the popularity that Gaskin holds among Boundary Waters visitors. The trail should be fairly dry in most places, but expect some rocks and occasional rough going. The forest you carry through has large numbers of dead and downed spruce, as well as a few old dead white pine sentinels along the way.

Gaskin is a large wilderness lake with nine designated campsites. Minnesota DNR lake surveys show it to have poor fish populations, but it still seems to draw fishermen all season long, perhaps an indication the DNR surveys are not foolproof. Gaskin will seem huge after the long, narrow lakes that defined most of the journey until here. Also, you are now entering lakes that are easily accessible from all the Poplar Lake entry points, as well as Morgan Lake and Brule Lake. The result is that you will certainly encounter more visitors on the coming segments of this trip than you did in the early segments. In peak periods all of the sites on Gaskin can be taken, so arrive early in the day.

Paddle and portage 3 miles from Gaskin Lake to Horseshoe Lake, including portages of 19 rods (L3) from Gaskin to Jump Lake, 16 rods (L3) from Jump to Allen Lake, and 5 rods (L5) from Allen to Horseshoe Lake. You will now travel from Gaskin Lake to Horseshoe. The *quickest* option is to head through the east end of Gaskin over a 97-rod portage directly to Horseshoe. The route suggested here, sticking true to the goal of staying off the beaten path, takes you on an alternative option over two short portages into and out of Jump Lake, and then on to Allen Lake, which has two designated campsites. This is certainly the least popular route out of Gaskin, and neither of the short portages gets much maintenance. The big advantage of this option is a chance to get off more popular Gaskin and Horseshoe for a night. The first portage follows the outlet of Gaskin into Jump, while the second, longer portage takes you right to Allen Lake. On Allen you have two designated sites to choose from, neither of which appears to get significant use. The 51-rod portage from Allen to Horseshoe is also infrequently used, following mostly through a mixed forest on a generally level trail.

Enchanted Horseshoe Lake is among the most appealing lakes on this journey. Its long, narrow bays curve around in a horseshoe-shaped northern portion, and two long bays branch off to the south. All but one of its seven designated campsites are on the north "horseshoe" portion of the lake, and one of them occupies highlands providing fine vistas over the lake below. Based on my experiences and Forest Service data, Horseshoe Lake is a tough location to find a campsite in July and August. This is certainly a lake where you want to arrive early if you expect to spend the night.

Important warning: One note about Horseshoe is that some commercial maps show three portages along the Brule River draining the south end of Horseshoe Lake. I paddled that stretch of the Brule during research for this guide and found no evidence of these portages. I was forced to bushwhack around difficult rapids without a hint of a trail. Other rapids appeared without warning, and many trees had fallen across parts of the river, making for perilous travel. It would certainly be possible to become wedged beneath a capsized canoe in one of the unexpected rapids. *I do not believe this river can be safely navigated by most paddlers, and strongly advise against attempting it.*

Paddle and portage 5 miles from Horseshoe Lake to your starting point on Poplar Lake, including portages of 21 rods (L2) from Horseshoe to Caribou Lake, 67 rods (L4) from Caribou to Lizz Lake, and 53 rods (L4) from Lizz to Poplar Lake. The final leg of this journey will take you out of the wilderness and back to your starting point on Poplar Lake. All of the lakes you encounter are connected by excellent portages. The portage from Caribou Lake to Lizz Lake is quite flat and easy to travel. On the Lizz Lake side a low-lying area has been built up with a corduroy log trail and a small log landing, a rarity in the BWCAW. Once on Poplar Lake head west back to your starting point.

Entry Point 49, Skipper and Portage Lakes (Map 39)

> Permit quota: 2
> Permit availability: moderate

Skipper and Portage lakes combine to form the third of three entries giving access to the Boundary Waters from Poplar Lake (along with Entry Points 47 and 48). You can start at Poplar Lake and then head to Skipper, or you can start at the Iron Lake campground a few miles to the west and head to Portage Lake and then portage to One Island Lake before entering the BWCAW at Rush Lake. The more common choice appears to be by way of Skipper Lake because it affords numerous loops that lead back to your starting point on Poplar Lake.

This entry gets relatively few visitors, no doubt a result of the long portages that must be taken to start your trip, and the fact that few loop routes are possible. This entry is reminiscent of the Bower Trout Lake entry (Entry Point 43), described earlier, because the number of travel routes is so limited. Two route options are described below. First is a simple trip to Skipper, Rush, and Banadad lakes, all of which are beautiful and isolated (Route 49A). The second route loops west through Banadad and on to Long Island Lake, before heading south and east to return to Poplar Lake by way of Meeds Lake (Route 49B).

To reach Poplar Lake, if you are entering by way of Skipper Lake, take the Gunflint Trail for 32 miles to a left at County Road 92. Drive just over a half mile down CR 92 until you come to the intersection with Forest Road 561, which you take for three-quarters of a mile to the Poplar Lake public access. You will need to portage from Poplar to Skipper to enter the BWCAW, as described below. Adequate parking is available for dozens of cars at the Poplar Lake landing. The Iron Lake campground, with seven campsites, is just another 3 miles down CR 92 and is a good spot to spend the night before entering the Boundary Waters. This campground is also how you enter if you are coming in from Portage Lake.

Route 49A: Exploration of Skipper and Rush Lakes (Map 39)

> Difficulty: intermediate
> Number of days: 2 or more
> Total miles (approx.): 9
> Number of portages: 4 to 6 depending on water levels
> Total portage rods: 740 to 780
> Greatest portage difficulty: 320 rods (L9)
> Navigation maps: Voyageur 9
> Fisher F13
> McKenzie 3

This route heads into the wilderness at Skipper Lake by way of Poplar Lake, then takes you on a short journey to Rush Lake and back again to Poplar. This is a good trip into a relatively remote portion of the BWCAW, but it requires long portages that will challenge unprepared visitors.

Detailed Route

Paddle and portage 4.5 miles from Poplar Lake to Rush Lake, including portages of 320 rods (L9) from Poplar to Skipper Lake, 20 rods (optional) from Skipper to Little Rush Lake, and 50 rods from Little Rush to Rush Lake. The portage from Poplar Lake to Skipper Lake is long, but fortunately the trail is very smooth and free of major obstructions, and you are not likely to encounter much mud along the way. The first half of the trail climbs slightly in elevation, but the second half levels off and travels along an easy needle-covered path. To a reasonably fit individual traveling with only a moderate amount of gear, this portage should pose no problem, but leave your cot and cooler behind.

Skipper Lake is low lying and is one of a few lakes in this immediate area hit heavily by the 1999 windstorm, along with Little Rush Lake and some of Rush Lake. The Forest Service will be conducting small-scale patch burns in this area, including Skipper, Rush, and Little Rush lakes, to remove excess burnable fuel accumulated during the windstorm. All of these burns should be completed by 2007. One designated campsite is located on the north shore of Skipper.

The portage from Skipper Lake to Little Rush Lake requires navigating through a shallow, boulder-strewn creek connecting the two lakes. The lakes are not joined by a well-maintained portage, so instead you must carefully pick your way through the rocks of a couple shallow stretches. Alternatively, try to beach on the south side of the connection, and portage along the grassy shoreline. This second option has been tried before, as is evidenced by the slightly worn path through the grass, but apparently not as often as the first. Little Rush Lake is fairly shallow, particularly on the western side, where emergent water plants can be seen growing. The slightly rocky shoreline is a mixed cedar and spruce forest. Camping is not allowed on Little Rush Lake, so press on toward Rush Lake.

The final portage of this leg, from Little Rush Lake to Rush Lake, follows through a low-lying cedar grove. You will portage over extensive roots protruding from the cedars and will encounter a great amount of mud if the weather has been wet. On Rush Lake you can camp at any of four designated campsites. Minnesota DNR surveys indicate a good number of northern pike in Rush but no other game fish.

Paddle and portage 4.5 miles from Rush Lake back to your starting point on Poplar Lake, including portages of 50 rods, optional 20 rods, and 320 rods (L9). Reverse the way you came to Rush Lake to get back to your start.

Route 49B: Loop through Banadad, Long Island, and Henson (Map 39)

Difficulty: challenging
Number of days: 4
Total miles (approx.): 29
Number of portages: 17
Total portage rods: 1,792
Greatest portage difficulty: 190 rods (L10)
Navigation maps: Voyageur 6, 8, 9
Fisher F12, F13
McKenzie 2, 4, 7

This route starts along the first leg taken in Route 49A but then extends with a great western loop to Long Island Lake before heading south and east by way of Henson Lake and back to its origin on Poplar. It is a wonderful trip for visitors seeking a real challenge.

Map 39 shows most of this route, and Map 34 shows the farthest west portions. The entire route is shown on Map 36.

Detailed Route

Paddle and portage 4.5 miles from Poplar Lake to Rush Lake, including portages of 320 rods (L9) from Poplar to Skipper Lake, 20 rods (optional) from Skipper to Little

Rush Lake, and 50 rods from Little Rush to Rush Lake. This journey starts with a repeat of the first half of Route 49A.

Paddle and portage 8.5 miles from Rush Lake to Long Island Lake, including portages of 10 rods (L4) from Rush to Banadad Lake, 92 rods (L9) from Banadad to Sebeka Lake, 165 rods from Sebeka to Ross Lake, 186 rods from Ross to Cave Lake, and 106 rods from Cave to Long Island Lake. The 10-rod portage from Rush Lake to Banadad Lake is rather difficult for its length because the last portion is very rocky and difficult to manage with a canoe. If this portage seems to be far longer than 10 rods, then you have mistakenly hooked up to the Banadad Ski Trail. Backtrack to the start, and continue the short distance to Banadad Lake. Banadad is a long, narrow, and isolated lake. Four designated campsites are scattered along its shores.

The 92-rod portage from Banadad to Sebeka is difficult. Expect an infrequently traveled trail with some mud and boulder obstructions, as well as a steep descent to Sebeka. At a few points along the way you will make hairpin turns among fairly thick trees while clambering over rough boulders. In addition, you will skirt along the south side of a rock slope, making it necessary to walk along an inclined rock face where footing is difficult when wet. Watch your footing on this portage. Camping is not permitted on Sebeka Lake, which is small and peaceful with numerous birch and aspen back from the shore and spruce lining much of the immediate shoreline.

The 165-rod portage from Sebeka to Ross Lake is generally free of mud and rocky obstructions. The trail winds through a stand of old birch and aspen intermingled with conifers and then drops 70 feet to Ross. This infrequently maintained portage is likely to be somewhat overgrown compared to more frequently traveled Boundary Waters routes. Ross Lake is small and narrow but very picturesque. The south side has a number of steeply inclined rock faces dropping off toward the water. In particular, on the far eastern end is a neat palisade rising about 70 feet above the forest.

The 186-rod portage from Ross Lake to Cave Lake follows along a winding, seldom-traveled trail. Some mud and dilapidated walkways will be encountered. The terrain alternates between flat sections and gently rolling hills. Cave Lake is lined almost exclusively by spruce, with a fringe of emergent plants on much of the shoreline of this boreal classic. From Cave, take the 106-rod portage to Long Island Lake, which is largely flat and free of obstructions.

Long Island Lake is an excellent BWCAW destination for almost every purpose. Good campsites are usually available among the fifteen Forest Service designated sites, and it contains lake trout and northern pike. Caution should be taken on Long Island Lake because it can develop substantial chop and rolling waves during windy days.

Paddle and portage 4.5 miles from Long Island Lake to Kiskadinna Lake, including portages of 25 rods (L4) and 4 to 12 rods (L2) to Muskeg Lake, and 190 rods (L10) from Muskeg to Kiskadinna. On Long Island, paddle southeast into a scenic narrow backwater containing the start to the 25-rod portage to Muskeg Lake. This portage has significant rock obstacles on both ends, particularly on the Muskeg Lake side, and slippery rocks along the way. Next, a 4- to 12-rod portage to Muskeg Lake changes dramatically depending on water levels. The portage follows a couple of different trails, depending on where you start and stop, but is generally passable.

Significant roots hinder your passage along parts of the portage, but otherwise this is an easy carry to Muskeg. Muskeg Lake is surrounded by a rich spruce forest. The sole designated campsite on Muskeg is quite nice because it overlooks a small private bay. Despite the name Muskeg, the lake's shores are fairly rocky, and it is not a particularly boglike lake.

Next, take the 190-rod portage to Kiskadinna from Muskeg. This portage appears to get a fair amount of use. Most of this portage is not too exceptional, but halfway through you will encounter a 20-rod climb that rises over 100 feet in elevation, making this one of the most difficult sub-200-rod portages in the Boundary Waters. Over all you will climb over 150 feet in elevation from the shores of Muskeg to the shores of Kiskadinna. You and your legs won't soon forget this portage. The trail is steep enough that a fall could result in serious injury, so take caution and don't overload yourself. Dismounting a canoe halfway up the steep section would not be fun or easy, so rest at the bottom, make a good haul up, and then rest at the top. Kiskadinna is long and narrow with a rocky south shore and a moderately flat north shore.

Paddle and portage 7.5 miles from Kiskadinna Lake to Meeds Lake, including portages of 35 rods (L6) from Kiskadinna to Omega Lake, 37 rods (L3) from Omega to Henson Lake, 53 rods (L5) from Henson to Pillsbery Lake, 93 rods (L7) from Pillsbery to Swallow Lake, and 110 rods (L7) from Swallow to Meeds Lake. The portage from Kiskadinna to Omega Lake is fairly short but climbs steeply and then descends very steeply with extensive rocks along the way. A portage of this length is rarely going to be more difficult than this one.

Omega Lake is unequivocally beautiful and a pleasant enough end to a day's journey, if you so choose. Numerous arms extend outward from the central axis, providing pleasant vistas for paddlers moving through, and a certain degree of solitude for those who stay at one of the four designated campsites. The shoreline is very rocky, with nice exposed bedrock. During busy times of the year do not expect to find a place on Omega for the night unless you get there early.

From Omega Lake you will take a 37-rod portage to Henson. The portage is reasonably well traveled and well maintained. Expect occasional muddy spots during wet times of the year, but these shouldn't be too bad. Henson is another long, narrow lake, with four designated campsites along its shores. Opposite the portage to Otto Lake is a nice stand of white pines, many of which are fairly mature. The western side of Henson has a number of well-exposed rock faces on its north shore, and a relatively large population of older white pines. One final note on Henson is that some BWCAW maps show a campsite on Henson in the north-pointed bay by Creeper Lake. This is an error; the campsite is actually in the main body of Henson on the north shore about 20 rods west of the north-pointed bay.

Next, take the 58-rod portage from Henson Lake to Pillsbery Lake and continue over the 93-rod portage to Swallow Lake. Pillsbery Lake is long, narrow, and low lying. The shoreline is dominated by spruce and a relatively dense population of cedars. A few old white pines puncture this cedar and spruce forest at intervals along the shoreline. This area was not heavily hit by the windstorm of 1999. The portage from Pillsbery to Swallow is very flat although also very low lying. If it has been a dry summer, you are likely to have few problems with mud, but if it has been a wet summer, expect a fair amount of the trail to be muddy. This is also a less frequently traveled route, so the trail tends to be a bit brushy. Expect a fair number of toaster-size rocks protruding from the trail.

Finally, the 110-rod portage from Swallow to Meeds Lake follows in part along an old wooden walkway constructed of pine and spruce logs. It has seen better days and warrants great caution lest you injure yourself. Along the portage, approximately 30 rods from Meeds Lake, is a spectacular old white cedar. The trunk is at least 30 inches in diameter at chest height.

Paddle and portage 4 miles from Meeds Lake to Poplar Lake, including a portage of 288 rods (L9). Head back to your origin on Poplar Lake. The portage from Meeds to Poplar Lake is not heavily used, probably because other, shorter routes to Poplar are possible. A number of slight uphills are found along the way, and you should expect a trail that is somewhat rocky. At least three spots on the first half of this portage are low lying. Near Meeds Lake you will come across an old log walkway constructed through this stretch many years ago, but many of these logs appear to be fairly well rotted. On Poplar paddle back to your starting point on the west end of the lake.

Entry Point 50, Cross Bay Lake (Map 40)

> Daily permit quota: 3
> Permit availability: difficult

Cross Bay Lake, Entry Point 50, is a great starting point for trips venturing south of the Gunflint Trail, particularly for visitors hoping to reach Long Island Lake without the long portages necessary when entering through Missing Link Lake. Many of the routes out of Cross Bay Lake involve frequent portaging, but the portages are typically not too long. Get your reservation early if you wish to enter through Cross Bay, because permits are usually reserved well in advance.

Three routes are described below. The first outing (Route 50A) is an excursion to Long Island Lake, avoiding tough portages yet reaching a fantastic interior lake with many day-trip options for further exploration. The second journey (Route 50B) is a nice loop through legendary Tuscarora Lake. You won't forget the beauty along this journey, but come prepared to portage: this route has a number of tough portages, including one that is over a mile long. The third trip (Route 50C) is a huge loop to the southern edges of the BWCAW and back again, well suited for visitors interested in a long, challenging adventure.

To reach Cross Bay Lake, take the Gunflint Trail for 47 miles from Grand Marais to County Road 47 (you will see a sign for Tuscarora Lodge), and turn left. Head down CR 47 until you reach a turnout and parking lot approximately a half mile from the Gunflint Trail. A short trail leads to a landing and dock on the Cross River. The small parking lot is adequate for the limited number of visitors who enter through

Cross Bay. From the landing on the Cross River you will paddle to Ham Lake and then on to Cross Bay Lake, where you will officially enter the BWCAW.

The nearest public camping location is the Trails End campground 9 miles farther up the Gunflint at Sea Gull Lake. Expect to pay a nightly camping fee. Be certain to make a reservation in advance because the campground is very busy during the summer months. If Trails End campground is full, consider staying at the smaller Iron Lake campground closer to Grand Marais. Also, a number of outfitters along the Gunflint Trail offer bunkhouse accommodations that are both convenient and economical.

Route 50A: Long Island Lake Excursion (Map 40)

> Difficulty: intermediate
> Number of days: 2 or more
> Total miles (approx.): 15
> Number of portages: 6
> Total portage rods: 478
> Greatest portage difficulty: 50 rods (L4)
> Navigation maps: Voyageur 6
> Fisher F12
> McKenzie 7

This route is a pleasant journey that takes six modest portages on the way to Long Island Lake. You should have no problem reaching Long Island in one day, and you will double back along the same lakes on your return. This is a relatively popular route well suited for first-time campers, so you will probably come across at least some other visitors along it. Nevertheless, this is a great wilderness journey and certainly an excellent introduction to the BWCAW.

Map 40 shows the start of this route, and Map 34 shows later portions. An overview of the entire route is shown on Map 36.

Detailed Route

Paddle and portage 7.5 miles from the landing on the Cross River to central Long Island Lake, including portages of 65 rods (L3) to a small pond, 35 rods (L3) to Ham Lake, 24 rods (L2) from Ham to Cross Bay Lake, 50 rods (L4) from Cross Bay to Rib Lake, 37 rods (L3) from Rib to Lower George Lake, and 28 rods (L2) from Lower George to Karl Lake and Long Island Lake.

Paddle upstream from the landing on the Cross River to a 65-rod portage that climbs along a nice path to a small pond. Paddle the length of the pond, and then take a 35-rod portage that follows another nice path around a set of rapids to Ham Lake. Paddle across Ham Lake, and take a 24-rod portage to Cross Bay Lake. This portage is mismarked on some maps, which show the portage located at the rocky

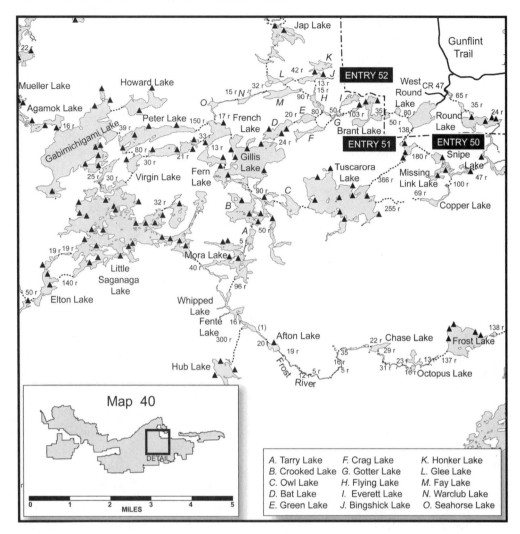

channel between the two lakes. In reality, the portage is about 200 yards to the west of the channel.

Paddling through the northern reaches of Cross Bay Lake, you will officially enter the BWCAW. Wind your way along the pleasant shoreline to the portage at the far south end of the lake. The diverse water plants growing along the shore give you an opportunity to identify such northern natives as blue flag iris and the carnivorous pitcher plant.

Continuing on, a 50-rod portage from Cross Bay Lake to Rib Lake is relatively flat until just before its end at Rib Lake, where it climbs a gentle hill. Rib Lake is surrounded by a mixed forest of jack pine, birch, aspen, and spruce extending up from rocky shores and marshlands. While no beavers were active on the lake the last time I traveled through, a long-abandoned beaver lodge clings to the east shore approximately 100 yards from the landing leading to Cross Bay Lake. The rich aspen forest will no doubt attract a new family of beavers in due time.

The 37-rod portage from Rib Lake to Lower George Lake is flat, wide, and typically free of any obstructions. The biggest challenge is finding the landing on the Rib Lake side, but this is accomplished by heading to the southeast corner of Rib and paddling up a small, slow-moving stream flowing into Rib. You will paddle about 200 hundred yards up the stream and find the landing on the right side of the stream. If you are observant, you will notice a number of timbers extending into the water on both sides of the portage—evidence of the heavier use that these lakes saw a generation ago.

Paddle through low-lying George Lake, past its predominantly spruce forest, and on to the 28-rod portage leading to Karl Lake. This easy portage begins with a brief uphill from a pool on the south shore of Lower George Lake and then follows a short, flat trail to Karl. You have two options for pressing forward after entering Karl Lake. The first option is to continue to the southeast to Long Island Lake without portaging or, if you are in a hurry to get to the west end of Long Island Lake, take the 35-rod portage over the peninsula from Karl to Long Island. This is a tough portage that climbs over a considerable hill, but it will save a substantial amount of time compared to going to the heart of Long Island Lake in order to meet up with the Long Island River. However, if you are paddling with a canoe full of loose baggage and detest portaging, this may be one to skip because it may be too difficult getting over the initial part of the portage. In addition, you will have more time to enjoy the island-studded waters of Long Island Lake and perhaps an opportunity to wet a fishing line. The end of the portage to Long Island Lake empties out onto a rare sandy Boundary Waters beach and is an ideal location for a short swim, a lunch break, or a foot soaking.

Long Island Lake is an excellent BWCAW destination for almost every purpose. Caution should be taken on Long Island Lake because it can develop substantial chop and rolling waves during windy days when the wind is coming from the west. Good campsites are usually available among the fifteen Forest Service designated sites, and it is a fine lake for trout and northern pike. Don't be surprised to see an occasional bald eagle or osprey overhead. Here, too, you will find the first significant stands of red and white pines since beginning your trip on Round Lake.

Paddle and portage 7.5 miles from Long Island Lake back to the landing on the Cross River, including portages of 28 rods (L2), 37 rods (L3), 50 rods (L4), 24 rods (L2), 35 rods (L3), and 65 rods (L3). Backtrack the same way you came, or design your own route based on the descriptions for Entry Points 51 and 52.

Route 50B: Tuscarora Loop (Map 40)

    Difficulty: challenging
    Number of days: 3 or more
    Total miles (approx.): 12
    Number of portages: 9
    Total portage rods: 1,099
    Greatest portage difficulty: 366 rods (L10)

Navigation maps: Voyageur 6
Fisher F12
McKenzie 7

A loop to Tuscarora is another excellent way to explore the beauty lying south of the Gunflint Trail and is well suited for someone looking for a trip more challenging than Route 50A. You will not be disappointed by Tuscarora Lake, and you will find some of the best lake trout fishing in the BWCAW. However, this is a route rich in portages: four are 100 or more rods, including one that is 255 rods and a massive 366-rod portage from Tuscarora to Missing Link. These portages should not dissuade a fit, experienced camper—just pack accordingly and lighten your load as much as possible.

Detailed Route

Paddle and portage 8 miles from the Cross River to central Tuscarora Lake, including portages of 65 rods (L3) to a small pond, 35 rods (L3) to Ham Lake, 24 rods from Ham (L2) to Cross Bay Lake, 47 rods (L4) from Cross Bay to Snipe Lake, 100 rods from Snipe to Copper Lake, 69 rods from Copper to Hubbub Lake, and 255 rods from Hubbub to Tuscarora Lake.

Paddle upstream from the put-in point on the Cross River to a 65-rod portage that climbs along a nice path to a small pond. Paddle the length of the pond, and then take a 35-rod portage that follows another nice path around a set of rapids before dropping to Ham Lake. Paddle across Ham Lake, and take a 25-rod portage to Cross Bay Lake. This portage is mismarked on some commercial maps, which show the portage located at the rocky channel between the two lakes. In reality, the portage is about 200 yards to the west of the channel.

Paddling through the northern reaches of Cross Bay Lake, you will officially enter the BWCAW. Wind your way along the pleasant shoreline to the portage at the end of the western bay of the lake. The portage from Cross Bay Lake to Snipe Lake follows along a creek draining Snipe. The trail is well traveled and should pose no problems.

Irregularly shaped Snipe Lake contains four designated campsites scattered along its shores. Consider spending a night on Snipe if your schedule allows it. All four campsites appear to get frequent use, so be sure to arrive early if you intend to spend an evening here. These are the last campsites before a 255-rod portage to Tuscarora Lake, which is at least two hours of paddling and portaging away, so allow yourself plenty of time to travel past Snipe. Legend has it that these shores provide some of the finest snipe hunting in the world. Keep your flashlights ready to lure them into camp, and tent bags ready to hold the bounty. As you are in a national forest, you must release all snipes unharmed.

The 100-rod portage from Snipe to Copper is moderately difficult but includes a decent small bridge over the only significant low area. If you are observant, you might see green copper oxide leaking out onto the exposed bedrock on the northern shore of Copper Lake, especially near the Hubbub portage, no doubt evidence of the basis for naming this lake. The 69-rod portage from Copper Lake to Hubbub Lake is generally easy, especially compared to other portages on this route.

Pressing on, take the long 255-rod trail to Tuscarora Lake that crosses the Howl Swamp. The path is likely to be in pretty good shape, despite its length, and has a boardwalk across the deepest portion of the Howl Swamp. I have crossed this portage when the boardwalk was partially underwater, so don't be surprised if you must get your feet wet on this carry.

This series of tough portages ends in Tuscarora Lake, which is a magnificent destination that you will find was well worth the effort. Tuscarora has eleven designated campsites and is known for a good population of lake trout, making it a popular destination for early-spring visitors. Tuscarora is an attractive destination, but the relatively long portages into it significantly limit the number of visitors. Nevertheless, campsites can be hard to come by during the two or three weeks after the fishing season opens in the middle of May.

Paddle and portage 4 miles from Tuscarora Lake to Round Lake, including portages of 366 rods (L10) from Tuscarora to Missing Link Lake, and 138 rods (L7) from Missing Link to Round Lake. When leaving Tuscarora, you will take a long portage to Missing Link Lake over a path well known to Gunflint Trail regulars. This portage will not be readily forgotten by anyone who has hauled their gear over its long, hilly path. Fortunately, you will find that the trail is generally in good shape, making this a reasonable carry for well-packed visitors.

Missing Link is another nice BWCAW lake and contains a good population of stocked brook trout that brings in fishermen year-round. I have sought trout through the ice on Missing Link in the middle of winter but without success. However, DNR lake surveys indicate the fish are present there, as well as at less visited and smaller Mavis Lake just to the east of Missing Link.

A 138-rod portage completes your carries for this trip, taking you from Missing Link Lake to Round Lake and out of the BWCAW. On this portage you will initially proceed past a short marshy area and then move along a rocky trail with extensive exposed roots and stones before paralleling a small stream for 30 rods until you drop to Round Lake. Scenic cliffs rise up on the west side of part of this portage.

Once on Round Lake, paddle up to the northwest shore, where a nice landing and large parking lot are located. This parking lot is just down the road from where you parked your car by the Cross River. Head out on the gravel road entering the parking lot, and take a left at the first junction (County Road 47). Your car will be down the road a few hundred yards.

Route 50C: Cherokee, Sawbill, Gillis Voyage (Map 40)

    Difficulty: challenging

    Number of days: 8 or more

Total miles (approx.): 62
Number of portages: 52
Total portage rods: 3,002
Greatest portage difficulty: 280 rods (L8)
Navigation maps: Voyageur 6, 8
                  Fisher F5, F11, F12
                  McKenzie 7, 20, 21

This superb route will take you clear across the BWCAW to its southern boundary and back again. Along the way you will pass through fantastic lakes of every shape and size, including such famous gems as Cherokee, Sawbill, Malberg, and Little Saganaga. You will also pass through less frequented areas, such as Anit, Pan, and Makwa. This route avoids the biggest and worst portages in this portion of the BWCAW, but it is not a good trip for the novice canoeist.

This trip is more about having enough time to complete it rather than having enough raw power. You will have excellent prospects for seeing moose, deer, beavers, otters, eagles, and other north-woods natives. Also, fishing can be great on many of the lakes along the way, but don't assume you will be catching any of your dinners— BWCAW fish can be very finicky. All things considered, this is a route that will not disappoint adventurous visitors.

Map 40 shows the start and end of this route, and Maps 32 and 30 show the remainder.

Detailed Route

Paddle and portage 7.5 miles from the Cross River to Long Island Lake, starting at the landing on the Cross River, including portages of 65 rods (L3) to a small pond, 35 rods (L3) to Ham Lake, 24 rods (L2) from Ham to Cross Bay Lake, 50 rods (L4) from Cross Bay to Rib Lake, 37 rods (L3) from Rib to Lower George Lake, and 28 rods (L2) from Lower George to Karl Lake and Long Island Lake.

Your journey starts from the landing on the western shore of the Cross River. Paddle upstream to a 65-rod portage that climbs along a nice path to a small pond. Paddle the length of the pond and then take a 35-rod portage that follows another nice path up around a set of significant rapids before dropping to Ham Lake. You will paddle across Ham Lake and take the 24-rod portage to Cross Bay Lake. This portage is mismarked on some commercial maps and is actually about 200 yards to the west of the rocky channel connecting these two lakes. Paddling through the northern reaches of Cross Bay Lake, you will officially enter the BWCAW. Wind your way along the pleasant shoreline to the far south end of the lake.

The portage from Cross Bay to Rib Lake is relatively flat until just before Rib, where it climbs a gentle hill. Rib Lake is surrounded by a mixed forest of jack pine, birch, aspen, and spruce extending up from rocky shores and marshlands. The trail on the 37-rod portage from Rib Lake to Lower George Lake is flat, wide, and relatively free of obstructions. The biggest challenge is finding the landing on the Rib Lake side, but this is accomplished by heading to the southeast corner of Rib and paddling up the small, slow-moving stream that flows to Rib. Head upstream about 200 yards, and find the landing on the right side of the stream.

Paddle through low-lying George Lake, past the predominantly spruce forest, and on to the portage leading to Karl Lake. This easy portage to Karl Lake begins with a brief uphill from a pool on the south shore of Lower George Lake, and then follows a short, flat trail to Karl. You have two options after entering Karl Lake: continue along a portage-free route to Long Island Lake to the southeast, or if you are in a hurry to get to the west end of Long Island Lake, take a tough little 35-rod portage over the peninsula from Karl to Long Island.

Long Island Lake is an excellent BWCAW destination for almost every purpose. Good campsites are usually available among the fifteen designated sites, and the lake has fine fishing for lake trout and pike. Here, too, you will find the first significant stands of red and white pines since beginning your trip up on the Cross River. Exercise caution on Long Island Lake because it can develop substantial chop and rolling waves on windy days when the breeze is coming the from west.

Paddle and portage 5 miles from Long Island Lake to Cherokee Lake, including portages of 8 rods (L3), 28 rods (L3), and 13 rods (L2). Continue south out of Long Island Lake, and enter the Long Island River. While traveling up the Long Island River, you will take three portages. The first, 8-rod portage bypasses a series of small rapids and a partially washed-out beaver dam. During high water you should be able to paddle your way through, and even if paddling doesn't work, this is an easy portage to wade through with your canoe. The second portage follows for about 28 rods along the banks of the river. The final, 13-rod portage is moderately traveled, so don't be surprised to see alder and hazel bushes growing out over the path. In some ways this portage amounts to an informal divide between the north and the south halves of the eastern BWCAW. Most visitors who visit Long Island Lake reach there by way of northern entry points, while most who visit Cherokee Lake reach there by way of southern entry points. You are crossing the divide as you head to Cherokee.

Cherokee Lake holds a special place in the hearts of many visitors to the BWCAW. Its large, island-studded surface includes nineteen designated campsites, and easy connections can be made to four neighboring lakes. Cherokee hosts an average northern pike population and some lake trout, although walleye are absent according to Minnesota DNR lake surveys. This route will take you out the southwest end of Cherokee Lake on to Cherokee Creek. If you want an additional diversion, consider heading to North Temperance Lake or east to Town Lake. Also, a loop can be made to Brule Lake by way of Cam and Vesper lakes, but this loop is very difficult due to the infrequent use of the portages and their extremely rocky conditions.

Paddle and portage 8 miles from Cherokee Lake to Sawbill Lake, including portages of 180 rods to Skoop Lake (L7), 96 rods from Skoop to Ada Lake, 76 rods from Ada Lake to Ada Creek, and 78 rods from Ada Creek to Sawbill Lake. You will find few Boundary Waters portages as clear as the 180-rod path south out of Cherokee Creek to Skoop Lake. Small footbridges have been constructed across the few low areas along the trail, making this a great all-weather crossing even though it has frequent short hills along the way.

The 96-rod portage between Skoop and Ada was historically a long, muddy, nasty trail, but in recent years it was modified by the Forest Service to become longer but much less muddy. An additional 76-rod portage leads to Ada Creek, followed by a 78-rod portage to Sawbill Lake. This 78-rod portage from Ada Creek to Sawbill Lake is relatively flat, free of obstructions, and well traveled because it is a main gateway out of the busy Sawbill Lake entry point. Sawbill Lake lies on the southern edge of the BWCAW and gets relatively heavy visitor use because it serves as a major gateway to the wilderness. You will certainly run across other visitors on Sawbill because as many as fourteen permits per day are issued to enter here.

Paddle and portage 8.5 miles from Sawbill Lake to Phoebe Lake, including portages of 29 rods (L2) from Sawbill to Alton Lake, 147 rods from Alton (L4) to Beth Lake, 280 rods (L8) from Beth to Grace Lake, and four portages of 12 (L1), 22 (L3), 5 (L2), and 88 rods (L5) to Phoebe Lake. When your time comes to leave Sawbill, head to Alton by way of an easy 29-rod portage. Alton Lake is big and relatively low lying, and provides you with a choice of sixteen designated campsites. Northern pike, walleye, and bass are all located beneath its 1,000-plus acres. While sixteen campsites are plenty for most areas, the busy Sawbill entry point is just a portage away, and it attracts large numbers of canoeists. You would be well advised to get an early start to Alton if traveling in July or August.

An easy portage from Alton to Beth Lake receives frequent use. The majority of the trail is level, having a couple of plank footbridges over low areas, and then climbs a short, steep hill before leveling off again before the Beth Lake landing. When you go over the top of the hill, you are crossing the Laurentian Divide. Water falling on the south side of the divide eventually flows to the Atlantic Ocean by way of the Lake Superior Drainage and St. Lawrence River. Water falling on the north side eventually drains to the Arctic Ocean by way of Hudson Bay.

Beth is a clear-water lake of approximately 180 acres, with a maximum depth of 20 feet. Tall hills rise up on the south shore and are much higher than most hills that you will come across in this portion of the BWCAW. Notice the predominantly birch and aspen forest covering these hills, evidence of youthful stands.

When you press on to Grace Lake, you should take the 280-rod portage, which rises and falls along the south shore of a marshy area. Don't be misled by your topographic map—this portage is high and dry. If you are observant, you will notice that the exposed rock is primarily a red granitic composition, evidence that it is from a different deposit than the primarily gray gabbro underlying most of this route, and in particular these southern lakes. I recommend taking this 280-rod portage directly to Grace Lake rather than the 93-rod and 151-rod portages by way of Ella Lake. The longer portage also appears to be more popular, based on the condition of the trail. You don't save much distance by splitting the trip into two portages, have an extra load and unload of your canoe, and have to canoe an extra mile and half on Grace

Lake to Phoebe. If you take the Ella Lake route, you will find the 93-rod portage is lower lying and less traveled than the 280-rod portage. Expect significant amounts of mud along the trail. Ella Lake is peaceful with a nice mixed forest and a fair number of young white pines surrounding the lake, particularly near the Grace Lake portage. The final, 147-rod portage to Grace from Ella Lake is fairly rocky, and portions of it are muddy. In addition, the landing on the Grace Lake side is rocky.

Grace is a great place to camp for a night, a weekend, or a week. You have seven campsites to choose from and can troll or cast for walleye and northern pike. The mixed forest is particularly scenic in fall when the colors are changing. After exiting Grace Lake, you will head down the Phoebe River to Phoebe Lake.

You next travel along the Phoebe River for approximately 1 mile, with four short portages along the way. The first portage starts on the western corner of Grace and is a flat, well-traveled path. The Phoebe River is very rocky, shallow, and slow-moving most of the year. You will need to cautiously pick your path through this obstacle course to the 22-rod portage, which is also very flat and dry most of the year. Continue along through a tamarack swamp past various bog plants to the 5-rod portage bypassing a 2-foot waterfall. On the upstream side you will notice an excellent exposure of dark gray gabbro that has been intruded by a subsequent lighter gray granitic rock. The intruding granite is readily apparent as inch-wide bands. The 88-rod portage to Phoebe has a few ups and downs but is generally not too strenuous. The most difficult portion is a short stretch where you must scurry down a rock face for a few feet. Exposures of intruded gabbro are also evident at numerous places. As you reach the Phoebe landing, a small waterfall cascades through the woods on your left. A trail leads back to the falls, which is a great place to refresh and soothe any mosquito bites you may have picked up along the way.

Well-loved Phoebe Lake has eight campsites scattered across the west shore and on three islands. The depths of Phoebe are home to walleye and northern pike. The early-growth forest of birch and aspen is an indication of disturbance to these hills not many years ago.

Paddle and portage 8 miles from Phoebe Lake to Lake Polly, including a portage of 144 rods (L6) to Hazel Lake, followed by portages of 57 rods (L4), 28 rods (L2), 91 rods (L6), 14 rods (L1), and 97 rods (L4) along the Phoebe River to Lake Polly. To leave Phoebe, paddle through the channel on the north shore and enter Knight Lake. The eastern shores of Knight are low lying and covered by a mixture of birch and spruce, with large areas of nonforested land that are more evidence of a recent disturbance to this area.

Paddle up the peaceful Phoebe River until you see a portage on your left side. Stretches of the river are quite shallow, so keep alert for rocks. You will be passing through fine beaver country and should keep your eyes peeled for signs of beavers. You will have no problem spotting beaver lodges but should also look for less obvious evidence such as skinned branches and matted-down grassy spots on the edge of the river where beavers have recently fed.

The trail to Hazel Lake is fairly level and free of most obstacles as it passes through an aging aspen forest. Stretches of fairly thick underbrush may make it feel somewhat overgrown and rugged if it has not been recently cleared. Head across Hazel Lake, or spend an evening at one of the three designated campsites.

You next travel by way of the Phoebe River to Lake Polly. Five portages must be crossed along the way. The 57-rod portage starts at a clear rock landing just to the right of the spot where the Phoebe River starts its journey from Hazel Lake. The portage covers a smooth, flat trail and soon winds down to the right and drops abruptly to a gravel landing. The Phoebe River then broadens out through a tamarack swamp, and glacial erratics stick up from the riverbed at various points.

Continue through shallow pools to the 28-rod portage, which is also flat and well traveled. Next, the 91-rod portage climbs a very gradual hill before once again dropping to the river. The 14-rod portage bypasses a short series of rapids. Expect a simple portage with only a few exposed roots and rocks. The upstream landing is a bit challenging because you will be scampering up an inclined rock face. The final portage is a straight 97-rod path through a spruce forest before descending to a rocky landing on Lake Polly.

Beautiful Lake Polly is another wonderful lake on this great route. Dozens of islands dot its surface, and it has fifteen designated campsites. Arrive early if possible because many visitors entering from Kawishiwi Lake make Polly their destination for their first day of paddling. Walleye and northern pike both inhabit these depths, and even sunfish can be caught on occasion. Some of the forest around Lake Polly was severely damaged by a windstorm in 1949. This natural event was used by the Forest Service as partial justification for ongoing logging operations in this area as part of the Tomahawk Sale in 1945, discussed earlier in the history section of this guide.

Paddle and portage 2.25 miles from Lake Polly to Koma Lake, including portages of 21 rods (L1), 48 (L3) rods, and 113 (L5) rods. The first, 21-rod portage is flat and wide, bypassing rapids. Head across the small pool on the Kawishiwi River to the 48-rod portage. This portage is also fairly flat and wide-open with few obstructions and two good landings. Point your canoe north and continue across another pool in the Kawishiwi. The 113-rod portage to Koma Lake is very easy considering its length. The path climbs over a slight hill when leaving Phoebe and then descends along the side of the river before gradually climbing another hill and making the final descent to Koma.

Paddle and portage 1.5 miles from Koma Lake to central Malberg Lake, including a 24-rod portage. The 24-rod portage leads from Koma Lake to Malberg, after which you will take a portage from the northeast corner of Malberg to the Kawishiwi River.

Paddle and portage 9.25 miles from Malberg Lake to Little Saganaga Lake, including portages of 48 rods from Malberg to the Kawishiwi River, 33 rods from the Kawishiwi River to Kivaniva Lake, 18 rods from Kivaniva to Anit Lake, 63 rods from Anit to Pan Lake, 50 rods from Pan to Panhandle Lake, 90 rods and 38 rods from Panhandle to Makwa Lake, 58 rods from Makwa to Elton Lake, and a pair of portages, 19 rods and 19 rods, from Elton to Little Saganaga. This stretch of paddling is the most remote segment of the BWCAW you will cover on this journey, and it will feel much more isolated than the segment you will have just passed through. In addition, the smaller lakes along this stretch have ten campsites scattered among them, allowing ample opportunities for a secluded place to spend one or more days with greater isolation than you will get along the rest of this route. If you are traveling early in spring or after Labor Day, you have a good chance of having complete solitude on these lakes.

Start by taking the 48-rod portage out of the north end of Malberg to the Kawishiwi River, and then take the 33-rod portage to Kivaniva. The portage from Malberg Lake to the Kawishiwi River is along a relatively flat trail. Paddle northeast through a narrow little channel before crossing a wide section of the Kawishiwi that will seem more like a lake than a river. This stretch of river is among the most beautiful areas in the BWCAW. The portage to Kivaniva is not heavily traveled but gets enough use from day-trippers out of Malberg and from through-trippers that it should be in decent shape. One designated campsite is located on Kivaniva, and it can be a good location from which to fish this pretty little lake. Follow up with a short portage to Anit Lake, and a 63-rod portage from Anit to Pan. If you are using older maps, you will notice that the Anit to Pan segment appears to be two portages separated by a small pond. This pond is now essentially overgrown with vegetation and doesn't look to be navigable at any time of year.

From Pan Lake you must portage to Panhandle and then to Makwa. The trail from Makwa to Elton follows along a streambed with a nice path. When traveling from Elton Lake to Little Saganaga, you have two options: either a 140-rod (L7) single portage, or two shorter portages of 19 rods each. The long portage from Elton to Little Saganaga follows a reasonably smooth trail but has a long climb and similarly long descent that are quite steep or slippery in parts. The two shorter portages appear to be the more popular route. The first 19-rod (L4) portage climbs above a stream before dropping to a bog. Wind through this bog to the second 19-rod (L2) portage down an easy trail.

Little Saganaga is an island-studded masterpiece. Few lakes in the BWCAW can compare with a misty morning on Little Sag, the islands floating before your campsite like a drifting pine flotilla. Twenty-four designated sites are available for camping, but they are popular with the canoeists coming in from the entry points at Missing Link, Round, and Cross Bay lakes.

Paddle and portage 5 miles from Little Saganaga to Crooked Lake, including portages of 40 rods (L4) from Little Saganaga to Mora Lake, 5 rods (L1) from Mora to Tarry Lake, and 50 rods (L6) from Tarry to Crooked Lake. The 40-rod portage to Mora bypasses a raging rapids that is completely impassable by canoe. The trail skirts to the north side of the rapids. Although it includes some relatively steep inclines, the trail is generally clear and provides nice views of the raging rapids below. Mora is an attractive BWCAW destination, with four fine designated campsites and good fishing prospects for northern pike. The irregular shoreline is lined with a mixture of jack pine, spruce, and birch.

The 5-rod portage from Mora Lake to Tarry Lake diverts you around a small series of rapids. The only difficulty with this portage is finding it, as some maps are confusing regarding the location. The portage begins at the end of the very narrow finger extending north from the main body of Mora. The portage itself is little more than a lift-over. Tarry Lake is low lying with a mixed forest of birch and spruce, along with stands of jack pine and an occasional white pine.

The 50-rod portage from Tarry to Crooked Lake follows the side of a stream obscured beneath a field of massive glacial boulder deposits. The portage begins with an uphill stretch through the boulder fields, and at one point skirts over the stream along well-placed boulders. After a 5-rod boulder scamper, the trail continues with an extended moderate climb before dropping along a stone face to Crooked Lake.

Crooked Lake is an excellent spot to slow down and relax for a few nights. The six designated campsites provide ample choices for pitching camp, and stands of white pines remain along the rocky shores. The 320-acre lake extends to more than 60 feet in depth and is home to a healthy population of lake trout.

Paddle and portage 1.25 miles from Crooked Lake to Gillis Lake, including a 90-rod (L6) portage. The 90-rod portage from Crooked to Gillis skirts along the east shore of a pond and small stream. Stay alert and you will see a 2-foot-high waterfall and remains of an abandoned cabin along the route. Most of the trail is reasonably flat, although short stretches climb up and down slight hills, and a few notable rocks protrude into the pathway. Magnificent Gillis Lake plunges some 180 feet in depth—plenty deep for the lake trout that inhabit this cold, scenic lake. Seven designated campsites provide plentiful places to pitch a tent, and more designated sites are nearby on Fern Lake, French Lake, and Bat Lake.

Paddle and portage 5.75 miles from Gillis Lake to Round Lake, including portages of 24 rods (L5) from Gillis to Bat Lake, 20 rods (L2) from Bat to Green Lake, 80 rods (L7) from Green to Flying Lake, 50 rods from Flying to Gotter Lake, 103 rods (L7) from Gotter to Brant Lake, 35 rods (L2) Brant to Edith Lake, 50 rods (L3) from Edith to West Round Lake, and 80 rods (L3) from West Round to Round Lake. The 24-rod portage to Bat Lake from Gillis is relatively hard considering its length because it is somewhat rocky and has a significant climb. Moving on to Green Lake, a relatively easy 20-rod portage follows a much more level path. Another difficult portage awaits you heading to Flying Lake, where the 80-rod portage has both a steep climb and a steep descent.

Head out through the southeast end of Flying Lake, where a staircase leads you to Gotter Lake. The normal length of this portage is about 50 rods, but it can be up to 80 rods if water levels are low. A false trail heads to the right into a marshy area after about 20 rods, but this appears to be a dead end except during unusually high water levels. Scout the portage first, but you will probably be best served by taking the full portage of 50 to 80 rods.

Your paddle across Gotter will be short because you soon portage 103 rods along a hilly path to Brant Lake, where you can spend an evening at one of three designated campsites. This portage has several difficult hill climbs and descents over rocky terrain on the Gotter side. Part of the shore of Brant has beautiful cliffs, with much of the rest being low lying, covered with a mixed forest of jack pine, birch, and balsam. Continue with the easy 35-rod portage from Brant to Edith.

All of these final portages of this segment are relatively flat and easy, but they can accumulate some water during wet periods and in early spring. A primarily low-lying spruce forest surrounds Edith Lake. Edith and her kin have a simple, remote beauty you will not find on the more elevated shorelines covered with pine, birch, and aspen. Tiny Edith does not have any campsites. Look for pitcher plants along the shore.

Once on Round Lake, paddle up to the northwest shore, where a nice landing and large parking lot are located. This parking lot is just down the road from where you parked your car. Head out on the gravel road entering the parking lot, and take a left at the first junction (County Road 47). Your car should be down the road a few hundred yards.

Entry Point 51, Missing Link Lake (Map 40)

> Daily permit quota: 5
> Permit availability: moderate

Missing Link Lake, nestled just south of the Gunflint Trail, provides excellent access to the stretch of remote wilderness east of Sea Gull Lake. Although five permits are issued to canoeists each day, the numerous small lakes and divergent routes allow you to seek a peaceful locale where you can enjoy true north-woods wilderness. If you prefer short loop trips that can be completed in a weekend, you can circle south from Missing Link Lake to Tuscarora Lake or east through Cross Bay Lake. Likewise, if you prefer longer, more remote trips, Missing Link Lake will please you with numerous interior options. Two routes are described below: Route 51A is a short trip to interesting, twisted lakes; Route 51B takes you into the maddening intricacies of the Frost River. Both routes offer great wilderness travel into beautiful lakes.

Missing Link Lake is located near the end of the Gunflint Trail, and access is made by way of Round Lake. To get to Round Lake, take the Gunflint Trail for 47 miles, and turn left on County Road 47, identified by a sign for Tuscarora Lodge. Drive a mile down CR 47, and turn right onto Forest Service Road 1495 at the first spur. Curve around the north shore of Round Lake until you arrive at a sizable parking lot. If you need to rent a canoe or other camping gear, Tuscarora Lodge is also on Round Lake. Just continue down CR 47, but to reach the lodge don't take the right onto 1495. The public landing on Round Lake includes outhouses and enough room for at least thirty vehicles. At the far end of the parking lot is a short staircase leading to Round Lake.

You cannot camp at the Round Lake landing. The nearest public camping is at the Trails End campground 9 miles farther up the Gunflint at Sea Gull Lake. Expect to pay a nightly camping fee. Be certain to make a reservation in advance because the campground is very busy during the summer months. If Trails End campground is full, consider staying at the smaller Iron Lake campground closer to Grand Marais. Also, a number of outfitters along the Gunflint Trail offer bunkhouse accommodations that are both convenient and economical.

Route 51A: Snipe, Cross Bay Weekend (Map 40)

Difficulty: easy
Number of days: 2 or more
Total miles (approx.): 7
Number of portages: 6
Total portage rods: 489
Greatest portage difficulty: 180 rods (L5 to L8)
Navigation maps: Voyageur 6
                  Fisher F12
                  McKenzie 7

This weekend trip is a really enjoyable introduction to the BWCAW. The lakes are small but deep and home to a variety of wildlife. I have come across otters, beavers, and moose while paddling these scenic waters.

Detailed Route

Paddle and portage 2.5 miles from Round Lake to Snipe Lake, including portages of 138 rods (L7) from Round Lake to Missing Link Lake, and 180 rods (L5 to L8) from Missing Link to Snipe Lake. As many as nine groups can enter the wilderness by way of Round Lake each day, divided between Entry Points 51 and 52, so do not be startled to see other people unloading on Round. Fortunately, the maze of lakes south and west of Round quickly disperses visitors. For this route paddle southwest until you reach the 138-rod portage to Missing Link Lake. While this is a fairly easy portage to locate, be alert not to take the 80-rod portage to West Round Lake, which is used for Entry Point 52 (Brant Lake). The proper portage is best spotted by aiming for the low spot between the two hills at the south end of the lake. This low spot is visible even from the parking lot and provides a good navigational aid.

The portage to Missing Link Lake begins with a rocky boulder field paralleling an intermittent stream for 30 rods. The trail soon levels out but remains rocky with extensive roots and exposed stones at numerous points. Halfway through the portage a sign indicates you have officially entered the BWCAW. Continue past the sign, proceed along a short marshy area, and then drop to Missing Link Lake.

A fine campsite greets you immediately to the left as you enter Missing Link, and its sloping rock outcropping may make a fine home for the weekend. Alternatively, continue to one of the other two sites to the south. Missing Link Lake has been regularly stocked with brook trout. The brookies have outwitted me in all seasons, but perhaps you will prove more skillful at catching a couple. If you are moving on, continue across Missing Link to the landing for the 180-rod portage to Snipe Lake.

The portage connecting Missing Link with Snipe follows a reasonably flat trail through a spruce forest carpeted with patches of bunchberry. Try your hand at identifying this common north-woods plant. Remember to look for little white flowers in spring, green berries in summer, and red berries in fall. In dry weather, the portage is average in difficulty, normally warranting only an L5 rating. However, a low spot in the middle of the portage is likely to be wet after heavy rains and early in spring, thus warranting an L8 rating at these times.

Once you hit the deep, cool waters of Snipe you will have already portaged over 300 rods—a full day's share by most standards. Consider spending the night at one of the four excellent campsites available on this sinuous little lake. Alternatively, or if all sites are occupied, continue to the portage to Cross Bay Lake.

Paddle and portage 1.5 miles from Snipe Lake to Cross Bay Lake, including a 47-rod (L4) portage. The portage from Snipe Lake to Cross Bay Lake follows downstream along a creek draining Snipe. This is a well-traveled and uneventful portage that opens into the marsh forming the western side of Cross Bay Lake. Upon entering Cross Bay Lake you initially wind your way through the shallow marsh. In summer you are likely to be treated to a display of flowering blue flag iris. An extensive carpet of pitcher plants also grows here—a peek inside one might reveal an unfortunate insect or two that were unable to resist the tasty but deadly nectar.

Paddle and portage 3 miles from Cross Bay Lake to the Cross River, including portages of 24 rods (L2), 35 rods (L3), and 65 rods (L3). Paddling through the northern reaches of Cross Bay Lake, you will officially leave the BWCAW. Wind your way along the pleasant shoreline to the portage at the far south end of the lake. Take a 25-rod portage from Cross Bay Lake to Ham Lake, and then take a 35-rod portage, which follows another nice path around a set of significant rapids before leaving Ham Lake. Finally take a 65-rod portage to the Cross River. About a third of a mile along the Cross River you will come to a landing on the west (left) where you can haul your gear out to County Road 47. Your starting point is just a mile by car or foot back down the road.

Route 51B: Frost River Loop (Map 40)

> Difficulty: challenging
> Number of days: 4 or more
> Total miles (approx.): 30
> Number of portages: 35
> Total portage rods: 1,717
> Greatest portage difficulty: 180 (L8)
> Navigation maps: Voyageur 6, 8, 9
>   Fisher F12, F13
>   McKenzie 7, 8

This demanding route travels through the very heart of the BWCAW along the twisting Frost River and the numerous small lakes lying south of the Gunflint Trail. You will have over a dozen small portages and beaver dam lift-overs on the Frost River, so don't bring your Dutch oven or 96-quart cooler on this journey. The Frost River is arguably the most remote navigable stream in the BWCAW, competing with the Little Indian Sioux River South for that distinction (see Entry Point 9).

Map 40 shows the western portions of this route, and Map 31 shows the eastern portions. An overview of the entire route is shown on Map 36.

Detailed Route

Paddle and portage 2.5 miles from Round Lake to Snipe Lake, including portages of 138 rods (L7) from Round to Missing Link Lake, and 180 rods (L5 to L8) from Missing Link to Snipe Lake. The first leg of this journey repeats the first portion of Route 51A.

Paddle and portage 1.5 miles from Snipe Lake to Cross Bay Lake, including a 47-rod (L4) portage. The portage from Snipe Lake to Cross Bay Lake follows downstream along the creek draining Snipe to Cross Bay. See Route 51A for additional information on this leg.

Paddle and portage 4 miles from Cross Bay Lake to Long Island Lake, including portages of 50 rods (L4) from Cross Bay to Rib Lake, 37 rods (L3) from Rib to Lower George Lake, and 28 rods (L2) from Lower George to Karl Lake. The portage from Cross Bay to Rib Lake is relatively flat until just before Rib Lake, where it climbs a gentle hill before arriving at Rib. Rib Lake is surrounded by a mixed forest of jack pine, birch, aspen, and spruce extending up from rocky shores and marshlands. While no beavers were active on the lake the last time I traveled through, a long-abandoned beaver lodge clings to the east shore approximately 100 yards from the landing leading to Cross Bay Lake. The aspen will no doubt attract a new family of beavers in due time.

The trail on the 37-rod portage from Rib Lake to Lower George Lake is flat, wide, and relatively free of any obstructions. The biggest challenge is finding the landing on the Rib Lake side, but this is accomplished by heading to the southeast corner of Rib and paddling up the small, slow-moving stream that flows into Rib. Head upstream about 200 yards, and find the landing on the right side of the stream. If you are observant, you will notice a number of timbers extending into the water on both sides of the portage, evidence of the more developed portages common in earlier decades.

Paddle through low-lying George Lake, past the predominantly spruce forest, and on to the portage leading to Karl Lake. This easy portage begins with a brief uphill from a pool on the south shore of Lower George Lake and then follows a short, flat trail to Karl. You have two options after entering Karl Lake: continue along a portage-free route to Long Island Lake to the southeast, or if you are in a hurry to get to the west end of Long Island Lake, take the tough 35-rod portage over the peninsula from Karl to Long Island.

Long Island Lake is an excellent BWCAW destination for almost every purpose. Good campsites are usually available among the fifteen designated sites, and the lake has fine fishing for lake trout and northern pike. Here, too, you will find your first significant stands of red and white pines since beginning your trip on Round Lake. Caution should be taken because Long Island can develop substantial chop and rolling waves during windy days when the breeze is coming from the west.

Paddle and portage 3.5 miles from Long Island Lake to Frost Lake, including portages of 8 rods (L2), 28 rods (L3), and 138 rods (L7). Continuing south out of Long Island Lake, you will cross the western bay of Long Island and enter the Long Island River. You now travel deep into the wilderness. While traveling up the Long Island River, you will navigate two portages: a first of 8 rods and a second of 28 rods. The first portage bypasses a series of small rapids and a partially washed-out beaver dam. During high water you should be able to paddle your way through. The 28-rod portage is a bit more difficult to bypass, and you will be wise to take the flat trail.

When the Long Island River widens out and forms a broader body of water known as Gordon Lake, turn to the west and hit the 138-rod portage to Unload Lake. The portage from Gordon Lake to Unload Lake appears to be just 140 rods on the map but will no doubt feel substantially longer. The trail begins with a long sloping uphill followed by a relatively level path through thick brush that ultimately concludes at the landing to Unload Lake.

Just before you reach Unload Lake, on your left is a small growth of exceptional white cedars, one of which is nearly 2 feet in diameter at chest height. This tree is certainly hundreds of years old and has been spared from the intermittent forest fires by its low-lying, moist environment. These trees are worth the 50-foot hike back from the landing if you happen to reach the end of the portage without noticing them. Head across tiny Unload Lake, and pull your canoe over the beaver dam leading to Frost Lake.

Frost Lake is an excellent stopover spot as you prepare to paddle the Frost River. A sand beach lines portions of the north shore, and majestic old white pines sprout up from a number of spots along the lake. You will notice that Frost Lake has five designated campsites, while the next 7 miles of the Frost River have no campsites before you reach a lone campsite on Afton Lake. Needless to say, you must not start the Frost River late in the day, because you will not have a place to camp. The Frost River is best started early in the morning when you can be certain to have adequate time to navigate its winding path. You do not want to figure out around seven at night that the going was slower than you expected.

Paddle and portage 7 miles along the Frost River to Afton Lake, including portages of 137 rods to the Frost River, 13 rods to Octopus Lake, and portages along the Frost River of 16 rods, 23 rods, 31 rods, 29 rods, 22 rods, 35 rods, 16 rods, 5 rods, 5 rods, 12 rods, and 19 rods. The stretch of the Frost River and intermediate lakes to Afton Lake may have twelve or more portages, depending on water levels and beaver efforts. If water levels are low and beavers have been busy, expect a long slow go at it. The majority of the Frost River is only about two canoe lengths wide, which allows plenty of room for the occasional canoes and more frequent moose that travel along it.

Octopus Lake is one of the more interesting lakes along this stretch and gives you access to the challenging Hairy Lake Primitive Management Area (PMA) and such lakes as Fetters, Iris, Mass, and Sora, none of which are connected by maintained portages but can be reached by bushwhacking through rugged terrain. I have not explored this area, but I have talked to one crew who reached Sora Lake and confirmed that it is rough going but possible to reach Sora. As with all PMAs, only extremely experienced visitors should attempt to enter them, and you will need a special authorization from the Forest Service to stay overnight in one. In this case, such authorization can be obtained from the Gunflint Ranger district. See the discussion on PMAs earlier in this guide to learn more about these PMAs.

Getting back to the journey from Frost Lake to Afton Lake, of special note is the portage from Pencil Lake back to the Frost River. This portage avoids an extended portion of dangerous rapids that should not be attempted in a canoe. The portage is difficult to spot, in part because few travelers come this way. Look for a seldom-used landing on the south side of the Frost River that goes up a steep hill through rugged and somewhat overgrown territory.

After Pencil Lake, the Frost River becomes increasingly twisted and narrows substantially. Numerous beaver dams cross the river, and many of these are not marked as portages on maps yet still require lift-overs. Also, map distances can be deceptive on the Frost River. For example, the stretch between Pencil and Afton looks like only 2 miles at first glance at a map, but the "stretched out" length of this portion of river is probably more like 5 or 6 miles. Budget your time and energy accordingly.

The Frost River can challenge the friendship of any pair of canoeists. Based on my experience, the stern paddler will spend the hours on the Frost River preoccupied by its twists and turns, hoping to minimize the number of accidental beachings. At the same time, the bow paddler will spend the hours generating alternate names for the river, such as Stream of Thoughtlessness, River of Tears, or Pauly Grave Creek. Spotting a few beavers or moose, as we did, tends to ease the toil. Fortunately, you have a good chance of seeing both.

Paddle and portage 2.75 miles from Afton Lake to Mora Lake, including portages of 20 rods from Afton to Fente Lake, an optional 1 rod, 16 rods (L2) from Fente to Whipped Lake, and 96 rods (L5) from Whipped to Mora Lake. The portage between Afton Lake and Fente Lake is only 20 rods long but is very challenging. The trail requires a climb up a steep hillside followed by a descent down an equally steep and seemingly more perilous downside. Continue along narrow Fente Lake. Halfway up Fente you will come to a point where the lake narrows and rushes over a rock obstruction—dropping about 1 foot in the process. Expect to pull your canoe over this short cataract.

Next, a 16-rod portage from Fente to Whipped Lake is flat and relatively clear of obstacles—an easy haul after what you have been through on the Frost River.

The 96-rod portage (L5) to Mora Lake is well traveled, although it feels significantly longer than 100 rods to muscles that battled the Frost River. Nothing more than an occasional deadfall is likely to obstruct you and your load. Mora is a particularly beautiful BWCAW destination, with four fine campsites and good fishing for northern pike. The irregular shoreline is carpeted with a mixture of jack pine, spruce, and birch. The very edges of the lake are fringed with numerous white cedars—most of which have no green branches below 6 feet from the ground, evidence of the length of a white-tailed deer's winter reach.

Paddle and portage 1.5 miles from Mora Lake to Crooked Lake, including portages of 5 rods (L1) from Mora to Tarry Lake, and 50 rods (L6) from Tarry to Crooked Lake. The 5-rod portage from Mora Lake to Tarry Lake diverts you around a short series of rapids. The only difficulty with this portage is finding it, as some maps are confusing regarding the location. The portage begins at the end of a narrow finger extending north from the main body of Mora. The portage itself is little more than a lift-over or pull-through. Tarry Lake is low lying with a mixed forest of birch and spruce, along with stands of jack pine and an occasional white pine.

The 50-rod portage from Tarry to Crooked Lake is low lying and follows the side of a stream obscured beneath a field of massive glacial boulder deposits. The portage begins with an uphill stretch through the boulder fields, and at one point skirts over the stream along three well-placed boulders. After another 5-rod boulder scamper, the trail continues with an extended moderate climb before dropping along a stone face to Crooked Lake.

Crooked Lake is an excellent spot to slow down and relax for a few nights. The six designated campsites provide ample choices for pitching camp, and relatively extensive stands of white pines remain along the rocky shores. This 320-acre lake extends to more than 60 feet in depth and is home to a healthy population of lake trout, making it a popular destination in May for people seeking lakers just after ice-out.

Paddle and portage 1.25 miles from Crooked to Gillis Lake, including a 90-rod (L6) portage. The 90-rod portage from Crooked to Gillis skirts along the east shore of a pond and small stream. Stay alert and you will see a 2-foot-high waterfall and remains of an abandoned cabin along the route. Most of the trail is reasonably flat, although short stretches climb up and down slight hills, and a few notable rocks protrude into the pathway. Magnificent Gillis Lake plunges some 180 feet in depth— plenty deep for the lakers that inhabit this cold, scenic lake. Seven designated campsites provide plentiful places to pitch a tent, and more designated sites are nearby on Fern Lake, French Lake, and Bat Lake.

Paddle and portage 5.75 miles from Gillis Lake to Round Lake, including portages of 24 rods (L5) from Gillis to Bat Lake, 20 rods (L2) from Bat to Green Lake, 80 rods (L7) from Green to Flying Lake, 50 rods from Flying to Gotter Lake, 103 rods (L7) from Gotter to Brant Lake, 35 rods (L2) from Brant to Edith Lake, 50 rods (L3) from Edith to West Round Lake, and 80 rods (L3) from West Round to Round Lake. The 24-rod portage to Bat Lake from Gillis is relatively hard considering its length because it is somewhat rocky and has a significant climb. Moving on to Green Lake, a relatively easy 20-rod portage follows a much more level path. Another difficult portage awaits you heading to Flying Lake, where the 80-rod portage has both a steep climb and a steep descent.

Head out through the southeast end of Flying Lake, where a staircase leads you toward Gotter Lake. The normal length of this portage is about 50 rods, but it can be up to 80 rods if water levels are low. A false trail heads to Green Lake after about 20 rods into a marshy area, but this appears to be a dead end except during unusually high water. Scout the portage first, but you will probably be best off taking the full portage of 50 to 80 rods.

Your time on Gotter will be short because you soon portage 103 rods along a hilly path to Brant Lake, where you can spend an evening at one of three campsites. This portage has several difficult hill climbs and descents over rocky terrain on the Gotter side. Part of the shore of Brant has beautiful cliffs, with much of the rest being low lying, covered with a mixed forest of jack pine, birch, and balsam. Continue with an easy 35-rod portage from Brant to Edith.

All of these final portages of this segment are relatively flat and easy, but they can accumulate some water during wet periods and in early spring. A primarily low-lying spruce forest surrounds Edith Lake. Edith and her kin have a simple, remote beauty you will not find on the more elevated shorelines covered with pine, birch, and aspen. Tiny Edith does not have any campsites. Look for pitcher plants along the shore. Once on Round Lake paddle to the northwest shore to your starting point.

Entry Point 52, Brant Lake (Map 40)

Daily permit quota: 4
Permit availability: easy to moderate

Brant Lake is the third of the three entries originating at Round Lake and gives you direct access to many small lakes to the west of Round. When starting at Brant Lake, you enter a maze of interconnected lakes with an especially large number of route options. Most visitors appear to head directly to Gillis Lake by way of a southern route through Flying, Green, and Bat lakes. Once on Gillis, loops to Little Saganaga and Gabimichigami are relatively easy. It is also possible to take a more northern route from Brant Lake by way of Fay, Warclub and Seahorse lakes, a segment that gets considerably less activity than the one through Flying, Green, and Bat.

Excellent loops can be taken by dropping south through Gillis and Tuscarora before returning to Round Lake (see Route 52, below). The adventurous will head farther south to take the Frost River to Long Island Lake before returning to Round Lake (see Route 51B, described above). A one-way trip to Sea Gull Lake is also possible by heading through Gabimichigami, Ogishkemuncie, and Jasper lakes. This route is connected by good portages. A much shorter route appears to lead through Glee and Jap lakes to Sea Gull. However, the Jap to Sea Gull portage is one of the toughest in the BWCAW, often all but impassable in the early season before it has been cleared. Take that route only after checking with the Forest Service at the Gunflint Ranger Station to confirm the portage is passable.

Brant Lake is located near the end of the Gunflint Trail, and access is made by way of Round Lake. To get to Round Lake, take the Gunflint Trail 47 miles and turn left on County Road 47, identified by a sign for Tuscarora Lodge. Drive a mile down CR 47, and turn to the right onto Forest Service Road 1495 at the first spur. Curve around the north shore of Round Lake until you arrive at a sizable parking lot. If you need to rent a canoe or other camping gear, Tuscarora Lodge is also on Round Lake. Just continue down CR 47, but to reach the lodge don't take the right onto FS 1495. The public landing on Round Lake includes outhouses and enough room for at least thirty vehicles. At the far end of the parking lot is a short staircase leading to Round Lake.

You cannot camp at the Round Lake landing. The nearest public camping location is the Trails End campground 9 miles farther up the Gunflint at Sea Gull Lake, which charges a nightly camping fee. Be certain to make a reservation in advance because the campground is very busy during the summer months. If Trails End campground is full, consider staying at the smaller Iron Lake campground closer to Grand Marais. Also, a number of outfitters along the Gunflint Trail offer bunkhouse accommodations that are both convenient and economical.

Route 52: Loop through Gillis and Warclub (Map 40)

Difficulty: intermediate
Number of days: 3
Total miles (approx.): 20
Number of portages: 26
Total portage rods: 1,181
Greatest portage difficulty: 150 rods (L9)
Navigation maps: Voyageur 6
Fisher F12
McKenzie 7

This loop takes you west from Round Lake to a pocket of small lakes north of Tuscarora, Gillis, and Little Saganaga. The route emphasizes heading to small, intimate lakes that get significantly fewer visitors than their larger neighbors to the south. Many visitors to the BWCAW take the easiest portages between the biggest lakes, hoping to cover as much territory as possible. This "contrarian" route takes you to lots of small lakes connected by less frequently traveled portages.

Detailed Route

Paddle and portage 2 miles from Round Lake to Brant Lake, including portages of 80 rods (L3) from Round to West Round Lake, 50 rods (L3) from West Round to

Edith Lake, and 35 rods (L2) from Edith to Brant Lake. This journey starts with an easy set of portages to Brant Lake. See the last segment of Route 51A for a detailed description.

Paddle and portage 4 miles from Brant Lake to Gillis Lake, including portages of 103 rods (L7) from Brant to Gotter Lake, 80 rods from Gotter to Craig Lake, 42 rods from Craig to Green Lake, 20 rods (L2) from Green to Bat Lake, and 24 rods from Bat to Gillis Lake. This 4-mile segment travels along relatively short portages, but you will find some of them challenging, especially the 42-rod carry from Craig to Green over a modest hill.

Paddle and portage 4.5 miles from Gillis Lake to Peter Lake, including portages of 26 rods (L2) from Gillis to Fern Lake, 13 rods (L1) from Fern to French Lake, 33 rods (L4) from French to Powell Lake, 21 rods (L2 to L4) from Powell to West Fern Lake, 30 rods (L2) from West Fern to Virgin Lake, and 80 rods (L6) from Virgin to Peter Lake. You will now travel from Gillis Lake to Peter Lake, exploring a series of interesting little lakes that get far fewer visitors than most lakes in this vicinity. The first portage from Gillis to Fern has a modest hill but otherwise is an easy trail. One campsite is located on Fern, and it appears to get little use. Pressing on from Fern, the portage to French is also quite easy. Two designated campsites are located on French Lake. French gets as deep as 130 feet at its maximum and contains some lake trout, but according to DNR surveys the trout population is relatively low.

From French Lake you will press on to Powell Lake along a 33-rod portage. This trail appears to be along a substantially new route after the 1999 blowdown and involves a moderate climb. Like many of its neighbors, Powell contains lake trout and apparently a more robust population than is found next door in French Lake. You can also spend the night on Powell Lake, which has two designated campsites. When your time comes to leave Powell, take the 21-rod portage to West Fern Lake. This short portage is a bit lower lying than most on this route and appears to be fairly muddy after major rains, giving it an L2 difficulty rating in dry periods but an L4 difficulty rating during wet periods. West Fern also has two designated campsites and contains lake trout. Continuing on, a nice flat trail leads from West Fern to Virgin Lake.

This route next takes you to Peter Lake, but if you are planning your own trip, you can portage to Little Saganaga Lake. The portage begins with a modest uphill followed by a flat portion and a dip into a lowland swamp, from which it climbs and then enters a final downhill to a quiet bay. This portage too is also fairly overgrown and does not appear to get a tremendous amount of use, since most people take the Rattle Lake/Gabimichigami route when traveling to the north end of Little Saganaga.

The last portage of this leg is an 80-rod carry that twists and turns its way from Virgin Lake to Peter. This portage does not appear to get much maintenance, so expect a brushy trail unless one of the infrequent maintenance crews has been through recently. Peter is one of the deep lake trout waters encountered on this journey, and according to DNR surveys it has historically held one of the more substantial trout populations. These same DNR surveys indicate that the trout on Peter are slower growing than average for Cook County, so catch-and-release fishing is perhaps especially appropriate. Four designated campsites are located along the shores of Peter Lake. In early spring, especially from fishing opener until the middle of May, Peter is a popular lake for trout fishing, and these four sites may all be occupied on many nights. Not only do visitors like to fish Peter Lake, but it offers easy access to the big trout waters of Gabimichigami, which are reached by way of a slightly rocky 39-rod portage starting from an old, decaying boat landing on the Peter Lake side.

Paddle and portage 5 miles from Peter Lake to Bingshick Lake, including portages of 150 rods (L9) from Peter to French Lake, 17 rods (L2) from French to Seahorse Lake, 15 rods (L4) from Seahorse to Warclub Lake, 32 rods (L6) from Warclub to Fay Lake, 22 rods (L3) from Fay to Glee Lake, and 42 rods from Glee to Bingshick Lake. This route will now head along a neat set of lakes north of Gillis and south of Sea Gull. Although both of these large lakes are relatively popular, this stretch of small lakes in between them is well off the main travel corridor and gets far fewer visitors. You will travel through prime moose habitat, so with luck you will get a chance to view one feeding in the shallows along the way. Once you leave Peter Lake you will encounter just two campsites before Bingshick, both on French Lake, so this segment is more likely to be paddled through without stopping to spend an evening.

Head out the east end of Peter Lake, and take the challenging 150-rod portage to French Lake. The trail climbs considerably from Peter Lake before eventually leveling out and descending to a boardwalk over a low area that leads to French. Next, the portage from French to Seahorse follows a nice trail along a pretty cascade. The trail is rather steep at the start but is then quite easy. Seahorse is shallow and has lots of aquatic vegetation. Here you may see your first moose of the trip!

Press on from Seahorse to Warclub Lake over a rocky trail that appears to get very little maintenance. Take a careful look at the rock on the Seahorse side of the portage, and you will notice clear signs of iron ore in the rusty rubble. This iron ore is from the Gunflint Iron Formation, which also formed the deposits unsuccessfully mined at the Paulson Mine a few miles to the east, described in the history section of this guide. Be careful to stick to the low-lying portage, and don't climb out of the valley along the Kekekabic Trail, which runs by these lakes.

Warclub Lake is shallow throughout its length and covered extensively by water lilies. The shoreline, particularly the north shore, is covered by bog plants including pitcher plants and numerous small tamaracks. Midway through the lake, you will pass over a shallow portion that is the remains of an old beaver dam. This lake is a fine example of the latter stages of lake evolution as it fills in. The portage from Warclub Lake to Fay Lake is very challenging because most of the trail is along boulder-covered paths and tends to become somewhat overgrown. After approximately 20 rods the trail will fork, with part going straight and part going downhill to the right toward a stream. You should take the turn to the right since this goes approximately 20 rods to the put-in point on Fay Lake, while the other trail is a portion of the Kekekabic Trail.

Fay Lake has wooded shores with predominantly spruce and fir and some birch, and few rocky outcroppings. The portage between Fay Lake and Glee Lake begins with a fairly steep uphill followed by a shorter up-and-down increment. The portage path is relatively rugged, particularly in the first portion. The portage from Glee Lake to Bingshick begins with a climb up a steep hillside approximately 3 rods long followed by a winding path through a forest that was heavily hit by the 1999 windstorm. Once on Bingshick you can spend the night at one of the two designated campsites, which appear to get few visitors.

Paddle and portage 4.25 miles from Bingshick to Round Lake, including portages of 13 rods (L3) and 15 rods (L3) from Bingshick to Flying Lake, 50 rods from Flying to Gotter Lake, 103 rods (L7) from Gotter to Brant Lake, 35 rods (L2) from Brant to Edith Lake, 50 rods (L3) from Edith to West Round Lake, and 80 rods (L3) from West Round to Round Lake.

On your way to Round Lake you will start with a pair of portages from Bingshick Lake to Flying Lake. The first portage is 13 rods long and climbs up a rock platform from Bingshick and then drops to a level stretch before descending to a tamarack swamp. Paddle south, rounding a bend to reach a second portage concealed in a small bay. This second portage, approximately 15 rods long, starts with a short but very steep 2-rod uphill and then follows a rocky and muddy trail leading to the north end of Flying Lake.

Head out through the southeast end of Flying Lake, where a staircase leads you to Gotter Lake. The normal length of this portage is about 50 rods, but it can be up to 80 rods if water levels are low. A false trail heads down to the right into a marshy area after about 20 rods, but this appears to be a dead end except during unusually high water. Scout the portage first, but you will probably be best served by taking the full portage of 50 to 80 rods.

Your paddle across Gotter will be short because you soon portage 103 rods along a hilly path to Brant Lake, where you can spend an evening at one of three designated campsites. This portage has several difficult hill climbs and descents over rocky terrain on the Gotter side. Part of the shore of Brant has beautiful cliffs, with much of the rest being low lying, covered with a mixed forest of jack pine, birch, and balsam. Continue with an easy 35-rod portage from Brant to Edith.

All of these final portages of this segment are relatively flat and easy, but they can accumulate some water during wet periods and in early spring. A primarily low-lying spruce forest surrounds Edith Lake. Edith and her kin have a simple, remote beauty you will not find on the more elevated shorelines covered with pine, birch, and aspen. Tiny Edith does not have any campsites. Look for pitcher plants along the shore. Once on Round Lake, paddle up to the northwest shore and the landing from where you started.

Entry Point 54, Sea Gull Lake (Map 41)

Daily permit quota: 13
Permit availability: moderate

Sea Gull Lake is located near the end of the Gunflint Trail and has much to offer its visitors. It is a wonderful, island-covered lake perfectly suited for exploring for a few days, yet it also offers easy access to numerous lakes to the south, west, and north. You can head south to Alpine Lake and to the interior of the BWCAW, or you can loop north to Saganaga, allowing you many more areas to explore. For hardy souls there is even a grueling portage to Jap Lake, known for a good population of lake trout.

When reserving a permit, you can request one either for Entry Point 54 or Entry Point 54A. Both start at Sea Gull Lake, but 54A does not allow you to camp on any lake other than Sea Gull. Most visitors prefer a permit for Entry Point 54 rather than 54A since it gives greater flexibility.

Three different routes are described below. The first (Route 54A) is a nice trip to explore Sea Gull Lake, requiring no portages. The second trip (Route 54B) takes you in a loop to Saganaga Lake along a few backwoods lakes that see far fewer visitors than most lakes in this area. The third journey (Route 54C) takes you all the way to Kekekabic and Little Saganaga lakes on a wonderful journey full of challenges and rewards.

To reach Sea Gull Lake, follow the Gunflint Trail north 54 miles from its start at Lake Superior on Highway 61. Sea Gull Lake has two public accesses. The first lies just west of the Gunflint Trail at the end of a short road appropriately labeled "Sea Gull Lake Access" and marked with a prominent Forest Service sign. If you reach Sea Gull Creek, you have gone too far. An excellent landing and dock and ample parking are provided. A pay phone is available for calling home when you leave the wilderness, a potentially useful feature since cell phone coverage is not available on most of the Gunflint Trail as of the publication of this guide.

The other access is located farther down the Gunflint Trail at the Sea Gull River just south of the public parking lot near the Trails End campground. This second access is generally less desirable because it requires that you paddle upstream through the Sea Gull River. To get to this second access point, drive to the end of the Gunflint Trail and follow the loop through the Trails End campground (which has a one-way circular layout) past a large parking lot, a landing for Gull Lake and Saganaga Lake (Entry Point 55), and a number of spur roads to campsites. As you complete the circle, you will come to the Sea Gull Lake landing. After unloading you will have to drive your car around to the parking lot, which is just a hundred yards away as you start to recircle the campground.

Consider spending a night at Trails End campground before you enter the wilderness, but definitely reserve a campsite in advance. You can also choose to stay at one of the outfitters along the Gunflint Trail, many of whom have reasonably priced bunkhouse accommodations.

Route 54A: Exploration of Sea Gull Lake (Map 41)

> Difficulty: easy
> Number of days: 2 or more

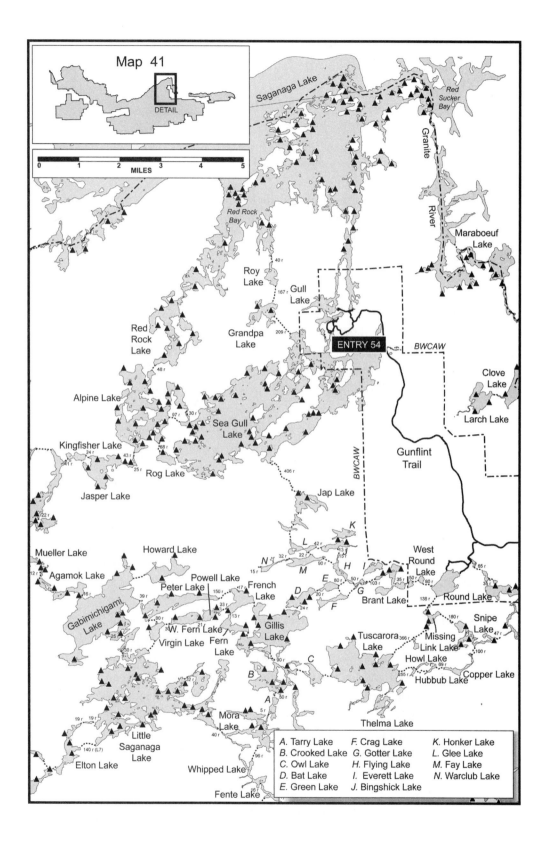

Map 41

DETAIL

0 1 2 3 4 5
MILES

Saganaga Lake

Red Sucker Bay

Granite River

Maraboeuf Lake

Red Rock Bay

Roy Lake

40 r

167 r   Gull Lake

209 r

Grandpa Lake

Red Rock Lake

ENTRY 54

BWCAW

Clove Lake

Larch Lake

48 r

Alpine Lake

97 r 30 r

Sea Gull Lake

BWCAW

Gunflint Trail

Kingfisher Lake

24 r   43 r

21 r   25 r   68 r

Rog Lake

406 r

Jap Lake

Jasper Lake

22 r

K

L   42 r

N   32 r   22 r   13 r
15 r   90 r

H   I

West Round Lake

Mueller Lake

Howard Lake

M

E   80 r   50 r   103 r   35 r   80 r   65 r

Agamok Lake

12 r

16 r

Powell Lake

39 r

150 r   17 r

French Lake

D   20 r

G

Brant Lake   138 r   Round Lake

Peter Lake

33 r

Snipe Lake

180 r

Gabimichigami Lake

80 r

13 r

Gillis Lake

F   24 r

C

Tuscarora Lake   366 r   Missing Link Lake

47 r

35 r

3   21 r

W. Fern Lake

Howl Lake   69 r   100 r

25 r   Virgin Lake   Fern Lake

Copper Lake

50 r

90 r

255 r

Hubbub Lake

B

19 r   19 r

Mora Lake

A   5 r

Thelma Lake

Little Saganaga Lake

40 r

140 r (L7)

Elton Lake

Whipped Lake

6 r

Fente Lake   16 r

A. Tarry Lake	F. Crag Lake	K. Honker Lake
B. Crooked Lake	G. Gotter Lake	L. Glee Lake
C. Owl Lake	H. Flying Lake	M. Fay Lake
D. Bat Lake	I. Everett Lake	N. Warclub Lake
E. Green Lake	J. Bingshick Lake	

Total miles (approx.): 5 or more
Number of portages: 0
Total portage rods: 0
Greatest portage difficulty: N/A
Navigation maps: Voyageur 6
                      Fisher F32
                      McKenzie 6

This route sends you to Sea Gull Lake for one or more days of exploring, relaxing, and perhaps fishing. This huge lake has much to offer and is a fine destination for your first trip into the Boundary Waters.

Detailed Route

If you want good fishing, great scenery, and *no portages,* this might be the trip for you. Much of Sea Gull was heavily hit by the 1999 windstorm, but this wonderful lake remains a magnificent destination. After you enter Sea Gull Lake, you can stay at one of the thirty-eight designated campsites scattered among the islands and bays. If you prefer, a 97-rod portage leads you to equally scenic Alpine Lake with another twenty-two campsites to consider.

Sea Gull Lake's location at the end of the Gunflint Trail and the multiple ways in and out of this huge gem make it an attractive intersection of many fine routes. Although this route starts and ends at Sea Gull, you can craft fine routes to neighboring lakes. Most people who leave Sea Gull will do so by way of the 97-rod portage to Alpine Lake or by the Sea Gull River to Gull Lake and then Saganaga. Less frequently traveled is the route south to Rog Lake by way of a moderate portage, where you will find a single designated campsite as well as brook trout in the depths (if you are lucky). An alternative journey to Saganaga is by way of Grandpa and Roy lakes. The three portages you will encounter, described below in Route 54B, are not heavily traveled but are passable.

Some visitors will also want to climb the long 406-rod portage to Jap Lake. This portage would make Darwin proud. Only the fittest will make it over, and even then not without a struggle. Two times I have been forced back by an impassable trail of downfalls, both times in the spring before the winter blowdowns had been removed. This portage was burned in 2003 by a prescribed burn, eliminating some of the trees that would periodically fall onto the trail. It is likely to be open more often in the future but is still a tough carry.

The Forest Service conducted a prescribed burn on Sea Gull Lake just south of Fishhook Island (next to Meditation Lake) in September 2002. The forest south of Sea Gull Lake, extending toward Jap Lake, was burned in a prescribed burn in late 2003. Three Mile Island has long been known to naturalists for being home to some of the oldest stands of red pine in the BWCAW. Many of these pines were blown down in the 1999 windstorm, but some still stand, as do younger white pines. Much of Three Mile Island was burned in a prescribed burn in fall 2002. The fires removed some of the accumulated wood from the blowdown, although surprisingly large amounts of wood did not burn. Consider exploring these blowdown and burned areas regularly over the coming years, photographing the changing forest each time.

Route 54B: Loop through Sea Gull and Saganaga Lakes (Map 41)

> Difficulty: easy to intermediate
> Number of days: 3
> Total miles (approx.): 25
> Number of portages: 6
> Total portage rods: 571
> Greatest portage difficulty: 209 rods (L9)
> Navigation maps: Voyageur 6
> Fisher 32
> McKenzie 6A, 7

This short loop is not overly taxing yet takes you through some spectacular island-dotted border country lakes. Much of this route is well traveled, so you will not have quite the degree of solitude available on journeys deeper into the wilderness. Still, these big lakes provide plenty of room for everyone, and you are unlikely to feel overwhelmed.

Detailed Route

Paddle and portage 3 miles to the heart of Sea Gull Lake. From the landing on Sea Gull Lake paddle south to its island-covered heart. See Route 54A for more ideas on Sea Gull Lake, perhaps exploring the remaining old pines of Three Mile Island or making a hard haul to Jap Lake.

Paddle and portage 3 miles from Sea Gull Lake to Grandpa Lake, including a portage of 209 rods (L9). Pressing on from Sea Gull, head north over a 209-rod portage to Grandpa Lake, where you may want to wet your line for smallmouth bass. This is a tough portage with two low sections that tend to accumulate a bit of water. Three routes connect Sea Gull Lake to Saganaga (the others being west through Red Rock Bay and east through the Sea Gull River), and this is the most difficult by far. In return for your toils, you will be treated to far more solitude than is available from the other two options, the first of which is taken later in this route. Grandpa has two designated campsites, but allow yourself enough time to press on to Saganaga in the unlikely event both are occupied.

Paddle and portage 4 miles from Grandpa Lake to the heart of Saganaga Lake, including portages of 167 rods (L7) from Grandpa to Roy Lake, and 40 rods (L4) from Roy to Saganaga. You will have a bit of a climb just as you head out of Grandpa Lake, but then the trail gets quite a bit easier. The final portage to Saganaga is also not well traveled but is reasonably short and should pose no significant problems.

Paddle and portage 8 miles from Saganaga Lake to Alpine Lake, including portages of 10 rods (L2) from Red Rock Bay of Saganaga to Red Rock Lake, and 48 rods (L4) from Red Rock to Alpine Lake. The 10-rod portage from Red Rock Lake to Red Rock Bay of Saganaga Lake may be avoided during high water by paddling your canoe through the narrows. Alternatively, or in dry times, on the east shore is a rocky landing and trail leading a few rods to another small rocky landing. The 48-rod portage from Red Rock to Alpine drops you to a cedar-ringed bay on the north arm of Alpine Lake. The trail is average in difficulty with a simple uphill climb that levels out halfway across the portage before dropping to Alpine. There are abundant exposed rocks along the way, and you will notice that the rounded boulders come in many colors and textures, an indication that these boulders are glacial deposits from various types of bedrock north of this area.

Paddle and portage 7 miles from Alpine Lake to your starting location on Sea Gull Lake, including a portage of 97 rods. The portage rises up from Alpine before descending to Sea Gull. The Forest Service has constructed a simple rock and log staircase leading up from Sea Gull. The portage was leveled by the 1999 windstorm and has subsequently been swept by a prescribed burn in fall 2002. Look for evidence of the regenerating forest, including progression from initial colonizers (such as fireweed) to aggressive early growth (such as aspen). This portage is a very popular entry and exit from Sea Gull Lake and thus gets a lot of use.

Route 54C: Loop through Kekekabic and Little Saganaga (Map 41)

> Difficulty: challenging
> Number of days: 7
> Total miles (approx.): 40
> Number of portages: 37
> Total portage rods: 1,853
> Greatest portage difficulty: 160 rods (L9)
> Navigation maps: Voyageur 6
> Fisher 32
> McKenzie 6A, 7

This is a fantastic route through the heart of the BWCAW. You will paddle along small, remote lakes that have few visitors each summer, as well as along a few larger lakes likely to attract numerous campers. If you hate portaging, I suggest reading no further—you will be portaging a total of thirty-seven times over this trip for a total of nearly 6 miles.

Map 41 shows the first portion of this trip, and Map 43 shows the additional areas. An overview of the entire route is shown on Map 36.

Detailed Route

Paddle 3 miles to the heart of Sea Gull Lake. This journey starts with the same first leg as Route 54A to Sea Gull Lake. See that route for information about Sea Gull Lake.

Paddle and portage 9 miles from Sea Gull Lake to Ogishkemuncie Lake, including portages of 97 rods from Sea Gull to Alpine Lake, 43 rods from Alpine to Jasper Lake, 24 rods from Jasper to Kingfisher Lake, and 41 rods from Kingfisher to Ogishkemuncie Lake. These portages are described below in Route 55C.

Paddle and portage 6.75 miles from Ogishkemuncie Lake to Kekekabic Lake, including portages of 16 rods, 14 rods, 17 rods, 18 rods, 1 rod, 20 rods, 15 rods, and 10 rods through Annie Lake, Jenny Lake, Eddy Lake, and the Kekekabic ponds. These portages are described below in Route 55C.

Paddle and portage 6.5 miles from Kekekabic Lake to Fraser Lake, including portages of 85 rods (L8), 10 rods (L2) to Wisini Lake, 90 rods (L7) from Wisini to Ahmakose Lake, 30 rods (L6.5) from Ahmakose to Gerund Lake, and 15 rods (L2) from Gerund to Fraser Lake. See Route 27B for more information about Kekekabic Lake.

Paddle and portage 8.5 miles from Fraser Lake to Makwa Lake, including portages of 68 rods (L4) from Fraser to Sagus Lake, 32 (L4) rods from Sagus to Roe Lake, 61 rods (L4) from Roe to Cap Lake, 186 rods (L8) from Cap to Ledge Lake, 160 rods (L9) from Ledge to Vee Lake, 80 rods (L6) from Vee to Fee Lake, 47 rods (L5) from Fee to Hoe Lake, and finally 86 rods (L5) from Hoe to Makwa Lake. You will now press on from Fraser Lake into some of the most remote wilderness in the BWCAW. Details on these portages are found in the description for Route 37B, found earlier in this guide. Your last portage of this leg is a good downhill trail to Makwa Lake. Makwa is not a heavily visited lake, but due to its location as a junction allowing connections in three directions, it probably gets more visitors than any other lake on this route since Fraser. Pay attention to the exposed bedrock on Makwa, especially an interesting large cliff with layers of intruded gabbro.

Paddle and portage 4 miles from Makwa Lake to Little Saganaga Lake, including a 58-rod portage from Makwa to Elton Lake, and portages of 19 rods (L4) and 19 rods (L2) from Elton to Little Saganaga Lake. As you travel from Elton Lake to Little Saganaga, you have two options: either a 140-rod (L7) single portage or two shorter portages of 19 rods each. The long portage from Elton to Little Saganaga follows a reasonably smooth trail but has a long climb and similarly long descent that are quite steep and slippery in parts. The two shorter portages appear to be the more popular route. The first 19-rod (L4) portage climbs above a stream before dropping into a bog. Wind through this bog to the second 19-rod (L2) portage down an easy trail.

Paddle and portage 3 miles from Little Saganaga Lake to Gabimichigami Lake, including portages of 30 rods from Little Saganaga to Rattle Lake, and 25 rods from Rattle to Gabimichigami Lake. The portage from Little Saganaga to Rattle Lake was damaged by the 1999 windstorm but is wide-open. Farther down, the portage from Rattle to Gabimichigami (also known as "Gabi") follows along a nice trail beside a raging stream.

Paddle and portage 4 miles from Gabimichigami to Ogishkemuncie Lake, including portages of 16 rods from Gabimichigami to Agamok Lake, 112 rods (L7) from Agamok to Mueller Lake, and 103 rods (L8) from Mueller to Ogishkemuncie Lake. The first portage on this leg follows along a low-lying trail beside a channel flowing from Gabimichigami into Agamok. The trail may be a bit wet in spring but is otherwise likely to be in good shape. Pressing on, take the 112-rod portage to Mueller, covering a fairly rocky trail. Finally, take the 103-rod portage to Ogishkemuncie, which is moderately traveled. The blowdown of 1999 took the trees down on the top of this portage, giving you a great view of the islands spread out before you on Ogishkemuncie. Although this portage descends a total of 50 feet, it requires that you first climb about 50 feet, making it a difficult portage for its length.

Paddle and portage 12 miles from Ogishkemuncie to Sea Gull Lake, including portages of 41 rods, 24 rods, 43 rods, and 97 rods. Once on Ogishkemuncie Lake, retrace your trail back to Sea Gull Lake.

Entry Point 55, Saganaga Lake (Map 42)

> Daily permit quota: 20
> Permit availability: easy

Saganaga Lake is the last entry point on the Gunflint Trail and one of the most popular. Saganaga's appeal lies in its size, beauty, and location. At over 17,000 acres, it is one of the largest lakes in the BWCAW. The southern half of Saganaga is dusted with islands of every shape and size, making it a beautiful paddling haven and navigational adventure.

With up to twenty permits allowed per day it is usually possible to get a permit for Saganaga, even during peak travel times. When requesting a permit, you can reserve one for either Entry Point 55 or Entry Point 55A. Both start at Saganaga Lake, but 55A does not allow you to camp on any lake other than Saganaga. Most visitors prefer a permit for Entry Point 55 rather than 55A because it gives greater flexibility for trip planning. The great majority of permits (seventeen out of twenty) available each day are for the more liberal Entry Point 55.

Saganaga has great connections to Boundary Waters lakes to the west, south, and east, and access by way of Cache Bay to the Quetico Provincial Park for visitors with appropriate permits. The routes described below include a trip exploring Saganaga (Route 55A); a great little route to Sea Gull Lake (Route 55B); a long, looping journey west over ancient portages to Kekekabic Lake (Route 55C); a trip to less frequented lakes west of Saganaga, including Cherry, Topaz, and Amoeber lakes (Route 55D); and an epic journey retracing the route to Lake Superior (Route 55E).

Most of the lakes near Saganaga are readily accessible and thus get a fair number of visitors. The 1999 windstorm cut down marginally on visitor use, but usage will likely go back up to historical levels as time passes. The farther you get from Saganaga and Sea Gull lakes, the fewer people you will encounter. Based on visitor surveys conducted by the Forest Service, as well as my own experience, you are most likely to see other paddlers along the border corridor to Knife Lake, south toward Alpine Lake to Ogishkemuncie, and down the Granite River east of Saganaga. The wedge of smaller lakes west of Saganaga, including Ester, Hanson, Topaz, and Amoeber, have historically seen the fewest visitors.

The maze of lakes around Saganaga Lake also allows you to use this guide to design your own route. Routes 55A to 55E cover most lakes in the vicinity of Saganaga, and you can use the index and maps throughout this guide to make further plans. If designing your own trip out of Saganaga, a few points should be kept in mind. First, if you are heading to the west, you will encounter some of the most significant blowdown in the BWCAW from the 1999 windstorm. Part of this area has been subject to prescribed burns, and other areas will be burned in coming years, making it a fascinating area to observe regenerating forest. You will likely have fire bans for much of the paddling season, so be prepared to cook on a camping stove, which is generally superior anyway. You may also have some difficulty finding a good place to hang your food pack, so consider renting or buying a bear-proof container to store your food. A few local outfitters on the Gunflint Trail have started to make these containers available at reasonable prices.

To get to Saganaga, follow the Gunflint Trail north 56 miles from Grand Marais to the intersection of County Road 11 (the Sag Lake Trail). A public access is located at the end of County Road 11. An alternative access is located at the end of County Road 81, a bit before County Road 11 (55 miles up the Gunflint Trail). A parking fee is charged at each of these public parking lots.

Access to Saganaga Lake can also be made by way of Gull Lake and the Sea Gull River at Trails End campground. Take the Gunflint Trail all the way to Trails End campground. Just after the entrance to Trails End is a landing on Gull Lake as well as an entry point kiosk for Saganaga Lake. After unloading your vehicle, you will need to drive your vehicle back to the large parking lot. The Trails End option is particularly good for loops that exit through Sea Gull Lake.

Trails End campground is also an excellent place to spend the night before entering the wilderness and has thirty-three campsites. You should get a reservation if you will be visiting this popular campground in the busy summer months. You can also stay at one of the other Forest Service campgrounds along the Gunflint Trail or at an outfitter's bunkhouse.

Route 55A: Exploration of Saganaga Lake (Map 42)

>   Difficulty: intermediate
>   Number of days: 2 or more
>   Total miles (approx.): 6 or more
>   Number of portages: 0
>   Total portage rods: 0
>   Greatest portage difficulty: NA

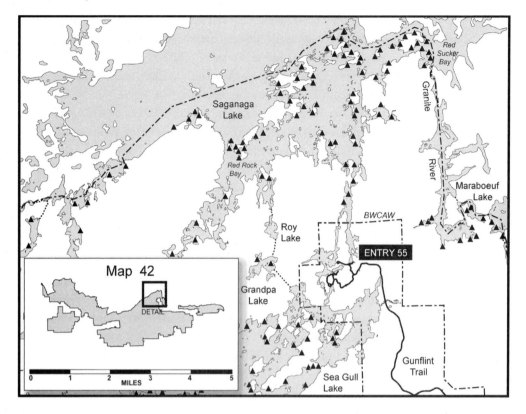

Navigation maps: Voyageur 6
Fisher 32
McKenzie 6A

Massive Saganaga is a great destination in its own right, worthy of as much time as
you can give it. Although you will not portage on this route, be sure to keep careful
track of your position on a map. The dozens of islands and bays can prove confusing.
This route is suitable for most visitors, but less experienced canoeists should be careful on the big stretches of open water during windy conditions.

Detailed Route

From your start at one of the public landings (or from an outfitter's dock), head
north to the main body of Saganaga. The campsites immediately north of where the
Sea Gull River widens into Saganaga Lake are a good spot to spend the first night, although they are not very private because of boat traffic into and out of the main lake.

Don't forget that Saganaga is big water and can get very rough if it is windy. The
biggest wave hazards are usually in areas that have a large open stretch of west–east
water. For example, the area north and west of Munker Island can be very rough, as
can the stretch of water on the Canadian border west of American Point.

Motors up to 25 horsepower are allowed on the American side of Saganaga east of American Point. If you intend to fish heavily on Saganaga, you may want to bring along a portable depth finder. This is one of the few lakes within the BWCAW that has not been sounded by the Minnesota DNR. Thus, there are no lake contours available for Saganaga from any public source, with the exception of portions near Red Rock Bay.

Saganaga is one of the most fascinating lakes in the BWCAW from the standpoint of diverse natural and human history as well as recreational opportunities. Native Americans made Saganaga home for centuries, and prehistoric archaeological sites have been discovered at a number of locations on Saganaga. French traders established at least one post on Saganaga in the eighteenth century, and later the British had a trading post on these waters, connecting them with the activities at Grand Portage on Lake Superior. Certainly thousands of canoes full of voyageurs with furs or trade goods passed over Saganaga's waters two hundred years ago.

A century after the voyageurs, in the 1870s and 1880s, miners prospected for gold on aptly named Gold Island along the western shores of Saganaga. The miners hoped to exploit a gold-containing quartz vein across the island. State geologists were able to find some evidence of blasting when they surveyed this area in the 1890s, although I did not locate evidence of these early mining efforts. As you can guess, the miners made no major gold discoveries. Had viable gold deposits been present, the Boundary Waters would probably not exist in anything resembling its current form.

In the 1900s Saganaga became a recreational destination. One of the more interesting stories from that time is the chance meeting in 1921 on Saganaga between Sigurd Olson and Arthur H. Carhart. Olson is now well known for the decades he spent laboring to preserve the wilderness and his wonderful books about the border country. Less well known is Carhart, an early advocate for turning the border lakes into a paddling wilderness. Apparently Olson and his friends were target shooting on a Saganaga island when Carhart, a Forest Service employee, dressed them down. You can read about both these men in the chapter on natural and human history in this guide. Outfitters and lodge owners also operated on Saganaga, including Justine Kerfoot, the well-known proprietor of Gunflint Lodge, who had a camp on an island north of Saganaga Falls.

Route 55B: Loop through Saganaga and Sea Gull Lakes (Map 42)

Difficulty: easy to intermediate
Number of days: 3
Total miles (approx.): 19
Number of portages: 3
Total portage rods: 155
Greatest portage difficulty: 97 rods

Navigation maps: Voyageur 6
Fisher 32
McKenzie 6A

This popular route is the easiest loop out of Saganaga. You will head north into Saganaga, eventually coming out through its southwest corner by way of Red Rock Bay, Red Rock Lake, and Alpine Lake. Your final destination is mighty Sea Gull Lake, which you will cross to exit at Trails End campground. All of the portages along this route are frequently traveled and well maintained. You will be visiting lakes with relatively heavy visitor usage, but their mazes of bays, islands, and narrows provide plentiful opportunities to seek out a private refuge.

Detailed Route

Paddle 3 miles from the Saganaga landing north to the main body of Saganaga Lake, walking your canoe through a short stretch of shallows if water levels are low. Start your journey at one of the Saganaga public access points, and paddle north. Once on Saganaga you have opportunities to explore its depths for all of the game fish native to the Boundary Waters, and you can spend days paddling among its various islands and bays. See Route 55A for details of the natural and human history of this great lake.

Paddle and portage 9 miles to Alpine Lake, including portages of 10 rods (L2) to Red Rock Lake, and 48 rods (L4) to Alpine Lake. When your time comes to leave Saganaga, head southwest out through Red Rock Bay to Red Rock Lake. Much of the shore along Red Rock Bay and east to the Granite River was burned in large forest fires in the last few decades of the twentieth century. The Roy Lake fire in 1976, caused by lightning, burned 3,400 acres of forest. Twenty years later, the huge Saganaga Corridor fire burned 12,000 acres of forest along the shores of Saganaga to Maraboeuf Lake in the east. That time the fire was started at an illegal campfire on a warm, windy day.

An easy 10-rod portage travels from Red Rock Bay to Red Rock Lake. It can be avoided during high water by paddling or pulling your canoe through a narrows. Alternatively, or in dry times, on the east shore is a rocky landing and a short trail leading a few rods to another small rocky landing.

Red Rock Lake is an excellent place to spend a day and is an attractive destination for many canoeists coming from Saganaga because motorboats are not permitted. Eight designated campsites are scattered along its shores. To leave Red Rock Lake, take a 48-rod portage to a cedar-lined bay on the north arm of Alpine Lake. The trail is average in difficulty, with a simple uphill climb that levels out halfway across the portage before dropping to Alpine. Abundant boulders are exposed along the trail, and a quick observation reveals that the rounded boulders come in many colors and textures, an indication that these rocks are glacial deposits from various types of bedrock north of this area.

Alpine Lake is a popular destination for short trips out of Sea Gull Lake, so you might see a fair number of its campsites occupied. The blowdown of 1999 seems to have lightened the visitor load a bit, at least temporarily. Alpine has historically held a good population of walleye and some northern pike and smallmouth bass.

Paddle and portage 7 miles across Alpine and Sea Gull lakes to the Trails End campground, including a portage of 97 rods from Alpine Lake to Sea Gull Lake. The 97-rod portage between Alpine Lake and Sea Gull Lake was leveled by the 1999 windstorm and has subsequently been swept by a prescribed burn in fall 2002. Look for evidence of the regenerating forest, including progression from initial colonizers (such as fireweed) to aggressive early growth (such as aspen).

You can also attempt to paddle from Alpine Lake down Alpine Creek to Sea Gull Lake. This is not a maintained route, and you will want to carefully scout the creek by shore before attempting to shoot the shallows and rapids along it. Be prepared to dump your canoe, and certainly wear a life jacket if attempting this "shortcut." Yet another option is to head from Alpine to Rog Lake, which has been stocked with brook trout in recent years, and then to Sea Gull. Two moderate portages connect to Sea Gull, although neither trail is particularly well traveled. One campsite is located on Rog Lake.

Sea Gull Lake is another Boundary Waters jewel. Parts of it were hit quite hard by the winds of 1999, including many old red pines on Three Mile Island. These trees were some of the oldest in the BWCAW and were snapped off like toothpicks by the straight-line winds. Fortunately, some of these old trees survived to be enjoyed as you paddle past. More importantly, these surviving trees will hopefully produce a new generation of saplings following a prescribed burn conducted by the Forest Service on Three Mile Island in fall 2003.

If you want to extend your trip and want a real challenge, consider taking a spur to Jap Lake on the southeast shore of Sea Gull. A tough mile and a half portage climbs the long hill out of Sea Gull before rolling to Jap. In the early spring this trail can be a challenge to cross because of downed trees, although a prescribed burn in 2003 appears to have removed some of the borderline trees that would have fallen in winter.

Continue on to the landing at Trails End campground, and then walk back to your vehicle. If you prefer, you can portage around a set of rapids into Gull Lake and then on to Saganaga Lake and your waiting vehicle.

Route 55C: Loop through Knife Lake and Kekekabic Lake (Map 42)

        Difficulty: challenging
        Number of days: 7
        Total miles (approx.): 46
        Number of portages: 19
        Total portage rods: 588
        Greatest portage difficulty: 97 rods

Navigation maps: Voyageur 6
                   Fisher 32
                   McKenzie 6A

This route will appeal to anyone wishing to cover lots of miles with minimal portaging. You travel out of Saganaga Lake and then along the Canadian border by way
of Ottertrack Lake to Knife Lake. You then drop south into Kekekabic Lake before
working your way back along Ogishkemuncie and Alpine lakes. This route is along
relatively popular lakes. You will be circling a series of smaller, less frequented lakes,
which are described in Route 55D, which is perhaps a better route for anyone seeking
more challenges and fewer people.

Map 42 shows the beginning of this route, and Map 43 shows the remainder.

Detailed Route

*Paddle 3 miles along the Sea Gull River to the main body of Saganaga Lake, walk-
ing your canoe through a short stretch of shallows if the water levels are low.* Once in
Saganaga you have opportunities to explore its depths for all of the game fish native
to the Boundary Waters, and you can spend days paddling among its various islands,
points, and bays. See route 55A for details of the natural and human history of this
great lake.

*Paddle and portage 11 miles from Saganaga Lake to central Ottertrack Lake,
including portages of 5 rods (L2) from Saganaga to Swamp Lake, and 78 rods over
the Monument Portage from Swamp Lake to Ottertrack Lake.* A 5-rod portage from
Saganaga leads to Swamp Lake. Rocky landings on both sides provide adequate
spots to load and unload your canoe. While very short, this portage is a bit difficult
because rocky landings can make it a challenge to load and unload gear. Swamp
Lake provides no designated campsites along its shores.

The Monument Portage from Swamp Lake to Ottertrack Lake is a bouldery mix
of glacial erratics, ending with an improvised staircase descending to Ottertrack.
The landing on the Swamp Lake side includes a lengthy boardwalk to help you over a
low, marshy area. Along the portage you will find four border monuments establishing the boundary between the United States and Canada: a small modern marker,
two 4-foot-high brass obelisks, and a larger round monument. Small border markers
are common along the border, but the three larger ones on this portage are special.
Similar large border markers are found only at the Height of Land Portage between
North and South lakes (east of Gunflint) and on the Watap Portage. A total of nine
of these larger markers are located at these three portages and are numbered one to
nine from west to east. In contrast, the small marker is one of 1,279, also numbered
from west to east.

*Paddle and portage 5.5 miles from Ottertrack Lake to east-central Knife Lake,
including a portage of 5 rods (L1).* Ottertrack Lake is a lovely, long border-country

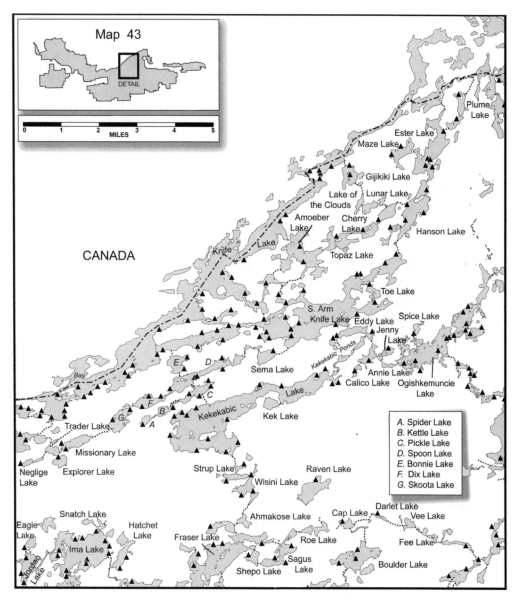

classic. Much of Ottertrack's shore is rocky palisades hovering over the water, and the Canadian side is marked by extensive stands of white pines. On the south shore is the old homestead of Benny Ambrose, who, along with "Root Beer Lady" Dorothy Molter, was one of the two last year-round inhabitants of the BWCAW. At the west end of Ottertrack is a small rapids descending into Knife Lake. Take an easy 5-rod portage to get around the rapids. Some older maps also show a 20-rod portage to the east across a low spot between the lakes, but this portage is exceedingly overgrown and does not appear to get much use or maintenance. You are better off traveling farther west to the main (and shorter) portage.

Paddle and portage 7.5 miles from Knife Lake to Kekekabic Lake, including portages of 42 rods (L4) from Knife to Bonnie Lake, 31 rods (L4) from Bonnie to Spoon Lake, 24 rods (L3) from Spoon to Pickle Lake, and 78 rods (L6) from Pickle to Kekekabic Lake. Press on westward through Knife Lake to the portage to Bonnie Lake. The forest along this portage was heavily hit by the 1999 windstorm, but the trail should be wide-open and easily traveled. Bonnie has two designated campsites and is a significantly quieter lake than Knife. Old DNR surveys show a population of northern pike in this little lake.

From Bonnie, travel 31 rods to Spoon Lake, along a trail that climbs nearly 40 feet in elevation. Spoon Lake also has three campsites. Although Spoon Lake is surprisingly deep at 85 feet maximum, it does not hold lake trout, according to the Minnesota DNR. It does, however, contain some northern pike. Head out the south side of Spoon Lake to Pickle Lake along a trail next to a nice, bubbling stream. Maps show a portage from Pickle Lake to Kettle Lake, where another campsite is believed to be located, and a portage to Spider Lake from Kettle, where another Forest Service designated campsite is located. However, the blowdown was so severe on the south end of Pickle that the portage could not be located in 2003 during research for this guide. Forest Service maps of the blowdown area show that these two campsites were searched after the storm, but they are not identified as being inhabitable. Thus, even if your maps show a portage to Kettle and then on to Spider, you are likely to have trouble reaching either lake. The last part of this trip is a 78-rod carry to Kekekabic, requiring that you climb about 40 feet in elevation along a decent trail.

Kekekabic is a deep and remote lake known for its lake trout population, and sixteen designated campsites are located along the shores of this fine wilderness lake. Kekekabic lies about midway between Snowbank Lake on the west and Sea Gull Lake on the east, making it reasonably far from the nearest road. However, good paddle routes allow approaches from many directions, so it sees significant numbers of visitors all canoeing season.

The Kekekabic Trail runs south of Kekekabic Lake, having originally been built for fire control. A lookout tower was also constructed on the prominent hill south of the east bay of the lake (one of just four placed within the boundaries of the current BWCAW), and a Forest Service cabin was built on the south shore of Kekekabic for crews staffing the tower. The tower was removed decades ago.

If you have time to explore Kekekabic, be sure to circle the two largest islands on the westernmost bay, and then paddle down to the southern shore of the lake itself. You will notice a significant difference in geology between these areas because the islands are composed of granite (formed by cooling molten magma) that is rare in these parts, while most of the rest of Kekekabic's shore started as mud and sand deposits that were formed into rock by heat and pressure.

Paddle and portage 8 miles from Kekekabic Lake to Ogishkemuncie Lake, including portages of 10, 15, 20, 10, 18, 17, 14, and 16 rods through the Kekekabic ponds, Jenny Lake, and Annie Lake to Ogishkemuncie. Your route continues on through the Kekekabic Ponds to Ogishkemuncie. You start by traveling over five portages to Eddy Lake, a couple along the side of a raging rapids. The portage out the east side of the smallest pond is frequently passable by water and is generally easy even if it cannot be paddled.

From Eddy Lake you have a rocky 17-rod uphill climb to Jenny Lake, relatively hard for its length, followed by a well-traveled and generally flat 14-rod portage from Jenny to Annie. If you are observant, you can see the remains of an old landing in the water on the Jenny Lake side. The final, 16-rod portage from Annie to Ogishkemuncie is along a straight, flat path free of any sizable obstructions.

Ogishkemuncie Lake is a well-loved crossroads lake that draws visitors from all directions. Eleven designated campsites are scattered along its shores, and you can also head to a number of neighboring lakes for more solitude. The primary entrances in and out of Ogishkemuncie are by way of Annie Lake to the west, Mueller Lake to the south, and Kingfisher Lake to the east. All of these portages are well traveled and likely to be in good shape. The portage to Annie Lake, which you take on this route, is quite easy and gives access to Kekekabic and the South Arm of Knife Lake. The portage south to Mueller Lake is moderately traveled. The blowdown of 1999 took the trees down on the top of this portage, giving you a great view of the islands spread out before you on Ogishkemuncie. Hike this portage for the view, even if you are not going to Mueller. The northern exit to Kingfisher Lake, described below, is a wide clear path up next to a creek. You will take this portage if you are heading to Sea Gull Lake.

Ogishkemuncie has three additional portages to "dead-end" lakes, and you might want to explore these jewels. Based on the condition of the infrequently traveled portages, these lakes appear to get very few visitors. The first such destination is Spice Lake, over a 10-rod portage from Ogishkemuncie. The portage trail passes through a nice cedar grove spared by the 1999 windstorm. The portage landing is located on the east side of the stream from Spice Lake, not the west side as shown on many Fisher and McKenzie maps. The second short excursion is found on the northeast side of Ogishkemuncie, where a seldom-used 22-rod portage runs to Skindance Lake, which has two designated campsites along its shores. You can also portage 146 rods to Holt Lake. This portage has poor footing, with rocks, roots, and undergrowth along the way, but skirts nice moose habitat along a marsh and creek. Holt Lake reaches depths of nearly 80 feet, enough for it to sustain lake trout, which have been identified in DNR surveys. However, it does not have any designated campsites.

Don't fail to spend a little time on Ogishkemuncie examining the bedrock under your feet and exposed along the shoreline. Knife Lake slate can be found in many places, such as on the portage to Annie. Ogishkemuncie conglomerate can also be seen in many spots, such as in the boulders on the Annie side of the portage between Annie and Ogishkemuncie. This conglomerate is among the most interesting rock in the BWCAW. It looks much like concrete because it contains many rocks of various sizes put together and formed in part from molten masses ejected from volcanoes north of here millions of years ago. Some of the rock in this conglomerate originated in the same formations as found to the north at Saganaga Lake, and was expelled by volcanoes miles from its origins.

Paddle and portage 4.5 miles from Ogishkemuncie Lake to Alpine Lake, including portages of 41 rods (L4) from Ogishkemuncie to Kingfisher Lake, 24 rods (L4) from Kingfisher to Jasper Lake, and 43 rods (L3) from Jasper to Alpine Lake. The 41-rod portage from Ogishkemuncie to Kingfisher meanders through a mixed forest along the edge of a stream before dropping down a short hill to a rock landing on the western lobe of Kingfisher. Kingfisher Lake has no campsites and is relatively low lying. The 24-rod portage between Kingfisher and Jasper rises and descends along a slightly rocky trail with a fair number of exposed roots. Jasper Lake has seven designated campsites. A 25-rod portage from Jasper heads to Tern Lake, but this portage is a tough trail with few visitors and still has blowdown obstructing parts of it. Having no designated campsites and no known fish population, Tern Lake attracts few visitors.

The 43-rod portage between Jasper and Alpine travels along the east side of a raging steam that is impassable by canoe. The trail is generally free of obstructions. Along the portage is exposed metabasalt bedrock localized to this area, and on the upstream side of this portage are the remains of a landing from decades past when the Forest Service permitted and maintained such structures.

Paddle and portage 6.5 miles across Alpine and Sea Gull lakes to the Trails End campground, including a portage of 97 rods from Alpine Lake to Sea Gull Lake. The main portage between Alpine Lake and Sea Gull Lake was leveled by the 1999 windstorm and has subsequently been swept by a prescribed burn in fall 2002. Look for evidence of the regeneration of the forest. You can also attempt to paddle down Alpine Creek to Sea Gull Lake, or head from Alpine to Rog Lake and then to Sea Gull. Review route 55B for details about these two options, both of which will be harder than the 97-rod portage for most visitors.

Route 55D: Remote Western Loop to Amoeber Lake (Map 42)

> Difficulty: challenging
> Number of days: 4 or more
> Total miles (approx.): 30
> Number of portages: 17
> Total portage rods: 870
> Greatest portage difficulty: 110 rods (L9)
> Navigation maps: Voyageur 6
> Fisher 32
> McKenzie 6A, 8, 26

This route contrasts sharply with Route 55C, taking you off the most popular lakes to visit a challenging and wonderful corner of the BWCAW. You will head west along the Canadian border from Saganaga Lake and then leave the border to travel through Ashdick, Ester, and Hanson lakes, moving on to more remote Cherry, Lunar, and Gijikiki before venturing to Amoeber and Topaz on your way back to

Saganaga. Some of the lakes you will visit get significantly fewer visitors than most other areas reachable from Saganaga, perhaps because they have some of the more difficult portages. This route is not the fastest way through the BWCAW but will reward an adventurous spirit who doesn't shy from a challenge.

Map 42 shows most of the route, and Map 43 shows additional portions. An overview of the entire route is shown on Map 36.

Detailed Route

Paddle 3 miles from the Saganaga landing north to the main body of Saganaga Lake, walking your canoe through a short stretch of shallows if water levels are low. Start your journey at one of the Saganaga public access points and paddle north. Once on Saganaga you have opportunities to explore its depths for all of the game fish native to the Boundary Waters, and you can spend days paddling among its various islands and bays. See route 55A for details of the natural and human history of this great lake.

Paddle and portage 10 miles from Saganaga Lake to Ashdick Lake, including portages of 5 rods (L2) from Saganaga to Swamp Lake, and 167 rods (L9) from Swamp to Ashdick Lake. This first leg starts by heading west out of Saganaga to Swamp Lake, taking a 5-rod portage from Saganaga to Swamp that bypasses a shallow stream connecting the two lakes. Rocky landings on both sides provide adequate spots to load and unload your canoe. While very short, this portage is a bit difficult because the rocky landings make it hard to load and unload gear.

Swamp Lake has no designated campsites along its shore, so you will need to portage to Ashdick. The portage trail follows the eastern bank of a large swampy area, is at times rooty and rocky, and can be wet in spring due to the low-lying trail. While some of the trail includes an aging log walkway, the logs are in a state of significant decay and provide marginal improvement over the muddy alternatives. Ashdick Lake is a neat off-the-beaten-track lake with two designated campsites, either of which should make a nice place to spend a night. The northern lobe of Ashdick has a mixed forest of cedars and pines, while cliffs on the western shore have some particularly nice stands of young white pines.

Paddle and portage 3 miles from Ashdick Lake to Hanson Lake, including a portage of 55 rods (L6) to Ester Lake. When leaving Ashdick, a 55-rod portage leads to Ester Lake along a rocky, winding trail. This portage provides a great geology lesson. On the Ashdick side, near the landing, you will notice that the rocks are greenish, with flat broken sides. These rocks are part of the Knife Lake slate formation and started as sedimentary deposits laid down by erosion of older rock. Intrusion of molten magma into these sedimentary deposits cooked, or metamorphosed, them into their present form. The rock has flat surfaces because the sedimentary deposits were laid down in layers. Farther down the trail are additional tantalizing historic hints: granitic boulders, probably part of the Gunflint Formation to the north and east. These boulders, with a completely different color and texture, are readily distinguishable from local bedrock and were probably carried here over 10,000 years ago during the Wisconsin glaciation.

Ester is a big lake with five designated campsites, including four clustered to the south on or near a large island. These sites are attractive because some of the shallows between the island and the mainland are just a few feet deep and sandy bottomed—ideal for swimming. If these campsites are all occupied, paddle south through the channel connecting to Hanson Lake, which has four additional designated campsites and also provides a nice place to spend a few days.

Paddle and portage 3 miles from Hanson Lake to Gijikiki Lake, including portages of 110 rods (L9) from Hanson to Cherry Lake, 40 rods (L6) from Cherry to Lunar Lake, 10 rods (L3) from Lunar to Lake of the Clouds, 75 rods (L7) from Lake of the Clouds to Rivalry Lake, and 35 rods (L4) from Rivalry to Gijikiki Lake. You will now press deeper into an even more remote portion of the wilderness. A 110-rod portage from Hanson Lake to Cherry Lake climbs steeply from the shores of Hanson, dips once, and then goes over a peak before descending to Cherry Lake. This is a rather steep and somewhat rocky trail. Except for the small flat portion in the center, this trail is essentially straight up and straight down. Cherry Lake is impressive, with 70-foot cliffs along portions of its western shore and a towering island in its southern lobe. Two campsites are located on Cherry Lake, and they appear to get relatively few visitors because of the difficult portage to Cherry. Your next camping opportunities are not until Gijikiki Lake, which is a few tough, short portages away.

The 40-rod portage from Cherry Lake to Lunar Lake is a rugged haul that starts with a sharp climb from Cherry to an old beaver pond that appears long abandoned but still has evidence of cutting in the woods and flooded pines in the pond. Hike along the western side of the pond until you reach an intermittent streambed. Climb along the south shore of the streambed, and you will soon arrive at Lunar Lake. Lunar is small but attractive, with a shoreline that is primarily jack pine with some birch and aspen along the western end. No designated campsites are located on Lunar, so press on to Lake of the Clouds.

A steep but solid 10-rod portage leads from Lunar Lake to Lake of the Clouds, climbing approximately 20 feet in elevation. Lake of the Clouds is famous in natural history circles as one of the first places where lake bottom sediments were used to study historic plant populations. The deep, relatively undisturbed sediments of Lake of the Clouds contain thousands of annual layers of pollen that were deposited year after year. These pollen layers have been used to determine forest plant populations over time in this area.

A 75-rod portage connects Lake of the Clouds to tiny Rivalry Lake. This seldom-traveled trail is rockier than most and likely to have a fair number of wet areas during spring. Expect the trail to be somewhat overgrown. Finally, a 35-rod (L4) portage leads from Rivalry Lake to Gijikiki Lake. The trail, rugged in places, includes a significant descent to Gijikiki and plenty of exposed portions of the Knife Lake slate formation. Gijikiki is also a nice place to spend an evening at one of two designated sites.

Paddle and portage 4 miles from Gijikiki Lake to Amoeber Lake, including portages of 50 rods (L7) from Gijikiki to Ottertrack Lake, 5 rods from Ottertrack to Knife Lake, and 20 rods (L3) from Knife to Amoeber Lake. You will leave Gijikiki by way of a 50-rod portage to Ottertrack Lake. This portage climbs steeply from Gijikiki before descending sharply and following eastward over a short switchback. Much of Ottertrack Lake's shore is a rocky palisade towering over the water, and the Canadian side is marked by extensive stands of white pines.

A 5-rod portage connects Ottertrack to Knife Lake. This portage is little more than a lift-out, a carry around a small but fierce stream, and then a set-in on Knife. The next portage is a 20-rod trail from Knife Lake to Amoeber Lake, following uphill along the banks of a stream. You will see plenty of damage from the 1999 windstorm along this portage, but the trail is generally clear. Although there are some exposed rocks along the route, the trail is generally clear and reasonably heavily traveled. Amoeber Lake has two designated campsites and is a nice place to enjoy a few peaceful days. The depths of Amoeber contain walleye and lake trout, although historically only in limited numbers.

Paddle and portage 2.5 miles from Amoeber Lake to Cherry Lake, including portages of 20 rods (L2) from Amoeber to Topaz Lake, and 5 rods (L2) from Topaz to Cherry Lake. The 20-rod portage from Amoeber to Topaz Lake follows along a small rivulet connecting the two lakes that is too narrow and shallow to navigate. You will need to follow the trail through a grove of cedars. A 5-rod portage runs from Topaz to Cherry. Although short and flat, the trail tends to get wet in spring, so don't be surprised if it is muddy.

Paddle and portage 4.25 miles from Cherry Lake to Ottertrack Lake, including portages of 110 rods (L9) from Cherry to Hanson Lake, and 80 rods (L7) from Ester Lake to Ottertrack Lake. Continue to Hanson Lake along the tough 110-rod portage you took earlier in this trip. Next, a challenging 80-rod portage leads you from Ester Lake into Ottertrack. Although the trail is well traveled, it is quite hilly and has a swampy interior stretch and short but steep climbs and descents at each landing.

Paddle and portage 13 miles from Ottertrack Lake back to your start on Saganaga, including portages of 78 rods over the Monument Portage to Swamp Lake, and 5 rods (L2) from Swamp to Saganaga. The Monument Portage from Ottertrack to Swamp Lake is a boulder mix of glacial erratics. The first few rods out of Ottertrack follow an improvised staircase. Along the portage you will find four border monuments establishing the boundary between the United States and Canada: a small modern marker, two 4-foot-high brass obelisks, and a round monument. Your route finishes by taking the 5-rod portage back to Saganaga and then paddling back to your starting point.

Route 55E: One-Way Challenge to Lake Superior (Map 42)

Difficulty: very challenging
Number of days: 7 or more

Total miles (approx.): 83
Number of portages: 23
Total portage rods: 4,966 rods (15.5 miles)
Greatest portage difficulty: 2,720 rods (8.5 miles)
Navigation maps: Voyageur 6, 9, 10
Fisher N/A
McKenzie 6A, 5, 4, 2, 1, 98

This is the longest one-way trip presented in this guidebook, and it takes you all the way from Saganaga Lake to Grand Marais along the historic voyageurs' highway. This long and challenging route has few portages relative to its total distance, although the 8.5-mile Grand Portage at the end of the trip will be memorable. Unlike most other routes in this book, this journey has an extended portion outside of the Boundary Waters as you head down the Pigeon River to the Grand Portage. The historic significance of the route and its beauty justify including it in a Boundary Waters guide.

Map 42 shows the start of this route, and Maps 43 and 44 show the sequential eastern sections. The last segment of this trip on the Pigeon River is outside of the BWCAW, but it is shown on McKenzie Map 98 and Voyageur Map 10.

Detailed Route

You will need two vehicles for this journey or will at least need assistance from an outfitter in moving your car because a car must be left in Grand Portage for when you complete your trip. The best option, and one I have used, is to have an outfitter at the end of the Gunflint Trail drive your car to Grand Portage while you are on your trip. The outfitter can keep your car in their parking lot for most of your trip and then drive it to the Grand Portage Monument the day you are expected to cross the portage. This way your car is not unattended for an extended period of time.

Paddle 5 miles to Saganaga Lake. The first day of this journey is an easy paddle to Saganaga Lake. I recommend spending a first evening on Saganaga because of its history and beauty. See Route 55A to learn more about the interesting history of Saganaga and opportunities for side trips.

Paddle and portage 5 miles from Saganaga Lake to Maraboeuf Lake, including portages along the Granite River of 39 rods (L5) and 27 rods (L5). You will now start a long stretch of travel toward Magnetic Lake, traveling along some of the most beautiful wilderness stretches in the BWCAW. You will wind through scenic rocky channels and lakes, taking portages that have carried travelers for centuries. On this relatively easy leg, you will paddle into the eastern end of Saganaga and take a 39-rod portage leading from Red Sucker Bay of Saganaga along the east side of Saganaga Falls. The trail is generally flat but tends to be rocky and muddy in places.

Paddle down the Granite River for 1 mile until you reach the Horsetail Rapids.

Both shores of the river show lasting signs of the Saganaga Corridor fire of 1995. This is a great area to pull over and examine the regenerating forest. The 27-rod Horseshoe Rapids portage follows along a rocky trail on the east side of the Granite River. This is a relatively difficult trail not because it changes in elevation but because the rocky path follows along a steep riverbank. Also, part of the trail is prone to flooding in spring but should still be passable. The Horsetail Rapids are one of many along this route that were portaged around or paddled through by voyageurs more than two centuries ago. The Minnesota Historical Society conducted a thorough underwater archaeology project in the early 1970s along many of these portages, uncovering numerous artifacts of the fur trade years.

In addition, you should use either Voyageur or McKenzie maps for this route because Fisher does not produce a complete set of maps covering the entire route. In particular, the eastern end of this route is not on current Fisher F-series canoeing maps.

Maraboeuf Lake is a big, wide stretch in the Granite River. According to the Minnesota Historical Society, the name *Maraboeuf* is believed to be an anglicized French word meaning "marsh deer" or "marsh buffalo," perhaps a reference to moose. This name was assigned at least as early as 1801, but state geologist N. H. Winchell temporarily gave Maraboeuf the name "Banks' Pine Lake" in 1880 for its population of jack pine, known by its Latin name *Pinus banksiana*. Later it was called Granite Lake after its bedrock geology, before the name Maraboeuf was finally restored.

Paddle and portage 6.5 miles from Maraboeuf Lake to Clove Lake, including portages of 27 rods (L3), 34 rods (optional), 25 rods (L2), 72 rods (L8), and 48 rods (L4). You will now head south toward Clove Lake. Keep paddling until you come to the 27-rod Gneiss Lake portage, which is relatively flat and goes around a set of shallow rapids. The trail has a fair number of rocks pointing out. This portage was hit by the 1999 windstorm. You can wind around the Devils Elbow without having to portage into Gneiss Lake, or take a rocky 36-rod (L5) portage that cuts around the eastern peninsula in Maraboeuf Lake.

Pressing on, you will take a 34-rod portage that bypasses a section of double rapids. It is possible much of the year to walk or paddle your canoe through this stretch of stream. You will then come to a 25-rod portage that is reasonably flat with good landings on each side. The next carry is the 72-rod Swamp Portage, which avoids a stretch of very hazardous water. Aptly named Swamp Portage is not long but is difficult because it gets very muddy in the middle. A final, 48-rod portage leads you to Clove Lake.

Clove Lake has three campsites, all of which are reasonably popular. Visitors coming in from Gunflint Lake (to the south) often try to make their first night's stay on Clove Lake. If you want more solitude or these sites are not open, consider taking the portage out the east end of Clove Lake to Larch Lake, where you will find three more designated campsites.

Paddle and portage 6 miles from Clove Lake to central Gunflint Lake, including portages along the Granite River of 115 rods (L7), 30 rods (L5), 20 rods, and 20 rods. A 115-rod portage leads from Clove Lake to the Granite River. It climbs quickly for the first 20 rods up a well-traveled trail, levels off, and then rises two more times before dropping to the Granite River. The 30-rod portage is generally easy but might have some mud, as well as a very difficult landing on the north side, where you have to climb through a rocky gully. Finally, you will take 15- and 20-rod portages leading to Magnetic Lake, paralleling magnificent rapids. Alternatively, there is a 100-rod portage that combines these two shorter portages.

You will now paddle across Magnetic Lake to Gunflint Lake, temporarily leaving the BWCAW. Magnetic Lake retains a very remote wilderness feel, with the exception of a little island in its north end with a collection of small cabins. This island is certainly pricey real estate, and an outfitter on Gunflint Lake suggested that but for this island, perhaps Magnetic Lake would also be in the Boundary Waters. The cost of acquiring the island would have been too high to make it a practical purchase.

You must paddle through a narrows when going from Magnetic Lake to Gunflint Lake. As you do so, look down for submerged pylons from the railroad trestle bridge that once crossed the narrows. Read the history section in this guide to learn more about the Port Arthur, Duluth & Western Railway (PAD&W) that ran across this narrows, as well as about the Paulson Mine destination of the railroad. Old photos and historical accounts show the bridge to be over 100 feet long and at least 20 feet high.

Paddle and portage 12 miles from Gunflint Lake to South Lake, including portages of 15 rods (L1) from Little Gunflint Lake to Little North Lake, and 8 rods (L6) from North Lake to South Lake. The first segment of this journey sends you east through long, deep Gunflint Lake.

Gunflint Lake's length and east–west orientation make it highly susceptible to developing large, rolling waves when the wind is out of the west or northwest. An early morning start is therefore advised, because this is usually the calmest part of the day. The PAD&W railway, built in the late 1800s to serve Paulson Mine (just southwest of Gunflint Lake), once ran along the north shore of Gunflint. The shore still contains some remnants of that old railway, including bread-making ovens and a cross carved into the bedrock where a railway construction worker died.

Continue east from Gunflint Lake toward Little Gunflint Lake. No portage is necessary when crossing from Gunflint to Little Gunflint because the two lakes are joined by a shallow waterway. However, the eastern end of Gunflint has a fine sand beach well worth a stop for a swim or lunch.

The level portage from Little Gunflint to Little North Lake was once the location of a mechanized portage where boats were pulled on small rail-mounted cars to Little North Lake. Some authors report that these rails or their predecessors were probably first laid down in 1890 or 1891. Today, the rusted remnants of the tracks still remain, as does the decaying cable mechanism used to manually advance the small rail cars. This portage can usually be avoided by pulling your canoe upstream along the channel between the lakes, or in the downstream direction by floating it. Paddle along Little North Lake and through a narrows to North Lake.

North Lake is gorgeous, with high hills rising from its deep Canadian arm. This lake is entirely outside of the BWCAW, and therefore motorized boats are allowed everywhere. You should travel across North Lake and then head over the Height of Land Portage to South Lake. The Height of Land Portage is one of the truly historic border-country portages. Thousands of voyageurs traveled across this portage, and Native Americans had been following the same path for at least centuries before the voyageurs. Rain falling on the west side of the portage eventually flows to Hudson Bay, while rain falling on the east side of the portage eventually flows to the Atlantic Ocean. Intuitively one would expect that this portage would have some of the best drainage in the world, yet the trail on the Height of Land Portage is actually quite low lying and muddy most of the year.

Paddle and portage 6 miles from South Lake to Rose Lake, including portages of 65 rods (L3) from South Lake to Rat Lake, and 4 rods from Rat to Rose Lake. The South Lake Portage leading to Rat Lake is quite level with little mud, making for an easy trail. The 4-rod portage from Rat Lake to Rose Lake diverts around an impassable little rapids over a rock exposure. With a strong crew, you should be able to lift fully loaded canoes up and over this short, rocky portage.

Paddle and portage 4 miles from Rose Lake to Rove Lake, including a portage of 665 rods (L10). The first part of this 2-mile-long trail is flat and smooth, following along an excellent trail elevated above the narrow Arrow River. The final 200 rods travels through a hilly mixed forest of ancient red and white pines. Many of these great old trees were brought down by the 1999 windstorm, but even more still stand.

Paddle and portage 6.25 miles from Rove Lake to Mountain Lake, including a portage of 110 rods (L5). Rove Lake leads to Watap Lake without a portage, and then Watap Lake leads to Mountain Lake via a fine 110-rod trail, dropping you to Mountain Lake at Monument Border Marker No. 9. Despite being quite large and over 3 miles long, Watap Lake contains no designated campgrounds along its shore. Mountain Lake is a magnificent, big border-country lake with crystal clear waters and towering hills on both shores. The eastern end of the Canadian side was hit hard by the storm, as were parts of the U.S. side, particularly some of the campsites. Mountain has a healthy lake trout population and also a good smallmouth bass population. Remember that you cannot fish Canadian waters without a Canadian fishing license. For a side trip out of Mountain Lake, consider hauling over an 86-rod (L6) portage on the south shore to little Pemmican Lake, home to a stocked population of brook trout.

Paddle and portage 7 miles from Mountain Lake to Moose Lake, including portages of 90 rods along the Lesser Cherry Portage to Fan Lake, 40 rods along the Vaseux Portage to Vaseux Lake, and 140 rods over the Greater Cherry Portage to Moose Lake. The flat 90-rod Lesser Cherry Portage is likely to be very muddy during all but the driest years. In addition, the landing on the east end has hazardous boot-eating muck, so use caution. Paddle across shallow Fan Lake, and then take the 40-rod Vaseux Portage, which is a big improvement over the Lesser Cherry Portage but still potentially quite muddy. The flat, moderately muddy trail is a tad more difficult than most. Paddle across lily pad–covered Vaseux Lake, and land at the 140-rod Great Cherry Portage. This portage drops steeply down a clean trail for the first third and then levels off along a somewhat rocky trail for its final two thirds, ultimately depositing you on the shores of Moose Lake.

Paddle and portage 4.75 miles across Moose Lake, including a portage of 130 rods to North Fowl Lake; paddle across North Fowl Lake. The Moose Portage continues the line of relatively muddy portages, although there are a few Forest Service–constructed footbridges along parts of the trail. This portage is still quite muddy after rains and somewhat muddy during all but the driest years. However, the trail is otherwise in generally good shape. The landing on the North Fowl side is relatively muddy, and you should take the north fork in the trail (at the BWCAW sign) to reach the best landing.

After taking the Moose Portage, you pass out of the BWCAW for the last time. The Fowl lakes are well named, with extensive rice beds attracting great numbers of migrating waterfowl in the fall. Continue along the shores of North Fowl, through the island-studded marsh, and into South Fowl. If continuing on to the Pigeon River and Grand Portage, it would be best to camp at one of the campsites on North Fowl Lake or South Fowl Lake and allow a full day to cover the Fowl Portage and Pigeon River, both of which can be quite challenging.

Paddle and portage 3 miles across South Fowl Lake and over the 320-rod (L10) Fowl Portage to the Pigeon River. The Fowl Portage is long and difficult. You will initially climb steeply uphill on a fine trail for about 40 rods before dropping gradually to the Pigeon River. Allow yourself at least a couple of hours to cover the portage, even if you normally single-trip portages.

Paddle down the Pigeon River for 8.5 miles until you reach Partridge Falls. The first couple of miles down the Pigeon River are easy, flat water. After about 3 miles the pace picks up, and you travel along a 2-mile stretch of intermittent rapids. Be absolutely certain that your gear is fully waterproofed before heading downstream, because a tip-over can easily occur. No established campsites exist along the shores of the Pigeon until you reach the site of Fort Charles at the end of the Grand Portage. The wet, wooded shoreline provides very few sites to temporarily camp. Therefore, it is essential that you allow yourself adequate time before starting the Fowl Portage to complete both the portage and the Pigeon River before sundown. I recommend starting the Fowl Portage in the morning to guarantee adequate time.

Navigation down the Pigeon River is interrupted by the cascades at Partridge Falls. Here, you have two options, both requiring that you haul your canoe out of the water upstream from the falls at an abandoned log cabin. The first option is to portage around the falls and then head another three-quarters of a mile downstream to the top of the Grand Portage. Alternatively, if you have made arrangements, you can leave from Partridge Falls along the rough jeep trail heading to Lake Superior. You can camp at Fort Charlotte, which has two backwoods campsites.

Hike 8.5 miles down the Grand Portage. The last segment of this trip is a hike down the 8.5-mile Grand Portage. The trail crosses old Highway 61 after about 4 miles and then crosses the modern Highway 61 after about 8 miles, just before Lake Superior. Primitive camping is permitted at Fort Charlotte. A backcountry camping permit is required and can be filled out at a self-service kiosk at Fort Charlotte. No other camping is permitted within the Grand Portage Monument.

Entry Point 57, Magnetic Lake (Map 44)

> Daily permit quota: 3
> Permit availability: moderate

Route 57: Granite River Journey to Saganaga (Map 44)

> Difficulty: easy to intermediate
> Number of days: 3
> Total miles (approx.): 21.5
> Number of portages: 11
> Total portage rods: 391
> Greatest portage difficulty: 115 rods (L7)
> Navigation maps: Voyageur 6
>   Fisher F32
>   McKenzie 6A

This route goes from Gunflint Lake though Magnetic Lake and the Granite River along the Canadian border. It follows along stretches of twisting streams, portages around beautiful waterfalls and rapids, and leads you to legendary Saganaga. Well-suited to visitors of every skill level, it will produce memories for a lifetime.

Detailed Route

As a warning, late in the summer and fall parts of this route can have very low water, seeming as if someone turned off the tap upstream, making the portages significantly longer. If you are taking this route during these times, you may want to call the Gunflint Ranger Station in Grand Marais to confirm that water levels are sufficient for normal paddling.

Paddle and portage 5 miles from Gunflint Lake through Magnetic Lake and then on to Clove Lake, including portages along the Granite River of 20 rods, 20 rods, 30 rods (L5), and 115 rods (L7). You will start on Gunflint Lake and then paddle through a narrows into Magnetic Lake. You may want to start your journey exploring Gunflint Lake. See Route 58A for interesting notes about this historic lake. As you

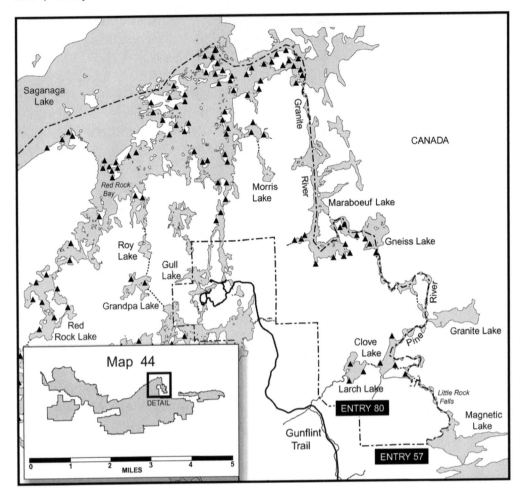

paddle into Magnetic Lake, look down for submerged pylons from the railroad trestle bridge that once crossed the narrows. Read the history section in this guide to learn more about the Port Arthur, Duluth & Western Railway (PAD&W) that ran across this narrows, as well as the Paulson Mine destination of the railroad. Old photos and historic accounts show the bridge to be over 100 feet long and at least 20 feet high. See Route 55E for details about the portages along this stretch.

Clove Lake has three campsites, all of which are reasonably popular. Visitors coming in from Gunflint Lake (to the south) often try to make their first night's stay on Clove Lake. If you want more solitude or these sites are not open, consider taking the portage out the east end of Clove Lake to Larch Lake, where you will find three more designated campsites.

Paddle and portage 6.5 miles from Clove Lake to Maraboeuf Lake, including portages of 48 rods (L4), 72 rods (L8), 25 rods (L2), 34 rods (optional), and 27 rods (L3). See Route 55E for details about the portages along this stretch.

Paddle and portage 5 miles from Maraboeuf Lake to Saganaga Lake, including portages along the Granite River of 27 rods (L5) and 39 rods (L5).

Paddle and portage 5 miles to Saganaga Lake. The final day of this journey is an easy paddle to Saganaga Lake. See Route 55A to learn more about the interesting history of Saganaga and opportunities for side trips. In addition, Routes 55B, 55C, and 55D give you additional options for interesting extensions of various lengths from Saganaga.

Entry Point 80, Larch Creek (Map 44)

> Daily permit quota: 1
> Permit availability: moderate to difficult

Larch Creek provides a unique entry to the great Granite River system and gives an opportunity to travel a tiny, winding stream to Larch Lake. You should expect to frequently pull your canoe over beaver dams and through shallows on Larch Creek, particularly when water levels are low.

To get to the Larch Creek entry, take the Gunflint Trail (County Road 12) from Grand Marais for 51 miles, and turn right onto a gravel road immediately past the Sea Gull Guard Station. The entry is on the north side of unmarked Larch Creek. The parking lot is limited to space for just a couple of vehicles.

Route 80: Exploration of Larch Lake (Map 44)

> Difficulty: moderate
> Number of days: 2 or more
> Total miles (approx.): 3.5
> Number of portages: 0
> Total portage rods: N/A
> Greatest portage difficulty: N/A
> Navigation maps: Voyageur 6
>   Fisher F32
>   McKenzie 6A

Detailed Route

After you put in on Larch Creek, you will wind 1.75 miles through this little creek toward Larch Lake. Three designated campsites are located along the shores of low-lying Larch Lake, which is more than enough for the few people who enter from Larch Lake each week. However, people also come to Larch Lake by way of Clove Lake to the west, typically people who started at Saganaga or Magnetic lakes. Thus, you cannot assume a campsite will be available during the peak travel seasons of July and August. Get an early start at the Larch Creek land if you are traveling during these months in order to give yourself time to press farther if necessary to find a campsite.

ENTRY NORTHEAST
OF THE GUNFLINT TRAIL

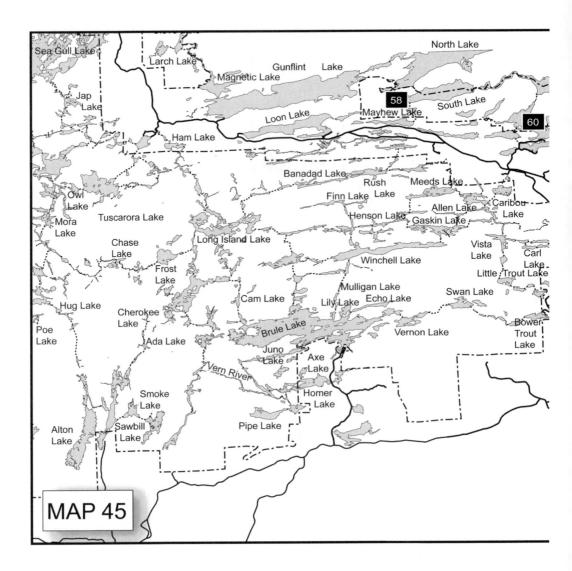

MAP 45

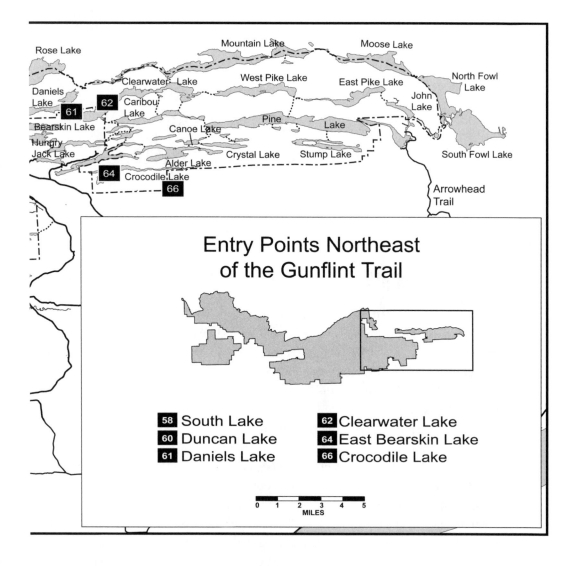

Rose Lake

Mountain Lake

Moose Lake

Clearwater Lake

West Pike Lake

East Pike Lake

North Fowl Lake

Daniels Lake

61 **62** Caribou Lake

John Lake

Bearskin Lake

Pine Lake

Hungry Jack Lake

Canoe Lake

Crystal Lake

Stump Lake

South Fowl Lake

Alder Lake

64 Crocodile Lake

66

Arrowhead Trail

Entry Points Northeast of the Gunflint Trail

58 South Lake

60 Duncan Lake

61 Daniels Lake

62 Clearwater Lake

64 East Bearskin Lake

66 Crocodile Lake

0 1 2 3 4 5
MILES

ENTRY NORTHEAST
OF THE GUNFLINT TRAIL

- -

The area north of the Gunflint Trail has a look and feel very distinct from the rest of the BWCAW. This region encompasses long, deep lakes lined up in a generally west–east orientation, in contrast to the many irregular-shaped lakes in the central and western BWCAW. Some of these lakes harbor healthy populations of lake trout in their deep, cold, clear waters. In addition, tall hills rise up between them, adding a topographic relief unique in the BWCAW and also producing a few notably long, hard portages.

The most popular entry points to this portion of the BWCAW are Duncan Lake (Entry Point 60), East Bearskin Lake (Entry Point 64), and Clearwater Lake (Entry Point 62). Each of these three entries offers good prospects for long explorations to excellent lakes, and all of them have good options with relatively modest portages. Additional entry points north and east of the Gunflint Trail are South Lake (Entry Point 58), Daniels Lake (Entry Point 61), and Crocodile Lake (Entry Point 66). South Lake offers great travel opportunities along the Canadian border and crosses into the wilderness at the Height of Land Portage, one of the most famous and historic portages in all of canoe country. Many of the lakes accessible from South Lake allow motorized boats, lessening the appeal to some visitors. Daniels Lake is a good entry for short trips, but any extensions far beyond Daniels require quite long portages. Finally, Crocodile Lake is a little dead-end lake perfect for a weekend trip but with limited travel options.

Keep in mind a few considerations if you are starting at any of these six entry points north and east of the Gunflint. First, travel over portages oriented from east to west is typically significantly easier than travel over portages oriented from north to south. The reason for this difference in difficulty is that the geology of this area has resulted in huge hills on many of the north and south shores of these lakes, and lowlands connecting their east and west ends.

Second, a major challenge in planning a loop through these lakes is that most loop routes require at least one portage exceeding 200 rods, often over one or more high hills. Trips of longer distances usually require that you be fit or pack especially lightly.

Third, many of the lakes north of the Gunflint Trail lie on the Canadian border, and motors are allowed on watercraft on the Canadian side of these lakes. Some routes in this area also take you to American waters out of the BWCAW, and motors are allowed on the entire surface of these lakes.

Fourth, the orientation of many lakes north of the Gunflint Trail and their large size allow winds to race across the lakes unhindered by landforms and trees. If your route calls for travel down one of these large lakes, try to travel early in the morning, and perhaps allow yourself an extra day of travel in the event you get wind bound.

Observant travelers in the northeast BWCAW are likely to see the effects of decades of these winds. The western ends of most long lakes, such as Pine, East Pike, West Pike, Caribou, and Alder, are relatively free of floating natural debris—logs, branches, leaves, beaver cuttings, and so on. In contrast, the eastern ends are often the last resting spot for massive tree trunks and other floating objects propelled by the winds over the decades. Also observe that many of the old pines, especially old white pines, have windblown tops with significantly more branches on their downwind east sides than their upwind west sides. Entire trees inclined slightly to the east are relatively common.

Entry Point 58, South Lake (Map 46)

> Daily permit quota: 3
> Permit availability: easy

Entry Point 58, South Lake, lies along the Canadian border north of the Gunflint Trail and is reached from the west by water from Gunflint Lake. You must paddle nearly 12 miles across four lakes before you even enter the BWCAW. The South Lake entry is notable because you cross into the Boundary Waters at the Height of Land Portage. Water on the west side of the portage flows to Hudson Bay, while water on the east side flows to Lake Superior on its way to the Atlantic Ocean. This portage has been in use for centuries and was a place of initiation for new voyageurs on their first journey inland, making it one of the more interesting and historic of all Boundary Waters portages.

Your travel options are somewhat limited when entering at South Lake, which explains why relatively few permits are issued for it each year. Fortunately, an excellent out-and-back route takes you from Gunflint Lake to South and Rose lakes, returning you back to your start along the reverse route. This short trip, described below as Route 58, avoids long portages and follows through long lakes bordered by towering hills. It also allows you to hook into routes starting at Entry Point 60 (Duncan Lake) in the event that you would like a longer journey.

To reach South Lake, take the Gunflint Trail 43 miles from Grand Marais until you reach the South Gunflint Lake Road, which is County Road 50. Take County

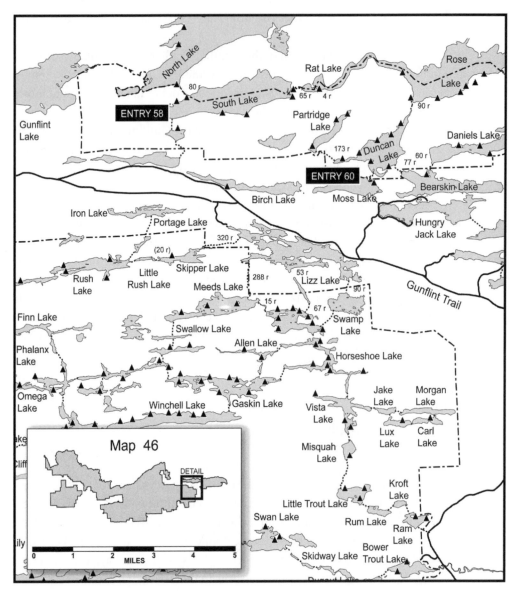

Road 50 for just a half mile to the public access on Gunflint Lake, where you should find ample parking. If you need a place to spend the night, the Trails End campground is located 12 miles farther down the Gunflint Trail, or you can rent a bed in a bunkhouse at one of the outfitters or campgrounds along the trail.

Route 58: Rose Lake Round-Trip (Map 46)

> Difficulty: moderate
> Number of days: 3 or more
> Total miles: 36
> Portage number: 8

Total portage rods: 328
Greatest portage difficulty: 80 rods (L6)
Navigation maps: Voyageur 9
                 Fisher F13
                 McKenzie 1, 4

This route takes you along a little piece of the historic voyageurs' highway. You will see a few interesting artifacts of earlier days and some of the best scenery in the BWCAW.

Detailed Route

Paddle and portage 12 miles from Gunflint Lake to South Lake, including portages of 15 rods (L1) from Little Gunflint Lake to Little North Lake, and 80 rods (L6) from North Lake to South Lake. The first segment of this journey sends you east through long, deep Gunflint Lake. Gunflint's length and orientation make it susceptible to developing large, rolling waves when the wind is coming from the west or northwest. An early morning start is advised because this is usually the calmest part of the day to travel down Gunflint.

Gunflint Lake is a serene and peaceful north-woods gem, with a handful of resorts along its south shore and an occasional boat or floatplane on its surface. A century ago this was a much different place, bustling with activity from loggers, fishermen, and even the small village of Leeblain on the Canadian shore. At least one small steamboat plied the water, and trains from the Port Arthur, Duluth, and Western Railroad (PAD&W) ran down tracks along the north shore to Thunder Bay, Canada. Much of this activity focused on the new Paulson iron mine being developed 6 miles southwest of Gunflint Lake (near present-day Mine Lake). The mine did not succeed, and the tracks and town of Leeblain were abandoned within years, left to surrender their territory back to the forest.

Upon entering Gunflint Lake you can paddle north for a 2-mile diversion to the mouth of Magnetic Lake. Here you will spot submerged pilings from a trestle bridge where the PAD&W crossed the U.S.-Canadian border. Old photos and historic accounts show the bridge to have been over 100 feet long and at least 20 feet high. The north shore of Gunflint Lake still contains other remnants of the old railway, including bread-making ovens and a cross carved into the bedrock at the spot where a railway construction worker died.

Continue east across Gunflint Lake toward Little Gunflint Lake. In the winter of 1902–3 loggers built a second, much smaller railway spur from the main PAD&W line. This spur ran from north of Gunflint Lake south to Crab Lake, a distance of about 4 miles. This small spur was proudly named the Gunflint and Lake Superior Railway. You can still identify its old route at a few spots, including an area near Bridal Falls on the south side of Gunflint Lake, where logs were stacked side by side to raise the grade, after which gravel was added to make the rail bed. The Pigeon River Logging Company operated out of the southeast bay on Gunflint Lake near Saucer Lake, using the Gunflint and Lake Superior line to move their logs to sawmills. A fire in 1909 destroyed a big PAD&W trestle bridge on North Lake, ending the operations of the main PAD&W railroad and its little cousin the Gunflint and Lake Superior Railway.

The eastern end of Gunflint has a fine sand beach well worth a stop for a swim or lunch. A shallow channel joins Gunflint Lake to Little Gunflint Lake, so no portage is necessary between them. Paddle on to the level 15-rod portage from Little Gunflint to Little North Lake. This was once a mechanized portage where small rail-mounted cars pulled boats to Little North Lake. Historians report that these rails or their predecessors were probably first laid down in 1890 or 1891. Its rail car is said to have come from the short-lived Bishop sawmill on North Lake. Today, the rusted remnants of the tracks still remain, as does the decaying cable mechanism formerly used to advance the small rail cars. This portage to North Lake can usually be avoided by pulling your canoe upstream along a channel between the lakes, or in the downstream direction by floating your canoe.

North Lake is gorgeous, with high hills rising from its deep Canadian arm. This is a big lake built on a large scale. North Lake is entirely outside of the BWCAW, and therefore motorboats are allowed everywhere on both sides of the border. You should travel across North Lake and then head over the 80-rod Height of Land Portage to South Lake, where you will officially enter the BWCAW. This portage received its name because of its location on the continental divide. Rain falling on the west side of the portage eventually flows to Hudson Bay, while rain falling on east side eventually flows to the Atlantic Ocean. The Height of Land Portage is one of the most significant historic sites in the border country. Countless voyageurs traveled across this very portage, and for thousands of years before them Native Americans probably followed the same path.

One would expect that the Height of Land Portage would be bone dry because it has some of the best drainage in the world. You might even hope to find a prominent outcropping high on a hill where you and your mud-free boots could pose for pictures with lakes rolling off into the distance on both sides of you. Actually, and ironically, the trail on the Height of Land Portage is low lying and likely to be muddy most of the year.

It may take you a while to reach South Lake from the Gunflint landing, in which case you will want to camp along the way. You can camp at one of thirteen campsites scattered outside of the BWCAW along the U.S. side of Gunflint, Little Gunflint, and North lakes, but remember that you need to cross into the BWCAW on the Height of Land Portage on the date of your permit. Factor this into your travel plans. If you are entering Gunflint Lake late in the day, you might want to spend a night outside of the BWCAW and have your permit reserved and issued for entering the wilderness the following morning.

Paddle and portage 6 miles from South Lake to Rose Lake, including portages of 65 rods (L3) from South Lake to Rat Lake, and 4 rods (L1) from Rat to Rose Lake. Press on from South Lake when you are ready for more travel and exploration. The 65-rod South Lake Portage leading to Rat Lake is quite level with very little mud, making for an easy carry. The 4-rod portage from Rat Lake to Rose Lake diverts around an impassable little rapids. With a strong crew you should be able to lift fully loaded canoes over this short, rocky trail.

Rose Lake is a nice destination, with towering hills along its south shore and seven designated campsites spread along the American side. Remember, unless you have a Remote Area Border Crossing (RABC) permit (see "Planning Your Trip"), you cannot camp on the Canadian side of this or other border lakes. You should certainly take a trip south to the Stairway Portage leading to Duncan Lake. A fine pair of waterfalls tumble down the side of this old portage trail. You can also hook up to the Border Route Trail, which crosses the Stairway Portage, to do a bit of hiking.

Paddle and portage 18 miles from Rose Lake to Gunflint Lake, including portages of 4 rods (L1), 65 rods (L3), 80 rods (L6), and 15 rods (L1). When your time comes to leave Rose Lake, return by the same way you came. If you want to press farther ahead, look to good routes heading east from Entry Point 60.

Entry Point 60, Duncan Lake (Map 47)

> Daily permit quota: 4
> Permit availability: moderate

The Duncan Lake entry is a relatively popular gateway to lakes on the Canadian border, requiring just two portages before reaching Rose Lake. Over a dozen campsites can easily be reached on Duncan and Rose lakes. In addition, you can access the Border Route Trail from Duncan Lake, giving you an opportunity for a nice day hike along hills high above the border lakes.

You will need to head north to Rose Lake and then west toward Gunflint Lake or east toward Rove Lake if you intend to travel on an extended journey beyond Duncan Lake. The western route, described below as Route 60A, is a relatively easy one-way trip without challenging portages. The eastern route, described below as Route 60B, covers one of the longest portages in the BWCAW but offers nicely varied trip options after that monster carry.

To reach Duncan Lake, take the Gunflint Trail 27 miles from Grand Marais to County Road 66, which is on the right side of the road. You will see signs for Bearskin Lodge, among others. Take County Road 66 for 3.2 miles until you reach Bearskin Lake on your left. A good parking lot and landing are located there. Paddle across Bearskin Lake to reach the portage to Daniels. In the alternative, you can enter from Hungry Jack Lake. Overnight camping options are available at Flour Lake campground and East Bearskin Lake campground, as well as at local outfitters.

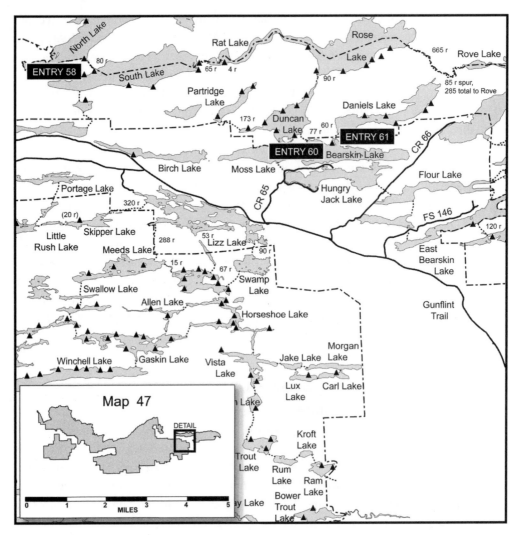

Route 60A: Gunflint Lake One-Way (Map 47)

>Difficulty: easy to intermediate
>Number of days: 3 or more
>Total miles: 23.5
>Portage number: 5
>Total portage rods: 254
>Greatest portage difficulty: 90 (L8)
>Navigation maps: Voyageur 9
>   Fisher F14
>   McKenzie 1, 4

This one-way route sends you north to the Canadian border and then west to your destination on Gunflint Lake. You will avoid hard portages but will need to cross a few large lakes where wind and waves can pose a challenge. This one-way trip requires that you leave a vehicle at your exit point, the public access landing on Gunflint Lake.

Map 47 shows most of this route, and Map 46 shows areas to the west.

Detailed Route

Paddle and portage 3 miles from Bearskin Lake to Duncan Lake, including a portage of 77 rods (L3). From the landing on Bearskin Lake, paddle west to the 77-rod portage leading to Duncan. While crossing the portage you will enter the BWCAW. This portage is about as easy as a trail of this length can get in the Boundary Waters. The path should be in good condition unless the weather has been very wet, in which case it will be a bit muddy.

Duncan Lake is a nice place to spend an evening, particularly if you are getting a late start. If you are staying for a while, consider an adventurous side trip over to Partridge Lake by way of an infrequently used 173-rod (L9) portage. The trail ascends more than 100 feet in elevation. Partridge Lake hosts a population of lake trout, which is probably the primary reason most people make the difficult journey. An easier diversion is to connect to the Border Route Trail and Caribou Rock Trail on the north end of Duncan, reachable from the portage leading to Rose Lake. You can take the Border Route Trail to the west or east. Both directions are nice, but the best views are probably from the portion of the trail to the west of the portage.

Paddle and portage 2.5 miles from Duncan Lake to Rose Lake, including the 90-rod (L8) Stairway Portage. The aptly named Stairway Portage follows two sequential staircases to Rose Lake along a well-traveled trail. It has probably been in use for centuries, considering the strategic location. The Civilian Conservation Corps did reconstruction work on this portage in the 1930s.

Six designated campsites are located on Rose Lake, and they make another nice place to spend an evening. Remember that you are not authorized to camp on the Canadian shore without a Remote Area Border Crossing (RABC) permit (see "Planning Your Trip"). No Quetico permit is required because Rose Lake is outside of Quetico Provincial Park.

Paddle and portage 7 miles from Rose Lake to South Lake, including portages of 4 rods (L1) and 65 rods (L3). In the next segment of this journey you head west toward South Lake. Start by paddling to the western bay of Rose Lake and then taking a 4-rod portage from Rose Lake to Rat Lake that diverts around a small, impassable rapids. Rat Lake is quite shallow. Paddle across little Rat Lake and then take the 65-rod portage from Rat to South Lake, known as the South Lake Portage. The path is quite flat and typically free of mud, making for an easy trail, unless it has been very rainy or you are entering in early spring.

Paddle and portage 11 miles to Gunflint Lake, including portages of 80 rods (L6) and 15 rods (L1). The final stretch of this trip takes you to North Lake before winding across two smaller lakes to your takeout point on Gunflint Lake. You will start by crossing the Height of Land Portage between South and North lakes. The Height of Land Portage separates the Hudson Bay watershed from the Lake Superior watershed. Rain falling on the north side of the portage travels eventually to Hudson Bay, while rain falling on the south side of the portage travels to Lake Superior and eventually to the Atlantic Ocean. Ironically, the Height of Land Portage is actually low lying and can be muddy much of the year, so expect to encounter a wet trail as you climb over the continental divide!

When you finish the Height of Land Portage and arrive at North Lake, you are leaving the BWCAW, so do not be surprised if you come upon motorboats anywhere during the rest of this trip. North Lake is a huge, gorgeous lake with high hills rising from much of its shore. If you did not camp on South Lake, you may want to stay at one of the six designated sites on North Lake's American shore. Otherwise, paddle through the narrows to Little North Lake and on to the 15-rod portage to Little Gunflint Lake. This portage can usually be floated in the downstream direction. Remains of a mechanized boat-carrying railway are found along this portage. Today, the rusted rails are still present, as are the rotting portions of the cable mechanism used to manually advance the cars.

No portage is necessary when crossing from Little Gunflint Lake to Gunflint Lake, where your vehicle will be waiting. Evidence suggests that Gunflint was long used as a source of flint, thus its name. Gunflint Lake is one of the most historic lakes in the Superior National Forest, so be sure to read the description in Route 58. Paddle to the west end of Gunflint if you would like to see old submerged pilings from a trestle bridge still located in the shallows between Gunflint Lake and Magnetic Lake. More recently, Gunflint Lake was the home of Justine Kerfoot, who ran the Gunflint Lodge with her family for decades prior to her death in 2001. If you wish to extend your stay, consider staying at one of a handful of designated campsites near the eastern end of the lake.

Route 60B: One-Way from Duncan to Clearwater (Map 47)

>   Difficulty: difficult
>   Number of days: 3 or more
>   Total miles: 19.5
>   Portage number: 6
>   Total portage rods: 1,122
>   Greatest portage difficulty: 665 rods (L10)
>   Navigation maps: Voyageur 9
>   Fisher F13, F14
>   McKenzie 2

For centuries, canoeists seeking game, food, and trade goods have traveled the same lakes as you will on this route. You will also have the opportunity for a number of interesting day hikes. This route crosses the Border Route Hiking Trail at three points, giving you a chance to head ashore on a day hike if you choose. Such hikes are a rarity in the BWCAW, where the dense forests make bushwhacking all but impossible, and where relatively few hiking trails are maintained. Of these limited hiking trails, the Border Route is one of the finest.

The biggest challenge of this route is a 2-mile portage from Rose Lake to Rove Lake. Although this portage is one of the longest in the Boundary Waters, the trail is mostly level and generally in good shape. Fit visitors with light gear should have no problem crossing it. Also, since this is a one-way trip, you will need to leave a car at your exit point, the public boat access on Clearwater Lake. Make sure to bring two sets of keys in case one gets lost!

Map 47 shows most of this route, and Map 48 shows the eastern portions.

Detailed Route

Paddle and portage 3 miles from Bearskin Lake to Duncan Lake, including a portage of 77 rods (L3). Duncan Lake is a nice place to spend an evening, particularly if you are getting a late start. Consider making an adventurous side trip over to Partridge Lake by way of an infrequently used 173-rod (L9) portage that ascends more than 100 feet in elevation to its peak, perhaps to seek out lake trout. Alternatively, make an easier diversion to the Border Route Trail and Caribou Rock Trail on the north end of Duncan.

Paddle and portage 2.5 miles from Duncan Lake to Rose Lake, including a portage of 90 rods (L8). When you are ready to leave Duncan, take the Stairway Portage to Rose Lake. This aptly named portage follows a well-traveled trail believed to have been in use for centuries. This portage saw significant reconstruction by the Civilian Conservation Corps during the 1930s. Six designated campsites are located on Rose Lake. Remember that you are not authorized to camp on the Canadian shore without a Remote Area Border Crossing (RABC) permit (see "Planning Your Trip").

Portage 665 rods (L10) from Rose Lake to Rove Lake. The first part of the 2-mile-long trail from Rose to Rove is flat and smooth, following an excellent path elevated above the narrow Arrow River. This straight, clear path still shows indications that it was once briefly used as a logging railroad bed. The final 200 rods travels through a hilly mixed forest of ancient red and white pines. Many of these great old trees were brought down by the July 4, 1999, windstorm, but even more still stand.

A century ago Rove Lake was at the end of the Gunflint Trail (known then as the Mayhew Wagon Trail) and had a small trading post along its shore. Obviously the Gunflint Trail no longer reaches here, and the exact location of the post is no longer known.

Paddle and portage 7 miles from Rove Lake to Watap Lake and then to Mountain Lake, including a portage of 110 rods (L5). Rove Lake leads to Watap Lake without a portage, and then Watap Lake leads to Mountain Lake via a fine 110-rod trail. Allow yourself time to press on to Mountain Lake because Watap Lake contains no designated campgrounds along its shores.

Mountain Lake is a magnificent, big border-country lake with crystal clear waters and towering hills on both shores. The eastern end of the Canadian side was hit hard by the 1999 windstorm, as were parts of the U.S. side, particularly some of the campsites. Mountain Lake has a healthy lake trout population and also contains a good smallmouth bass population. Remember that you cannot fish Canadian waters without a Canadian fishing license. For a side trip out of Mountain Lake, consider hauling over a tough 86-rod (L8) portage on the south shore to little Pemmican Lake, home to a stocked population of brook trout.

Paddle and portage 5 miles from Mountain Lake to the public access on Clearwater Lake, including a portage of 90 rods (L8) from Mountain to Clearwater. Head out through the southwest end of Mountain Lake over the 90-rod (L8) portage to Clearwater. This neat portage climbs steeply uphill before dropping steeply, but a great stand of red and white pines towers over the trail. If you are carrying a canoe on your way across, you should hike back and take in these grand old trees. Paddle across Clearwater Lake to the public landing, where your vehicle should be waiting.

Entry Point 61, Daniels Lake (Map 47)

Daily permit quota: 1
Permit availability: moderate

Entry Point 61, Daniels Lake, gets relatively few overnight visitors compared to neighboring entry points. Only one overnight permit is available per day, and many of these go unused. The limited permit number is due in part to the fact that just four designated campsites can be reached from Daniels Lake without portaging at least 285 rods to Rove Lake, and two of these campsites are sometimes occupied by hikers on the Daniels Spur of the Border Route Trail.

Although not in great demand, the Daniels Lake entry offers good wilderness canoeing opportunities. A pleasant weekend can be spent exploring the shoreline, trolling the depths for lake trout, or connecting to the Border Route Trail for a day hike. If you seek a longer trip with greater challenges, fantastic areas to the east are available for your exploration, including a memorable loop to South Fowl Lake and back again, described below as Route 61.

To reach Daniels Lake, you will need to travel from neighboring Bearskin Lake, which lies entirely outside the BWCAW. To get to Bearskin, take the Gunflint Trail 27 miles to County Road 66. Head north on 66 for 3.2 miles until you see a public landing on the left side of the road. Adequate parking is available for at least a dozen vehicles. The Flour Lake campground is a nice place to spend a night before embarking on your journey and is located off Country Road 66 before you reach the Bearskin Lake public access. The East Bearskin Lake campground is also an option, but be certain to make reservations in advance. A number of area outfitters rent bunkhouses where you can spend a night, and they are often a good option that allows you to get out quicker in the morning, without having to break camp.

Route 61: South Fowl Loop (Map 48)

> Difficulty: challenging
> Number of days: 7
> Total miles: 49
> Portage number: 14
> Total portage rods: 1,254
> Greatest portage difficulty: 285 rods
> Navigation maps: Voyageur 9, 10
>   Fisher F13, F14
>   McKenzie 1, 2

This journey makes for a wonderful week-long trip. Good paddlers can cover it more quickly, but a week allows sufficient time to relax, explore sites of interest, enjoy the fantastic views, and even be wind bound for a day or two. Side trips can be made to a number of brook trout lakes, and good fishing is found in many of the lakes along the journey.

Map 48 shows the western portion of this trip, and Maps 50 and 51 show the remainder.

Detailed Route

Paddle 3.5 miles across Bearskin Lake, and cross the 60-rod portage to Daniels Lake. Your journey starts with an easy leg to Daniels Lake. Daniels is a fine place to spend a day or two, either for fishing or hiking. Unless you made a very early start, you will want to stay on Daniels for a night because the next campsites are more than 5 miles away and require crossing a 285-rod portage.

Paddle and portage 9.25 miles from Daniels Lake to Mountain Lake, including a portage of 285 rods to Rove Lake; paddle along Watap Lake, and portage 110 rods (L5) from Watap to Mountain Lake. When you leave Daniels Lake, you will need to paddle all the way to Mountain Lake because neither Rove nor Watap lakes have any designated campsites.

The first portage from Daniels to Rove is quite long, nearly a mile, so it is a tough haul if you have overpacked. Rove Lake is of interest to historians because it was the site of a fur trading post in the late 1800s developed by Henry Mayhew, who is known as one of the founders of the Gunflint Trail. In fact, the Gunflint Trail originally ended at Rove Lake and was known as the Mayhew Wagon Trail. The exact location of Mayhew's trading post on Rove Lake is not known, but it is believed to have been on the west end.

Rove Lake leads to Watap Lake without a portage. Despite being over 2 miles long, Watap Lake contains no designated campsites. Watap Lake leads via a fine 110-rod trail to Mountain Lake. Mountain Lake is a magnificent, big border-country lake with crystal clear waters and towering hills on both shores. The eastern end of the Canadian side was hit hard by the 1999 windstorm, as were parts of the U.S. side, particularly some of the campsites. Mountain Lake has a healthy lake trout population and also contains a good smallmouth bass population.

Paddle and portage 6.75 miles from Mountain Lake to Moose Lake, including portages of 90, 40, and 140 rods through Fan Lake and Vaseux Lake. You will now head out the east end of Mountain Lake to Moose Lake. The flat, 90-rod Lesser Cherry Portage is likely to be very muddy during all but the driest years. In addition, the landing on the east end has hazardous boot-eating muck, so use caution. Paddle across shallow Fan Lake, and then take the 40-rod Vaseux Portage, which is a big improvement over the Lesser Cherry Portage but still potentially quite muddy. The flat, moderately muddy trail is a tad more difficult than most. Paddle across lily pad–covered Vaseux Lake and land at the 140-rod Great Cherry Portage. This portage drops steeply down a clean trail for the first third and then levels off along a somewhat rocky trail for its final two-thirds, ultimately depositing you on the shores of Moose Lake.

Moose Lake is a fine north-woods lake with five designated campsites. Motorized watercraft are allowed on the Canadian side but not the American side. Moose Lake holds lake trout, walleye, and smallmouth bass in depths that reach down to 117 feet. Serious fishermen might want to bring along their own depth finder or sonar for Moose Lake because this is one of just two large BWCAW lakes that has not been fully sounded by the Minnesota DNR (the other is Saganaga Lake). Thus, none of the maps of Moose Lake contains bathometric lines (which are underwater topographic lines).

Paddle and portage 14 miles from Moose Lake to Pine Lake, including portages of 130 rods to North Fowl Lake, 96 rods to the Royal River, 61 rods to John Lake, 10 rods to Little John Lake, 16 rods to McFarland Lake, and 5 rods to Pine Lake. The 130-rod Moose Portage continues the string of potentially muddy portages encountered on this route, although a few footbridges have been built along part of the trail. The landing on the North Fowl side is relatively muddy, and you should take the north fork in the trail (at the BWCAW sign) to reach the best landing.

After taking the Moose Portage you temporarily pass out of the BWCAW to enter North Fowl Lake. This lake is well named because its extensive rice beds attract good numbers of migrating waterfowl in fall. North and South Fowl lakes have been inhabited, at least seasonally, for thousands of years. Some of the earliest human artifacts found in the BWCAW originated along the shores of South Fowl, including chipped points made of jasper believed to be 7,000 to 10,000 years old. Archaeologists have also found artifacts from the "Old Copper Complex" here, evidence of possible trade with Isle Royale 3,000 to 5,000 years ago. These copper complex tools include stone and copper gouges believed to have been used to hollow out red and white pines to make dugout canoes, long before development of more modern birch-bark canoes.

You will continue on to Royal Lake, which is more royal marsh than royal lake and can be royally full of emergent plants in late summer. However, it should always be navigable. The 96-rod and 61-rod portages are not well traveled and a bit low lying. Next, a 10-rod portage from John Lake to Little John Lake bypasses a shallow stretch of slow-moving water. During most of the year you should have no problem paddling your canoe upstream through this shallow stretch. Even if the water is too shallow to canoe through, you should be able to easily pole through. If you are intent on portaging, head slightly west about 50 feet from where the stream connects the lakes, and you can take a seldom-used portage to Little John. This portage is short and level but hard to find because it receives so little use.

Next, a 16-rod portage heads from Little John Lake to McFarland Lake, bypassing a stretch of quick-moving water running under a bridge at the end of the Arrowhead Trail. You have two options here: you can either try to paddle and pull your canoe through the water under the bridge, which is very easily done much of the year, or land at the boat access to the east and hike across the Arrowhead Trail before dropping in on the McFarland side.

Finally, a 5-rod portage leads from McFarland to Pine Lake, bypassing a short stretch of shallow water running from Pine to McFarland. You should have no problem shooting this little stretch of rapids when going from Pine to McFarland, but it may be a little bit rough going in the opposite direction. Alternatively, about 5 rods south of the rapids you can portage across an infrequently used trail.

Nearly a dozen designated campsites are available on Pine Lake, most on the sunny north shore. Beware of waves on Pine; they can become very large if a strong wind comes out of the west. Prudent visitors will allow themselves a "makeup" day on their schedule in case winds prevent travel down Pine. Consider trolling for lake trout in the deep waters. If the trout on Pine Lake don't catch your fancy or you don't catch theirs, weigh the benefits of hauling your gear and pride to Vale or Gadwall lakes on the south side of Pine Lake for a showdown with brook trout. These two little lakes are not available for overnight camping but have been regularly stocked with brook trout by the Minnesota DNR. You can also portage to Long Lake and Stump Lake, which have one campsite that appears to be very infrequently used, located at the narrows on the peninsula separating the two lakes. Finally, and best of all, on the west end of Pine is a network of trails leading to Johnson Falls, a 20-foot waterfall that is one of the prettiest in the BWCAW.

Paddle and portage 6.5 miles from Pine Lake to Caribou Lake, including portages of 80 rods (L6) to Little Caribou Lake, and 25 rods (L4) to Caribou Lake. The 80-rod portage from Pine Lake to Little Caribou Lake climbs steeply and then follows a nice trail crossing a small stream on a simple bridge. At the bridge you should pause to observe the exposed Rove slate bedrock formations of loosely attached flat layers of stone. This exposed slate is significantly older than the hilltop rocks in this area but was more easily carved out by glaciers to become lake beds while the harder rock became hills. Originally deposited as layers of mud and silt, the slates were cooked at high pressure when the neighboring gabbro bedrock formed from molten magma.

Little Caribou was heavily hit by the 1999 windstorm and has significant numbers of downed trees along much of its shore, as do parts of Caribou Lake, particularly along the east end. The 25-rod portage between Caribou Lake and Little Caribou Lake is very flat, but small rocks stick out along much of the trail. The portage ends on the Caribou side north of a pile of windblown pine and cedar trunks. The prevailing westerly winds assure that many of the downed trees that fall into Caribou Lake wash ashore at its end. Some of these logs are probably quite old, perhaps dating back to big-pine logging a century ago, preserved as waterlogged artifacts.

Paddle and portage 3 miles from Caribou Lake to Clearwater Lake, including a 200-rod (L10) portage. The portage trail from Caribou to Clearwater climbs over a tough, tall hill. Along the way you will notice a couple of additional rocky outcroppings composed of the Rove slate formation. Once you reach Clearwater, paddle west to the public access. You will have a modest walk down the Clearwater Road to your starting point on Bearskin Lake.

Entry Point 62, Clearwater Lake (Map 48)

> Daily permit quota: 4
> Permit availability: moderate

Entry Point 62, Clearwater Lake, is one of the three most popular entries to the BWCAW north of the Gunflint Trail and is also one of the most beautiful. Crystal clear water fills the depths, and fine cliffs rise up along the south shore. The deep waters are home to a healthy population of lake trout. Motorboats are allowed on all of Clearwater Lake, even inside the BWCAW. The western end has no motor size limits, although the large portion of the eastern side of the lake within the BWCAW has a 10-horsepower limit.

Four portages lead out of Clearwater Lake, one north to Mountain Lake, one east to West Pike Lake, and two south to Caribou Lake. All of these portages are relatively long or challenging, which is why a fair number of visitors simply stay on Clearwater. Three routes of various difficulty are described below: a trip to explore Clearwater Lake (Route 62A), a longer loop to Caribou and Pine lakes (Route 62B), and a great trip through West Pike and East Pike lakes and then to Pine Lake (Route 62C).

Numerous outfitters operate in the area, including Clearwater Outfitters on Clearwater Lake. They have bunkhouse facilities for spending the night before you head into the wilderness. The lodge at Clearwater Outfitters was built in 1926 by local legend Charlie Boostrom, which was the same year that an upgraded "car" road reached Clearwater. The Flour Lake campground and East Bearskin Lake campground are also close by and excellent places to spend a night before you enter the wilds.

To get to Clearwater Lake, take the Gunflint Trail for 27 miles until you reach County Road 66 (the Clearwater Lake Road). Turn right (north) onto 66 and drive just over 5 miles to the end of the road at the public landing. You can spend a night at the Flour Lake campground, which you will pass on County Road 66 as you head

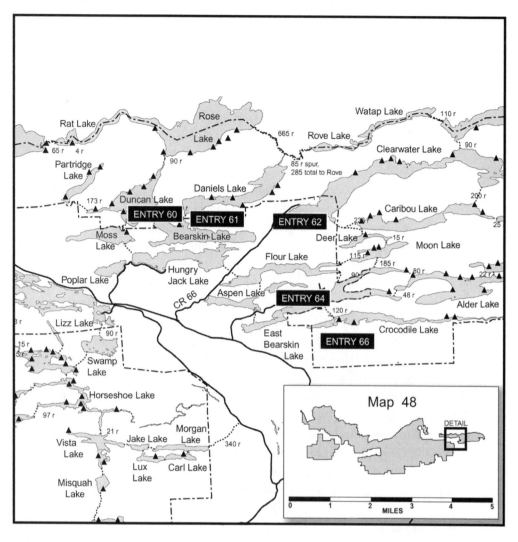

Map 48

to Clearwater. This campground has thirty-seven sites, and one should be reserved in advance to be certain of availability.

Route 62A: Clearwater Lake Weekend (Map 48)

      Difficulty: easy
      Number of days: 2 or more
      Total miles: 4 or more
      Portage number: none
      Total portage rods: N/A
      Greatest portage difficulty: N/A
      Navigation maps: Voyageur 10
                           Fisher F14
                           McKenzie 2

This basic trip keeps you on Clearwater Lake without any portages and provides a good introduction to the BWCAW for first-time visitors and anyone interested in a less strenuous trip. It offers fantastic scenery, good trout fishing, and opportunities for a couple nice day trips by paddle or foot. Motorized boats are legal on the entire lake, so do not expect complete privacy or silence. Fortunately, the majority of the lake is limited to boats of 10 horsepower or less.

Detailed Route

Put in at the public access at the end of County Road 66 and paddle east. The western-most portion of Clearwater is outside the wilderness, but after a quarter mile you will be entering the large expanse of Clearwater Lake within the BWCAW. Seven designated campsites are located on the north shore of Clearwater, many providing nice views of cliffs on the south shore and also offering maximum sunlight. Four permits are available each day for overnight visitors, so the seven designated camp-sites can fill up relatively quickly if people don't move on to neighboring lakes.

If you get a late start and cannot find a campsite, your best bet is probably to head over the 90-rod portage to Mountain Lake or the 218-rod portage to West Pike. Both portages are quite challenging: the 90-rod carry because it climbs over a tough hill, the 218-rod carry because of its length. I am partial to the 218-rod portage because West Pike is completely motor free, unlike Mountain Lake, which allows motorboats on the Canadian side.

You have numerous options for exploring the area around Clearwater. A nice day trip out of Clearwater Lake is to take the 200-rod portage on the southeast bay of Clearwater to Caribou Lake, and then paddle east to Little Caribou and the west end of Pine Lake, where you can hike a short trail to beautiful Johnson Falls. This trip is about 9 miles if you start from the middle of Clearwater Lake. It requires over 2 miles of portaging, but they will be relatively easy if you pack light.

An alternative option is a day hike to the Border Route Trail, which runs along the north ridge of Clearwater. You can reach the trail along a spur next to the west-ernmost campsite on Clearwater, or at the portages to Mountain Lake and West Pike Lake. Any of these locations will take you into beautiful forest with occasional vistas sweeping over the vast Canadian wilderness to the north.

Route 62B: Caribou and Pine Lake Loop (Map 48)

    Difficulty: intermediate/challenging
    Number of days: 3
    Total miles: 21
    Portage number: 5
    Total portage rods: 840
    Greatest portage difficulty: 317 rods (L10)

Navigation maps: Voyageur 10
Fisher F14
McKenzie 1, 2

This journey takes you south from Clearwater Lake to Caribou Lake, then east to massive Pine Lake, finally climbing to West Pike Lake and your return to Clearwater. An excellent sightseeing detour can be made to Johnson Falls on Pine Lake. Packing light is essential for this trip because it crosses three very long portages, two of which involve significant hill climbs. The busiest lakes are likely to be Clearwater and Caribou, and your greatest opportunities for solitude are on West Pike. If you want to extend your trip by a day or two, consider hauling your gear to three smaller lakes on the south side of Pine Lake for real backcountry fishing.

Map 48 shows the western portion of this trip, and Maps 50 and 51 show the remainder.

Detailed Route

Paddle and portage 5.5 miles across Clearwater Lake to Caribou Lake, portaging 200 rods (L10). Your journey starts with a nice paddle down the length of Clearwater Lake to its southeast bay. Continue along the 200-rod portage from Clearwater Lake to Caribou Lake, which has length, hills, and a relatively rough trail. The portage climbs nearly 150 feet over the first 75 rods before dropping nearly 250 feet over the final 125 rods. The path has a fair number of exposed rocks and roots, and the potential for small mud holes. Near the top of the climb you will intermittently traverse areas of exposed bedrock. At these places you are scurrying over the top of ancient gabbro bedrock that withstood the last ice age better than the slates down below at the lakeshore. Notice how the exposed rock on the top of the portage is rounded and smooth, in contrast to the straight-faced and jagged slates forming the shoreline of Clearwater and Caribou.

Caribou is one of the most popular destinations in this part of the BWCAW and is an easy trip from the nearby East Bearskin Lake entry. Seek a campsite early if you intend to spend the night. If the designated campsites on Caribou are taken, you will probably need to press on to Pine Lake because the solo site on Little Caribou Lake is also quite popular. Little Caribou was heavily hit by the 1999 windstorm and has significant numbers of downed trees along much of its shore. Parts of Caribou Lake, particularly along the east end, were also heavily hit.

Paddle and portage 6 miles from Caribou Lake to the heart of Pine Lake, including a 25-rod portage (L4) from Caribou Lake to Little Caribou Lake, and an 80-rod portage from Little Caribou to Pine Lake. The 25-rod portage between Caribou Lake and Little Caribou Lake is very flat, but a fair number of small rocks stick into the trail. The portage begins on the Caribou side just to the north of a pile of windblown old pine and cedar trunks.

The 80-rod portage from Little Caribou Lake to Pine Lake follows a nice trail over a small stream on a simple bridge built by the Forest Service. It then drops quickly to Pine Lake, which is about 100 feet lower in elevation than Little Caribou. At the bridge you should pause to look at the exposed slate formations, arrayed in layers of flat stone. Notice how the layers seem to almost fall apart. This structural weakness was exploited by glaciers 10,000 years ago, which carved out much of the slate in this area to form present-day lake beds. I also recommend paddling a couple hundred yards south to the landing on Pine Lake leading to Johnson Falls.

After visiting Johnson Falls you will have Pine Lake to explore. Ten designated paddling campsites are located along Pine Lake, all but one on the north shore. The south side of Pine Lake was heavily hit by the July 4, 1999, windstorm, but fortunately the campsites on most of the north shore were not nearly as damaged. Consider trolling for lake trout in the deep waters. If the lake trout on Pine don't cooperate, consider hauling your gear and pride over to Vale or Gadwall lakes on the south side of Pine Lake. These two little lakes have been regularly stocked with brook trout, but overnight camping is not allowed on either lake. You can also portage to Long Lake and Stump Lake, which have one campsite.

Paddle and portage 9.5 miles from Pine Lake to Clearwater Lake, including a 317-rod (L10) portage from Pine Lake to West Pike Lake, and a 218-rod (L8) portage from West Pike Lake to your starting point on Clearwater Lake. When the time comes to leave Pine Lake, prepare yourself for one of the toughest portages in the BWCAW: the 317-rod trail to West Pike Lake. This long portage is generally free of mud and large rock obstructions, but very few stretches are level. Starting at Pine Lake you will climb the first 190 rods before dropping steeply to West Pike. The trail sees fewer visitors than any other portage on this route, so expect it to be more overgrown. Fortunately, even with relatively little use, the trail through an aging aspen and birch forest is easy to follow.

Shortly after leaving Pine Lake you will find a hike-in campsite on the right-hand side of the trail, nestled in a grove of old white pines. If the canoeing sites on Pine are taken, this may be a good place to spend the night. However, the site is fairly shielded from breezes, so don't get your hopes up for wind to keep away mosquitoes or blackflies. As you descend toward West Pike Lake, the trail will cross over the Border Route Trail. Remember to stay on the central trail going downhill. When you get to the bottom near West Pike Lake, you will come to a fork in the trail. Take the left fork (heading west), and continue a short distance over a boardwalk to reach the landing on West Pike Lake. West Pike Lake is the most remote lake on this route. It sees fewer visitors than any of its neighbors and is your best bet for relative isolation.

The final portage from West Pike to Clearwater is substantially flat, except for a first portion that climbs for about 30 rods. Near the start of the portage you will come to a fork in the trail. You should stay to the left (which is the more worn path) leading to Clearwater Lake. The trail to the right is part of the Border Route Trail. Be alert for this junction. If you take the wrong fork, you will portage an extra 2 miles on the Border Route Trail until it connects again to Clearwater Lake!

Once on Clearwater you can spend another night at one of the designated campsites, or you can head to your starting point at the public access on the west end.

Route 62C: Pike and Pine Loop (Map 48)

Difficulty: moderate
Number of days: 4 or more
Total miles: 33
Portage number: 9
Total portage rods: 958
Greatest portage difficulty: 200 rods (L10)
Navigation maps: Voyageur 9, 10
Fisher F13, F14
McKenzie 1, 2

This challenging route enters the BWCAW at Clearwater Lake, heads east to John Lake on the edge of the BWCAW, and then briefly turns south before heading west across Pine Lake to your start on Clearwater. The operative word on this magnificent journey is "big." It is a big loop with big lakes connected by big portages. Depending on wind strength and direction, it may also have big waves. If you have little experience and huge packs, it is also a big mistake! Strong paddlers with light packs will have a great trip.

Map 48 shows the first portion of this trip, and Maps 50 and 51 show the eastern portions.

Detailed Route

Paddle and portage 8.5 miles from Clearwater Lake to West Pike Lake, including a 218-rod portage (L8). Put in at the public access on Clearwater Lake at the end of County Road 66 and paddle east. After a quarter mile you will be entering the majority of Clearwater Lake within the BWCAW. Seven designated campsites are located on the north shore of Clearwater, many providing nice views of cliffs on the south shore and also offering maximum sunlight. Four permits are available each day for overnight visitors, so the seven designated campsites can fill up relatively quickly.

The 218-rod portage from Clearwater Lake to West Pike Lake is substantially flat except for a final segment that dips down gradually for about 30 rods. Toward the end of the portage you will come to a fork in the trail. You should stay to the left on the more traveled route, which leads directly to West Pike. The trail to the right is part of the Border Route Trail.

Paddle and portage 7 miles from West Pike Lake to John Lake, including portages of 161 rods from West Pike to East Pike Lake, and 207 rods from East Pike to John Lake. The 161-rod portage to East Pike Lake is almost perfectly level, but it has a significant low spot on the first half of the portage, creating the potential for a major mud hole in spring or after big rains. A pair of Forest Service boardwalks traverse the wettest portions, but there are plenty of other potentially muddy sections. The landing on East Pike Lake is less than ideal, being shallow and rocky. You may need to walk out into the water a few paces to set your canoe down, unless you are comfortable dragging it across rocks with you in it. The aluminum-colored tops of many of the rocks at this landing indicate that many people prefer the drop-and-drag method, which is absolutely not recommended for a Kevlar canoe.

Upon entering East Pike Lake you will be treated to two memorable sights. To the east is a looming diabase hill covered with a mixed forest. Few places in the Boundary Waters offer such significant topographic relief. In addition, on the north side of this bay is a significant growth of nearly solid white pines. The water in both East Pike and West Pike lakes is very clear. A healthy population of fish inhabiting the depths provides good hunting for ospreys and bald eagles, and these lakes are as good as any in the Boundary Waters for spotting these great birds.

The 207-rod portage from East Pike Lake to John Lake has steep sections on either end, although they are not particularly long. Other than that, the heart of the trail is up a gradual incline, across a flat portion, and then down a gradual decline. The landing on East Pike Lake is a massive gabbro outcropping that extends up the trail. The landing on John Lake is not bad but a bit rocky. The south side of John is a steep, tree-covered bluff. The opposite shore is low lying and covered with many spruce.

Paddle and portage 7 miles from John Lake to central Pine Lake, including an optional portage of 10 rods, a portage of 16 rods, and another optional portage of 5 rods. The 10-rod portage from John Lake to Little John Lake bypasses a shallow stretch of slow-moving water. During most of the year you should have no problem paddling your canoe upstream through this shallow stretch. Even if the water is too shallow to canoe through, you should be able to pole through it very easily. If you are intent on portaging, head slightly west about 50 feet from where the stream connects the lakes, and you can take a seldom-used portage to Little John. This portage is short and relatively level but somewhat poorly marked because it receives so little use.

The 16-rod portage from Little John Lake to McFarland bypasses a stretch of quick-moving but shallow water running under a bridge on the Arrowhead Trail. You have two options here: you can either try to paddle and pole your canoe through the water under the bridge, which is very easily done much of the year, or land at the boat access to the east, hike across the road, and then drop in on the McFarland side. Choose the option that suits you best.

The 5-rod portage from McFarland to Pine Lake bypasses a short stretch of shallow water running from Pine to McFarland. You should have no problem shooting this little stretch of rapids when going from Pine to McFarland, but it may be a little rough going in the opposite direction, and in low water you will have to pole your way through. Alternatively, on the south side of the rapids you can travel across an infrequently used portage. This portage starts approximately 5 rods south of the stream.

Once you get to Pine Lake, eleven designated campsites are available, most on the sunny north shore. Beware of waves on Pine; they can become very large if a strong wind comes out of the west. You can troll for lake trout in the deep waters. If the lake trout are stubborn, consider hauling your gear and pride to Vale or Gadwall lakes on the south side of Pine Lake. These two little lakes are not available for overnight camping but have been regularly stocked with brook trout. You can also portage to Long Lake and Stump Lake, which have one campsite. On the west end of Pine is a network of trails leading to Johnson Falls, a 20-foot waterfall that is one of the prettiest in the BWCAW. The south side of Pine Lake was heavily hit by the July 4, 1999, windstorm, but fortunately the campsites on most of the north shore were not nearly as damaged.

Paddle and portage 7 miles from Pine Lake to Caribou Lake, including portages of 80 rods (L6) to Little Caribou Lake, and 25 rods (L4) to Caribou Lake. The 80-rod portage from Pine Lake to Little Caribou Lake climbs steeply and then follows a nice trail that crosses a small stream on a simple bridge built by the Forest Service.

The 25-rod portage between Caribou Lake and Little Caribou Lake is very flat, but a fair number of small rocks stick into the trail. The portage ends on the Caribou side just to the north of a pile of windblown old pine and cedar trunks. The prevailing westerly winds assure that many of the downed trees that fall into Caribou Lake wash ashore at the eastern end of the lake. Many of these logs are probably quite old, some perhaps dating back to big-pine logging a century ago.

Paddle and portage 3 miles from Caribou Lake to Clearwater Lake, including a 200-rod (L10) portage. The portage trail from Caribou to Clearwater has occasional small rocky outcroppings and a few minor low muddy spots but significant hill climbing. The landings on both sides have exposed rock, although they are otherwise flat and shallow. Along the way you will notice a couple of additional rocky outcroppings composed of the Rove slate formation. See the geology section in "The Natural and Human History of the Boundary Waters" in this guide to learn how the bedrock of this area greatly influenced lake shape and depth.

Entry Point 64, East Bearskin Lake (Map 48)

> Daily permit quota: 5
> Permit availability: moderate

Entry Point 64, East Bearskin Lake, provides access to the northeast section of the BWCAW. This corner of the wilderness is an area of long, narrow lakes and towering hills. No other portion of the BWCAW encompasses such high hills and cliffs. These hills make for great scenery but of course also make for challenging portages.

East Bearskin is a nice entry because it gives you access to Moon Lake, Caribou Lake, and Alder Lake without too much difficulty. You also have access to excellent lakes well off the beaten path, including Pierz and Crystal to the east. If you want a long loop route, you will need to take at least one tough portage exceeding 200 rods.

Consider elevation changes between lakes when planning a trip out of East Bearskin. Although elevation changes are always a factor in planning a trip, they are particularly important in this portion of the Boundary Waters. For example, the Pine to Canoe portage is 232 rods long but doubly hard because it climbs nearly 250 feet from Pine Lake.

Two excellent routes starting at East Bearskin are described below. Route 64A is a fine, short trip to Caribou Lake, where you will have a number of excellent day-trip options. Route 64B is a moderate loop east through Alder Lake and then to Pine Lake before returning through Caribou Lake. This route also allows relatively easy extensions to interesting areas with few visitors. You can also design your own routes through this area and can make a much longer route heading toward Mountain Lake, East and West Pike lakes, or John Lake.

The entry to East Bearskin Lake starts at the East Bearskin campground. To get to the campground, take the Gunflint Trail 26 miles from Grand Marais, and turn right onto Forest Service Road 146. Continue down this road for just over a mile to the East Bearskin campground, and follow the signs to the boat launch on East Bearskin Lake. This campground is a good place to spend a night, as is the nearby Flour Lake campground.

Route 64A: Caribou Lake Weekend (Map 48)

> Difficulty: intermediate
> Number of days: 2
> Total miles: 11
> Portage number: 6
> Total portage rods: 356
> Greatest portage difficulty: 115 rods (L6)
> Navigation maps: Voyageur 10
> Fisher F14
> McKenzie 1, 2

This moderate route takes you to beautiful Caribou Lake and provides an opportunity to head to Pine Lake and visit Johnson Falls on a day trip, or to head to Clearwater Lake to see the palisades rising up from its south shore. The only reason this route doesn't get an "easy" rating is because of the relatively steep hill you encounter between East Bearskin and Moon Lake.

Detailed Route

Paddle 3 miles across East Bearskin Lake, and portage 115 rods (L6) to Moon Lake. Your route starts on East Bearskin Lake, which is a popular fishing destination. You are likely to encounter fishermen in motorboats trolling and jigging the depths for pike and walleye. Only the two eastern bays of East Bearskin are within the BWCAW. The shores of East Bearskin are covered by a predominantly aspen and birch forest fringed with white cedars.

Head east from the landing on East Bearskin, and navigate into the left (north) bay at the fork on the eastern end of the lake. Continuing three-quarters of a mile, you will see the landing for the 115-rod portage leading to Moon Lake. The portage starts with a relatively rocky landing and continues along a generally flat but rocky and somewhat muddy trail for the first 60 rods. The portage then continues down a steep incline for the last 20 rods. At one point the Forest Service has constructed a short staircase to improve the trail. You will switch back a couple of times before dropping the last few rods to Moon Lake. It will come as no surprise that Moon is approximately 60 feet lower in elevation than East Bearskin.

Paddle and portage 2.75 miles from Moon Lake to Caribou Lake, including portages of 15 rods (L3) from Moon to Deer Lake, and 48 rods (L5) from Deer to Caribou Lake. This is a great opportunity to practice your tree identification skills as well as to enjoy the forest. The 15-rod portage to Deer Lake travels along a nearly flat, low-lying trail. The trail is covered with boulders, and the landings on both sides are fairly rocky. Nevertheless, the portage is not too difficult, because of its short length. Deer Lake is very scenic, and you will notice here that the forest has changed and has far fewer old white pines. The General Logging Company constructed a logging railroad to the west ends of Moon and Deer lakes in 1929, and some big-pine logging occurred in this area during that time. However, the low quality of the trees for lumber and national economic conditions significantly slowed this logging.

On the portage to Caribou you should be careful to head right (east) at the fork in the trail. The left fork heads 200 rods to Clearwater Lake. This portage, like the earlier one to Moon Lake from East Bearskin, begins relatively flat, then drops steeply for the final one-third. You will go through a nice grove of cedars on this trail. The landing on the Deer Lake side is relatively open, although the landing on the Caribou Lake side is fairly rocky.

Caribou Lake is long and narrow, with a mixed forest of early-growth trees, particularly spruce, aspen, and birch, as well as cedar along the shore. Portions of the lake are more than 50 feet deep, and a nice variety of game fish inhabit the depths. Six campsites are positioned on the north shore of Caribou, and another is available 25 rods away to the east on Little Caribou Lake, although the site on Little Caribou is popular due to its relative privacy.

Two great day trips are possible out of Caribou to either Pine Lake and Johnson Falls or to Clearwater Lake and its palisades. To get to Pine Lake, take the 25-rod portage to Little Caribou Lake and then the 80-rod portage to Pine Lake. On the far western shore of Pine, near where you enter from Little Caribou, is a trail heading to Johnson Falls. This half-mile trail is well worth the hike. The falls drop 20 feet off a slate ledge. To get to Clearwater Lake, take a 238-rod portage on the west side of Caribou. You can then head to the east, following the south shore and its impressive palisades, dropping back to Caribou over a 200-rod portage to make a nice loop.

Paddle and portage 5.5 miles from Caribou Lake to East Bearskin, including portages of 48 rods (L5), 15 rods (L3), and 115 rods (L8). To return to your starting point, follow the route back to East Bearskin Lake the same way you came. The portage from Moon Lake to East Bearskin increases in difficulty from L6 to L8 because of its significant climb in this direction.

Route 64B: Alder to Pine Loop (Map 48)

     Difficulty: moderate
     Number of days: 3 or more
     Total miles: 23.5
     Portage number: 6
     Total portage rods: 549
     Greatest portage difficulty 232 rods (L9)
     Navigation maps: Voyageur 10
                          Fisher F14
                          McKenzie 1, 2

This route will take you on a wonderful little loop through Alder and Canoe lakes. You will travel along one of the most demanding portages in the wilderness, but fortunately it will be mostly downhill. This route offers the best chance to see small, peaceful lakes in the BWCAW northeast of the Gunflint Trail. It is also one of the best routes in this region for fit campers capable of difficult portages but less confident about navigating the big waters of nearby lakes.

Map 48 shows the beginning of this route, and Maps 50 and 51 show the eastern portions.

Detailed Route

Paddle and portage 5 miles from East Bearskin Lake to Alder Lake, including a 48-rod portage (L3) from East Bearskin to Alder. Start from the same East Bearskin landing used for Route 64A, but follow the south bay of East Bearskin to a 48-rod portage leading to Alder Lake. This portage is very level with only a slight incline on either side. The trail is about as free of obstructions as you can expect in the Boundary Waters, although there are some exposed roots and a few rocks. On the East Bearskin side you can still see the remains of a boat landing, including timbers and piled rocks just below the surface of the water. The landings on either side are not perfect but pose no real obstacles.

Alternatively, you can take the 80-rod (L7) northern portage from East Bearskin to Alder Lake. This is also a great portage and not as heavily traveled as the 48-rod route, although it is rigorous. The portage is well worth the extra effort for one reason: you will travel through old-growth cedars, some of which are well over 2 feet wide at their base and even close to 2 feet wide at shoulder height. No doubt these trees are hundreds of years old. In addition, the trail is punctuated by a handful of grand old white pines.

Alder Lake and Canoe Lake (described below) are both quiet waters free of motorized watercraft, a reflection of legislation in 1997 that removed motors from these lakes in exchange for allowing trucks to haul boats from Vermilion Lake to Trout Lake (see Entry Point 1) and from Moose Lake to Basswood Lake over the Prairie Portage (see Entry Point 25). This legislation also retained a phase-out of motors west of Three Mile Island on Sea Gull Lake (see Entry Point 54) and kept trucks off the Four Mile Portage from Fall Lake to Basswood Lake (see Entry Point 24).

Paddle and portage 6.5 miles from Alder Lake to Pine Lake, including portages of 22 rods (L2) to Canoe Lake, and 232 rods (L9) to Pine Lake. The 22-rod portage to Alder Lake is generally flat except for a short, steep hill at the Canoe Lake side. Three sites are available for camping on Canoe lake: two in the main body of the lake, and one in the bay near the Pine Lake portage. Any one of these sites makes a nice place to camp, but their proximity to a major route between East Bearskin and Pine makes them popular stops. Do not count on an open site late in the day, or you may be back-tracking to Alder or attempting a long portage to Pine to find an open campsite.

The 232-rod portage from Canoe to Pine Lake winds down a steep hillside. You will climb a rocky trail out of Canoe Lake and then drop down a long path with switchbacks through two little swampy areas before finally settling down to Pine Lake. This portage is among the hardest in the BWCAW when coming from Pine Lake, but from Canoe Lake it is considerably easier.

Pine Lake stretches 8 miles from west to east. You will notice that white pines grow in considerable numbers on the north side of the lake but not on the south side. The north shore gets a full dose of sun each day, while the south shore is in shade all day. The south side of Pine Lake was heavily hit by the July 4, 1999, windstorm, but fortunately the campsites on most of the north shore were not nearly as damaged. You may want to explore Vale or Gadwall lakes on the south side of Pine Lake. These two little lakes are not available for overnight camping but have been regularly stocked with brook trout. You can also portage to Long Lake and Stump Lake, which have one campsite.

Paddle and portage 12 miles to East Bearskin Lake, including portages of 48 rods (L5) from Caribou Lake to Deer Lake, 15 rods (L3) from Deer to Moon Lake, and 115 rods from Moon to East Bearskin Lake. The portage to Deer Lake is a mere 48 rods long, but the first third is very steep. The landing on the Caribou side is fairly rocky, while the Deer Lake side is more open. The last two-thirds of the portage pass through a nice grove of white cedars.

Deer Lake is scenic, but you will see far fewer white pines than on neighboring lakes, perhaps a reflection of the logging railroad that once reached these shores and the big-pine logging in these parts in the 1920s. The white pines have been replaced by a mixed forest of black spruce, white cedar, birch, aspen, and small white pine. One campsite is located on Deer Lake, but it is often occupied during the busiest months of the year.

The portage to Moon Lake is nearly flat. Numerous boulders will challenge you, and both landings are fairly rocky. Still, considering the length, this is an easy portage. Moon Lake is the last lake before you reach your start at East Bearskin. Three designated campsites are available for camping, but do not count on them being available if you get a late start. Their location near East Bearskin makes them a popular first-night location for people starting at East Bearskin and heading toward Caribou and Clearwater lakes. You will conclude with the 185-rod portage to East Bearskin.

Two additional route options are described below and give nice diversions out of East Bearskin from major routes.

Option 1: Paddle and portage from Alder Lake to Pierz Lake, including a 19-rod (L3) portage (see Map 50). The portage to Pierz Lake is located on the most easterly point of Alder. The 19-rod portage follows along a mostly level, relatively infrequently traveled trail with a few rocky outcroppings. A steep hill provides a backdrop to the southern shore of Pierz, and three designated campsites are located on the north shore.

Option 2: Paddle and portage from Canoe Lake to Crystal Lake, including a 48-rod portage (L2) (see Maps 50 and 51). For a second option, traverse the 48-rod portage from Canoe Lake to Crystal Lake. The trail is wide and free of obstructions, but expect it to be a little more overgrown than most portages in this area. The west end of Crystal, where you will put in your canoe, is relatively shallow. To reach its two campsites, continue a half mile up the south shore for the first site, and 2 miles up the south shore for the second site.

Head to Spaulding and Bench lakes from Crystal if you are feeling adventurous, although campsites are not available on either lake. Spaulding is an interesting side trip because on the far east end of the lake lie the remains of the tiny Spaulding Mine, started in the 1880s by Captain William Spaulding. Captain Spaulding believed a rich vein of silver lay beneath the site. The only vein he found played out quickly, and he soon abandoned the mine. The well-decayed walls of a log cabin can still be found, as well as a boiler, winch, and other remains.

You can portage past Spaulding to Bench Lake, which is notable for being regularly stocked with brook trout. The 100-rod portage to Bench is challenging because it gets little use, was heavily damaged by the 1999 windstorm, and drops down a remarkably steep trail over the final 25 rods. This is a lot of work to fish a small lake. Remember that fish are indifferent to the struggle you take to reach them, so don't be upset (at this author) if the brookies decline your bait despite your toil.

Entry Point 66, Crocodile Lake (Map 48)

Daily permit quota: 1
Permit availability: easy

Crocodile Lake is a little getaway lake that has just one overnight permit allowed per day and no other large lakes reachable from it. However, the busy waters of East Bearskin bring many people to Crocodile on one-day fishing trips, which do not require an advance permit but only a day-use permit that can be self-issued at the East Bearskin landing.

To reach Crocodile Lake, take the Gunflint Trail 26 miles from Grand Marais, and turn right onto Forest Service Road 146. Continue down this road for just over a mile to the East Bearskin campground and follow the signs to the boat launch on East Bearskin Lake. This campground is a great place to spend a night, as is the nearby Flour Lake campground. You will need to paddle to the south-central shore of East Bearskin, where a tough 120-rod portage leads to Crocodile. The first 25 rods of this portage climb quite steeply. The trail then levels out before dropping you to Crocodile.

Head east and find a place to spend an evening among the four designated campsites. You can test the waters for walleye, which have been regularly stocked. Some old maps show a portage out the east end toward Kiowa and Bean lakes, but this portage is too overgrown to readily find and does not appear to be maintained at the present time.

ENTRY FROM THE ARROWHEAD TRAIL

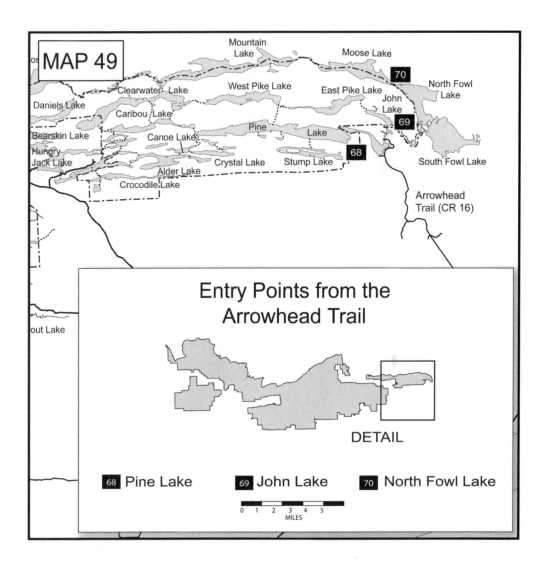

MAP 49

Mountain Lake

Moose Lake

70

North Fowl Lake

Clearwater Lake

West Pike Lake

East Pike Lake

John Lake

69

Daniels Lake

Caribou Lake

Pine

Lake

68

Bearskin Lake

Canoe Lake

Hungry Jack Lake

Crystal Lake

Stump Lake

South Fowl Lake

Alder Lake

Crocodile Lake

Arrowhead Trail (CR 16)

out Lake

Entry Points from the Arrowhead Trail

DETAIL

68 Pine Lake   69 John Lake   70 North Fowl Lake

0 1 2 3 4 5
MILES

ENTRY FROM THE ARROWHEAD TRAIL

Your eastern-most option for entering the BWCAW is from three entry points at the very tip of Minnesota's "Arrowhead" region. These three entries are Pine Lake (Entry Point 68), John Lake (Entry Point 69), and North Fowl Lake (Entry Point 70). These three entries allow just four overnight permits total per day, making the Arrowhead Trail an infrequently used origin for visitors to the BWCAW. Pine and John each has a permit quota of one group per day, while North Fowl Lake has a quota of two groups per day.

You reach all three entry points at the end of the Arrowhead Trail, which is County Road 16 and originates at the town of Hovland on Lake Superior. Hovland is located on Highway 61 about 19 miles northeast of Grand Marais. To reach Pine Lake, take the Arrowhead Trail for 18 miles until you reach a bridge crossing the creek connecting McFarland and Little John lakes. If you are heading to Pine Lake, you will paddle up McFarland; if you are heading to John Lake, you will paddle down Little John Lake; and if you are heading to North Fowl Lake, you will paddle through Little John Lake and on to the Royal River.

All of the Boundary Waters lakes reachable from these three entry points are described in the sections for the East Bearskin entry (Entry Point 64) and the Clearwater entry (Entry Point 62), each of which has at least as many permits available per day as these four entries *combined*. The Arrowhead Trail is not well served by outfitters and does not have any permit issuing stations along its length. Thus, the most convenient location to pick up your permit is at the Gunflint Ranger Station in Grand Marais.

Even many diehard visitors to the BWCAW have never made a trip up the Arrowhead Trail to enter at one of these lakes. To keep this guide manageable in size, the benefits and idiosyncrasies of each of these entries are described below but not specific lakes and portages. For these descriptions, see the route descriptions for Entry Points 64 and 66, in "Entry Northeast of the Gunflint Trail."

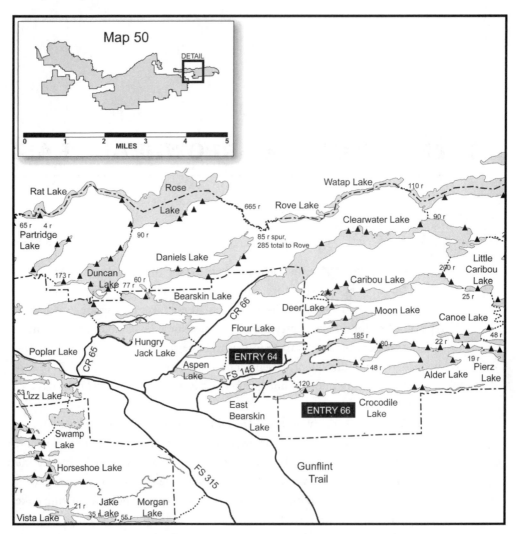

Entry Point 68, Pine Lake (Maps 50 and 51)

> Daily permit quota: 1
> Permit availability: difficult

Pine Lake provides easy access to interior lakes by way of a paddle across McFarland Lake and a short portage or pull-through to Pine. The daily permit quota is just one, so reservations are essential during the entire paddling season.

Various trips are possible starting at Pine Lake. Many visitors will be content simply enjoying Pine, fishing the depths for walleye, northern pike, and lake trout and paddling to Johnson Falls at Pine's west end. If you wish to cover more territory, good loops are possible by circling west through Caribou Lake and then back east by way of either Mountain and Moose lakes on the Canadian border, or West Pike and East Pike lakes just to the south of the border. Both loops offer fantastic scenery.

To reach Pine Lake, put in at the public landing on McFarland Lake, and then

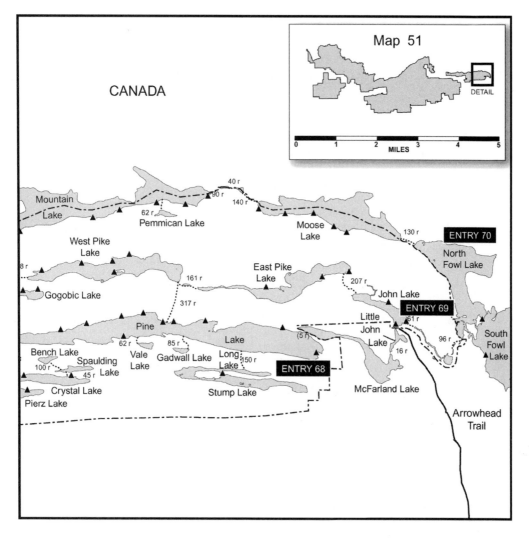

paddle through McFarland to its western connection with Pine Lake. McFarland is entirely outside of the BWCAW, and much of the shoreline is privately owned. There are no motor size restrictions on McFarland, nor do there appear to be many zoning restrictions on some of the free-form homes built along the shore.

After paddling across McFarland, find the small channel on its west end where Pine Lake empties into McFarland. You should be able to paddle up this channel in high water or pull your canoe through during lower water. A 5-rod portage is located near the channel but appears to be seldom used and will probably not be needed.

See routes out of Entry Points 64 and 66 for ideas on exploration from Pine Lake.

Entry Point 69, John Lake (Map 51)

> Daily permit quota: 1
> Permit availability: difficult

Entry Point 69, John Lake, is an excellent "back door" to the eastern BWCAW. Like Entry Point 68 to Pine Lake and 70 to North Fowl Lake, this entry point is reached by way of the Arrowhead Trail from Hovland. The permits are popular and often reserved well in advance—so a bit of planning is in order.

Perhaps one of the best features of Entry Point 69 is that it provides two excellent routes along the historic voyageurs' highway: first, a loop through the Pike lakes and then back along the historic route from Mountain Lake to North Fowl Lake; second, a one-way excursion from John Lake to South Fowl Lake and all the way to Lake Superior by way of the Pigeon River and the Grand Portage. This latter route is only briefly within the BWCAW but is nevertheless an excellent high-quality wilderness trip.

By entering the Pigeon River system by way of John Lake, you can make an easy one-way trip with two cars and a minimum of driving, since your automobile shuffle is only up and down the Arrowhead Trail rather than up and down the Gunflint Trail if you were to enter at East Bearskin or another Gunflint entry point.

See routes out of Entry Points 61, 62, and 64 for ideas on exploring from John Lake. In particular, look at Route 55E for descriptions of the Pigeon River and the Grand Portage.

Entry Point 70, North Fowl Lake (Map 51)

> Daily permit quota: 2
> Permit availability: easy

Entry Point 70, North Fowl Lake, is located along the portage separating Moose Lake from North Fowl Lake. This is not one of the entry points where your park your car and dip your canoe into the BWCAW. You must paddle by way of Little John and John lakes and the Royal River to reach North Fowl Lake and then take the Moose Portage to Moose Lake.

While a fine entry point in many regards, North Fowl Lake is one of the most infrequently reserved entry points in the BWCAW. This may be due to the fact that motorboats are permitted on all of North Fowl Lake, and the desire by many canoeists to find smaller, more intimate lakes. However, North Fowl, Moose, and the other lakes forming the international boundary have at least two great advantages: one, they are almost all long and connected by infrequent small portages; and two, they traverse the historic voyageurs' route traveled by thousands of trappers and traders hundreds of years ago, thus providing a unique historic trail.

See routes out of Entry Points 61 and 62 for ideas on exploration from North Fowl Lake.

RECOMMENDED READING

Boundary Waters Camping Tips and Suggestions

Furtman, Michael. *A Boundary Waters Fishing Guide* (Minocqua, WI: Northword Press, 1990). A thorough treatment of fishing gear and techniques for the Boundary Waters.

Furtman, Michael. *Canoe Country Camping: Wilderness Skills for the Boundary Waters and Quetico* (Minneapolis: University of Minnesota Press, 1992). A useful how-to book from a respected Boundary Waters author.

Jacobson, Cliff. *Canoeing and Camping: Beyond the Basics* (Guilford, CT: Globe Pequot Press, 2000). A trusted camping guide to the canoe country from a long-time Boundary Waters explorer.

Natural History

Ahlgren, Clifford, and Isabel Ahlgren. *Lob Trees in the Wilderness: The Human and Natural History of the Boundary Waters* (Minneapolis: University of Minnesota Press, 2001). A natural history text that is a good supplement to Heinselman's *The Boundary Waters Wilderness Ecosystem*.

Heinselman, Miron. *The Boundary Waters Wilderness Ecosystem* (Minneapolis: University of Minnesota Press, 1996). This book gives perhaps the best, most complete natural history of the Boundary Waters and is highly recommended.

Mead, Kurt. *Dragonflies of the North Woods* (Duluth: Kollath-Stensaas, 2003). An authoritative text on a very rich order of insects.

Ojakangas, Richard W., and Charles L. Matsch. *Minnesota's Geology* (Minneapolis: University of Minnesota Press, 2001). A thorough text on Minnesota's geology with interesting discussions about the Boundary Waters.

Stensaas, Mark. *Canoe Country Flora: Plants and Trees of the North Woods and Boundary Waters* (Minneapolis: University of Minnesota Press, 1996). A great entertaining description of plants of the Boundary Waters; highly recommended.

Stensaas, Mark. *Canoe Country Wildlife: A Field Guide to the North Woods and Boundary Waters* (Minneapolis: University of Minnesota Press, 1993). The companion to Stensaas's flora book, also eminently readable and enjoyable and highly recommended.

Stensaas, Mark, and Rick Kollath. *Wildflowers of the BWCA and the North Shore* (Duluth: Kollath-Stensaas, 2003).

Weber, Larry. *Spiders of the North Woods* (Duluth: Kollath-Stensaas, 2002). An authoritative text on spiders, well written and complete.

Human History

Backes, David. *Canoe Country: An Embattled Wilderness* (Minocqua, WI: Northword Press, 1991). An interesting book that explores the evolution of an environmental ethic in the Boundary Waters.

Barr, Elinor. *Thunder Bay to Gunflint: The Port Arthur, Duluth & Western Railway* (Thunder Bay: Thunder Bay Historical Museum Society, 1999). This text details the fascinating development of the PAD&W railroad built through Canada west from Thunder Bay and then along Gunflint Lake to the Paulson Mine. Great reading for anyone entering the Boundary Waters from the Gunflint Trail.

Bishop, Hugh. *By Water and Rail: A History of Lake County, Minnesota* (Duluth: Lake Superior Port Cities, 2000). A good book about Lake County history, especially outside the BWCA.

Furtman, Michael. *Magic on the Rocks: Canoe Country Pictographs* (Cambridge, MN: Birch Portage Press, 2000). A good book with a full listing of BWCAW pictographs, although many listed in this guide are quite faded and difficult to see.

Gilman, Carolyn. *Where Two Worlds Meet: The Great Lakes Fur Trade* (St. Paul: Minnesota Historical Society, 1982). A good scholarly review of the world of the voyageurs. Adds wonderful details to any trip along the Canadian border.

Proescholdt, Kevin, Rip Rapson, and Miron Heinselman. *Troubled Waters: The Fight for the Boundary Waters Canoe Area Wilderness* (St. Cloud, MN: North Star Press, 1996). A detailed look at the three years of legislative activity leading to passage of the Boundary Waters Wilderness Act in 1978. This book picks up where Searle's *Saving Quetico-Superior* ends.

Raff, Willis H. *Pioneers in the Wilderness: Minnesota's Cook County, Grand Marais, and the Gunflint in the Nineteenth Century* (Grand Marais, MN: Cook County Historical Society, 1988). This interesting book provides great details about the Paulson Mine and its colorful local history. Great reading for anyone entering from the Gunflint Trail.

Searle, R. Newell. *Saving Quetico-Superior: A Land Set Apart* (St. Paul: Minnesota Historical Society, 1977). This book, which is out of print but available used and in libraries, provides a rich explanation of the history of the Boundary Waters until 1977. It is a particularly interesting account written before the Boundary Waters Wilderness Act of 1978 and not influenced by later events.

Wilderness Literature

Gruchow, Paul. *Boundary Waters: The Grace of the Wild* (Minneapolis: Milkweed Editions, 1997).

Jaques, Florence Page. *Canoe Country and Snowshoe Country* (Minneapolis: University of Minnesota Press, 1999).

Olson, Sigurd F. *The Singing Wilderness* (Minneapolis: University of Minnesota Press, 1997); and *Listening Point* (Minneapolis: University of Minnesota Press, 1997). Two classics that are now back in print and should be in every Boundary Waters visitor's library.

Olson, Sigurd F. *The Meaning of Wilderness: Essential Articles and Speeches* (Minneapolis: University of Minnesota Press, 2001). Good reading for anyone interested in leaning more about Sigurd Olson.

Biographies

Backes, David. *A Wilderness Within: The Life of Sigurd F. Olson* (Minneapolis: University of Minnesota Press, 1997). A well-written biography of Sigurd Olson and a great companion to Olson's books.

Cary, Bob. *Root Beer Lady: The Story of Dorothy Molter* (Minneapolis: University of Minnesota Press, 1993). A good biography of Dorothy Molter, giving readers a broad understanding of her. An easy read, this book will be particularly interesting to anyone going through Moose or Knife lakes.

Kerfoot, Justine. *Woman of the Boundary Waters: Canoeing, Guiding, Mushing, and Surviving* (Minneapolis: University of Minnesota Press, 1994). Stories of a pioneering resident of the Gunflint Trail.

Paddock, Joe. *Keeper of the Wild: The Life of Ernest Oberholtzer* (St. Paul: Minnesota Historical Society, 2001). A great biography of one of the leading environmentalists who fought for the preservation of the wild areas along the Minnesota and Ontario boundary waters. Oberholtzer's contributions are often overlooked, and this text identifies his many contributions.

OUTFITTERS, LODGES, SUPPLIES, AND EQUIPMENT

The Boundary Waters Canoe Area Wilderness is served by numerous high-quality outfitters and lodges. These organizations can give you up-to-date information about businesses in their vicinity. In addition, go to www.BoundaryWatersGuide.com for a current list of outfitters, lodges, and resorts.

Lake Vermilion Resort Association
P.O. Box 159
Cook, MN 55723
800-648-5897
www.lakevermilionresorts.com

Crane Lake Visitor and Tourism Bureau
Crane Lake, MN 55725
800-362-7405
www.visitcranelake.com

Gunflint Trail Association
P.O. Box 205
Grand Marais, MN 55604
800-338-6932
www.gunflint-trail.com

Ely Chamber of Commerce
1600 East Sheridan Street
Ely, MN 55731
218-365-6123, 800-777-7281
www.ely.org

Lutsen-Tofte Tourism Association
Box 2248
Tofte, MN 55615
218-663-7804, 888-616-6784
www.61north.com

Minnesota Office of Tourism
320 West Second Street, Suite 707
Duluth, MN 55802
218-723-4692, 800-657-3657
www.exploreminnesota.com

Tower-Soudan Chamber of Commerce
Box 776
Tower, MN 55790
800-648-5897

FOREST SERVICE
CAMPGROUND LOCATIONS

- -

The following U.S. Forest Service campgrounds are located within the Superior National Forest. Many charge fees. Reservations can be made at www.reserveusa.com or by calling toll free 1-877-444-6777. Camping is not allowed at entry points, except those adjacent to Forest Service campgrounds.

Name	District	Sites	Fees/ Reservations
Trails End	Gunflint	32	Yes/Yes
Iron Lake	Gunflint	7	Yes/Yes
Flour Lake	Gunflint	35	Yes/Yes
East Bearskin Lake	Gunflint	33	Yes/No
Kimball Lake	Gunflint	10	Yes/No
Two Island Lake	Gunflint	38	Yes/No
Devil Track Lake	Gunflint	16	Yes/No
Crescent Lake	Tofte	33	Yes/No
Temperance River	Tofte	9	Yes/No
Sawbill Lake	Tofte	50	Yes/No
Ninemile Lake	Tofte	24	Yes/No
Divide Lake	Tofte	3	Yes/No
Little Isabella River	Tofte	11	Yes/No
McDougal Lake	Tofte	21	Yes/No
Cadotte Lake	Laurentian	27	Yes/Yes

Name	District	Sites	Fees/ Reservations
Whiteface Reservoir	Laurentian	53	Yes/Yes
Pfeiffer Lake	Laurentian	16	Yes/Yes
Birch Lake	Kawishiwi	28	Yes/Yes
South Kawishiwi River	Kawishiwi	32	Yes/Yes
Fall Lake	Kawishiwi	66	Yes/Yes
Fenske Lake	Kawishiwi	16	Yes/Yes
Echo Lake	La Croix	24	Yes/Yes
Lake Jeanette	La Croix	12	Yes/Yes
Baker Lake (rugged)	Tofte	5	No/No
Kawishiwi Lake (rugged)	Tofte	5	No/No
Poplar River (rugged)	Tofte	4	No/No
Cascade River (rugged)	Gunflint	4	No/No
Clara Lake (rugged)	Tofte	3	No/No
Eighteen Lake (rugged)	Tofte	3	No/No
Fourmile Lake (rugged)	Tofte	4	No/No
Harriet Lake (rugged)	Tofte	3	No/No
Hogback Lake (rugged)	Tofte	3	No/No
Section 29 Lake (rugged)	Tofte	3	No/No
Silver Island Lake (rugged)	Tofte	6	No/No
Toohey Lake (rugged)	Tofte	5	No/No
Wilson Lake (rugged)	Tofte	4	No/No
White Pine Lake (rugged)	Tofte	3	No/No
Whitefish Lake (rugged)	Tofte	3	No/No
Windy Lake (rugged)	Tofte	1	No/No

FOREST SERVICE INFORMATION

Superior National Forest
8901 Grand Ave. Place
Duluth, MN 55808
218-626-4300, 218-626-4399 TTY

Gunflint Ranger District
2020 West Highway 61
P.O. Box 790
Grand Marais, MN 55604
218-387-1750, 218-387-1750 TTY

Isabella Work Station
759 Highway 1
Isabella, MN 55607
218-323-7722

Tofte Ranger District
North Highway 61
P.O. Box 2159
Tofte, MN 55615
218-663-8060, 218-663-7280 TTY

Kawishiwi Ranger District
118 South Fourth Avenue East
Ely, MN 55731
218-365-7600, 218-365-7602 TTY

LaCroix Ranger District
320 North Highway 53
Cook, MN 55723
218-666-0020, 218-666-0020 TTY

Laurentian Ranger District
318 Forestry Road
Aurora, MN 55705
218-229-8800, 218-229-8800 TTY

INDEX

- - - - - - - -

Daniel Pauly has been a frequent visitor to the Boundary Waters for more than two decades and has explored the lakes, rivers, and portages in all seasons. The Boundary Waters Canoe Area Wilderness has long been special to him—it is where he became engaged to his wife and spent his honeymoon—and is now his favorite place to explore with his two sons.